Report Upon The Basin Of The Upper Nile: With Proposals For The Improvement Of That River

Sir William Garstin

REPORT

UPON THE

BASIN OF THE UPPER NILE

WITH PROPOSALS FOR THE IMPROVEMENT OF THAT RIVER

BY

SIR WILLIAM GARSTIN, G. C. M. G.
Under Secretary of State for Public Works in Egypt.

TO WHICH IS ATTACHED

A REPORT UPON LAKE TSANA AND THE RIVERS OF THE EASTERN SOUDAN

BY

Mr. C. DUPUIS
Egyptian Irrigation Service.

WITH MAPS AND APPENDICES.

CAIRO:
NATIONAL PRINTING DEPARTMENT
1904.

CONTENTS.

LIST OF ILLUSTRATIONS.

PART III.

LIST OF PLANS

REPORT

UPON THE

BASIN OF THE UPPER NILE

WITH PROPOSALS FOR THE IMPROVEMENT OF THAT RIVER

BY

SIR WILLIAM GARSTIN, G.C.M.G.

Under Secretary of State for Public Works in Egypt.

INTRODUCTORY REMARKS

The present report, although it embodies the results of five consecutive years' observations on the Bahr-el-Gebel, and presents the general conclusions at which I have arrived regarding future schemes in connection with the improvement of the White Nile, has been written, mainly, with the object of describing my recent visit to the Equatorial lakes.

To my own note is added another, by Mr. C. Dupuis, of the Egyptian Irrigation Service, giving an account of his expedition to Lake Tsana, and the rivers of the Eastern Soudan (1).

Since my last report was written (2), a substantial advance has been made in the direction of acquiring knowledge of the respective volumes of the two main rivers throughout the year. The chapter upon "River discharges" contains, I venture to think, fuller information on this subject than has ever before been published. Monthly discharges have been made of the Blue and the White Nile, during a period of nearly two years, and the flood discharge of the Bahr-el-Gebel, above and below the "Sudd," has been measured during the years 1902 and 1903 (3). These observations have resulted in a considerable modification of the schemes, proposed in 1901, for the improvement of the Upper Nile.

The present note is, in no sense of the word, intended to be a record of travel. The countries, which I visited, have been described by many more competent pens than mine, while, as regards the Protectorate of Uganda—the magnificent volumes, which bear Sir Harry Johnston's name, leave little, or nothing, unsaid regarding that region. My report is a purely technical one, written with the intention of presenting the information collected, regarding the Nile basin, in a convenient form, and with the view of assisting, in some degree, the comprehension of the diverse questions connected with the hydrography of that river. Some description of the country traversed has been, of course, inevitable, but in any detailed account of a long river, or of a great lake, it is difficult to avoid constant repetition, and wearisome reiteration. In my desire not to omit information, that might one day be of use, I have probably erred in the other direction.

In order to make this account of the Nile basin as complete as possible, I have compiled (for those portions of the area that I was unable, personally, to visit) the accounts of various travellers and explorers, and added them to my own. In such cases the references have invariably been given. Again, with the same object, I have reproduced certain portions of the description of the "Sudd" and the affluents of the White Nile, which have already appeared in my previous report. These descriptions I have revised and corrected, from the latest information obtainable. I have given no account of my visit to the East African Protectorate, and to the "Great Rift" valley. My stay in that most interesting

(1) Throughout this report, I have spelt the name of the Abyssinian lake, as "Tsana," not "Tana." As there appeared to be a difference of opinion, as to which of these two names was correct, I asked Sir John Harrington, the British Minister at the Court of the Emperor Menelik, to enlighten me. He very kindly obtained the information I required.

The following is an extract from a letter written to me, by Mr. G. H. Clerk, who was acting for Sir John, during last summer.

British Agency
Adis Ababa, 29th August, 1903.

" In Amharic, it is as follows :—

" ጻና : which is *TSANA* ጻ = *TSA* and ና = *NA*."

" It is true, that even many of the Abyssinians call it *TANA*, but the *true* name is *TSANA*."

Signed: George H. Clerk.

(2) Foreign Office Blue Book, Egypt (No. 2) 1901.

(3) The regular monthly discharges were observed by Messrs. Barron, Hume, Beadnell and Wood, of the Egyptian Survey Department, while the "Sudd" discharges were measured by Mr. J. Craig, of the same Service.

country was but a short one, and the special object of my journey related more directly to the Nile, and the regions forming its catchment area.

It has only been possible for me to write this report in those intervals of the day, left free by my administrative duties. This fact must be the excuse for its many shortcomings.

I have but little more to add.

Although a series of observations was made with the hypsometer, throughout a great portion of the Nile valley, but little use has been made of the results obtained; for the following reasons (1).

From the Victoria lake to Khartoum, no levelled altitudes are available, and barometric and hypsometric determinations furnish the only data for the relief of the country. The altitude of Gondokoro was discussed by Hann (2), who pointed out that the atmospheric pressure at that station, during certain months, increases, while, at the same time, it falls at Khartoum; and *vice versa*. Again, in the months of June and July, the pressure at the two places is practically identical, although they are eleven degrees of latitude apart, and the one is some eighty metres lower than the other. All determination of altitude, by means of aneroids, or hypsometers, can therefore only be regarded as approximate (3).

A compass-traverse, of the route followed, was made from the head of the Semliki river, at the Albert Edward lake, down the Nile bank, (with one break), to Gondokoro. The break in this line was that portion of the river between Lake Albert and the head of the cataracts at Nimuli. For this reach, the map prepared by Lt.-Colonel Delmé Radcliffe has been made use of.

In conclusion, I wish to acknowledge the invariable kindness and assistance that I received, throughout my long expedition, from every single official whom I met.

To Sir Charles Eliot, and to Colonel Hayes Sadler, the Commissioners of the Protectorates of East Africa and Uganda respectively, and to Sir George Whitehouse, the Chief Engineer of the Uganda Railway, my grateful thanks are due. Had it not been for the very complete arrangements made by these gentlemen, the journey would have been far more difficult than was the case, and it would probably have been impossible to complete it within the space of time allowed. From them, and from every district officer, my whole party received the most generous hospitality, and the most ungrudging assistance.

On each occasion that I have visited the Soudan, the Governor General, Sir Reginald Wingate, has invariably extended to me the most cordial, and the fullest, help. On this last occasion, I have to thank him for having so kindly placed a steamer at my disposal, to await my arrival at Gondokoro, and bring me back to Khartoum.

It now only remains for me to thank those who accompanied me in my journey, and rendered my task possible.

Of the original members of my party, the health of two, Mr. E. M. Dowson, of the Survey Department, and Dr. H. W. Beech, of the Sanitary Service, unfortunately broke down. I was consequently, obliged to leave the one behind at Entebbé, and the other at Hoima.

Captain R. A. Markham, Coldstream Guards, whose services were kindly lent to the expedition by the Sirdar, accompanied me for the entire distance. My debt to him is a heavy one. He took entire charge of the caravan and the commissariat, and any one who has had experience of African travel, and the African porter, will understand what this means. He never spared himself in the slightest degree, and relieved me of all trouble. To his hard work, is largely due the successful completion of the journey.

(1) Although in the descriptive chapters, I have made use of the altitudes given on the most recent maps, I have not attemped to give a longitudinal section of the Bahr-el-Gebel, as was my original intention.

(2) "Über das Klima und die Seehöhe von Chartoun und Gondokoro." Pet. Mitt. 1875, p. 342.5.

(3) Mercury barometers are now installed at Mongalla, (latitude 5° 12' north) and at Kodok. When two or three years' observations are available, the distribution of pressure, in this part of Africa, will be better understood. By that time, however, spirit-levelling will probably have been carried up the White Nile, and the Bahr-el-Gebel.

Captain H. G. Lyons, the Director General of Surveys in Egypt, met me at Gondokoro, and returned with me to Cairo. His services, in connection with the study of the Upper Nile, have been invaluable. Besides superintending the preparation of the maps and sections, with the checking of discharges and calculations, he personally corrected the traverse survey of the Bahr-el-Gebel, (north of Gondokoro), which was published in 1901; bringing it up to date. He has made a special study of the levels of the Victoria lake, and his conclusions are appended to my report, in the shape of a most interesting note. He has, further, largely assisted me in the collection of different records regarding the Nile basin.

Mr. J. Craig, who replaced Mr. Dowson, and who accompanied me from Hoima to Khartoum, rendered much assistance, both on the journey, and in the preparation of the discharge tables. His calculations are appended to this report.

In consequence of the large number of maps which required preparation, the work of the drawing office of the Survey Department has been much augmented, during the last few months.

Mr. J. S. Beresford, late Inspector General of Irrigation in India, has, from the commencement, taken the keenest interest in the objects of my journey. He and I have, at different times, discussed the whole question of the Upper Nile, and my present proposal, for a new channel for the river, north of Bor, is the result of a suggestion made by him during one of my many conversations with him on the subject.

Lastly, I have to thank Mr. Herbert Samuel, M.P., Mr. G. Butcher, late of the Uganda Civil Service, and Major Loughlin, of the Uganda Rifles, for kindly permitting me to publish the photographs to which their names are attached (1).

W. E. Garstin.

Cairo, March 14th, 1904.

(1) Of the other photographs, those of the lakes, and of the Upper Nile, were taken by me; those of the rivers, north of Gondokoro, by Mr. Kearney, of the Survey Department.

Note.—Since the above was written, I have again visited the Upper Nile. The observations made during this journey are recorded in Appendix No. VI of the present report.

W. E. G.

Cairo, June 10th, 1904.

PART. I.—DESCRIPTIVE.

GENERAL DESCRIPTION OF THE LAKE AREA.

A study of the map of East Central Africa, reveals the existence of two remarkable depressions, or "Rifts," running north and south—both of great length, and embracing between them a very considerable area of the earth's surface. The geology of this region has formed the subject of much discussion, and the list of contributors to the literature regarding it is a full one, containing many names of the highest authority in this branch of science. (1)

Under these circumstances, any further attempt at a description, however summary, of the changes which have taken place in this area, may seem to be superfluous. The excuse for making it must lie in the fact that the sources of the Nile are inseparably connected with the existence of these two great "Rifts" and that, consequently, in any note purporting to describe the hydrography of this river, some allusion to their conformation and origin is unavoidable.

These two "Rift" valleys have a common starting point in Lake Nyassa, and bifurcate at the northern end of this sheet of water, in latitude 10° 15′ south. From this point, they follow a northerly direction, more or less parallel to one another, and at an average distance apart of some six degrees of longitude. The eastern branch follows, very closely, the 36th meridian east of Greenwich, and either disappears at Lake Rudolph, latitude 4° north, or skirts the southern limits of the Abyssinian highlands, until it joins the similar depression now occupied by the Red Sea. The western valley lies, generally, between the meridians of 29° and 30° E., but its course is not so straight as is that of the eastern branch. It appears to die away in the neighbourhood of Gondokoro; latitude 4° 30′ north. Both these great lines of fracture contain an almost continuous chain of lakes. Thus, in the eastern "Rift," are situated the Lakes of Manjara, Natron, Naivasha, El Menteita, Nakuru, Hannington, Baringo, and Rudolph. In the western, or as it is sometimes called, the Albertine "Rift," lie Lakes Tanganyika, Kivu, Albert Edward and Albert, while its northern course forms the valley of the Upper Nile, for a length of several hundred kilometres.

In neither of these valleys is the slope uniform throughout, or in one direction. In each of them a ridge occurs, which forms the parting of the waters, and from which the streams flow in opposite directions. In the east "Rift" valley, the highest elevation is attained in the vicinity of Lake Naivasha, but here the ridge is, in no sense, an abrupt one. In the Albertine "Rift," on the contrary, the separation is very marked, as, between Lakes Kivu and Albert Edward, a chain of mountains, containing several active volcanoes, bars the valley across, and divides the lake series into two distinct systems.

These two "Rifts" form a striking feature in the conformation of the country, and run through many degrees of latitude. Their width varies from 30 to 70 kilometres, and they are bounded, on either side, by continuous lines of steep, scarped cliffs, which, in places, attain a height of 700 metres above the bed of the valley below. Along the line of these fractures are found many isolated, extinct craters, such as those of Kilimanjaro, Kenia, Elgon and Langonot, while the extruded masses of newer volcanic rocks in each "Rift" are intimately connected with the great earth movements to which these fissures are due.

(1) In "The Great Rift Valley," by J.W. GREGORY, London, 1896, one of the most recent works on this subject, these names are given at length: page 214.

Geologists are of opinion that the whole area lying between these depressions, as well as those to the east and west, once formed a high plateau, extending in all directions in a rolling expanse, and reaching its highest elevation somewhere about the 32nd meridian east of Greenwich. A series of great convulsions and upheavals took place, which effectually changed the face of this region, and altered its physical features in a most remarkable degree. According to Gregory (1), after the great outpouring of lava which now covers so large an area, a period of quiescence set in, and a slow depression of the country took place, east and west of certain lines. These dividing lines were left as ridges, and as the areas on either side continued slowly to subside, parallel cracks opened along the flanks of the dividing ridges. Gradually, their summits were let down, and formed the commencement of the "Rift" valleys. With these new movements, volcanic disturbances recommenced, and along the lines of weakness formed by the "Rifts" accumulations of lava and other volcanic materials were piled up. These movements interfered with the existing drainage of the area, and lakes soon formed in the depressions. During a portion of the time when these changes took place, the climate was one of much heavier rainfall than at present, as the remains of the old glaciers on Mount Kenia and Ruenzori show. This helped the growth of these lakes, whose waters once stood at a much higher level than is now the case. The subsidence of the great central plateaux, lying between the lines of fracture, resulted in a great depression, covering many thousands of square kilometres. This area received the drainage of the surrounding high lands, and eventually formed a large sheet of water, which is now known as the Victoria Nyanza. In the course of time, the different lakes overflowed, and their waters, passing their barriers at the lowest point, formed rivers, which again followed the slope of the country. In the case of Lake Victoria, the outflow took place at the northern end, and formed the Victoria Nile, while the waters of the Albert Edward Lake found their way, by the medium of the Semliki river, into the Albert Nyanza, meeting those of the Victoria Nile at the north end of the lake, from whence they issued in one single stream. This stream is the Bahr-el-Gebel, known further north as the White Nile.

Although all violent action has, for many ages, ceased, it cannot be stated with any certainty that it has ceased altogether, or that, at some further time, eruptive forces may not again make themselves felt, at any rate over a portion of this region. The volcanoes north of Lake Kivu are still active, and there is evidence throughout the entire area that this part of the crust has not yet reached a condition of equilibrium. The steam jets in the neighbourhood of Lakes Naivasha and El Burro, the geysers at the south end of Lake Albert Edward, and the chain of hot springs which surrounds Ruenzori, and is also met with near Lake Albert, and in the Upper Nile Valley, bear witness to this fact. Again, the shocks and earth movements which are of such frequent occurrence in many places, are unpleasant reminders, to the dwellers in this region, that it lies within the zone of seismic disturbance. It may well be then, that, one day, another upheaval may take place, and a fresh development of volcanic force may make further startling changes in the configuration of this portion of the earth's surface.

Such possibilities belong entirely to the sphere of conjecture, and a mere allusion to them is sufficient. There are, however, other changes which may be predicted with a certain degree of confidence. These last follow natural laws, and, although the action which causes them may be slow, and almost imperceptible within the limits of a generation, it is nevertheless constant and resistless, and must in the end produce an inevitable result. The changes alluded to are those caused by the degradation of the mountain ranges, and by the erosion of the river beds, due to the action of water. It is unnecessary to remark that similar effects are occurring everywhere, throughout the world's surface, but, in this

(1) "The Great Rift Valley."

particular area, it seems probable that they will eventually have a very important effect upon the sources of the Nile supply. This fact is sufficient excuse for alluding to such a well-known truth in the present note.

The locality more immediately affected, and at the same time most intimately connected with the Nile sources, is that portion of the western "Rift" valley which comprises the Albert Edward and Albert lakes, and the Semliki river. It is beyond question that the first mentioned lake, at one time, covered an immensely greater surface than that occupied by its present limits. The different levels at which its waters once stood can be traced without difficulty by the deposits which they have left upon the terraces and high lands surrounding it. Moreover, the configuration of former bays and headlands, and successive levels, are as plainly marked, in the lake basin, as if they were outlined upon a contoured map. Some of this shrinkage is of comparatively recent date, and it is probable that the rate of fall is rather more rapid than has been supposed. What caused the first great lowering of the lake surface, is difficult to understand. That the valley to the north of the lake must at one time have been blocked across, and the water thus held back, appears to be certain, but by what means this block was removed, is as yet undetermined. Whatever may have been the cause, the disappearance of this barrier has resulted in a very marked shrinkage in the area once covered by the water of the lake. The outfall channel, in time, has worked its way down through the material, and formed a river, which follows the slope of the country, and discharges its waters into the Albert lake, thus connecting the two lake systems. This river is the Semliki. By degrees, this river has eroded its bed and sides, until finally its present levels have been reached. A study of the general cross-section of the upper Semliki valley affords proof that this is what must actually have occurred.

As the river bed worked down, more water was discharged from the lake, and the levels of the reservoir fell. As the Semliki is still eroding its bed, the process of the lowering of the levels must be continuing. The only restraining force appears to be the rocky bar, which stretches across its central course, and over which its waters tear, in a series of rapids and cataracts. This acts as a regulator, and arrests the too rapid degradation of the bed slope. Nevertheless, in the course of time, even this obstacle must yield to the slow, but continuous, cutting back of the bed, due to the steep slope and the action of the water. When this disappears, then the Albert Edward lake must disappear with it.

In the Albert Nyanza, a different process is at work, equally resistless, and equally certain in its effects. The glaciers and atmospheric agencies on Ruenzori cause a continual degradation of the mountain sides, and the detritus thus formed is borne down by the torrents which scour out its ravines into the channel of the Semliki, which, again, conveys them into the Albert lake, together with the alluvium which its waters have brought down from the upper portion of its course. At the south end of Lake Albert, the slope of the river bed becomes flatter, and the velocity of the current consequently lower. Its waters are therefore unable to carry these matters further, and deposit them on the adjoining country. In this way, a great plain has been formed, and is still forming, at the southern extremity of Lake Albert, which is slowly, but surely, encroaching upon its water surface, and raising the levels of its bed. At the north end, the Victoria Nile is producing a similar effect, and is, by degrees, pushing out its delta across the lake and contracting its width. In a minor degree, the many torrents which pour in from the boundary cliffs on the east and west, are each and all of them, bringing large quantities of deposit into this lake, and assisting in the raising of its bed. In the fullness of time, the Albert lake, like the Albert Edward, will disappear, and all that will remain of these two great sheets of water, will be a river, draining the northern slopes of the Kivu range, and the "Rift" valley itself, and joining the Victoria Nile at the point where that stream now discharges into Lake Albert.

It is possible that what has taken place in the Upper Nile Valley will be repeated here, and that, as the lakes disappear, immense swamps, similar to those in the "sudd" region, will be formed, through which the river will wander in a series of channels.

Naturally, similar changes to those taking place in the Albert lake, are occurring in Lake Victoria. The rivers, which drain into it from the uplands, must bring down large quantities of deposit in their waters, which must gradually tend to fill up its bed, and reduce its area. Such changes, however, taking into consideration the area of this lake, as compared to the volume of its affluents, must be extremely slow in their effect, and, unless the ridge at the Ripon Falls gives way, or should be lowered, must take an indefinite period of time before they produce any visible diminution in the water surface. It seems probable, then, that long after the Albertine lakes have disappeared, the Victoria lake will remain the great reservoir for, and the true source of, the waters of the White Nile.

THE VICTORIA NYANZA (1).

This lake, which is the largest sheet of fresh-water in the old world, is situated between the parallels of latitude 0° 20′ north and 3° 0′ south, and the meridians of 31° 40′ and 35° east of Greenwich. Its elevation is 1129 metres above mean sea level at Mombasa. The equator traverses the lake towards its northern end, and the Anglo-German boundary, which follows the parallel of latitude 1° 0′ south, approximately divides its area into two equal portions. In shape, it is an irregular quadrilateral, but its shores, more especially on the north and south, are deeply indented by large bays, or gulfs. On the western shore, the coast line is straighter, as it closely follows the line of the great fault which runs north and south, from the mouth of the Kagera river.

Lake Victoria is remarkable for the numerous groups of islands which break the surface of its waters, most of them not very far from the coast line (2). Of these islands, the principal groups are those comprised in the Buvuma archipelago in the north, the Sessé archipelago in the north-west, and those in the vicinity of Ukerewe island in the south-east corner. Another small cluster of islands is that known by the name of Komé, in the south-west. The largest island in the lake is Ukerewe, in German Territory. This is almost a peninsula, and is connected with the mainland by a narrow strip of shore, traversed by two small channels known as Rugeshi (3). Most of these islands are inhabited, chiefly by a fishing population, but in many of them considerable areas of cultivation exist. Coffee of a particularly fine quality is grown upon the Sessé islands (4). The scenery of many of these islands is of fairy-like beauty, notably in those of the Buvuma and Sessé groups. Most of them are mountainous, and, in some of them, the ranges attain a height of 500, and 600 metres above the lake. Nearly all are densely forested. Their formation is generally ironstone, overlying quartzite and crystalline schists (5). Of the depth of Lake Victoria, except in the northern half, not very much is known. According to the latest chart, the deepest sounding yet obtained is 73 metres, close to the Lolui islands, on the northern coast (6). As a general rule, the depth, within a distance of 15 to 20 kilometres from the shore, is very variable, the soundings showing depths ranging from 15 to 60 metres (7). In the bays and creeks, the water is shallow. Of the depths in the centre of the lake, no information as yet exists. The nature of the bed appears to vary between stretches of coarse-grained sand and fine grey mud. It is, however, full of reefs, many of which are just below the surface, and navigation is consequently attended with a certain risk.

The water of Lake Victoria is singularly clear and limpid, and very sweet and fresh. In this last respect, it is a great contrast to that of the lakes in the two "Rift" valleys. In fine weather, when the sun is shining, the colour is a beautiful azure blue, but when the sky is clouded, it assumes a dark steel-grey tint, almost black at times. This lake is very liable to severe squalls and storms, and at such times, its surface is lashed into waves of very considerable height. It is rarely safe for the small craft which navigate it to venture far from the vicinity of the islands; in the lee of which they can run for shelter, should a sudden storm arise (8). Water-spouts are occasionally seen (9). The area of Lake Victoria is some 68000

(1) "Nyanza" means "a sea" in the language of Waganda.

(2) The centre portions of the lake have not as yet been explored, so it is quite possible that groups of islands may exist, which are at present unknown.

(3) "Uganda and the Sudan," London 1882, by the Rev. C. T. Wilson, F.R.G.S.

(4) The population of the Sessé islands has suffered very severely of late years from the ravages of the sleeping sickness.

(5) Stuhlmann states that these islands are a rib of the primitive slate formation of which the great plateau once consisted

(6) From the chart prepared by Commander Whitehouse, R.N., and published by the Admiralty.

(7) Idem.

(8) In the spring of 1903, a steamer of 600 tons burden was launched at Port Florence, and another is under construction. With boats of this size, it ought to be quite safe to cross the lake in almost any weather, and it should be found possible to explore these portions which are at present unknown.

(9) "Uganda and the Sudan," by the Rev. C. T. Wilson.

square kilometres, or nearly the same size as Scotland. Its greatest length is 400 kilometres, and greatest breadth 320 kilometres. Many rivers feed it, but it has only one outlet; the Victoria Nile, which discharges from the Ripon Falls, in the Napoleon gulf, on the northern shore.

The principal affluents on the north, are the Sio, Nzoia and Lukos, or Yala. West of the Sio, no other rivers drain into the lake on its northern shore, the watershed here being close to the coast and the streams in this area actually rise within a few kilometres of the lake, and flow *away from it,* to the north, and eventually into the Nile. On the eastern shore, in British territory, the rivers are the Nyando, the Tuyayo and the Sondo. On the west, north of the Anglo-German boundary, the lake is fed by the Katonga and the Ruizi rivers, and, at the point where this boundary touches the coast, the Kagera river, which is its most important tributary, enters it. A brief description of these rivers will be given later on, but the information regarding most of them is as yet extremely meagre. Concerning the streams which feed this lake within the limits of German territory, a considerable amount of information is available (¹). Very excellent maps, corrected up to date, have been published by the German Government. The names of the principal rivers appear to be: on the east, the Mara Dabash, or Mara, the Ruwana and the Mbalaasti, all of which drain the high eastern plateau. On the south, are the Mtuma, the Suiuya, the Moami, the Wami, the Lokungati and the Ruiga. Some of these are said to be tolerably large streams, and it is stated that the Mara Dabash ranks next in volume and importance to the Kagera (²). There is one point of difference between the rivers in English, and in German territory, namely, that, whereas, the former are, one and all, perennial streams, some of the latter, more particularly in the south-east, are torrents, which bring down considerable volumes in the rainy season, but are dry during a portion of the year.

The principal gulfs are those of Kavirondo, Berkeley, Napoleon and Murchison, in the north, and those named after Emin Pasha, Smith and Speke, in the south. In addition to these, there is an infinite number of smaller bays and creeks, in which the water is, as a rule, shallow and muddy. Their shores are frequently surrounded by wide swamps, full of papyrus and high reeds, the home of numberless hippopotami, crocodiles and water birds. The waters of the lake teem with fish of many varieties, and fishing forms a large part of the occupation of the inhabitants in the neighbourhood of the coast.

The character of the lake shores varies considerably. On the northern coast, it is generally high, consisting of rounded hills from 100 to 150 metres above the water, running down in a succession of rocky headlands to the shore. The valleys behind these hills are thickly wooded. In the north-east corner, it is flat and bare, with but little bush and few trees, and stretches, a wide table-land, to the foot of the Nandi hills. To the west, the hills continue as far south as the Katonga river. From this point, to the junction of the Kagera with the lake, the levels gradually fall, and flats, with sandy beaches, border the water. This shore is marked by a continuous fault line, which runs parallel to the lake from the south-west corner, at a distance of a few kilometres, as far north as the Katonga estuary. On nearing the Kagera, the hills recede from the water, and dense swamps, full of ambatch and papyrus, stretch inland for some distance from the coast. South of this river, the land again rises in a series of high downs some of them 300 metres above the water, with sheer precipices, often 100 metres in height, running down into the lake. In the south-west corner, barren and stony hills stand up, with long bare ridges of rock running out in reefs into the water. The southern coast is more generally mountainous than any of the other shores. At the south-east end, the masses of the Majita and Magu mountains rise to a height of some 700 metres above the lake, and to the north stretches a fine, bold rocky coast,

(¹) This is to be found in the sixteen published volumes of "Abhandlungen der deutschen Schutzgebiete," and in the works of Fischer, Baumann, Stuhlmann, Von Götzen and others.

(²) KOLLMANN. "The Victoria Nyanza, London", 1902.

in a succession of bluffs and headlands, to the Lumbwa ranges which border the Kavirondo gulf. On the eastern coast, the water is, as a rule, deep, close in shore, but on the west, more particularly between the Katonga and Kagera rivers, the shallows extend for a considerable distance (¹).

A current sets across the lake from the Kagera river to the Ripon Falls. How much of this is due to the volume of that river, and how much to the effect of the prevailing trade wind, it is impossible to say.

The catchment basin of Lake Victoria is some 240000 square kilometres in area, including the lake itself. It is of extremely irregular shape, and very difficult to trace, more particularly to the north and north-west.

Allusion has already been made to the fact that, on the north, between the Sio river and the Nile, the watershed is on the shore of the lake itself, and that the drainage lines running northward have their sources in the hills which border the coast. West of the Nile outlet, a ridge runs in a north-westerly direction, until it meets the foothills of Ruenzori, whence it runs south to the Ruampara chain, which forms the northern watershed of the Kagera river. This area is drained by the Katonga and Ruizi rivers. The basin of the Kagera is a large one, as it extends south-west to the hills bordering Tanganyika lake. To the south, the area is again narrow, but to the east it is wider and stretches in a high stony plateau, for a long distance from the lake. In the north-east, the dividing ranges are the Lumbwa hills, and the Mau escarpment, and, further north, the Nandi plateau.

The records regarding the mean annual rainfall, throughout this large area, are as yet most incomplete, and consequently any attempt to determine the amount of water entering the lake annually must be nothing but a mere approximation, based upon the limited information existing. Moreover, it is evident that, in such a large tract of country, nearly four times the size of Scotland, the variations in the climate and in the amount of rainfall must be considerable. Thus, while the rainfall, in the vicinity of Ruenzori and the Nandi and Mau plateaux, is very heavy, in the south-east it is said to be comparatively scanty, and an arid tract extends for a long distance east of the Victoria lake. Meteorological stations are few and far between and, in many of those existing, registers have only been commenced very recently. Until, then, full records of the rainfall, lasting over a series of years, are obtainable for the southern half of the lake, as well as for the north, any definite assertion regarding the volume of water by which the lake is increased annually, must necessarily be very misleading. Even the area of the catchment basin is but an approximation, and until accurate maps are prepared and an improved knowledge of the levels obtained, this figure can be nothing else.

Rain-gauge statistics have been obtained from a certain number of places, but, unfortunately, the returns are incomplete and only in a few instances do they show the entire rainfall for the year. Those for Entebbé and Natete, in the north-west corner of the lake, cover the longest period of time, and give an average rainfall, for 14 years, of 1267 millimetres. At Kisumu, in the Kavirondo gulf, the average for five years is 1242 millimetres, and at Mumias, in the same district, but on the high plateau, the average for six years was 1832 millimetres. Rain gauges have been erected at Masaka, and at Mbarara in the Ankoli district; also at Fort Portal, near the Ruenzori mountains, but their records as yet do not cover a period of one year. In German Territory, observations are recorded at Bukoba, on the west shore of the lake; at Muanza, on the south, and at Tabora, a station in S. lat. 5° 3′ and at altitude 1230 metres. This last station is due south of lake Victoria, and some 280 kilometres from the lake (²). Of these three, Bukoba registers the largest fall, an average of 2181 millimetres having been obtained in four years, while Tabora

(¹) The description of the coast lying south of the Anglo-German line is largely taken from that given by the REV. C. T. WILSON, "Uganda and the Sudan." London, 1882.

(²) Observations are also recorded at Shirati, on the east of the lake, but nothing has as yet been published from this station.

in a similar period, was only 734 millimetres. Muanza in one year, 1894-95, registers 1375 millimetres, but in 1902 the rainfall was 2800 millimetres. All these returns are more or less fragmentary, and a comparison, between most of them, is impossible, as they refer to different years. They show, however, as far as they go, that the rainfall on the western and southern shores of the lake is heavier than on the northern coast, while in the extreme south it is again less. No records exist for the eastern shores. Again, they prove that although rain falls more or less throughout the year, the two periods of heaviest rainfall take place in the months of March, April and May, and in September, October and November. June and July are the driest months of the year. Lastly, they show how very variable is the fall, according to the locality. Thus, while at Muanza, in 1902, the rainfall was 2800 millimetres, in the same year, at Tabora, only 280 kilometres distant, it was only 353 millimetres (1).

The study of the geology of the table land, surrounding Lake Victoria, shows that the general formation consists of gneiss, quartz and schistose rocks. These are covered with red clay and marl, on the higher lands, and in the valleys, with a rich black loam. Throughout the entire region, more particularly in the vicinity of the lake shores, there is a large outcrop of piscolithic ironstone. This, by disintegration, gives the remarkable red colour to the soil which is such a characteristic of the locality (2).

The following pages give a rather more detailed description of the northern and western shores of the lake, as compiled from notes made during a recent visit.

The north-eastern boundary of the lake basin is the Mau escarpment, which reaches a height of 2740 metres above the sea, and is distant, nearly 150 kilometres, from its shores. From this point, the slope of the country is very rapid, and, between the edge of the plateau and Mubaroni, a distance of only 94 kilometres, the drop is as much as 1350 metres. The country here is stony, and generally treeless, with deep and wide valleys. At Mubaroni, 160 metres above the present lake-level, gravel and boulder beds are found in the cuttings of the Uganda railway, and similar indications of water-worn deposit are found at other places round the lake towards the north. They are at a very considerable height above the level at which it now stands.

Descending the slopes, in the direction of the lake, the country gradually flattens out into an undulating expanse of scrub and grass, broken, at intervals, by low wooded ridges and by numerous shallow ravines. To the south, the grand masses of the Nandi cliffs tower like a great wall. Their face is bare and rugged, and long spurs run out into the valley below. As the descent is continued, the trees and bush get thicker, and for the last 35 kilometres, a generally flat plateau is traversed which, in places, is very swampy and extends with an easy slope to Port Florence, the terminus of the Uganda Railway, on the Victoria lake. Kisumu, or Port Florence, is situated on the small bay of Ugowe, at the eastern extremity of the Kavirondo gulf. This bay is about 1½ kilometres across. Port Florence, with the station and offices of the railway staff, is situated upon the southern shore, while Kisumu, the head-quarters of the civil district officials, is immediately opposite, on the north side of the bay. The point of land upon which Port Florence is situated is 53 metres above lake level, while the elevation of Kisumu is 32 metres lower. Kisumu bears an evil reputation for malarial fever, and is one of the most unhealthy spots upon the lake shore. Port Florence on the other hand is high and well drained, and favourably situated with regard to the prevailing winds. It has consequently been decided to transfer the Government offices from Kisumu to Port Florence, and the erection of the necessary buildings has been for some time in progress. Port Florence is a good site for a station

(1) January and February are, as a rule, dry months, as are June and July. August is very variable as regards rainfall, and in December there is frequently a large amount of rain. In this last month, it is largely a question as to whether the autumn rainy season begins early or late.

(2) STUHLMANN. "Mit Emin Pasha im Herz von Afrika." Berlin, 1894.

VICTORIA NYANZA
PORT FLORENCE

VICTORIA NYANZA
KAVIRONDO GULF

and consists of a promontory of land running out into the lake. The soil is a mass of piscolithic ironstone, which is the prevailing formation throughout the whole extent of lake shore. This material forms a useful building stone, as, although soft when first quarried, it rapidly hardens with exposure to the air. It is used in the construction of all the new buildings. It forms an important ingredient in the rich loam which covers so large an area of the lake basin (1). Good progress is being made with the new station, both as regards the offices and the roads. Should the Uganda Railway ever realise the hopes entertained of its future, and develop an appreciable trade, Port Florence will doubtless one day become a place of considerable importance. It must always be the port through which all commerce, brought from different points on the lake, must pass for conveyance to the sea at Mombasa.

Kisumu, the present civil station, and headquarters of the Kavirondo district, consists of a few buildings, surrounded by trees, standing on a gently rising plain, covered with rich and short grass. This plain extends north to a low range of hills called Korando. This range is a spur of the Nandi mountains, which runs west for a considerable distance at some 6 to 7 kilometres from the lake shore. The plain affords excellent grazing and the numerous villages show that this portion of the district supports a considerable population. On the top of the Korando hills, a wide plateau extends for a long distance to the north. This plateau consists of a lava bed, varying in thickness from 16 to 30 metres. It is reputed to be very highly cultivated and, beyond it, the country slopes up to the Nandi plateau, covered by dense forests, containing many valuable timber trees (2).

The market at Kisumu is a curious sight. It is thronged with a good-humoured crowd of Kavirondo (3). The chief articles exposed for sale appear to be sweet potatoes and dried fish. Both sexes are entirely destitute of clothing. The women wear nothing but a fringe of small beads in front and a curious decoration, made of fibre, behind, which exactly resembles a cow's tail. The men wear a few beads, with anklets and bracelets of iron. They dress their hair in fantastic fashion and are fond of decorating it with hippopotamus teeth. Both men and women are inveterate smokers, and all carry short, straight pipes. The Kavirondo are a large tribe, but those dwelling in the vicinity of the lake have of late suffered heavily from the sleeping sickness. Although given to intertribal quarrels, they are, on the whole, peaceful and easy to govern. They employ rainmakers and medicine men, and possess considerable herds of cattle. They call themselves the Jalua. Under the very capable administration of Mr. Hobley, local trade seems to be making a good beginning among these people. They already understand the value of the rupee, and prefer to take money instead of beads, as payment for their goods. They are expert fishermen, and on this portion of the lake canoes are very numerous. These canoes are from 8 to 10 metres in length, and one metre in breadth. No nails are used in their construction and the planks are attached to one another by fibre. A hard wood called "amvule" is used. The prows are peculiar. Beyond the bow of the canoe, and on a level with the keel, a sharp, straight point projects horizontally for a metre or more. This is the "war prow," and is used for ramming

(1) The following is the analysis of a sample of this ironstone, made by Mr. Lucas, Director of the Public Works Laboratory, at Cairo.

Appearance, etc.	Analysis.	
		Per cent.
Limonite looking material, yellowish-brown to black in colour with traces of piscolithic structure.	Silica and Insoluble..	32·78
	Iron oxide with a little aluminium-oxide..	56·62
	Combined water (by difference)	10·60
	Total..	100·00

(2) Mr. Hobley, the collector of the Kavirondo district, states that the two most valuable timber trees in these forests are the Juniper and the Podocarpos. These are both conifers, the former with a red, and the latter with a white wood. Some of these trees exceed one metre in diameter.

(3) The Kavirondo on the lake belong to the Nilotic branch of this tribe and are quite distinct from those inhabiting the higher plateau, who belong to the great Bantu race.

an enemy's canoe. Upon this is lashed the "peace-prow," which turns up vertically, almost at a right angle. This last is usually decorated with feathers, or with antelope's horns. The fishing and trading canoes carry a crew of from 16 to 18 men, who sit facing the direction in which the canoe is travelling. They use short, narrow-bladed paddles. In Busoga, and in the Buvuma islands, the canoes are much larger, being sometimes 23 metres in length, with a crew of 40 men and more.

The crocodiles in the neighbourhood of the Kavirondo gulf are reputed to be especially bold and dangerous, and exact a heavy yearly toll upon the population (1).

On leaving Kisumu for the northern shores of the lake, the view, on looking back, is a very fine one. The Lambwa mountains extend along the southern shore of the gulf, though at some distance from it, while in the east, the Nandi range forms a magnificent background. The Kavirondo gulf has a length of some 70 kilometres, and a maximum width of 24 kilometres. Its average breadth, however, is much less than this, being not more than from 9 to 10 kilometres from shore to shore. The general direction from Kisumu is south-west, until the Rusinga channel is reached, when it turns sharply to the north-west. Many floating islands of papyrus dot its surface. Its depth is nowhere great, the deepest soundings obtained being rarely more than 15 to 20 metres. At 29 kilometres (2) from Port Florence, a promontory, low, rounded and grassy, rises above the flat plain which has hitherto extended along the northern shore. This plain is bare and treeless, but covered with numerous "bomas" or small villages. In the distance beyond it, stretches the line of the Korando hills, before mentioned. On the south shore of the gulf, the scenery is wild and picturesque, a broken stretch of bush-covered country extending to the Lumbwa hills. At kilometre 37, the high extinct crater of Homa, juts out into the gulf, in an imposing mass, joined to the mainland by a long, low and sandy strip of shore. At this point, the width of the channel contracts, and is not more than 9 kilometres. A little further on, to the south and south-west, the group of peaks, known as Usau, stands out, at no great distance from the shore. Of these, Ruri is the highest, and is some 600 metres above the lake level. These hills are of very irregular outline. Some of the peaks are conical in shape, while others have rounded summits. All are of volcanic origin. This part of the coast is wild and bleak looking. The country to the north is still flat, but high above water level, and stretches, in an expanse of scrub and grass, far to the north. A few kilometres further on, the straits narrow still more, and the promontory of Uyoma, ending in the low, flat-topped headland of Mtara, projects into the channel from the northern shore. Close to this point is a basalt block, which projects out of the water and is known as the "Sentinel Rock." It is the haunt of numerous water-birds. The width of the gulf here is barely 5 kilometres. Shortly after passing Mtara, the mountain range of Kasagunga, on the south coast, towers above all else, and its northern masses approach very near to the water. These mountains are said to be higher than any others bordering the entire lake. The highest peak, near the Kavirondo gulf, is Gembi, and is 800 metres in height, but further south, in the same range, the Gwasi peak attains an elevation of 1200 metres above the lake level. The outlines of these mountains are remarkable for their wildness. The summit of the range, with its succession of pointed peaks, resembles an exaggerated saw, which rises in the centre to a tall and very ragged-edged cone. In front of these hills, a flat bush-covered shore extends to the water's edge, and the whole combines to make a very striking bit of scenery. After passing these mountains from Port Florence, the mouth of the Kavirondo gulf is reached, flanked on its southern side by the large island of Rusinga. This island consists of

(1) Previous to the spring of 1903, the voyage across the lake between Port Florence and the northern station was generally made in a small steamer called the *William Mackinnon*. In rough weather, which is the rule rather than the exception, this voyage is scarcely a pleasure trip, as the accommodation is very limited, and the capacity of this steamer for rolling and pitching is unlimited.

(2) The distances given in the following pages, were obtained by noting the speed of the steamer. They have been checked and revised from the excellent chart, prepared by Commander Whitehouse, R.N., and published by the Admiralty.

a series of low hills, the highest not more than 400 metres, and is separated from the southern mainland by a narrow strip of water. The northern channel is some 5 kilometres wide, and is guarded on the right hand by a thickly-wooded bluff. On Rusinga, limestone is found, embedded between layers of volcanic ashes and detritus. It is of inferior quality, but is sufficiently good to be used in the construction of the buildings at Port Florence. To the south-west of Rusinga, and separated from it by a narrow channel, is another island, known as Mfwanganu. It is higher and more abrupt than Rusinga, and contains four or five small peaks. All these islands are inhabited by fishermen. The entrance to the gulf is cleared at 70 kilometres from Port Florence, and the open lake is reached. Two small rocks are found here, one of them, from its peculiar formation, being christened "Bridge Island." The colour of the water now changes. In the Kavirondo gulf it is dirty and muddy, but in the lake itself it is remarkably clear.

From this point to Jinja, the general course is north-westerly. To the south, no land is visible, but on the north, many reefs and small islands are found, and in the extreme distance the high country on the mainland can be faintly seen. At 50 kilometres from the Kavirondo gulf, always on a north-west course, the group of islands known as Lolui are reached. These consist of one large, and three small, low, rocky masses, covered with dense vegetation and thickly wooded. These islands, from their position, form a convenient anchorage for vessels wishing to obtain shelter from the heavy storms which so frequently occur. They lie some 50 or 60 kilometres to the south-east of Port Victoria. Off these islands, the deepest sounding yet obtained in the lake, viz., 73 metres, has been measured. On leaving Lolui, and proceeding on the same course, i.e., north-west, all land, with the exception of a few very distant islands to the north, is speedily out of sight. The resemblance to the sea is complete, and, in bad weather, this is heightened in more ways than one, as the waves, which are often of considerable height, render the voyage, to indifferent sailors, one of extreme discomfort. The next anchorage is at the island of Bugaia, some 48 kilometres north-west of the Lolui group. Bugaia covers a fairly large area, rising in a series of low round-topped hills which slope gently from the centre to the water. The higher elevations are bare of trees and are covered with short grass. The lower, as a rule, are well-wooded. Many villages are hidden away in the glens of this island and it appears to be well populated. The remains of the stone entrenchments, formerly used by the islanders during their long warfare with the Waganda, are still visible. On the flats near the shores, are extensive cultivations of millet and sweet potatoes. Banana plantations are numerous. The people appear to be prosperous and contented. They are all neatly clothed, and in this respect are in strong contrast to the Kavirondo. The lower slopes of this, and all the other neighbouring islands, are covered with an extensive outcrop of ironstone. On the hills, the soil is poorer and blocks of gneiss and quartz everywhere crop up. The shore is not swampy, but, inland, large marshes exist. Due north of Bugaia, lies the large island of Buvuma, a channel, 5 or 6 kilometres in width, separating the two. As this channel is practically landlocked it makes an excellent harbour in rough weather.

Buvuma island is one of the largest on the lake. In shape it is triangular and its area is some 450 square kilometres. The coast scenery much resembles that of Bugaia, but, in the interior are mountains, some of which are said to attain a height of over 650 metres above the lake (1). Portions of it are forested. The Buvuma have always borne the reputation of being one of the most powerful among the lake-dwelling tribes. They attacked and drove off Sir H. Stanley's expedition, when attempting to land upon the island. In former times, they possessed a large fleet of canoes and, for a long period, waged a continual warfare with the Waganda from the mainland. The latter never succeeded in conquering them.

(1) "The Uganda Protectorate" by Sir Harry Johnston, G.C.M.G., K.C.B., London, 1902.

The scenery of this portion of the Victoria Nyanza is charming and peaceful looking in its character. The calm lake, the rounded outlines of the wooded hills, the neat thatched huts, and the large groves of bananas, all combine to give an air of repose and prosperity to the scene and the traveller finds it difficult to realise that he is in Central Africa, and not in Europe.

The channel followed by boats going from Bugaia to Jinja, runs nearly due north; passing west of Buvuma and between it and the mainland. It has an average breadth of from 5 to 6 kilometres, and winds about through a chain of islands, presenting a succession of beautiful pictures. Both on these islands and on the mainland the scenery is very similar. Rounded low hills and deeply wooded valleys, border the water's edge, and behind the eastern hills, extends an open and undulating expanse of country. Some 65 kilometres north of Bugaia, the entrance to the Napoleon gulf is reached. This is a large, irregularly shaped inlet, deeply indented by small bays, one of which runs north-west, leading to the Ripon Falls and the Nile outlet, while another, of considerable size, stretches north-east. This last is known as Thruston Bay, in memory of the late Major Thruston. Between these two bays the Usoga heights stand up, some 100 to 120 metres above the lake. Many small islands dot the surface of this fine sheet of water. On the right hand, or east, stands the Fort known as Luba's. This is the spot where Major Thruston and his companions were murdered in 1897, by the mutinous Sudanese troops. To the left, a high bluff stands out prominently on the mainland and in the distance two high saddle-backed hills rise in the north-west.

The station of Jinja is situated on the right of the long bay leading to the Falls. This bay runs up for some 3 kilometres between wooded cliffs, narrowing gradually as the outlet of the Nile is approached. Jinja, the headquarters of the Busoga district, is a small station, well situated on the high cliffs which rise abruptly from the water. At this point there is a small landing stage, to which the Nile gauge is attached. The gauge itself is not a very good one, as it is difficult to read and very roughly made. It is, however, the best situated gauge on the lake, being in a completely landlocked sheet of water and well sheltered from the effect of storms or waves. As regards Egypt, this gauge is the most important register on the lake, being close to the point where the Nile has its source. The Government offices and stores are enclosed within a large rectangular stockade. There is much cultivation in the district, the principal crops being sweet potatoes, Indian corn, millet and the universal banana. The soil is very rich, being composed of the red loam which covers the crystalline rocks throughout this whole area. The view from Jinja is very fine; in one direction commanding an extensive panorama of the lake and its islands, and in another, of the fertile plateau which extends to the north and east. This district, as a whole, is flat and open, but the country has a heavy slope to the north, where lies a region of extensive swamps and dense forest. Iron ore is said to be plentiful in certain localities, and slate and copper are also found. It is said that limestone exists in some parts of the district. It has already been mentioned that the drainage of Busoga is to the north, and *away from* the lake. All the rivers which traverse it rise close to the hills which border the Victoria Nyanza, and flow through the great swamps and eventually into the Nile.

The people of this district, who are known as the Basoga, much resemble the Waganda in appearance. They are tall and dark, and many of them are fine looking men. They are expert boatmen. They wear curious head-dresses made of black and white hair (1).

Although Jinja is high above the lake level, it is the reverse of a healthy spot, and malaria is very prevalent.

The district of Busoga has suffered more heavily than any other from the sleeping sickness, with perhaps the exception of the Sessé islands. According to Mr. Grant, the

(1) Probably from the skin of the Colobus monkey.

VICTORIA NYANZA
BUGAIA ISLAND

VICTORIA NYANZA
WAGANDA CANOES

RIPON FALLS

Plan and Section

Scale 1 : 6000

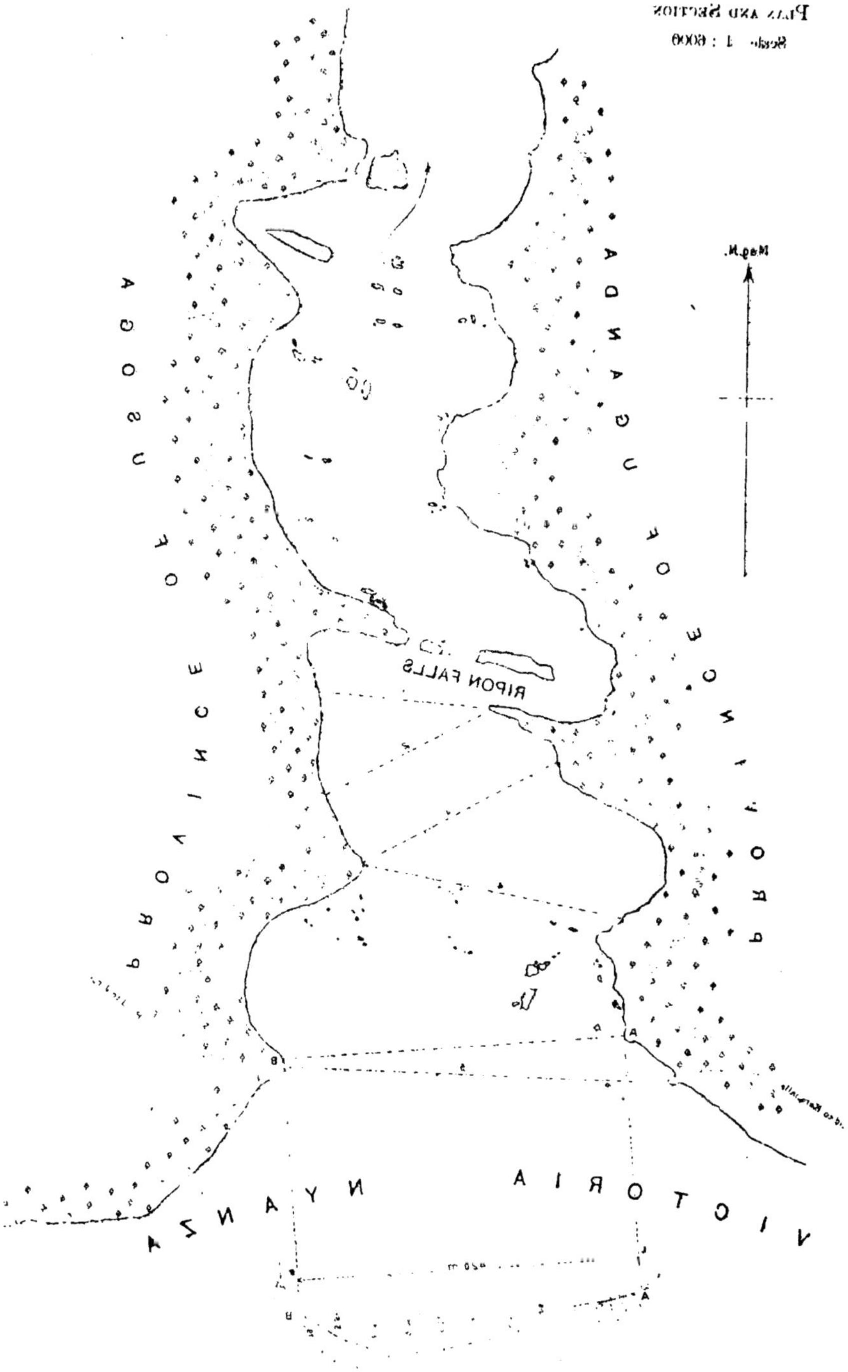

RIPON FALLS

PLAN AND SECTION

Scale 1 : 6000

PLAN I a

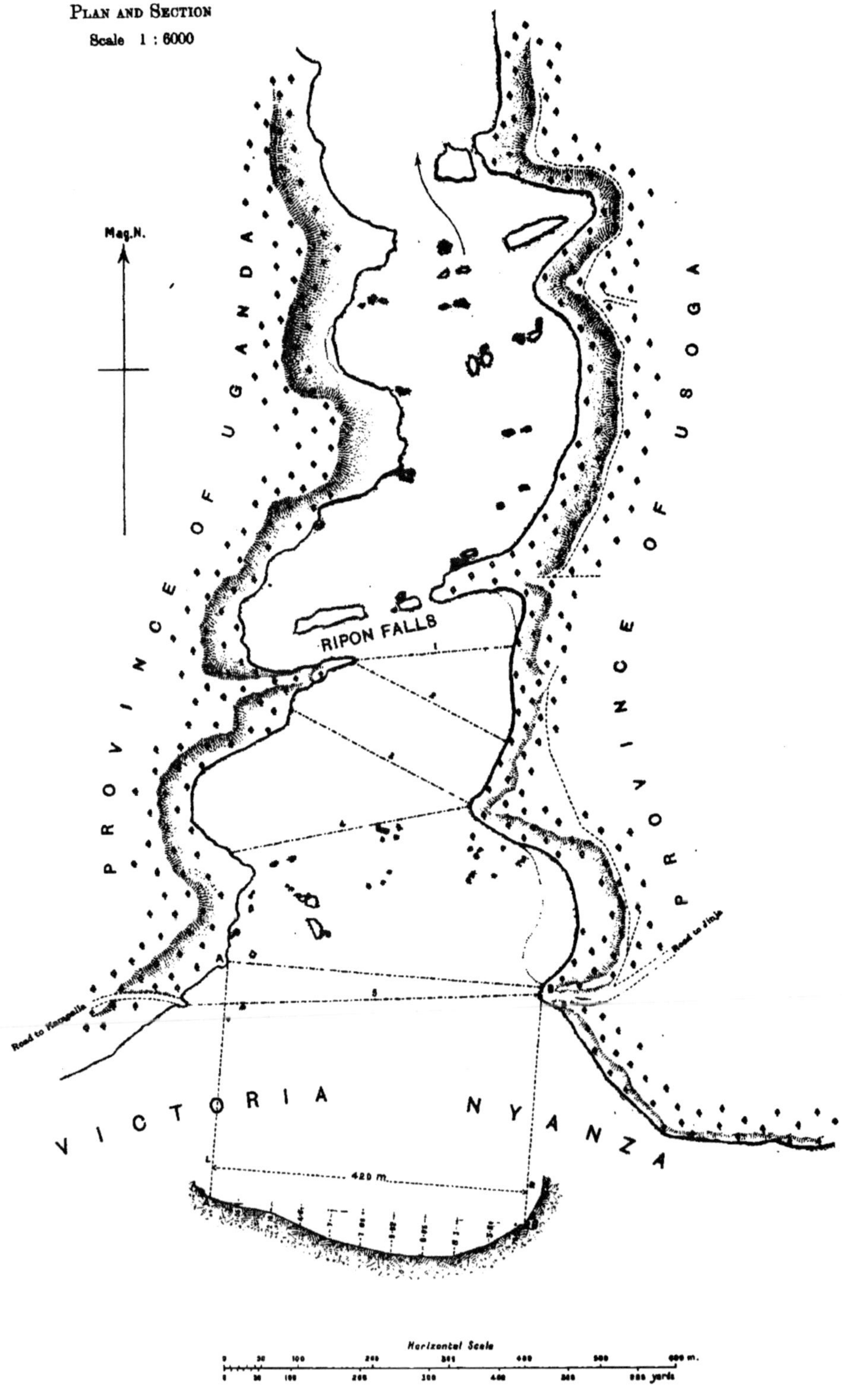

Dept. P.W.M. Cairo

RIPON FALLS - CROSS SECTIONS - 1903.

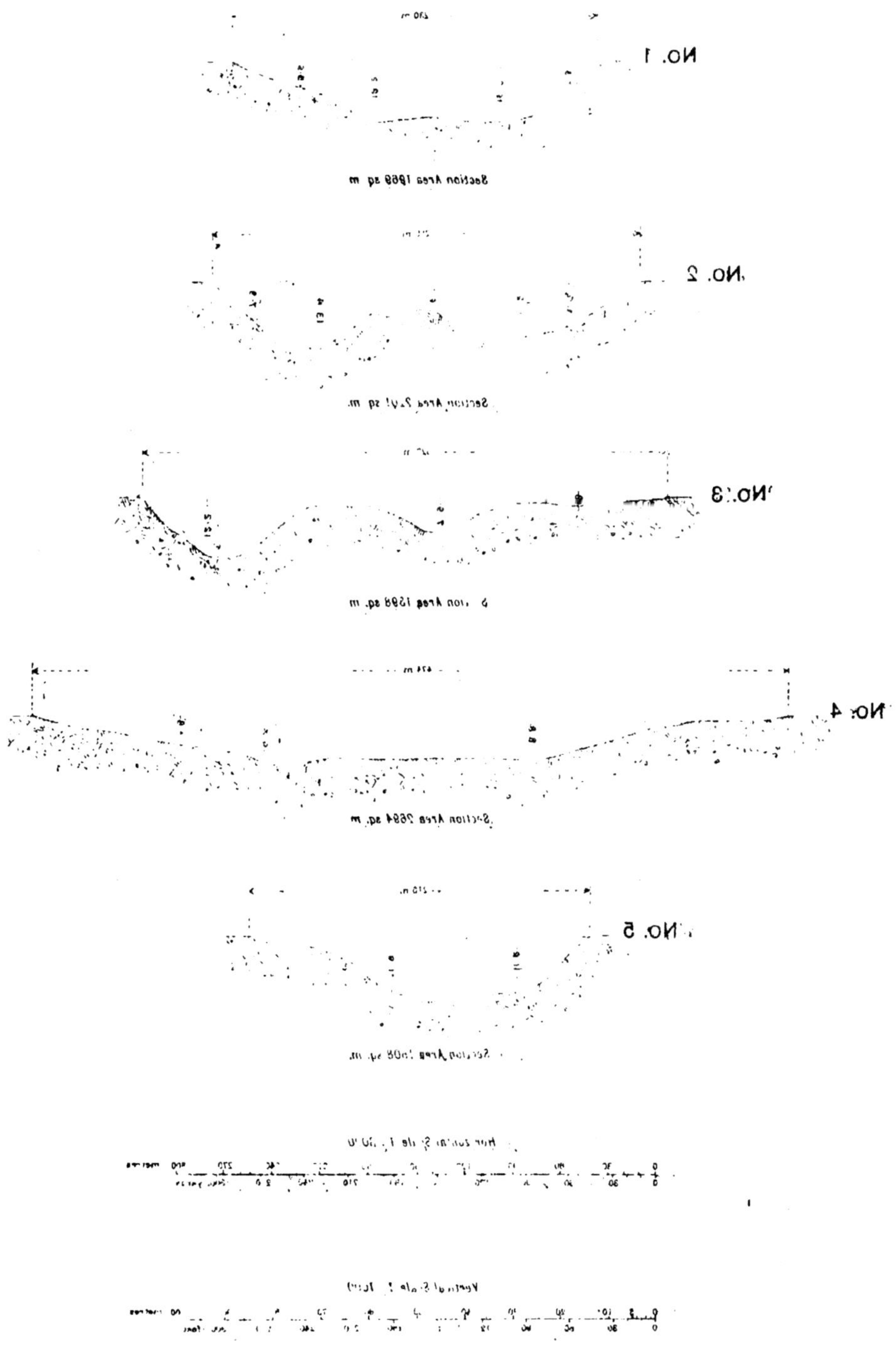

RIPON FALLS - CROSS SECTIONS - 1903.

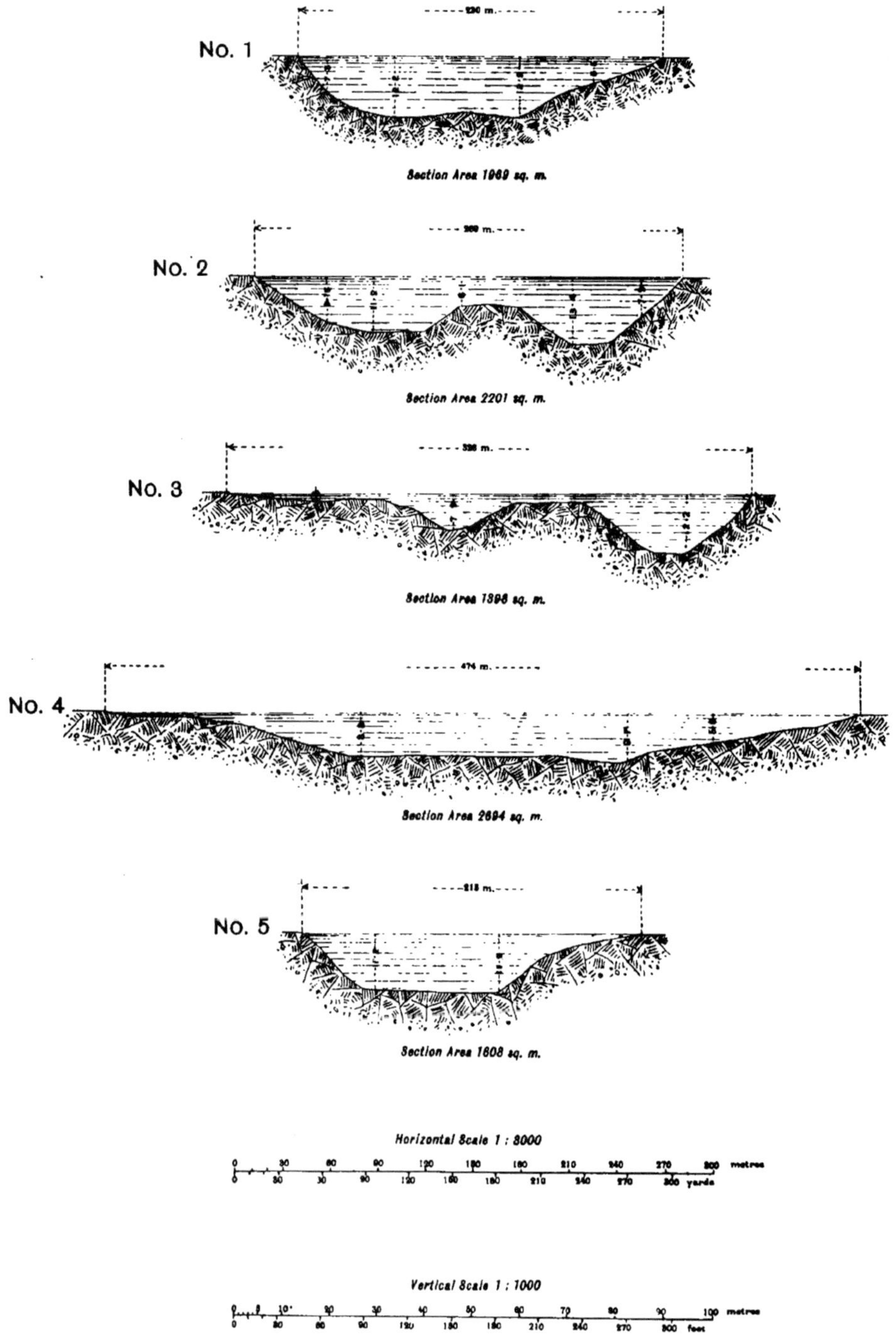

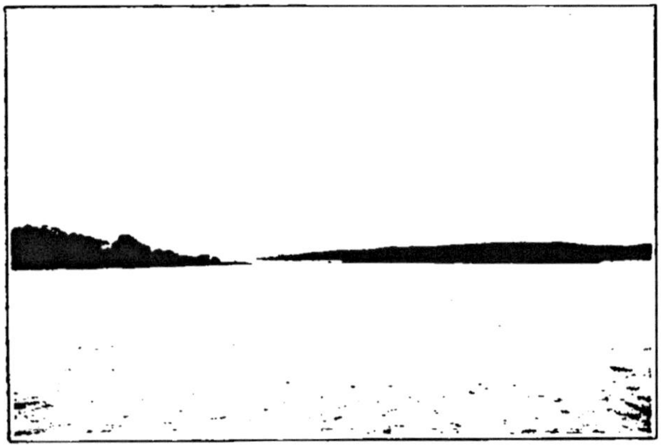

VICTORIA NYANZA
NAPOLEON GULF

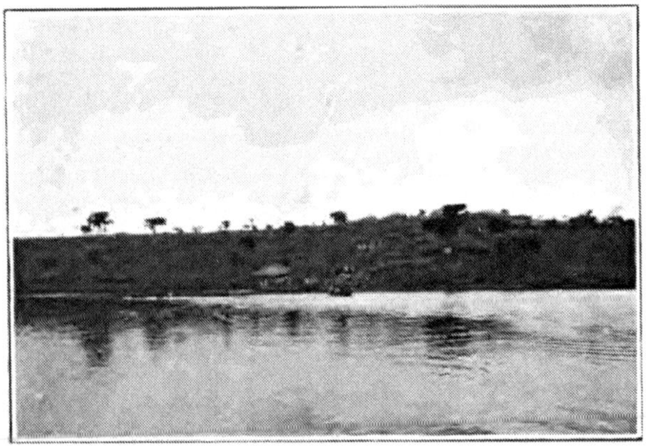

VICTORIA NYANZA
JINJA CIVIL STATION, BUSOGA DISTRICT

sub-commissioner, over 14000 people have succumbed to this disease, and in some localities from 75% to 80% of the population have died. It is said to have commenced during the great famine which prevailed thoughout the Upper Nile Valley, and the lake districts, in 1899.

A very short distance below Jinja, a distinct current, flowing north, is visible on the lake surface and the sound of the falls is distinctly heard. On rounding a high bluff, the reef of rocks which projects out of the water, upstream of the cataract, becomes visible. The channel gradually narrows, like a funnel, between high cliffs, from 60 to 70 metres above the water. The face of these cliffs is densely covered by vegetation, and, on the summit, with bush and forest. The red soil of which they are composed gives a dash of brillant colour to the generally sombre tints of the landscape. The sharp-edged reefs stand out, like gray sentinels, above the surface of the water. The river glides down to the barrier in a glassy expanse, until it thunders over the fall in three separate channels, parted by rocky ridges, and breaks, below the leap, into a white and foaming expanse of raging and seething water. The whole scene is of singular beauty, and wild to an extreme degree. It is one of the most beautiful in the whole Protectorate, and, indeed, is one which would be hard to surpass anywhere. Looking downstream from the falls, the picture is, if possible, even more beautiful. The Nile flows northward in a deep gorge, formed by wooded cliffs, on either side. Through this the river tears, in a succession of swirling rapids. The colour of the water is a deep blue, almost approaching a purple, but its surface is broken into endless threads by the snow-white streaks of foam which indicate the existence of the rocks. Occasional small islands separate it into one or more channels, and the dark-green outline of the wooded highlands forms an effective frame. No one who has visited the Ripon Falls is likely to forget them, as, apart from the sentiment associated with the spot, as being the source of the Nile, the landscape itself is so exceptionally beautiful that it must impress itself deeply on the memory.

The accompanying plan and cross sections, give a good general idea of the falls themselves, and the channel above and below them (1).

Some 370 metres upstream of the ridge of rocks (2), the width of the channel is 515 metres, with a maximum depth of 6 metres. It quickly narrows after passing this ridge, to 355 metres, while the depth increases to 13 metres. At this point, the stream divides, the strongest and deepest following the eastern shore. Between these two streams is a shoal, 70 metres in width, of comparatively still water. The depth here is not more than 1.5 metres. Rather less than 60 metres above the actual fall, a long, narrow point of rock juts out from the western branch, forcing the water on towards the further shore, but a little lower down, another and larger spur projects from the eastern branch which drives the stream back again, and across the channel. The main volume of water consequently passes over the falls by the western opening. The reef which forms the actual fall has three passages by which the water passes over. That on the west is the largest, being 70 metres in width, while the central opening is 40 metres wide, and the eastern, and smallest, only 17 metres. The actual drop is a clear fall, of five metres, but what the depth of water is, passing over the crest, it is impossible to say. Below the fall, the water swings sharply to the east bank, round a rocky projection, only to be diverted, equally sharply, back to the west again. Its general course at this point is north, and the average width of the channel, for some distance, is 250 metres. The slope is very heavy, and the rapids continue as far as the river can be traced. The section, as observed in connection with the discharge measurements of the 22nd of January 1903, was taken 400 metres above the falls,

(1) The survey of this site was made at my request, by Sir George Whitehouse, K.C.B., the Chief Engineer of the Uganda Railway.

(2) These rocks are at the same distance, i.e., 370 metres above the falls.

and 100 metres upstream of the first reef. The measured width, at this point, was 406.9 metres. The greatest depth of water here was 9.20 metres, but, on the west side of the channel, the section was comparatively a shallow one. The greatest mean velocity, obtained in any one section, was 0.350 metres per second, and the lowest, 0.041 metres per second. The mean worked out to 0.237 metres per second. The discharge of the river was 548 cubic metres per second, with the Jinja gauge registering a height of 2ft. 7in., or 0.79 metres.

As the only boats available in this part of the lake were extremely crank "dug-out" canoes, made from a single log, considerable care had to be observed in stretching the rope across and in attaching the canoes to it. The Basoga boatmen are experts in their trade, but, had any of the fastenings given way while making the measurements in the strong stream, the canoe must inevitably have been carried over the falls. This part of the river swarms with crocodiles.

With regard to the question as to whether the Ripon Falls are a suitable site for a regulating work, putting other considerations for the moment aside, it may be briefly stated that there ought to be comparatively little difficulty in barring the river across at this point. The rock is a hard and compact diorite, and appears to be sound and suitable for such a work. The river could be turned through one of the openings, while the masonry in the others was in progress. When this portion of the work was completed, the river could be passed through the sluices and the remaining opening similarly closed. To lower the reef would be rather more difficult, as it would not be so easy to manage the diversion of the stream, and a considerable amount of blasting would be necessary in the channel below, to ensure a clear outfall for the water. Still, even to this proceeding, there would be no insuperable difficulties.

In making for Entebbé, from Jinja, the same channel, i.e. the Buvuma passage, as was used in the voyage from Bugaia, is followed for a distance of 40 kilometres. At this point, the Roseberry channel is reached. This passage is a broad sheet of water, from 6 to 8 kilometres in width. The mainland of Uganda is on the right hand, and a continuous chain of islands protects it from the open water on the left. The general direction is south-west. This channel is so well sheltered that nothing but a strong south-westerly breeze could raise a sea in it. The islands on the left all form a portion of the Buvuma archipelago, but for revenue purposes, they are now classed with those of the Sessé group. The scenery of the Roseberry channel is monotonous. Bay alternates with headland, in wearisome regularity. The hills are low, flat-topped and bare, without any bold or striking outlines. None of them are more than 100 metres above the lake. The shores of the bays and inlets are all well wooded. This rather bleak looking country extends back from the lake shore, in a band of some 7 or 8 kilometres in width. Beyond this is a highly cultivated and thickly populated area. In the vicinity of the lake there is but little marsh, but in the valleys inland, extensive swamps extend. After following the Roseberry channel for some 55 kilometres, it widens out and is called the Damba channel; from the large island of that name to the east. Opposite to this point, the hills on the mainland rise up more abruptly from the water and the rocks crop up on their slopes, through the grass. There are no landing places in this portion of the coast. The general direction now is due west and, further on, the mainland becomes flatter and the hills recede from the lake. One curious feature of this scenery is the extraordinary number and size of the anthills. They cover these hills right up to their summits. The Damba island has a low coast line, but in the interior, the hills rise to a considerable height. On arriving opposite to the mouth of the Murchison gulf, the line of islands left of the channel ceases, and open water stretches to the horizon. Only in the extreme south can the faint outlines of the Sessé islands be seen. The Murchison gulf, or bay, extends inland from the lake for a distance of some 24 kilometres. The shores in parts are very swampy and fringed with a thick belt of papyrus. On either side of it, the

VICTORIA NYANZA
RIPON FALLS, THE SOURCE OF THE WHITE NILE

VICTORIA NYANZA
VIEW LOOKING DOWNSTREAM FROM RIPON FALLS

Pl. V

RIPON FALLS
FROM A PHOTOGRAPH BY HERBERT SAMUEL, Esq., M.P.

fine weather, when the lake is calm, the glassy surface of the water reflects the colours of the brilliant sky above, and each reef and island is mirrored with perfect accuracy. The deep green foliage makes a lovely foreground and, as a rule, the views of the lake are framed between groups of beautiful forest trees, or are seen through a vista of the feathery "Raphia" palms. Beautiful as Entebbé is, it has, however, its drawbacks. The climate at all seasons is damp and hot, and the place can hardly be considered as a sanatorium. Although the chief rainy seasons are in the spring and autumn, there are few days in the year when rain does not fall. Everything, even indoors, speedily becomes covered with a white mould, and white ants are a pest. Earthquakes are very numerous, and the locality is subject to frequent and very violent thunderstorms. These storms generally occur at night, and once seen are not easily forgotten. They generally commence with a strong gust of wind which bends the tree tops and raises a wall of dust and sand in its course. This is followed by the thunder which keeps up a prolonged roll, varied at times by a terrific crash, and the flashes of lightning follow one another with such startling rapidity that the glare is almost continuous. These flashes appear to be in every quarter of the sky at the same time (1). Meanwhile, the rain comes down in a solid wall, and this avalanche of water, lighted up by the blue flashes of the lightning, produces a most weird scenic effect. Such storms are extremely dangerous, and the lightning has been known to pass right through the thatched roof of a house, and set fire to objects in the room below. In this manner, one of the military offices at Entebbé was, not long ago, burnt to the ground.

The Botanical Gardens lie to the north-east of the station, and are well worth a visit. They cover an area of some 200 acres, upon the slope of the hill, overlooking a small bay. This was once all forest, and is now being cleared as required. The soil of these gardens is composed of leaf-mould, mixed with decomposed rock, and is the richest loam possible to imagine. The gardens are beautifully laid out, and contain a fine collection of trees, shrubs and plants. Mr. Mahon, the Director, is experimenting in the cultivation of different tropical products, such as cocoa, coffee, tea and the different kinds of rubber-bearing trees. All these, and there are many varieties, appear to be succeeding well. Fruits in profusion are grown, such as pine apple, mango, paw paw, passion fruit and the different kinds of banana. English roses and vegetables of all kinds grow luxuriantly, but the white ants do considerable damage, more especially to the eucalypti. In these gardens, nearly all the varieties of forest trees met with in the Protectorate are to be found (2).

Neither the Podocarpus, nor the Juniper, thrive well at Entebbé, as these conifers do not flourish at a lower elevation than 1700 metres above the sea. One of the commonest and the most beautiful of the Uganda forest trees is the "Piptadinia Africana," of which there are many fine specimens in Entebbé. This is a lovely tree, growing in a single, straight boll to a great height, and throwing out large buttresses at the base. Its striking feature is the mass of chocolate-coloured flowers which cover its upper foliage. It is a good timber tree. The Incense tree, "Pachylobus," is common, and its timber also, is of good quality. The incense is made from the bark. The "Canarium" and the "Sapota" are frequently met with. The former yields good timber, but the latter does not. All round the northern lake shore, the "Raphia" palm grows in profusion. It is a very graceful variety. Fibre is made from the young trees. In some of the forests, the indiarubber creeper, "Landolphia," is common. There are many kinds of "Ficus." That variety from which the bark cloth is obtained, is plentiful both in Uganda and in Busoga. The process of making the cloth is simple. The Waganda strip the bark from the trunk in large sheets, and hammer it out until it becomes quite pliable. The girdling appears to have

(1) In January 1903, during a storm at Entebbé, 26 flashes of lightning were counted in one minute, and this after the first violence of the storm had passed.

(2) The Uganda forests, as regards the different species of trees and creepers found in them, much resemble those of the Congo.

no injurious effect upon the tree, and the stripping takes place when the foliage is at its prime. The best bark is obtained from the Uganda district, and the trees used are nearly always raised in gardens. The wild tree is rarely made use of. It is propagated by cuttings. This is a handsome tree, some ten metres in height, and affords excellent shade.

Among other beautiful shrubs in these gardens is the Congo coffee tree. This is a most lovely variety, with masses of dazzling white flowers, and very dark green leaves. It is much larger than either the Indian or the Uganda coffee plant. The coffee grown in suitable localities in the Protectorate, is very good. That produced in the Sessé islands is remarkable for its delicious fragrance and taste. Most of this coffee is exported to Italy by a Milanese firm ([1]).

The Entebbé lake gauge is erected in the small bay below the Botanical Gardens. The place selected is not absolutely perfect, as, although sheltered from storms, a swell, even in calm weather, runs up the bay and causes a variation in the readings. It would be difficult, however, to find a better place anywhere near the station, and the gauge is protected by a fringe of high reeds and tall ambatch.

The soil of the country round Entebbé is ironstone, right up to the summit of the highest hills. This again, is covered by a rich red loam, or marl. Nowhere does the rock appear on the surface. The swamps contain a blue plastic clay, possibly a washing from the ironstone.

Proceeding south, by boat, from Entebbé, the western shore of the lake is closely followed. For a considerable distance beyond the promontory upon which the station is built, wide flats and marshes extend. These marshes are full of papyrus and ambatch and, at this point, the coast line is very broken and indented. Twenty-four kilometres south-west of Entebbé, what is known as the Salisbury channel is entered. This is a broad stretch of water, perhaps 15 to 18 kilometres in width, running between the western mainland and the Sessé islands. The coast continues low and swampy, and the hills here are at a considerable distance from the lake. The flats contain marshes of large extent. This is the basin of the Katonga river, which runs into the lake, some 50 kilometres south of Entebbé. It enters near the wooded island of Bunjako, in latitude 0° 4′ south. After passing the estuary of the Katonga, the western coast-line rises, and is marked by a line of low flat-topped hills, from 100 to 120 metres above the water. Between these hills, a broad plateau extends, and a thick belt of dense forest extends parallel to the lake, at a few kilometres distance, from the Katonga to the Ruizi river mouth. South of the Katonga, the coast-line is fairly straight. There are few bays, and those existing are of small size. The cliffs, as a rule, come down to the water, and there is but little foreshore, although occasional wooded flats are met with. The Sessé islands flank the eastern boundary of the Salisbury channel. This is the largest group of islands in the lake. It consists of 62 islands, 42 of which are inhabited ([2]). In the Salisbury channel, the nearest islands are those of Lulamba and Buvu. Neither of these is of large extent. Both are low and well forested, rising gently from the coast, which is indented by many small bays and creeks. On the latter is a small hill, ending in a picturesque bluff, some 150 metres above the water. The channel at this point is not more than 10 or 11 kilometres in width. At some 60 kilometres from Entebbé, the largest island in the Sessé group is passed. This island is called Bugala, and next to Buvuma, covers the greatest area of any island lying within the British territory. It approaches to within five kilometres of the mainland, making a narrow channel called Bugoma. The shore of the island, in the northern end,

([1]) The greater part of the foregoing information, was obtained from Mr. Mahon, the Director of these gardens. He very kindly devoted an afternoon to showing me over them. W.E.G.

([2]) This statement is made on the authority of Mr. Martin, the Collector of Entebbé, under whose charge these islands are placed.

land is low, until its further end is reached, where hills border its northern shores. There are two very small islands near the outlet ([1]). After passing the bluff known as Murchison Point, the rounded hills upon which Entebbé stands are clearly visible. The coast here is low, and thickly wooded with masses of "Raphia" palms. Another small bay, called Kissubi, extends inland for some 5 kilometres, and then the landing stage of Entebbé, 103 kilometres from Jinja, is arrived at.

Entebbé, or, as it was formerly called, Port Alice, is the residence of the Commissioner of the Uganda Protectorate, and the headquarters of the Government. The situation of the station is a good one, on a hill, or rather two hills, forming a peninsula, surrounded upon three sides by the lake. The highest point is 113 metres above water level. The promontory occupied by Entebbé, is joined to the mainland by a low strip of land, some 5 kilometres in width. North-west of the station hill is another and higher elevation, upon which Sir H. Colville's old fortifications were erected. The outline of these works can still be traced, and, from this point, an extensive view is obtained, both of the lake itself and of the mainland. The landscape here is very typical of the Uganda district. In every direction, as far as the eye can see, an expanse of flat, or rounded, hills, perhaps 100 metres high, alternating with wide valleys, extends. The summits of these hills are covered with bush and grass and their slopes by continuous plantations of bananas. The valleys are well wooded and invariably contain wide swamps, filled by a dense growth of papyrus and reeds. Except in the immediate vicinity of the lake, there is scarcely a square mile of level ground in the district. It is very thickly populated, and the villages surrounded by cultivation dot the hill sides. The soil is extremely rich and this district is one of the most fertile and prosperous in the whole Protectorate.

The station of Entebbé is prettily laid out, with broad, well-kept roads running between avenues of trees. The Residency and the house of the Commandant, are situated upon the high land overlooking the lake, each in extensive grounds and commanding lovely views. The houses occupied by the other officials, are scattered about upon the slopes, up to a height of 80 metres above the lake. These houses have all either thatched, or corrugated iron roofs, and each stands in its own enclosure, surrounded by a high hedge. The general appearance of the station much resembles that of an Indian cantonment. Besides the Government offices and stores, there is a church, an hotel, and a fair number of shops and trading stores, chiefly owned by Parsee and Indian merchants([2]). A new hospital is in course of construction upon the highest point above the lake ([3]). Near the public gardens are situated the cricket ground and tennis courts. It is intended to bring the water supply of Entebbé from Malin Point, a long tongue of land stretching out into the lake, south of the station. Upon this point, the French mission buildings are situated. A fine, straight and broad road leads from Entebbé to Kampala. The distance between the two places is some 30 kilometres. At the port of embarkation, a small, stone quay has been built, and a winding road ascends through beautiful forest trees to the station. Wherever the hill sides have been left untouched they are covered with dense vegetation. In the quarter occupied by the town, this has been cleared away, but continual work is required to keep down the undergrowth, which, in this damp, tropical heat, springs up with extraordinary rapidity. As at Port Florence, ironstone is much used in the masonry of the buildings.

It is difficult to describe the beauty of the views obtainable from Entebbé. Looking over the lake, the Sessé islands, in many irregular shapes, break the horizon to the south and south-west. To the east, and nearer, the Damba and Korne islands stand out, while between the two groups, to the south-east, open water stretches, apparently in all directions. In

([1]) Kampala, or Mengo, the residence of the King of Uganda, and the headquarters of the Church of England, and Roman Catholic Missions is situated inland of this bay, at a distance of some 12 kilometres from its southern shore.

([2]) There are a few German and Italian traders in Entebbé.

([3]) A special hospital has been erected for the treatment of patients suffering from the sleeping sickness, and attached to this is the laboratory where Dr. Castellani conducts his researches, regarding the bacillus of this disease.

RIPON FALLS
FROM A PHOTOGRAPH BY HERBERT SAMUEL, Esq., M.P.

March 1897, gives its width, at the point where it is joined by the Akanyaru, as 43 metres; a depth varying from 1·75 to 3·75 metres, and an approximate discharge of between 40 and 50 cubic metres per second.

The Akanyaru is reported to be in volume nearly as large as the Nyavarongo.

Two measurements exist of the Ruvuvu, one made by Baumann, in September 1892, at the Ruanilo ford. The width was 35 metres, the depth 3 metres, and the discharge 250 metres cube per second; the river being then in partial flood. The other measurement was made by Ramsay, in March 1897, at its junction with the Nyavarongo. The width at this point was 29 metres, the depth 5·5 metres, and the velocity 0·92 metres per second; corresponding to a discharge of some 150 metres cube per second. The Ruvuvu has two main tributaries, the Luvironja and the Muwaresi, both of which rise to the south, in the Kangosi hills which form the eastern boundary of Lake Tanganyika (1).

Downstream of the junction of the Nyavarongo and the Ruvuvu, the Kagera flows northwards, along the line of the great fault, for some 170 kilometres, falling 20 metres in this distance. Throughout a great portion of its course here, it passes through a succession of very large swamps, which, again, are connected with the marshy lakes of Ikemi and Kasingeni. Its breadth is given as varying from 2 to 5 kilometres and, in flood, it submerges the valley. These lakes and swamps most probably act as a regulating force, and reduce its discharge considerably At Latoma, latitude 1° 2′ south, it turns abruptly to the east, and flows in this direction for another 130 kilometres, eventually discharging into Lake Victoria, about latitude 0° 55′ south. In this portion of its course, its basin is bounded to the north by the Ruampara mountains, and it is described by Langfeld a sflowing in a series of rapids, through a valley, from 15 to 20 kilometres in breadth and bounded by high hills as far as Kitangulé. Below this point, it crosses a level, alluvial plain, into which it has deeply cut its channel, having banks 20 metres high which reduce in height as the lake is approached. In August 1894, Scott Elliott measured the Kagera at Latoma, as having a channel 36·5 metres wide, and a velocity of 1 metre per second. He describes it as "very deep." Assuming that its depth was 8 metres, this would give a discharge of 300 metres cube per second. At Kitangulé, the width is given as from 60 to 70 metres, the depth from 9 to 11 metres, and the velocity varying from 1·5 to 2 metres per second, between February and April (2). These data work out to a minimum discharge of 600 metres cube per second, and a maximum of 1500 metres cube per second. In October 1892, Count Von Schweinitz gives the width as varying between 80 and 100 metres, and the depth from 10 to 12 metres. The velocity, he describes as "rapid" (3). Assuming this velocity to be 1·5 metres per second, the discharge would be about 1500 cubic metres per second. The latest discharge of the Kagera was measured by Colonel Delmé Radcliffe, of the Anglo-German boundary Commission, on the 26th February 1903. The site of the discharge was within ten kilometres of the mouth. The width of the section was 105 metres, the greatest depth 7 metres, the greatest velocity 0·526 metres per second, and the discharge 143 metres cube per second. Colonel Radcliffe considered this to be nearly a minimum discharge. The discharge of the Kagera may then be considered as varying between 140, and 1500 metres cube per second. Probably, were it not for the loss of water which must occur in the long length of its channel which passes through the marshes and lakes, the volume in flood would be considerably greater (4).

No note upon the Victoria Nyanza would be complete without some reference to the steady fall in the levels which is alleged to have occurred during the last 20 or 30 years. The subject is one of great interest, more particularly to Egypt, whose main source of water supply is drawn from this lake for many months of the year. That there has been a fall

(1) Baumann.
(2) Fitzner, from data compiled from writings of Speke. Grant, Stanley, Stuhlmann and von Trotha.
(3) "Uber eine Fahrt auf dem Kagera" Deutsch Kol-Blatt, 1893.
(4) Mr. Lionel Decle informed me that when he visited the Ruvuvu in 1900 it was much blocked by "sudd". [W.E.G.]

for several years is undoubted. Whether this lowering of the levels is but a temporary one, due in great manner to a failure of rainfall over the catchment basin, or whether it is a slow, but steady, shrinkage of the water surface, similar to that which is stated to have occurred in others of the Central African lakes, is a question which is very difficult to answer. The consensus of opinion among the officials of the district is in favour of the latter hypothesis. At the same time, it must be remembered that, except for the gauges which now record the daily rise and fall of the water levels, and which have only existed for a very few years, no definite records exist to prove the difference, if any, between the former and the present, mean level of the lake.

A summary of the information collected on the spot, in January and February 1903, is given below ([1]). To this may be added the testimony of Stanley, Stuhlmann, Baumann, and others, but the evidence given is, in some instances, rather conflicting. There is not doubt that, during the last 7 years, there has been a decided lowering of the lake levels, but during this period, the rainfall was much below the average and, in the northern half of the lake, in 1899, failed almost completely. It must always be borne in mind when discussing this question, that the period of time, during which this lake has been known to Europeans, is not a long one, and is nothing in comparison to the time usually required by nature when completely changing the face of a large portion of a continent. It is true that, in certain of the other lakes, there has been a lowering of the water levels. The shrinkage of Lakes Albert Edward and Albert can, as it has been endeavoured to show, be explained from natural causes, and in the case of the lakes in the eastern "Rift" valley, it is possible that the extraordinary variations in their levels, if substantiated, are due to slight tilting of the "Rift" valley floor ([2]). In the case of Lake Victoria Nyanza, no such explanations are possible and, if there is a permanent fall, it can only be accounted for, either by a general reduction in the annual rainfall, or by the lowering of the bar at the Ripon Falls. A careful examination of the last-named site showed no signs of any degradation of this ridge. The rock is hard and compact, and shows no signs of any special wear, beyond that due to the gradual action of water. That this ridge must be lowered in time, is no doubt true, but the process must be extremely slow and can in no way account for the very considerable fall which is reported to have taken place in recent years. It is difficult then not to arrive at the conclusion that this fall is not a permanent one, and will, should another period of heavy rainfall set in, disappear, and the lake rise to its former level ([3]).

Before leaving this subject, it may be mentioned that Captain Lyons, the Director General of Surveys in Egypt, himself a geologist of repute, has been studying the question in connection with the formation of the lake plateau, and also with reference to the remark-

([1]) (*a*) Père Bresson, of the French Mission at Entebbé, states there had been a considerable lowering of the levels in Kisubi bay (between Entebbé and Murchison gulf) and that the lake area had been reduced by a width of from 7 to 10 metres, during the last seven or eight years.

(*b*) Mr. Pordage, of the Uganda Public Works Department, pointed out that the reef of rocks, a short distance from the shore at Entebbé, was covered in 1896; while in 1903, it was 0·16 metres out of water.

(*c*) Mr. Martin, the Collector of Entebbé, who has known this lake since 1889, stated the following : "At Kisumu, there are" "now villages and pasture, where, when he first saw the lake, it was all water. He is of opinion that the rainfall throughout the" "catchment basin is getting less. Places which used to be swamps are now dry land. At the Ripon Falls, the water surface" "used to cover a horizontal width greater, by 10 metres, than it does now. As the land slopes sharply from the water here, this" "would mean a vertical height of at least 1·5 metres. On the large Sessé island, the Sabala Point, in the south-west corner, is" "now dry land. Formerly the natives used to cross it in canoes."

There were also once two small islands, a little distance from the larger one, which are now connected with it. Between the islands of Kaianja and Lulamba, there was formely a channel, through which canoes used to pass. This no longer exists, and the two form one island.

(*d*) Lastly, there is the statement of Mr. McAllister, sub-commissioner of the Nile Province, quoted in a former report (Egypt, No. 2, 1901,) that the French Fathers at Muanza, in the south of the lake, had a register, showing, from marks on the rocks, that there has been a fall of some 2·4 metres during the last 25 years.

([2]) Lakes Naivasha, El Menteita, and Baringo are all said to have fallen, while Nakuro, on the contrary, has risen in level.

([3]) Since the above was written, information has been received, which goes to bear out this conclusion. Mr. Pordage, of the Uganda Service, arrived in Cairo on the 19th December 1903, having left Uganda in early October. He stated that the lake had risen so high, that the reef (mentioned in Appendix III, p. 24,) at Entebbé, was covered to a depth of nearly one metre, and that the water had risen, at the Entebbé quay, to within 0·50 metres of the top. This quay was designed to stand 1·8 metres above an ordinary maximum level. He further stated that, everywhere, the land gained from the lake in the last few years had been flooded.

able, and apparently inexplicable, results recorded by the different lake gauges, during the short period of their existence ([1]). What puzzled every one who made a study of these gauges, was the extraordinary difference between the lake levels, as recorded at Entebbé, and those at Kisumu and Jinja. When the water level fell at these last two places, at Entebbé it steadily rose! Captain Lyons is of opinion that the land at Entebbé sank slightly, from an earth movement, during the years 1898 and 1899, when this difference occurred, but that the movement did not affect the Napoleon gulf and Jinja, nor the Kavirondo gulf and Kisumu. Again, in 1901, a rise was shown on the Entebbé gauge, some 0.30 metres higher than that at either Jinja or Kisumu. This would certainly look as if something unusual had happened at the former place. The Entebbé gauge is in a sheltered spot, where it cannot be disturbed by canoes, or by fishermen. It is, moreover, carefully watched and read by Mr. Mahon, the Superintendent of the Botanical Gardens. Commander Whitehouse, in his note, verifies the fact that, at the Kisumu gauge, during this period, there was no fall, while the Entebbé gauge was rising.

From the data available, Captain Lyons puts forward the theory that there has been a local, interrupted earth movement at Entebbé, which has disturbed the gauge records and rendered them valueless for recording the oscillations of the lake level. It is difficult to account for what happened in any other way, as the Kisumu and Jinja gauges do correspond, and apparently afford a reliable register of the rise and fall ([2]).

The general results go to show that the maximum annual oscillation of the lake is from 1 to 3 feet, (0.30 to 0.90 metres) and that, during the last seven years, there has been a fall, amounting to 0.76 metres, in the *average* levels of the lake. Nothing, however, proves that this fall is a permanent one. On the contrary, a study of the rainfall and available data, shows that:—

The year 1878 was one of high level.

From 1880 to 1890, the level was falling.

In 1892 and 1895, it was again high ([3]).

From 1896 to 1902, there has been a steady fall.

All these periods correspond fairly well with the amount of the annual rainfall, as far as this is known ([4]).

The last question to be considered is that of the relations between the amount of water entering the lake annually, the amount drawn off by the Nile at the Ripon Falls, and the quantity lost yearly by evaporation. It has already been explained how insufficient are the existing data with regard to the rainfall in the vicinity of this lake, and how variable is its distribution throughout the vast area of country comprised within its catchment basin. No accurate estimate of the quantity of water annually added to the lake is consequently possible. Nevertheless, an attempt at such calculations may be made, which, even with the limited knowledge available, may be of interest, and which, moreover, will, in all probability, err on the side of being below, rather than above the actual figure. A reference to pages 13 and 14 of this report, will show that the mean annual rainfall, as far as is known, is, at the north end of the lake, over 1.2 metres, and on the south and west, over 2.0 metres. Consequently, for the purposes of the present calculation, it may be assumed that it is not less than 1.25 metres ([5]) throughout the whole lake area.

([1]) Captain Lyons's note, which is of great interest, is printed as an appendix to this Report, as is another note by Commander Whitehouse, R.N., on the same subject.

([2]) The difference between the registers of Jinja and Kisumu, in December 1901, was apparently inexplicable, until it was discovered that the officials had themselves *lowered* the former gauge, by 0.28 metres, and had forgotten, either to mention the fact, or to register the change in their records.

([3]) There is no good record of the years 1893 and 1894.

([4]) Captain Lyons's study of the rainfall and gauges on Lake Victoria, has produced a very interesting fact, viz. that upon the intensity of the rainfall in the months of November and December depends the mean height of the lake in the year following. The maximum level is generally reached in July, and the rainfall statistics go to prove that, if there was heavy rain in the catchment basin in November and December, of any one year, the mean of the whole year following would probably show an increase.

([5]) 1.25 metres equals 50 inches.

The catchment area, excluding the lake, is 172000 square kilometres, and of the lake itself, 68000 square kilometres.

The question of the "run off," i.e., the proportion of the rainfall which runs off into the rivers, etc., must next be considered. A considerable area of the basin is under forest, but, again, a large tract, particularly to the south and south-east, is said to be sparsely wooded. In thickly wooded countries, it is customary to assume that 25% of the rain which falls on the surface is carried off by the streams and drainage lines. In thinly wooded country, the proportion is greater. It will then be safe to assume that at least, 25% of the total annual rainfall enters the lake.

The calculation thus becomes :—

(i) In catchment basin = 172000 square kilom. $\times \overset{\text{Metres}}{1.25} \times \frac{25}{100}$

(ii) On the lake surface = 68000 „ „ $\times$ 1.25

Therefore (i) = 53750,000,000 metres cube.

(ii) = 85000,000,000 „ „

Total 138750,000,000 metres cube.

This represents the total amount of water that annually enters the lake, in an average year.

The next calculation is that of the amount of water annually drawn off by the Nile in a year of mean supply. According to Mr. Craig's calculation, the mean discharge of the Victoria Nile, at the Ripon Falls, is 575 cubic metres per second. This is equivalent to a daily discharge of 49,700,000 metres cube, or to an annual amount of 18140,000,000 metres cube.

The proportion of water drawn off is small as compared to that entering the lake, being only about 13% of the above amount.

The question next to be considered is, what becomes of the remainder, i. e., 87% ?

In order to solve this, it is necessary to study the gauge registers which record the daily rise and fall of the lake level. For this purpose, the Kisumu gauge has been selected, as presenting the most unbroken, and the most satisfactory, record.

Taking account of the returns for the last eight years, i.e., from 1896 to 1903, but omitting 1897 and 1898, the mean annual range of the lake for the whole period is 0.66 metres (¹). Owing to the mutiny, the returns for 1897 and 1898 are incomplete.

The maximum rise, during this period, was in 1901, when it was 0.89 metres (²).

It is self-evident that this rise, multiplied by the area of the lake surface, must represent the total cubic content of the water added to it, in one year, *after the loss by evaporation, and the amount drawn off by the Nile have been deducted.*

The figures thus give :—

(i) for a low year like 1902 ; a cube of 21760,000,000 metres.

(ii) for the mean of 6 years, omitting 1897-98, a cube of 44880,000,000 metres.

(iii) for a high year like 1901, a cube of 60520,000,000 metres.

In the present calculation, the figure representing the mean of the six years' period will be used, viz., 44880 millions of metres cube. This is reasonable, as mean figures have been used all through.

(¹) By "range" is meant the difference between the highest and lowest levels.

(²) The following are the figures :—

Year.	Range in Feet & Inches.		Range in metres.
	ft.	in.	
1896	1	6 1/4	0·46
1899	2	7 1/4	0·79
1900	2	3	0·69
1901	2	11	0·89
1902	1	0 1/2	0·32
1903	2	8	0·81
Mean	2'	2"	0·66

The extreme range was 1.16 metrès.

It now only remains to ascertain the amount of water lost by evaporation, and for this a very simple calculation is necessary.

Let a be the amount of water entering the lake in one year—138750 millions of metres cube.

Let b be the amount of water discharged by the Nile in one year—18140 millions of metres cube.

Let c be the amount by which the lake is increased in one year, after deducting evaporation and discharge—44,880 millions of metres cube.

The amount of water evaporated in the year must then be equal to $a-(b+c)=138750-(18140+44880)=75730,000,000$ metres cube.

This means that 55% of the water which enters the lake, in an average year, is lost by evaporation (1).

In other words, evaporation would reduce the lake level by 1.113 metres annually, or by 0.003 metres per diem.

In reality, the daily rate of evaporation must vary largely throughout the year, and, during the rainy season, when rain is falling and the sky is cloudy, it must be practically nil. Probably the greater part of the loss occurs during the five driest months, i.e., in January, February, June, July and August. If this be so, then the daily rate during these months would be 0.007 metres.

With reference to the foregoing, it may be argued that the whole calculation is based upon assumptions, regarding:—

(1) The catchment area and that of the lake,

(2) The average annual rainfall,

(3) The average run-off,

(4) The mean annual discharge of the Nile,

and further, that all these figures may be found, with improved knowledge of the subject, to require considerable modification.

This is quite true, and yet each of these assumptions is based upon certain data, and upon, what may be termed, *probabilities*.

Thus, the areas of the catchment basin and lake have been calculated from the most recent maps.

The rainfall has been taken from a certain limited number of observations.

The average run-off is of course very doubtful, but the figure used is that generally applied to forest country.

Lastly, the mean annual discharge has been calculated from a measured section, and from velocities actually observed.

This being so, the figures may be allowed to stand, at any rate, until subsequent information shall prove by how much, or in what way, they should be modified.

Before leaving the subject, it may be of interest to calculate what would be the effect of closing the Ripon Falls by a regulator, and thus possibly raising the level of the lake.

The mean daily discharge of the Nile is 49700,000 metres cube. This volume of water, if retained in the lake, would, in theory, raise its level by 0.00072 metres per diem, or by 0.2628 metres in one year.

It would therefore require 1388 days, or 3 years, 293 days, to raise the lake level by one metre.

In reality, it would take much longer than this, as the calculation is based upon the assumption that the area of the lake surface would not be increased by the raising. It would be increased, as the swamps and low ground would be flooded, over a very large extent of country. The evaporating area would of course be proportionally increased.

Meanwhile, during this whole time, the Nile supply would be entirely cut off.

(1) No account has been taken of loss by percolation.

THE COUNTRY BETWEEN THE VICTORIA AND THE ALBERT EDWARD LAKES, COMPRISING THE DISTRICTS OF BUDDU AND ANKOLI.

The caravan track between these two lakes starts from Bujaju, on the western shore of the Victoria Nyanza and, passing through the stations of Masaka and Mbarara, the headquarters of the districts of Buddu and Ankoli respectively, finally arrives at Kazinga, on the north-east corner of Lake Albert Edward, having traversed a distance of 298 kilometres (1). The general level of the plateau at Bujaju, (N. lat. 0° 13′), is some 40 metres above the water, rising from the shore in a steep incline. Bujaju itself consists of an open grass plain, surrounded by forest. This forest extends in a belt, from 4 to 5 kilometres in width, from the Katonga river in the north, to the Ruizi river in the south, i.e., for more than 100 kilometres. It runs parallel to Lake Victoria throughout its course. It is full of fine trees and thick undergrowth. The trees are festooned by huge creepers, which hang in loops from the branches. Palms are not uncommon, and beautiful wild flowers exist in profusion. One flowering tree is a feature in this forest, and indeed throughout the Uganda Protectorate. It is covered with clusters of bright scarlet flowers and, as the tree itself is very common, brilliant patches of colour are produced all over the landscape in a most effective way (2).

West of the forest belt, a swamp, 9 kilometres, or more, in width, extends north and south, and parallel to the lake for some 65 to 70 kilometres. This swamp drains into the Ruizi river, and within it is situated the small lake of Nabu Gabu, a circular sheet of water, from 7 to 8 kilometres in diameter. To the south, the grass in this marsh is very high and dense, but to the north, it is lower, and clumps of fine trees and "Raphia" palms are scattered about, giving it a park-like appearance. Beyond this swamp, proceeding west, the land rises in a ridge of low, basalt cliffs. This line of cliffs, which is that of the great fault bordering the western shore of Lake Victoria from the Kagera to the Katonga, runs nearly due north and south. Gravel beds are found here, at more than a hundred metres above the present lake surface, and it is reported that caves, worn by water action, are also to be met with. The whole of this district is covered with a layer of ironstone, similar to that described in the districts of Uganda and Kavirondo (3). Beyond the range of cliffs, a wide, open, and undulating plateau extends, the surface broken by copses and clumps of trees. This part of the Protectorate is prosperous-looking and highly populated, with a fertile soil. The Bahima own many cattle, but, as a rule, these are carefully hidden away in secluded pastures (4). In Buddu, there are no villages, in the sense of a collection of dwellings grouped together. The huts are scattered about through the forest and grass, either singly, or in pairs, each close to its own patch of clearance, containing bananas or sweet potatoes. These huts are circular, with bee-hive roofs, very neatly made. The sides are of elephant-grass, and the eaves come down close to the earth all round. The entrance is shaded by a high grass fence, and the jungle is cleared for a considerable space in front. The people of Buddu are very dark-coloured, but are not of a pronounced negro type. Many of them have oval faces and good features. All of them are clothed. Nearly two-thirds of the population of the province have embraced the Christian religion, most of them being Roman Catholics. There are also

(1) Between Masaka and Mbarara, a cart-road has been constructed, which, again, connects Masaka with Entebbé. This road, being graded for wheeled traffic, follows the easier slopes of the hills. The caravan route is shorter and more direct, but with very steep gradients at times. Both roads are made by native labour, given in lieu of payment of the hut-tax. They are fairly well kept up, particularly in the Buddu district.

(2) Erythrina Tomentosa.

(3) The iron ore in this region is not found in sufficient quantity to pay for the working, as is the case in Kavirondo.

(4) The Bahima form the aristocracy, so to speak, of the Uganda Protectorate. They are large cattle owners, and their name is most probably derived from the arabic word for cattle.

BUDDU DISTRICT
TYPICAL SCENERY, SHOWING ANTHILLS

BUDDU DISTRICT
A CAUSEWAY ACROSS A SWAMP

some Protestants, and a few Mohammedans (1). Most of the women, and many of the men, wear a chain round the neck to which is attached a cross.

West of the plateau, the country assumes the character which is so typical of Uganda, i.e., a succession of hills and hollows, which may be compared to a gigantic switch-back. In each hollow is a swamp, varying in width from a few hundred metres to three or four kilometres. These swamps are filled by a dense growth of papyrus and ambatch, among which purple-coloured creepers twine. The water surface is generally hidden by a mass of lovely blue water-lilies. The hills, which are low and rounded, are covered with bush, and on the slopes bananas are cultivated. On the line of the track, the swamps are crossed by means of cleverly constructed causeways (2). On the tops of some of the hills are small level spaces, or table-lands, but more often than not the descent commences as soon as the ascent is completed. These continual ups and downs make a journey through Uganda hard upon the porters and fatiguing for the traveller.

At 30 kilometres west of Bujaju, the station of Masaka is reached. The small fort is situated on the top of a flat-topped hill, some 300 metres above the level of Lake Victoria. In this fort are the Government offices and the residence of the English Assistant Collector. It is surrounded by an earthen bank and a deep ditch. The lines are lower down, on the western face of the hill. The garrison consists of police and a small detachment of the Uganda Rifles. From the top of this hill, a fine view is obtained in all directions. The rounded hill-tops appear in endless succession and a good idea is arrived at of the network of swamps which fill the valleys.

Between Masaka and Mbarara, at 10 kilometres west of the former station, a range of low hills is crossed. The country now rises in level and the hills are higher than further to the east. The valleys are also wider. Cultivation is more scanty, and the scenery generally wilder (3). At Kiboyo, 49 kilometres from Lake Victoria, the land is high, but the ridges are flat and the swamping less. Every now and again, a steep dip and rise is met with, but as a whole this plateau resembles a series of rolling downs more than anything else. There are few trees—nothing but bush and scrub. The yellow flowers of the young mimosas, at a distance might be mistaken for gorse and, were it not for the presence of numerous high anthills, the landscape would bear a singular resemblance to a Scotch grouse-moor. The inhabitants are few in number and beyond an occasional banana plantation, there is little cultivation. No cattle are to be seen, but small flocks of goats are occasionally met with. Ironstone crops out everywhere. The soil in the swamps is generally sandy and the hills are covered with a thick layer of red, volcanic earth. A few euphorbia trees are scattered about on the slopes of the hills. At Imbrezi, 67 kilometres west of the lake, the hills rise more abruptly from the valleys. Rock, chiefly quartz and gneiss, is everywhere close to the surface and great blocks stand out upon the hill sides. In the valleys, high grass replaces the papyrus and the swamps are wider than before. What trees there are, are confined to the euphorbia or the acacia species (4). The wild flowers in this region are very numerous and of singular beauty. One variety, resembling a marsh-mallow in shape, is found of many colours—orange, rose, yellow, purple and white. Another tall plant, apparently of the thistle species, has a vivid, purple flower and is some 2½ metres high, while another, and very common flower, bright red in colour, is found upon a stem running through a series of small spike-covered balls, about 20 centimetres apart.

Near Marongo, 93 kilometres from Lake Victoria, a great, bare, hog-backed mountain rises in the north, to a height of some 1,400 metres above the sea. To the west, long valleys

(1) This does not comprise the Bahima, who, it is said, rarely become converts to either Christianity or Islamism.

(2) These causeways are made as follows :—A layer of brushwood bundles is placed on the surface of the marsh. Over this is laid a layer of larger logs, and the whole is confined between vertical stakes, driven through the mud, with openings left to permit of the passage of the water. On the surface of the logs, is placed a layer of clay and sand, which forms the roadway.

(3) These hills mark the second rise, or step, up from Lake Victoria.

(4) The acacias here are stunted, and many of them are destroyed by a woolly looking parasite which covers the branches.

run up, enclosed between ranges of hills, the colours melting in the distance into lovely shades of blue and purple. In the near foreground, the golden balls of the mimosas contrast well with the dark green of the foliage and the brighter green of the short thick grass. The valleys and the ravines of these hills are thickly wooded and the former contain large swamps, all of which drain to the south into the Kachera lake. Very few inhabitants are met with here. Nine or ten kilometres further to the west, the character of the country, in the vicinity of the route, again changes. The hills are lower and the valleys, and consequently the swamps, are broader. Marshy streams traverse them, all flowing to the south. Heavy grass, anthills, mimosas and euphorbias fill the valleys, and an occasional rocky hill stands out above the low ranges on either side. At kilometre 110, a swampy river forms the boundary between the districts of Buddu and Ankoli. A signpost, on the side of the track, announces this fact. Five kilometres beyond this point, the camp of Nsongi is reached. It is situated on a small plateau, surrounded on three sides by low hills. To the south, a wide valley extends which, during the rainy season, is a large marsh. In the dry weather, the water supply is very scanty and the villagers take their cattle elsewhere (1). Throughout this country, signs of elephants are very numerous and the damage these animals do to the forests is amazing. Large trees are snapped off near the roots and others are uprooted and tossed about, apparently wantonly, as frequently the branches are not even stripped of their leaves.

For the next forty kilometres or so of the journey to the west, the character of the scenery is extremely uninteresting and most monotonous. Low ridges and broad swamps alternate with maddening regularity. These ridges are sparsely wooded and the reedy swamps generally border a sluggish stream, flowing in a channel blocked by tall grass. The soil of these swamps is black clay and coarse sand. The former becomes very greasy in rain. At kilometre 150 from Lake Victoria, a welcome change appears in the landscape. The hills are high, and more resembling mountains than any met with since leaving the lake. They are bare and grass-covered. The absence of trees is very striking. The valleys are full of dense jungle and, in the dry season, water, in this part of the route, is a serious difficulty. A few kilometres further on, banana plantations recommence, on the lower slopes of the hills. In the extreme south, the Ruimpara mountains are visible (2). After making a rather long and steep ascent and descending another valley, the hill upon which Mbarara is situated is arrived at.

Mbarara is the headquarters of the Ankoli district. The station is built upon the summit of a flat-topped hill, 1600 metres above the sea, and 178 kilometres west of the Victoria Nyanza. It is a pretty place, well kept and neatly laid out, with good roads, lined on either side by trees. The bungalows are comfortable and well built. They are each enclosed in large compounds. With the exception of Entebbé, Mbarara is by far the pleasantest and the most civilised station in the whole of the Uganda Protectorate. The military lines, the magazine and the fort, are on the highest point of the hill. A little lower down, are the Civil Offices and quarters and, on another hill opposite, are the Police lines, the hospital, jail, etc. The English Officials consist of a Sub-Collector and a Doctor, with two Officers in command of the troops. The detachment stationed at Mbarara is formed by two Companies of the Uganda Rifles (3). There are also 100 Police.

The Ruizi river runs in a deep gorge, about 800 metres to the south of the station. The country all round is very bare of forest. Wood, both for fuel and for building purposes is a great difficulty. From the top of the hill, on a clear day, a lovely panorama extends The Ruimpara mountains bound the southern horizon, at a distance varying from 16 to 19 kilometres. This range runs nearly due east and west and some of its peaks rise to a

(1) The water at Nsongi is obtained from the swamps. It is black in colour, and filthy to the taste.
(2) These mountains form the northern boundary of the valley of the Kagera river.
(3) In these Companies, are 180 Soudanese, and 70 Waganda.

ANKOLI DISTRICT
THE RUIZI RIVER

ANKOLI DISTRICT
MBARARA, HEADQUARTERS OF DISTRICT

height of 2,000 metres, and more, above the sea. The length of this chain is perhaps 70 kilometres and beyond it, to the south, the Kagera flows (1). In exceptionally clear weather, Ruenzori is visible to the north-west, but at a great distance, and in all directions ranges of low hills are to be seen. Unfortunately, except during a break in the rains, such extensive views are rarely to be obtained. During the dry season, while the grass is being burnt, the smoke forms a thick haze which obscures everything (2). For some distance round Mbarara, the country is largely cultivated. The chief crops are sweet potatoes and terebon, for the use of the garrison, but bananas are also planted over a considerable area. About 1½ kilometres to the west of the station, the palace of the King of Ankoli occupies the summit of an isolated hill. The palace consists of a large thatched hut, with a collection of smaller ones, for the King's women and his suite. These huts are surrounded by a high reed fence and all over the hill are banana plantations. The English Mission Church is also situated upon this hill. The King himself is a pure-blooded Bahima. He is a young man of 19 years. He is of exceptionally tall stature, being over 6 feet 6 inches in height. His complexion is very dark, but he has good features and a pleasant face. He wears a long white dress and a white skull-cap, but over the former he wears a cloth coat, of European manufacture. The Church of England Mission buildings are on the low ground to the west of this hill and those of the Roman Catholic Mission upon another low hil adjoining. The climate of Mbarara, during the winter months, is delightful and the station is said to be one of the healthiest in the Protectorate (3).

Proceeding west from Mbarara, in the direction of Lake Albert Edward, after descending from the hills, an extensive plateau is crossed (4). This table-land, which is 1,400 metres above the sea, is open and generally flat, but broken by gently swelling elevations which rise above the plain at intervals. Anthills are very numerous and stand up above the grass, which averages 0·70 metres in height. The soil has the appearance of being volcanic, but in the swamps clay is found. This plateau, to the south, is bounded by the Ruimpara mountains, along the base of which the Ruizi river runs. Several swampy streams cross the plain, all of which discharge their waters into the Ruizi. Their beds are filled with papyrus and reeds, through which the water filters slowly. Some of these channels are deep, one in particular, being 40 metres wide and 10 metres deep. Near the western end of the table-land, a solitary round-topped hill rises from the plain, to a height of over 200 metres. At 190 kilometres, west of Lake Victoria, the plateau ends and the land rises sharply. Here is the Rusasa camp. From this place, the mountains which form the eastern boundary of the Albert Edward valley are visible in the extreme distance. In the north, and much nearer, the square mass of the Chinyeni mountain stands out prominently (5). Between Rusasa and Kaniamatabara, at 236 kilometres, many low ridges, mostly running north and south, are crossed. The character of the country changes altogether. The valleys are narrow and deep and the hills, which may well be called mountains, are high and rugged. On their lower slopes, is much cultivation, but their summits are bare. Kaniamatabara camp is on a small plateau, 1700 metres above sea level. From this point, a lovely view is obtained. The Chinyeni mountain fills the northern background. This is a long flat-topped hill, attaining an elevation of some 2500 metres. Its southern face is precipitous and bare. Between it and the plateau above mentioned, is a wide valley full of fine forest trees. To the south-west, another valley stretches, with clumps of small trees scattered about and ending in two

(1) This river, at its nearest point, is not more than 50 kilometres from Mbarara, in a direction due south.

(2) These grass fires cause the atmosphere to be hot and oppressive, besides creating a haze, or fog, which hangs over the whole country.

(3) The maximum mean temperature is 81° F. and the minimum 55° F. The first rainy season begins at the commencement of February, and lasts to the end of May The second commences in the middle of September, and lasts to the end of November.

(4) All cultivation stops at a few kilometres to the west of the palace.

(5) At kilometre 203, the Koja river is crossed. This stream, which rises in the low hills to the north, has a channel 103 metres wide and 2 metres deep. The depth of water, in February 1903, was 1 metre, but there was hardly any current, owing to the reeds. It discharges into the Ruizi.

picturesque conical hills. Water is very scarce here and has to be brought from a long way ([1]). West of Kaniamatabara, the mountain ranges which extend to the eastern escarpment of the Albertine "Rift" valley, commence ([2]). This portion of the journey is very trying to porters. The ascents are long and steep and the descents equally bad. There are very few level bits. As soon as one hill is ascended, it must be descended on the other side and immediately across the narrow valley another and still higher hill commences.

These mountains cover the whole area, from this point to the Albert Edward valley. Their direction is generally north and south. In the north, they eventually merge into the high ridges which break the plateau extending through Toro and Unyoro, and which separate the Victoria and the Albert lake water-systems. To the south, they extend until the range, north of Lake Kivu, is reached. The highest point crossed by the route between Mbarara and the Albert Edward lake, is at 229 kilometres from Lake Victoria, where the pass has an elevation of 2000 metres above the sea ([3]). The scenery here is lovely, resembling that of the Alps, or of the lower Himalayas. Tier upon tier of mountains rise, one above the other, in all directions, the ranges being higher towards the west and the north. Great ravines, running down into deep valleys, score their sides. Large blocks of quartz and basalt project from the upper slopes, some of them of fantastic shape. In the valleys, there is some cultivation, but at the highest elevations there is a remarkable absence of wood. The climate, at this elevation, is delightful. Although the sun is hot, the air is cool and bracing. The hill sides are covered with rich grass and many wild flowers ([4]). Occasionally, beautiful pictures of the plateau below are obtained. In the early morning, looking eastward, the near hills are in shadow, while the plains and the distant mountains of Ruimpara glitter through the mist, in the rays of the rising sun. The track leading to the Albert Edward lake winds along the spurs of these mountains in a continual series of ascents and descents. Three kilometres beyond the pass, after a sharp descent of 300 metres, the Kayangi river is crossed ([5]). Beyond this stream, the gradients, in crossing the valleys, get steeper and steeper. Few of them are less than 1 to 1, and many of them are as much as ¾ to 1. The unfortunate porters, with their loads, frequently have to descend these slopes in a sitting position.

At kilometre 239, the watershed is crossed, and the streams, instead of flowing from the north to the south, beyond this point, follow the reverse direction ([6]). From here there is a gradual descent and two kilometres further on the Walaga river is crossed ([7]). West of this river, the country is easier to traverse, as the route follows a series of elevated table-lands, or plateaux, between high mountain ranges and only crosses a ridge where this is unavoidable. At some of the many glens, through which the streams run, the crossings are very steep and difficult, but on the whole the gradients are less trying than was the case in the vicinity of the pass. In all these glens, fine forest trees are met with, the "Piptodinia" being especially remarkable for its great height, its buttresses, and the crown of brown flowers on the top ([8]).

([1]) Some lovely birds are to be seen here One variety has a brilliant scarlet head, breast, and tail, with black wings, and another, a black head and back, with an orange breast.

([2]) At 1 kilometre from Kaniamatabara, the Kandeki river crosses. It is a swampy stream, flowing round the western slope of Chinyenj and discharging into the Ruizi. It has a channel 94 metres wide, and 2½ metres deep, with much papyrus.

([3]) The highest mountains here are said to be 2700 metres above the sea.

([4]) One particularly striking and common flower, in shape and colour, somewhat resembles a gigantic daisy. Some of these flowers are 5 inches in diameter.

([5]) The Kayangi flows from north to south. Its channel is 49 metres wide by 3 metres in depth. In the dry season, the water is 0·60 metres in depth, and of a clear amber colour. The flow is much checked by the reeds and papyrus in the river bed.

([6]) East of kilometre 239, the drainage is to the Ruizi river. West of this, it finds its way into some of the streams that feed the Katonga.

([7]) This is a rapid stream, 12 metres wide and 0.30 metres deep, with clear water.

([8]) Allusion has already been made to the wild flowers of this locality. In every meadow or prairie, they are of quite exceptional beauty. They are all of considerable height, so as to top the grass, some of them being as much as 1.75 metres. The mixture and variety of colours is extraordinary, but, as Sir Harry Johnston remarks in his recent work, the absence of blue is remarkable. Some of the flowers resemble monkshood, with white or lilac cups. Some are like yellow daisies, and some of the colour of the marigold. Others are not unlike heliotrope, while everywhere the large white flower already mentioned and the scarlet bells of the Erythrina Tomentosa are found in luxuriance.

ANKOLI DISTRICT
MOUNTAINS FORMING EASTERN BOUNDARY OF ALBERTINE RIFT VALLEY

ANKOLI DISTRICT
MOUNTAINS FORMING EASTERN BOUNDARY OF ALBERTINE RIFT VALLEY

After passing the small plateau of Kisara, at kilometre 257, the Kibasi range of mountains stretches along the north-eastern horizon, at a distance of from 16 to 18 kilometres from the track. These mountains are flat-topped and precipitous on their western face. Between them and Kisara is a series of low hills, covered with grass and with rounded or conical summits. In the north-west, two sugar-loaf peaks are visible and in the nearer distance, an open and park-like country extends—very broken in its surface and studded by numerous clumps of large trees. The grass is replaced by tall bracken. Proceeding in a westerly direction, the track passes through the park-like country above mentioned, on a gentle descent, and gradually draws nearer to the Kibasi range. Some of the trees are magnificent, one in particular, with very dark green leaves resembling those of the "Poinciana Regia" or "Gold Mohur" tree. Upon each of the darker clusters are apparently laid bunches of lighter coloured leaves, of a greyish-green, or almost white, hue. The effect, at a little distance, is as if the foliage were covered by a sprinkling of hoar-frost, or snow. Further on, the forest becomes more continuous to the west and the track approaches to within three kilometres of the Kibasi mountains. At kilometre 254 from the Victoria Nyanza, the great forest belt is arrived at. This forest extends in an unbroken line for many hundred kilometres to the south, bordering the cliffs of the great fault which form the eastern boundary of the Albertine "Rift" valley ([1]). The Kibasi range bars it at the north end, not far from the point where the route under description crosses the spurs of these mountains. Although its length, in the direction of north and south, is considerable, the width of this forest, i.e., in a line from west to east, is nowhere great. It is rarely more than from 5 to 6 kilometres and, at the north end, only 3 kilometres. The belt is, however, extremely thick and, in its tropical luxuriance, possesses all the characteristics of the great Congo forest which covers so large an area to the west of the Semliki valley. The trees are straight and very tall, like the columns of a vast cathedral. The resemblance is heightened by the buttresses, most of which throw out from the lower stem. The branches spread in all directions and intertwine, making a thick covering, or roofing, which, except in rare instances, completely shuts out the sun's rays. All over these trees hang great creepers, in multitudinous folds, with fantastic loops and festoons. These creepers are frequently 4 and 5 inches in diameter and, like the trees themselves, are covered with mosses and lichens. Sometimes a creeper has so encircled a tree that it has sapped its life away, leaving nothing but the hollow shell, round which the cause of its death, like a huge python, twines and flourishes. Some of the trees in this forest are of wonderful size and girth and many of them must be of great age. One beautiful tree has leaves of a rose colour, blending into brown. Another resembles a large horse-chestnut. The undergrowth is extremely thick and tall; a species of gigantic nettle, and a shrub with leaves like those of the tobacco plant, being very common. Within this forest, it is very dark and the contrast with the bright external light is a strong one. Here and there, the sun's rays do manage to pierce through the leafy roofing of the overhanging foliage and in such places a lovely green light pervades over a limited area, making the surroundings look darker and more gloomy by the contrast. In the interior of the forest, the atmosphere is damp and heavy and, during the rainy season, the place must be depressing beyond words. No sign of either animal or bird life is visible and an intense stillness reigns. One or two small streams cross this forest, tumbling over rocky beds in a series of small rapids, with beautifully clear water ([2]).

At kilometre 257, the track emerges from the forest and, after a very steep ascent, a low spur of the Kibasi hills is surmounted ([3]). This ridge, or spur, strikes off from the

([1]) Further south, it approaches close to the shores of Lake Albert Edward.

([2]) The largest of these streams is called locally the "Nillia Mama." It has a bed width of 12 metres, but in the dry season the depth of water is not more than a few centimetres.

([3]) This ascent, of about 100 metres, is nearly vertical, and more resembles a ladder than a road. The large tree-roots, which cross it, heighten the resemblance.

Kibasi mountains and runs north-west, more or less parallel to the main range. Between the two is a deep valley, or amphitheatre, which was once the crater of a large volcano. The hills forming the western ridge of this crater are called Kisangua, and among them are the two sugar-loaf peaks before alluded to. This crater is from four to five kilometres in diameter. The valley is very deep, crags rising all round it in a series of precipices, their faces seamed by the scars of great slips. The landscape is wild and desolate, the entire enclosure being surrounded by a rocky wall. The bottom of the crater is filled by heavy grass, with occasional small glades of trees (1). At the north end is situated a small lake, known as Kogoto. This lake is from 1 to 1.5 kilometres in diameter. The water washes the foot of the rocky mass of Kisangua, which here comes down, from summit to base, in one sheer precipice, several hundred metres in height. On the other side, a steep headland from the Kibasi range stands out close to the lake edge. To the north, the rim of the crater is lower, and not more than 100 metres above the water. The narrow shores are thickly wooded, and many palm trees are grouped near the water's edge. The surface of the lake is calm and glassy, and the palms and foliage, with the background formed by the mountains, are reproduced as if in a mirror.

At kilometre 267, the Kibasi range comes to an end, in a high, bold-looking bluff. From this point, a long and wide valley stretches for several kilometres, enclosed between low hills and full of banana plantations and tall grass, averaging from 4 to 5 metres in height. Beyond this valley is another crater, also containing a lake, but smaller than that of Kogoto (2). Cliffs, 40 to 50 metres in height, enclose it. West of this point, craters are to be seen in every direction, and close to one another. The track winds along between them, often on a high narrow ridge, not more than a few metres wide, which forms the rim, or separation, between two of these strange valleys. These craters are generally circular enclosures, with steep and, occasionally, vertical sides, forming inverted cones. Many of them are 300 metres deep. In some cases, a lovely little lake nestles at the bottom. In others, they are dry and one or two have been planted all over the sides with bananas. The effect of these plantations, viewed from the height of some 200 metres above, is curious, and reminds the observer of a large strawberry bed. The hills here are of very irregular shape, bare, and full of crags and precipices. The landscape is a unique one, as the entire area, as far as the eye can see, is riven by these craters, as close together and as regular, as the cells of a gigantic honeycomb.

At 275 kilometres from Bujaju, the crest of the escarpment is attained, and an extensive view of the great "Rift" valley, lying some 500 metres below, is obtained. In the north, the mountain mass of Ruenzori is plainly visible. On the edge of the escarpment, the village of Kichwamba is situated among large banana plantations. The descent of the cliffs of the eastern fault-line commences from this place (3). The path down these cliffs is a very steep one, and runs in zigzag lines down the face of the escarpment. Near the bottom, at a height of 100 metres above the valley, a small plateau, formed by a sinking of the mountain side, extends (4). Here is the camping station known as Mkorotoveza. Just below, a small river, the Kiambura, has its rise, and crosses the valley in a north-westerly direction to the Dueru lake. The temperature at Mkorotoveza is much higher than on the summit of the cliffs, and the air is damp and oppressive (5). From this plateau, the descent into the valley is easy. The plain here is swampy and covered by high grass, with many anthills.

(1) On some of these trees there is a curious parasite, with large leaves, exactly like those of a cabbage.
(2) There are no outlets for any of these craters.
(3) The strata of this fault all dip at an angle of 60°.
(4) Lake deposit is found all over this plateau.
(5) At 4 p.m. on the 12th February 1903, the temperature was 80° F.

ANKOLI DISTRICT
KOGOTO CRATER LAKE NEAR EASTERN ESCARPMENT OF ALBERTINE RIFT VALLEY

ANKOLI DISTRICT
CRATER LAKE NEAR EASTERN ESCARPMENT OF ALBERTINE RIFT VALLEY

At kilometre 280, a branch of the Kiambura river is crossed. It is very shallow, with a bed-width of 30 metres. It flows to the north, its course being marked by a thicket of bush and low palms, on either side. Beyond this river, a wide alluvial plain extends, crossed by numerous shallow depressions. Some of these are as much as 600 metres wide and 2 metres deep. This plain is covered by low grass and scattered bush. At kilometre 287, a belt of low forest crosses, and extends north and south, for some distance. On approaching Kazinga, the surface of the plain alternately rises and falls, forming a succession of low dips and ridges. These follow the contours of different levels of the lake in former times. The bays and headlands of the shores are marked in successive terraces, one above the other, and show that the fall in the water-levels must have been a very gradual one (1). The entire area is covered by lake deposit and small shells. A few Euphorbia trees are dotted about through the plain. Looking back, i.e., to the east, the outlines of the mountains forming the fault-line, are very plainly seen. Some of the peaks are of great height. The point where the track from Mbarara crosses these mountains is lower than any other, for a long distance both to the north and to the south. Beyond kilometre 296, the level of the valley rises gently and on this elevation the village of Kazinga is situated. Kazinga is a large, but scattered, collection of huts, forming a nearer approach to the general idea of a village than any met with since leaving Entebbé. These huts are built of reeds and are circular in shape. Each one is surrounded by a small hedge of Euphorbia shoots and of thorny bush, from 1 to 1.25 metres in height. The Church is a singular-looking structure, with open lattice-work walls, and a thatched roof. At kilometre 299 from Bujaju, on the Victoria Nyanza, the shore of the Albert Edward lake is reached. This lake is generally hidden by a veil of thick haze which, during the dry season, is but seldom lifted. The climate at Kazinga during the month of February is dry and pleasant, the temperature ranging from 60° to 90° F.

(1) At kilometre 296, there is a very marked line of a former lake shore. The drop is some 25 metres, and the ridge extends north and south for many miles, showing distinctly the position of what were once bays and creeks.

LAKE ALBERT EDWARD.

This lake, which was discovered by Stanley in 1875, has been explored by many travellers, notably by Stuhlmann, Moore, Scott Elliott, Grogan, Lugard and Gibbons, all of whom have described in some detail those portions of it which they visited. Lake Albert Edward lies between latitudes 0° 8′ and 0° 40′ south, and the most recent maps show its limits as bounded by the meridians of 29° 32′ and 30° 6′ east (1). In shape, it is a rough oblong and at the north-eastern corner, a long and narrow channel connects it with a smaller lake, marked on some maps as Ruisamba, but more generally known as Dueru (2). The present area of Lake Albert Edward is some 2100 square kilometres, comprising that of Lake Dueru. Its greatest length is 70 kilometres, and breadth 50 kilometres. Dueru lake is 30 kilometres in length, but narrow, averaging only from 16 to 17 kilometres at its widest part. The connecting channel is some 40 kilometres in length. The catchment basin is of very irregular shape and covers some 18000 square kilometres in area, including the area of the lake itself. The now generally accepted value for the height of its water above the sea, is 965 metres.

Both these lakes are, like Kivu and Tanganyika to the south, and the Albert Nyanza to the north, bounded by the fault-lines of the great meridional "Rift" valley in which they lie (3). Formed by the sinking of the strip of country between these fault-lines, they are overlooked by the steep cliffs of the plateaux on either side, which rise to 600, and even to 900 metres, above the level of their water surface. To the north, the huge mountain mass of Ruenzori towers, and these lakes receive the entire drainage of its southern and eastern slopes.

Geologically, the whole country is situated in the great area of crystalline schists, through which, in the "Rift" valley, eruptive rocks have been extruded at numerous points, such as the recent lavas and basalts to the north of Lake Kivu and south of the Albert Edward lake. Between these two lakes, the floor of the "Rift" gradually rises, until in south latitude 1° 30′ it is finally blocked by the mountain chain, which contains the volcanoes of Mukavurre, Kirunga-cha-mia-Gongo and Karisimbi, in the district of Ufumbwiro. Some of these are still active, and rise to a height of 5000 metres above the sea. On the northern slopes, a stream of lava has spread, covering them and the upper end of the valley as well. This range completely closes the "Rift" valley at this portion of its length and forms the watershed between the lake-systems lying to the north and south of its mass.

With reference to this block in the valley, Moore says (4) "it seems clear that, at some" "previous period, not very remote, the volcanic eruptions, which took place in the "Rift" "valley to the south of the Albert Edward lake, filled this valley up with a dam of volcanic" "detritus, and generally so altered the contour and general level of the country, that the" "drainage of all the Lake Kivu area was cut off from the lakes lying to the north of it and so" "from the Nile system, being diverted into Lake Tanganyika."

This comparatively recent outburst has undoubtedly reduced the supply of water flowing to the Albert Edward and Albert lakes.

At the south end of Lake Albert Edward, the country is flat and stretches in a broad alluvial plain to the northern slopes of the Kivu range. This plain is treeless and barren, and contains numerous salt-pans, while many geysers are met with in the south-eastern

(1) Later observations would seem to prove that the longitudes, hitherto accepted, are incorrect, and that this lake, with the upper Semliki valley and the Ruenzori mountains, lies considerably further to the west than had been supposed.

(2) The Albert Edward lake is called Dueru by the Wanyoro. Ruisamba is a mountain west of Lake Dueru, in the Ruenzori range.

(3) Vide page 7 of this report.

(4) "The Mountains of the Moon," London, 1901.

LAKE ALBERT EDWARD JUNCTION OF DUERU CHANNEL WITH LAKE AT KAZINGA

DUERU CHANNEL LOOKING NORTH FROM LAKE ALBERT EDWARD

corner [1]. The flats extend along the eastern shore as far as Kamarangu, about half-way between the northern and southern limits of the lake. North of this point, a high plateau borders the water in a succession of flat-topped and rounded bluffs, averaging 100 to 120 metres in height. This plateau extends as far as the southern spurs of Ruenzori. All along this coast, at no great distance from the lake, a thick belt of forest stretches, while in the north-eastern area, numerous crater-lakes are met with.

Although at the southern end, the eastern fault-line approaches the lake very closely, towards the north it recedes far from it, and opposite Kazinga, in the north-east corner, the width of the valley is some 18 kilometres. It continues thus broad to the north, enclosing Lake Dueru in its expanse, until at some 140 kilometres from the south end of Lake Albert Edward, the cliffs trend sharply to the west and meet the eastern foothills of the Ruenzori range.

On the west of Lake Albert Edward, the great range of mountains, known as Wakondjo, (in the Congo Free State), which forms the western boundary of the "Rift," follows the coast line closely. On this side the flats are small and there is but little swamping. These mountains close in on the lake, in its north-west corner, and approach near to the point where the Semliki river has its exit, in latitude 0° 8′ 30″ south.

To the north of the lake and west of the Semliki, the country is a high alluvial plain, rising towards the shore in similar bluffs to those on the east, but with this difference, that on the northern coast, a wide border of swamped flats separates the high land from the water. This plateau extends north, to the most southerly spurs of Ruenzori, from one of which a subsidiary range runs south to the lake. This range, known as the Kipura, forms the eastern boundary of the upper Semliki valley. The whole of this plateau, as well as that to the south, was undoubtedly once covered by the waters of Lake Albert Edward. All round its shores, as well as those of Lake Dueru, there are evidences to show that, at one period, this lake covered a very large area and that its waters stood at a very much higher level than they now do. This period was probably anterior to that of the outburst which blocked the "Rift" north of Lake Kivu, and the Albert Edward lake must once have washed the base of the cliffs forming the fault-lines on either side, as well as that of the foothills of Ruenzori. It may possibly have extended to the south, and comprised the Kivu lake as well, but this is conjectural. On the north and east, and probably on the west side also, lake deposit is everywhere found, at a height of 100 metres and more above the present water level of the lake. On every adjacent ridge, such as that of the Katwe salt lake, below this level, such deposit is found. It is also to be met with on the Kipura hills and on the spurs of Ruenzori, and, again, on the eastern escarpment of the "Rift" itself. In addition to this, the whole of this area bears trace in its conformation, of having once been the bed of a great inland sea. In almost every part of it, the high land slopes down to the lake in a series of terraces, at different levels, but at parallel heights. These terraces are indented by bays and creeks and show clearly the elevation at which the lake waters once stood, during successive periods of its history. How to account for the great change which has taken place is not easy. Moore's explanation that the water-supply from the south was largely cut off, when the mountains rose in the valley floor, is hardly sufficient to account for such a lowering of the water surface. It seems probable that, at one time, the valley, north of the lake, and at the point where it is narrowest, was filled by a dam of detritus, washed down from the western slopes of Ruenzori. This dam was, by degrees, cut through by the overflow of the lake, thus forming the Semliki river, which in time worked down, lower and lower through the loose material, and in this way drained the waters of the lake. There is no reason to conclude that this lowering of the levels has entirely ceased. The general opinion of those who are acquainted with the

[1] "From the Cape to Cairo," by E.S. Grogan, London, 1900.

district, and of the natives, is that it is still continuing. In any case, the forces which caused the Kivu upheaval are still existent, as the active volcanoes on this range, and the hot springs which encircle the entire base of Ruenzori, testify. Moreover, the whole of this area lies within the region of seismic disturbance. Earthquakes and earth-movements are of frequent occurrence, and of considerable severity, throughout the whole of this portion of the "Rift" valley.

Several rivers enter the Albert Edward lake, which has only one outlet, the Semliki (¹).

Regarding the annual rainfall over this area, but little is known. It is probably not less than 1·50 metres per annum. The rainy season is divided into two periods. The heavier rainfall occurs during the months of March, April and May, and the lighter in October, November and December.

One noticeable characteristic of this lake is the haze which hangs over it throughout the dry season. This haze is so thick that it is often impossible, from the shore, to see more than a few hundred yards out into the lake. It is rarely, except during the rainy season, that the magnificent panorama of mountains which encircles it, to the north and west, can be seen, and the traveller visiting it during the early months of the year, might stay in the neighbourhood for a week and be utterly unaware of the near vicinity of these great ranges, or even that he was close to a large lake. Now and then, particularly when the sun is setting, a golden light pierces the mist and irradiates the water surface with a peculiarly lovely effect. When the mist lifts, the view is worth waiting for. To the south, the volcano of Karisimbi stands out with its top clouded in smoke. To the west, the range of the Congo mountains stretches like a wall, while in the north, the snow peaks, which form the summits of Ruenzori, can be distinctly seen. Again, in the east, the cliffs of the great "fault" extend and form the horizon. Such views are rare, however, and the general impression of the scenery round this lake is extremely disappointing.

Except in the south-west corner, and in the north, the shores of Lake Albert Edward contain but few bays of any size. Of these, Katwé and Witshumbi are the largest. There are only three islands in this lake, in the Katwé bay, on the north-east corner (²).

The colour of the water is a light green and, although very clear, it has a distinctly brackish taste. Like Lake Albert, the shore surrounding it is strongly impregnated with salt. Except to the north and south, where broad swamps extend, the shores of the lake are generally well above the water surface and fringed by a narrow band of reeds. The bed of Lake Albert Edward is covered with a layer of slimy, grey mud. There are but few rocks anywhere, either in the bed or on the coast. The lake abounds with fish and, in certain parts, with crocodiles. Hippopotami are said to be plentiful in the southern swamps and there are many water birds. A current, or drift, exists from the south to the north, and the natives assert that, if a canoe be set adrift from the mouth of the Mtungi river, in the south-east corner, it will, after two or three days, arrive at the outlet of the Semliki in the north. This is probably due to the influence of the prevailing trade wind. No information exists regarding the depth of Lake Albert Edward, but, according to native report, it is nowhere great. All along the northern coast, it is extremely shallow for a considerable distance from the shore, and along the north-eastern limit the depth is also insignificant. During the rainy season, Lake Albert Edward is subject to violent storms which render navigation in dug-out canoes, which are the only craft on the lake, very dangerous. The fishermen rarely venture far from the shore and when going from one distant point to another, invariably hug the coast.

The following pages contain a description of the northern shores of this lake in rather fuller detail than the foregoing account and also of the country adjacent to Lake D ueru.

(¹) These rivers will be briefly described later on.
(²) In that portion of it known as Lake Dueru there are several islands, the largest being those of Chikalero and Naukavenga.

LAKE ALBERT EDWARD, KATWE BAY

LAKE ALBERT EDWARD, LOOKING SOUTH FROM KATWE

Kazinga, the point where the caravan track from Mbarara reaches Lake Albert Edward, is a village in Ankoli, situated on the eastern bank of the Dueru channel and about 1½ kilometres north of its junction with this lake. It contains some 500 houses, but there is little cultivation, the people obtaining their supplies from Kichwamba, on the eastern escarpment. There is a trade in salt between this place and Katwe. The principal occupation of the inhabitants is fishing. There is a ferry at Kazinga and the passage of the channel is made in canoes, hollowed out of a single tree. The crossing is a very tedious business for a large caravan, as there are but few canoes and these are not sufficiently stable to permit of their being heavily laden. Fortunately, in this part of the lake, there are few crocodiles.

The Dueru channel, at Kazinga, is 420 metres in width, with a mean depth of 4.16 metres, and a maximum depth, at low water, of 5.25 metres. This channel has been described by some travellers as a river, but this is incorrect. It is merely a connecting arm between the two lakes. There is no current at all. In the early morning, when the wind, as a rule, blows from the north, there is *apparently* a slight velocity *towards* the Albert Edward lake (1). When the wind changes, which generally happens before mid-day, this stream sets in exactly the opposite direction, i.e., *from* the Albert lake *towards* Lake Dueru. It may be confidently asserted that, in the dry season, when the lakes are at a low level, there is no stream at all. In the rains, it is, however, different. Lake Dueru is the receptacle of the entire drainage of eastern Ruenzori. When all the torrents and streams from these mountains are discharging large volumes into this sheet of water, its level must quickly rise, more especially as its only outlet is the channel between the two lakes, and this is throttled, so to speak, by its narrow width. It is natural to suppose that, at such times, the level of Lake Dueru rises quicker than does that of the larger area of Lake Albert Edward, and that consequently there is a distinct and, possibly, a considerable discharge from the former into the latter lake (2). On either side of the Dueru channel are cliffs from 80 to 100 metres in height. These are not precipitous, but slope sharply up from the water's edge to the table-land on either side. There is but little swamping along this channel, but a fringe of reeds marks the water edge (3). The eastern shore of the Albert Edward, for a long distance south of Kazinga, is bounded by cliffs of the same character as those which border the Dueru channel, varying from 70 to 100 metres in height. Their sides are steep and bare of everything but short grass and small Euphorbia trees (4). The strip of land, between these cliffs and the lake, is not wide, being rarely more than 200 or 300 metres, but rises in steps, or terraces, marking distinctly the different levels at which the lake, in recent times, has stood (5). About seven metres above the present level, is a water mark, showing that the lake must have once washed the base of these cliffs, apparently at no very remote period (6). The cliffs themselves are covered with lake deposit and must have been below the water surface at the time when it extended over the whole valley and was bounded by the eastern fault-line. On this side of the lake, (the east), the high land stretches close to the water, in a line of low headlands, one succeeding the other with most monotonous regularity (7). Along the water's edge is a

(1) So apparent was this current, on the morning of the 14th February 1903, that preparations were made to measure the discharge of the supposed river. In the afternoon, however, the wind changed, and the drift was reversed, so that the floats moved *from* the lake and *up* the Dueru channel.

(2) Most probably the assertion that this was a river is due to the fact that it has been visited by travellers at such times.

(3) The eastern cliffs rise with a slope of from 4, to 5 to 1. Those on the west are steeper, being from 2, to 3 to 1.

(4) The Euphorbia is one of the most marked features of this district. It is met with everywhere.

(5) There are two terraces. One from 1 to 2 metres above the water, and the other from 3 to 5 metres above the lower one.

(6) Stuhlmann records a layer of shells, one metre thick, on the plain west of Witshumbi (in the south) at an estimated height of eight metres above the present level of the lake. The inhabitants of this village have a tradition that, in the days of their forefathers, it was situated at the foot of the hills. It is now on the shore of the lake. "Mit Emin Pasha im Herz von Afrika," Berlin, 1894.

(7) The valley to the east of this lake, between it and the eastern escarpment, is described in the chapter on the country between Lakes Victoria and Albert Edward.

fringe of reeds (1). The point of junction between the Dueru channel and the lake is indicated, on its western shore, by a fine bold bluff, wooded at its southern end. From this, a flat, 100 metres in width, stretches to the water. On the further side of this bluff, is the Katwe bay. The water level of Lake Albert Edward, in February 1903, was very low, and probably at its lowest, as there had been a long period of drought prior to this date. The marks on the shore appeared to show that the maximum rise of the lake did not exceed one metre above its level at that season. The curious light-green colour of the water in this lake has been already alluded to. It is covered at times, with a white scum which extends from the bank to a distance of several hundred metres. The water in the Dueru channel is of the brightest emerald-green possible to imagine, and even when poured into a basin preserves its colour. It, like the water of the lake itself, has an unpleasant taste and is slightly brackish.

The lake canoes are hollowed out of a single log. Their average length is 15 metres, by 1 metre in width, and 0.75 metres in depth. The paddles used are very small.

After crossing the Dueru channel, the country between it and the lake, is a high, flat plateau, about 1.5 kilometres in width, covered with thin grass, scattered bush and Euphorbia. A good view of the Katwé bay is obtained from the high land here. This bay, or gulf, is some 4 kilometres across, and 8 kilometres in length. It contains three wooded islands, two, Rulimba and Kerrisaba, near the mouth, and the third, close to the northern shore. This last is so close to the mainland that, at first sight, it appears to form a portion of it. It is, however, separated from it by a narrow channel, from 160 to 180 metres in width. None of these islands are of any great height, and one of them, Kerrisaba, exactly resembles in shape the island of Inchkeith, in the Firth of Forth. Below the eastern cliffs, which are here 80 metres above the water, low flats extend for some two kilometres, to the edge of the bay. The calm lake spread out below, the wooded islets, and the foreground of dark Euphorbia contrasting with the yellow grass, make a charming picture, the beauty of which is enhanced by the background of low, broken hills on the further side of the bay. To the east of the lake, the country stretches in a high grassy plain as far as, and across, the Dueru channel. The Euphorbia here are very numerous and this tree is certainly one of the most marked features of the landscape in the vicinity of the Albert Edward lake. It grows luxuriantly and there are few other trees, although many thorny bushes (2).

Proceeding north, along the eastern shore of Katwé bay, the flats get narrower and the slope of the cliffs flatter. Many ravines run down from the high land to the water. At 8 kilometres from Kazinga, the northern extremity of the bay is reached. Here the flats extend back from the lake in a succession of terraces, rising one above the other, to the north, eventually bounded by a high ridge, from which the land slopes gradually up to the southern spurs of Ruenzori. The lake, at one time, must have extended five kilometres further to the north than it now does and lake deposit and shells are found on the ridge, at a height of quite 100 metres above the present water surface. The Dueru channel, at this point, is some 7 or 8 kilometres to the east of the lake, separated from it by a high ridge of land (3).

Turning west, along the northern shore and following the ridge, which at this point is only 60 metres above the water, at 10 kilometres from Kazinga, a curious amphitheatre, or hollow, surrounded by a low ridge, is reached. This was probably once a crater and now contains a small salt lake. This circular hollow is about 1.75 kilometres in diameter,

(1) Further south, a line of dense forest approaches the lake, separated from it by a belt of swamp.

(2) Some of these Euphorbia grow in a curious way. A straight boll rises from the ground, to a height of from 10 to 12 metres. The top then spreads out horizontally, something like a fir tree. Often, there is a second top, half-way up the stem. The holes, made by the old shoots are visible all the way up the trunk.

(3) The whole district in the vicinity of Katwe has a very bad reputation for malaria. Mosquitoes are very numerous, but the climate in the month of February is not unpleasant. The days are hot, but the nights very cold.

NYAMGASHA RIVER, PRESENT FRONTIER BETWEEN UGANDA PROTECTORATE AND CONGO FREE STATE

CONGO FREE STATE
LAKE ALBERT EDWARD, HEAD OF SEMLIKI RIVER

and the surrounding ridge varies from 35 to 100 metres in height. The lake, in the centre, is, in the dry season, an expanse of crusted salt. It is surrounded by mud flats covered with scrub, and a few stunted Euphorbia. The only sign of life in this desolate and lonely spot is an occasional flock of pelicans. This crater receives the drainage of the surrounding high lands and the flood marks show that the area of the water surface, at times, increases by one-third. There is no outlet and the level of the bottom is rather below that of the water in the Albert Edward lake. The ridge, to the west of this depression, is some 80 metres high and of calcareous formation—covered with lake sand and shell deposit. After a small dip and rise, the village of Katwé is reached, at 13 kilometres from Kazinga, measured round the shore of the bay. This is a collection of huts, upon a hill facing the lake. The chief's house stands alone and has a pent, thatched roof. There are no signs of cultivation in the neighbourhood, but the villagers keep large flocks of sheep and goats. At 14 kilometres from Kazinga, still going due west, Fort George, latitude 0° 8′ 15″ south, is reached. This fort consists of a small rectangular enclosure, surrounded by a stone wall and containing a few huts. It is now occupied by half a dozen local police. From this point, the road to Fort Mbeni on the Semliki starts.

Just beyond Fort George, a remarkable scene presents itself. A knife-edged ridge, not more than fifty metres in width, and with almost sheer sides, extends for a length of 500 or 600 metres and connects the high land on the west with that on the east. On the south side of this ridge and just underneath it, is the Albert Edward lake, while on the north, or right side is a large circular hollow, containing the Katwé salt lake. The total distance between the two sheets of water cannot be more than 800 or 900 metres, and the contrast between them is very striking. The colour of the water in the Albert Edward lake is a greenish blue, while that of the salt lake is a pale rose. This last is surrounded by high cliffs, and along its shores is a thick fringe of palms. The shadows of these hills and trees, reflected, in an almost crimson shade, upon the rosy surface of the water, give a peculiar and very beautiful effect to this unique scene. The level of the salt lake is certainly lower than that of Lake Albert Edward, but how much lower it is difficult to say exactly (1). The Katwé salt lake is almost circular in shape and was doubtless once a crater. Its diameter is some 2 kilometres, and high and steep cliffs entirely surround it. This lake is the great centre of the salt trade of the district and traders come from long distances to obtain this article of commerce.

After crossing the ridge and leaving the salt lake behind, the country, for the next four or five kilometres, is fairly level, with easy undulations. It is covered with much bush. All along the shore of the Albert Edward Nyanza, a line of high bluffs extends, similar in character and height to those described as forming the eastern shore of the Katwé bay. Between these bluffs and the water are wide flats, which in some places form papyrus swamps.

At 15 kilometres from Kazinga, the Nyamgasha, or Nyamgashani, river is reached (2). This river is, for the present, considered as the boundary between the Uganda Protectorate and the Congo Free State. It flows from the Ruenzori mountains, across the plateau, in a generally southerly direction, joining Lake Albert Edward on the western shore of Katwé bay. On its left bank, on the Mbeni-Katwé road, is situated the village of Nyababari. In the neighbourhood is a good deal of cultivation, consisting of bananas, maize and sweet potatoes. The crossing of the river is a matter of some difficulty, as, even in the dry season, it is deep, with a swift current, and almost perpendicular banks.

(1) Stanley makes the salt lake some 50 metres below the crest of the ridge, and the Albert Edward lake some 07 metres. These heights were measured with an aneroid. With such an instrument, and for these small heights, it is difficult to correctly judge the differences of level. I should put them at 70 to 80 metres for the salt lake, and at 50 to 60 metres for the Albert Edward. [W.E.G.]

(2) This river will be described in that part of this chapter, which is devoted to the streams which feed Lake Albert Edward.

After crossing this stream, the same type of landscape continues, but the bush and trees get thinner. West of the junction of the Nyamgashi with the Albert Edward Nyanza, the coast of the lake becomes much more indented by bays and creeks than was the case on the eastern side. The high land continues along the edge, to which the plateau behind slopes up. Bay succeeds bay and promontory succeeds promontory. Many of these headlands, although rarely more than 80 metres above the water, form bold and striking bluffs, but of rounded outline. The flats vary in width. In many places they are several kilometres broad, with a wide swampy belt near the water, full of papyrus and reeds. Behind, is an extent of slightly higher land, covered with a thick growth of small acacia trees. The alluvial plain which stretches north of the lake, from the high coast-line to the Ruenzori hills, is, at times, park-like in aspect, with clumps of fine trees. At others, it is open and bare, with low grass and a few scattered thorn bushes, or Euphorbia. With the exception of an occasional fishermen's hut, on the ridge bordering the lake, there is no sign of human habitation in this part of the country. At 20 kilometres from Kazinga, the road leading to the Belgian fort at Mbeni strikes off to the north-west and travellers, wishing to visit the head-waters of the Semliki, must leave it and go across country in a westerly direction. From this point no track exists. The plateau is now a dreary-looking expanse of dead-flat plain, traversed by an occasional shallow depression. The lake shore, at this point, is low and very swampy. A few kilometres further on, a series of extraordinary dips and rises commences. These run north and south and are all more or less parallel to one another. The country resembles a gigantic ploughed field, the furrows being from 400 to 800 metres in width and the ridges between them from 2 to 3 metres in height. These depressions extend some 5 to 6 kilometres from the lake and beyond them the flat plateau which they drain, stretches to the north. Six kilometres further west, these peculiar depressions cease and the character of the country changes. The ridge bounding the lake recommences, but it is not so high as before, being not more than 50 to 60 metres in height. The lake shore is a succession of swampy bays and creeks, all full of papyrus and all bounded by a belt of acacias. The country behind the ridge is fairly high and open, with glades of exceptionally tall mimosa trees scattered about it. The general elevation of this plateau is from 30 to 40 metres above the lake. Its level is generally high, but it is traversed at intervals by many swampy depressions, full of tall reeds and averaging 60 to 70 metres in width.

At 31 kilometres from Kazinga, the valley of the Dibirra river is reached. It is a broad belt of very deep swamp, some two kilometres wide, in the centre of which the river winds (1). This river is even more difficult to cross than the Nyamgasha, as its current is very swift and the banks both steep and high. On the west side of the swampy valley, broken ground, covered with thick bush, rises to the foot of the Kipura range of mountains, which is reached at 35 kilometres from Kazinga (2). These hills are a continuation of the Ruenzori chain and form the only break in the flat and low plateau which extends north of the Albert Edward lake. The range runs nearly due north and south and continues right to the lake shore (3). The Kipura hills form the eastern boundary of the valley of the Semliki. This is a beautiful range, full of picturesque peaks, some of them rising to 1600, and even 1800, metres above the sea. The eastern slopes are rugged and steep, the western flatter, and more wooded. On the east face, except in clefts and in the deep ravines, there are but few trees, and grassy slopes alternate with sheer precipices, which stand out, masses of bare rock, rising abruptly above the lower portion of the range. Behind the first line of hills, a second and higher one, towers. Along the base, and parallel to the Dibirra valley, a

(1) This river will also be described further on.

(2) On the maps this range is called Kitoro, but this name appears to be unknown to the inhabitants of this locality. According to the District Officers, further to the north it is called Kakoni.

(3) Here the maps are wrong. They show these hills as ending some distance to the north of lake Albert Edward.

long flat-topped ridge, or terrace, continues for some distance, at a height of some 70 metres above the river. These mountains extend south to the Albert Edward lake, and end in a low rounded hill. The lake shore here is low and flat, swampy in places, and everywhere covered with a very thick growth of acacia forest. Some of the ravines upon the eastern face are very deep and precipitous, extending nearly from the top of the range to the valley itself. All of them are densely wooded. One very striking ravine has sheer sides, several hundred metres in depth. A large portion of the hill-side has slipped into this chasm and the section shows distinctly the different strata. Lake deposit and shells are found here, at an elevation of more than 100 metres above the present lake level; a strong proof that, in former times, its water stood at a much greater height than is now the case.

There are several passes by which these hills can be crossed. One, the best known and the easiest, is to the north, and at this point, the road from Katwé to Fort Mbeni crosses. In the centre of the range is another pass, crossed by Lugard in 1891. The third and the most difficult, lies at the southern end of the chain. The ascent from the east is very steep and is made by mounting a succession of terraces, on a long spur, flanked by deep ravines on either side. At different elevations, small plateaux are reached, generally surrounded by a wall of peaks, some rounded, and some of jagged and conical outline. Most of these secluded plateaux are well wooded, and are tenanted by large herds of waterbuck (Cobus Defassa), the males of which bear horns of exceptional length and spread. The top of the pass is attained, after an ascent of six kilometres in length. This point is some 350 metres above the lake. On either side, the summits of the adjacent hills stand up for another 100 or 150 metres. Further north, the mountains increase in height and the highest peaks in this range must be quite 600 metres above the valley, or 1600 metres above sea-level. From the summit of the south pass, a far-reaching and lovely view of the Albert Edward lake is obtained. The many bays and promontories which mark the coast line of its northern shore are, with the swamps and wooded flats, spread out below the observer, as if on a large scale map. To the west, the Semliki valley extends, the Congo mountains bounding its further side. The descent, on the western face of the Kipura mountains, commences through a gap of 800 metres width between two hills, and the route follows a long spur; a wide and gently sloping valley lying below it to the north. This valley is full of scattered mimosas and occasional little granite knolls stand out on its further ridge. At 5 kilometres from the summit of this pass, the descent into the Semliki valley is achieved [1].

It is now necessary to give a brief description of the Dueru channel and lake, which form a portion of the larger sheet of water. The channel, from Kazinga, is some 40 kilometres in length. For nearly 11 kilometres from the point where it leaves Lake Albert Edward, it runs between high cliffs, with an average width of 500 metres and a very winding course. From here, it widens out, following the valley in a north-westerly direction, with a width of from 2 to 2·5 kilometres. At 25 kilometres from Kazinga, and near Katangula, the small Kiambura river which rises at the foot of the eastern escarpment, joins it. At the point where this channel widens out into the Dueru lake, the village of Maonga is situated on its eastern bank and not far from this, a small river, the Katabera, enters the lake from the east. At the junction of this river, a large expanse of swamp stretches far to the south-east and four small streams drain across the eastern valley into the lake [2]. The Dueru lake, for some 20 kilometres of its length, is a roughly-shaped parallelogram, with a maximum width of 16 to 17 kilometres. At its north-western end, a long arm, 6 to 7 kilometres wide at the mouth, but gradually narrowing, stretches for

(1) This valley will be described, in some detail, in the chapter relating to the Semliki river. It has a width of some 25 kilometres.

(2) These are the Kitanda, the Kinteya, Bagao and Kikumi.

another 10 or 12 kilometres. On the western shore, is a large bay known as Luanka, and not far from the entrance of the Dueru channel, are two large islands, called Chikalero and Naukavenga. Throughout the western shore, wide swamps of papyrus and reeds extend, and the northern arm is more like a huge marsh than a lake (1). On the eastern coast, the cliffs of the great "fault" line approach the water closely, but, north of the Mpango river, they recede from the lake. The shores here, and all along its northern extremity, are covered by dense forest, tropical in its vegetation, and inhabited by large herds of elephants. In the extreme north, the country rises sharply in a series of plateaux, formed by the eastern spurs and foothills of the Ruenzori mountains (2). Lake Dueru receives the water of numerous rivers, all of which, with the exception of the small streams at the south end, rise in the Ruenzori mountains and some of which are fed by the glaciers of this range.

The principal rivers, commencing from the south end of this lake, are as follows :—

The Makokia, the Nuisamba, the Lokoku, the Sebu, the Mbuku, the Hima, the Ruimi or Nsongi, and the Mpango, with its branch the Manobo.

All these rivers rise on the eastern face of the Ruenzori mountains, and the Lokoku, Sebu and Mbuku, are glacier-fed streams (3).

With the exception of the Ruimi and the Mpango, all these rivers flow into Lake Dueru, on the western shore. None of them are of great length, as the Ruenzori chain is nowhere very far to the west of this lake and, after their issue from the mountain gorges, the width of valley to be traversed is rarely more than from 8 to 10 kilometres. The Ruimi and the Mpango, although like the others, they rise on the eastern slopes of Ruenzori, take a long sweep to the north, and passing round the northern end of the lake enter it on its eastern shore. Between them runs a high range of hills, connected with the Ruenzori range, which rise towards the south, into the great mass of Mount Lobaba (Mt. Edwin Arnold). This mountain attains the height of 1700 metres above the sea. Of all these rivers, the Mpango is the most important, and is the largest of all the feeders of the Albert Edward lake, not even excepting the Rutshuru, in the south.

The following pages give a brief description of these streams.

The Makokia river issues from the mountains, about 29 kilometres due north of Katwé. In the dry season, it is a very small stream, with a width of 3 metres, and a depth of 0·40 metres. Its discharge, on the 23rd February 1903, was only 0·455 metres cubes per second. In flood, it is a formidable obstacle to travellers. At the point where it leaves the hills, it flows through a fine gorge, 100 metres in width, and from 10 to 12 metres deep, with vertical sides. This gorge is full of high reeds. At its western end is a bold mountain peak which stand sout from the surrounding hills. The total length of the Makokia is under 20 kilometres (4), and it joins the lake at the north-western extremity of the bay of Luanka.

The Nuisamba river crosses the plain, between the mountains and Lake Dueru, at 41 kilometres north of Katwé. At this point, a wide valley runs up into the hills, and the plain, of about 1·5 kilometres in width, is a succession of dry torrent-beds. The beds of these streams are strewn with boulders, many of them very large. Some of these torrents are of considerable size, one being 30 metres in width, by 2·25 metres in depth. All these channels show signs of severe water-action, and the way in which the boulders have been tossed about, shows how violent must be the force of the stream, when in full flood. The channel of the Nuisamba, in the dry season, is only 4 metres wide, by

(1) The western shore will be described in some detail in the chapter on the country between Lakes Albert Edward and Albert.

(2) A belt of forest stretches north from this lake, through Toru to Unyoro.

(3) The whole of the drainage of the Ruenzori mountains falls, eventually. into Lake Albert, inasmuch as the streams, on the east, discharge into the Dueru lake, and their waters pass into Lake Albert Edward ; from which the Semliki is the only outlet. The rivers, on the west of Ruenzori, all fall into the Semliki, which, again, discharges its waters into the Albert lake.

(4) Map of "Albert und Albert-Edward Seen," by Dr. F. Stuhlmann, compiled by Max Moisel.

0·30 metres deep. The discharge of this river, on the 23rd February 1903, was only 0·636 metres cube per second. The flood channel is 100 metres in width, by 1·25 metres deep, and is filled with dense reeds and grass. The length of the Nuisamba is about 33 kilometres (1).

Eight kilometres further to the north, the Lukoku river is arrived at. Although so close to the Nuisamba, this stream issues from the mountains by a different gorge. The Lokoku is a glacier-fed river, running in a channel 10 metres wide, 4·8 metres deep, with nearly vertical sides. On February the 23rd 1903, its water-width (near the point where it leaves the hills) was 10 metres. The depth was 0·95 metres, and the mean velocity 0·53 metres per second. The discharge was 2·8 metres cube per second. Its flood rise, at this point, is 1·7 metres, as marked on the banks, but in heavy floods, it is possible that this height is considerably exceeded. On either bank of the Lokoku, flats extend, to some 80 or 90 metres in width, covered with a growth of very tall reeds. Its course after leaving the mountains, is very winding, and there is much erosion. The water is very clear and has all the appearance of snow water. The bed is alternately sand and boulders. The general course of the Lukoku is south-easterly (2).

The Sebu river leaves the hills, five kilometres to the north of the Lukoku, or 53 kilometres north of Katwé. At this point, the western foothills recede from the Dueru valley, forming a wide valley, flanked, on the right hand, by three low, conical peaks. Through this gorge, the Sebu flows. This river, with the Lokoku, rises in the eastern glaciers of Ruenzori and, like all the streams which have their rise in this portion of the chain, has a perennial flow. Its valley is wide and, in flood, must be traversed by many torrents, as throughout it there are marks of severe water-action and boulders are strewn about in all directions. The low-water channel of the Sebu is very small, being only 2 metres wide, by 1·75 metres deep. The banks stand up vertically above the water. Its discharge, as measured on the 25th of February 1903, was only 0·53 metres cube per second. The width was 2 metres, the depth 0·49 metres, and the mean velocity 0·50 metres per second. The length of the Sebu is given on Stuhlmann's map, as only 20 kilometres (3). Just before it reaches the lake, the Sebu joins the Mbuku river, of which it is really a tributary.

Between the Sebu and the Mbuku, the entire valley is filled with a dense covering of very tall reeds, through which numerous dry channels, full of boulders, wind about. During the rainy season, independently of the two river crossings, this valley must be impassable for caravans.

At 58 kilometres north of Katwé, the Mbuku, or Mpuku, as it is sometimes called, crosses the valley from the foothills, on its way to Lake Dueru. This river, which derives its supply from the large glaciers of the Ruenzori mountains, is by far the most important of the streams which feed Lake Dueru, on the west. Its general course is westerly, and it has a length of some 40 kilometres, its sources being situated in a range nearly 4,000 metres above sea-level (4). Where it issues from the mountains, it tumbles in a succession of small falls, over rocks and boulders. Its water is clear, and icy cold. The width of its channel, at low water, is 8 metres, by 1·5 metres deep, with perpendicular rocky sides. The discharge was measured on the 25th of February 1903, and, with a depth of 0·83 metres, and a mean velocity of 1·16 metres per second, was equivalent to 7·05 metres cube per second. The flood rise, at this point, is 2·75 metres above the lowest level, and its width, when in full flood, is 120 metres. It is very difficult to estimate the flood discharge of this river, but when at its maximum, it cannot be much less than 300 metres cube per second. Its floods do not, however,

(1) Map of "Albert und Albert-Edward Seen," by Dr. F. Stuhlmann, compiled by Max Moisel.

(2) As regards the Lukoku, Moisel's map appears to be wrong. The course is marked as very short, only some 16 or 17 kilometres. It is really one of the largest of the rivers entering Lake Dueru in the west, and rises in the glaciers of Ruenzori. This would give it a length of, at least, 30 or 35 kilometres.

(3) Here again, the map appears to be wrong, as the Sebu, like the Lukoku and the Mbuku, is glacier-fed, and must have a length of more than 30 kilometres.

(4) Stuhlmann's map.

last long, coming down in a series of rushes, which sometimes render the crossing impossible for as much as six or seven days, and then subside again.

Proceeding northwards, the next river to enter the Dueru lake, on the west, is the Hima, 63 kilometres north of Katwé. The Hima runs in a deep channel, 130 metres in width, between extremely steep banks. The southern, or right bank, is 24 metres above the river bed, the northern is 16 metres. Both have very nearly vertical sides. Within this deep gash, the stream runs in two separate channels, that on the right hand, being 10 metres from the bank, and that on the left, 31 metres from the further side of the valley. Of these, the right-hand channel is the more important, being 4 metres wide, by 3·5 metres deep. The section of the smaller channel is 3 metres, by 2·5 metres. The intervening space, as well as those between the channels and the banks, is filled with an extremely thick growth of very tall reeds. A few large trees stand up among the grass, at intervals. On the 26th of February 1903, there was practically no discharge in the left-hand channel, while in the larger one to the right, it was only 0·728 metres cube per second (1). The water is very clear, and passes over a rocky bed. It is not easy to ascertain the rise of the floods in this river. The natives of the locality assert that it never rises over the top of the two small channels. This is probably true, as the existence of the trees and bushes seems to prove that no heavy rush of water passes down the valley. Moreover, the slope of the bed is very considerable. The maximum rise may be considered as between 2·0 and 3·0 metres. The direction of the Hima river is nearly due east and, according to Stuhlmann's map, its length is some 25 kilometres. It is not glacier-fed, but rises in the secondary ranges of Ruenzori. On the top of the cliffs, a calcareous deposit, much resembling "Kunkur," is found. The Hima is the most northerly and the last, of the rivers running into the western shores of Lake Dueru. Between it and the next tributary of this lake, the Ruimi, a spur runs out east from the mountains and approaches the northern extremity of Lake Dueru, thus turning the drainage to the north, and round the head of the lake, whence it finds its way into the valley on its eastern shore. This spur, although of considerable elevation, is not a wide one and a distance of only six kilometres separates the Hima from the Ruimi.

The Ruimi, called in its lower reaches the Nsongi, rises in latitude 0° 28′ north, in the ranges which bound the high plateau, at the north-eastern end of Ruenzori. Upon this plateau, Fort Portal is situated, and here the Mpango river has its source. This portion of the Ruenzori mass is known as Kiriba, and has a height of some 2400 metres above the sea (2). Its direction, for the first portion of its course, is nearly due south, but on reaching the above-mentioned spur, it is deflected to the east, and follows this course until it has skirted round the head of the lake valley, when it again turns south. Near its mouth, it is joined by another river, the Dura, and their combined waters flow into the lake, on its eastern shore, in latitude 0° 11′ north (3). The length of the Ruimi is some 50 kilometres (4). Not far above the point where it makes its last turn to the south, the Ruimi runs through the hills, in a deep and winding gorge, 70 metres across, with a sheer drop of 35 metres. The stream here, is a series of rapids, flowing over large boulders and rocky falls, worn into numerous pot-holes by the action of the water. This gorge is densely wooded and full of tall trees, some of them remarkable for the beauty of their foliage. The wildness of the scene is enhanced by the high hills which enclose this gorge on either side. The left bank is much higher than the right and is quite 100 metres above the water. In its course through the hills, the slope of the Ruimi is very heavy, and there are numerous falls. In its lower reaches, where it is joined by the Dura, it passes through wide and deep swamps (5).

(1) The depth of water was 0.60 metres, and the mean velocity 0 25 metres per second.

(2) Stuhlmann's Map.

(3) The Dura rises in the same range as the Ruimi, but further to the north, i.e., in north lat. 0° 40′. It has a length of some 70 kilometres.

(4) Stuhlmann's map

(5) Stanley, who crossed it a good deal lower down, gives the width as 17 metres, and the depth as 0·75 metres.

The discharge of the Ruimi, as measured on the 26th of February 1903, gave the following results: Width of water 11 metres, with a maximum depth of 9·90 metres, and a mean velocity of 0·77 metres. The volume was 4·3 metres cube per second. The Ruimi water is very clear and cold, although not fed by the Ruenzori glaciers. Its main tributary, the Dura, is made up of the combined waters of three mountain rivers, the Yeria, Balariba and Msongi, all of which lie within a distance of 83 and 92 kilometres north of Katwé. Of these the Msongi is the largest and the most important (1). The valleys in which these streams run, average from 70 to 100 metres in width, and from 20 to 25 metres in depth. They are all swampy and filled with high reeds, and some trees. Their flood-rise appears to average 2·75 metres, and the Msongi must, when running full, have a width of quite 35 metres.

The last of the series of rivers, which supply the Dueru lake, is the Mpango. This is by far the most important of all the affluents of this lake, and probably carries a larger volume than any of the streams which enter the Lake Albert Edward. Some travellers have considered it to be as large a river as the Semliki, but this is certainly not the case. It may, occasionally, carry a volume exceeding that of the Semliki, but only for a very short period of time, and its mean annual discharge cannot be compared to that of the former river. It has two main branches, the most southerly rising in the Kiriba range, south-west of Fort Portal, and the other far to the north, near Nssororo or Fort Wavertree (2). Of these, that rising in the south is the larger and the most important. The Mpango, in its upper reaches, has an easterly direction, and passes close to Fort Portal, the headquarters of the Toru district (3). Not very far from here, it is joined by its northern branch and, below the junction, flows for the rest of its course in a very deep and wide valley, between high cliffs. Some 50 kilometres from its source, it turns due south and continues in this direction for another 40 kilometres. It then turns sharp to the west and enters Lake Dueru, in latitude 0° 7′ north, after a total length of some 110 kilometres (4). The Mpango receives the waters of numerous small streams and drains a considerable area of country. Throughout its southern course, it flows through tropical forest, between the Lobaba mountains and the high plateau, to the east, which forms the watershed between the streams flowing to Lake Albert Edward and those feeding Lake Victoria (5). In its upper reaches, although the fall of the bed levels is very heavy, the section of the channel carrying the supply during the dry season, is not very great. Near Fort Portal, it runs in a rocky bed full of large boulders, and 5.0 metres wide, by 2.60 metres deep, with the usual vertical banks. The maximum flood-rise, at this point, is 3.3 metres above low water-level, which would make its depth in flood equal to 4.10 metres. A discharge of the Mpango, measured on the 6th of March 1903, gave a total of 2.64 metres cube per second (6). The width of the river in flood, at this point, is 114 metres, with a flood section of 91 square metres. Allowing that the mean velocity for the whole area was 2 metres per second (7), this is equivalent to a discharge of 182 metres cube per second. As these measurements refer to the upper portion of the Mpango, which, between Fort Portal and the Dueru lake, receives many tributaries, some

(1) The following are the measurements of these three streams, as made at the points of crossing, on the 28th February 1903.

The Yeria. The channel was 3·0 metres by 3·0 metres, depth of water 0·49 metres, and mean velocity 0·38 metres per second.

The Balariba was dry, but the channel was 2·75 metres by 2·5 metres.

The Msongi, has a bed, 4 metres wide by 1·25 metres deep. The depth of water was only 0.30 metres, but the mean velocity was 0·51 metres per second. The combined discharge of the Msongi and the Yeria was 1·494 metres cube per second.

(2) The south branch has several tributaries, the principal of which are the Igasha, the Nakatera and the Malluna.

The Igasha has a bed-width of 3 metres, with vertical rocky sides, 1.5 metres high. The water on 1st of March 1903, was 0.60 metres deep and the discharge was 0.99 metres cube per second. The Nakatera was dry in March 1903. It is a smaller river than the Igasha.

The Malluna has a bed-width of 3.0 metres by 1.0 metre deep. The discharge on the 1st March 1903 was only 0.33 metres cube per second.

(3) Fort Portal is 114 kilometres north of Katwé.

(4) Stuhlmann's map.

(5) Near its entrance to Lake Dueru, it is described by Lugard as passing through a gorge 250 metres in depth, with precipitous banks, and full of dense forest.

(6) The water width was 5.0 metres, depth 0.80 metres and mean velocity was 0.88 metres per second.

(7) On the flats, the depth is shallow and the velocity cannot be very great.

of them of considerable size ; it is probable that its flood discharge, where it enters the lake, is quite three times the above amount.

Before leaving Lake Albert Edward, some description of the rivers entering it is necessary. This must necessarily be a brief one, as very little information exists regarding them (1).

On the southern shore, the two principal streams are the Rutshuru and the Ruendu. The latter enters the lake in the Witshumbi bay. It is described by Stuhlmanu as having "a width of from 5 to 6 metres, a depth of 1 metre, and a strong stream." The Ruendu, like the Rutshuru, drains the northern slopes of the great ridge, or block, in the "rift" valley, which forms the separation between the Albertine and Tanganyika systems. The Rutshuru is the most important of all the affluents of Lake Albert Edward, as considered apart from Lake Dueru (2). In its southern reaches, it is known as the Keku, and is described as "a large body of water, deep and quite unfordable, passing through dense forest." It rises in latitude 1° 25′ south. Stuhlmann, who crossed it in May 1891, describes it as "nearly 60 metres in width and 1 metre deep, with a very strong current" (3). It must, however, in flood, be a river of considerable volume, as Moore, who visited it in the winter of 1899, describes it, as "a mighty stream of muddy yellow water, as wide as the Thames at Westminster, and whirling in eddies and rapids to the north" (4). In its lower course, it passes through the marshy plains to the south of the lake, which it enters in latitude 0° 24′ south.

On the western shore of Lake Albert Edward, no rivers of importance enter. The Wekondjo mountains run parallel to, and close to its shores, throughout its entire length. Although numerous rain torrents drain off their eastern faces, these are all of short length and heavy slope, and can none of them be classed as rivers.

Turning to the eastern shore, here again the fault line approaches within a short distance of the lake, and the width of the intervening plain, except in the north-east corner, is not more than 5 to 6 kilometres. The length of the drainage lines is consequently not great, and none of them are important (5).

In the south-eastern corner, however, there is a river of some size, viz., the Muwengu, or Mtungi. This stream crosses the southern plain and receives the drainage of the eastern escarpment. According to native statements, a current runs across Lake Albert Edward, from the mouth of this river to the outlet of the Semliki, and a canoe, set afloat from the former, would drift across in time to the latter. Not very much information exists regarding the Muwengu. It is said to be, at times, of considerable volume, but to run very low during the dry season of the year. Its length is not great, being not more than 35 kilometres.

On the north of Lake Albert Edward, only two rivers enter, viz., the Nyamgasha and the Dibirra. Both of these streams rise in the southern ranges of Ruenzori, and, crossing the great alluvial plain lying to the north of the lake, enter it to the east of the Kipura hills.

Of these the Nyamgasha is the more important (6). This river rises in latitude 0° 11′ north and has a length of some 55 kilometres. Its junction is some five kilometres west of Katwé, at the end of the promontory on the western side of the Katwé bay. At the point where the Katwé-Mbeni road crosses it, it has a width of 8 metres, and runs between

(1) With the exception of the Nyamgashi and the Dibirra, on the north of the lake, none of the tributary streams were crossed during the expedition made in the spring of 1903.

(2) The Mpungo is a larger stream than the Rutshuru.

(3) "Mit Emin Pasha im Herz von Afrika," Berlin.

(4) "The Mountains of the Moon," London.

(5) Stuhlmann, on his map shows four streams in this length of lake, viz., commencing from the south, the Intwara, the Kaissa, the Dwampono and the Wissegwe. None of these are more than 7 to 8 kilometres in length.

(6) It is also called locally, the Nyamgashani.

steep, vertical banks, 2.80 metres high. On either side of its channel, which is very winding, are wide reed-covered flats. These are topped, to a depth of 0.50 metres, by the water, when the river is in flood ([1]). It has a rapid stream and is not fordable in many places. The bed of the Nyamgasha is sandy, and there is much erosion where it cuts its way through the alluvium of this plain. The entire valley, which averages 5 to 6 kilometres in width, is full of calcareous deposit and is much cultivated. Its general direction is south, or south-westerly. For some distance above its junction with the lake, it passes through dense, reedy swamps, much frequented by elephants, who levy a heavy toll upon the banana plantations in the vicinity. Its waters are clear and very cold. On the 16th of February 1903, a discharge of the Nyamgasha was measured, a little upstream of the ford on the Katwé-Mbeni road. The width of the water at this point was 1 metre, the greatest depth 1.50 metres, and the mean velocity 0.55 metres per second. The discharge was 4.9 metres cube per second. The area of its flood section is 125 square metres, and its discharge, when running full, must be, at least, 250 metres cube per second.

The Dibirra river is a smaller stream than the Nyamgasha, but has a course nearly parallel to it. It crosses the plain, some 10 kilometres west of Katwé, and the Kipura hills form the western boundary of its valley. It has a short course, of not more than 30 kilometres, and for some distance it runs close under the mountains. Its valley averages from 2 to 3 kilometres in width, and, for the lower half of its course, is swampy and full of high, very thick reeds. Through this valley, the stream winds in a succession of loops, changing its course continually, as it cuts through the soft alluvial soil ([2]). In places, the bed of the Dibirra is covered with a layer of soft clay, which makes crossing it a matter of difficulty. In most parts of its course the bed is gravel. It is only fordable at a few points and is full of deep pools, the haunt of wild buffaloes. The banks are extremely steep, and, in some places, as much as 3 metres over the water. The average width of the low water channel is 7 metres, and at the ford, some 7 or 8 kilometres upstream of its junction with the lake, its depth was 0.75 metres. As a rule, it is considerably deeper than this. As it approaches the lake, the marsh gets wider and more impenetrable ([3]). The discharge of the Dibirra was measured, at the above ford, on the 17th February 1903, and gave a total of 3.19 metres cube per second ([4]). It is very difficult to say to what extent the Dibirra valley is flooded during the rainy season. The marks on the banks indicate a rise of 1.75 metres above low water level, but it must, at times, spread its waters over the marshes on either side. At the same time, it certainly does not carry anything like the same volume as does the Nyamgasha, probably not more than half, even at its maximum.

([1]) The total width of the water-surface, when in flood, is 211 metres, and the depth, in mid-stream, 3.30 metres.

([2]) In many places dry channels are met with, marking former courses of the Dibirra.

([3]) Travellers who have crossed the Dibirra, or camped in its vicinity, have cause to remember it, owing to the presence of a small, black, and peculiarly vicious mosquito, which bites by day as well as by night. The bite leaves a smart for a considerable time.

([4]) Width 7 metres, depth 0.75 metres, and mean velocity 0.60 metres per second.

GENERAL DESCRIPTION OF THE COUNTRY BETWEEN THE ALBERT EDWARD AND ALBERT LAKES IN THE DISTRICTS OF TORU AND UNYORO.

The easiest, and the most frequented, route, between these two lakes, has a general direction from the south to the north. For a considerable portion of its course, it skirts the slopes of the eastern foot-hills of the Ruenzori range, which rises, a snow-capped mass, partially blocking the "Rift" valley and, for more than 70 kilometres north of Lake Albert Edward, dividing it into two distinct portions. Before describing the route to the Albert lake, it may be well to relate the part which this chain of mountains plays with regard to the Nile supply.

To the west of Ruenzori, runs the valley of the Semliki river, bounded on its further side by the Wakondjo mountains, which here form the dividing ridge between the waters of the Nile and the Congo river. This valley, although in parts very narrow, is continuous, and runs without a break from the southern to the northern lake. That portion of the "Rift" which lies to the east of Ruenzori forms a large loop, once a bay, or a gulf, of the great lake which at one time covered this entire area. Its further boundary is the line of cliffs marking the great eastern fault. All that now remains of the great sheet of water which once covered the surface of this portion of the valley, are the lakes of Albert Edward and Dueru, with the narrow channel which connects them. To the north of the latter lake, the faultline deflects to the west and is merged in the high plateau which stretches eastward from the northern ridges of Ruenzori. The valley is thus completely barred across. The "Rift," or fissure, is, however, continued to the north, in the line of the Semliki valley above mentioned, and, although contracted in its limits for a considerable distance by the projecting mass of the Ruenzori chain, this obstacle once passed, it again spreads out and forms the wide valley in which is situated the Albert lake. Throughout this portion of its course, the eastern boundary is the escarpment of the high plateau already referred to. It will thus be understood that the whole of the rainfall of Ruenzori, together with the supply derived from its glaciers, must necessarily drain into one or other of the two great lakes lying to the south and to the north, and consequently helps indirectly, to feed the Nile supply. The streams draining its eastern slopes, without exception, flow into Lake Dueru, which again is a portion of Lake Albert Edward. Those on the west flow directly into the Semliki, and their waters are thus carried into the Albert lake.

The following is a more or less summary description of the general features of the country lying adjacent to the "Rift," along the line of route which would be followed by a traveller making his way from Lake Albert Edward to Lake Albert. The boundary between the districts of Ankoli and Toru lies a few kilometres to the north of the village of Katwé, on the bay of that name, in the north-east corner of the Albert Edward lake (¹).

Proceeding north, the land rises gradually from the lake, in a couple of terraces or steps, one above the other. These terraces are broad, and of calcareous formation, and mark distinctly the shores of the lake at different periods, when its water stood very much higher than is now the case. The upper terrace is some 100 metres above the present lake-level, and the bay, which it once enclosed, runs north for three kilometres from Katwé. Beyond this, the high land continues and is in reality a prolongation of the southern spurs of the Ruenzori mountains. On the east, the valley of the Dueru runs parallel and stretches across to the Kichwamba escarpment, which here is some 17 kilometres distant. This

(¹) See the chapter upon Lake Albert Edward.

TORU DISTRICT
A CRATER SALT LAKE, EAST OF RUENZORI

valley is generally flat, with occasional low ridges running north and south. At 8 kilometres north of Katwé, the high land bordering the valley rises suddenly into a range of low hills, along the base of which a terrace runs. This again, throws out a succession of spurs running east and west, and sloping down into the Dueru valley below. These spurs make the journey a fatiguing series of continual ascents and descents. Between them, the low land is swampy and the black clay soil makes walking in wet weather a matter of some difficulty. The terrace averages 150 metres above the valley and on it, as well as on the hills adjoining, many extinct craters are met with. The most southerly of these craters is called Kiandru. It is circular and some 800 metres in diameter, by 100 metres in depth. Its bed is full of trees. Behind it to the west, and separated from it by a very narrow ridge, is another and deeper crater (1). Behind this again, and bordering its western edge, rises a sheer precipice of bare rock, many hundred metres in height. To the north and south of this cliff are high hills, out of which a deep gash has been cut, probably caused by a subsidence of the hill-side. Some two kilometres further north and on the same terrace, two more cavities, once craters, are met with. These, like the first pair, are separated from one another by a narrow wall of rock, which forms a rim common to both. These two inverted cones are from 600 to 700 metres in diameter, and from 100 to 150 metres deep. Their sides are very steep, and in places descend about vertically. In one of them is a salt lake, evidently a favourite resort of water-buck and other antelope. From the cliffs above, numbers of these animals can be seen, licking the salt encrusted on the shores of this weird-looking and lonely tarn. North of this lake, the terrace extends for some distance and the general cross-section from the western hills, is a flat plateau, from 800 to 1000 metres in width, and 150 metres above the valley. This plateau ends in a sharp drop, on to another and lower terrace. Finally, the valley stretches east, to the distant escarpment. At the 18th kilometre, the upper terrace disappears and the Kikerungu crater-lake is passed, on the second, or lower, step. This lake, which is close to the foot of the hills, is nearly circular, with a diameter of 1300 metres. The water is brackish and undrinkable, but it is tenanted by hippopotami. The beach is pebbly and sloping and the rise of the water-level never exceeds one metre. There are no reeds in the vicinity of this lake, but there is a marshy strip all round, some 40 metres in width, marking the extent of the flooded area. To the north, a broad, low and bush-covered plateau extends from the foothills to the marshes of the Dueru lake, which here is not more than two kilometres from the western mountains. Kikerungu is remarkable for the violence and the frequency of the thunder-storms which sweep over the face of the adjacent mountains. Opposite this lake, a great mountain towers high in the air (2). Its skyline is extremely jagged in outline. So serrated is it, that it resembles the vertebrae of some prehistoric monster (3).

For several kilometres further north, the route continues in the near vicinity of the hills, which at times, run down in a long slope to the valley, and at others, are flanked by one or more terraces, similar to those already described. On all of these terraces are plentiful signs of lake deposit, at heights varying from 80 to 100 metres above the valley. At kilometre 29 from Katwé, the Makokia river is crossed. It flows through a fine gorge, headed at its western end by a high, bold peak (4). Beyond this river, the ground is high and covered with thick forest, which extends into the valley, to the shores of the Dueru lake. Between kilometres 41 and 49, a wide gorge runs up into the mountains, through which the Nuisamba and the Lokoku (5) rivers issue from the hills. These streams are at a distance

(1) Many of these crater bowls contain small lakes. Others are dry.

(2) By some, this mountain, which is a portion of the Ruenzori chain, is called Ruisamba, and to this is probably due the fact that Lake Dueru is sometimes called by this name.

(3) Thirty-three distinct small peaks can be counted in this block alone.

(4) This river, as well as all those rising in the Ruenzori hills, has already been described in the chapter upon the Albert Edward lake.

(5) This is a glacier-fed stream.

of 6 kilometres apart, but between them is an expanse, scored by many dry channels and covered by boulders, showing that at times it is crossed by torrents. A few kilometres to the north of the Lokoku another and wider gorge is met with, flanked on the right by three conical hills. This is the outlet of the Sebu river, another glacier-fed stream. From this point north, the valley is very flat and the hills rise suddenly without any intermediate steps or terraces. This flat valley continues as far as the Mbuku river, which leaves the mountains (kilometre 58) and crosses the plain on its way to the Dueru lake. This stream, which is the largest of all those flowing into the lake on its western side, has, like the Sebu and the Lokoku, its source in the Ruenzori glaciers. The scenery in the Mbuku valley is superb, and from this point, in clear weather, a magnificent view of the snow peaks of Ruenzori is obtained. North of this river, the terrace formation recommences along the foot of the lower hills and continues, until at kilometre 63, the Hima river is arrived at. This river runs in a deep and wide valley and, like all those previously described, has a course to the lake, nearly due east. The scenery of the Hima is extremely wild and high ranges encircle it on the west and north-west, some of the peaks rising to a great height. Beyond it, the plateau rises to 150 metres, and more, above the valley of the Dueru, and further north, as the mountains rise more abruptly, a continual succession of long spurs run out into the plain below. Between each of these is an expanse of rank grass, which, in the rainy season, is all marsh. These swamps render travelling, at that period of the year, a work of difficulty. At kilometre 66 from Katwé, the northern extremity of the Dueru lake is reached and a few kilometres north of this, ridges, low at first, but rising steadily, run up north and south. These ridges are covered with dense forest and increase in elevation until the level of the plateau which bounds the northern end of the great loop, previously alluded to, is attained. From this point, the eastern valley ceases and the country becomes a high expanse of table-land and ridge, all forest-covered, from which isolated ranges of low hills rise at intervals (1). At kilometre 67, the route rises on to the Ruenzori lower ranges and, after several extremely sharp rises and equally sharp descents, crosses the Ruimi river, at kilometre 69. The Ruimi here, runs in a deep gorge, 70 metres wide and 35 metres deep, with sides almost vertical. The crossing is an exceedingly difficult one for porters (2). Beyond this river, the track runs through bush-covered hills and gradually rises until the summit of the outer range of hills is attained. The tops of these hills are rounded and bare of trees, but there is much heavy grass. To the east, a solitary, conical hill, called Kyatura, rises above the level of the surrounding lower ranges. At kilometre 84, Kisaia Camp, 1500 metres above the sea, is reached. From this elevation, the whole of the lower ranges of hills are spread out to the east, below the observer. The effect is that of a panorama of rolling downs, quite devoid of trees, and with no very marked elevations or depressions. Turning to the west and north-west, the Ruenzori mountains stretch, in imposing grandeur, like a huge wall, their faces deeply furrowed by wide ravines (3). North of Kisaia, within the next nine kilometres, three small rivers are met with (4). These streams all flow in an easterly direction and eventually find their way into the Dura, a tributary of the Ruimi river. After crossing the Msongi, the most northerly of these three streams, the character of the vegetation changes and the high grass, which has for so long covered the hills, gives place to a thick undergrowth, in which a few trees are interspersed (5). Between kilometres 97 and 100, the Igasha and Malloma

(1) The north-eastern end of Dueru is covered with forest, which stretches in an almost unbroken sheet across to the Budonga forest, on the cliffs adjacent to Lake Albert.

(2) The Ruimi joins Lake Dueru on the east bank.

(3) Moisel, in his map, calls this portion of the range Kiribi. He gives the height as from 4000 to 5000 metres above sea level.

(4) The Yerin, Balariba and Msongi.

(5) The great defect of the Ruenzori scenery is the absence of trees. In this respect, it compares unfavourably with that of the Himalayas. Moreover, the snow peaks of the former appear small and insignificant to anyone who has seen those of the latter.

TORU DISTRICT
THE RUIMI RIVER, FLOWING INTO LAKE DUERU FROM RUENZORI

TORU DISTRICT
FORT PORTAL. HEAD-QUARTERS OF DISTRICT

rivers are crossed. Neither of these streams are large, but both run in deep valleys, with very steep and high ridges between them (1). These valleys are from 400 to 500 metres in width, and are densely wooded. The intervening ridges are bare of anything but bush. North of the Malloma, the plateau rises and a level of 2000 metres above the sea is attained. The ridges are now bare and there is much outcrop of granite and basalt. Cultivation recommences and, on the lower slopes, there is a good deal of millet grown, and a few banana plantations. On approaching that portion of the plateau upon which Fort Portal is situated, the valleys become wider and their slopes flatter, while the hills are more scattered and isolated. After crossing two small streams, the Nakatura and the Nyamhanawi, both tributaries of the Mpango, at kilometre 110, a broad straight road is reached. This road passes through Kabaroli, the residence of the King of Toru, and continues to Fort Portal, the headquarter station of this district. This road is fairly straight and runs nearly due north. It has an average width of 12 metres and is fenced in on both sides by curious reed fences, three metres high (2). Cultivation extends on either side of this road, for a considerable distance. The chief crops appear to be peas, millet, sweet potatoes and tobacco. Banana plantations are very numerous and cover a large area. Many huts and houses line the road on either side and, on approaching the hill upon which the King's palace is situated, it passes through an avenue of eucalyptus trees. On the right-hand side here, is the Roman Catholic Mission, a large, walled enclosure, full of well-built houses, with a tall wooden cross in front of the gate-way. A little further on, are the Church of England Mission buildings, also consisting of comfortable-looking buildings. On a round-topped hill, about 80 metres high, to the left of the road, is the palace of the King (3). The hill-sides are covered with bananas, which surround the buildings on the summit. After passing this hill, the road dips sharply down into the valley of the Mpango river and, after crossing this stream by a wooden bridge (4), rises equally sharply to the top of another hill. Upon this hill, at 114 kilometres from Katwé, the station of Fort Portal is built. The situation is a good one, being high and well drained (5). The country round is open and free from bush and it ought to be a comparatively healthy spot. The fort consists of a rectangular enclosure, surrounded by a deep ditch. Within this, are the residences of the English officials, the stores, and office buildings. The police lines lie to the west of the fort and on the slope of the hill. Beyond this, again, is the native bazaar. There are two English civil officials at Fort Portal, and an English non-commissioned officer. The garrison consists of 180 police. A hospital building exists, but there is no medical officer of any kind, not even a hospital assistant. Were any of the officials to fall dangerously ill, it would be impossible for them to obtain medical advice under 5 or 6 days and, in the rainy season, when the rivers are in flood, it might take very much longer (6). The climate at Fort Portal is temperate, and there is no very great heat (7). It is, however, very wet and, owing to the vicinity of the mountains, is subject to continual heavy storms (8). The view of the Ruenzori mountains from the fort, is an extensive one. Some of the snow peaks are plainly visible in clear weather, particularly in the mornings and evenings. The nearest point, on these mountains, is some 11 kilometres from Fort Portal, but, between them is a range of low conical hills, containing the craters of several extinct volcanoes. The western slopes of

(1) These rivers both find their way into the Dura.

(2) These fences are very neatly made, the reeds crossing one another and interlacing in diagonal lines. They appear only to mark the road boundaries, as there are no cross fences on the properties adjacent.

(3) The King of Toru is a Bahima named Kasagamma. He is 45 years of age.

(4) The Mpango, which is the most important of all the tributaries of the Dueru lake, joins it on the east bank, near the north-east corner.

(5) The altitude of Fort Portal is about 1500 metres above the sea.

(6) There is a good deal of malaria at the end of the rainy season.

(7) In March 1903, the temperature, even at mid-day, did not exceed 74° F. or 24° Centigrade.

(8) The driest months are January and February, but a day rarely passes without a rainstorm of some sort.

Ruenzori are thickly forested, up to a height of some 2000 metres above sea-level. Those on the east are bare. This side of the mountains is inhabited by the Bakonja, a race of hill-men, also met with at both Katwé and Kasinga. On the west are found the Bwamba (1). To the north, north-west, and east of Fort Portal, a high rocky table-land extends to the horizon. It is much broken by valleys and low ridges.

Before describing the route from Fort Portal, through Unyoro, to the Albert lake, it may be of interest if a brief account is given of the area lying to the west of this station, and of the country at the north end of Ruenzori, as far as the great drop into the valley of the Semliki (2). Proceeding west from the fort, cultivation extends for a few kilometres from the station and then ceases. Beyond this point, the country is a succession of ridges, hardly deserving the name of hills, but separated by valleys, which, though not wide, are frequently very deep. The ascents and descents are steep. The surface of this area is covered by a layer of what appears to be lava, which is met with in curious stratified slabs, a few centimetres thick, somewhat resembling slate (3). On many of the ridges, are low elevations, some conical and some almost perfect pyramids. Extinct craters are very numerous and, at 5 kilometres from Fort Portal, is a crater-lake, surrounded by a ridge of round-topped hills. This lake is about 1.5 kilometres in length, by 700 metres wide. West of this lake, the country rises up to the edge of the escarpment cliffs, which here form the eastern boundary of the Albertine "Rift" and which overlook the valley of the Semliki. The scenery here is very wild. There are no trees—nothing but an expanse of bleak moorland, occasionally intersected by deep valleys running east and west. At 8 kilometres due west from Fort Portal, the top of these cliffs is reached, at an elevation of some 1570 metres above the sea. From here, a magnificent view is obtained of the northern spurs of Ruenzori and of the wide valley below. In the extreme distance, the range of the Congo mountains can be traced. These form the western boundary of this valley. In the north, a glint of silver indicates the presence of the Albert Nyanza.

The descent into the Semliki valley is very steep indeed, and there are but few tracks by which porters can descend from the plateau above. Of these, one of the easiest is that leading from Fort Portal to Mboga, (on the Congo State frontier) which crosses the Semliki by a ferry. The drop into the valley is in three portions. The first, and by far the most difficult, is about 450 metres in depth. It passes between two cone-shaped hills and down a long, and extremely steep, spur, flanking a deep gorge, down which a stream dashes, over sharply sloping rocks, in an endless series of cascades. On either side of the narrow and difficult track, the cliffs rise almost perpendicularly. At the foot of this first descent, the detritus, brought down by the subsidence of the land, at the time when the slide occurred, has formed a long extent of mounds, or low ridges, resembling large tumuli and extending far into the valley. The total drop, from this point, is about 100 metres, but it is a gradual one, the going being comparatively easy. After this descent, a fairly level plateau, covered with high grass, extends, until at 16 kilometres from Fort Portal, the Washa river is crossed. This stream, which rises on the northern face of Ruenzori, flows in a north-westerly direction into the Nyabrogo river, which again is a tributary of the Semliki (4).

The Washa is a small stream, flowing in a shallow valley. Its width is 3.5 metres, and in March 1903, its depth was 0.70 metres, and its velocity 0.28 metres per second. Its flood rise is 2 metres. On its western bank, the plateau is higher, and covered with low forest. On either side of it run deep valleys. At 21 kilometres from Fort Portal

(1) This is the "ape-like" race of men, described by Sir Harry Johnston and Mr. Grogan.

(2) The description given in the following pages, is, in many respects, very typical of the country bordering the cliffs of the eastern escarpment, throughout the entire length of the Albert lake valley.

(3) All the strata in this part of the country dip sharply.

(4) It is not quite certain whether the Washa actually joins the Nyabrogo, or loses itself in the marshes of the lake. The swamps are so wide, that it is impossible to traverse many parts of them.

TORU DISTRICT
A CRATER LAKE NEAR FORT PORTAL

TORU DISTRICT
VIEW OF RUENZORI MOUNTAINS

the Nyabrogo river is crossed. This is a much more important stream than the Washa and runs through a deep and wide valley. At the point where the track crosses it, this valley is 500 metres in width, by 90 metres in depth. It is full of very dense forest. Through this cleft, the Nyabrogo winds about. Its summer channel is 22 metres wide, but in March 1903, the depth of water was only a few centimetres. It is a succession of pools, of very clear water. The bed is sandy. The flood-mark shows a rise of 4 metres and it must, when running thus deep, be a stream of considerable size. It rises in the northern spurs of Ruenzori and flows, generally, in a northerly direction. After a length of some 30 kilometres, it joins the Semliki river, some 45 kilometres upstream of the point where the latter enters Lake Albert.

Beyond this river, the track runs more or less in a northerly direction, along the plateau, which continues high and thickly wooded. It is intersected by numerous deep ravines, which run into the Nyabrogo valley, with, as a rule, precipitous sides. This plateau is, in reality, the lowest of the spurs of the Ruenzori mountains, which run down north into the lake valley. Between some of the ravines are ridges of only 20 metres in width. The average width of these ravines is 400 to 500 metres, and the depth varies from 50 to 80 metres. They have evidently cut back, and are still cutting back from the valley below, through the surface of the level plateau. The soil on the surface appears to be a conglomerate of lava, clay and quartz pebbles. Below this are the crystalline rocks (1).

After crossing a small branch of the Nyabrogo, called the Kikeya, which follows a deep and very steep ravine, the path turns sharply to the west and, after a steady descent, the last drop into the Semliki valley commences (2). This portion of the descent is a very sharp one and the difference of level, between the top of the cliffs and the valley below, is some 250 metres. The track follows a very narrow ridge, running between two deep valleys, and winds between high masses of rock. Precipitous cliffs stand up on either side. A very extensive view of the valley is obtained here. Looking south, along the line of the escarpment, the rugged masses of the Ruenzori mountains extend, towering one behind the other, as far as the eye can see. Right in front, the valley of the Semliki stretches west and the river itself can be traced, in a winding course, by the line of reeds which marks its banks. Patches of forest alternate with swamps, on the eastern side of the valley—the green of the latter contrasting with the brown colour of the burnt, grassy plain. In the distance, the Congo mountains form the boundary, and to the north, the marshes which border the southern extremity of Lake Albert, can be traced through the haze which lies over them. The descent of these cliffs continues to be very steep, until the valley is reached. It will be seen from the foregoing, that the total drop, from the summit of the plateau on which Fort Portal is situated to the valley of the Semliki, is some 870 metres, (3) in a distance of 23 kilometres.

In order to describe the country north of Fort Portal, it is necessary to start again from that station. The route now follows a course, generally parallel to the line of the "Rift" valley. This region is very similar in its character to that lying to the south of Fort Portal, being a high table-land, broken by ranges of low hills, which rise above swampy valleys and stretch to the north and east, as far as the eye can see. Few of these hills are of any height, and most of them are of rounded outline. The general level rises gradually

(1) This long plateau consists of four terraces, at different elevations, running from the Ruenzori foot-hills into the Albert lake valley.

(2) The total fall in the levels, between the Washa river and the top of the last descent, is about 70 metres.

(3) This is divided somewhat as follows:—

The first and longest drop	450 metres
The second, along the spur of Ruenzori	170 "
The third and last, into the valley	250 "
	870 metres

Further to the north, when the Albert lake is reached, the height is less, not more than 600 metres.

from the east to the west, i.e., to the edge of the escarpment. A good deal of scattered cultivation is met with, for some distance after leaving Fort Portal. In some of the valleys, the grass is very high and in others, there is a thick growth of papyrus among which creepers are intertwined. All this country forms a portion of the catchment area of the Mpango river. Looking back, a good view of Ruenzori is obtained. From six to seven snow peaks are visible.

At kilometre 125 (1) from Katwé, outlying portions of the great Budonga forest are passed and at the 133rd kilometre, the northernmost branch of the Mpango—the Manobo—is reached (2), in a valley 50 metres wide. Six kilometres further on, the watershed is crossed, and north of this point, the entire drainage passes into the Msisi river and thence into Lake Albert. At kilometre 142, the Budonga forest commences and follows the line of the "Rift" for many kilometres to the north. This forest, which lies west of the track, is full of fine timber and, in its tropical luxuriance, resembles the great forest on the west of the Semliki valley. It, like the Budoma, further north, is the home of large herds of elephants, which ascend and descend to the lake valley, by ravines in the cliffs (3). The whole of the Toru district being a game reserve, elephant shooting is strictly prohibited. The result has been that, along the shores of Lake Dueru, and everywhere in the vicinity of these forests, the people are deserting their villages, owing to the impossibility of preserving their banana plantations from the ravages of the elephants (4). As bananas form the staple food of the population, their case is a hard one, and the revenue of the district, as a matter of course, must suffer. The elephant is now so effectively preserved throughout the Uganda Protectorate, that there does not appear to be the slightest danger of its numbers being seriously diminished. Vast herds must roam through this country, as their tracks are everywhere to be met with, although they themselves are not often seen.

For the next 20 kilometres or so, there is no change in the general features of the country. Valleys and ridges alternate with extreme regularity. In the east, several distant ranges of hills are to be observed and the Kagorara mountain (some 500 metres high) stands out prominently by itself, some 16 or 17 kilometres east of the cliffs which bound the lake valley. In this distance, four tributaries of the Msisi are crossed (5). Of these the Asua, at kilometre 161, is the most important. It flows nearly due north, in a valley 300 metres wide, but the width of the actual channel is only 60 metres, with vertical banks 1 metre in height (6). Its rise appears to be 2.25 metres and it must bring down a large volume of water when in flood.

At kilometre 174, the Msisi river is reached (7). This river forms the boundary between the districts of Toru and Uganda and, with the exception of the Victoria Nile, is the most important of all the feeders of the Albert lake. Its valley is both wide and deep, and full of thick forest. The cliffs on the right, or north bank, rise in two flats, or steps, through forest, to a high table-land, some 200 metres above the bed of the river. These cliffs are formed by one of the great fault-lines which traverse the plateau from east to west (8). The high land, north of the Msisi, extends for a considerable distance and is covered with bush. There is a little cultivation at first, but, further on, the character of the

(1) In the following pages, the kilometrage, from Lake Albert Edward, has been carried right through to Lake Albert.

(2) The Manobo is a much less important stream than the southern branch at Fort Portal. It rises near Nsororo (Fort Wavertree), close to the source of the Msisi. Its general course is south-east. In its upper reaches, it is a wide swamp, full of muddy water, and horrible slime. On the 8th March 1903, the discharge was 0.337 metres cube per second.

(3) In all this part of the country, as well as near Lake Albert, the elephants cover their bodies with the red volcanic dust. The effect is peculiar, as their colour, in consequence, resembles that of a chestnut horse.

(4) This statement is made upon the authority of the English civil officers of the district.

(5) The Yumzaka, the Nakatiwya, the Yakwisi and the Asua. The two first flow over rocky beds. The third is a swamp.

(6) On 9th March 1903, the water in the Asua was 6 metres wide, and 0.35 metres deep. The velocity was 0.80 metres per second, and the discharge, 1.68 metres cube per second.

(7) The Msisi is described in the chapter on the Albert lake.

(8) The Msisi valley is notorious for the prevalence and violence of its thunder-storms. These occur almost daily. They seem to follow the line of the river. These storms are generally accompanied by a deluge of rain, and not infrequently by hail. The discomfort caused to a camp by one of them is indescribable.

country changes and the scenery becomes wild and desolate-looking to an extreme degree. There appear to be no inhabitants and no signs of either dwelling places, or cultivation. The hills are higher and thus vary the monotony of the dreary landscape. The valleys are deep and in each of them are swamps, consisting of an expanse of red, fœtid slime, full of high papyrus and reeds. Through these swamps, small rivers, like the Kitabi and the Kamaranjoju, wander. This part of the country has one feature which appears to be peculiar to it—the shape of the anthills. Instead of the conical mounds met with elsewhere, here they resemble gigantic toadstools. The stems are vertical, round in section, averaging 0.35 metres in diameter. The top is also circular, but overhanging—very much like the head of a mushroom. This top is probably constructed as a shelter against rain. The height is rarely more than 1 metre.

After passing Magalika, at kilometre 198, the country is more wooded and some cultivation, in the shape of bananas and millet, is met with. The hills are high and several streams flow from the east to the west, the principal being the Mponbi and Kamubo, both tributaries of the Ngusi (1). After a long succession of steep rises and dips, another table-land is reached, at kilometre 214. This plateau is covered with forest and from here there is a long descent, through Pachwa, to the valley of the Ngusi river (2). This river is the boundary between the districts of Uganda and Unyoro. It is reached at the 218th kilometre. The width of the valley is 3 kilometres. Its surface is most uneven and it is full of rocky ridges and much bush and grass (3). The Ngusi is an important stream and, in flood, is quite impassable. Even in the dry season it is difficult to cross, as its current is extremely strong. On the right bank of the valley, at the point where the track crosses it, are two high hills, that on the west being a conical peak, known as Kibrara. The eastern hill is flat-topped, and is called Isunga. These hills are about 140 metres above the valley of the Ngusi and are connected by a high ridge. From this ridge, an extensive view is obtained. Seen from this height, the surrounding country presents the aspect of an expanse of nearly flat woodland, with an occasional hill rising above the general level. On descending and traversing it, the traveller speedily finds out how deceptive this appearance has been. It is extremely uneven and ridges succeed valleys with most tiresome regularity. In fact, there is hardly a square kilometre of level ground throughout its entire extent. From the ridge above mentioned, the line of the "Rift" eastern escarpment makes a very flat horizon, only broken by the gaps where the different rivers cross it, in descending to the valley of the Albert lake. In clear weather, the hills on the far side of Lake Albert can be distinctly seen. In the next 20 kilometres or so, there is but little variety in the landscape (4). This part of Unyoro differs from both Uganda and northern Toru, inasmuch as it is very thickly forested. Even the hills which rise above the plateau are wooded to their summits. At kilometre 238, the route passes between two hills, forming a gap between two low ranges. The right-hand hill is called Kikunda and that on the left, Bigogo. Both of them are visible for a very long distance and form striking landmarks. In the gap between these hills flows a river called the Nyakabari, the valley between them being 600 metres across and densely wooded (5). North of these two hills, the number of isolated peaks and small ranges increases. From the top of a ridge at kilometre 244, no less than 14 different, and separate, elevations can be counted. These solitary hills run north and south, in two almost parallel lines, that to the west being within 3 or 4 kilometres of the edge of the eastern escarpment, while the other is about 16 kilometres to the

(1) The Mponbi has no flow during the dry season. Its valley is 50 metres wide, by 17 metres deep. The flood-rise is 2 metres. The Kamubo is still smaller.

(2) Pachwa is a hot, steamy and mosquito-haunted spot in the forest.

(3) For a description of the Ngusi, see the chapter on Lake Albert.

(4) The Kiswaga river, a branch of the Ngusi, is crossed in this distance. It is unimportant in the dry season.

(5) Kikunda is some 250 metres high, and has a fine peak. Bigogo is of rounded outline. For information regarding the Nyakabari river, see the chapter on Lake Albert.

east. None of these ranges are continuous, but all rise separately and at some distance apart, out of the plain (1).

Far to the east, and a long way beyond the eastern hills, the distant ranges which mark the watershed between the two great sources of the Nile, can be distinguished. The country between these two lines of low hills is a wooded plateau, much cut up by deep valleys, crossing from east to west, and conveying the drainage of the country into the Albert lake. These valleys generally contain small streams, most of them choked by a thick growth of tall reeds, through which the water slowly filters without any perceptible flow. Even in flood, this vegetation must check any very sudden rush of water (2). These channels vary in width from 3 to 6 metres, and the depth of water, in the dry season, is from 0.50 to 0.60 metres. Their flood-rise is from 1.5 to 2 metres. Their slope is feeble. Beyond kilometre 257, the flat plain of Chikubi is reached. This plain is not a very extensive one and after crossing the Kikitima river, the ridges and furrows recommence. In almost every dip, there is a sluggish marshy stream, flowing west to the lake, through high reeds and papyrus (3). Between each of these rivers, small plateaux rise, covered with bush and low forest. North of the Wambabia river, the forest ends and is replaced by grass-covered plain.

At 273 kilometres from Katwé, the station of Hoima is reached. This is now the headquarters of the Unyoro district; Masindi, the former station, having been abandoned on account of its unhealthiness. Two kilometres to the west of the station, is the palace of the King of Unyoro. The palace consists of a collection of large thatched huts, surrounded by a high reed fence (4). Not far from the palace are the English Mission buildings and the Church. A little further on are the market, stores and the telegraph office (5). The houses of the English officials are upon a low rounded hill, 1.5 kilometres to the east of the palace. Still further east, and across a wide valley, are the military lines. The garrison consists of a company of the Uganda Rifles. Hoima itself is at an elevation of 1270 metres above the sea, or nearly 600 metres above the level of the Albert Nyanza. The nearest point on the lake is Kibero, 16 kilometres west of the station. In clear weather, the mountains on the further side of Lake Albert can be clearly seen. The climate of Hoima is hot and damp, but singularly free from mosquitoes. This is surprising, as the jungle, which is only partially cleared as yet, is very thick in close proximity to the station. Hoima is still in its infancy and the Government buildings are still under construction. The staff consists of an English sub-collector and a doctor, also an English officer in command of the troops. Close to the station, on the north side, a small river, called the Lukajuka, runs down the valley. Beyond this river, is a range of hills, with two principal peaks. One of these peaks is flat-topped and is called Palijoku; the other, which is pointed, is known as Impalu. In the gorge between these mountains, the Wambabia river runs to the south-west (6). On the southern slopes of these hills was formerly situated the palace and kraal of King Kabarega (7). The cart-road from Hoima to Butiabu, on the Albert lake, runs nearly due west, and skirts the base of the Palijoku hill. On the right

(1) In the western line, the most prominent hills are those of Kidoma (with 8 peaks), Rubanga, Kikanja and Kikunda. To the east, are Yekoba, Kikgerama, Lukanja, Makabara and a bold rounded mass, resembling the Bass Rock in shape, called Msaigamkuru.

(2) The principal of these streams, are the Balbona, the Jimangawu, the Kagaradindu and the Kikituna. In flood, their width is considerable; that of the last named being 285 metres.

(3) These streams are the Mtaria, the Kaberogola, the Kajradindi, the Migo, the Grika and the Wambabia. These all combine a little further to the west, and cross the escarpment, in one single stream, the Wahamba.

(4) The King of Unyoro, Andrea by name, is a young and intelligent-looking man. He is a son of the famous King Kabarega. Like all the other chiefs in Uganda, he is a Bahima by race. He has embraced the Protestant religion.

(5) There is a telegraph line from Hoima to Entebbé, following the cart-road between these two places. From Hoima to Butiabu, on Lake Albert, there is a telephone line.

(6) This is not the Wambabia met with to the south of Hoima. Both the Lukajuka and the Wambabia unite further west, and form the Wahamba river, described in the chapter on the Albert lake.

(7) Kabarega was deposed after the Soudanese mutiny, and is now, with King Mwamba, of Uganda, a prisoner in the Seychelles Islands.

bank of the Lukajuka is the Catholic Mission. There is much cultivation around Hoima and this portion of the district appears to be thickly populated. The huts are neat, with eaves reaching to the ground and verandahs in front. At kilometre 275 from Katwé, the Lukajuka river is crossed (1). Its channel is 45 metres wide, by 8 metres deep, but in the dry season, the water is only 12 metres broad and a few centimetres in depth. A kilometre further on, the Wambabia crosses the road. It is a smaller stream than the Lukajuka. Both these rivers, however, have a rise of over 2 metres and must be serious obstacles when in flood. The road now runs parallel to the Palijoku hills, at a distance varying from 1 ½ to 2 kilometres. In the south, is a broad table-land, fairly level and covered with bush.

At kilometre 283, the Hoima river is reached. This is a small stream at this point, as its source is close at hand, but further down it receives the drainage of numerous ravines and valleys and its volume, where it drops over the escarpment, is, at times, considerable. After the Hoima river is crossed, the country becomes very broken and its surface is deeply scored by large ravines. The vegetation now is very thick and there are many fine trees (2). One common variety has large leaves, shaped almost exactly like the ear of an African elephant. There are also many very beautiful palms. These resemble the ordinary date-palm of Egypt in appearance, except that they are taller and the stem much more slender. They do not bear fruit.

At kilometre 289, the Palijoku range of hills comes to an end, the spurs running out for some distance to the north (3). At kilometre 296, a river called the Kajurra crosses the road. It is apparently a branch of the Wakki river, which is met with a little further to the north. Its valley is wide, being 380 metres across and on its right bank is a line of wooded hills, some 70 metres above the valley. In the dry season, it shrinks to very small limits and its channel is filled with trees, papyrus and undergrowth. West of this river, the road ascends the range of flat-topped hills above mentioned and winds about through valleys and ridges, covered with forest and thick bush.

At kilometre 309, the valley of the Wakki river is arrived at. This is a different type of stream altogether from the swampy and sluggish channels which have hitherto been met with in the Unyoro plateau. In the Wakki, clear, sparkling water rushes over a rocky bed, in a succession of small falls. At the point where the road crosses it, its valley is 60 metres wide and 10 metres deep. Its banks are thickly wooded. In the dry season, its width shrinks to some 3 metres, with a depth of 0.80 metres and a high velocity (4). After crossing the Wakki, the road takes a northerly direction, passing through very broken ground. To the west, the river runs in a deep gorge quite 100 metres in depth. At the point where it falls over the cliffs, the scenery is wild and beautiful. All round is thick forest and bush and many ravines break the level of the country. The escarpment descends to the valley like a great wall, and down its sheer sides the river drops, in a sheet of foaming water; a white streak on the dark face of the cliffs.

At kilometre 312, the top of the great eastern fault-line is reached (5). From this point a wondrous view is obtained. The Albert Nyanza is spread out, a great sheet of water, several hundred metres below. The difference between this lake and those of Albert Edward and Victoria is remarkable. The two last-named lakes, with certain local exceptions, are bounded by a wide table-land of no great height and broad flats, as a rule, extend between this high land and the water's edge. The Albert lake is long and narrow and enclosed, throughout its length, by high mountains and cliffs on either side. There is but little

(1) To avoid confusion, the kilometrage from Lake Albert Edward has been carried on, in this note, to the Albert lake.

(2) All this country is on the southern limits of the Budonga forest, which borders the Albert lake valley further to the north.

(3) It was impossible to find out the real name of these hills. They have therefore been called, in this note, after the peak at Hoima. They are a portion of the great central ridge of Unyoro.

(4) The Wakki is more fully described in the chapter on the Albert lake.

(5) On the top of the escarpment is a rest house, and the office of the signaller in charge of the telephone line to Hoima, This line stops here, but the cart-road continues down to the small jetty on the lake.

beach and, in places, the cliffs rise up straight from the water. Viewed from the top, it is a beautiful scene.

The total drop to the lake here is some 400 metres. The road descent is rather a steep one, but easy compared to that into the Semliki valley. The land slopes gently down to the lake from the foot of the cliffs and, at 317 kilometres from Katwé, Butiabu, on the shore of Lake Albert, is arrived at.

CONGO FREE STATE
SEMLIKI RIVER, LOOKING DOWNSTREAM FROM HEAD

CONGO FREE STATE
VIEW ON SEMLIKI RIVER

CONGO FREE STATE
VIEW ON SEMLIKI RIVER

THE SEMLIKI RIVER.

The Semliki is the only outlet for the surplus waters of Lake Albert Edward. It takes off from this lake, near its north-western corner, in latitude 0° 8′ 30″ south. From this point, it follows the line of the Albertine "Rift" valley and, skirting the western flanks of Ruenzori, after a course of some 260 kilometres, eventually discharges its waters into the south end of Lake Albert Nyanza, in latitude 1° 9′ north. It is thus the connecting channel between the waters of these two lakes and consequently plays an important part in the complicated system of supply from which the White Nile derives its origin.

It has been visited by many travellers and crossed at several points, but, so far as is known, no European has as yet succeeded in following its banks, throughout its entire length. Such a journey would be an enterprise of considerable difficulty, as, for some 120 kilometres, the river runs in a deep, narrow valley, closed in, on one side, by the cliffs of Ruenzori and, on the other, by those of the Congo mountains. In this distance, it falls some 254 metres and receives the waters of numerous torrents which feed it from the ranges on either side. To add to the difficulties of the explorer, throughout this reach, the great Congo forest stretches across the valley and ascends the Ruenzori spurs to an elevation of 3000 metres above the sea. The entire area is thus covered with an almost impenetrable hedge of tropical vegetation, which flourishes here in its densest and most luxuriant form. Through this forest, on both sides of the river, the tributary streams rush down the slopes, through steep and rugged valleys. The rainfall, below the snow peaks of Ruenzori, is extremely heavy and practically continuous throughout the year. The climate is hot and steamy to an extreme degree. Beyond the fact that there are rapids in this part of its course, and, according to native report, falls of considerable size, nothing is known of the Semliki between its first plunge into the forest a little to the north of Fort Mbeni, and the point where it issues again into the open, in the wide valley to the south of the Albert Nyanza (¹). In its upper reaches and again in its lower course, this river flows through broad alluvial plains and its course is comparatively easy to follow (²).

Using the generally accepted values for the levels of Lakes Albert Edward and Albert Nyanza, of 965 metres and 680 metres, respectively, above the sea, the total fall in the Semliki, from its head to its mouth, is 285 metres.

According to the heights observed and recorded, at different points in its course, this fall would appear to be distributed somewhat as follows:— (³)

From	To	Distance in kilometres	Fall in metres.	Fall in metres per kilometre.
Albert Edward Lake	Kilom. 75	75	15	0·20
Kilo. 75	„ 196	121	254	2·09
„ 196	Albert Lake	64	16	0·25
	Totals ...	260	285	

The above slopes are necessarily but approximations, as the information available is extremely scanty. In any case, the difference of level, between the 75th and 200th kilometre, is so great, that it seems about certain that, in its course through the forest, the Semliki must fall in a succession of drops, or very severe rapids. Upstream of kilometre 45, no stream enters this river from the east, but below this point, the tributaries on both sides are numerous (⁴). North of Ruenzori, the Nyabrogo river joins the Semliki on the east, 45 kilometres upstream of its junction with Lake Albert. Further down, somewhere in the

(¹) Stanley, in 1889, followed a course parallel to the Semliki, along the lower ranges to the west of Ruenzori. His route, however, was confined to the hills, and he rarely descended into the actual valley of the river.

(²) The main difficulty for the traveller is supplies. For long distances, the banks of the Semliki are quite uninhabited.

(³) The slopes in the upper and lower reaches have been calculated from observed discharges.

(⁴) According to Stuhlmann's map, there are 45 torrents coming in from the west, and 23 from the east.

impenetrable swamps which border its lower reaches, the little river Washa adds its discharge to that of the main stream. Throughout its entire course, the western boundary of the Semliki valley is the great mountain range, which here marks the line of the "Rift." On the east, in the upper reaches, the boundary is the Kipura hills, while further north, the limit is fixed by the Ruenzori mountains. These again give place to the cliffs of the fault-line which borders the Albert Nyanza, on the eastern shores.

For the first 20 kilometres from the head, the average width of the Semliki valley varies between 12 and 15 kilometres. Beyond this point, it widens out, but contracts again from the point where the spurs of Ruenzori divert its course and force its channel to the north-west. North of this range, the valley again broadens and, in the lower reaches, has a width of from 25 to 35 kilometres. The upper valley is covered with a thick layer of lacustrine deposit, grey loam, and sand, forming a high plateau between the mountain ranges. This plateau is arid and bare and much impregnated with salt. Through the alluvium, the river has cut a deep channel, traversing the country in a huge trench, from 500 to 800 metres in breadth and from 50 to 70 metres in depth. It has a very winding course and the slope of the western bank is invariably steeper than that of the east.

The general section of the upper valley is as below :—

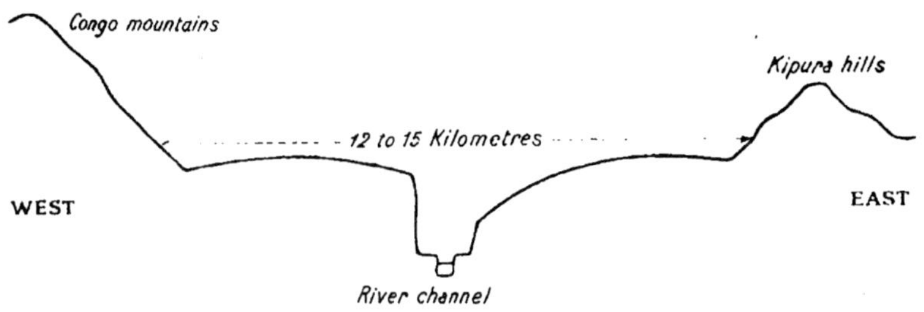

The actual channel has two typical sections, as below. In No. 1, the eastern side of the valley slopes gently down to the dip, and in No. 2, it descends in two, or more, terraces.

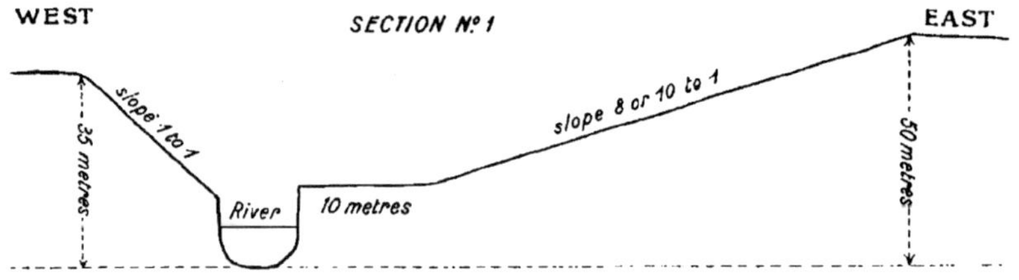

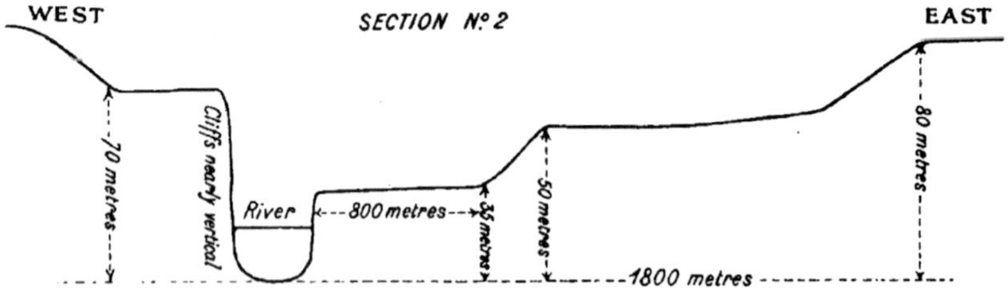

The coast of Lake Albert Edward, west of the Kipura hills, presents the same characteristics as those existing in the vicinity of Kazinga and Katwé. A high, but rounded, ridge, from 30 to 100 metres above the waters, borders its shores. The flats are narrow. The land behind this ridge slopes from the lake, to the north. All the drainage of this plateau drains *away* from the lake and *towards* the Semliki (1).

The Semliki river takes off from the lake almost at a right angle and between wide stretches of high reeds. On the right, or east bank, steep cliffs, from 90 to 100 metres in height, flank the channel. On the left, at this point, they are lower and not more than 20 metres above the river. It runs due north, for some 800 metres and then turns sharply to the north-west, but, after traversing a similar distance, it turns north again. The right-hand cliffs are sheer and covered, on the top, with calcareous deposit. Those on the left are of easier slopes and, beyond them a flat, bush-covered plain extends for a long distance to the west. To the east, the valley is undulating and slopes gradually up to the Kipura hills, some 5 to 6 kilometres away. It is covered with short grass and there are but few trees. Along the water's edge, the fringe of papyrus and reed is often very wide, particularly where the stream, in crossing from one bank to the other, leaves a large loop, or amphitheatre, of swamp at the foot of the cliffs. Beyond the Semliki head, the Albert Edward lake trends in a south-westerly direction. The view here is magnificent. It is, on the whole, finer than any met with in the country lying between the Victoria and Albert Edward lakes. To the north and north-west, a noble range of mountains towers, apparently to the skies. The base of these mountains is not more than eight kilometres distant from the west bank of the river, and between them and it, a high, wooded plateau slopes gently down to the water. Looking downstream, from the high bluff at the head of the Semliki, the river can be traced, winding beneath a grand sweep of cliff. To the south, the lake stretches into space and looking west, headland after headland runs down from the mountains to the water's edge. These mountains, which form the boundary of the "Rift" valley, run nearly due north and south. They rise into the clouds, in range upon range of peaks, many of them of irregular and beautiful shapes. Unfortunately, the haze which is so prevalent throughout the neighbourhood of this lake, prevents this range from being seen, except at rare intervals, most often in the early mornings, and in the evenings (2). Sometimes, at sunset, when the sun dips behind these mountains, the peaks stand out in deep, purple masses, against a sky flaming in crimson and orange, and again, blending into tints of rose and salmon colour. Under such conditions the scene, with the reed-fringed river in the foreground, is one of quite exceptional beauty.

Near to the head of the Semliki, and on the left bank, is a collection of huts, forming one of the villages of the Congo Free State. The right bank is entirely uninhabited. The canoes are very small and few in number, and, for the discharge operations, had to be brought round by lake, from Katwé. The swarms of small flies on the water here present a very curious effect. They rise from the lake surface in black clouds, exactly resembling the smoke of a large fire.

There are but few water-birds in the lake, in this locality and neither hippopotami nor crocodiles seem to be common. The temperature in this part of the valley, in the month of February, is delightful. The air is dry and cool and the thermometer rarely rises above 86° F., or sinks below 70° F., at night.

The section of the Semliki, at the head, as measured on the 19th of February 1903, gave a total width of 170 metres, from bank to bank. Of this, only 100 metres is clear stream, the other 70 metres consisting of stagnant, shallow water, full of tall reeds and papyrus. The

(1) The name "Semliki," is utterly unknown to the natives of Katwé, or to any of the inhabitants of these parts. Stuhlmann's name of "Issango" is equally unknown. The people always talk of this river as the "Kakoonda," and know it by no other name. Further north, it is called the "Kakini," but never the "Semliki," until Fort Portal is reached, and Ruenzori has been traversed. As, however, the name "Semliki," has been generally adopted by geographers, it has been used throughout this report.

(2) The photographs of the Semliki river, except in very rare instances, show no trace of these mountains. In fact, a traveller, visiting this place, might possibly remain for a day or so and leave it, without being aware that he was in the vicinity of a range, some 2000 metres in height.

depth of the river here, is not great, the deepest sounding only giving 1·60 metres (¹). The greatest mean velocity obtained, in any section, was 0·784 metres per second. The discharge was 96·60 metres cube per second. The flood-rise is very clearly marked here, both on the reeds and on the cliffs. It is the same as that of Lake Albert Edward and appears never to exceed one metre above low-water level.

The water of the Semliki river is very clear, but of a slightly greenish colour. It is brackish and unpleasant to the taste (²).

After the first bend to the north-west, just below the offtake from the lake, the Semliki takes another considerable sweep to the west and follows this direction for some six kilometres. After this point, its course is, in general, northerly. The river valley (³), in places, is as much as 1000 metres in width and deeply-wooded ravines run down from the high lands on either side. The eastern plateau is bare and devoid of trees. That on the west, is covered with bush and slopes up to the mountains with a very broken surface. The summits of these mountains are bare, but their lower slopes are clothed by thick forest. The average width of the Semliki, is from 70 to 80 metres. It winds about continually between the high banks. The Kipura range runs parallel to the river on the east, at a distance of from 5 to 6 kilometres. The Congo mountains are further away, perhaps 8 to 9 kilometres. The eastern plateau appears to be totally uninhabited, but, on the west, there are occasional villages, and a little cultivation (⁴).

At ten kilometres from the head, a village called Kusabbia is situated on the left bank. Here, a few bananas are grown. At certain points, high cliffs from 60 to 70 metres in height, project over the water, on the west side. On the east, the land rises in a succession of terraces, to the plateau, which is here very bare and covered with gravel and the remains of shells. Where the ravines have cut through the surface, the soil, in places, resembles marl, and, at others, is white, like lime. Behind Kusabbia, the western plateau widens out, as the rivers recedes further from the western mountains. A solitary, dome-shaped hill stands out by itself, separated from the main range by a wide gap. At 15 kilometres from the head, the Congo mountains stretch away to the north-west, while the Semliki pursues a northerly course in the direction of Ruenzori. A deep ravine crosses the eastern plain here and runs down from the high land to the river, with a very heavy slope. Its depth is quite 35 metres, with vertical sides. It is filled with dense bush, and is fast cutting back in the direction of the Kipura hills. The section is thus laid bare and shows very plainly the lake deposit of which this plateau is composed. It consists of alternate layers of shells, pebbles and sand, and, on the top, a layer of loamy clay, some 2 metres in depth (⁵). For many kilometres north of this ravine, the Semliki varies but little in its general characteristics and winds about in the channel with an even section and velocity. At Mkorongo, 53 kilometres from the head, but south-west of the main mass of Ruenzori, Stuhlmann describes it as having a depth of from 6 to 10 metres, in June 1891 (⁶). If these depths are correct, it must, at this point, pass through a very narrow gorge, as, at 3 kilometres downstream, it appears to have resumed its general section, for he says that, "the bed width was 60 metres, and depth only 1·25 metres, with light yellow water, flowing very rapidly over a sandy and gravelly bed" (⁷). It would certainly appear as if the depth of the Semliki varied much in this

(¹) Both river and lake were then at their lowest.

(²) A specimen of this water was taken, and brought away, with the intention of having it analysed. Unfortunately, the bottle broke and all the water escaped.

(³) That is, the actual channel cut out by the stream, as apart from the wide valley, lying between the two mountain ranges.

(⁴) With the exception of a few miserable-looking natives on the Kipura hills, there appear to be no inhabitants at all between the Nyamgasha and the Semliki.

(⁵) At this point, last year's expedition was obliged to abandon the original intention of following the river throughout its course, and to return to Katwé, owing to failure of supplies. The description of the river between kilometre 15, and the point where it issues from the Ruenzori valley, is consequently borrowed from the account of travellers. North of Ruenzori, the river was again visited.

(⁶) "Mit Emin Pasha im Herz von Afrika."

(⁷) Ibid.

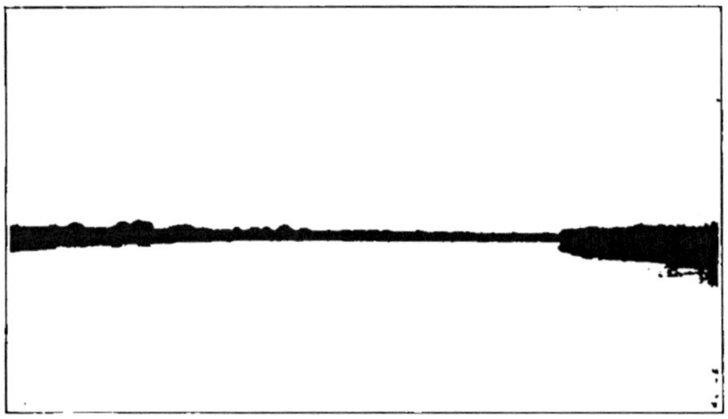

TORU DISTRICT
VIEW ON SEMLIKI RIVER NORTH OF RUENZORI, SOME 48 KILOMETRES ABOVE JUNCTION WITH LAKE ALBERT NYANZA

reach, as Stairs, who crossed it a little lower down, describes its width as 38 metres, its depth as 3 metres, and the banks as from 15 to 13 metres in height. He gives the velocity, as 1·33 metres per second, which is equivalent to a discharge of some 152 metres cube per second (1).

The photographs of the Semliki, given by Sir Harry Johnston, in his recent work (2), were taken at the ferry opposite Fort Mbeni, at a distance of 75 kilometres from the head-waters of the river. These picture it as apparently from 90 to 100 metres in width, and flowing, with a swift current, between high banks, thickly covered by bush and low forest. The river here is said to swarm with crocodiles, and large canoes are necessary for the transport of both men and live stock, the depth being far too great, and the stream too strong to permit of wading (3). At a short distance downstream of this ferry, the river plunges into the depths of the great Congo forest and the rapids and falls commence (4).

At 196 kilometres from the Albert Edward lake, the Semliki emerges from the gorges of the mountains and enters that portion of the "Rift" valley, lying between the two great fault-lines, which, continued further north, form the boundaries of the Albert Nyanza. This valley speedily widens out and becomes an expanse of plain, covered with grass and bush and, in many places, very swampy. The level of this plain has been raised by the detritus brought down from the mountain slopes. At some remote period, the waters of Lake Albert must have extended as far as the foothills of the mountains and covered the whole area (5), but the process which has been at work for so long, and which is still continuing, has gradually raised the bed levels and converted what was once a large sheet of water into an elevated plain. Through this plain, the slope of the river is easier, although the stream, until it reaches the Albert marshes, is still a strong one. Stuhlmann, in July 1891, crossed the Semliki, not far north of the point where it issues from the hills. He describes it as being from 60 to 80 metres wide, 15 metres deep, and with a strong current (6). A little further downstream, it had cut a passage through a cliff of laterite, 30 metres in height (7).

The valley of the Semliki, at 210 kilometres from its head, is from 17 to 18 kilometres in width (8), but rapidly widens to the north. The eastern escarpment here is very steep and some 700 metres above the level of the valley (9). Along the base of these cliffs, a wide swamp runs north and south, generally parallel to the range of mountains. This swamp is some 4 metres below the general level of the valley and probably marks the channel followed by the river, at some former period. Its average width is 1·5 kilometres and although, in some places, a low terrace, covered with mimosas, extends from the foothills, the general line of its course is close to the base of the fault-line cliffs. This marsh is full of high reeds and in the rainy season, must be well-nigh impenetrable (10). The track to Barango, 24 kilometres to the south, branches off in the middle of this swamp. At Barango, hot sulphur springs bubble up to the surface, in a bare and open space, with a temperature of nearly boiling heat. The water is much used by the natives for medicinal purposes.

At the point where the Mboga track crosses the valley, a fine view of the Ruenzori range is obtained. The peaks stand out boldly, above, and behind, one another. Some of the precipices are extremely fine and descend several hundreds of metres, sheer down into the valley below. After crossing the eastern swamp, the plain is fairly high, and

(1) "Darkest Africa," by Sir H. M. Stanley, G.C.B., London, 1890.
(2) "The Uganda Protectorate" by Sir Harry Johnston, G.C.M.G., London, 1902.
(3) Ibid.
(4) Between kilometres 75 and 196, the course of the Semliki is practically unknown.
(5) This valley is entirely covered by a layer of lake deposit and alluvium, brought down by the stream.
(6) "Mit Emin Pasha im Herz von Afrika."
(7) Ibid.
(8) At this point, the track from Fort Portal to Mbonga, on the Belgian frontier, crosses the valley.
(9) For a description of this escarpment, see the chapters on the country between Lake Albert Edward and the Albert Nyanza.
(10) An effort has been made to mark the track, by blazing the low trees which stand up in the swamp, but even with this assistance, travellers must find the crossing of this marsh extremely difficult.

covered with grass. As a rule, it is open, but clumps of thick bush are scattered about in all directions. Small drainage lines wander through it and, at 5 kilometres from the eastern cliffs, a reedy stream runs from south to north. This stream has a width of 5 metres, and a depth of 1·5 metres, but in March 1903 there was no current at all. West of this little river, the country is rather higher and the bush becomes thicker. Occasional "Borassus" palms are seen. At 7 kilometres from the foot of the eastern escarpment, the Semliki is reached. At this point, there is a ferry for travellers journeying to Mboga. The river here is a very fine stream, averaging 70 to 80 metres in width, and flowing, with a strong current, between vertical banks, some 2 metres above low-water level. Its course is very winding and some of the bends are extremely sharp. There is considerable erosion of the banks everywhere, and its waters, even at the period when the river is at its lowest, are turbid and charged with deposit. On either side of the channel, and in all the loops and bends, there is a thick bed of very tall reeds. On the west side, the flats extend, for another 3 to 4 kilometres. From here, the ground rises in a succession of terraces, and low forest begins. The rise continues steadily to the base of the foot-hills of the Congo range, which, at this point, are from 7 to 8 kilometres west of the river.

The discharge measurements of the 4th of March 1903 gave the following results:— The width of the water surface was 68 metres, and the average depth 1·90 metres. The deepest sounding was 2·30 metres. The strongest stream was in the centre, and along the right, or east, bank. The mean velocity in the section, where the current was swiftest, was 1·20 metres per second, and the total discharge, as measured, was 124.23 cubic metres per second. The maximum flood-rise, above the water level in March 1903, was 2·30 metres. This would give a water surface of nearly 100 metres in width (1). This discharge was measured at a time when the Semliki was at its lowest, i.e., after a drought which had lasted for some months. It has been shown that the discharge, entering the river from Lake Albert Edward, on the 19th of February 1903, was 96·6 cubic metres per second (2). As there had been no rain, to speak of, between the dates of these two discharges, it may be presumed that the lake-level had not altered in the interim; consequently, the added volume brought down by the different tributary streams, in its course through the hills, was only 27·3 cubic metres per second. In flood, the difference between the volume of water, leaving Lake Albert Edward, and that entering Lake Albert, must be very considerable, as the numerous torrents, which bring in the drainage of Ruenzori and the Congo range, must discharge, when full, immense quantities of water. An approximation of the flood discharge of the Semliki may be arrived at by making use of Stanley's figures (3). He crossed it, in May 1889, some 217 kilometres from the Albert Edward lake, and upstream of the point where the Nyabrogo river joins it. He gives the width, as ranging from 55 to 90 metres, with a current equal to 2·20 metres per second. These measurements were made during the spring rainy season, when the river was presumably in flood. Unfortunately, no details of the depth are given, and it is merely described as "a fine, deep, promising stream."

The flood section of the river, at the point where the discharge of March 1903 was measured, was 277·5 square metres. If to this section, Stanley's velocity be applied, the flood discharge would, approximately, equal 610·5 cubic metres per second. To this volume must, however, be added the flood discharge of the Nyabrogo and Washa rivers, on the east, and those of one or two streams which come in from the west, north of the Nyabrogo junction. There is no means of ascertaining the flood discharge of these tributaries, but some of them, more particularly the Nyabrogo, must be of considerable importance. It seems safe then to assume, that the volume of water entering the Albert lake, by the

(1) The canoes are merely dug-outs, very small and entirely unstable. Getting the rope across the strong current was a work of considerable difficulty. The river swarms with crocodiles.

(2) Vide page 68.

(3) "Darkest Africa," by Sir H. M. Stanley, G.C.B., London, 1890.

channel of the Semliki, when in flood, is not less than 700 metres cube per second, and that the minimum and maximum discharges of this river are, respectively, 125 and 700 cubic metres per second.

The distance from the Mboga ferry to the mouth of the river, at the Albert lake, is 50 kilometres. At the 220th kilometre from Lake Albert Edward, it is joined by the Nyabrogo (1), and for another 10 or 15 kilometres, its course is open, and the valley continues similar in its characteristics to those already described, except that its width varies considerably. For the last 25 to 30 kilometres of its length, the Semliki passes through wide papyrus swamps, which stretch across the valley from the southern end of the Albert Nyanza. Passage through these swamps is well-nigh impossible, and none of the existing maps give any idea of their extent. They cover several hundreds of square kilometres, and the junction of the river with the lake is so masked by high reeds that it is very difficult to find (2). The detritus brought down by its waters is gradually pushing its delta out into the lake and filling up the bed. The shoals are therefore gradually extending northward, and the swamps with them, while the dry land, raised above the waters south of these marshes, is simultaneously extending its frontier in this direction. The width of the valley of the Semliki, at its mouth, is from 35 to 40 kilometres. It is bounded on the west by the cliffs of the great fault-line, through which the Msisi river finds its way to the lake. The climate of the northern portion of the Semliki valley is extremely hot, damp and unhealthy, even in the dry season. Throughout the year, heavy rainstorms, accompanied by thunder and lightning, are of almost daily occurrence and, as they generally occur at night, or in the early hours of the morning, they cause much discomfort to travellers in this locality. The change of temperature, from the high plateau of Toro to this low and swampy valley, is very trying, and the heat of the sun is extremely powerful. There is no shade, as, beyond a few Euphorbia and Borassus palms, there are no trees whatever. Mosquitoes are very numerous (3). During the rainy season, it must be practically impossible to travel in the Semliki valley, owing to the swamps. The long grass is full of ticks. The few inhabitants met with have an unhealthy look and appear to be badly fed (4). Large herds of elephants inhabit the swamps near the mouth of the Semliki, passing to and fro, up ravines in the eastern cliffs, to the Budonga forest, on the plateau above. The late Lieut. Wylde, in a note upon this region, stated that he once saw a procession of these animals here which took more than an hour to pass (5). The whole valley abounds with game, chiefly waterbuck (6), the Uganda cob (7), and a dark-coloured variety of reedbuck (8). Buffalo are also found in the swamps (9).

(1) For a description of this river, see the chapter on the country between the Albert Edward and the Albert lakes.

(2) None of the earlier travellers, such as Gessi and Mason, discovered the existence of the Semliki, although they must have passed close to its entrance, in their navigation of the lake. Even Emin never actually saw it, although, in one of his letters, he relates that he has been told of the existence of a great river, entering the Albert lake at the south end.

(3) Dr. Walker, who visited this portion of the valley in December 1901, states that he found the Tsetse fly here. If this is the case, it must probably be of that variety which, according to the latest discoveries, conveys the poison of the sleeping sickness, as there has never been a case of cattle being attacked by the Tsetse in this region.

(4) Their principal food is fish, of which they catch large numbers. There is no cultivation whatever.

(5) "Notes upon the Semliki Valley," by the late LIEUT. WYLDE, December, 1901.

(6) Cobus Defassa.

(7) Cobus Thomasi.

(8) Probably, Cervicapra redunca wardi.

(9) Both Bos caffer æquinoctialis and Bos caffer nanus are said to be found in this valley. The latter are confined to the western shores of the Semliki.

THE VICTORIA NILE.

Below the point where it issues from Lake Victoria, at the Ripon Falls, the general direction of this river, for many kilometres, is north-westerly. It runs between high, wooded cliffs, averaging from 50 to 70 metres in height, with a channel varying in width, between 300 and 500 metres. The bed, throughout this reach, is seamed by a succession of rocks and reefs, among, and over which the water tears in a series of rapids. At 6 kilometres from the lake, it falls over another and similar ridge to that at the outlet. This drop is known as the Owen Falls. From this point to Kakoji, 64 kilometres from the Ripon Falls, rapids and broken water are continuous. North of Kakoji, the stream is navigable, and flows on, in a smooth broad sheet, gradually widening until it reaches Lake Choga, at the 112th kilometre from its head (1).

Lake Choga, 1106 metres above the sea, is a long, irregularly-shaped sheet of water, running generally east and west, but with two long branches, or arms, stretching north-east and south-east. It lies between the parallels of 1° and 2° north latitude, and the meridians 32° 15′ and 33° 30′, east of Greenwich. At its south-eastern end, the Gogonio river enters, and due south, but to the west of the Victoria Nile, another long, narrow and marshy lake, formed by the river Sensiwa, joins it. This Sensiwa lake is some 80 kilometres in length, and is fed entirely by streams rising at the north of the Victoria Nyanza, their sources being barely 9 kilometres from the lake shores.

Lake Choga, is the most westerly of a large chain of shallow sheets of water, which cover the northern portion of the Busoga district, and which extend from Mruli nearly to the foothills of Mount Elgon (2), covering rather more than a square degree in area. It is joined by Lake Kwania, another long and narrow sheet of water, supposed to connect with the Choga lake at its eastern, as well as its northern end (3). All the lakes in this region, are surrounded by wide marshes and in many places their shores are invisible on account of the dense growth of papyrus, ambatch and reeds which completely blocks all access. This chain of swamps runs nearly due east and west for some 200 kilometres and receives the drainage of the north-western slopes of Mount Elgon, as well as that from the low hills bounding the northern shore of Lake Victoria. The Choga lake is generally shallow, being rarely more than from 4 to 6 metres in depth. To the east, as has been mentioned, it extends in a chain of marshes, but to the north and south it is thickly wooded; the trees being chiefly Euphorbia (4). The surface is full of papyrus islands and lotus and water-weeds cover the shallows and creeks. To the south, the country is thickly populated. Many isolated hills rise out of the plains which surround it. Of these, Ungera is the largest, and is 500 metres above the water (5). The greatest length of the lake is 136 kilometres, and the greatest width 16 kilometres.

The Nile runs through the western end of this lake for some 80 kilometres, and with a perceptible current. At its junction with the lake, it widens out into a large lagoon and winds round the base of the Pegi hills, 100 metres high, which flank its east bank here. At its point of issue, the Kwania lake connects with that of Choga, south of the Mahori hills (6). 1170 metres above the lake. These lagoons form an immense evaporating surface, and

(1) The description of Lake Choga, is largely derived from the report of the late Captain R.T. Kirkpatrick, D.S.O., published in the Geographical Journal, 1899.

(2) The country to the east of Lake Choga, has not yet been thoroughly explored. The maps show another lake, called Salisbury, lying to the east, but this has only been seen from Elgon, and at a long distance.

(3) KIRKPATRICK.

(4) Ibid.

must undoubtedly have a regulating effect upon the flow of the Victoria Nile. Although a very considerable volume of water must enter from the east and south, it is probable, as will be shown later, that the discharge of the Nile, entering the Albert lake during the dry season, is not materially increased, even although augmented by the supply brought down by the rivers which join it, north of the Choga lake. It would seem then that the loss by evaporation on the surface of these large sheets of shallow water, must, *at least*, compensate for the additional volume added by the Nile tributaries and that, most probably, the discharge of the Victoria Nile, at the point where it leaves Lake Choga, is rather less than that which it pours into it.

The Nile leaves this lake at the 192nd kilometre below the Ripon Falls. At this point, it turns due west and, after some 22 kilometres, reaches Mruli, latitude 1° 39′ north. Its average width at this point is from 800 to 900 metres. The west bank here is low and fringed with papyrus. The east bank is high and steep, being covered with open, forest (1). There is much "sudd" in this portion of the channel. Mruli is low and unhealthy. The site of Gordon's old fort is visible on the right bank of the Kafu river, which joins the Nile from the west, at this point (2).

The Kafu river, which is the most important tributary of the Victoria Nile, rises in Unyoro, in the high plateau on which are situated Forts Lugard and Grant, about latitude 1° north. At its source, the watershed which separates the water flowing east, into the Nile, from that flowing west, into the Albert lake, is very narrow; in fact, the Musisi river rises within a few kilometres of the sources of the Kafu. This last river has a total length of some 120 kilometres. For the first half of its course, its direction is north-west. It then turns due east and follows this direction until its junction with the Nile at Mruli. On issuing from the high ground, it runs, with a low slope, over a flat plain, and through a series of dense marshes, with an average width of from 50 to 60 metres (3). Where it crosses the road between Hoima and Entebbé, Mr. Craig, in March 1903, found it to be only 10 metres wide. For some distance above its junction with the Nile, during the dry season, it is dead-water, but, in flood, it becomes a raging torrent, and is difficult to cross. It has three tributaries from the south, the Dubengé, Lugogo and Maanja. The latter rises, just north of Kampala. All these three streams flow in a north-westerly direction (4).

Below Mruli, the Victoria Nile turns, nearly at a right angle, to the north and at 88 kilometres from Mruli, (302 kilometres from the Ripon Falls) reaches the station of Foweira, 1060 metres above the sea. Between Mruli and Foweira, the banks are low and swampy, the right being the higher of the two; gently rising and covered with trees (5). Between these two places, the Titi river joins it from the west, not far north of Mruli. The Titi, although unfordable in the rainy season, is dry at times, its bed being a wide expanse of sand. It rises in the Kisoga hills, some 1300 metres above the sea, between Masindi and Mashudi.

Foweira, which used to be a post of some importance, is a village of considerable size. It is situated on a steep bank on the west of the Nile, which here has a width of 500 metres, and a strong stream (6). Opposite to Foweira, the Lenga river joins it from the east (7), and some 15 kilometres downstream, another river, the Dukhu, enters it from the same direction (8). Neither of these are important streams, except when in flood.

(1) "Uganda and the Egyptian Sudan," by the REV. C. T. WILSON, F.R.G.S., 1882.
(2) The late LT. COL. VANDELEUR. D.S.O. Report published in Geographical Journal, April 1897.
(3) Baker, in "The Albert Nyanza," describes the difficulties of crossing these swamps.
(4) VANDELEUR.
(5) Ibid.
(6) Felkin, "Uganda and the Egyptian Sudan," gives the breadth as 850.
(7) VANDELEUR. Felkin calls this river the Kubuli.
(8) Ibid.

Very shortly below Foweira, navigation ends, as the Nile begins to dash down to the Karuma Falls, which are reached at 321 kilometres from the Victoria Nyanza. These falls are described by Sir Samuel Baker (1) as insignificant, dropping 1·15 metres over a ridge of rock which crosses the bed. This ridge occurs just below the point where the Nile bends from the north to the west, which latter direction it maintains, from the falls to the Albert lake. Its width here is 150 metres and it runs between cliffs of 50 metres in height (2). From this point, the Nile, as in the earlier portion of its course, runs between high cliffs, and in a succession of rapids and falls. At 48 kilometres downstream of the Karuma rapids, the island of Patooan is reached. This island is some 800 metres long, by 150 metres wide, and the channel of the river is from 180 to 200 metres in width. It is full of reefs, rocks and small islands (3). The fall between this point and Karuma, is, according to Baker, some 24 metres. Downstream of Patooan, the gorges become wilder and more rugged and the country on either side is covered with much forest. The slope increases and the channel narrows, until at 370 kilometres from its source in Lake Victoria, the Nile, after a sharp bend to the north-west, turns west again and leaps over the escarpment, in the cascade, named by its discoverer, Sir Samuel Baker, the Murchison Falls (4). The width of the river, just above the falls, is only 70 metres and this gradually decreases, until, at the actual fall, the water passes through a narrow cleft, less than 6 metres in width. The fall is in three steps, the first 3 metres, and the second 1·70 metres. From this point, the cleft, alluded to above, is passed through and the final drop, into the valley below, is nearly 40 metres (5).

A reference to the accompanying illustration, shows that these falls, as seen from below, are, on the whole, disappointing, except as regards the impression produced by the power and force of the water. It is impossible, from any point near to the falls, to get the full effect due to the height of the drop.

Mr. Stewart Belton, in a letter to a scientific paper (6), gives what is perhaps the best account of these falls, yet published. He describes the intermittent roar of the water, and shows how this peculiar phenomenon is produced, by an obstruction in the bed, just below the point where the long water-slide, between the second and last fall, ends. The water in front strikes this obstacle and rebounds. Meanwhile, the body of water behind, which is confined between high walls of rock, has to find an outlet, and is forced over the fall below, while the back wave, repulsed by the obstruction and now a boiling mass, follows quickly after it. Seen from below, the effect is of a mass of water, tumbling headlong into the pool, immediately followed by an enormous broken wave. Each wave is succeeded by a short lull. The cleft through which the Nile rushes, before taking its last drop, has been measured and was found to be only 5·45 metres in width.

At the summit of the fall is a rocky plateau, much worn into deep pot-holes, over which the river evidently at one time passed. The cliffs are some 70 metres in height and covered with a luxuriant vegetation, constantly drenched by the spray, which rises like a cloud of steam, and upon which a double rainbow plays. Mr. Belton describes the rocks forming these falls, as consisting of biotite gneiss, mica schist and quartz (7).

Just below the Murchison Falls is the village of Fajao. At this point is the ferry, by which the caravan route from Uganda, down the Nile, used to cross. The boatmen take advantage of a double swirl, or eddy, in the river here, to work their canoes straight across the channel, which is not more than 80 metres wide (8). The passage is attended

(1) Baker. "The Albert Nyanza."
(2) Ibid.
(3) Ibid.
(4) Ibid.
(5) Ibid. This last drop is not quite a vertical one.
(6) "Nature." June 19th 1902.
(7) Ibid.
(8) Ibid.

VICTORIA NILE
MURCHISON FALLS LOOKING UPSTREAM
FROM A PHOTOGRAPH BY G. BUTCHER, Esq.

VICTORIA NILE, FAJAO
LOOKING DOWNSTREAM FROM MURCHISON FALLS
FROM A PHOTOGRAPH BY G. BUTCHER, Esq.

with some risk, as the river is infested by crocodiles, which may be seen in scores on the rocks below the falls.

For several kilometres downstream of Fajao, the river winds between high wooded cliffs, from 70 to 80 metres above the water. The channel is very twisting and, at the bends, occasional flats are formed. The right, or north, bank is, as a rule, higher than that on the left. The stream is clear and free from all obstructions, with a depth varying from 3 to 4 metres, and an average mean velocity of over 0·80 metres per second [1].

At 19 kilometres below Fajao, the discharge of the Victoria Nile was measured on the 20th of March 1903. The width of the channel here, was 289 metres, and the depth of water varied between 2 and 4 metres. The mean velocity varied between 0·513 and 0·865 metres per second, and the discharge was 577 metres cube per second, or only 29 metres cube per second more than the discharge of the river at the Ripon Falls some two months earlier [2].

At the discharge site, the right (north) bank is vertical, and 0·70 metres above the water surface. The left bank slopes gradually from the water. On this side a band of papyrus, from 100 to 200 metres in width, extends. The marks on the trees show that the maximum flood rise at this point has not (at least for some years) exceeded 1·0 metre above the level in March 1903. This gives an approximate flood section, of 1200 metres square, and, applying the mean velocity, throughout the section, of 0·70 metres per second, this would be equivalent to a flood discharge of 840 metres cube per second. The flood velocity is, doubtless, much greater than that of the dry season, and the flood discharge of the Victoria Nile is probably quite 1000 metres cube per second [3].

Below this point, it is rare to find the river entirely in one channel. Branches take off to the left and right, forming islands. Nearer to the mouth, as the delta is approached, these branches run direct into Lake Albert. The general course now is slightly north-west. At 25 kilometres downstream of Fajao, the banks are much reduced in height and the bands of swamps on either side increase in width. All through this portion of its course, the Victoria Nile is a noble stream, passing through an endless succession of lovely scenes, the beauty of which is enhanced by the colouring of the foliage and the exquisite tints of the water. On the left bank, which averages 7 metres in height and which is thickly wooded, many huts are to be seen, and a few canoes which the people attempt to hide on the approach of a boat. The right bank is lower, and the high land is from 1, to 1·5 kilometres distant from the river. Bananas grow luxuriantly, on small ridges, among the ambatch and papyrus [4]. The average width of the main stream here is about 180 metres, but there are many side channels. The depth varies, at the deepest point, from 3 to 4 metres. To the north, at some distance from the river, stretches a high, bare, plateau, which extends from the foot of the eastern escarpment, to the shores of the Albert lake. This plateau has a steady slope from the hills to the lake. It is covered with grass and, at 3 kilometres from the lake, is 70 metres above the water surface. At 30 kilometres from Fajao, the river begins to shoal, and the depth is rarely more than 1·5 to 1·75 metres. Many "sudd" islands occur and a broad band of swamp stretches on either side, while the high land recedes to the left, and to the right [5]. The river bank now is rarely more than 1·25 metres above the water and is covered with a mass of creepers, resembling a bright green velvet carpet. Among these creepers, a lovely purple flower is to be seen. The islands and

(1) This gradually decreases as the estuary is approached.

(2) On the 22nd January 1903, this discharge was 548 metres cube per second. The question of this difference will be discussed in the chapter upon river discharges.

(3) Mr Craig, of the Egyptian Survey Department, has worked out, from the above discharge, a table of discharges for the Victoria Nile, (see appendix), with a flood rise of 1·0 metres, he makes the discharges equal to 1005 metres cube per second, or 353 metres cube per second greater than the maximum discharge at the Ripon Falls.

(4) The ambatch on the Victoria Nile is the largest and thickest to be seen anywhere on the river. Some of the trunks are as much as 0·30 metres in diameter, and the trees are often from 8 to 10 metres high.

(5) Two kilometres lower down, the depth suddenly increases to 5 metres, but this is only local, and it speedily is reduced again to 2·5 metres.

channels increase in number, and curious-looking fish-traps are to be observed, placed in the mouth of the different outlets. These traps consist of dome-shaped, circular baskets of wicker, open at the bottom, two metres wide, and from 2·25 to 2·50 metres in height. They are placed in a semi-circle across the entrance to a channel, with their open ends pointing downstream. The people appear to drive the fish into these traps. Hippopotami are extremely numerous in this river.

At some 400 kilometres from Lake Victoria, the river has formed a delta of its own and passes through a mass of "sudd" islands, covered with papyrus and reeds, with numerous branches, running into the lake on either side. The high land, to the left, is some two kilometres from the river and, on the right, the swamps stretch for a long way. On approaching the lake, the current is much reduced and for some distance before the lake is arrived at, the channel is apparently full of dead-water. The main stream, until the bar is reached, is, however, fairly straight, with easy curves. At one kilometre from Lake Albert, the depth shoals very rapidly and a wide bar, stretching far out into the lake, is met with. It is extremely difficult to find a passage across this bar. In most places, the depth is barely 0·30 metres and only at one point is there a depth of 0·60 metres. From the lake, it is even more difficult to find the entrance to the river, as there are endless channels winding through the reeds and, without a guide, it is next to impossible to find that by which boats can ascend the Victoria Nile. This river enters Lake Albert Nyanza at 408 kilometres from the point where it left Lake Victoria. The delta, which is fan-shaped, is some 7 kilometres wide at the mouth and is covered, throughout its area, by tall ambatch and thick papyrus. Beyond this fringe, the shoal water extends for several kilometres into the lake. The name of this locality is Magungo, from the old station and fort, which once existed on the left bank of the river, at the junction. This, with the ground on which it stood, has long been washed away by erosion.

The view, looking down the Victoria Nile, for some distance before entering the lake, is ideally beautiful, more especially at sunset. Looking west, and across Lake Albert, three ranges of mountains tower one above the other, in a series of fantastic and irregularly shaped peaks, while, to the south, a line of lofty headlands stands out, the furthest melting into the violet haze of the evening. As the sun sets, the nearest hills become a deep purple, whilst the higher ranges are bathed in a rose-pink glow. The water is full of opalescent tints and reflects each one of the many hues of the sky. The broad river channel is framed by lines of feathery papyrus, in dark green borders and, beyond, the calm lake stretches, a deep shade line reflecting the distant ranges. As the sun sinks behind the mountains, the rosy tints of the western sky deepen into flame, while the outlines of the hills are marked in indigo, in a strong and gorgeous contrast.

THE ALBERT NYANZA. (1)

This lake, discovered by Sir Samuel Baker in 1864, lies within the parallels of latitude 1° 9′ and 2° 17′ north, and between the meridians of 30° 35′ and 31° 30′ east of Greenwich (2). In shape it is, roughly, an ellipse, with the northern end more pointed than that to the south. Its general bearing is to the north-east and, in its characteristics, it differs considerably from either Lake Albert Edward or the Victoria Nyanza. It is long and narrow, and bounded on the east and west shores by high cliffs which verge closely upon its waters. The greatest length of Lake Albert is some 160 kilometres, and its breadth averages from 30 to 45 kilometres (3). Since its discovery by Baker, the Albert lake has been visited by many travellers (4). Both Gessi Pasha and Mason Bey circumnavigated the lake and produced rough maps of its configuration, but no accurate survey has as yet been made of its waters. At its southern end, wide swamps exist and, towards the north, the boundary walls formed by the mountains on either side, recede to some distance from the lake. With these exceptions, it has but little foreshore and, in many places, its waters wash the base of the cliffs. Its main tributary is the Semliki river, which enters it at the southern end and adds to its volume the overflow of the Albert Edward lake, and the entire drainage of the Ruenzori mountains, together with that of a considerable portion of the great western chain of hills which here skirt the confines of the Congo Free State. Besides the Semliki, it receives the water of many perennial streams both on the east and on the west (5). All these rivers leap over the high escarpment in a series of cascades and waterfalls, some of which are of very considerable height and volume. Near its northern end, the Victoria Nile enters Lake Albert, in north lat. 2° 17′ and, although it is generally accepted that the lake ends, and the Bahr-el-Gebel begins at this point, in reality, the former continues for a good many kilometres to the north before it narrows into the channel of the Bahr-el-Gebel, which is its only outlet.

The area of the catchment basin of the Albert Nyanza, including the valley of the Semliki river, is some 32000 square kilometres. The level of its waters above the sea is 680 metres (6).

The depth of this lake, in the centre, has never yet been sounded (7), but, for a long distance from either shore, it rarely exceeds 10 to 12 metres (8). Its bed is covered, to a very considerable depth, by a layer of soft mud and slime, the deposit brought in by the Semliki, and the streams upon either side. At the mouth of the Victoria Nile, a large delta has been formed which extends for a long distance out into the lake.

The southern end of Lake Albert is a vast swamp of papyrus and ambatch, several hundred square kilometres in extent. The mouth of the Semliki is completely masked by the water-weeds through which it runs. The depth, at this end, is shallow near the shore—rarely exceeding 1 metre, and being, as a rule, very much less. A few small islands still

(1) The native name is "Mutanzigi," or "Lutanzigi," i.e. "Dead Locust."

(2) These latitudes and longitudes are taken from the most recent maps.

(3) De Martonne gives its dimensions as 200 kilometres long, by 50 kilometres in breadth, but later investigation has shown that these figures exceed the reality. Opposite Kibero, the width of the lake is about 45 kilometres. and this is its widest part.

(4) Of these, the most notable names are those of Gessi, Emin, Stuhlmann, Stanley, Jephson, Felkin and Grogan.

(5) The eastern streams drain the high plateau of Unyoro, lying between the Victoria Nile and the Albert lake. Some of them, like the Msisi and the Ngusi, are of considerable importance. On the west, the catchment area is remarkably narrow, and the watershed very close to the lake. As the bounding ridge of mountains is almost knife-edged, these streams must be of short length, and be more of the nature of torrents than of rivers bringing in a steady discharge

(6) This is the value now generally accepted for this lake.

(7) This is due to the frequency and violence of the storms upon this lake. Squalls arise so very suddenly, and with such little warning, that it is highly dangerous for the existing small craft to attempt to cross from the east to the west. Navigation at any distance from the shore is but rarely attempted.

(8) The deepest soundings recorded are those given by Emin, for the west coast, i.e. 16 to 17 metres.

exist on the western shore, but these are merely shoals which have gradually risen above the water. They are being by slow degrees, connected with the mainland (1).

Its waters throughout are, for some distance from the coast, although very clear, brackish and of an unpleasant taste. In the centre of the lake, the water is sweet and good. The soil of the surrounding flats is highly impregnated with salt and, at Kibero, lat. 1° 41′ north, on the east shore, there are extensive salt workings, supplying an extensive trade. Hot sulphur springs exist at this place and also on the western shore. The general colour of the waters of the Albert Nyanza is a dark sea-green. To the south, it is of crystal clearness, but in the northern half, more particularly along the eastern shore, it is covered by a thick green scum, or slime, evidently composed of minute algæ. This scum, when the lake is calm, gives its surface a curiously marbled and streaky appearance (2).

The scenery of this lake is, in parts, very beautiful. The western mountains (3) are of irregular shape, with many conical and pointed peaks. Their slopes are abrupt and deeply ravined. Three tiers of hills, one rising behind the other, can be observed. The foreshores, where they exist, are thickly wooded. On the east, the cliffs rise sharply, for many hundred metres above the water surface, to the Unyoro plateau. They are often covered with abundant vegetation and, seen from the lake, form a succession of noble headlands, the masses of towering rock being broken, at intervals, by wild gorges, through which the rivers dash down in cascades of white foaming water. These gorges are densely forested and are used as tracks to, and from, the lake, by the large herds of wild elephants which frequent the whole region upon either side. North of Kibero, on the west, the cliffs recede and wide flats extend from the water until at the junction of the Nile with the lake, their width is as much as 40 kilometres. No current was observable in Lake Albert, in March 1903, and, even to the north of the Victoria Nile junction, the water was dead for several kilometres. It was not until the shores had narrowed very considerably that any stream, flowing to the north, was apparent (4).

The following is a rather more detailed description of the general characteristics of the lake shores on either side (5).

Commencing at the southern end of the lake, and following the western shore, large flats, covered by grass and a few trees, extend inland for some 2 or 3 kilometres from the lake. These flats are bounded by a high wall of lofty and rugged mountains, ranging in height from 700 to 800 metres above the water. At intervals, large valleys run down to the shore, in each of which there is a stream, falling in a succession of beautiful cascades (6). In this reach of lake is the promontory of Nyamsassee, formerly an island and separated from the mainland by a narrow channel (7). At Kakanama, 48 kilometres from the south-west corner or the lake, the plains end and the mountains, turning sharply to the east, come down to the lake in one great headland. From this point, the scenery is extremely wild. The hills rise abruptly to a height of 800 metres and great rocks stand out into the water, which dashes against these giant walls with a noise like thunder, sending up showers of spray (8). On these rocks, every gully is full of trees and creepers, and cascades of clear water leap down and dash hundreds of feet into the lake below. Most of these streams form small deltas of their own in the lake, some of them being as much as 5 acres in extent (9). The soundings, along this coast, give a depth varying from 5 to 17 metres,

(1) Gessi in 1876, observed some small islands on the east side. These no longer exist, but form a portion of the foreshore.

(2) A specimen of this water was brought down in 1903, and has been sent to England, for analysis. At the time of writing, the results of this analysis had not been received.

(3) These have been called by Emin, the Luri mountains, as the country, west of the lake, is inhabited by the Luri tribe.

(4) Felkin, "Uganda & the Egyptian Sudan," London 1882, notes, in the month of December 1878, two currents at the mouth of the Victoria Nile: one flowing north towards the Bahr-el-Gebel, and the other S.S.W. into the lake itself.

(5) The description of the western and south-eastern coasts has been compiled from the narratives of different travellers. The north-eastern shore is described from personal observation, and from notes made in March 1903.

(6) "Emin Pasha in Central Africa," by R.W. Felkin, London, 1888.

(7) "Emin Pasha" by A.J. Mounteney Jephson, London, 1890. He found it an island, in 1888.

(8) Ibid.

(9) Ibid.

ALBERT NYANZA
VIEW OF WESTERN COAST

ALBERT NYANZA
VIEW OF EASTERN COAST

but close inshore the water is extremely shallow. The bed of the lake is covered with a thick deposit of black mud (1). At Mahagi (Mswa) (latitude 1° 52′ north), 100 kilometres from the south end of the lake, the cliffs again recede and a large plain, covering some 5000 acres, extends back from the water (2). It is surrounded by an amphitheatre of high mountains, the highest of which is Gebel Nydea (800 metres high) (3). This was Emin Pasha's station, the fort being placed upon a small hill in the centre of the plain. Jephson describes it, in April 1888, as being highly cultivated and densely populated. Mahagi, or Mswa, was formerly the most important station on the west shore of the lake. In more recent times, it was occupied by a garrison of the Congo Free State (4). The plain at Mahagi is alluvial and extends for some three kilometres back from the water. It is watered by a stream which drains a valley between the surrounding hills. North of Mahagi, the hills run close to the lake, with occasional flats, until at 29 kilometres, a grand headland stands out close to the water. After rounding this, in another 16 kilometres, Tunguru (little Mahagi) is reached (5). This place is situated some 146 kilometres from the southern end of the lake, and 10 kilometres south of the point, on the western shore, opposite to the junction of the Nile with Lake Albert, at Magungo. The village is on a peninsula, formerly an island and separated from the mainland by a flat strip of sand. Between this strip and the shore is a series of broad shallow lagoons. Tunguru was formerly Gordon's old station, and from this point, north, the mountains deflect suddenly, leaving a broad plain which extends along the Nile valley. Landing on the western coast is by no means easy, except at Mahagi, and one or two other spots. Mr. Grogan, who attempted to follow this coast on foot, describes the difficulties he encountered with his porters, in trying to pass round the innumerable headlands (6). Parallel to the lake, and at no great distance from it, a range of foothills, from 200 to 300 metres in height, runs. Behind this rise two other and higher ranges, one towering above the other, with many fantastically shaped peaks. These hills are sparsely wooded and even the foothills are devoid of much vegetation (7). The mountains at the southern end of Lake Albert are considerably higher than those to the north end and, after Mahagi is passed, the outlines of the western ranges are much flatter than they are south of this place. As a whole, there are very few large bays, or indentations, upon either shore of the Albert lake. Of these, the Kibero bay is the most important, but even this does not extend back far from the shore. The lake is practically enclosed, for quite half its length, between two straight walls of rock which only vary the monotony of the coast by a succession of headlands, separated by narrow beaches, on which the fishing population resides.

The eastern coast of Lake Albert, commencing from the south end, for a very considerable distance, resembles that of the western shore, as the face of the escarpment drops down to the water in a series of precipitous cliffs, averaging 500 metres in height. At the south-eastern corner, the Msisi river enters the lake through a long and narrow bay, some 16 kilometres in length and 1 ½ kilometres in width, at the entrance. This river drops over the escarpment here in a magnificent waterfall, some 200 metres in height (8). Between this place and Mbakovia (9), lat. 1° 15′ north, a distance of some 16 kilometres, the cliffs run sheer down into the lake. Mbakovia is a fishing village, on the level flats, 1 ½ kilometres

(1) FELKIN "Emin Pasha." Hot springs are met with at the foot of these cliffs.

(2) JEPHSON.

(3) FELKIN.

(4) It is reported that Mahagi has been abandoned on account of its unhealthiness, and another station formed more inland.

(5) Between Mahagi and Tunguru. Jephson reports sulphur springs. He describes the water as too hot for the hand to bear, and of a bright yellow colour in the basin.

(6) "From the Cape to Cairo," by E. S. GROGAN, London, 1900.

(7) Throughout this region, the western slopes of all ranges running north and south, are, as a rule, less steep, but more thickly forested than are those of the eastern face.

(8) "Exploration du lac Albert Nyanza," by ROMOLO GESSI, Société de géographie, Paris, June, 1876.

(9) This is the Vacovia of Baker, the place where he first reached the Albert lake on March 14th, 1864. "The Albert Nyanza," London, 1892.

in width, between two headlands which are some 8 kilometres apart. The beach here is of coarse sand and, according to Baker, a rise of $4\frac{1}{2}$ metres in the lake surface would flood the flats, right up to the base of the eastern hills (1). For another 48 kilometres to the north, the cliffs border the lake shore, often rising direct out of the water, but occasionally a narrow strip of beach separates them from the lake. The Hoga promontory is high and rocky and covered with dense jungle (2). North of Hoga, the flats widen out and a few villages are located near the lake, but some 15 kilometres further north the cliffs again approach the water and the Kibero bay commences. Between Mbakovia and Hoga, two rivers enter the lake. The first, or southernmost, is the Ngusi (3), the third largest tributary of the lake, while the second is the Nyakarangu river. The coast is now a succession of headlands, ending in the promontory which forms the southern boundary of the Kibero bay. This is the largest bay in the lake. Its width is 16 kilometres. In this bay are situated the village and salt works of Kibero, 88 kilometres from the south end of the lake. The Wahambu and Hoima rivers enter the lake within this bay. All along the eastern plateau here, the forests of Bugoma and Bidonga stretch for a long distance. These forests, which are tropical in the luxuriance of their vegetation, are the home of innumerable elephants.

The old fort at Kibero was situated on the cliffs opposite this bay, some 600 metres, or more, above the lake. From this place there is a road to Hoima, the headquarters of the Unyoro district and distant some 14 kilometres from Kibero. Before the cart road from Entebbé to Butiabu was completed, this used to be the starting point for travellers proceeding down the Nile. Opposite the Kibero bay, the lake attains its greatest breadth of 45 kilometres. At the foot of the cliffs, wide flats extend to the water and here are the headquarters of the salt industry. Kibero formerly used to supply the districts of Uganda and Unyoro with salt. Hot sulphur springs are met with in the neighbourhood. The lake here is very shallow for some distance from the shore, owing to the large quantities of alluvial deposit brought down by the rivers, which have thus formed the flats upon which the village of Kibero is situated. These flats are gradually pushing out into the lake, in the shape of long, narrow spits of land. Emin describes the hot sulphur springs as gushing forth at the foot of the lofty mountain chain. They are situated in a deep ravine, in which blocks of stone and debris lie scattered about. The floor of this ravine, and the stones which cover it are so hot that the bare foot cannot be placed upon them without pain. On every side is heard the bubbling and hissing of the water. Hundreds of tiny steam jets and springs burst out and fill the air with sulphurous gases. The water is very clear, with a temperature of 185° to 195° F. It has a slight smell (4).

The whole soil of these alluvial flats, as is the case all round Lake Albert, is impregnated with salt. The salt is extracted by pouring water upon the earth and by evaporating the liquid when drained off. It is coarse-grained, grey in colour, and has a bitter taste.

The eastern hills, at this place, are in a succession of terraces, one above the other like bastions. A small river, the Kachoro, 2 metres wide and 0.45 metres deep, drops down through them in a series of cascades. Beyond Kibero, the cliffs deflect to the east, and wide flats begin. These get wider and wider until the Victoria Nile is reached. At 20 kilometres beyond Kibero is the jetty of Butiabu, the terminus of the road from Entebbé to the Albert lake. From this place, the boat service to Nimuli, on the Bahr-el-Gebel, now starts. At Butiabu, the distance across the lake, from east to west, is some 30 kilometres. Not far south of the pier, a long and narrow spit of land runs out into the water. Its length is some three kilometres and it curves, in a crescent shape, to the north. A few palms

(1) "The Albert Nyanza," London, 1892.

(2) Ibid.

(3) Baker calls this the Kaligiri, but this must be a local name, and he only saw it at its junction with the lake. He describes its waterfall as being over 300 metres in height. It is the finest of all the many falls which adjoin the Albert lake.

(4) "Emin Pasha in Central Africa," by Dr. R. W. Felkin, London, 1888.

mark the extremity. This spit is caused by the alluvium brought down by the Wakki river which enters Lake Albert a little to the north of this point. A small settlement of natives, occupied in fish-curing, is located on this point of land. The eastern flats at Butiabu are from 5 to 6 kilometres in width, sloping up, in a succession of terraces, to the foot of the cliffs which here form the east boundary of the Albertine "Rift" valley. These flats are alluvial and must once have been covered by the waters of the lake, as the presence of numerous lake shells testifies. Nearer the hills, the detritus washed down from the slopes has raised them considerably. They are much scored by deep drainage lines, some of which are 3 metres in depth and from 4 to 5 metres in width. The sides of these channels are vertical and, as well as the beds, show signs of severe water-action. In many places, large-sized trees have been uprooted by the force of the torrent. Commencing at a height of 1 metre, this plain, for a long distance from the water, is some 1.5 metres above the lake. It gradually rises to a second terrace, some 3 metres above water level, while the third and last, may be as much as 5 metres, higher than the lake surface. The entire surface of these flats is covered with very high and dense bush. Nearer the hills, occasional large trees are met with. Everything points to the fact that, at one period, the lake waters must have covered the whole area, probably to the base of the eastern foot-hills.

The Wakki river, which enters Lake Albert some 5 kilometres to the south of Butiabu pier, after dropping down the escarpment in a series of the waterfalls, pursues a tortuous course through the flats to the lake. Its banks are covered with a thick belt of forest, which is a favourite haunt of wild elephants. The escarpment, at this point, although not absolutely precipitous, is exceedingly steep and rises directly from the plain for some 250 metres. Behind the first ascent stretches an extent of steep rounded hills covered with forest, which rise in a series of steps, until the full height of the plateau is attained, at some 500 metres above the lake. The ravines are very deep and, in some places, form great chasms. Between these ravines stand up stony and bare spurs which run down to the valley below. The flood marks on the shore at Butiabu, show plainly that, for some years previous to March 1903, the water surface in Lake Albert had not risen more than 0.30 to 0.45 metres above its lowest level. Previous to 1903, there had been a series of years of deficient rainfall throughout this area. The months of December 1902, and January, February and March 1903 were practically rainless. Consequently, all the tributary rivers were, in March, at their lowest and the entire volume discharged into the lake, by those crossing the eastern escarpment, did not exceed 16 or 17 metres cube per second. The Semliki discharge at the same time was only 124 metres cube per second, and it seems certain that the western streams must have been discharging even less than those on the east. Taking all these facts into consideration, it seems fair to assume that the water surface of this lake, in March 1903, was at as low a level as is ever reached. In years of abundant rainfall, it is possible that the rise of the lake is considerably more than that given above, but it is incontestable that, within any recent period of time, its waters have never topped the eastern flats [1]. The depth along the eastern shore, for several kilometres from the bank, is but small and rarely exceeds 2 to 2.5 metres.

North of Butiabu, the same scenery continues and the eastern flats widen out, as the hills recede from the lake. 16 kilometres further on, a second spit of land, similar to that previously described, juts out into the water for a long distance. This projection is formed by the deposit brought down by the Waiga river which enters Lake Albert not far from here. The spit has the same crescent shape as that formed by the deposit of the river Wakki. Opposite to this point, the eastern cliffs which, throughout their whole extent to the south, present a singularly flat skyline, rise into four low peaks, two being round, and

[1] Since the above was written, it has been confirmed that this lake does, in years of good rainfall, rise considerably above the level recorded. Mr. Pordage, of the Uganda Public Works Department, arrived in Cairo in December 1903. He reported that the Albert lake level, at the end of October 1903, was 0.83 metres above its level in March, of the same year. The rainfall from April to August 1903, was exceptionally heavy and very general.

two conical in shape. These peaks break the horizontal line and are visible for a long distance. The width of the flats here is some 15 kilometres and the terrace formation is always preserved. The lake itself now decreases considerably in width and the western hills are lower, and less rugged in outline. They are, however, still very steep in their eastern face. Proceeding north, the lake still further contracts and the flats upon either side get wider. On the west, near Tunguru (Mahagi Sogheir), they average 5 kilometres in width and slope sharply up to the foot-hills (1). They are thickly wooded with acacias and bush. The width of the lake, at this point, is not more than 11 to 12 kilometres. At 40 kilometres north of Butiabu, the delta of the Victoria Nile is reached, at a distance of 148 kilometres from the southern extremity of Lake Albert. For the next 7 or 8 kilometres, nothing is visible to the east but a wilderness of ambatch, papyrus and high reeds. This locality is known as Magungo, but, beyond a few fishermen's huts, there is now no sign of any human habitation (2). The old site of Magungo, which was occupied by Gordon, and which was formerly a post of importance, has long been washed away and no trace of it now remains. It was situated upon the southern bank of the Victoria Nile. It is difficult to account for the disappearance of this place and of the considerable area of land upon which it stood. It can only be concluded that, at times, there is a strong current, running south from the river, into the lake and along the eastern shore, and that the action of the water eroded the alluvial bank and gradually washed away the entire area (3). From the lake, there is no sign of the vicinity of a great river, beyond the change in the colour of water which here assumes an olive-green tint, similar to that of the Bahr-el-Gebel and the White Nile. No current at all is perceptible here (4), but the delta is gradually pushing out into the lake from the eastern shore and shoal water extends to from 4 to 5 kilometres, to the west of the ambatch fringe. The depth is nowhere more than 1.5 metres and the bottom of the lake is covered with a thick layer of very soft mud. Close to the reeds, the depth is rarely more than 0.60 metres and, in many places, it is much less. Looking east from the lake, it is a singularly desolate scene, as the eastern ridge is very far away and the tall vegetation completely shuts in the view (5).

The width of Lake Albert, at the Nile junction, is barely 9 kilometres. The delta of this river extends for a width of some 7 kilometres along the eastern shore of the lake and, throughout this entire reach, the ambatch and reeds continue. On the northern bank of the Nile, the land rises in a flat plateau, bare and covered with low grass. This plateau extends, in a series of low terraces, to the high land in the east. The formation, north of the Nile, is very similar to that described for the flats of the south, with this difference, that, whereas the latter are covered with thick bush, the former is entirely destitute of trees. This plateau, at some distance from the lake, rises to a height of some 70 or 80 metres above it and carries on this level to the eastern escarpment (6).

All along the water's edge, a thick belt of reeds and ambatch extends; and the height of the bank above the water is from 1 to 1·25 metres. For several kilometres downstream, the shoal water continues and landing anywhere along the eastern coast is very difficult,

(1) Mahagi Sogheir (now abandoned) was situated on the flats, between a high bluff of the secondary range, and the smaller hills nearer the lake. The gorge here looks as if a river enters from the north-west.

(2) Felkin, who visited the lake in December 1878, describes Magungo as a well-built town, surrounded by a strong earth fortification, and a moat 3 metres deep: "Uganda and the Egyptian Sudan," by Dr. R. W. Felkin, London, 1882.

(3) Felkin, as has been already stated. mentions the existence of this current, which he himself observed flowing up the lake. In March 1903, it was an expanse of dead water.

(4) i.e. in March 1903.

(5) The bar at Magungo across the mouth of the Nile is a wide one. It is caused by the river meeting the still water of the lake and consequently depositing the material which it had hitherto carried in suspension. The Nile has a very high velocity from the Murchison Falls, to within some 7 or 8 kilometres of Lake Albert. At this point, the current gradually slackens, and, before the lake is arrived at, it is an expanse of still, or nearly still, water, spreading in every direction, in a labyrinth of channels, until the lake is reached. There is no "draw," so to speak, from the Nile outlet to this point. It is more than probable that, at times, the river water runs south, up the lake. as well as north, to the outlet

(6) It is very difficult to find a name for this particular tract. The officers of the boat-service call it Okelu, but Okelu is, in reality, a village on the western shore of the lake.

ALBERT NYANZA
JUNCTION OF VICTORIA NILE WITH LAKE

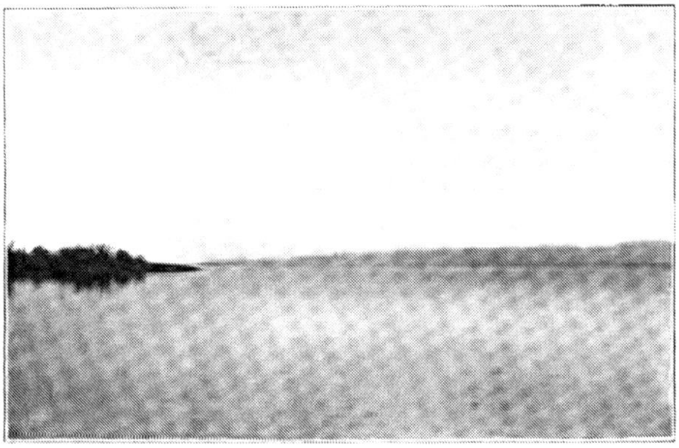

ALBERT NYANZA
VIEW LOOKING SOUTH FROM MAGUNGO

more especially as the bottom is covered with several feet of ooze. Allusion has already been made to the uncertainty as to the point where the lake ends, and the Bahr-el-Gebel commences. For several kilometres north of the junction of the Victoria Nile, the lake is still 5 to 6 kilometres in breadth and there is no difference in the general characteristics of the shore. The width narrows very gradually and it is only at 8 kilometres north of Okelu that it is so far reduced as to be fairly called a river. At the same time, as there is a faint, but perceptible current a few kilometres below the junction, the Bahr-el-Gebel may be considered as commencing from this point, even although the lake formation is continued for a considerable distance downstream.

Before discussing the question of the lake levels, a brief description of the principal rivers which feed the Albert lake may be of interest. Besides the Semliki, which has been already described, many streams pour their waters into Lake Albert, although few of them are anything but torrents which bring down large volumes during the rainy season, and sink to insignificant limits during the rest of the year. Of those on the western side but little is known, beyond the very meagre descriptions given by the travellers who have followed that side of the lake. It is evident, from the close vicinity of the Nile-Congo watershed to the western shore throughout, that none of these streams can be of great length and, as there is no plateau on the mountain tops here, they can only drain the eastern faces of the range parallel to the lake. Their floods cannot be of any long duration and in all probability they come down in a succession of heavy "spates" rather than with a steady and lasting supply. To a certain extent, this is true of the eastern rivers, but on this side of the lake, the catchment basin is considerably wider than on the west and comprises a much larger area. This basin is of singularly irregular shape, wide to the south, but narrowing sharply at the northern end of the lake. The line of the watershed is a remarkably twisting one and is extremely difficult to follow. Its height above sea level varies from 1200 to 1500 metres and, although generally running north, or north-east, it winds about in a most perplexing manner, following the ridge (consisting of alternate hills and high plateaux) which divides Western Unyoro from Uganda and Busoga. In some places, the distance which separates the head-waters of the streams running east into the Victoria Nile and west into the Albert lake, is only a few kilometres in width.

Commencing from the southern end, the principal rivers and streams which feed Lake Albert from the east are the following:—The Msisi, the Ngusi, the Nyakabari or Horo, the Wahamba, with its branch the Lukajuka, the Hoima, the Wakki and the Waiga (1). Of these rivers, the Msisi and the Ngusi are the most important and rank only second to the Semliki in importance. All of these streams cross the eastern escarpment and drop down into the lake valley in a series of fine cascades, many of them being of great height. Even in the dry season, these falls are very fine and when the rivers are in full flood they must form a magnificent sight. They have rarely, if ever, been seen by Europeans at this period, as during the rains it is almost impossible to travel in Western Unyoro. None of the rivers are bridged and the tall grass, which flourishes at that period, makes progress extremely difficult.

The Msisi river has its source in latitude 0°45′ north, near to Fort Grant, on the plateau rising above the hills to the south of the Embaia river (2). This plateau extends along the right, or northern, bank of the Msisi, broken by occasional peaks, as far as the escarpment of the "Rift" valley. It has several tributaries, mostly from the south. Of these, the most important are, the Ravasanja (3), and another stream which rises near the Lomaja mountains (4). The Msisi, throughout the greater portion of its length, turns and twists

(1) All these rivers are perennial. There are many other smaller streams, but during the dry season they are mere swamps trickling down to the west, and draining the plateaux and forest lands.

(2) A tributary of the Kafur.

(3) Vandeleur describes the Ravasanja, as 30 metres wide, and 1·3 metres deep.

(4) These mountains, which are 1840 metres above the sea, form the watershed of three different systems, thus:— the branch of the Msisi above mentioned, flowing to the Albert Nyanza, the Mpango, flowing into Lake Albert Edward, through the Dueru lake, and lastly, the Katonga, which is a tributary of the Victoria lake.

between high rocky hills, passing close to Fort Nakabunda on its way. Even in the dry season, it is unfordable at this place. It is crossed by a causeway (1). In flood it is a raging torrent. The total length of the Msisi is some 150 kilometres. In the first 110 kilometres, the river has a westerly course. It then turns north-east and, following a deep and wide valley, which scores the country like a large trench, it leaps over the eastern escarpment in a series of falls, some of which are of great height. It finally joins the lake in a bay known as the Dueru Gulf (2). The valley of the Msisi, for a long distance upstream of the escarpment, is some 4 kilometres in width and from 150 to 200 metres in depth. Its northern boundary is the transversal fault-line which forms a branch of the main ridge, or watershed, between the Albert and Victoria lake systems. The width of this river, when in flood, is considerably over 100 metres, and its depth in midstream, at this season, is 5 metres. During the dry season, it shrinks greatly in size, but even then is a formidable obstacle for a caravan. The discharge measurements, made at a point 10 kilometres upstream of the falls, on the 9th of March 1903, gave a water-width of 10 metres, and a depth, at the deepest point, of 1·4 metres. The water-section was 6·70 square metres. The mean velocity was 0·40 metres per second, and the discharge 2·68 metres cube per second (3). The total rise in flood above this level, is 3·6 metres. The flood-section, as measured, is 143 square metres, but portions of it are very shallow. Its mean velocity, throughout the whole section when in flood, cannot well be less, taking its slope into account, than 2 metres per second. This would be equivalent to a discharge of 286 metres cube per second (4). The Msisi ranks next to the Semliki in importance among the tributaries of Lake Albert Nyanza.

Next to the Msisi, comes the Ngusi river, which rises near Mawenda, in latitude 1°10′ north, on the ridge which forms a continuation of the plateau drained by the Msisi. Here again, the ridge is very narrow and the source of the Ngusi is not far distant from that of the Embaia, a swampy river which is a tributary of the Kafur, and thus helps to swell the volume of the Victoria Nile. The length of the Ngusi is not more than 65 kilometres. It runs nearly due west and falls into Lake Albert to the north of Mbakovia, in a series of magnificent cascades. The most important tributary of the Ngusi is the Mponbi (5), which joins it from the south-east. The total fall of the Ngusi is some 540 metres. Allowing 300 metres to be absorbed in the falls, this would leave 240 metres for the remainder of its course, or an average fall of some 3·6 metres per kilometre. Its bed is very rocky and full of boulders, and it rushes down in a series of rapids and small falls. Like the Msisi, this river, even in the dry season, is very difficult to cross and its depth is, at all times, considerable. Its discharge was measured on the 12th of March 1903, at a point some 15 kilometres upstream of the escarpment. The width of the stream was only 6 metres, but it had a depth of 1·85 metres, and a mean velocity of 0·50 metres per second. The water section of the river was 12·45 square metres, and the discharge 6·22 metres cube per second (6). The flood-rise of the Ngusi is 3·5 metres, and its depth in midstream, at that period, is 5·75 metres. Its width in flood is 69 metres, and its flood-section is 129 square metres. Allowing a velocity in flood of 2 metres per second (7), this is equivalent to a discharge of 258 metres cube per second. It is very probable that, at times, the Ngusi is discharging a greater volume than the Msisi, but its floods come down in a series of rushes, and run off much more quickly than do those of the larger river.

(1) Vandeleur.

(2) Gessi gives the height of the lowest fall, as nearly 200 metres.

(3) The river was at that time at its lowest.

(4) It is probable that the Msisi discharge, at times, exceeds these figures. The total fall of the river is 688 metres. Of this, some 500 metres may be presumed to be taken up in the falls, leaving 188 metres, an average fall of 1·4 metres per kilometre, for the remainder of its course. On the other hand, its catchment basin is of no great extent.

(5) This is called "Mpongi" on some maps, but its local name is as given above.

(6) Between the 9th and 12th of March 1903, there had been heavy rains, and it is probable that there had been a slight rise in the Ngusi, which would account for it, a smaller river, having a larger discharge than the Msisi. Its waters, at the time of the discharge, were turbid, and much charged with sediment.

(7) It is probably more than this at times.

WAKKI RIVER
LOWER FALL
FROM A PHOTOGRAPH BY G. BUTCHER, Esq.

WAKKI RIVER
UPPER FALL
FROM A PHOTOGRAPH BY G. BUTCHER, Esq.

The Nyakabari, or Horo, is made up of a number of small streams such as the Balbona, Jimangawu, Kagarandindu, and others which rise in the Kikonda hills. It finds its way, through the Bugoma forest, into the lake ([1]), in latitude 1° 27′ north. During the dry season, these different streams are mere swamps, oozing through deep valleys, and choked by dense vegetation. It is impossible to measure their volume at this period, as their velocity is almost nil, and they rather resemble quagmires than rivers. In flood, it is possible that the volume of the Nyakabari may be of importance, but it is difficult to obtain any information regarding this river, which has but a short course of hardly more than 40 kilometres.

Proceeding north, along the lake, the next tributary of importance from the east is the Wahamba. This river rises in the Kidoga hills ([2]) not far from the station of Hoima and in latitude 1°28′ north. Near its source, it is known as the Wambabia and its main tributary is a river called the Lukajuka, rising in the same hills. Their combined waters are known as the Wahamba. This river has a course of some 48 kilometres and, for a considerable portion of its length, it traverses the Bugoma forest, which covers so large an area of the eastern plateau. It enters the lake at the southern end of the Kibero bay. Several streams join the Wahamba from the south, among them being the Kaberogota, the Meego and the Greeka. Its most important affluent, however, is the Lukajuka. This river, like the Wambabia, rises to the north of Hoima, in that portion of the Kidoga range marked by the peaks of Palijoku and Impala. A little further to the north, a third stream, the Hoima, rises in the same range and, after a length of some 35 kilometres, enters Lake Albert in the Kibero bay. All these rivers have a heavy slope, considerably over 3 metres per kilometre. In flood, they must at times bring down large volumes of water, but their discharge is intermittent and these "spates" rarely last for more than a day or so. In the dry season, they shrink to very small limits and their united discharges, as measured in March 1903, at the point where they cross the road from Hoima to Butiabu, barely exceeded 2 cubic metres per second. Their united flood-section amounts to only 70 square metres and their maximum flood-rise at this point is only 1·6 metres. It is probable that the Wahamba, and Hoima streams carry, as a maximum, from 100 to 150 cubic metres per second, of which the Wahamba discharges considerably the larger share. These rivers flow over gravelly and rocky beds. The water in each of them, is very clear.

The Wakki river joins Lake Albert a few kilometres to the north of Butiabu. It rises not far from Masindi, and near Mount Fumbi. It has a north-westerly course, and is some 50 kilometres in length. Although, in the dry season, its discharge is very insignificant, in flood it brings down a large volume of water. On the 18th of March 1903, it was discharging some 2 metres cube per second, at the Hoima-Butiabu road-crossing. Its total rise at this point, does not exceed 2 metres and its flood-section is 65 square metres. Its flood discharge is probably, at times, from 100 to 130 metres cube per second, but, like the Ngusi, Hoima and Wahamba, it is a torrential stream. The Wakki flows with a heavy slope, over a very rocky bed, in a series of falls. Its water is particularly clear and limpid. Its valley is full of dense undergrowth, and, in places, of fine forest trees. As it traverses the escarpment, the slope of its bed becomes heavier and it runs in a very deep gorge, between almost precipitous cliffs, until at last, it makes its final descent into the lake valley, in a very beautiful, double fall, some 150 metres in height. Through a portion of its course, the Wakki traverses the Budonga forest.

The last, and most northerly of the eastern tributaries of the Albert Nyanza, is the Waiga, or Waija river. This stream joins the lake, 15 kilometres to the north of Butiabu,

(1) It is very difficult to arrive at the correct names of these rivers, every inhabitant giving them the name of his own chief.

(2) These are a continuation of the great central ridge, or backbone, of Unyoro, which separates the water-systems of the Albert lake and the Victoria Nile.

in north latitude 2° 16′. It rises in the Kerota hills, latitude 1° 58′ north, and has a length of some 60 kilometres. In section and discharge, it is very similar to the Wakki, but owing to the width of the flats where it joins Lake Albert, its slope, in the lower reaches, is easy. It is navigable for canoes at certain seasons of the year, as far east as the escarpment hills.

It will be seen from the foregoing, that, although all these rivers must at times add a large volume of water to the lake, the increase due to this supply cannot, owing to their short length, heavy slope and restricted catchment basin, be a steady one. Their discharges must be brought down in a series of violent rushes, lasting for a limited period of time, and quickly subsiding (1). All local information bears out this statement (2). In the case of the smaller streams, the floods probably only last for a few hours (3).

To calculate the amount of water which really enters Lake Albert Nyanza during the year is practically impossible, with the very limited information that exists. There is no gauge upon this lake as yet, and rainfall observations have but recently been instituted, and only at one station. This is Fort Portal, some 60 kilometres south of the lake, but not far from the northern end of the Semliki valley (4). The register has, however, only been commenced within some 7 or 8 months, and does not yet record the rainfall of an entire year. At Hoima, the civil station of Unyoro, which is within 16 kilometres of Lake Albert, there is as yet no rain gauge. It is much to be desired that an observing station should be established here as soon as possible. As there are three Europeans at Hoima, there should be no difficulty in keeping up the register. It would be invaluable, as affording information regarding the annual rainfall in the plateau to the east of the lake. Another rain gauge should be erected at Butiabu, at the telephone station on the crest of the escarpment. This gauge could be read by the signaller in charge. As regards the west of Lake Albert, the Belgian authorities might be asked to co-operate and observe the rainfall at certain of their stations. Lastly, a gauge for recording the daily rise and fall of the lake should be erected at Butiabu. The site is far from being a good one, owing to its exposed position, but is the only one where it would be possible to have the gauge read daily, as there seems to be no likelihood, in the near future, of Europeans being stationed at any other point of the lake. The Butiabu gauge, taken in conjunction with that on the Nile at Wadelai, would afford valuable information as to the relations existing between the lake and the river.

The problems regarding the supply of Lake Albert are still further complicated by the fact that the Victoria Nile discharges its waters into this lake.

The Albert Nyanza undoubtedly forms a great reservoir for the river, and most probably acts as a regulator to its supply. The two discharges of the Nile, measured in March 1903, the one, *above* its junction with Lake Albert, and the other, at Wadelai, *below* its outfall, prove, so far as they go, that when the river and lake are low and their levels not far above the minimum, there is a very inappreciable increase, if any, in the volume escaping from the lake, over that which enters it by the Victoria Nile (5). Although, in

(1) Of course, the Semliki discharge is excepted in the above remarks. This river, at all times, brings in an appreciable supply, and its floods are steadier and more lasting than are those of the other tributary streams.

(2) It was a frequent observation on the part of the Uganda Officials, when describing their journeys through the district, that, such and such a river being in flood, they were obliged to wait on its banks, for perhaps five or six days, before the water subsided, and they could cross it.

(3) It is apparently of rare occurrence for any of these rivers, except the Semliki, to be in full flood more than once or twice in a month. As the heaviest rain falls within two periods, of three months each, i.e., in the spring and autumn, this would mean that these highest floods only occur, at most, twelve times in the year.

(4) This station is too far from the Albert lake to be of much use as regards the rainfall in the lake itself, or on the adjoining plateau. It is, however, of use as recording the rainfall of northern Ruenzori, and a portion of the Semliki valley.

(5) The actual increase of the discharge at Wadelai, measured on the 22nd March 1903, over that measured below the Murchison Falls, on the 20th March of the same year, was only 69 metres cube per second. From this, the discharges of the Achwa and Umi (joining the Nile above Wadelai) 31 metres cube per second, must be deducted, and there are one or two streams which flow in on the western side. It may fairly be assumed, then, that, in the dry season, at all events, the amount leaving the lake is practically the same as that which enters it.

March last there was no current flowing south from the river at Magungo into the lake, it has already been stated, on the authority of Felkin, that at certain seasons, the Nile water does flow south and supplement the lake supply (1). This must be so, as the draw on the Victoria Nile at its mouth, must be more or less equal in all directions, and it is not for several kilometres to the north of the junction, and until the lake has contracted very considerably in width, that any current leading to the Bahr-el-Gebel is apparent.

What the relations between the incoming and outgoing discharges may be, during the rainy season, when both lake and river are at their highest, it is difficult to say. The information, even as regards the range of the lake, is extremely limited and, beyond the statements of a few travellers derived apparently from native sources, no records exist. Until a gauge has been erected on the lake and a register kept for some years, any theories hazarded must be purely speculative (2). As regards one single year, viz., 1903, a solitary piece of information has lately been afforded, and from this, incomplete as it is, an approximate idea of the amount of water stored in Lake Albert *during that year*, can be obtained. Mr. F. W. Pordage, of the Uganda Public Works Department, who visited this lake several times in 1903, has supplied the information that the level of Lake Albert, at Butiabu, as measured by him, was 2 feet 1½ inches, or 0·83 metres, higher on the 20th of October 1903 than it was in the month of April of the same year. This observation is incomplete, inasmuch as there is nothing to prove that the level reached in October, was the *highest* attained during the intervening period. Still, as the Wadelai gauge reached its highest level in October, it is not unfair to assume that the lake did the same. It may then be stated with some confidence, that, in 1903, after deducting the amount lost by evaporation, and that discharged by the Bahr-el-Gebel, and assuming the area of Lake Albert to be 4500 square kilometres, a total cube of water, equal to 3735,000,000 metres, was available for storage purposes.

It has already been shown that no statistics of the rainfall, over the catchment basin of the Albert lake, exist. At the same time, it is fair to assume that it is *not less* than that which falls over the area of the Victoria lake. It is in fact, probably heavier, as the Toro and Unyoro districts are notoriously wetter than that of Uganda, where the mean annual rainfall, as registered at Entebbé and Nateté, averaged 1·2 metres per annum in a period of fourteen years. Sir Harry Johnston, in his map of the rainfall which accompanies his recent work upon Uganda (3), includes the eastern and part of the western basin of the Albert lake, as falling within the zone of rain, amounting to from 40 to 60 inches per annum. As regards the Semliki valley, he includes the upper, or southern half, within the zone of over 60 inches, while the northern half, as well as the north-western shore of the lake, falls within that in which the average annual fall varies from 20 to 40 inches (4). It may then be safely asserted that the average, for the entire basin of the Semliki and Albert Nyanza, is not less than 50 inches, or 1·25 metres per annum. The catchment basin is some 32000 square kilometres and the entire area is more or less thickly forested. It may

(1) "Uganda and the Egyptian Sudan," London, 1882. Felkin, on 23rd December 1878, observed two currents at Magungo, one flowing north to the Bahr-el-Gebel, and the other S. S. W. across the lake, drawn in from the Nile. He considers the Albert lake to have an immense influence upon the Nile as a backwater. He says that, in the dry season, less water is brought in by the Victoria Nile, and the level of the lake, consequently sinks until the rainy season sets in, and the usual current of water is brought in by the Victoria Nile. Felkin seems rather to exaggerate the influence of the Nile upon this lake. It is very doubtful whether the rise and fall in its surface is caused, in any degree, by the discharge of the river. Evaporation must be so largely in excess of the Nile supply, that it, and it alone, must regulate the levels of the lake That Lake Albert has a large influence upon the Nile is undoubted, but the converse can scarcely be the case.

(2) The rise and fall at Wadelai gauge, although only 54 kilometres distant, cannot be considered as corresponding with that of the lake. Between this place and the outlet there are several rivers which enter the Nile. These must certainly cause the gauge to rise. During the dry season, the differences of levels are possibly very similar, but the range of the lake is very probably less than that of the river. Thus in 1902, a very dry year, the range of the Wadelai gauge was 0·86 metres. In 1903, an exceptionally wet year, it was 1·50 metres, while in the lake, according to Mr. Pordage's observations, the range last year was only 0·83 metres or 0·61 metres less than that of the river at Wadelai.

(3) "The Uganda Protectorate," London, 1902.

(4) Sir Harry does not show from where this information was derived, but as it is published in his book, it has been made use of in this note.

therefore be assumed that the "run off" of the rain which falls over this area, is not more than one quarter of the total amount. In other words, only 25 per cent of the mean annual rainfall reaches the lake. On these assumptions, the calculation would stand thus :—

		Sq. kilom.	metres.	
Rainfall from catchment basin excluding lake area. ..	=	27500	× 1·25	× 0·25
Rainfall at the lake surface itself.	=	4500	× 1·25	

This is equivalent to a total of 14219,000,000 metres cube. Now the mean discharge of the Bahr-el-Gebel, at Wadelai, as worked out by Mr. Craig [1], is 769 metres cube per second. This equals a total of some 24250,000,000 metres cube per annum. It has been shown that, in 1903, the amount of water stored, over and above that lost by evaporation and discharged by the river, was, in seven months, 3735 millions of metres cube [2].

Lastly, the Victoria Nile, according to Mr. Craig's calculation, brings in a mean discharge of 706 metres cube per second, or some 22265,000,000 metres cube per annum. The calculation would then stand :—

Annual increase due to rainfall	= 14219		millions of metres cube.	
" " " " Victoria Nile ..	= 22265		" " "	
		36484	millions of metres cube.	
Deduct amount discharged by the Nile .	= 24250		" " "	
And surplus, remaining in 1903	= 3735		" " "	
		27985	" " "	
Balance remaining	=	8499	" " "	

and this would represent the loss by evaporation, which is about 60 per cent of the total amount added by the rainfall, and by all rivers, except the Victoria Nile.

If we omit the mean discharges of the Victoria Nile and of the Bahr-el-Gebel, which are very nearly equal, the calculation is as follows :—

Annual increase	= 14219	millions of metres cube.
Amount available for storage	= 3735	" " "
Difference	= 10484	" " "

In other words, from 60 to 70 per cent of the water entering Lake Albert is lost by evaporation. These calculations are, it is true, based almost entirely upon assumptions. At the same time, like the calculations made for the Victoria Nile, they have a certain foundation in fact, and are interesting as far as they go.

The last question to be considered, with regard to the Albert lake, is that of the shrinkage of its present area and levels, below those of a former period. That the waters of this lake once covered a much larger surface, and stood at a greater height than they now do, admits of no doubt. What that height was, is difficult to assert with any confidence. The great alluvial flats, which stretch to the south, and again to the north of the lake, were certainly once under water. Those on the eastern shore are covered with the remains of shells, and all bear trace of lake deposit [3]. It seems then to be certain that the waters, at one time, washed the base of the cliffs bounding the lake throughout its length, but to what height they stood, above the foot of these hills, there is now no proof to be obtained. In this respect, the Albert lake shore differs from that of the Albert Edward, where lake deposit is found at a considerable height up the face of the surrounding cliffs. All that can be said with regard to the Albert Nyanza is that its waters must have, at one time, covered the eastern flats, as far as the hills, and that, to do this, they must have stood at a level, at

(1) Appendix IV.

(2) This is probably below the total for the year, as although the months of January and February are as a rule dry, those of November and December are periods of heavy rainfall, more particularly the former. As, however, there is no means of ascertaining the additional rise, if any, due to the fall of these months, the figures given must stand for what they are worth.

(3) The terrace formation, again, of these flats, marks the different levels at which the waters stood.

least 6 metres higher than they do at present. Even this elevation must have meant that the lake stretched far to the north, probably indeed to the head of the rapids at Nimuli. There is no gorge at the point where the Nile leaves the lake. The river, the whole way to the cataracts, flows between alluvial banks of no great height. In certain reaches, the high land comes close to it on either side, but such contractions are of no great length and, as a rule, immediately after passing through one of these reaches the river widens out below into a broad lagoon. The whole, or part, of its course is that of a long, narrow and shallow lake. What has caused this fall in the levels it is very difficult to say. There are no signs of any barrier which may have been cut through, neither is there any marked erosion of bed or banks. On the contrary, the velocity of the current is low, and the river flows north, in a broad and quiet stream. It is possible that the rainfall over its basin was, at one time, much greater than is now the case, and the evaporating surface of the wide expanse of shallow water, which is now an alluvial plain, must have been very great. It is possible indeed that this is the real cause, and that the evaporation conquered the volume of water brought into the lake, and that its area gradually diminished in this way. There appears to be warrant for the assertion that, within very recent times, the lake-level has fallen. Emin Pasha, in describing the western shore, states that, in 1885, an island, rising 2 metres above the lake, was met with S. S.-E. of Mahagi, where, in 1879, there had been an expanse of shallow water. Stuhlmann, who visited the south-western end of the lake in 1891, discusses this question at some length (1). In his opinion, the lake must formerly have stood at a much higher level than it does to-day and, in ancient times, must have reached the foot of the hills (2). He considers this fall in the level to be independent of the periodic variations, spreading over a cycle of years, which are common to all the Central African lakes (3). He mentions two islands on the western shore, Rassenye and Nyamssansi which, in 1891, were promontories connected with the mainland, while at the time of Stanley's visit they were surrounded by water. He further states, upon the authority of Emin Pasha, that in 1876, near Tunguru Island, in the north end of the lake, a shallow existed, over which the native boats used to pass easily. In 1880, this had become a sandbank (4). He mentions that another small island which, in 1886, was separated from the shore by water, had, in 1891, become a promontory of the mainland, and stood 2 metres above the lake surface. Lastly, he quotes Emin Pasha as informing him that he had observed a line on the rocks of the western shore, showing that the water had formerly stood from 2 to 3 metres higher than the level in 1891.

All these statements go to show that, between the years 1876 and 1891, there had been a decided fall in the levels. There is nothing, however, to prove that this fall is a permanent one, in fact, the evidence collected is to the contrary.

Of one fact there is no doubt, viz., that the bed of the Albert Nyanza is gradually rising owing to the deposit brought in by the streams and rivers which feed it. At the south end, this is very evident in the great marshes which were once lake, and are now a shallow expanse of swamp, surrounding the lower reach of the Semliki. Again, at the mouth of the Victoria Nile and, in a lower degree, at the junction of each river on the eastern bank, the deltaic formation is gradually working out into the lake, and the bed, throughout, is covered with a layer of alluvium and slime. The same phenomenon is said to be visible in the case of the western streams (5), and almost every traveller who has visited it has remarked this.

(1) "Mit Emin Pasha im Herz von Afrika," Berlin.

(2) Vide ante. This would mean a rise of nearly 6 metres on the eastern coast.

(3) Lake Albert, previous to 1891, had been falling steadily. In that year it began to rise again, until 1896, when the fall recommenced. These variations correspond with those of Lake Victoria and are doubtless due to the amount of the annual rainfall

(4) Jephson states that Tunguru was an island in 1886, but when he visited the lake in April 1888, it was joined to the mainland, by a narrow strip of land, 1·5 metres above the water. He asserts that this spit is constantly increasing in area, owing to the fall of the lake. "Emin Pasha," London, 1890, by A. J. Mounteney Jephson.

(5) Grogan remarked the shoals which extend for a long way in front of every tributary river, and both Felkin and Jephson give instances of similar encroachment of the land upon the lake.

The process is continual, and in time the bed, over the whole area, must rise, and the depth decrease proportionately.

With regard to the annual rise and fall of the lake, the evidence is scanty. Sir Samuel Baker gives the whole range as 4 feet, or 1·25 metres, while Mr. Wilson, the Deputy Commissioner of Uganda, quoting native authority, gives this as 5 feet, or 1·51 metres. In March 1903, the flood-mark of the previous year, and probably that of the period of drought which existed since 1895, was only 1 ft. 9 in. or 0·50 metres. In 1903, it has been shown that the rise was 0·83 metres. These differences probably represent the extremes between years of heavy, and of scanty rainfall.

THE UPPER NILE, OR "BAHR-EL-GEBEL."

The exact point at which the Albert lake may be said to end, and the Upper Nile to commence, is not very easy to determine; in fact, it is purely a matter of choice. For several kilometres north of the Victoria Nile junction, there is no marked decrease in the breadth of the lake, which contracts very slowly. Moreover, for some distance below Magungo, whatever current there may be is barely perceptible (1). As, however, on most maps, the Bahr-el-Gebel is shown as a continuation of the Victoria Nile, it will be considered as such in the present report, and all the distances, given in the following pages, will commence from the point of intersection, between the right bank of the latter river and the eastern shore of the Albert Nyanza.

The width of the lake, at this point, is from 5 to 6 kilometres, from shore to shore. On the left, or west bank, the Luri mountains, which have bordered Lake Albert throughout its length, gradually recede to the west, until, at a few kilometres downstream, they are out of sight. Between them and the river is a broad area of broken country, covered with bush and scrub. The strip of flooded land is narrow, and is marked by a belt of reeds and ambatch (2). Behind this, the dry land is from 1.0 to 1.25 metres above the water. On the east, the ambatch belt is continuous, and beyond it the land is high and bare. At 9 kilometres from Magungo, the width is not more than 1000 metres and a current is distinctly visible. The bottom is muddy and the depth varies from 4 to 6 metres. The water in the Bahr-el-Gebel is very green in colour and is covered with a bright green scum, which presents on the surface a curiously streaky appearance (3). It may be that the brackish water and shallow depth of Lake Albert, under a hot sun, foster the growth of these algæ. However this may be, the fact remains that the Nile water, as far north as Dufilé, is heavily charged at certain seasons, with vegetable matter and, at such times, is hardly drinkable. The surface of the river is covered with detached plants of "Pistia Stratiotes," floating down with the stream.

For some kilometres downstream, the character of the scenery shows but little change. At certain points, the swampy fringe widens and, at others, the high land comes down to the water's edge (4). The general direction is north-easterly. At the 10th kilometre, the Luri village of Otiak is passed on the east bank. The huts form a continuous line for some distance and a few trees are scattered about. The bank here is nearly 70 metres above the water, but this is merely a local elevation. At 15 kilometres, a high, wooded bluff approaches the water on the west. This bluff is from 10 to 11 metres in height (5). The east bank here, is also high, and this place would undoubtedly be the best site for a regulating work in the river, if it ever be decided to hold up the waters of the Albert lake. The width of the Bahr-el-Gebel here, is not more than 800 metres, and the depth of section varies from 5 to 5.5 metres at low water. The bottom is muddy, but this is the case everywhere until the cataracts are reached. The chief advantage of this site is, that, owing to the high land on either side, the flanks of the work could not easily be turned and heavy embanking would be saved. There is no rock, near the surface anywhere on this river, until shortly above Dufilé, but, as such a work would not be required to stand any remarkable head of water, there should be no difficulty in constructing it at this point.

(1) The channel of the Nile first assumes the character of a river, at some 9 kilometres north of the junction at Magungo.

(2) The ambatch on both sides of the river is remarkably high and thick.

(3) This green water comes from Lake Albert, and not from the Victoria Nile, which is quite clear. It is full of minute algæ.

(4) The flood marks, in March 1903, only showed a rise of 0.49 metres, but this indicated the levels of a series of low years, as, in the autumn of 1903, the water rose to a height of over 0.90 metres above the minimum level.

(5) The camp of the Belgian railway survey was located here.

It is not an ideal site for a regulator, but it is by far the best to be found anywhere south of Dufilé. The main difficulty of construction would be found in the absence of building materials, as there is no stone in the vicinity. It would probably have to be quarried on the shores of the Albert lake and boated down here ([1]).

The soil of these cliffs is a red marl, probably weathered gneiss. The colour is very vivid and contrasts in a striking manner with the green of the vegetation which clothes them. One and a half kilometres downstream of this gorge, the high land on the west recedes from the river and wide flats recommence. The village of Paraketo is situated on the eastern bank, on a flat plateau covered with many trees. At kilometre 21, a wide depression extends inland on the west, for a long distance. It probably marks the course of a "khor," or drainage line, from the western mountains which are now from 19 to 21 kilometres distant from the Nile([2]). Five kilometres downstream, the left bank rises again and is covered with forest trees. The depth of water is from 3, to 3.5 metres. The absence of all life on this reach is very striking. There are no birds and, although there are many huts and cattle on the east bank, the west shore appears to be entirely deserted. Not a single canoe is to be seen and the inhabitants do not seem to use the river as a water-way. At the 26th kilometre, the Tangi river joins the Nile from the east. This is a small stream, from 10 to 15 metres wide at the mouth which drains the eastern plateau. Its length is only some 19 kilometres. It enters the Nile at a right angle, through a dense swamp of high papyrus, some 600 metres in width. The flats on both sides are thickly wooded. Below the Tangi junction, the width of the river decreases and it runs through a narrow gut, about 250 metres wide. The current here is proportionately swifter, but the depth is nowhere more than 4 metres. The west bank is high, but on the east low flats extend for a long distance from the water. At the 31st kilometre, the right bank rises again, while the left is now low. To the east, a terrace extends for some 500 metres from the water and beyond it is a high, well-wooded elevation, from 100 to 130 metres above the river. There are many villages on this plateau. On either side, the ambatch belt continues and is now exceptionally high and thick. A few "Deleb" palms are to be seen on the left bank. There is a small island here. As the width of the channel increases, the velocity of the stream decreases. At kilometre 34, the Nile turns sharply to the north-west. On the right hand are cliffs, 100 metres over the water, but the left is low and flat ([3]). The general character of the country is a high and flattish plateau on both sides, with rounded outlines and ravines, or depressions, where the drainage makes its way into the river. These plateaux are covered with grass and low trees; that on the east averaging rather higher that on the west. In both cases, except where an occasional bluff abuts on the water, the high land is at some distance from the river channel and the intervening space is low, flat and often swampy. At the 35th kilometre, the width increases to 800 metres. The average depth is from 3.5 to 1 metres. From kilometre 35 to kilometre 44, both banks are high and well wooded, and the average breadth of the water channel is 700 metres. The scenery of this portion of the river is extremely monotonous, although occasional charming bits are met with.

At kilometre 46, the Achwa river joins the Nile, on the eastern bank. It has several mouths, as it passes through a wide extent of papyrus marsh. The high land, on the right bank, recedes here for some 5 kilometres from the river, forming a triangular plain from the point where the Achwa leaves the hills.

The Achwa rises near Mount Guruguru, in the Lamogi range, in lat. 2° 40′ north. Its total length is some 110 kilometres, and it drains a considerable area of country. At times, it is quite dry, but, in the rainy season, it rises very suddenly, a depth of 4 to 4.5 metres

([1]) A regulator, constructed at, or near the cataracts below Dufilé, would entail the flooding of a immense area upstream, and would, consequently, largely increase the evaporating surface.

([2]) Owing to the swampy nature of the foreshore, it was impossible to land and verify this

([3]) Wherever there is high land on one side of this river, on the other side there are flats and generally, swamp. It is quite exceptional to find a spot where the land is high on both banks.

having been observed. When in flood, its average width is some 40 metres; and it often remains unfordable for a week at a time. Its valley is deep and scored by large ravines on either side. There are several fine water-falls in its course. As the country through which it runs consists of stony hills, mostly bare, this river fills up very quickly. The discharge of the Achwa, in the month of March 1903, after some heavy storms in the hills, was, approximately, 18.55 metres cube per second. The Nile, at this point, contracts to a width of only 300 metres, with an average depth of 3.5 metres. Opposite to the Achwa junction, a small stream comes in from the west.

Below kilometre 46, the river widens out into a large lagoon, known locally, as Lake Rubi. This lake has a length of some 13 kilometres, and ends not far upstream of Wadelai. It varies in width from one to five kilometres. On either side of the main channel, reedy swamps, full of papyrus and ambatch, extend for a long way. The high land is, as a rule, at a considerable distance from the water, but at kilometre 54, a cliff some 30 metres high approaches the lake on the west and follows the shore for nearly two kilometres. The soil of this cliff is composed of the same bright red marl that was observed further to the south. The surface of Lake Rubi is covered with floating plants of "Pistia." Here the green water disappears, the colour of that of this lake being a steely grey. At kilometre 62, Lake Rubi ends and, at this point, the River Umi enters from the east.

The Umi is very similar in size to the Achwa, though it carries a slightly less volume when in flood. It, also, rises in the Lamogi hills, in lat. 2° 50′ north. Its length is some 90 kilometres and its valley is deep and wide, making a gash in the high and stony plateau through which it runs. The two rivers follow a nearly parallel course throughout, at a distance of some 20 to 30 kilometres apart. The Umi is subject to very sudden rises and is quite unfordable when in flood. On the 22nd of March 1903, its water width was 16 metres, with a depth of 1 metre, and a discharge of 12.32 metres cube per second. Its maximum rise is 4 metres, and in passing through the plains at the foot of the plateau, the width of its flood section is 150 metres.

Shortly below the Umi junction, and at 64 kilometres from the Victoria Nile, the station of Wadelai is reached (1). It is situated on a rounded hill, on the east bank of the Nile, from 50 to 68 metres above the river.

Wadelai is the head-quarters of a district, and here an English collector and a European medical officer are stationed. The collector's house, the offices, and the hospital are upon the top of the hill, while the lines are rather lower down and to the east (2). A few fig trees are scattered about and lines of bananas mark the roads. It does not possess a good reputation for health, and malarial fever, of a severe type, is said to be prevalent during the rainy season. From the station hill, an extensive view is obtained in all directions. That to the south is of great beauty, looking across Lake Rubi to the Albert Nyanza mountains, which are plainly visible in the distance. The country to the east of Wadelai is, for some distance, park-like in its character, with grassy glades alternating with open forest. Some 14 kilometres from the river, it changes altogether and is traversed by a series of high stony ridges, separated by deep ravines, all covered with thick low bush. This type of country extends for a long distance to the east. On the west, or Belgian side of the river, a generally flat plain extends, also bush-covered. In the extreme distance, a chain of mountains, the continuation of those which border the Albert lake, bounds the horizon.

Opposite Wadelai, the channel of the Nile contracts into very narrow limits, and, at one place, the width, from bank to bank, is only 147 metres. Through this contracted opening, the river rushes with a high velocity and a considerable depth (3). The deepest sounding here, in March 1903, was 9.25 metres. On the right the bank is high, and, on

(1) Felkin gives the height of Wadelai, as 666 metres above the sea.
(2) The garrison consits of police only.
(3) This is the narrowest point on the river, between Lake Albert and Nimuli.

the left, the flats are 1 metre above low-water level. The total flood-rise at this point, as registered in 1903, was 1.25 metres. The discharge of the Nile at Wadelai, as measured on the 22nd of March 1903, was 646 metres cube per second. The highest mean velocity obtained was 1.144 metres per second, and the mean for the whole section was 0.894 metres per second (1). This discharge represents that of the Nile, when very nearly at its lowest.

Below Wadelai, the river quickly widens again and flows in a long double curve, first to the north-east and then to the north-west. On the right bank is a line of low rounded hills, on the left are wide flats. At kilometre 66, Emin Pasha's old head-quarters are passed on the left bank. The remains of the earth-works are still visible, close to the river (2). Here there is a large island in the Nile, 1.5 kilometres in length; downstream of it are several smaller ones. At kilometre 69, the high land on the west borders the water, while that on the east is about a kilometre distant. The channel here is some 370 metres in width, with a depth of 5 to 6 metres, and a very strong stream. North of this place, the width of the Nile increases and it passes through a broad lagoon, which continues for many kilometres. This lagoon is full of large reedy islands, and much papyrus and ambatch. Through these islands, the channel winds, in some places being not more than 30 to 40 metres in width. Proceeding downstream, the number of islands increases, until, at kilometre 80, they form a perfect maze of channels, wandering through the high reeds (3). At the same time, the high land recedes from the Nile on either side, and the papyrus gets taller and taller. Only at one point, at kilometre 82, a bank, 7 metres high, borders the lagoon shore on the east for a short distance. On the flats beyond it, many villages are located, and palms are to be seen. This was the old Egyptian station of Bora. The land on the east bank rises in two terraces. The one nearest to the river is perhaps 5 to 6 kilometres in width, and beyond it, the second plateau, which is much higher, rises abruptly (4). At kilometre 87, a range of low, irregularly-shaped hills follow the eastern plateau at a distance of some 5 kilometres from the river (5). Six kilometres downstream, these hills approach to within 2000 metres of the Nile. At this point, they are higher and more broken in outline. From the water's edge, the ground rises to these hills, covered with low forest and much bush. On the left of the Nile, the country is low and flat. At kilometre 108, the lagoon is 5 kilometres in width. Here, it is more open and the islands are fewer, but the water surface is covered with large lilies that extend in all directions, like a green sheet. The depth is shallow, being nowhere more than 2.5 metres, even in the main channel. On either side of this it is much less. At the 116th kilometre, Abu Karar, on the east bank, is reached. The Jeifi hills, at this place, are of very rugged outline, with many small peaks, their faces scored by many deep ravines. They are covered with low bush. On the plain between them and the river which is here about 1.5 kilometres in width, is a thick growth of low forest. About 800 metres to the north of the Abu Karar camp, a small river joins the Nile from the eastern hills. It runs through a deep ravine which cuts through the intervening plain. This ravine has a width of 120 metres, and a depth of 15 to 16 metres, with vertical sides. Through this cleft, the stream wanders, forming a series of pools and surrounded by thick forest and bush. Its average width, in the dry season, is about 5 metres, but in the rains it must be a formidable torrent. The forest on these flats is largely composed of acacias and of a tree which is very common throughout the Unyoro and Toro districts, in Uganda. This tree is not very tall and the stem is very crooked. It is covered with bright green leaves, much resembling those of an

(1) The Nile gauge is situated on the east bank, at the landing stage. It is the best and most reliable of all the gauges erected south of Gondokoro. It is placed in a brick-lined pit. The late flood has, however, shown that the gauge-rod wants lengthening.

(2) This place has recently been reoccupied by the Belgians.

(3) Felkin states that the river here was blocked by "sudd" in 1878. The obstruction was swept away in 1879. It must always be a likely place for a block.

(4) From the river this plateau looks like a range of low hills.

(5) Emin calls these the Jeifi hills.

apple-tree. Outside the forest line here, a few baobabs and some exceptionally fine "Deleb" palms are met with. For many kilometres downstream of Abu Karar, the same scenery continues. The lagoon averages 3 kilometres in width and the depth varies from 3 to 4 metres, while the current is extremely feeble. At intervals, high land approaches the water, on either side alternately, but only to recede again. The green water which disappeared in Lake Rubi, reappears in this lake and continues as far as Nimuli. Very few water-birds are to be seen, and not many hippopotami (1). Elephants are occasionally viewed, drinking and bathing in the shallow water.

At kilometre 137, a small river, called Jokka, comes in from the east. It is a very unimportant stream (2). The Jeifi hills are here 5 kilometres from the river on the east. At kilometre 140, the lagoon widens out into a great sheet of water, some 6 kilometres broad. Opposite this point, a low isolated hill stands up on the right bank, at two kilometres distance and the Jeifi range ends in a long sloping spur which runs north-east for some distance. The lagoon continues up to kilometre 158, where it ends (3). Throughout this distance, it varies from 3 to 5 kilometres in width, at one point reaching a breadth of 6 kilometres. Although occasionally open water, its surface, for the greater part of its length, is a sheet of water-weeds, or papyrus. Through this great swamp, the river winds, with a width varying from 40, to 200 metres.

On issuing from the lake, at kilometre 158, the depth of the Nile increases to from 5 to 6 metres, but the current is very moderate. The shores on either side are low, but, at a kilometre or two from the water, they rise into a high table-land which, on the east bank, takes the form of a rocky ridge. In the extreme distance, the high range of the Kuku mountains which approach the river near Dufilé, is now, for the first time, visible. At the end of the great lagoon, a long promontory, or spit of land, runs out into the Nile on the west, or Belgian side of the river. It averages from two to three kilometres in width and is some 10 metres above the water. On either side of it are wide swamps. It is covered with forest, bush and grass. Traces of the Belgian railway survey are visible here, in the shape of lines cut through the forest (4). On the east bank, a line of low rocky hills runs parallel to the river, at from 1 to 1·5 kilometres distance.

The Nile water here, although not so green as to the south, is full of vegetable matter and dirty in colour; much resembling marsh water. The actual channel is not more than 220 metres wide, but the swamps extend on either side for a considerable distance. In the early morning, before rippled by the wind, the dark, glassy surface of the water in this reach forms a marvellous mirror. Every cloud in the sky and even each small bird flying across, is reflected with the most startling accuracy. Sitting in the bows of the boat and looking down into the water, it is difficult not to imagine that the observer can see through it, and, that these reflections are really objects at an immense depth below the surface.

The water is very deep and marked with curious, oily-looking streaks. Some 5 kilometres downstream of Mosquito Camp, the width increases and a few grassy islands are found. Some birds are now met with, chiefly geese, cormorants and darters.

At kilometre 168, the Kuku mountains are only some 5 kilometres to the west, and two large villages, called Tekaroli, are passed, on the high terrace to the east. The Nile is now a grand stream, from 500 to 600 metres in width, and from 5 to 6 metres in depth. There is comparatively little swamping and it flows, in long sweeping curves, in a well-defined channel. The land on both sides is higher and wooded. At kilometre 170, a spur from the eastern ridge runs down to the river bank. It is very rocky and marked by two singular

(1) These animals, which most travellers have described as being so numerous on the Upper Nile, as almost to constitute a danger to navigation, are now rarely to be seen.

(2) It is said to be called after a local chief.

(3) Its total length is consequently 79 kilometres.

(4) This place has been christened by the officials, who camp here during the river journey, "Mosquito Camp." It certainly well deserves its name, as these plagues are more numerous, and more venomous, at this spot, than at any other point in the whole Nile, not even excepting the "sudd" country.

looking granite knolls, which are visible for a long distance upstream and make striking land-marks. The most southerly of these two elevations is right on the edge of the water. It has nearly vertical sides and a rounded top, upon which a few bushes find nourishment. The height is 25 metres above the water (1). Five kilometres downstream, the second rocky knoll is passed. This is flatter than the first and lower, being not more than 15 or 16 metres high.

The scene looking down the Nile here is wild and beautiful. The Kuku mountains, and the high eastern bank, form a background to the river, which runs down to them in a long straight reach, its course being apparently barred across by the mountain range. The outlines of this chain are very striking and many tall peaks stand out above the general level. Their height above the water varies from 500 to 1000 metres, and the highest mountain on the range is estimated to be 1700 metres above the sea. Their eastern faces are precipitous and much indented by deep ravines. They are sparsely covered with bush (2).

At kilometre 175, the river channel suddenly contracts to a width of 250 metres, but swamps extend for a long way on either side. On the west bank, an isolated granite hill, or rock, 20 metres in height, stands up close to the water's edge, surrounded, on three sides, by swamps. The rocks are very jagged and broken, and a few trees and bushes find root in the cracks and interstices. On the right bank, a solitary boulder gives evidence that the reef extends across the river, and some 70 metres downstream, a third projects out of the water; the first indication of the vicinity of the rapids. The flood-level is marked very clearly upon these rocks, showing a maximum rise of 0.49 metres, above the level of the river (3).

For several kilometres further north, a wide swamp stretches to the left of the river, while, on the east bank, the land is some 3.5 metres above water level and extends in a flat grass plain to the stony ridge, 3 kilometres away. At kilometre 185, the channel contracts to some 160 metres and a long boulder spur juts out from the land, on the right bank. The depth of the Nile here is about 7 metres. At this point, the Kuku mountains are barely a kilometre and a half from the river. The great mass, called on the maps, Mount Otzé (4), dominates the landscape and towers above all else, in one principal, and several secondary peaks. In front of this striking mountain is a range of lower hills, separated from it by a deep valley, or gorge. This secondary range approaches the river in a bluff, shaped like a pyramid, but with a rounded apex. This hill, which is known as Mount Elengua, rises to some 400 metres above the river, which circles round it for some 15 to 20 kilometres (5). Throughout this reach, the swamped belt is narrow and the land adjoining the river on both sides, is high. On the west, it slopes up from the water, to the base of the mountain and on the east, it rises in high stony terraces, to the main ridge, which runs north and south, at some 3 kilometres' distance from the Nile. The width of the channel varies from 200 to 500 metres, and the current is now much stronger than it was further to the south.

At kilometre 209, from Magungo, the Belgian station of Dufilé is passed, upon the west bank of the river, overshadowed by the mass of the Elengua mountain, which here stands

(1) This answers to Felkin's description of the rock that he calls "Arbatasha," so called because 14 chiefs used to pay taxes there. There is no village now.

(2) It is very difficult to give one general name to this important chain of mountains. In none of the existing maps has this been done. Travellers appear to give this range different names, at different points of the Nile valley. Even those of the most important peaks are hard to fix. Emin Pasha frequently calls them the Kuku mountains, and. as the Kuku country lies behind, and adjacent to them. for a considerable portion of their course, this name will be used in describing them throughout this report. The whole question of nomenclature, in this part of Africa, is very puzzling. The local names of mountains, hills and even rivers, differ in a bewildering way, according to the locality, while those of villages appear to follow that of the local chief. They are, apparently, rechristened at his death, by the name of his successor.

(3) During the flood of 1903. this maximum was much exceeded. The observation given above, was made in the month of March, after a series of several years of very poor flood.

(4) Mount Otzé or Meto, is some 800 metres above the river.

(5) Felkin, in "Uganda and the Egyptian Sudan" says, that these mountains form two, almost parallel chains, running from the Niambari mountains, west of Lado, and ending near Dufilé. He calls the eastern range, i.e., that bordering the Nile, by many different names, thus; Gebel Nyefo at Kiri, Gebel Nyiri at Muggi, and Gebel Kuku at Dufilé.

THE BAHR EL GEBEL
SCENE SOUTH OF DUFILE

THE BAHR EL GEBEL
BELGIAN STATION AT DUFILE

up, an apparently solitary peak, above the surrounding plateau (1). The station is situated on the river bank and, behind it, the land slopes sharply up to the base of the mountain.

Dufilé, lat. 3° 34′ 35″ N, and long. E. 32° 30′ (2), consists of a collection of thatched houses, within a fortified enclosure. The earthworks, which bound three sides of the rectangle, consist of a bank some 2.5 metres high, with a ditch in front, 5 metres broad by 4 metres deep. The armament consists of Krupp guns. The river face is open and undefended. In the centre of the enclosure is the historic group of fig trees, associated with the name of Emin Pasha and his lieutenants, and under whose shade successive Governors of the Equatorial Provinces transacted business. On the plain outside, and to the north of the walled enclosure, are the native lines. The slope behind is covered with low bush and a few "Deleb" palms are dotted about. Dufilé is a dreary-looking spot and, during the rainy season, must be the reverse of a paradise for Europeans. It has the reputation of being extremely unhealthy and black-water fever is said to be prevalent. Opposite to the station, a small river called Ayugi, joins the Nile on the east bank. This stream rises in the northern face of the Lamogi hills, in lat. 2° 40′ N. Its length is about 60 kilometres. Its mouth is situated in the middle of a papyrus swamp. The ambatch on either side of the river, here, is exceptionally tall and resembles a line of poplar trees. Throughout the intervening distance between Dufilé and Nimuli, the river channel averages 220 metres in width, with a depth of from 3.5 to 4 metres. The stream is very strong and the water surface is covered with floating masses of "Pistia Stratiotes." On the west of the Nile is a high and stony plateau; on the east, a flat plain, covered with trees, extends for a very long distance. At kilometre 216, the landing stage of Nimuli is reached, and immediately downstream of this the river bends sharply to the north-west, making an angle of about 75°. Here, the rapids of the Bahr-el-Gebel commence, the first reef being barely 200 metres downstream of the landing stage.

Just above this staging, the river Unyami comes in on the east bank of the Nile. This river, like the Ayugi (3), rises in the Fatika plateau, and on the slopes of the Lamogi hills. It is the main artery of this region and, in flood, is a stream of some importance. Its width, at the junction, is 20 metres, and its depth 1.25 metres. In the dry season, it shrinks to very small dimensions, but, in the rains, it rises very rapidly and comes down in a torrent. The flood-marks at Nimuli indicate a maximum rise of 0.75 metres, above the level in March 1903 (4).

Nimuli, on the east bank of the river, is the head-quarters of the Nile Province. It is occupied by an Assistant-Commissioner and by the Commandant of the military force stationed upon the Nile. The military station is situated on an elevation, some 70 metres high and 800 metres from the river bank. Behind it, to the north-east, a range of stony hills, called Arju (5), commences. This range runs parallel with the Nile, all the way to its junction with the Asua. On the plateau above the river are placed the military lines, the Commandant's house and office, and here also, is the parade ground. At the foot of the eastern hills are the quarters of the other officers. The civil station is some 2½ kilometres to the south-east, and on the plain. It is separated from the military lines by the dry channel of a stream (6). The soil on which Nimuli is built, is extremely stony and bare of vegetation. Except to the south-east and south, few trees are to be seen. The country is generally flat

(1) The main chain, of which Elengua is the south-eastern extremity, runs north-west, and is met with again, down the river, north of the Fola rapids. The Nile at Dufilé, has a north-easterly direction.

(2) Emin Pasha. The height of Dufilé is given as 610 metres above the sea.
Felkin gives the altitude of Dufilé as 609 metres above the sea.

(3) The Ayugi and the Unyami run parallel to one another, at a distance of from 15 to 20 kilometres.

(4) This flood-level, like all others measured in the beginning of 1903, on the Nile, is too low. Judging from the flood levels of October 1903, at Wadelai and Gondokoro, it is probable that 1.0 metre represents the maximum rise at Nimuli.

(5) Felkin.

(6) It is difficult to understand why the Government civil offices, which are only now being commenced, should have been located so far from those of the military, and at such a low level above the river. The military buildings are on high ground, and well drained. The reverse is the case as regards the civil buildings. There is ample room for both on the plateau.

and high. A few isolated low hills break the level, at some distance from the river. The station, although high and well drained, is far from being a healthy place. The climate at all seasons is excessively hot, and heavy storms are of frequent occurrence.

The river at Nimuli runs between high banks and in a series of rapids. The width of the valley is about 1000 metres and the plateau on either side, is from 50 to 70 metres above the water. On the right, or east bank, a terrace, some 1200 metres wide, stretches from the edge of the river valley to the base of the Arju hills, which are here about 130 metres in height. These hills are round-topped, very bare, and stony. Two kilometres downstream of Nimuli, a dry channel, 4 metres wide by 2.5 metres deep, crosses the plateau from the eastern hills. The river bed is full of rocky islands and is divided into many channels. These islands are covered with much reed and papyrus. At kilometre 221, the hills on the right bank close in upon the river, in a rounded headland. The channel here is 200 metres in width, with many rocks and reefs. The Kuku mountains, which approached the river south of Dufilé, now run generally parallel to it, at a distance of some 5 kilometres from the west bank. Between them and the Nile, the land is high, but very broken on its surface. At kilometre 223, the Fola rapids commence. Just above these falls, the river widens to 400 metres, with many papyrus-covered rocks intersecting it. A large island divides these rapids into two channels.

The Fola rapids constitute the most formidable obstacle to the flow of the Nile, in the whole of its course between the Albert Nyanza and Khartoum. It is doubtful whether, in the cataracts between Shabluka and Aswan, any such demonstration of the force and power of water is to be seen. The main volume of the river passes down the right-hand, or eastern, channel. Except in flood, the amount of water in the channel to the left of the central island, is insignificant (1). The scene from the rocks on the right bank is an extraordinary one. At the south end of the island, the rapids commence, in two or more falls, with a drop of some 5 or 6 metres, and a total width of about 60 metres. These break the surface of the river into a sheet of foam, but it is only after they have been passed that the real struggle commences. Below the falls, the stream rushes down an extremely narrow gorge, with a very heavy slope, enclosed between vertical walls of rock. This can best be compared to a gigantic mill-race, or water-slide, one hundred metres in length. The water tears through this channel, in a glassy, green sheet, with an incredible velocity. The width of this "gut" is nowhere more than 16 metres across, and in places it is less! What the depth of the water may be, it is impossible to say. At the foot of this race, the river leaps into a deep cauldron, or pot, which it fills with an, apparently, boiling mass of white water, lashed into foam and affording a remarkable example of the rage with which water attacks any serious obstacle to its course. The length of this cauldron is only 50 metres, but its width is not more than 12 metres across! Immediately below this, the channel widens out to some 30 metres and, eventually, more, while the river thunders down, in a series of rapids, for a considerable distance. It is difficult, in words, to give even a faint idea of this unique scene. The best photographs do not satisfactorily reproduce it. They cannot show the colouring of the picture, or really depict the wild beauty of the surroundings. On either side of the channel, are vertical walls of rock, from 7 to 10 metres above the water. These rocks are polished like black marble, and stand up in vertical ribs, indicating how severe must have been the dislocation of the strata, at the time when they were originally forced to the surface. In many places, they are hidden by masses of vegetation and creepers hang down in graceful festoons, forming a curtain resembling green velvet. The island and river banks are covered with a thick growth of mimosa trees. The inky blackness of the rocks, and the variegated greens of the folinge contrast vividly with the seething mass of white water, above which the spray is tossed high in the air in a misty cloud.

(1) This island which is very rocky, with steep banks covered with vegetation, is some 17 metres high by 500 metres in length.

THE BAHR EL GEBEL
FOLA RAPIDS, LOOKING UPSTREAM

THE BAHR EL GEBEL
FOLA RAPIDS, LOOKING DOWNSTREAM

Above all, a deep blue sky, and a brilliantly clear atmosphere, add to the effect of an exceptionally lovely scene. In the distance, but a long way downstream, the pointed peaks of the Kuku mountains form an effective background to this enchanting picture.

Some three hundred and fifty metres below the lower drop, the central island ends and the two channels of the river reunite. The course is now, for some distance, a straight one between deep and thickly-wooded banks, and a continued succession of rapids (1).

Proceeding down the Nile bank, at kilometre 225, a dry channel, 5 metres wide by 2 metres deep, comes in from the east, and a flat, rocky plateau, 600 metres in width, extends from the river to the eastern range of hills. On the west, the banks are stony and some 70 metres above the water. The valley here is not more than 800 metres across and, a little further downstream, contracts to 500 metres. At this point, the river channel is 100 metres wide, and a mass of rocks and reefs. Both banks are high, from 80 to 100 metres above the water. At kilometre 226, the banks get lower and the rapids come to an end. The reach of calm water is not of very long extent, as at kilometre 228 the rapids recommence and the river becomes a sheet of tumbling water. On either side of the channel, are many wide and deep ravines, some of them being as much as 80 metres in width and 17 metres in depth. Just below the head of these rapids is the Sabaka camping ground. Here, there is a pretty fall, of some 5 metres, but not all in one drop. Below this fall are many rocks and islands, all covered with thick vegetation and reeds. North of this point, the eastern bank is 100 metres in height and the table-land stretches for some 800 metres, to the foot of the Arju hills which still run generally parallel to the river. At kilometre 229, these hills throw out a high spur which extends to the edge of the river. The track crosses this headland and, from its summit, an extensive view is obtained. The western banks average some 70 metres above the river, and the Kuku mountains are barely 5 kilometres distant. To the east, what is, apparently, a rolling plain extends and, in the far horizon, the peaks of the Agoro mountain are dimly visible (2). The word, "apparently," has been used advisedly, as to call this expanse of country a plain, is a misnomer. In reality, it is an immense tract of high, undulating country, covered with forest and bush, and much broken by deep ravines. Between these ravines are flat or rounded plateaux, and the effect, looking at it from an elevation, is that of a generally level area. Although thickly wooded, the soil is very stony. At different points, solitary peaks stand up, the nearest being some 10 kilometres from the river.

At kilometre 231, a grand view of the Kuku mountains is obtained. These now form an immense wall, bounding the western slopes of the Nile valley. Their outline is strikingly irregular and the sky-line is broken by a succession of jagged-looking peaks. From the summit, sheer precipices descend for several hundreds of metres and, even below these, the slopes, down to the river valley, are both steep and bare. Between these mountains and the Nile is a secondary range of very low hills, separated by a wide valley (3). To the right, or east, the first sight of the Asua river is obtained, far below the observer. This river here runs in a gorge, averaging from 40 to 50 metres in depth, and from 80 to 100 metres in breadth. This gorge is densely wooded and, through it the Asua flows over a rocky bed. In the dry season, it forms a succession of pools. From this point, there is a steady descent from the spur before mentioned and the Arju hills are now to the left of the track, or between it and the river. After a still sharper descent, the Asua

(1) It is difficult to say exactly what is the total drop at Fola. It is impossible to get very close to the edge of the stream and measurements of the water itself are out of the question. By the eye, it would seem that the fall was 10 to 12 metres, divided into three, or more drops, but this is merely an approximation.

The maximum flood-rise appears to be about 1·0 metre.

(2) Agoro mountain is in the Lamoga range, which runs north and south. This mountain rises to some 3400 metres above sea level. It is some 100 kilometres to the east of the Bahr-el-Gebel, in north latitude 4°. To the east of this range, the great "khors" Kos and Tu flow to the north, finally losing themselves in the marshes near Bor.

(3) Felkin calls this portion of the Kuku chain, Gebel Wadi Locquoi. He gives the height as nearly 800 metres above the river.

river is crossed, at the 237th kilometre. At this ford, it is some 58 metres in width, but nowhere more than 0·60 metres in depth (1). The bed is a mass of rocks and boulders, all of pink basalt. Along the right bank, the strata are vertical, as at Fola, and much broken. The flood-marks show a rise of some 1·25 metres (2), above the level of the water at its lowest. The left bank is high and wooded, being the continuation of the Arju range which terminates at the point where the Asua joins the Nile, at kilometre 239. The right bank slopes up more gently, until it rises to a height of 50 metres above the water. The width of the flood-section here, is about 80 metres, and the area, approximately, 113 square metres. Although the rise of the Asua, near the Nile junction, is not great, the stream, when in flood, is so strong that it is quite unfordable. A ferry boat, to work upon a wire hawser, is under construction at the junction. Some means of crossing the river is indispensable, as, when the Asua is in flood, all communication between the stations of Nimuli and Gondokoro is cut off.

The Asua, which is by far the most important tributary of the Nile south of Gondokoro, has a total length of some 270 kilometres. It rises in lat. 2° 20′ N, in the Suk mountains, which form the dividing ridge between the drainage of the Nile and of Lake Rudolph (3). It drains a large area of country and receives the waters of numerous affluents, of which the Bugger (4) and the Atappi, are the most important. It is a perennial stream and, although it shrinks, at times, to a very insignificant limit, it never actually runs dry, and, in flood, discharges a very large volume of water into the Nile. The slope is very heavy, and it is said to be subject to very sudden increases, rising as much as 5 metres in a very few hours. It is torrential in its character and its floods subside almost as quickly as they rise. In its upper course, it is described by Emin as being 40 metres wide, with broad sand-banks and numerous granite boulders in the bed. Some 25 kilometres above its junction with the Nile, the same writer found it to be 29 metres broad, and 1 metre deep, with banks 2·5 metres high (5). Near this point, the Odiri hot springs are met with, on the left bank, and also in the river bed itself. After flowing past the Gebel Dhomi, an isolated rocky hill upon its right bank, it is joined by the Atappi from the north-east, 6 kilometres upstream of its junction with the Nile.

The Atappi is a much smaller stream than the Asua, but it too, is subject to very rapid increases. A rise of 3 or 4 metres, in a very short space of time, frequently occurs. This river rises in the Lumoga mountains, at the south end of the Lobull chain, about lat. 3° 15′ N. It has a length of over 70 kilometres and its course is generally east and west (6). During the dry season, the Atappi is dry, except for numerous pools. Downstream of the Atappi junction, the Asua flows in the deep gorge already described. This gorge, and the whole of its valley, as well as that of the Atappi, is very densely wooded. Immense herds of elephants roam in the country, between and, on either side of these two rivers.

The scene where the Asua joins the Nile, is a beautiful one. After a low fall, the river, which above the junction has swung to the west, comes down in a north-easterly direction, in a broad sheet of water, undisturbed by rocks, but full of swirls and eddies, meeting the Asua at an obtuse angle. Immediately below the junction, it turns north, and follows the same general direction as that of the Asua itself upstream of this point. To the west of the Nile, the peaks of the Kuku mountains form a fine background (7).

(1) Many of the pools are much deeper than this.

(2) The discharge of the Asua at this ford, on the 28th of March 1903, was only 2·43 cubic metres per second. The river was then at its lowest, and there was a very small discharge between the pools.

(3) Some maps show it as having its source in a lake, called Kirkpatrick, N. lat. 2° 20′, and long. 34° E., but this point is not definitely determined.

(4) Emin describes the Bugger as from 17 to 20 metres in breadth, flowing over a boulder bed, between banks 3·0 metres high, and with a flood-rise of 2 metres above its level in May (FELKIN).

(5) Ibid.

(6) Emin describes the Atappi as 17 metres wide, with swampy approaches, and with gently sloping banks on either side (FELKIN).

(7) The long narrow and high point between the Asua and the Nile is the termination of the Arju range of hills which form the eastern limit of the Nile valley from Nimuli north.

THE BAHR EL GEBEL
RAPIDS AT SABAKA

THE BAHR EL GEBEL
JUNCTION OF THE ASUA RIVER WITH BAHR EL GEBEL

300 metres downstream of the junction of these two rivers, a ravine, over 20 metres in depth and from 30 to 40 metres wide, crosses from the eastern ridge, making a deep V-shaped cleft in the country. This ravine is full of trees and must be a torrent during the rainy season. North of this point, the width of the channel varies from 80 to 100 metres, and flats, averaging 100 metres in width, border the right bank for some distance. These flats are from 3 to 7 metres above the water level and the river bank is fringed with a thick belt of bush. Behind them, the land rises abruptly for about 50 to 60 metres, being the edge of the high plateau which lies to the east of the river. Both the flats and the high bank are thickly wooded and some fine trees are to be seen. The left bank is high and covered with dense bush. At kilometre 241, the track leaves the river altogether and rises on to the eastern plateau (1). The course of the Nile is fairly straight and the valley averages 5 to 6 kilometres in width. All along the western edge, the mountains form the boundary, never being more than 3 or 4 kilometres distant from the river. Their top is serrated, in a succession of small rounded peaks. Walls of rock, forming sheer precipices, descend for some hundred metres below the crest-line. They stretch in a continuous line, resembling a huge wall, and no openings, or passes, through them are apparent. Between them and the river is a rocky waste, but at kilometre 243, the fort of old Dufilé was stationed (2).

Behind these mountains lies the Kuku country which is said to be extremely fertile, and to form the granary, supplying the garrisons, of a great portion of the Lado Enclave (3).

At kilometre 245, a range of hills commences on the eastern bank of the Nile, and follows its course for more than 20 kilometres. These hills, known as Gebel Kurdu, are, in their highest points, some 300 metres above the river. Their shape is very irregular and their slopes are covered with thick bush and forest. The valley here contracts to a width of not more than 2 kilometres and the river runs between deep banks, in a series of rapids, but with a fairly straight course to the north. The Kurdu hills are separated from the eastern plateau by a broad valley which runs parallel to them and carries off the drainage of the plateau itself which is intersected by numerous ravines. The majority of these ravines are dry, except in the rainy season, but many of them contain water-holes. Their beds show signs of severe scour and are alternately sandy reaches and masses of boulders. Here, for the first time, the bamboo is met with. These trees do not grow to a great height, but follow the lines of the ravines and streams, forming very thick belts. The high land between the ravines is, as a rule, stony and bare, but, in parts, it is covered with low forest and occasionally fine trees are met with. A few Madi villages are scattered about this plateau, but the cultivation which is scanty, is only carried on during the rainy season (4). The whole of this district which is known as Kirefi, is the home of large herds of elephants. These animals are probably more numerous here than in any other portion of the Uganda Protectorate, except in the Toru Reserve and in the forest bordering the Albert lake.

The eastern plateau covers an immense area and may be said to border the Nile valley, throughout its course to Gondokoro. Its characteristics are much the same throughout, being high and stony, with much bush and forest, and deeply scored by ravines and torrent lines. Occasional ridges and low hills break its surface, but its level does not rise much, until a long distance has been traversed in an easterly direction.

At kilometre 261, a conical hill stands out, separate from the main range on the west bank of the Nile, forming a land-mark which is visible for a long distance. Three kilometres north of this, the Kurdu hills end in a series of low wooded spurs. Some 8 or

(1) The river bank is impossible for caravans here.

(2) The garrison has been withdrawn from this fort. In its vicinity, the Khor Ayu, joins the Nile, on the west bank.

(3) The Kuku country commences near Dufilé and extends to the west for six days' journey from the river. Its northern boundary is some 10 kilometres below Labori.

(4) The Madi huts are of circular shape, with pointed thatched roofs, and low walls of wicker-work. Their diameter is about 3 metres, and the height from the peak of the roof to the floor, the same.

Granaries, like miniature huts, are erected on platforms about a metre above the ground, and the villages are invariably surrounded by a high thorn fence, or "zariba," generally with only one entrance.

10 kilometres to the north-east, a curious double-peaked hill rises above the level of the plateau and small rounded elevations project on many of the ridges between the ravines. At kilometre 266, the Madi village of Mougi is reached on the right bank (1). This village is situated on a grassy open slope above the river. Near to it is a magnificent specimen of the fig tree, affording a splendid shade. Downstream of Mougi, the eastern bank consists of a succession of low flats, varying from 400 to 800 metres in width, and bounded on the east by the high bank which here averages from 20 to 30 metres in height. On these flats, a little millet is cultivated. The course of the Nile here is straight and generally north-west. The stream is very strong and the breadth varies from 90 to 120 metres. The scenery is very beautiful, more especially looking upstream through the gorge to the south of Mougi. At kilometre 270, Labori, Emin's old fort, is passed. It is situated on the west bank of the Nile and in a very commanding position, some 80 to 100 metres above the river (2). It was here that Emin had his severe fights with the powerful Kuku tribe. Opposite Labori, there is a low wooded island in the channel and, two kilometres further downstream, another and smaller one. The channel here is very twisting and winds between rocks forming long and strong rapids, known as Yerbora (3). On the east, many ravines cut their way down from the high bank to the river. Some of these are both deep and wide and all must be torrents during the rainy season. At kilometre 274, the Madi village of Kuio is passed on the high ridge to the right and, at kilometre 276, the Umi river joins the Nile on its eastern bank.

The bed of the Umi, at this point, is 40 metres wide. It is an expanse of sand, with basalt rocks projecting at many points of its surface. The banks are vertical and 4 metres deep, while the valley of this river has a total width of 100 metres and a depth of 15 metres. In the month of March 1903, the Umi was dry, except for a succession of pools of clear water. It has a rise of 1.25 metres and, as it has a heavy slope, it must, at times, bring down a large quantity of water. It has great length and is one of many similar streams which bring the drainage of the eastern plateau into the Nile. Its banks, and whole valley, are covered with thick bush, among which are some forest trees. The Umi forms the boundary between the countries of the Madi and the Bari.

The Yerbora rapids continue for a long distance below the Umi junction. All the rocky strata in the river here slant upstream. The Nile now has a breadth of 150 metres and masses of reed-covered basalt rocks break its surface. Close to the water-edge, the banks are very steep and 3 metres high. Beyond these, grassy flats extend on either side, a heavy fringe of reeds bordering the water. The Kuku mountains here, are nearly 500 metres above the river (4). They are flat-topped and there is an absence of any marked peaks.

After crossing the Umi, the eastern bank rises in a long, flat slope, for about 500 metres, until a height of 50 metres is attained. It then rises again in a rocky ridge, covered with thick forest. On the west, the secondary range borders the Nile and beyond it, is a valley which separates it from the mountains (5). A curious slip has taken place in the face of the western cliffs here, about one-third from the summit of the range. Throughout this reach, many deep ravines and stream channels traverse the eastern slopes, all of which are dry except during the rainy season. At kilometre 280, the character of the west bank changes. The ridge and the valley disappear and the land rises in a long and well-wooded slope from the river channel to the foot of the mountains. The east bank becomes more open and, although numerous ravines cross it, some of them very deep, with reedy pools

(1) This is quite distinct from Emin's old station of Muggi, which is on the left bank of the Nile, and north of Labori.
(2) Emin gives the height of Labori, as 567 metres above the sea.
(3) It is difficult to give a name to any of these particular rapids. They are almost continuous.
(4) This altitude was measured by Mr. Craig, in March 1903, as 470 metres.
(5) Down this valley, the cart road from Gebel Akaju to Rejaf runs.

THE BAHR EL GEBEL
THE GOUGI RAPIDS

in the bed, the general slope to the river is much less abrupt than further to the south. The country is very stony and thinly wooded. Bari villages are occasionally met with (1).

At kilometre 285, the inland road to Gondokoro leaves the river bank and strikes off to the north-east (2)

Throughout this country, there is a remarkable outcrop of granite dykes which project above the surface for perhaps 0.25 to 0.30 metres. These dykes are so very straight and occur at such regular intervals, that they resemble ordinary village boundary marks.

At kilometre 290, the village of Lakki is reached, on a grass plain, some 500 metres from the Nile. The land slopes gently to the river which is here 100 metres in width and at the tail of a rapid (3). The channel is full of small rocky islands, covered with high grass. The flood-rise is very clearly marked on these rocks and shows a maximum of 1 metre above the level, in March 1903. The Kuku mountains now present rather a curious formation on their eastern slopes. There appears to have been a slip, all along the top face of the range, leaving a continuous line of sheer precipice several hundred metres in depth. Below this point, the debris which has fallen, has formed a steep slope to the base of the hill. Vertical ravines score the face of this slope, at almost equal distances. Between these hollows, the faces are rounded and resemble huge bastions. The distances are so regular and the spaces between the clefts so similarly rounded, that it looks exactly as if they had been artificially constructed. The small secondary range (due of course to this slip) now reappears and follows the western bank of the Nile to the north.

North of Lakki, the country east of the Nile, becomes more and more open and the general slopes and undulations are flatter. The rock is everywhere close to the surface and quartz and basalt crop out. At about 4 kilometres from the river, a high stony ridge runs north and south. This marks the limits of the Nile valley here. The face of the high land is much scored by ravines, some of them very wide and most of them containing water-holes, even in the dry season. The beds and sides of these ravines are rock and the channels are generally filled by a growth of tall reeds. Along the ridge are a few Bari villages and solitary trees (mostly of the fig species) of great age, size and beauty are occasionally met with (4).

At kilometre 293, the Karpeto river joins the Nile on the eastern bank. This stream, which comes from a considerable distance, has a valley 300 metres wide, with an average depth of 12 to 14 metres. The stream-bed itself is 35 metres in width and 4 metres in depth. The bed is very rocky, but with sandy patches. The reeds are very dense. The flood-mark shows a rise of 1 metre. The general course of the Karpeto is from the south-east. A round-topped and wooded hill rises on its left bank, at a kilometre and a half from the Nile.

From kilometre 296, the Kuku mountain chain which has bordered the Nile valley since Dufilé, deflects to the north-west and recedes from the river. The character of this range has now changed. The mountains are much lower and instead of resembling a flat-topped wall, with a nearly vertical face, their summits are broken into a series of rounded peaks, from which the slope to the valley is comparatively long and easy. The ridge along the river bank also gets lower and has a flatter slope than before.

The Nile in this reach is generally quiet in its course, although occasional reefs are met with. The stream is very strong and the width averages 120 metres.

The Gougi rapids begin at kilometre 297, and a rocky hill, about 80 metres high, rises above the eastern plateau, at one kilometre from the river. The river widens to 200 metres and is separated into several channels by small islands, on some of which are very fine

(1) The Bari huts are smaller than those of the Madi. They use flat stones, about 0.45 metres high, for the walls and line the interstices with wattle. The roofs are pointed and thatched, the peak being some 2.5 metres above the floor.

(2) This road is shorter, and much easier than that along the river bank, but in the dry season, water is sometimes difficult to obtain.

(3) This is the end of the Yerbora rapids.

(4) Throughout this country there are numerous remains of old villages, some of them very large. These were destroyed when the Dervishes invaded this portion of the Nile valley.

trees. Near to this place, on the west bank, are the ruins of Emin's old station of Muggi. This post has long been abandoned. Below Muggi, the river-bed is a mass of rocks and small wooded islands. On either side of the channel, deep ravines run down to the water and on the east bank there is thick forest, at some two kilometres' distance from the river. The straightness of the general course of the Nile, all through this portion of the valley, is very noticeable. There are occasional bends and curves, it is true, but none of these are sharp and it is remarkable that a river of this size and volume should follow such a direct line of flow. At 5 kilometres from the Nile, on the east bank, a range of hills, marked by six peaks, (one a double one), runs more or less parallel with the river (¹). Between them and the valley, the country is fairly open, with patches of forest at intervals.

The Gougi rapids are very fine. In one spot, there is a drop of 1.5 metres in a very short length of channel. Some of the islands are inhabited and all of them are covered with large trees.

At kilometre 308, the Kuku mountains are visible in the extreme distance on the west, and between these and the Nile, is a rolling expanse of wooded plateau, occasionally rising into a low ridge.

At kilometre 311, Kaniye is reached (²). The principal village is a large one, about 2 kilometres to the east of the Nile and on high land. It draws its water from a "khor" in the neighbourhood. From this village, the country slopes up, through bush and very broken ground, studded by many rocky crags and small projections. The trees are chiefly mimosa. North of Kaniye, the general characteristics of the Nile landscape change completely and much more resemble the scenery of the southern Soudan than that hitherto met with. Mimosa, bush and grass cover the country and the mountains are replaced by low rocky ridges and by isolated hills which break the general level. An aromatic plant grows abundantly here. It much resembles wild thyme in appearance and smell. The Bari call it "Raham," and boil the leaves with fat, thus making an ointment with which they anoint their persons.

Immediately downstream of Kaniye village, a river, called Niumbi, comes in from the east. It has a bed-width varying from 40 to 45 metres, and vertical banks, 2·5 metres high. In the bed are granite masses, piled up in great confusion and stretches of very coarse sand. This river is dry for a considerable portion of the year, but is a torrent in the rains. The flood-marks only, however, indicate a rise of 0·70 metres. A thick belt of mimosa borders it on either side. None of these torrents appear to come from any great distance. They drain the forest land which covers the high plateau lying to the east of the Nile. Their slope is very heavy and they doubtless, at times, bring down large rushes of water, but their floods cannot be of long duration.

At kilometre 315, the Gougi rapids terminate and the river flows between fairly wide flats, bordered by high, stony and wooded ridges, some 800 metres from the water on either side. Most of these flats are high and even at the water edge, are from 3 to 4 metres above the river. On the left bank, the line is broken at kilometre 316, by a high ridge which rises abruptly to a height of 100 metres. Opposite this point and at 1·5 kilometres east of the river, are hot springs. These bubble out of a rocky pool, at a very high temperature, almost that of boiling water and, even at 500 metres from the source, the heat is too great for the hand to bear comfortably. The water is clear and sparkling and has no taste whatever. It flows in a channel 1 metre wide by 0·20 metres deep. The Bari call these springs the "Khor El-Harr" or "Khor of heat," and use the water medicinally.

At kilometre 319, another small river, the Kweh, runs into the Nile on the east bank. It flows through a deep ravine, 30 metres wide by 3 metres deep. It was dry in March 1903. At this point, the western mountains have disappeared from sight. The country is covered,

(¹) Felkin gives the names of these peaks as Fochi, Kokuge and Moni.
(²) This is really a collection of villages, not one village, and the name is applied to an area of country.

on both sides, with thorny bushes, among which the "Heglik," so well known in the Soudan, is very common.

At kilometre 320, the Nile flows between two granite hills, averaging from 120 to 130 metres in height. That on the left bank is downstream of the other, and lower. On the western hill was the site of the old fort of Kiri and the remains of the walls are distinctly visible from across the river (1). Between these two hills, the rapids known as Makedo commence (2). Immediately downstream of the Kiri hill, the right bank rises in rocky, precipitous crags to a height of 70 to 80 metres above the water. On the top of these crags are some very fine trees and, to the east, forest covers the whole area and, apparently, stretches unbroken into space. Signs of elephant are very numerous here. The river has a width of only 90 metres and runs between high banks in a series of rapids. Many deep ravines break through the banks on either side, most of them full of large boulders. On the west side is much forest, but thinner than on the east. Remains of old villages are numerous and this country must at one time have been thickly populated.

At kilometre 325, the country is more open and the banks of the river lower, but high rocky ridges stretch in all directions. The Makedo rapids cease and the river channel is now open (3). Further downstream, flats recommence and, at kilometre 339, the village of Armoji is arrived at. This, like all the Bari villages, is a collection of small groups of huts, scattered over a large area. The river channel here is 200 metres in width and straight, with several islands in mid-stream. At 341 kilometres, the torrent Khurru joins the Nile on the east. It has a bed-width of 20 metres and a depth of 4·5 metres. In the dry bed are many pools of water. This stream forms the boundary between Armoji and Mongi, which last village is situated on the eastern ridge, some 30 metres above the river, amid some grand old fig trees. At kilometre 345, a very large ravine, containing a river called Laumôkh, crosses the country from the east. It has a width of 67 metres and a depth of 3 metres, at the junction. Higher up, the width is only 20 metres and the depth increases to 7 metres. The bed is full of coarse sand, dense grass and occasional water-holes. It shows signs of heavy scour and, in the rainy season, must be a succession of cascades. This ravine makes a remarkable fissure through the forest land. The right-hand cliffs are vertical and form precipices, quite 50 metres in height. The general course of this river is from the south-east and it evidently comes from a long distance. It must be a very formidable torrent when in flood. The whole country here, is a wilderness of rock and stone. Small granite peaks project from every ridge, between the dividing ravines. As the whole area is covered with thick, but low forest, or dense undergrowth and bush, it is extremely difficult to find a way through it in any direction, except on the river bank itself. Just below this river junction, there are a few small rapids in the Nile (4) and many islands, nearly all of which are inhabited by the Bari (5).

At kilometre 346, the Lagogolo river comes in on the east and at kilometre 351, another river, the Peki, joins the Nile on the same side. Both of these streams are dry, except in the rainy season. The former has a bed-width of 75 metres and a depth of 2 metres; the latter is 15 metres wide by 2·5 metres deep. Both are full of reeds, rocks and pools, and both flow through valleys of from 300 to 400 metres in width. North of the Peki, the right-hand ridge borders the Nile for several hundred metres, rising to a height of 70 metres above the water. Beyond this the flats recommence. On the west, at a considerable distance, is a line of low hills (6).

(1) Felkin gives the altitude of Kiri, as 515 metres above sea level.

(2) Makedo is a district.

(3) Felkin made the journey from Kiri to Bedden in a boat.

(4) It is difficult to understand how Felkin made his boat journey down this reach, unless the river was in flood.

(5) The Bari appear to have a predilection for islands on the Nile, probably, because they afforded protection against the Dervish raids. It is curious that, although so many of these islands are inhabited, nothing in the shape of a canoe, or boat, is ever to be seen.

(6) This range consists of three blocks, or small ranges, and two solitary hills, one like an inverted bowl and the other resembling a pyramid. All are a long way from the river.

After passing very similar country to that already described, the head of the Bedden rapids is reached, at kilometre 355 from the Albert lake (1). The stream, here, is very strong and many rocks project above the water surface. The banks, on both sides, are from 5 to 6 metres over the river which here swings to the north, after a rather wide bend to the west, caused by the projecting ridge on the right hand, above mentioned. The country to the left of the river is stony and, at a kilometre away, a succession of rocky and broken ridges stand up. On the right hand, wide flats extend for about 800 metres, after which the land rises in a bush-covered slope. The Nile at Bedden is separated into two channels, (each full of rapids) by a high and rocky island. At the southern end is a sheer cliff 20 metres high, rising vertically from the water in a wall of bare rock. The island, which is about 30 metres high at its highest point, is covered with trees and bush. The left hand channel is 60 metres wide, but the great mass of the water passes down that to the right which has a breadth of 90 metres. A little lower down, it contracts to 40 metres. The stream here is very deep. The water-marks, as measured in March 1903, show a maximum flood-rise of 1 metre. The scene at these rapids is a very impressive one, particularly in the early morning, when the sun is shining full on the eastern face of the cliffs. At that time, the black rocks are mirrored with an accuracy that brings out each small detail in the water which, although calm on the surface, indicates by the swirls and eddies which risê continually from the depths below, how strong is the force by which it is being urged down the narrow channel which lies before it. After passing through this contraction, the river, in the right-hand channel, widens out to 100 metres and a multitude of rocks fill its entire extent. The Bedden island is both broad and long, in places having a breadth of nearly 300 metres. It is well wooded and some fine lime trees, planted in the time of Emin Pasha, still bear fruit. In this reach, papyrus is rare and ambatch is not met with (2). At kilometre 360, the Bedden island ends. Others separate the channel to the north, but none of them as large as that at the south end of the rapids.

For the next three kilometres, the river passes between wide flats and at the 363rd kilometre, Fort Berkeley is reached. It is situated on the right hand ridge, about 800 yards from the Nile. The present fort is nothing but a collection of straw huts, surrounded by a zeriba, forming an enclosure of from 70 to 80 metres square. It is garrisoned by retired Soudanese soldiers who cultivate a little maize and millet. The Commandant is a pensioned native officer who lives in a small hut of his own (3). A very extensive view is obtained from this ridge which is some 70 metres above the river. The Nile here makes a long swing to the north-east. To the west, as well as to the north, forest and bush extend to the horizon, in an undulating expanse of dark green, the level being broken by occasional peaks and by a distant range of hills of beautiful outline. To the south, the bush, which covers the ridge, blocks all view and, looking to the east, the wooded valley of the Kit river can be distinctly traced. Descending from the ridge to the Nile, a dry "khor" is passed on the eastern bank. This "khor" has a width of 126 metres and a depth of 2.25 metres. It was evidently once a channel of the river, but, except for a narrow strip on its western edge, is now never flooded (4). The river, opposite Fort Berkeley, is divided into three channels by two wooded islands which are situated at the northern end of the Bedden rapids. Down-stream of these islands, the Nile is a fine stream, varying from 400 to 500 metres in width and, except for occasional sunken rocks, clear of all obstacles(5). The stream is strong and

(1) These are the last rapids on the Bahr-el-Gebel, and the last on the Nile, until Shabluka, north of Khartoum, is reached.

(2) Although both these water-plants flourish luxuriantly in the river south of Nimuli, throughout the cataract region, i. e. from Nimuli to Bedden, they almost disappear. After the cataracts are passed, they reappear.

(3) At 500 metres to the east, are the ruins of the abandoned fort, and the quarters once occupied by the English Officers. This fort was situated on the highest point of the ridge, but a long way from the river. The remains of four round buildings, which formed a quadrangle, still exist. Some burnt stems of palm trees stand up in the centre of the square. It is a melancholy looking spot.

(4) The land between this "khor" and the river was once an island, 225 metres wide. It now forms the eastern bank.

(5) These sunken rocks continue, at intervals, as far as Gondokoro and render navigation, south of that place, difficult, if not dangerous.

THE BAHR EL GEBEL
HEAD OF BEDDEN RAPIDS

THE BAHR EL GEBEL
REJAF HILL

the general direction is north-easterly. The banks average 5 metres in height above the water and broad flats extend upon either side. Many islands, some of considerable size, are met with. To the west, the land rises very gradually from the river. On the east, the ridge runs north, at a distance of about a kilometre.

At kilometre 374, the Kit river is reached. This, which ranks next in importance to the Asua, of the tributaries north of Nimuli, enters the Nile on its eastern bank, almost at a right angle. Its section is as follows:—

The bed-width is 169 metres, with a sharply-defined channel and banks 1.6 metres high. On the right bank, is a berm, 6 metres in width and on the left, a similar step, 38 metres broad. Both of these berms are covered with heavy grass and, beyond them, the land rises in another step, about 1.25 metres in height. The flood-level, as shown by the marks on the banks, appears to be only 1 metre above the bed, but it seems probable that, in high floods, the berms are, if not covered, on a level with the water. This would mean a rise of at least 1.6 metres (1). During the dry season, the bed of the Kit is an expanse of coarse sand and not a drop of water, or even of moisture, is visible. About 0.30 metres below the surface, however, water is met with. The yellow colour of the sand, the flatness of the bed and the regularity of the banks give this channel, when dry, a singular appearance.

The Kit rises in the Lumoga mountains (2), in latitude 3° 53′ north and has a length of some 145 kilometres. Its general direction is north-westerly. At times, it is quite unfordable and it must bring down a large volume of water during the rainy season. Further to the south, the bed is rocky and is said to contain pools of water all the year round (3).

Four kilometres downstream of the Kit junction, the Rejaf hill and the Belgian settlement of that name are passed. The western ridge here comes down to the Nile, marked by two small rocky eminences, about 15 metres in height. It terminates in the conical hill of Rejaf which is only a few hundred metres from the water's edge. The Rejaf hill is a perfect cone (4). On the top is a mass of rock, resembling the ruins of an old castle. It was possibly once a volcano, the rocks on the peak forming the crater and the outer surface of the hill being disintegrated by the weather (5). On the slope is the mushroom-shaped rock, mentioned by Sir Samuel Baker (6). The Nile, opposite Rejaf, has a width of between 500 and 600 metres. On the west, the land slopes up from the river and immediately to the north of the hill, the Belgian fort and station, are situated. The houses are neat-looking and have thatched roofs and verandahs. Some of the huts extend to the base of the hill. There are no trees and the country all round is very open and bare of bush. Rejaf is very subject to earthquakes (7). On the plain, upstream of Rejaf, the troops of the Congo Free State defeated the Dervishes. Just above Rejaf and close to the east bank, are two tiny rocky islets and, below the station, is a large one, covered with grass and reeds. Some Bari huts and villages are located on the right bank of the Nile, close to the water.

North of Rejaf, the character of the country, adjoining the Nile, completely changes and what may be called the "marsh" formation commences (8). A low ridge follows the water's edge on either bank. Beyond this again, on both sides, is a wide depression, full of tall elephant-grass and very swampy. This depression is of varying width and extends to the high forest-land which marks the border of the Nile valley. Downstream of Rejaf

(1) It must be remembered that, previous to April 1903, when these notes were made, there had been a long period of drought and, moreover, the rainfall had been exceptionally scanty for several years in succession. This accounts for all the flood marks, registered during this journey, being so much below those shown by the gauges, in the latter months of last year.

(2) Its sources are not very far from those of the Atappi.

(3) Kit, pronounced "Keet," is the Bari name for this stream. The Arabs call it "Bahr Ramlia," or, "Sandy river." In its upper reaches it is called the Gomoro.

(4) Felkin gives the height of this hill as 114 metres.

(5) Baker "Albert Nyanza."

(6) Ibid.

(7) According to Felkin, the name "Rejaf" means "Earthquake" in the Bari dialect.

(8) This formation characterises the Bahr-el-Gebel for many hundred miles to the north.

the river is very wide and the channel is full of large islands which split it up into several passages. From this point to lake No, i.e., to the end of Bahr-el-Gebel, this river never, even at its lowest, flows in one single channel.

At kilometre 376, the Lungwi mountain is passed on the east bank, 1·5 kilometres from the river. The swamps here have a width of 1·25 kilometres. Lungwi is a round-topped hill that stands up some 150 metres, or more, above the surrounding country. Like all the hills in this region, it is thickly forested, but with great blocks of granite projecting through the trees. A little further downstream, the river approaches to within 300 metres of its base. The eastern flats present the aspect of an almost continuous line of Bari huts here and, at kilometre 379, the village of Ibrahimia is arrived at. From this place, two separate ranges of hills are visible in the western plain. The nearest, called Kurrak, is some 5 to 6 kilometres west of the Nile. It is a group of irregularly-shaped peaks. The other, Kajur, is a good deal further to the west and has two peaks only, both of them conical in shape. For several kilometres north of Ibrahimia, the river alternately approaches and recedes from the eastern high land, thus forming a series of swampy bays between the successive headlands of the ridge. Into all of these bays, drainage lines run down from the forest which here covers the high table-land in all directions. At kilometre 385, this ridge is high and masses of granite project above the surface. From here, a range of low hills, with four peaks, is visible on the east, some 6 kilometres away and another, lower, but with the same number of peaks, rises above the forest, at a distance of between 2 and 3 kilometres. At kilometre 392, the Lokadero river joins the Nile on the east. This river is a miniature edition of the Kit, with a similar, dry, sandy bed and well-defined channel. The width of this stream is 35 metres and the banks are 1 metre high. It has a north-westerly course. Beyond the Lokadero, the land rises into a high, flat plateau, covered with pretty open forest, containing some fine trees. This stretches to the east as far as it is possible to observe and, above it, the Belinian mountain rises in the distance, forming a striking land-mark, visible for many kilometres. On either side of the river are wide marshes, covered with a thick growth of tall reeds and occasional clumps of papyrus. The islands continue in the channel which is here extremely wide. The plateau averages from 7 to 8 metres above the marshes. At kilometre 395, on the above plateau, the station of Gondokoro on the east bank of the river, is reached (¹).

Since 1901, much progress has been made in the direction of improving Gondokoro. New lines have been selected for the troops, to the south of the old ones and good huts have been erected for the men. At the same time, comfortable houses have been built for the English officials, both civil and military. The roads are good and the jungle has been cleared away. Altogether, the station now shows but little resemblance to the desolate spot visited in 1901 (²). There appears, however, to be a possibility of difficulty in the future, with regard to Gondokoro. The river has made a severe set on the cliff, upon which the station is situated and the action of the current is to gradually eat away the high clay bank. Much of it has already gone, including the site on which the Austrian Church and Mission formerly stood. It is to be feared that, unless protective works are undertaken, those portions of the bank, upon which some of the houses are situated, will share the same fate and disappear into the river. The Nile gauge at Gondokoro, is situated not far from the Collector's house. That erected in 1901 was carried away by a boat. In 1903, a new one was put up by Captain Lyons, of the Egyptian Survey Department, of the pattern which he has introduced all over the Soudan, i.e., a gauge following the slope of the river bank, and lying flush against it.

(¹) Gordon gives the latitude of Gondokoro as 4° 54′ 29″ north. and the longitude as 31° 43′ 46″ east. The altitudes given by different authorities differ very greatly.

(²) Writing in 1901, the following remarks were made: "Gondokoro, although a healthy-looking station, has a deserted" "appearance. The buildings contrast but poorly with those of the Belgians at Lado and Kiru. What is required, is a wholesale" "clearance of the forest and bush, for a considerable radius, drainage of the swamps and hollows, and the construction of houses" "suitable to the climate." Egypt N° 2-1901. Foreign Office, Blue Book.

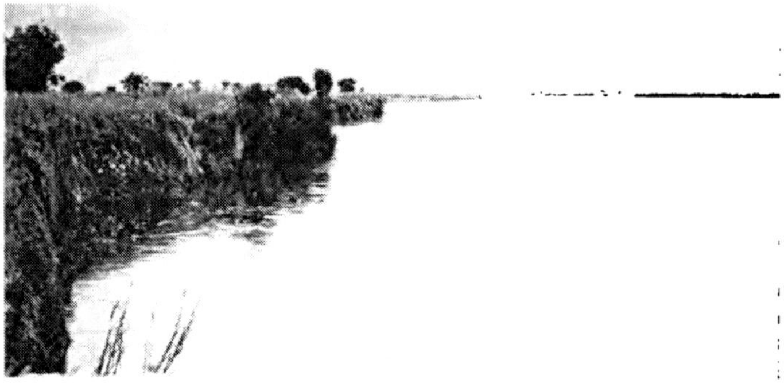

THE BAHR EL GEBEL
GONDOKORO

THE BAHR EL GEBEL
LADO

Proceeding down the Bahr-el-Gebel from Gondokoro (1), the whole character of the river speedily changes (2). In the place of a rapid stream, flowing in a narrow channel, with a heavy bed-slope and between high banks, the Nile, north of the cataracts, winds its way between vast marshes, with a low velocity, in a broad channel, and between numerous islands. The banks are low and the width, both of the valley and of the flooded area, is very great. Papyrus, reeds and ambatch replace the forest trees met with to the south and, except at a very few spots, throughout its course to Lake No, it passes through a country, probably, as dreary-looking and, as desolate as is to be met with anywhere in the known world.

On leaving Gondokoro, navigation is rendered difficult by shoals and the maze of channels and islands. For some distance, mountain peaks are still visible and the flat ugliness of the landscape is thereby relieved. On either side of the river bank, up to these ranges, extends a broad expanse of reeds and grass, bounded by the dark forest line. The Bahr-el-Gebel, between Gondokoro and Lado, has a width of from 250 to 300 metres and the depth ranges from 2, to 2·5 metres. Islands and side-channels abound, and in flood, it is difficult to say which is the main stream (3).

Lado is situated on the west bank of the Nile, at 407 kilometres from the Albert lake, in latitude 5° 1′ 33″ north (4). It is surrounded by swamps. The height of the bank is from 5 to 5·5 metres above the river and here, as at Gondokoro, the action of the water is very severe. The soil is light and sandy and a large portion of the bank is yearly eaten away by the current. Both Lado and Gondokoro are stations which have been in existence for years. With the present set of the river, it looks as if both would disappear before many years elapse. Lado was for long the capital of the Equatorial Provinces of Egypt, and it was here that Emin Pasha lived and governed. Traces of his old fortifications are still visible. The enclosure would seem to have been formerly, about 700 metres broad, but so much of the area, once comprised within it, has been cut away by the river, that it is difficult to say what were its original limits. The Belgians at Lado have done a great deal in the way of housing their troops. The majority of the houses are built of burnt brick, with conical thatched roofs. The latest approved type appears to be a circular hut, built upon brick arches, so as to insure that a current of air shall pass freely underneath the building. Although ugly, these houses are serviceable and well suited to the climate. The house of the Commandant is considerably larger than the others. Lado is a desolate looking spot, surrounded by a flat plain, covered with bush. It is swampy in places and stretches from the river for some 3 kilometres. Beyond, the forest commences and the land gradually rises to the spurs of Gebel Lado which stands out, a prominent land-mark, at a distance of from 15 to 20 kilometres west of the station. The country appears to be deserted by the inhabitants and the food for the troops has to be brought from a very long distance. In front of Lado is a low island, upon which vegetables, bananas and castor-oil plants are grown. This island is 1·25 metres above low-water level in the river. There appears to be no trade worth mentioning and but little cultivation. A little ivory is brought in. India-rubber is, apparently, not found within any reasonable distance of the Nile here. The riverain inhabitants have mostly migrated to the opposite bank. They suffered heavily from the drought in 1000 and 1000. Fever is very prevalent during the rainy months, but does not appear to be of such a deadly type as at Kiru, lower down the river.

At kilometre 410, a channel branches off to the west (5). The width of the valley now contracts to some 5 or 6 kilometres and the islands are very numerous. The flats, on either

(1) The following pages have been largely taken from the Report on the Bahr-el-Gebel, made in June 1901. Foreign Office Blue Book, Egypt N° 2-1901. The description of this river, as now given, where it varies from that of the Report in question, is based upon more recent knowledge.

(2) This portion of the journey is made by steamer, while between Nimuli and Gondokoro. it has to be made on foot.

(3) A point about 3 kilometres south of Lado, was selected as the discharge site.

(4) The altitude of Lado is given by Felkin as 462 metres. Junker gives it as 455 metres above the sea.

(5) The frontier between the Uganda Protectorate and the Egyptian Soudan touches the east bank of the Nile at kilometre 420, at a "khor," or lake, which runs up into the heart of the forest.

side, are wide. Such a labyrinth of streams winds through these grassy flats, that, without an experienced pilot, navigation is very difficult, more especially as the depth of water is nowhere great and rarely exceeds 3 metres. Hippopotami are numerous and particularly obtrusive. At kilometre 437, the river leaves the western bank and crosses the swamps to the east. Here the station of Mongalla has been formed. This is the most southerly of the outposts of the Soudan garrison on the Bahr-el-Gebel. The forest has been cleared away and huts erected for the troops, as well as houses for the British officials. Mongalla seems likely to be as healthy as it is possible for any of the stations on the Bahr-el-Gebel to be. The site is well chosen and the forest and bush have been removed for a long distance from the quarters of the troops. A Nile-gauge has been erected here. At kilometre 440, still skirting the eastern shore, the high land and trees come down close to the water's edge. Here is a good wooding station. Some two kilometres to the north, a large "khor" joins the river, forming a picturesque lake in the heart of the forest. Signs of elephant are very plentiful here. North of this place, the river averages from 250 to 300 metres in width. At kilometre 446, the western branch which bifurcated below Lado at kilometre 410, rejoins the main stream.

At kilometre 449, a large lake opens out in the western forest. At one end of it, the Lado mountain forms a background, making an imposing picture. A couple of kilometres further north, two more lakes on the same side of the river, are enclosed by forest. All along this reach, the main channel skirts the western bank and at kilometre 453, Kiru is arrived at.

Kiru is one of the Belgian stations in the Lado Enclave. It is on the west bank of the Nile, in latitude 5°12′, or 5°13′, north. It is a picturesque looking place, surrounded by forest, in which are some fine trees. The bank, on which the station stands, is from 5 to 6 metres above water-level. The erosion, caused by the current here, is greater even than at Lado and large masses of the cliff which is vertical, are constantly falling into the water. The huts at Kiru are well laid out and neatly built. The cantonment is surrounded by a wooden stockade, armed with Krupp guns. The Commandant's house is a comfortable-looking structure, with a good thatched roof and a deep verandah. Upon an island, opposite the station, are many Paw Paw trees and vegetables are grown. Beyond this, there appears to be no cultivation. The garrison is said to consist of 400 men. It possesses a small paddle steamer (the *Van Kerckhoven*) and several steel boats. The Negro soldiers of the Congo Free State forces differ largely from the inhabitants of the Nile valley. In figure they are short and squat and some of them are much tatooed. They are said to be largely recruited from the cannibal tribes.

North of Kiru, the river scenery is fine and luxuriant tropical vegetation abounds. Giant Euphorbia are a marked feature of the forest. The whole of the banks and most of the trees, are covered with a velvety looking mass of creepers. A bluff, 3 to 4 metres high, projects into the stream, but the action of the current is so strong that the friable soil is being rapidly eaten away. The face of this cliff is perforated by myriads of holes, made by a very beautiful and tiny species of bee-eater. These birds have rose-coloured wings, with bronze-coloured bodies. They add much to the beauty of a very lovely scene.

The trees on the west are, as a rule, finer than those in the eastern forest. The west bank, at the water's edge, is from 1 to 1·25 metres high, but rises rapidly to a height of 4 or 5 metres above the water. At kilometre 466, the river leaves the western forest which it has followed for so long and traverses the marshes again. Below Kiru, the depth of the stream increases. Upstream of that place, it has rarely been more than from 2 to 3 metres. This river varies immensely in width. In some places it is from 200 to 300 metres broad, in others, only 80 to 90 metres. At kilometre 479, the channel again bifurcates, the two branches re-uniting at kilometre 486. There are so many islands and so many side channels, that it is almost, if not quite, impossible to find the whole stream contained in one single

THE BAHR EL GEBEL
KIRO

THE BAHR EL GEBEL
MONGALLA

channel. At kilometre 492, the river which has wound about through the swamps for so long, approaches the eastern bank. In thus crossing the marshes, an excellent idea of the general section of the valley is obtained. In the centre, the flats on either side are perhaps 0·60 metres above the water; towards the water's edge, they rise to a height of 1·25, and sometimes 1·5 metres. The lower portions are marked by a series of lagoons. In moderate floods, the high lands are not topped by the water. In the flood of 1903, which was a very high one, the whole area of the valley, which is here from 12 to 14 kilometres in width, was under water.

At kilometre 493, a magnificent tree is situated on the eastern shore. It makes a striking land-mark and is on the extreme edge of a perpendicular bank, 3 metres above the water. As there is great erosion here, it is to be feared that this fine tree will not long remain. The forest rises rapidly from the water and, at its highest point, is quite 6 to 7 metres over river level.

For the next 12 or 13 kilometres, the river bends and winds in an interminable series of twists. There is hardly a straight reach anywhere. The average width is 80 metres, and the depth 3.5 metres. The banks are very sandy, as are the flats which show up above the water surface. Occasional small islands separate the channel into two, or more, branches. There is a decided ridge on either side of the main channel, upon which are located a few groups of Bari huts surrounded by dhurra fields (¹). The high land does not average more than 100 to 200 metres in width and, in exceptional floods, even this is topped. East and west of these ridges are wide depressions, in which lagoons are formed and winding channels wander. These flats are covered with high grass. The width of the valley is from 9 to 10 kilometres. At kilometre 506, the channel bifurcates, forming a grassy island, from 800 to 1,000 metres in width. At kilometre 533, these two channels reunite, the eastern being the deeper of the two (²). From here, for many kilometres, the river runs close to the eastern bank. It winds continually and there are occasional loops of swamp, but, as a whole, it follows the high land closely. The bank is from 2 to 2.5 metres high and, in places, is perpendicular. At such points, there is always great erosion. The scenery much resembles that of the Blue Nile. The forest close to the river, the high banks, the profusion of creepers and undergrowth, the boils and eddies of the water along the curves combine to form a picturesque scene, utterly different from that usually met with on this part of the Bahr-el-Gebel.

The Bari are now replaced by Dinka, and the difference is at once apparent. In the place of the untidy and badly built "Tukls" of the Bari, the Dinka huts are neat and commodious.

At kilometre 561, the Dervish "Dem," or fort, so long held by the Emir Arabi Dafallah, is passed on the east bank. The spot is well chosen for defence, as the river sweeps round it on two sides. The bank all round has been cleared of bush for a long way. The "Dem" is surrounded by a mud wall, forming a rectangle, of which the river forms one side. The enclosure is some 700 metres long by 400 metres deep. The bank is 1.5 metres high, with an outer ditch 1 metre deep by 1.5 metres wide. At the corners are small watch towers.

For the next ten or eleven kilometres, the river hugs the high eastern bank, which is from 2, to 2.5 metres above the water and is, of course, never flooded. The forest consists of thick bush, with a few large trees. A distinctive feature is the thicket of small "Deleb"

(¹) In the flood of 1903, these huts were submerged up to the roofs, and the people had to remove to the mainland.

(²) Since this was written, Mr. Craig, in the month of September 1903, navigated the western channel in a steamer. The flood, which was an exceptionally high one, was then at its highest. He describes this branch as a fine river, from 100 to 150 metres broad, and, except at the south end, where the depth was only 2.5 metres, it was 5 metres deep throughout. This channel is straighter than that to the east and should, when training works are undertaken, be selected as the true river. It follows the western high bank pretty closely, which, here, is well wooded. There are several villages, but the natives (Aliab) are miserably poor. The women wear a piece of quartz-crystal, stuck through the lower lip. The men shave the head. This was probably the channel followed by Baker in 1863.

palms which covers the ground. Not one in five hundred of these plants appears to develop into a tree, but they form an extremely dense undergrowth. The Bahr-el-Gebel here, is a fine stream, 80 to 90 metres wide, with a strong current. On the west, the marshes stretch into space. The valley in this reach must be quite 16 kilometres across.

At kilometre 570, Bor is reached on the east bank, in latitude 60° 12′ 46″ north. This is a collection of Dinka villages which stretches northwards, (outside of the swamps), almost to the Bahr-el-Zaraf. The forest stands back from the river, but the high bank comes close to the water, except where a large back-water, or lagoon, passes through it for some 2 kilometres (1). A few tall "Deleb" palms stand out as land-marks. Bor itself is neither large nor important, but, like all Dinka villages, it is well kept, neat and clean. The huts are circular in shape. They are plastered with mud and have conical, thatched roofs. Each has a small door, through which the inhabitants crawl. The people show no signs of shyness and appear comfortable and contented. They possess large herds of cattle.

North of Bor, the "sudd" country, properly so-called, commences, although the real swamps are not reached until north of Ghaba Shambé. The character of the marshes changes. North of this place, papyrus and ambatch, with those reeds which require to have their roots under water for a great portion of the year, take the place of the grasses met more to the south. The general level of the swamps too is much lower.

After leaving the high land on the east of Bor, and proceeding downstream, the banks are low and flat, rarely being more than 0.25 to 0.30 metres above the water. At kilometre 576, the high land on the east has receded to 3 kilometres' distance from the river (2). Many natives are to be seen fishing, and hippopotami are abundant. At kilometre 579, a large lake, or lagoon, 5 kilometres in breadth, is passed, the river winding round it, for a long distance, in a series of sharp curves. Large clumps of papyrus stand up in the marshes. At kilometre 614, another large lagoon, known as Lake Powendael, commences. The Bahr-el-Gebel circuits this lake for some 6 or 7 kilometres, separated from it by a belt of swamp. This belt varies in width, from a few hundred metres, to two kilometres. Lake Powendael, at its broadest point, is 3 kilometres in width, but is very shallow. Its surface is dotted with many small papyrus islets and it is connected with the river by several inlets.

Between this point and Kanisa, at kilometre 687, there is little to describe. The whole of this reach is desolate-looking and monotonous. The banks, where they exist at all, are flat and low, rarely being 0.50 metres over the water. Tamarisk is common and large clumps of papyrus commence. A line of trees on the eastern horizon, some 12 to 15 kilometres away, appears to mark the limits of the swamps. It is easy to see how the Bahr-el-Zaraf marshes are formed. At every few hundred metres, the river spills into them. These spill-channels are deeply cut, with vertical sides, as if dug by hand, and the amount of water discharged by them in flood, must be very great. In size, they vary considerably. Their average breadth is from 3 to 5 metres, but some are as much as 16 metres wide. Between Bor and Kanisa, a distance of some 117 kilometres, 129 spills were counted, of which 97 were on the east bank. Probably many more escaped observation.

Kanisa (3), or "Heiligen Kreuz," in latitude 6° 46′ north, is the site of the Austrian Mission Station which was located here for many years. The church and buildings were situated on the eastern bank and their traces are said to be still visible. A large fruit garden formerly existed on the west bank and some of the lemon and orange trees are still alive. The Mission was abandoned in 1864, or 1865, on account of the deadly effects of the climate. The only inhabitants now are a few Dinka. Kanisa is the principal wooding station for steamers making the journey through the "sudd." The forest is very

(1) Gordon mentions Bor as an inconvenient wooding station.

(2) The point where these marshes commence on the east, must be the head of the channel which Mr. Grogan has named the "Gertrude Nile." See Appendix VI.

(3) Kanisa, in Arabic, means a church.

THE BAHR EL GEBEL
RIVER BANK AT BOR

THE BAHR EL GEBEL
PAPYRUS

thick and consists of mimosa, nabak, and a few Euphorbia. It is continuous, as far as the banks of the river Rohl, 100 kilometres to the west of the Nile.

At kilometre 734, Abu Kika, north latitude 6° 54′, is passed. Here, the western forest again approaches the river and the bank is dry. Thick bush comes down to the water's edge, but the trees are about 1,500 metres away. The village of this name is inland and is not visible from the river. North of Abu Kika, the aspect of the landscape, for the next 12 or 14 kilometres, is extremely desolate, with papyrus-covered marshes stretching in all directions. The river itself, alternates between long, straight reaches, or easy curves, and a series of sharp twists and bends which form a regular maze through the swamps. The water-surface is covered with masses of detached plants of the "Pistia Stratiotes." The mean velocity of the stream, during the low-water season, is 2·5 kilometres per hour. The average depth is 5 metres and the average width from 50 to 60 metres. Throughout this reach, the same dreary scenery prevails. The river recedes a long way from the western forest and, on both sides, an expanse of reeds and water extends. The width of the swamped area here cannot be less than 30 kilometres (1).

At kilometre 742 and 744, two outlets, leading to the Bahr-el-Zaraf, take off from the eastern bank (2). For many kilometres, the river winds round the eastern edge of the great Shambé lagoon, separated from it by a band of marsh and reeds, about 600 metres wide. This lake is from 6 to 8 kilometres long, and more than 2 kilometres in breadth. Its depth averages 1·5 metres. At kilometre 766, the Shambé lake ends, joining the Nile by a wide and shallow opening. On the west bank of this sheet of water, is situated the post of Ghaba Shambé (3), in latitude 7° 6′ 12″ north. This station is some 2 kilometres from the river. It is a very dreary-looking spot, consisting of a few huts and offices, situated on the shore of the lake which is very flat. The western country is about 0·60 metres above the water, but rises as the forest is reached. Shambé is now an important place, as it is the Nile Post of the Bahr-el-Ghazal Province. East of the river here, the papyrus marshes stretch to the horizon.

Seven kilometres downstream of Shambé, i.e., at kilometre 773, the Bahr-el-Zaraf takes off the Nile, following a false channel of the river for some distance, before branching to the east. The width of this river, at the head, is some 30 metres and the outlet is surrounded by a sea of marsh and high papyrus. Just upstream of this point, there is a severe bend in the Bahr-el-Gebel which may one day give trouble in the shape of a block. As the steamer passes this place, decomposed "sudd" rises to the surface.

The average breadth of the Gebel river, throughout this reach, is from 50 to 60 metres. Its depth is some 5 metres. Between kilometres 772 and 788, occurred the four "sudd" obstructions which were removed in February 1901 by Lieut. Drury, R. N., and which were known as blocks Nos. 16, 17, 18 and 19. All along this portion of its course, numerous channels join the Bahr-el-Gebel on both sides. Many islands, covered with ambatch and papyrus, separate the stream into numerous branches and the whole country is a waste of swamp. The river itself is extremely narrow here, not more than 25 to 30 metres in width, but from 6 to 7 metres deep. The false channel, above mentioned, in all but its depth, far more resembles the main river than does the true one. It is hard to imagine that this narrow twisting stream can be the Nile. Its windings are bewildering. A tree, or the

(1) As the term "high land" is often used in describing the shores of this river, it should be explained that it is only "high" by comparison, inasmuch as it is drier than the surrounding swamps. The river banks commence, as a rule, at a height of about 0·25 metres above the summer water-level and the flats, after a central depression, gradually rise until the forest is reached. Most of this area is submerged in an ordinary flood, and all of it in a high flood. The ground, however, is firm, and rears a vegetation other than the "sudd" grasses. The swamps here differ from those to the north of Shambi, in that the deposit on their surface, formed by decayed vegetation, does not exist. One peculiarity of the river, in these parts, is, that it always seems to be approaching the higher land, but just before reaching it, turns away from it again, in a maddening series of loops, through the marshes. In each of these loops, is generally to be found a large lagoon. The points where the river touches the high bank and runs along it, are comparatively rare. Some of the loops are remarkable, and almost form a circle. In one, particularly, at kilometre 678, the width of the strip of land, between the two bends of the river, is only 50 metres.

(2) Later experience has shown that these are inlets from the River Awai, or Gertrude Nile, into the Bahr-el-Gebel Probably in a low year, water flows *from* the Nile, *into* this channel. See Appendix No. VI.

(3) "Ghaba" or "Gabt" means a forest.

mast of a boat may be visible at a comparatively short distance ahead and yet many kilometres of channel must be traversed before it is reached. The general course of the river here is due west. The false channel follows an easterly course, passing through numerous shallow lakes until it joins the main river again at kilometre 804 (1).

At kilometre 807, and again at kilometre 812, channels come in from the west, both of which bring water into the Bahr-el-Gebel. These streams may possibly be the mouths of the river Jei, or Yei, which is supposed to join the Nile somewhere in this locality (2). North of this point, the marshes extend in all directions and not a vestige of dry land is visible anywhere, until kilometre 844 is reached. Here the high land which is covered with thin bush, and is from 0·60 to 0·70 metres above the water, bounds the river channel on the east and touches it at intervals up to kilometre 882. There is one break in this line, viz., at kilometre 862, where two or three small channels, or spills, leave the Nile, in an easterly direction. These are said by the natives to be the most northerly feeders of the Bahr-el-Zaraf. In 1900, a fine "Deleb" palm stood on the water's edge at this point. It formed a land-mark that could be seen for a very long distance. It has now, unfortunately, disappeared, the current having cut away the bank upon which is stood (3).

After another interval of swamp, the eastern high land again approaches the river and runs parallel to it for 3 kilometres. A few Euphorbia are to be seen here.

At kilometre 893, a "khor" joins the Nile, on the west bank, bringing in a strong stream of water (4). Two villages (Nuer) are to be seen in the distance. These are probably Favor and Fatooah, of Perthes's map. Below this point, the Bahr-el-Gebel widens out. Its breadth, in places, is 200 metres, and its depth from 5 to 6 metres, with a mean velocity of 2.5 kilometres per hour. The swamps continue as before and large shallow lagoons extend on either bank, separated from the river by a belt of papyrus. At kilometre 894, high land is visible to the west, at 1.5 kilometres from the river and, on the east, a line of palms, perhaps 11 or 12 kilometres distant, not improbably indicates the banks of the Bahr-el-Zaraf. At kilometre 896, the width of the river is 90 metres, and the depth 7.5 metres, but very shortly below this point, the last of the remaining "sudd" blocks commences (5). It is consequently necessary for steamers, navigating the river, to leave the true channel and follow the false one, which takes off the west bank at an angle of nearly 90 degrees (6). The depth suddenly decreases to 1.5 metres. For some way, a network of channels confronts the navigator and very careful steering, with a knowledge of the passages to be followed, is required. Each year, these channels change. What is, in one season, the deepest channel is, perhaps, the next year impassable. For 8 kilometres, the stream is split up into many different branches, all winding through papyrus swamp, but at the 905th kilometre, a line of broad and shallow lakes is reached. These lakes have a depth of some 1.5 metres, at the deepest point, but shoal rapidly towards the shores. A feeble, but distinct current passes through them to the north. Their breadth varies largely. In some places, it is only a few hundred metres and in others, as much as 4 or 5 kilometres. Their shores are fringed by high papyrus and their surfaces are dotted by countless "sudd" islands. There are, however, indications on both sides, that the high land is not very far distant. The true channel of the Bahr-el-Gebel which lies to the east of these latter, is said, by the natives, to skirt the dry land (7). On the west, a line of fair-sized trees, at a distance of perhaps 3 kilometres, shows that the swamps in that direction also have a limit. A very

(1) Previous to the clearance of blocks 16 to 19, this false channel was the only navigable line for vessels going south This was the route followed, in 1900, by Major Peake and Lieut. Drury, in making the journey to Gondokoro. They found the passage very difficult. During the transit they bent their rudder twice, and went aground four times.

(2) Mr. Craig, who visited the Bahr-el-Gebel in the flood of 1903, does not think so, but believes that the channel which enters the Nile at kilometre 893, is the true mouth of the Yei.

(3) Petherick gives an illustration of this palm, in his book "Travels in Central Africa," London. 1869. He states that it, marked the boundary between the Nuer and Kytch countries.

(4) This is the stream supposed by Mr. Craig to be the mouth of the Yei.

(5) This is known as block 15 and continues for some 37 kilometres.

(6) In April, 1900, the head of this channel was blocked by sudd but it was light and easily removed.

(7) Recent investigation has proved that this is not the case.

noticeable feature of these lonely lakes is the absence of animal life. No birds are to be seen and even hippopotami appear to avoid them altogether. At kilometre 920, these lakes stop, and another maze of channels, similar to those met with at their south end, confronts the navigator. Branches cross and recross one another, forming, between them, a bewildering labyrinth of islands. The services of a competent pilot are indispensable. At kilometre 937, these channels converge, apparently from all points of the compass, and another small lake, about 2 kilometres in length and 500 metres wide, is reached. At the northern end of this lake, at kilometre 939, the block N° 15 ends and the true river is again met with. The entrance to the blocked channel is difficult to find, but once found, there is no doubt about its being the real river. The sounding-rod shows a depth of from 5 to 6 metres, as against 1.25 to 2 metres in the lake itself. The bed of this, the true channel, is filled to a considerable depth with decomposed "sudd." This rises to the surface, if disturbed, giving out bubbles and a noisome smell. The native "Reisses" who knew this channel when it was free from "sudd," state that one of the Dervish steamers, with boats containing ivory, was sunk in this part of the river (1).

For the next two kilometres, the Bahr-el-Gebel follows a series of sharp curves, its average width being 60 metres and depth 5 to 7 metres. At kilometre 941, Hellet en Nuer, or Eliab Dok, is reached, in latitude 8° 4′ 36″ north. At this point, the high land touches the west bank of the Gebel and stretches in a broad expanse to the horizon. The bank here is 1 metre above the water, but the land rises at a short distance from the river. This plain is evidently never swamped, even in flood. It is covered with a growth ot Euphorbia, "Deleb" palms and bush. It commences at the small lake above mentioned, and continues along the river, with swampy intervals in the loops, as far as kilometre 967.

At Hellet en Nuer itself, a branch of some size takes off the Bahr-el-Gebel on the west. This channel is not shown upon any existing maps and was first mentioned by Captain Gage, of the 7th Dragoon Guards, in his report upon his journey through the "sudd," in the winter of 1899-1900. It has a width of 66.5 metres at the head, of which 10 metres on either side, are filled by the swamp grasses. Its average depth, at low water, is 1 metre, and its mean velocity 0.60 metres per second (2). Captain Gage's channel leaves the Bahr-el-Gebel at a right angle, but, some 500 metres downstream, it turns in a north-westerly direction. Captain Gage followed its course for some 64 kilometres, but was then stopped by "sudd." It seems not improbable that this channel may form a junction between the waters of the Bahr-el-Gebel and those of the river Rohl, which discharges into the Bahr-el-Ghazal. It would be interesting if this stream could be followed up and its outfall determined (3). A few kilometres below the head, its banks are lined by a succession of Nuer villages and its width increases to 200 metres.

Proceeding downstream from Hellet en Nuer, the width of the Bahr-el-Gebel is very variable. In many places it is only 60 metres and, in others, as much as 150 metres. The general average may be taken as from 75 to 80 metres, and the mean velocity of the stream is over 2 kilometres an hour, at low water. The depth ranges from 5 to 9 metres, and, in places, is as much as 9 metres. Between kilometres 1028 and 1073, the "sudd" blocks Nos. 9 to 14 were met with, and removed by Major Peake, in 1900. At block 14, what may be termed the first series of "sudd" obstructions ended, and with its removal, through navigation between Khartoum and Gondokoro was restored. The worst place in the river, as regards giving trouble, was at block 10 (4).

(1) The above was written in 1901, and during the clearance of this channel in 1903, the statement of the Reisses has been verified, and the steamer and boats have been found. Major Matthews commenced the clearance of block 15, in 1902, but owing to the commencement of the rainy season, was obliged to abandon the work before completion. In the winter of 1903 and 1904. Lieut. Drury, R.N., made another attempt, but failed to complete the work owing to severe illness. The block to navigation on the Bahr-el-Gebel between Gondokoro and Khartoum, still, therefore, continues.

(2) Its discharge, as measured in March 1901, was 21.74 metres cube per second.

(3) It is of course possible that it again finds is way into the Bahr-el-Gebel through some of the large lagoons to the north.

(4) This place will be more fully described in that part of this report which deals more particularly with the "sudd."

Throughout the whole of this reach of river, shallow lakes or lagoons border the Bahr-el-Gebel in continuous lines (1). Some of them are of considerable area, as a reference to the map of the river will show. They form nurseries for the growth of water-plants and are the chief cause of the blocks which form in the channel. Their depth rarely exceeds 1 metre. The river frequently passes between two of these lagoons, separated from them by a strip of papyrus. In winter these "mayyehs" are open spaces of water, but, with the advent of the rainy season in April, their surfaces become covered with detached masses of floating vegetation. Many of them are connected by a series of openings with the river, and their water-level rises and falls with that of the latter. The loss of water, by evaporation on these shallow ponds, is very great.

It is difficult to say whether these lagoons are old courses of the Bahr-el-Gebel, long since filled up, or whether they are the remaining traces of the vast lake which, as some imagine, once covered this area. The latter supposition appears to be the more probable, as the channel of the river is so deep and well-defined, that it appears hardly possible that it should have utterly disappeared. On the other hand, there is at least one instance where the river has been actually in process of vanishing i.e., between kilometres 900 and 940, in what is called block 15. In this reach, the water was quite stagnant and the bed of the river filled, for several metres, with a layer of decomposed sudd ; so much so, that it was difficult to trace the channel by sounding. It is reasonable to suppose that, unless it had been cleared, this reach of the river would, in time, have disappeared and been transformed into a series of " mayyehs " or shallow lakes.

These lagoons are constantly changing their shape and, consequently, any map of the river attempting to describe them requires correction after every flood. New channels burst into the river and others fill up and disappear. North of kilometre 1058, these "mayyehs" are less numerous, and are smaller than they are upstream of this point. The average level of the banks, in March and April, varies from 0.20 to 0.35 metres above the river surface (2).

Between kilometres 1059 and 1079, the 5th, 6th, 7th and 8th "sudd" blocks were met with and cleared by Major Peake in 1900-1901. Here, swamps stretch to the horizon on both sides of the channel. At kilometre 1093, the ridge between the Bahr-el-Zaraf and the Bahr-el-Gebel is visible on the eastern bank. This ridge follows the latter river, to its junction with the White Nile at Lake No, at a distance varying from 1 to 3 kilometres. Between it and the river is deep swamp and high papyrus, while, to the west, the marshes extend to the horizon.

North of kilometre 1093, the first four "sudd" blocks, cleared by Major Peake's party, occurred. From kilometre 1146, Lake No stretches along the west bank, separated from the river by a broad area of papyrus and marsh. The width of the swamp, separating the river and lake, gradually decreases until, at kilometre 1156, it is merely a strip of papyrus, and the Bahr-el-Gebel joins the White Nile, or Bahr-el-Abyad, at the eastern corner of this lake, in north latitude 9° 29′, after having traversed a distance of 723 miles, from the Albert Nyanza lake. Its entry is effected in a long sweeping curve, its general direction at this point being to the north, or at right angles to the Nile, which here follows a course nearly due east and west.

The scenery of the Bahr-el-Gebel, throughout its course through the "sudd" region, is monotonous to a degree. There are no banks at all and, except at a few isolated spots, no semblance of any ridge on the water's edge. Reedy swamps stretch, for many kilometres upon either side. Their expanse is only broken at intervals, by lagoons of open water. Their surface is only a few centimetres above that of the water-level in the

(1) These lagoons are known as "Mayyehs."

(2) These levels are for 1901. In April 1903, the heights of these banks were some 0·33 to 0·45 metres above the water but with an equal volume passing down the river. This may mean that scour of the bed has set in.

THE BAHR EL GEBEL
HELLET EN NUER

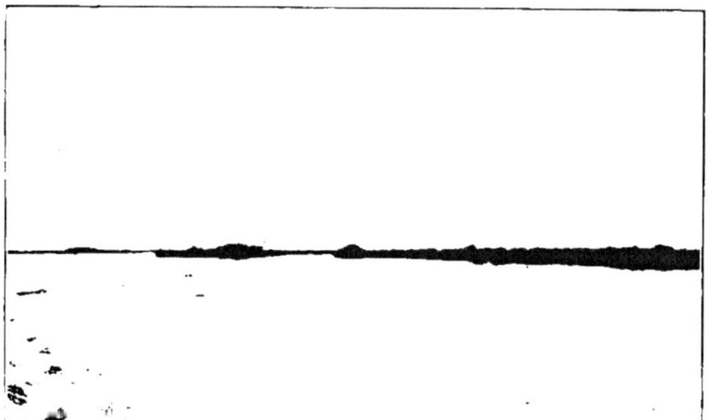

THE BAHR EL GEBEL
LAKE NO.

river, when at its lowest, and a rise of half a metre floods them to an immense distance. These marshes are covered with a dense growth of water-weeds, extending, in every direction, to the horizon. Of these reeds, the principal is the papyrus, which grows in extreme luxuriance. The stems are so close together, that it is difficult to force a way through them and the plants reach a height of from three to five metres above the marsh. In addition to the papyrus, large areas are covered with the reed called "Um-Soof," or "mother of wool," by the Arabs, another called "Bus," and the tall feathery-headed grass so well known to Indian sportsmen by the name of "tiger" grass. The extent of these swamps is unknown, but, more especially to the west of the river, it must be enormous. In all probability, the greater portion of the region lying between the Bahr-el-Gebel and the Bahr-el-Ghazal is, in the rainy season, a vast marsh. To the east, their area is more limited, as the country beyond the Bahr-el-Zaraf gradually rises into alluvial plains, covered with dense grass and intersected by numerous swamp lines. These plains, as a whole, are above the level of the Nile, even when in flood (¹). In the long island, lying within the loop formed by the Bahr-el-Zaraf with the main stream, there undoubtedly exists a ridge of comparatively high land. Upon this, a scanty population has settled. Except by occasional glimpses of trees and, more rarely, of a village, it is impossible to trace this ridge. Its limits are undetermined. It is surrounded on every side, by a belt of almost impassable marsh. Throughout this whole region, more especially between Bor and Lake No, it is extremely rare to see any sign of human life. Even hippopotami, which in the White Nile swarm, appear to shun the swamps of the Bahr-el-Gebel. Beyond a few night herons, bird life is unrepresented, especially in the lower part of its course. The water, on the contrary, teems with fish and crocodiles are constantly to be seen. The Bahr-el-Gebel has an evil name for mosquitoes and one that is well-deserved. With the disappearance of the sun, they come forth in countless myriads and make life a burden until the luminary reappears above the horizon. The whole region has an aspect of desolation, beyond the power of words to describe. It must be seen to be understood. The dark-green masses of the papyrus which hedge in the channel, although possessing a certain gloomy beauty, become monotonous to the eye, when kilometre after kilometre is passed without any change in the aspect of the landscape. Even on the rare occasions when it is possible to see over this hedge, no relief is experienced. In every direction, the sea of vegetation extends without a break.

An occasional stunted mimosa is welcomed as a land-mark. The air is hot and steamy, while the whole region is malarious to a degree. No one can remain long in this portion of the river without experiencing a feeling of depression. Through these dreary marshes, the river winds, in a continual succession of loops and curves. As soon as one is passed, another commences. So numerous are these twists, that the loss of slope caused by them must be very great. When it is considered that the mean velocity of the Bahr-el-Gebel, at dead low-water, averages at least 2 kilometres per hour, it is evident that, were it possible for the river to avoid these curves and to follow a straight course from Bor to the White Nile, the surface-slope, under such conditions, would be considerable. The water of the Bahr-el-Gebel is dark-coloured and contains little or no sediment. Very little ambatch is met with in its northern reaches.

(¹) See Appendix No. VI.

THE WHITE NILE, OR "BAHR-EL-ABYAD."

At the point where the Bahr-el-Gebel meets the waters of the Bahr-el-Ghazal, is the shallow lake, known as Lake No, or "Moghren El-Buhur" (1). The Bahr-el-Gebel does not pass through this lake, but skirts its eastern corner. From this point, as far as Khartoum, where it is joined by the Blue Nile, this river is known as the White Nile (2).

On issuing from the Bahr-el-Gebel, the change in the character of the stream is at once apparent. North of Lake No, it is a broad river, open and fairly straight. The marshes on either side of the channel are wide and, for a considerable distance downstream, the river is separated into two or more branches, by "sudd" islands. The papyrus and reeds are high and thick, but, (and here lies the difference between the White Nile and the Bahr-el-Gebel), beyond the swamps on either side, high land, often covered with forest, is visible. The marshes, in many places, are as much as three kilometres in width, but the dry land is always within sight.

At 5 kilometres from Lake No, or at 1161 kilometres from Lake Albert, a large lagoon, known as the "Mayyeh Signora," joins the Nile on the right bank (3). This channel, (which owes its name to the fact that it was explored by a Dutch lady, Madame Tinné, in 1863), is a flood-spill from the Bahr-el-Gebel, taking off this river from a point some 21 kilometres upstream of its junction with the White Nile, at Lake No. The "Mayyeh Signora" has a width, even at low water, of some 500 metres. It skirts the forest on the right bank for a great portion of its length. Opposite this "mayyeh," the left bank of the Nile is high and extends in a wide, treeless plain to the horizon. This plain, although in in places low and swampy, is generally above the river-level, except in excessive floods. Between it and the river, a belt of swamp extends, varying in width from a few hundred metres to over a kilometre. On the right bank, the swamps are much wider and are intersected by a labyrinth of "khors" and marshes. When the grass is burnt, the general aspect of the country is not unlike the Norfolk coast at low tide, but upon a very large scale. For some distance downstream of the "Mayyeh Signora" junction, a waste of swamps borders the channel on either side. It is difficult to tell, especially before the grass is burnt, where the solid ground begins and ends, or what is the distance which separates the river banks. In flood, the horizon is bordered by high masses of papyrus, ambatch and other swamp grasses. Through them, the main channel winds, in a tortuous course, at times 150 metres, and at others only 50 metres in width. The water-surface is covered with masses of floating "sudd," some of large size. These masses, on reaching a shallow, ground and form islands. The channel in this reach is constantly changing (4).

At 1222 kilometres from Lake Albert, the large island known as Tonga commences on the left of the main channel. In the low season it is not an island at all, but forms the left bank of the Nile. The channel, which separates it from the mainland, is dry at the southern end when the river is low. Tonga island is very low and its northern end is covered annually by the flood (5). Its width varies from 2 to 4 kilometres. Beyond the

(1) Lake No, or Nu, is probably a corruption of Nuer, and it should more properly be called the Nuer lake, as the inhabitants in its vicinity are of that tribe. "Moghren El-Buhur" is the Arabic name. It means the "Meeting of the Rivers."

(2) It, most probably, received this name from the white tinge given to its waters by the Sobat river. Some maps make the White Nile only commence from below the Sobat junction.

(3) The kilometrage from Lake Albert will, for convenience, be carried through, in this report, to Khartoum. Although they have different names, the Bahr-el-Gebel and White Nile, are one and the same river. Between Lake No and the Sobat junction, the course of the White Nile is nearly due east and west. It would be a misnomer. here, to talk of the east and west banks. For this portion of the river, therefore, the words, right and left banks only, will be used. The right bank being that on the right hand of the observer, facing downstream.

(4) In 1863, the While Nile was blocked by "sudd" downstream of Lake No.

(5) In 1903, the whole island was submerged during the flood, and the Shilluk navigated all over it in canoes.

"khor" on the left, the high land rises and a continuous line of Shilluk villages runs parallel to the river. The most southerly of these villages is called Tonga, whence the island receives its name. Except during the dry season, it is impossible to land anywhere, on account of the width and depth of the swamps between the high land and the river. The average depth of the water over these swamps, during flood, is 2 metres and in high floods, like that of 1903, is as much as 3 metres. The entire surface of the water is concealed by a dense, tangled covering of weeds, some floating, and some with roots extending to the bottom of the marsh. Through these weeds, neither steamer nor boat can force its way.

For many kilometres, downstream, the same scenery continues. On the right bank, the swamps extend, for from 2 to 3 kilometres. Beyond this, the ground rises and is covered with thick, thorn forest, which stretches in a narrow belt, some 2 kilometres wide, parallel to the river. On the left, the width of swamp is not more, as a rule, than 500 yards. Beyond this is the Tonga island and then, at some distance, the high grass plain, and the Shilluk villages.

At kilometre 1232, the Bahr-el-Zaraf joins the Nile, on its right bank (1). This river, previous to the cutting of the "sudd" in the Bahr-el-Gebel, used to bring down a considerable body of water. As soon as the Gebel was opened, the volume of the Zaraf was reduced and, even in the high flood of 1903, the discharge was a small one (2). There can be little doubt that, during the period when the Bahr-el-Gebel was blocked by "sudd," a considerable portion of the volume of water passing to the north, forced a passage through the Zaraf marshes. It is even possible that, had the "sudd" not been removed, in time, the Bahr-el-Zaraf might have become the main channel of the Nile through this region. It now brings in a very insignificant addition to the volume of the river. It is true that, in the years of 1900, 1901 and 1902, after the "sudd" was cut, the floods were far below the average, but even in 1903, which was a year of exceptional supply, in the Upper Nile, the discharge of the Bahr-el-Zaraf was but a small one.

For a long distance downstream of the Zaraf junction, the aspect of the country is monotonous in the extreme. Grass plains, of apparently endless expanse, extend on both sides of the river, separated from it by swamps of great width. The banks are very low. On the left bank, not a tree is visible, and beyond the Shilluk villages, nothing breaks the line of the horizon but the large ant-hills which dot the surface of the plain. On the right, a thin belt of thorn jungle and low forest extends in a more or less continuous line. At kilometre 1269, a large "khor," known as Gabt El-Megahid, discharges into the Nile on the right bank. A few hundred metres from the river, the channel widens out and forms a lake, some 1000 metres long by 500 metres wide. This sheet of water is surrounded by forest. The "khor" itself, runs up for many miles into the country and on either side of it is a thick belt of forest. It drains an immense, undulating plain, covered by a growth of high grass, with here and there a few scattered Dinka villages. Downstream of this "khor," the forest on the right bank of the river is continuous, and the swamp varies in width, from 500 to 300 metres. At kilometre 1275, the island of Tonga ends. The "khor" which bounds it on the left here is the so-called river Lollé, or Fanakama. The Lollé, at the point where it joins the Nile, has a width of 70 metres, and a depth, during the low-water season, varying from 0.50 to 0.60 metres. In April 1901, there was no current in the channel which had all the appearance of a back-water. In 1903, there was an apparent discharge from this "khor" and Mr. Craig's measurement resulted in a volume of 31 metres cube per second (3).

It is, however, uncertain whether this current was not really that caused by the Nile flood itself, passing over Tonga island down the boundary "khor," and thence into the

(1) The Bahr-el-Zaraf will be separately described.

(2) Writing in 1899, it was observed that "this affluent brings down a large body of water, even in the winter, and the "strong current causes a succession of whirlpools and eddies in the main stream." Egypt No. (2) 1899.

(3) The width, as measured on the 23rd September 1903, was 72 metres. The depth 4.4 metres.

Lollé channel. It is doubtful whether the Lollé has any claim to be called a river, more than any other of the many large " khors " which bring water, at certain seasons, into the Nile. Its sole claim to this distinction is, that, in Perthes's map, it is shown as a continuation of the Keila, or Keilak, a stream which, apparently, rises in Dar Nouba, latitude 11° north, but about which, little or nothing is known. Marno, who explored the Lollé in 1880, shows it on his map as running parallel to the Nile for some 50 to 55 kilometres, and connected by two branches, one of which forms the Tonga island. It seems probable that the Keilak, if it exists at all, discharges its waters into the Bahr-el-Ghazal and not into the Lollé. However this may be, this stream, or " khor, " can have no important influence upon the White Nile when in flood (1). Just below the Lollé junction, the river changes its direction completely. Between this point and Lake No, its course has been nearly due east and west, but from here it flows nearly due north, or north-east, until its junction with the Blue Nile at Khartoum.

At kilometre 1280 from Lake Albert, the Sobat river joins the Nile, upon the eastern bank. The country now is flat and open and the nearest bush is some fifteen hundred metres away. Between this and the river is an expanse of marsh. The old fort is situated on a knoll, on the south bank of the Sobat and is surrounded, on three sides, by swamp (2). The latitude of this place is 9° 22′ 8″ north, and the longitude 31° 31′ east. The Sobat meets the Nile nearly at right angles and, if anything, its direction at the junction is slightly to the south. The depth, even in the dry season, is considerable. The soundings show 6 or 7 metres, but at that time, the current is feeble, its waters being held up by those of the Nile. In the flood, the reverse is the case and the Sobat water, coming down in great volume and with a fair velocity, holds back the discharge of the White Nile, which, upstream of the junction, has a nearly horizontal slope and a feeble current (3). The colour of the Sobat water, when in moderate flood, is a milky-white and, in full flood, a pale brick-red. The effect of this volume of chalky-looking water, mingling with the greenish-grey waters of the Nile, is a very remarkable one. For a long way downstream, a sharp line separates the two.

North of the Sobat, the same scenery continues. The Shilluk villages line the western banks, separated from the river by a broad expanse of swamp. At kilometre 1288, the station of Taufikia is reached. This place is on the east bank of the river and on fairly high ground. Taufikia is Sir Samuel Baker's old station, where, in 1870, he passed the whole summer. The bank here is high and some 5 metres above low-water level. The cantonments cover about ten acres of land, from which the bush has been cleared. The lines are well laid out, in rows of neat thatched huts, including a hospital of ten beds. The Commandant's house is situated at the south end of the station, close to some large spreading trees. The high land does not extend to any great distance from the river and beyond it, the country is marshy, although never submerged, even in the highest floods. Nevertheless, it is far from being a healthy place and even in the winter months, there are many sick (4). White ants are a serious nuisance, as they destroy the wood-work of the huts, almost as soon as erected. The utmost that can be said in favour of Taufikia is that it is slightly more healthy than Kodok (5).

North of Taufikia, the same dreary landscape prevails. The line of Shilluk villages continues along the western ridge, parallel to the river. These villages are close together and almost continuous, each being separated from the next by a few hundred metres only.

(1) In 1899, Colonel Sparkes attempted to explore the Lollé, but was stopped by "sudd," some 40 kilometres from its mouth. In 1903, according to Mr. Craig, the natives agreed in stating that the Lollé was blocked by "sudd," some 2 or 3 days' journey from the White Nile, i.e., some 40 to 50 kilometres from the mouth.

(2) This fort has been abandoned, owing to the proximity of Taufikia.

(3) This holding up of the White Nile water by the Sobat in flood, is an important factor in the problem of the regulation of the river. It will be discussed more fully in that part of this report, relating to discharges.

(4) In the rainy season of 1900, 50 per cent of the small garrison were incapacitated from fever.

(5) The telegraph line from Khartoum, now extends to Taufikia. Giraffes are said to give a good deal of trouble, to those charged with the maintenance of the line, by breaking the wires.

THE WHITE NILE
TAUFIKIA

THE WHITE NILE
KODOK

They are surrounded by groups of the "Deleb" palm ([1]). The distance of these villages from the Nile varies with the width of the swamp. It averages from one to two kilometres, but is rarely as much as three kilometres. In the rainy season, the Shilluk migrate into the interior of the country, taking their cattle with them, to avoid the "Seroot" fly, which, always plentiful in this tract, is particularly so during the rains. On the east bank, the swamping is narrower, averaging from 800 to 1200 metres in width. The banks are very low and, with the exception of the palms above mentioned, absolutely treeless. Hippopotami are to be seen in great numbers, inhabiting the grass islands in the centre of the river ([2]). After passing the Austrian Mission Station of Lul (kilometre 1351) at 1371 kilometres from Lake Albert, Kodok is arrived at. This is the headquarters of the Mudiria of the Upper Nile. Much progress has been made in this station during the last two years. All the Government offices are well-built brick structures and the whole place bears a very different aspect from that which it presented in 1899.

Kodok is situated on the west of the Nile, in latitude 9° 55′ 20″ north, and longitude 32° 6′ east. The station is on a small peninsula which juts out into the river, and is connected with the ridge by a narrow strip of land. On three sides of this peninsula is a deep swamp and even the, so-called, dry land becomes a morass during the rainy season. Even in dry weather, it is an uninviting spot. A long, low island stretches in front of the station. This island is from 300 to 500 metres in width. During the season when the river is at its lowest, the channel, which separates it from the mainland, becomes dry. Water has, consequently, to be brought from a long distance. The western channel, between the island and the bank, is 50 metres in width, and in flood boats and steamers can pass up it and come close alongside the station. The main channel, east of the island, is some 500 metres in width. The view, looking across the river to the east, consists of a dead-flat expanse of grass and reeds, extending to the horizon. Not a tree is to be seen. On the west, the bush commences, at some 2 to 3 kilometres from the river. Kodok used to be a place of some importance, prior to the Mahdi's rebellion. Many of the roads from Kordofan converge upon the river at this point. It is, moreover, close to the residence of the Mek, or king, of the Shilluk tribe. It is not, and never can be, a healthy spot and, although much has been done to improve the place, it has still an evil reputation as regards malarial fever. The climate, even in the dry season, is steamy and damp, and the temperature in the month of March ranges from 98° to 105° F. in the shade. The rainy season commences in May and the sickness increases at this period, reaching its maximum during the autumn months. During the rains, mosquitoes are very bad.

North of Kodok, a constant succession of grass islands is met with. On the west bank, a double line of Shilluk villages is to be seen—the one on the edge of the swamp and the other, further inland. On this side of the river, occasional large "khors" run in. These depressions extend for many kilometres inland and their banks are marked by a thick growth of thorny trees. Until Kaka is reached, at kilometre 1479, there is but little variety in the Nile scenery. The channel averages from 300 to 500 metres in width and is blocked by many islands. The depth, at low water, varies from 4 to 6 metres and the flood rise is about 2 metres. The Shilluk villages cluster along the western ridge, but, in this reach of the river, a belt of thin forest separates them from the swamps which extend in front of them in a broad belt, varying in width from a few hundred metres, to over two kilometres. On the east, the swamp averages 500 metres in width. Behind it, the ground rises and, near the river, is fringed by a line of forest. Outside of this again, stretches an apparently endless plain of grass, dotted with clumps of trees and bush. In

([1]) Borassus Œthiopicus.

([2]) The width of the low-water section is about 600 metres and in flood 1000 metres. The depth varies from 2 and 5, to 4 and 7 metres.

flood, landing at any point of this reach is extremely difficult. The marsh is very deep and covered with thick grass and reeds, through which nothing but a hippopotamus can force its way.

In the spring, when the river is low and the grass burnt, the general section of these marshes is plainly observable. It varies but little throughout the whole swamp region. It consists of a broad depression, deep in the centre, and rising towards the river channel on the one side, and towards the high land and the forest, on the other. This depression varies in width, from a few hundred metres, to, perhaps, 3 kilometres, or more. Along the water's edge runs a ridge, averaging a metre higher than the lowest portion of the swamp. This ridge is from two to three metres in width and is broken by openings, through which the water passes in and out of the marshes. In high floods, this ridge is submerged. Thus, in 1903, when the levels of the White Nile were exceptionally high, the water stood nearly two metres above the ridge. Consequently, the depth at that time, over the lowest portion of the depression, must have been nearly three metres. In a year of average supply, these depths are reduced by about one metre. The entire space between the forest and the river, including the ridge itself, is covered by a dense growth of reeds and papyrus which utterly prevents ingress, even in a boat. When the reeds are burnt and the marshes are thus laid bare, it is possible to walk over these swamps. It is then seen that what looked, from a distance, like a flat surface, is intersected by deep "khors," or water-courses, one of which, more often than not, runs close under the high bank. This is generally covered with a belt of trees, mostly mimosas. The ground rises abruptly from the swamp and the forest, as a rule, stretches inland, for a width, varying from 500 to 2000 metres, but which is occasionally much more. The forest land is generally above water-level, but, in high floods, the water extends into it for some distance. South of Kaka, the general level of the marshes, relatively to that of the river, is considerably lower than is the case north of that place. Upstream of the junction of the Sobat river, they are lower again— only a few centimetres above the water-surface, even at the time of lowest level. As their width at the same time increases, the first rise of the river is largely wasted in spreading over these immense areas of swamps and in filling up the numerous depressions which seam their surface. Behind the forest belt, on both banks of the river, extend broad grass plains. These are rarely flooded. Through them pass numerous wide "khors," some of which, more particularly those on the eastern bank, bring water from an immense distance. They form the drainage lines of the higher land. Their channels are filled with reeds, through which a sluggish stream winds. As the river falls, the water in these "khors" falls with it. The higher land is covered by a growth of tall grass and in places, by thickets of mimosa trees. Until the grass is burnt, progress through the country is almost impossible, except by following the tracks made by the game. The villages are situated upon the ridges, as near to the river, or to the "khors," as is consistent with being above the level of the highest floods. Round these villages are patches of clearing, in which the people plant their crops. As soon as the rains cease and the grass is sufficiently dry to burn, the natives set fire to it, in order to obtain pasture for their cattle. In the early spring months, these grass-fires are to be seen, in all directions, some of them covering several kilometres in width.

Kaka, kilometre 1479, is a large Shilluk village, on the western bank. North of this point, the continuous line of villages ceases and they become scattered, eventually disappearing altogether. On the east bank, the high land, in one place, comes close to the water and a wooding station has been formed. Downstream of Kaka, except for a very occasional fishing village, the country, on both sides, appears to be absolutely uninhabited. The marshes, and the forest line, continue as before and large islands separate the stream into two or more channels. At kilometre 1549, a solitary granite hill, called Ahmad Agha, stands out above the plain, on the eastern bank. This hill is some 3 kilometres from the

THE WHITE NILE
GEBEL AHMAD AGHA

THE WHITE NILE
GEBELAIN

river. It is hog-backed in shape, and some 120 metres, or so, in height. All round its base stretches a dense thicket of mimosa trees. A wide and deep "khor" runs to the south of this hill, in an easterly direction. From this, another large "khor" branches off and runs north, and behind the hill. This last "khor" follows a course more or less parallel to the Nile, which it rejoins in the neighbourhood of Renk, some 87 kilometres downstream (1), North of Ahmad Agha, the forest belt, on both sides, is thick. The swamping continues, but is not so wide as it was further to the south. The west bank is generally lower than that to the east. The river channel is very wide, even at low water averaging 600 metres. The current is not strong and, even in flood, is barely 1.5 metres per second. Hellet el Renk is passed, on the east bank, at 1609 kilometres from Lake Albert. This is a Mamuria of the District and an English Officer is stationed here. The Government offices are situated close to the river, but the village is some 5 kilometres inland. The forest, up and downstream of this place, is very thick, but in the vicinity of the station it has been cleared away. On the west bank, the swamps are wide and the country beyond them, consists of alternate areas of forest and expanses of grass, intersected by broad depressions. At Renk, there was formerly a Dervish "Dem," or camp, which was captured in 1898. Here, the remains of the Emir Ahmed Fadil's force surrendered, in the same year. For the next 50 or 60 kilometres, the scenery of the river is most dreary and monotonous. A fringe of thick forest on either bank, marks the higher land. Between this the river winds through reedy islands, bordered by the eternal belt of swamp.

At kilometre 1734, the hills of Gebelain are passed upon the east bank. These hills are visible for a long distance, up and downstream, and are easily recognizable by the five, peculiarly-shaped, granite peaks which rise abruptly from the plain. The highest of these peaks is perhaps 100 metres. They form a sort of amphitheatre, the nearest being a kilometre and a half from the river, and the furthest, five kilometres. All round these hills, a wide expanse of prickly grass, interspersed with clumps of low mimosas, extends. The grass is about one metre in height. The soil is light and friable. Much of this area must be flooded in the rainy season. One or two ravines traverse it. The forest, on the east bank, is some 500 metres in width, and extremely thick. The remains of Ahmad Fadil's "Dem" are still visible here. There is a telegraph station at this place. On the west bank, the swamping is narrow and forest borders the river (2).

The tract, to the east of the river here, once formed part of the Dinka country, but is now generally uninhabited, most of the Dinka having migrated to the south to escape the raids of the slave-traders. Downstream of Gebelain, the marshes decrease in width and forest, on both banks, borders the river.

At kilometre 1782, the Abu Zeid ford is passed. This is the most serious obstacle to navigation, when the river is low, between Gondokoro and Khartoum. At this point, for a length of about 6 kilometres, the river has an immense width and spreads out, in a broad, very shallow, sheet. Upon the bed, masses of what are called "fresh-water oysters" collect (3). The broken shells form, with the shingle, a kind of "conglomerate," almost as hard as rock and which nothing but a specially adapted dredger could remove. In the months of March and April, 1900, when the river was abnormally low, the depth of water, at this point, was, in places, not more than 0·40 to 0·50 metres. Through steamer traffic was entirely suspended and a "portage," either by camel, along the shore, or by lightly-laden native boats, on the river, was necessitated. The inhabitants daily crossed the river on their donkeys and were to be seen, carrying their sheep across on their backs. 34 kilometres

(1) The width of the flood section at Ahmad Agha, in 1903, was 500 metres, with a maximum depth of 6.4 metres.

(2) Gebelain appears to be the northern limit of the "*Seroot*" fly, which has been a constant, and unwelcome, guest throughout the journey from the south. This fly, which is about the size of a wasp, has a sharp sting, and, if allowed to settle, speedily draws blood.

(3) "Ætheria."

upstream of Abu-Zeid, a reef of rocks, known as Dunkool, occurs in the channel (1). Here the reef runs right across the river bed, and the only method of passing safely, at low water, is to steer a course like the letter S. Many of the rocks are below the water-surface, and their presence is only indicated by the ripples which they cause.

Proceeding downstream, the country on either side, is higher and the swamping is less. Goz Abu-Goma, on the east bank, is reached at the 1807th kilometre. The width of the river varies from 700 to 900 metres. Here, there is a small Government station and a telegraph office. Opposite this place, is the southern end of the large island of Abba which, north of Goz Abu-Goma, divides the Nile into two channels, for a distance of 46 kilometres.

Goz Abu-Goma is the northern limit of the "sudd" vegetation. Downstream of this place, the papyrus and "sudd" grasses disappear and, although there is flooding on either side of the channel, there are no swamps, properly so-called. The country of the Negro has now been left behind and he is replaced by the Arab. The difference is almost at once apparent, as the foreshores and islands are cultivated.

Abba island is both long and narrow. It is higher at the southern, than at the northern end. Throughout its entire length, it is thickly wooded. The ruins of the house of Mohamed Ahmad, the Mahdi, are still visible. The western channel is the better for navigation and, when the Nile is at its lowest, the channel on the east is dry in places. At 1835 kilometres Fashi Shoya is passed, on the western bank of the river. The country here is open and high, with scattered bush and mimosa. There is no swamping. From this point, the expedition started in 1899, which ended in the defeat and death of the Khalifa Abdullah. Abba island comes to an end at the 1847th kilometre from the Albert lake. From here to Kawa, kilometre 1884, both banks of the river are covered with forest, and the land rises from the water on either side, in a long, very flat slope. In flood, the water extends for a considerable distance into the forest and the marks on the trees show that it rises to a height of 0·50 metres, and more. As the water recedes, the slopes are cultivated by the inhabitants. Upstream of Kawa is a low island, some 6 kilometres in length, which is richly cultivated with a variety of crops, comprising wheat, barley, onions, lubia, bamia and dukhn.

Kawa is a large village, on the east bank of the Nile. It is a prosperous-looking place, with neat Government offices, and a gum depot, with a small grain store. It is built on high land and the bush is open all round it. It is the headquarters of a Mamuria. Kawa has a moderately large market, at which grain and vegetables are exposed for sale. The inhabitants are a mixture of Hassaniyeh, Jaalin and Danagla.

North of Kawa, signs of returning prosperity are everywhere apparent, and the difference in the aspect of the river, between the years 1899 and 1903, is very striking. In the former year, there were few inhabitants to be seen and but little cultivation (2). Now, villages are springing up and a large population appears to have migrated to the river banks. As the waters recede and the mud-flats are exposed, the scene is a busy one. Huts are erected on the flats, and shadoofs, for the irrigation of the more valuable crops, such as wheat, barley, onions, summer-maize and millet.

Boat-building is in progress in many places, and the people cut and collect wood for fuel, for Khartoum and for the steamers. The inhabitants appear to be rich in cattle. Large herds are to be seen grazing on the banks. As the width of these flats and islands is considerable, the total area under cultivation, between Abba island and Khartoum, must attain a respectable figure (3). This river cultivation depends largely upon the maize crop of the previous flood. When this last is large, the inhabitants have secured their food

(1) In addition to Abu-Zeid and Dunkool, obstacles to navigation occur, in the shape of reefs, at Goz Abu-Goma, Ahmad Agha, and Kaka. South of Kodok, the White Nile is navigable, even in years of abnormally low supply.

(2) In the winter of 1899, the Khalifa's forces occupied the western bank of the river.

(3) This area naturally varies with the levels of the river. In a year of high water-level, it is small, compared with one in which the water sinks to a level below the average.

supply and, being naturally indolent, are disinclined for the labour entailed by the raising of a second crop. If the maize crop fails, as was the case in the year 1900, then the area, under cultivation on the flats, increases.

North of Kawa, the country on either side is high—flat on the east, and covered with bush—on the west, more broken, with a belt of high and thick, acacia forest near the river's edge. The width of the channel here is considerable. It is rarely less than 700 metres, from bank to bank and frequently much more. In flood, it increases to a maximum, as measured, of nearly 1300 metres. The current is feeble and the depth, at low water, is rarely more than four metres (1). Islands, submerged in flood, are very numerous and the mud-flats on either side are wide.

El-Duem is situated on the west bank, at kilometre 1917 from the Albert lake. An island separates the river into two channels, at this point. Here, the improvement in the last few years is very marked. The place is rapidly developing into an important trade centre. It is the principal mart for the export of gum from Kordofan, and is a busy station, with many store-houses and a large market. Substantial Government offices have been erected, including a hospital. El-Duem is the point from which the transport service to El-Obeid, the capital of Kordofan, starts. The gum is brought from the interior on camels, packed in large bales and covered with matting, made of the grass known as "Lahaw." At El-Duem, it is shipped by steamer, or by native boat, to Omdurman, where the Government royalty is imposed. The trade in gum is, at present, chiefly in the hands of Greek merchants. A Nile gauge has been erected at El-Duem and the river levels are daily recorded (2).

North of El-Duem, the landscape is monotonous and uninteresting. The banks on either side are low, except where an occasional ridge of sand-hills borders the flats. On the east, the plain is open, but covered with thick bush. On the west, a dense fringe of mimosa follows the line of the channel. This bank, during high Nile, is flooded to an immense distance. A good many villages are passed, more on the east than on the west and the flats and foreshores are largely cultivated. The river itself is of great width. At kilometre 1945, a ridge of hills, called Gebel Arashkol, at some distance from the river, breaks the deadness of the flat expanse. This range consists of several peaks, and is seen for a long distance. From kilometre 1982 north, the east bank is open, high and sandy. Beyond it, an immense flat plain stretches across to the Blue Nile.

Between kilometres 2069 and 2084, two isolated hills are seen. That on the east bank, is known as Gebel Mandara, and that on the right as Gebel Auli. Except for these two peaks, the country on either side is strikingly flat. The channel widens to 1000 metres, and, further on, to 1500 metres in width. It assumes the appearance of a lake, rather than a river, and north of kilometre 2098, the width increases to from 2 to 3 kilometres and, in places, more. This width is continued until Omdurman is sighted. The flats on either side are immense and the country low and treeless. The depth is very shallow and landing in boats of any draught is impossible, on account of the shelving banks. Large flocks of water-birds of many kinds are met with and crocodiles are numerous. When the wind is high, waves, of considerable size, rise in this reach. The western bank is generally lower than that on the east.

Proceeding north, the palms and trees of Khartoum are visible to the right front and the houses of Omdurman to the left. The foreshore gets flatter and the cultivated area on the flats gets larger, until at last, at Khartoum, the river is joined by its great eastern tributary, the Blue Nile, after having traversed a length of 2118 kilometres, from the point where it left the Albert Nyanza. If to this, be added the length of the Victoria Nile, the distance between Khartoum and its source at the Ripon Falls is 2526 kilometres.

(1) The maximum depth in the flood of 1903, at El-Duem, was 8·7 metres.

(2) The mean velocities of the White Nile as measured, at El-Duem, are 1·25 kilometres an hour, at low water, and 2 kilometre an hour, in flood.

LAKE NO, AND THE BAHR-EL-GHAZAL.

Lake No is situated in north latitude 9° 29′. It is a shallow expanse of water covering several square kilometres of area and surrounded on all sides by reedy marsh. It probably is a portion of the great lake which once covered this country. Through its eastern end the Bahr-el-Gebel passes and the Bahr-el-Ghazal enters it at its western extremity. Lake No acts as a reservoir for the waters of the sluggish streams which drain the extensive plateau, forming the watershed between the Congo and the Nile. These streams find their rise in an area, lying between latitudes 5° and 8° north, and longitudes 24° and 30° east. The channel, by which their united waters are delivered to the Nile, is the Bahr-el-Ghazal, or Gazelle River and, from it, the province through which it passes receives its name. Its chief affluents are the Rohl, the Jau, and the Tonj on the right, and the Bahr-el-Arab, the Bahr-el-Homr, and the Jur on the left.

The water, thus brought down, fills up the depression known as Lake No, over which area the water of the Bahr-el-Gebel spreads. The consequence is that this lake is an expanse of water, through which little or no current passes, but whose levels rise and fall with that of the Nile. The flooded area changes, according to the season of the year. It forms an important reservoir for the White Nile. The actual extent of Lake No is difficult to ascertain. It has been variously estimated at from 50 to 100 square, kilometres. These differences are probably due to the fact that the area was estimated at different periods of the year. During maximum flood, the extent cannot be much less than the larger estimate, but at the period of low supply, the area is much reduced and, in 1900 and 1901, could hardly have exceeded 20 square kilometres. In the early months of these years, the surface had shrunk to very small dimensions and more resembled a large river than a lake. The width, during the period of low Nile, is extremely variable. Thus in April 1901, in the first kilometre from the White Nile, the open-water surface was, at times, under 200 metres, and then suddenly widened out to perhaps, 3 kilometres; a little further on, it again contracted and for 6 or 8 kilometres more, varied from 300 to 600 metres. The depth, at the time, was nowhere more than 2·25 metres and, in places, only 1·5 metres. No current at all was visible, through any portion of the lake. Beyond the open water stretched a broad belt of flooded reeds. This belt was chiefly composed of "Um Soof," with clumps of ambatch. The open water itself was full of reedy islands. Lake No abounds with hippopotami and water-fowl. The former cause a good deal of trouble to the Nuer population, as they are unusually savage in this locality and are said to make a practice of attacking any canoe, or raft, crossing the lake. At 9 kilometres from the White Nile, a continuous line of Nuer villages runs parallel to the left bank of the channel, for many kilometres and marks the ridge, beyond which the swamping does not extend. Their average distance is some 3 kilometres from the river.

The villages appear to be thickly populated and the inhabitants possess large herds of cattle, sheep, and goats. The last few years have made a wonderful difference in their shyness; they now barter their fowls, etc., with readiness.

From 11 kilometres above the White Nile junction, the channel contracts to some 80 or 90 metres, and is styled on the map, the Khor Deleb.

At 25·5 kilometres the Bahr-el-Ghazal joins this "khor." The former comes in from the right, and the latter from the left. The nomenclature is rather puzzling. The Bahr-el-Ghazal, being the more important river, should certainly have given its name to the channel carrying the united waters of the two streams. As, however, this is styled the Khor Deleb on most maps, no change has been made and, in this note, the

Bahr-el-Ghazal is considered as commencing from this junction, and the kilometrage starts from this point.

The Khor Deleb is a wide expanse of channel, from 150 to 200 metres in breadth. It forms the outlet for the waters of the siver Rohl, coming from the south (1). In summer, no current at all is apparent and it is consequently impossible to measure the discharge. The Ghazal river, at this point, has a width of some 40 metres and in appearance, is a more insignificant stream than is the other. Its depth, however, is greater, averaging 4 metres, as against 2, or 2·5 metres in the Deleb. The Khor Deleb was explored by Major Peake for some 28 kilometres above this junction. At this point, it was blocked by "sudd" and reeds, so that further progress was impossible. It had, however, a decided stream. The transparency of the water differs in the two channels; that of the Khor Deleb being opaque, and of a whitey-grey colour, while that of the Bahr-el-Ghazal is clear and limpid, like that of the While Nile itself. Between the two rivers, which run parallel for some distance, is an expanse of low marsh, 3·30 metres above low-water level. This whole area must resemble a large lake when the rivers are in flood and the aspect of the country is desolate and monotonous to an extreme degree. It is absolutely treeless. The atmosphere is damp and warm, even in the winter months and the mosquitoes are of a peculiarly venomous variety.

Proceeding up the Bahr-el-Ghazal, for a long way there is little change in the landscape. The low banks continue and the stream winds about through the marshes with a very feeble velocity. At 5 kilometres from the junction, a large "khor" joins the Bahr-el-Ghazal, on the left bank. This is known as the Mayyeh Eleri and appears to come from a north-westerly direction. It is this "khor" which has been supposed to be the junction between the Bahr-el-Ghazal and the Lollé. From the slope of the country, however, it would seem that water flows, from the higher land, into the Bahr-el-Ghazal. It is possible that, in flood, there may be a spill in the opposite direction, This "khor," although 200 metres in width, is very shallow. At 9½ kilometres, the Khor Deleb approaches to within 1200 metres of the Bahr-el-Ghazal. A solitary "Deleb" palm (mentioned by Junker) forms a fine land-mark on the right bank. The Khor Deleb derives its name from this palm.

The left bank of the river, beyond the fringe of swamp, is an extensive grass plain, covered with ant-hills. These are so close together that they somewhat resemble a gigantic grave-yard. The Nuer villages are now a long way from the bank.

As the river is ascended, the country becomes more and more hopeless-looking. Flat grass plains extend to the horizon, and a wide band of swamp borders either side. The channel narrows, and in places is not more than 25 metres. The depth is from 4 to 5 metres and the turns and bends, though not as sharp as on the Bahr-el-Zaraf, are endless.

The difference between the Bahr-el-Zaraf and the Bahr-el-Ghazal is very striking. The water of the former, during the period of low supply, is considerably below its banks; in the latter, it is almost level with them. The rise of the former, even in ordinary flood, is not less than 1·65, to 2 metres. That of the Bahr-el-Ghazal, on the contrary, must be very small. It is difficult to imagine that, even in flood, the water can rise more than 1, or, at most, 1·20 metres, over its lowest level (2). Even with such a rise, the area of country under water would be enormous and the flooding would extend for a very long distance.

A few kilometres further up, the depth of water increases to 6 metres and in places to 7·5 metres. For the first time, forest appears in the distance on the left, but several kilometres away from the river. The right bank is now covered with low bush and scrub, beyond the flooded line. The country bordering the Bahr-el-Ghazal does not have the appearance of being under water for any length of time, even in flood. In this respect

(1) Felkin measured the Rohl, in October 1879: he gives the width as 120 feet, mean depth, 12 feet, and velocity, 1 knot an hour; approximate discharge—2,390 cubic feet per second=33·5 metres cube per second; he notes that both banks were flooded.

(2) Von Heuglin gives the mean difference between high and low water as from 3 feet to 4 feet, it is lowest in March and April.

again it differs from that traversed by the Bahr-el-Zaraf. It must, however, be saturated and resemble a sponge in the rainy season. There cannot be more than a very shallow film of water over these plains, or the bush and scrub would not flourish as it does; neither would ant-hills be found in such quantities. The general slope of the country is so low that the water must drain off extremely slowly.

At kilometre 24, the width is 60 metres and the reed-belt gets narrower; a very large "mayyeh," or "khor," comes in on the left bank here. This is known as the Mayyeh Nuer, or the Mayyeh Mahmoud Effendi. Its width near the junction is from 150 to 200 metres, and its general direction appears to be west. It is very shallow. This mayyeh is said to receive the waters of the Keilak river (¹), a stream about which little is known, but which is supposed to rise in the hills of Dar Nuba. Upstream of this junction, the Bahr-el-Ghazal takes a more southerly direction. The two streams run for some kilometres parallel to one another, from 700 to 600 metres apart. The country between the two is, perhaps, 0·60 metres over the water.

At kilometre 32, the first papyrus, seen since leaving the White Nile, is met with. From this point on, for many kilometres, a band of this reed fringes both edges of the water. It is never so high as on the Bahr-el-Gebel, nor does it here grow in such dense luxuriance as on that stream. The water surface is very narrow, often not more than 20 metres, but the depth is considerable, averaging from 5 to 6 metres. The reed-birds here are an extraordinary sight. They are to be seen in myriads and resemble a flight of locusts. The "Seroot" fly is very bad on the Bahr-el-Ghazal. The ant-hills certainly form a distinctive feature of the Ghazal scenery. Nowhere else are they so large or so numerous. They are generally from 20 to 50 metres apart.

The papyrus belt gets wider as the river is ascended and, at 67 kilometres, the forest on the left bank comes down close to the water's edge and the river skirts it for some 3 kilometres. The trees are large, but the belt is only a few hundred metres wide. The scenery here is beautiful, as the ground is high and glades of fine trees are scattered about the grassy plain. Many elephants are to be seen. On the right bank is a wide marsh, through which the river channel has evidently wandered at times. This is the beginning of the reach in which the Bahr-el-Ghazal is occasionally closed by "sudd." In 1880, Marno found his first block here. The channel is very narrow, deep, and winding. At present, it runs under the high bank, but it is clear that it could easily be blocked at one of the many bends and in such a case, it would doubtless form a series of lagoons and "mayyehs," in the adjacent papyrus marsh. After leaving the left bank forest for a time, the river, at kilometre 73·5, again returns to it.

The depth of the channel suddenly decreases to 1·8 metres, but soon deepens again to 3 and 4 metres. This shoal is doubtless caused by decomposed "sudd" which has sunk to the bottom. Such a bar is one of the frequent causes of a block. The "sudd" raises the bed-level and other masses floating down, ground upon the obstruction and the channel is speedily closed. The Bahr-el-Ghazal has evidently changed its course here very recently. It is now much closer to the left bank than it was in 1899. The change has probably been caused by a block of "sudd." It was near here, i.e., at kilometre 77, that Gessi Pasha had such a disastrous experience in January 1880. His steamers, on descending this river, were imprisoned in the "sudd" for some six weeks, and he lost over 100 men. Had it not been for the opportune arrival of Marno, in the *Bordein*, none of the party could have escaped. They were on the verge of starvation and it was impossible to obtain fuel for the steamers, being cut off from the shore by an impassable swamp.

These 9 or 10 kilometres of the Bahr-el-Ghazal, must always be more or less dangerous, as regards possible closure by "sudd," at certain seasons of the year. In 1900 and 1901, the channel was open, but in the spring of 1899 it was closed not far upstream of this point (²).

(¹) See note upon River Lollé.

(²) In 1903, it was again, temporarily, closed.

THE BAHR EL GHAZAL

THE BAHR EL GHAZAL
MOUTH OF RIVER ROHL

The channel is extremely contracted, having a width of only 12 metres and a depth of 4½ metres. The course is so tortuous that it is difficult to follow all the turns. The whole of this area must, in the rainy season, be a reedy lake. At kilometre 74·5, the river emerges from this dreadful marsh and the width increases to 30 metres. The banks average 0·75 metres above low-water level. The country on either side is generally higher. On the right, bush is dotted about and the ant-hills reappear to the left in a large grassy plain.

At kilometre 80 the river widens into a lagoon, some 400 metres broad, and 1½ kilometres in length. At the upstream end of this lagoon, a large "mayyeh" is said by the Arabs to form the outlet of the Jau river, which is another of the tributary streams that feed the Bahr-el-Ghazal from the south (¹). This channel, which is known as the Mayyeh Ahmed Arabi, runs more or less parallel to the Bahr-el-Ghazal, for some 64 kilometres, taking off it at Lake Ambadi, or 144 kilometres from the point where the Ghazal and the Deleb join. It is often at a considerable distance from the main stream, but glimpses are to be seen of it at times. A fine tamarind tree, close to the edge of the "mayyeh," assists recognition of this spot.

In 1899, the Bahr-el-Ghazal was blocked by "sudd" near this junction. The right bank continues to be fairly high, but the left is low and must be flooded for a long distance. The stream is now more rapid. The air in the mornings here, is cool and damp, but a strong marshy smell prevails.

At kilometre 85, the Euphorbia first appears. This shrub is fairly plentiful from this point upstream. For several kilometres there is little change in the conditions, but at kilometre 113, trees are visible on the right bank, about 1500 metres from the river. The intermediate country is flooded. A few Dinka are occasionally met with, but no villages. The absence of human habitation on this river is very striking. Since the Nuer villages were left behind, at kilometre 43, not a sign of life was visible. A small, but deep, "khor" joins the river on the left bank here.

At kilometre 120, a large and important "khor" comes in also on the left bank. This channel, which was asserted by the boatmen to be the Bahr-el-Arab and which was ascended under this supposition, flows in a north-westerly direction and evidently brings water from a long distance. Later experience has proved that the Bahr-el-Arab is several kilometres further upstream, but this khor must, nevertheless, bring down a large volume of water during the flood (²). It is quite possible that it forms a second mouth of the Bahr-el-Arab. It joins the Bahr-el-Ghazal through two small lakes, or lagoons, the largest about 1000 metres long by 800 wide, with an island in the centre. These lakes are swarming with hippopotami. The width of this "khor" is much greater than that of the Ghazal, being from 100 to 120 metres. It has a perceptible, though feeble, current, even in April, but its depth is shallow, averaging from 1·25 to 1·75 metres. It was ascended for some 13 kilometres above the junction, when shoal-water prevented further progress. Its general direction is north-west, but at the furthest point reached it turns sharply to the north, and its course can be traced for a long distance, winding through the country. Even here, its width is 100 metres, with wide-stretching mud-flats on either side. It runs between flat plains, covered with low grass, and averaging 0·70 metres over the water at the river's edge. It differs remarkably from the Ghazal in its characteristics, particularly in the absence of the reed fringe which distinguishes the main river. Its rise must be small, as the banks show no trace of flooding.

From 8 kilometres above the junction, a succession of Dinka villages lines both banks. Some of these are large, and appear to be thickly peopled. The principal village is called

(¹) Felkin crossed the Jau in October 1879. He gives the velocity as 1¼ miles an hour, and the width 420 feet; unfortunately, he does not give the depth.

(²) It seems evident from Marno's survey and map that this cannot be the Bahr-el-Arab. It is, however, such an important "khor," that it is curious it was not remarked by him.

Lau. This consists of a large collection of scattered huts, grouped together, and covering a large area. The Dinka suffered severely from the scarcity which ruled in 1900, and from the loss of their maize crop. They used to be extremely shy and fled at the approach of a steamer, but have now gained confidence and gladly accept the flesh of a hippopotamus, if one is killed. It would be interesting to explore this "khor" during high water, and ascertain whether it really is one of the outlets of the Arab river.

To return to the Bahr-el-Ghazal. From the point where this "khor" joins it, the general course is due west and fairly straight, with occasional long curves. It is bordered by a narrow strip of papyrus on either bank and traverses a country of flat, grassy plains. This river is placid and sluggish, throughout its entire length, and can never approach anything like a torrent, even when in flood. It meanders along slowly and gradually sucking away the moisture of the vast, water-logged flats through which it passes. Its width averages from 60 to 70 metres and its mean depth is 3·5 metres. At kilometre 136, trees and bush are found upon both sides. The banks are clear of reeds and continue, until kilometre 140, where the Bahr-el-Arab joins the Ghazal. This forest is known as the "Ghaba b'ta el Arab," and is one of the few wooding stations to be found on the river. The trees upon both banks are different from those found elsewhere. There are a few mimosas, but the bulk are very thorny trees, with bright green-leaves. The belt of wood extends for about a kilometre in width, back from the river. Behind it are open spaces of grass, through which broad and shallow lagoons wind. In this plain are many large clumps of trees. Except in the depressions, the country here is certainly not flooded, even in the rainy season. The marks on the banks show that the maximum rise of the river is not more than one metre.

The Bahr-el-Arab is a broad, well-defined channel, from 80 to 100 metres in width, and confined between well-marked banks. Its direction, at the junction, is due north, but, about 4·5 kilometres further up, it turns more to the west, and runs apparently through forest (1). It is impossible to investigate this river, as at some 1300 metres above the junction, it is closed by "sudd" and reeds. It has no current at the mouth and its depth is from 3, to 3·5 metres at low water. The water of the Bahr-el-Arab is singularly clear, and free from sediment.

Immediately upstream of the Bahr-el-Arab junction, the Lake Kit, or Ambadi, begins. The Bahr-el-Ghazal traverses this lake, but, from this point, its nomenclature changes and the river is known as the "Kit," or "Keit," by the natives, and as such is entered on many maps. At kilometre 421, Lake Ambadi is divided into two parts by a large grassy island, about 1 ½ kilometres in length, the right channel being 400 metres, and the left 150 metres wide. Half-way up the right channel, the large Mayyeh, Ahmed Arabi, previously alluded to, rejoins the Bahr-el-Ghazal. It has a width of 500 to 600 metres here. The swamps surrounding this lake are of considerable breath, especially on the left side. They are very low and reedy and a very small rise in the water-levels must increase the flooded area enormously. It is impossible to calculate the width of the swamps on the left bank. They appear to extend for many kilometres from the water's edge.

Lake Ambadi has an average depth of 3 metres, in the deepest parts of the channel, but shoals rapidly on either side. It is evidently the great reservoir of the Bahr-el-Ghazal, receiving the waters of the swamps and southern rivers, and slowly discharging them by means of the narrow, but deep, channel of the Ghazal itself. At low water, it has a length of about 16 kilometres, by an average breath of 1 ½ kilometres; in flood time, the area must be very much greater. It is a great nursery for certain of the "sudd" grasses, but chiefly those of the "swimming" variety. The "Agolla," "Utricularia," "Aldrovandia," "Otellia," and many other kinds are found upon its waters. The "Pistia"

(1) Next to nothing is known of this river. Felkin crossed it in December 1879, and found it 360 feet wide, with banks 15 feet above low water. He noted that in the rainy season, it flooded the surrounding country.

is conspicuous by its absence. Among the reeds in the swamps, a certain amount of "Vossia Procera," and "Saccharum Spontaneum" is met with, but not in such proportions as on the Bahr-el-Gebel.

The papyrus does not exist on this lake, nor does the ambatch. Except between kilometres 32 and 108, the former is not found at all on the Bahr-el-Ghazal, and it only grows in real luxuriance between kilometres 80 and 100. After Lake No is passed, ambatch also disappears from the Bahr-el-Ghazal. The absence of papyrus and "Um-soof" is probably the reason why the "sudd" in this river is so much less tenacious and so much lighter in consistency, than that of the Bahr-el-Gebel. Lake Ambadi is the home of large numbers of the rare "Balœniceps Rex."

The evaporation upon the lake must be very great, during the hottest months. With two large and shallow sheets of water, like Lakes Ambadi and No, the amount of water discharged by the Bahr-el-Ghazal must be largely reduced before it reaches the White Nile.

At kilometre 158, the lake stops and the river recommences. This is the Kit, properly so-called. Its width here is from 100 to 120 metres, and its depth 3 to 3½ metres. The current is so feeble as to be almost imperceptible. The Bahr-el-Homr comes in near this point (1). It appears to have no discharge in March and April, and the water shoals so that it is impossible to explore it.

From kilometres 158 to 162, the Kit has a mean width of 180 metres. The water-surface suddenly narrows to a width of 20 metres, the remainder of the channel being filled by "sudd." In this block are several reedy islands. The country is now a dead flat in every direction. Even on these African rivers, it is rare to see an expanse giving a greater impression of flatness than does this. On all sides, marshes extend, apparently to the horizon. It is quite impossible to arrive at an idea of their area. In these marshes are many large lagoons. A little further upstream, the channel widens again from 35 to 40 metres, with a depth varying from 3 to 4 metres. Occasionally it shoals to 2 metres, or less, probably owing to sunken "sudd" upon the bed. Navigation, at all seasons, must be very difficult, as the river winds and twists through the marshes. There are no tall reeds here; nothing but floating plants, and the water is choked with masses of decayed weed. It is a hopeless morass. During stormy weather, this place is one of those where blocks are often formed. There are no signs of life anywhere, with the exception of the "Balœniceps Rex," which are numerous. These horrible marshes continue for another 10 or 12 kilometres. "Sudd" islands separate the channel, in places, and the width varies greatly.

At one point of this reach, viz., at kilometre 169, the main channel of the Kit was quite closed in March 1900. The entire river was forced through a small opening, 10 or 12 metres wide, through which a strong stream was rushing and, in one place, it was actually barred for 50 metres. The total length of the block was about 500 metres. A more loathsome-looking swamp it is difficult to imagine. The "sudd" in this river is very different from that of the Bahr-el-Gebel. It is impossible to walk on its surface, which resembles slime, rather than "sudd," but which is bound into a mass by vegetable matter. The chief ingredients appear to be the long, trailing, swimming plants, described as found on Lake Ambadi. It is not difficult to force a way through it, but the stuff, when removed, does not float as does that on the Gebel, but sinks and decays. Opposite kilometre 174, the two groups of trees called Matruk-el-Baboor ("the landing-place of the steamers,") (*vide* Junker) are passed on the left, about 3 kilometres from the main stream. A channel, at present blocked by "sudd," leads to the landing-place. Matruk-el-Baboor is an island of dry land in a sea of swamp. When Major Peake visited it in 1898, the remains of the former French occupation were visible. The Egyptian flag was hoisted here on the 28th September, 1898.

(1) On the 1st October, 1900, the late Captain Sanders found the Bahr-el-Homr navigable for 8 kilometres, after which it was blocked by "sudd." Its width is 80 yards, and depth 6 metres; direction N.N.W.

Upstream of this point, for another 8 kilometres, the Kit winds about; the width of the channel increases, averaging from 180 to 200 metres; its surface is covered by myriads of water-fowl, the whistling duck being especially numerous. A few Dinka are to be seen, who come down to the river for the purpose of fishing, and hunting the hippopotamus. At kilometre 182, the channel bifurcates. The Kit itself runs due south, in the direction of Meshra-er-Rek. The other branch has a westerly direction, and receives the water of the Jur river, which again, forms the outlet for the Swei and Wau rivers.

The latitude of this junction, as observed in April 1900, was 8° 44′ 50″ north. The distance of the Meshra from this point is uncertain, but it was probably not very many miles away. The observations for the latitude of the Meshra-er-Rek vary considerably. In March 1863, Von Heuglin's observations were as follows :—

On	1st	March.	Latitude	8° 35′ 5″	north.
„	11th	„	„	8° 49′ 2″	„
„	13th	„	„	8° 35′ 2″	„
„	15th	„	„	8° 45′ 5″	„

The mean of these four observations, is 8° 41′ 35″ north and, if Heuglin's figures are correct, Meshra-er-Rek must be situated within a very few miles of the separation of the rivers Kit and Jur. Against this, Lupton Bey observed the latitude in 1869, making it 8° 17′ 30″ north. Lastly, Lieutenant Fell, R.N., observed it in November 1900, and gives it as 8° 24′ 12″. In any case, the Meshra cannot be very far from the point of junction, as the Dinka pointed out what they stated was the Kit island, and offered to show the way to the landing-place. The water, however, at the time (April 1900), was so shallow, that it was impossible for the steamer to ascend the channel, the width of which was from 600 to 700 metres, with a depth of 0·90 metres. The water coming down this stream was of a dark amber colour and was evidently the drainage of the marshes. A slight current was visible. The general direction of the Kit is south or south-west. It must at all times be difficult for a steamer to ascend this channel, and the natives state that for five months of the year it is dry. The late Captain Sanders, who visited this place in September 1900, found the Kit completely blocked by "sudd"; but Lieutenant Fell, R.N., ascended it in November of the same year, and reports that the water near the Meshra was "foul, stagnant, and very shallow." In March 1900, the "sudd" was very light, mostly floating, and easily removed.

Above this junction, the expanse of water into which the Jur discharges itself, has a width of 400 metres, a depth of 3 metres, and a fair velocity, even in the month of March. The marshes here, are bewildering in their extent. A few kilometres further up—i.e., at 190 kilometres from the junction of the Ghazal with the Khor Deleb—the water shoaled so rapidly that further progress was then impossible. This river has, however, since been repeatedly explored, and, at the time of writing, Colonel Sparkes's party is engaged in clearing the "sudd" in this channel, with a view to rendering it navigable as far as Wau, which place it is proposed to make the head-quarters of the Bahr-el-Ghazal Province (¹). The Jur, or Swei, joins this lagoon about 56 kilometres above the point where the steamer was stopped by shoal-water, in March 1900. Lieutenant Drury, R.N., who ascended the Jur in November 1900, describes it as a fine river, with a width of 60 to 70 metres, a depth of 3 to 3·5 metres, and a current of 2 knots an hour. This would be equivalent to an approximate discharge of 170 metres cube per second. It was at that time blocked by sudd some 18 to 20 kilometres further up. The Jur receives the waters of the Swei and Wau, both of which are important rivers. The former was the course followed by M. Marchand, in his journey to the White Nile; and Felkin, who crossed the Wau in October 1879, gives its width as 240 feet, and its velocity as 2 knots an hour. It is

(¹) In 1904, this work has so far advanced that it is expected to complete it before the flood of this year. It will, practically, be a new river channel that has been excavated.

THE BAHR EL GHAZAL
BLOCKED BY GRASS SUDD, 1903

THE BAHR EL ZARAF

evident from the foregoing that the Jur river must be the chief source from which the Bahr-el-Ghazal derives its supply. The volume of water brought down from the high plateaux must be largely diminished long before it reaches the Nile, owing to the low slope of the country and the enormous extent of the marshes traversed in its course.

This place, during the rainy season, must resemble an inland sea. Even in March 1900, after a failure of the annual rainfall, and with the river lower than it had been for years, it was a large lake, full of grassy islands. Swamp surrounds it in every direction. To the north alone trees are apparent, at some 5 kilometres from the river. These would seem to indicate the existence of higher land. Approach is impossible, owing to the intervening marshes.

The rivers which form the Bahr-el-Ghazal system more resemble large drainage depressions than anything else. Owing to their low slope, their velocity and discharge, even in flood, must be insignificant. Under no circumstances can the Bahr-el-Ghazal play an important part in the annual Nile flood. It certainly acts as a large reservoir, which slowly drains away, as the level of Lake No falls, and which is, consequently, a factor in preserving a constant supply in the Nile during the summer months.

The Bahr-el-Zaraf.

The principal channel by which the Bahr-el-Zaraf is fed leaves the Bahr-el-Gebel at 383 kilometres south of Lake No, and 8 kilometres downstream of Ghaba Shambé, in latitude 7° 6′ 22″ north. The water passes from the Nile into the Bahr-el-Zaraf by several outlets, but a large portion of its supply is derived from the drainage of the marshes which commence at Bor, and which form the eastern boundary of the Bahr-el-Gebel for a great portion of its course. Into these marshes, the latter river pours its waters, by a countless series of small openings in the bank. Even in summer, the amount of water thus wasted is very great and, in flood, the whole area becomes a lake. The outlet of this lake is the Bahr-el-Zaraf. A certain portion of this water thus finds its way back into the White Nile, as the Bahr-el-Zaraf rejoins the latter in latitude 9° 53′ 17″ north, 76 kilometres downstream of Lake No. In addition to the supply which this river receives from the Nile, it is also fed by the accumulated discharge of a series of large "khors" rising in the Latuka hills, such as the "Khor Too," the "Khor Khos," and the "Khor Kanieti." This last, which is an important stream during flood, apparently receives the united waters of the others. It flows through some two degrees of latitude and is described by Sir Samuel Baker as having abrupt banks, with a bed 5 metres below ground surface, and a width of some 50 metres. During flood, this "khor" must carry a large volume of water, but, in summer, it shrinks to very small dimensions. There is still considerable uncertainty as to its outfall, as the existing maps show it as stopping a little south of Bor. Mr. Grogan (1) is of opinion that it does not discharge its water into the Bahr-el-Zaraf, giving as his reasons the statement made to him by the natives that no water comes in east of the Nile for a long distance from Bor. This is a point which requires to be cleared up. These "khors" undoubtedly drain a large area of country, and their main line of flood is apparently parallel to the eastern banks of the Nile, within about half a degree of longitude (2).

Not much is known regarding the country traversed by the Bahr-el-Zaraf. It has been visited by but few travellers, and those who have ascended it by boat have been unable to land on either side owing to the swamps. To the east, grass plains extend, apparently as far as the Sobat (3). On the west, i.e., in the large island bounded by the loop made by the Zaraf with the Nile, swamps cover the southern area, and

(1) "From the Cape to Cairo," by E.S. Grogan. Hurst and Blackett, London, 1900.

(2) Recent information is to the effect that there may be a *possible* connection between Bor and the Sobat, by the "Khor" Filus, which runs into the latter river from the south. This has not yet been verified, and the report is only based upon the statement of the natives.

(3) See Appendix No. VI and map.

bush forests the northern region. Undoubtedly a ridge, of comparatively high land, does exist between the Bahr-el-Zaraf and the Bahr-el-Gebel, as glimpses of large trees and palms, which probably indicate the sites of villages, are visible from time to time, although at a long distance from either river. The inhabitants of this tract belong to the Nuer tribe. For a great portion of the year, they must be completely isolated, surrounded as they are upon every side by a wide expanse of almost impassable swamp. A very noticeable fact in the Bahr-el-Zaraf is the absence of almost any sign of human habitation for some 160 kilometres above its junction with the White Nile.

The difference in the flood-levels attained in the Zaraf, in the years 1899 and 1900, was very remarkable. In the former, the water spread over the country to an indefinite distance. The marks upon the tree-trunks show that the water must have covered the land adjoining to a height of nearly 1 metre. All trace of a river must, at that time, have been lost, and the entire area must have resembled a lake. In 1900, on the contrary, the flood water barely topped the river banks, except in the southern reaches where the banks are very low. The supply brought down by the Zaraf in that year must have been insignificant, as compared with that of 1899. The failure of the rains in the Upper Nile Valley is not an explanation of this fact. The drought in that region was as severe in 1899 as it was in 1900. The most plausible theory appears to be, that, the northern reaches of the Bahr-el-Gebel being blocked by "sudd," the flood waters of the upper Nile found their passage barred, and sought for some other outlet. The Bahr-el-Zaraf, offering an easy line for their escape, received a supply beyond its capacity to carry and consequently the water overflowed its banks and covered the adjoining country to an immence distanse. In 1900 a large portion of the "sudd" in the Bahr-el-Gebel had been removed and the flood waters, following the line of least resistance, selected this river rather than the Zaraf, for their discharge outlet. Consequently, the flood in the Bahr-el-Zaraf was an insignificant one and not much more than the channel was able to carry. If this theory be correct, it would seem probable that the Bahr-el-Zaraf, if left to itself, supposing the Bahr-el-Gebel be kept clear of "sudd," will gradually shrink to small limits and lose its importance as a relief channel for the flood-waters of the upper Nile. (1)

In order to describe this river, it will be necessary to commence at its junction with the White Nile and work upstream.

The width of the Bahr-el-Zaraf, at the point where it joins the Nile, is not more than 35 metres, but the channel widens a little higher up. It joins the Nile nearly at a right angle, and its waters, in the winter and spring, are held back for a very considerable distance from its mouth by those of the main river. No current at all is perceptible for some 10 to 11 kilometres above the junction and, for a long way upstream, the velocity is very feeble. The colour of the Bahr-el-Zaraf water is a slaty-grey and it is not transparent like that of the White Nile. It has a fair depth, averaging at low water, 6 metres. About 200 metres above the mouth, the channel turns sharply to the west. The west bank is, in general, higher than the east. The country, for many kilometres above the junction, is a wide plain of grass. At intervals, this is covered with mimosa forest. At certain points, this forest approaches the river, but, at times, recedes to a considerable distance. The flood-marks of 1899 showed a rise of 2·5 metres over the summer levels. The ground on the east bank is high at the river's edge, and slopes gradually away from the channel for about one kilometre. At this distance, a broad depression extends, similar to that which is found on the Sobat river, but rather less marked. On the west, this depression is not visible, the country extending in a flat slope, from the banks of the Zaraf to the swamp bordering the White Nile. Many wide and deep "khors" discharge on either bank, draining the country for a long distance. On the west, they are more numerous and more important than on the east.

The Bahr-el-Zaraf runs parallel to the White Nile for many kilometres, but eventually turns off in a south-easterly direction. Its windings are extraordinary. There are very few

(1) See Appendix No. VI.

straight reaches and the further it is ascended the more abrupt are the curves. The average width between the banks is from 50 to 60 metres and that of the water surface in summer from 30 to 35 metres. The banks are steep, with side slopes of ½ to 1, and their height varies from 2, to 2½ metres, over the summer water-level. But few villages are to be seen and there is a complete absence of any life on the banks. With the exception of the "sudd," region, the country traversed by the Bahr-el-Zaraf is, perhaps, the dreariest in appearance of any of the tracts bordering the White Nile and its affluents. On either side extend dry mud-flats and blackened plains of burnt grass. As a rule, these plains are treeless, and nothing breaks the monotony of the scenery.

For some distance above the junction, the four isolated hills, known as the Gebel-Zaraf, form a striking land-mark, as they rise above the flat plain. These granite masses, which are covered with scrub to a certain height, are situated some 9 kilometres on the east of the river. Their tops are conical, or rounded, and one of them, the highest, has two low peaks. At 27 kilometres from the mouth, a large Nuer village is situated on the west, at a distance from the river; large herds of cattle graze on the plain. This village is noticeable as being almost the only one met with on the river. The trees in the adjoining forests appear to be, as a rule, extremely young. Few of them are more than 0·30 metres in girth. Possibly the annual fires may account for this. The damage done to these forests by elephants is incredible. Their march can be easily traced by the broken trees. They break off the tops and main branches, until they produce the effect of a cut-and-laid hedge. These animals must be very numerous in this locality, as their tracks to the water are continuous. At 50 kilometres, a very large and long "khor" enters the river from the east. The bends here are sharper than ever. Nuers are now occasionally seen on the banks, but they have evidently come from a long distance in search of food, in the shape of fish. They are very shy and wild, and wave their hands with a peculiarly deprecating gesture, as the steamer passes. Neither the hippopotamus nor the crocodile appears to inhabit this portion of the Bahr-el-Zaraf.

The "khors" continue on both sides and these depressions, in a year like 1900 or 1901 must act as drains to an immense area of country. At 64 kilometres from the mouth, the forest and bush extends on either bank, for a considerable way. The trees are now smaller than was the case further north and the bush also is thinner. The water in the flood of 1899 must have stood quite 1 metre above the country. The average depth of the river in summer at this point is from 2·5 to 3 metres, but the water shoals at each of the numerous bends to considerably less than the above. This fact, with the sharpness of the curves, makes navigation of this river, for anything but a small boat, very difficult. At the 80th kilometre, a very large "khor" comes in on the west bank. It is dry at the point of junction with the river, but water is visible at some little distance. The banks at this point were from 1·75 to 2 metres above water-level (in March). The marks on the trees show that the depth of the river, during the flood of 1899, must have been from 6 to 7 metres. In the flood of 1900 the depth was much less and could not have exceeded 5 metres. On the other hand, the depth at low water in March and April of 1901 was some 0·60 metres higher than during the same period of 1900.

From kilometre 88, the real marsh country commences and continues, without a break, to the point where the Zaraf river takes off from the Bahr-el-Gebel, i.e., for a distance of some 370 kilometres. The bush and forest end here and the country consists of extensive grass plains, interspersed by large dry lagoons. The banks get lower as the river is ascended. The width between the banks varies from 40 to 45 metres and the average depth is 2·5 metres. The stream also is less strong and the whole aspect of the river is rather that of a sluggish drain, than of an important branch of the Nile. There are occasional high spots, even in this dreary waste of marsh. At kilometre 90, a fair-sized Nuer village is situated at about 1½ kilometres from the east bank of the river. To the west the swamping extends as far as the ridge lying between the Bahr-el-Zaraf and the Bahr-el-Gebel. At what distance this high land is situated, it is impossible to estimate. To the east, marshes extend to the horizon and, during the rainy season, they must cover a large area, The curves are so bad that, although the general direction of the stream is from the south, a boat ascending the river not infrequently has her bows pointing to the north, when rounding some of the sharpest bends.

This country is a hopeless expanse of swamp. Even the game appears to avoid this treeless waste which, for more than half the year, must be a marsh. At kilometre 104, it was found impossible in 1900 to proceed any further upstream. From this point the river shoaled rapidly and the bends got worse and worse.

Those who have ascended further ([1]) state that there is little or no change in the general conditions, except that the banks get lower and lower, and that eventually all semblance of a river disappears, until at 280 kilometres from the mouth, a large lake, or series of lakes, is encountered. These in 1898 were full of "sudd." They apparently extend up to the point where the Zaraf leaves the Bahr-el-Gebel, near Ghaba Shambé.

At kilometre 237, a "khor," or branch, comes in from the east, bringing a good deal of water. This may be the "khor" which Mr. Grogan ([2]) considers to be a possible connection with the Sobat. At kilometre 257, the "Moghren-el-Buhur-el-Zaraf," or "Meeting of the Zaraf Rivers," is reached. Two branches join at this point. One comes from the south-east, commencing in a large lagoon; the other runs due south and ends in the lakes already mentioned.

The only travellers who have, since Sir Samuel Baker's journey in 1871, explored the Bahr-el-Zaraf from end to end, are Mr. Grogan and Commandant Henri, of the Congo Free State Service. The former has described the river in his interesting book ([3]). The latter ascended it by boats, in February and March 1900. At that time, the water was so low, that, for the last 110 kilometres, he had to drag his boats over the dry marshes. This portion of his journey took him a month. He states that no channel at all exists through this portion of the swamps, but that shallow lagoons, in which he was able to float his boats, were occasionally met with. For the greater portion of the distance, however, they were hauled over dry land. It may then be taken for granted that, for the first 100 kilometres of its course, after leaving the Bahr-el-Gebel, the Bahr-el-Zaraf has no defined channel. It consists of a series of extensive marshes, which are sheets of water during the flood, and reedy swamps during the season of low supply. Below this point, a channel does exist and forms the drain for these marshes.

The eastern boundary of these swamps would appear to be the long "mayyeh," or lagoon, which leaves the Nile near Bor, and joins the Bahr-el-Zaraf some 230 kilometres further north. This channel, Mr. Grogan has christened the "Gertrude" Nile. Beyond it, to the east, he describes the country as being thickly populated by the Dinka tribe ([4]).

The Sobat.

The inspection lately made of this river, only extended to a distance of 50 kilometres upstream of its junction with the White Nile. The present note will consequently be a very brief one.

Allusion has been already made to the strong contrast between the colour of the water in the two rivers. That of the Sobat is, at times, a creamy white, and at others a

([1]) Major Peake and Captain Stanton in 1898, and Commandant Henri in 1900.

([2]) "From the Cape to Cairo." London, 1900.

([3]) Ibid.

([4]) Captain Liddell, R.E., of the Soudan telegraph service, has lately found a channel which would appear to correspond to Mr. Grogan's "Gertrude" Nile. It is described as flowing north, with a strong stream, and the Dinka state that it joins the Bahr-el-Zaraf near a village called Twi. See Appendix No. VI.

THE SOBAT RIVER
FROM DOLEIB HILLA

THE SOBAT RIVER
LOOKING DOWNSTREAM

they obstructed the channel in a very different manner from what had been generally supposed. Again, the nature of the "sudd" in the Bahr-el-Ghazal differs considerably from that in the Bahr-el-Gebel, and a visit to the former river alone gave an erroneous idea of the "sudd" in the latter.

In the Bahr-el-Gebel the main factors are the papyrus, the "Bus," and the "Um-soof" reeds. These three, with the earth adhering to their roots, form the real obstruction. Many of the smaller swimming plants, such as the "Azolla," the "Utricularia," and the "Otellia" are mingled with the others; but they certainly do not play an important part in the formation of the obstacle. The ambatch, too, has been unjustly accused of assisting in forming the barrier. This is not the case. This plant does not grow in any great quantity in the vicinity of the Bahr-el-Gebel, and its stem is so light and brittle, that it would break when subjected to great pressure.

On the Bahr-el-Ghazal, on the contrary, the "sudd" is chiefly composed of the swimming plants above mentioned. Their breeding places are Lake Ambadi and the other shallow lakes to the south.

The Ghazal "sudd" is much lighter in texture than that of the Gebel, and is consequently much easier to remove. At the same time, even in the former river, the "sudd" is at times dangerous, especially if it forms downstream of a vessel, and if the latter has to work upon it from its upstream end. The accident to Gessi Pasha's expedition in 1880 proves that even the Bahr-el-Ghazal "sudd" can be an impassable obstacle under such circumstances.

Before alluding to the work done in removing the "sudd," it may be as well to say a few words as to the principal causes of this remarkable barrier.

The Bahr-el-Gebel traverses the marshes, between Shambé and Lake No, for some 400 kilometres of its course. South of Shambé, the river has never been known to be blocked. On either side of the channel, in these immense swamps, extend large shallow lagoons, some of them covering several square kilometres of area. These lagoons are surrounded on every side by a luxuriant growth of aquatic plants, consisting chiefly of the papyrus, and the reeds known to the Arabs as the "Um-soof" and the "Bus" (1). All these plants grow in water, but not in any great depth. The "Um-soof" and "Bus," again, will not stand such a depth of water as will the papyrus. This last attains a height of from 5 to 6 metres, with fibrous roots which strike deep into the ground. The "Um-soof" rarely exceeds 1.5 metres in height, and its roots do not extend so deeply as do those of the papyrus. They are, however, very tough and difficult to break or cut through. These roots are bedded in the soil below the water, but the strong gales which blow in these regions, loosen their hold to a large extent. If such a storm be accompanied by any rise of the water-surface, large masses of these plants are set free from their original position, and begin to float on the surface of the lagoons. Their roots form such a tangled mass, that large quantities of the earth in which they were embedded, remain clinging to them. These act as ballast and, when the island of papyrus, or reeds is detached and, under the influence of the wind, is set drifting about the lagoon, the weight of this earth retains the plants in their vertical position. Their roots, the moment they reach a shallow, act as anchors, and speedily strike down again into the muddy bottom of the lake. Large masses constantly change their position in this way. If the storms cease, they remain where they are. Unfortunately, at the commencement and end of the rainy season, stormy weather is the rule, rather than the exception. At such seasons, large areas of the marsh vegetation are in motion, driven hither and thither by the wind.

The Bahr-el-Gebel has no banks whatever and is, as a rule, separated from the lagoons merely by a narrow belt of papyrus. In many places, it is in connection with them, and

(1) "Un Soof," *i.e.*, "the mother of wool." The Latin names of these plants are, according to Mr. Broun, Director of the Sudan Forests, for the "Um Soof," "Panicum Pyramidale," and for the "Bus," "Phragmites communis."

the water of the lakes flows in and out of the river, according to the level of the latter. As the stormy season in these latitudes heralds the approach of the annual rains, the rise of the river follows very speedily. The channel of the Bahr-el-Gebel being only of sufficient section to carry the low-water supply, with the first rise in the levels, the river spreads over the marshes, flooding them in all directions and increasing the depth of water in the lagoons. It thus causes the areas of reed, already detached by the wind, to float still more easily. The continuous gales which prevail set hundreds of acres of these floating masses moving in one direction. Eventually, they reach a point on the river where they are forced into the channel. Once there, the current speedily carries them downstream. Ere long, their course is arrested by a projection on the edge of the channel, or by a sharp bend. It may happen that an area of reed, several acres in extent, bursts into the river in a large sheet, and, in such a case, it must necessarily be arrested at the first point where the section is contracted. The result is, that the channel is quickly blocked, though, perhaps, not at first to any great depth. Masses of weed, however, follow one another in succession, brought down by the stream. The section of the channel being reduced by the first obstruction, the velocity of the water rapidly increases and these masses, following the easiest course, pass under the obstacle thus created. Each fresh mass arriving is sucked underneath those originally arrested, until at last, the whole becomes wedged into one solid block, composed partly of earth and partly of stalks and roots of papyrus and reed, broken up by the extreme compression into an inextricable tangle. So great is the pressure applied by the water, that the surface of the block is often forced several metres above the water-level, and is seamed by alternate ridges and furrows. The thickness varies greatly, according to the conditions and section of the channel. In some cases, it is not more than 1.5 to 2 metres, but it not infrequently obtains a thickness of 5 metres below water, and occasionally as much as 7 metres have been observed. Underneath this bar, the river manages to force an outlet, but with a velocity increased proportionately to the smallness of the aperture. At the same time, the upstream level rises, flooding the marshes in every direction, the water making use of any side channel that it can find. In time, doubtless, if left to itself, it would desert its original course and the stream would take an entirely new direction, the original channel becoming permanently blocked. It generally, however, happens from natural causes, such as strong winds, or increased heading-up of the water, that these blocks burst, and the obstacle is carried away. On such occasions, a great wave passes down the channel, carrying everything before it, and sweeping away any similar blocks which may have been formed downstream. Only in this way, can the self clearance of the "sudd" in certain years, which has undoubtedly occurred, be explained. Many of these blocks extend for a considerable length, some being as much as 1700 metres long. It is easy to understand that such closures of the river channel cause not only a complete bar to navigation, but also a very serious obstacle to the free passage of the water. More than this, each block thus formed assists in the formation of others, by raising the water-level upstream, and thus assisting the flotation of further areas of papyrus and reed, much of which eventually finds its way into the river.

The movement of these great masses of weed and the way in which they burst into the river bears a striking resemblance to the descriptions given of an ice-field, when in motion. Their steady and resistless movement, the manner in which the fields break up, and the way in which they pile upon one another when an obstruction is encountered to their course, recall irresistibly what travellers relate of the action of the ice-floes, when the pack is breaking up.

The "sudd" in this river and, in a less degree, that in the Bahr-el-Ghazal constitute a very real danger to navigation. Should a steamer happen to be surrounded by it, when the masses are in motion, the compression would certainly strain her framework, to the risk of crushing it. Even should she escape this, she will most probably be imprisoned for an indefinite time, owing to the river blocking on either side of her. During the stormy season, it should, if possible, always be arranged that two steamers should work in conjunction, one remaining downstream, so as to be able to go to the assistance of the other if necessary.

As no fuel is to be met with throughout the whole length of the "sudd" region, a solitary steamer, if detained for some time by a block, may find herself eventually prevented from proceeding, or from making any attempt to free herself, owing to the absence of any means of generating steam in her boilers.

The Bahr-el-Ghazal "sudd" is, as has been said, of a different kind to that of the Bahr-el-Gebel. It is, as a rule, much lighter in consistency and easier to remove. This is doubtless due to the fact that the velocity of this river is very low and, consequently, the pressure exerted by the water upon a block is small, compared with that caused by similar conditions in the Bahr-el-Gebel. Again, on the Bahr-el-Ghazal, the papyrus and reeds do not extend on either side to any distance, nor are continuous and large lagoons close at hand. Between kilometres 67 and 78, upstream of the junction with the Khor Deleb, there must, it is true, be always a risk of a block. In this reach, the river passes through papyrus swamps, which are miniature editions of the Gebel marshes. Even here, however, the obstruction can hardly attain to the same solidity as in the case of the Gebel "sudd," as the sluggish current of the Ghazal would fail to wedge the mass between the banks, as tightly as would the rapid stream of the other river. Lake Ambadi appears to be a great nursery for the smaller varieties of the "sudd" plants. In the beginning of the rainy season, these are carried downstream and, as the channel wanders and twists, they form small obstructions. None of these, however, appear to be lasting and it is rare that the Ghazal river is blocked for any length of time. It may be closed for a few months and then reopen itself. Thus, in Marchand April 1900, it was clear throughout its entire length, while in September, of the same year, it was blocked in more than one place. On this river, as on the Gebel, the "sudd" frequently sinks to the bottom and decomposes, gradually raising the bed of the channel. In this state it is very hard to remove.

Major Peake has fully described his "sudd"-cutting operations in a report to the Intelligence Department of the Egyptian War Office. I will only allude to his work very briefly. His party left Omdurman on the 16th December, 1899. By the 27th of March, 1900, they had removed fourteen blocks of "sudd," in a length of 131 kilometres of river. The lengths of obstruction, actually cleared by the party, amounted to nearly 8000 metres; but this does not at all represent the total length of "sudd" previously existing, as blocks Nos. 4, 8, and 14, broke away of themselves.

The thickness of the "sudd" varied much. In some blocks, it was only 2 metres, in others 5 and, occasionally, 6 metres.

The party worked with five gun-boats and a gang of 800 Dervish prisoners, guarded by 100 Soudanese. With them were five English and several Egyptian officers; also some English non-commissioned officers. The total cube removed was some 11850 cubic metres, but this does not include the large amount of stuff that came away by itself. How great this must have been, may be judged by the fact that, in one instance, when a block burst, the floating weed took thirty-six hours to pass a given point.

Major Peake states that the three most northerly blocks, viz., Nos. 1, 2, and 3, were the toughest and the thickest of all those removed by him. After these three had been cleared, the work became easier and the last four blocks, i.e., from Nos. 11 to 14, were very thin. The real block in the Gebel, or "plug," as it may be termed, occurred in the first 27 kilometres from the junction with the White Nile. Block No. 3 was incomparably the worst. It averaged over 6 metres in thickness and held up a large amount of water. This was proved by the fact that, after its removal, the upstream river-level fell 1·5 metres, in four days. This block was removed on the 7th of February. Its clearance drained the water as far as block No. 7, or to kilometre 81·5. On the 24th of February this block burst, bringing with it block No. 8. The large lagoons upstream of these blocks began draining into the river in consequence. Upstream of No. 8, the "sudd" was lighter and less water was held up. Block No. 10, which afterwards gave so much trouble, did not present any special difficulties at the time of its first removal.

The last block, viz., No. 14, was removed on the 27th of March, and this closed the work for the season of 1899-1900. Owing to the approach of the rainy season, it was deemed advisable to withdraw the men from the swamps. At this time, as far as was then known, there only remained two more blocks of "sudd" in the entire length of the Bahr-el-Gebel. These were registered as Nos. 15 and 16. The former is a long reach of river, apparently closed by "sudd," throughout the entire length of 36 kilometres (1). The latter was, at the time, supposed to be only some 5 kilometres long. As a matter of fact, it proved, when cleared, to be nearly 12 kilometres in length. This last block was removed in the month of January 1901 by Lieutenant Drury, R.N., with the assistance of one English sergeant of marines. It consisted of four separate blocks of "sudd," Nos. 16 to 19, the smallest being 600 metres in length, and the largest, 2 kilometres. Some of these blocks were very thick, and had evidently existed for a long time. Lieutenant Drury endeavoured to break up the mass of block No. 19, by means of explosives. The nitro-glycerine, however, was of little use, merely making deep holes, and having no further effect. The "sudd," although compact, is very elastic and has not sufficient resistance to permit of the full force of the charge being felt. There is little doubt that the most effectual way of removing the "sudd" is that practised by Major Peake, viz., cutting the surface into rectangular blocks, hauling these out by steamers, and then letting them float downstream.

There now remains only one block in the whole length of the river, viz., No. 15, with a length of some 36 kilometres. This block offers special difficulties to removal, inasmuch as there is no current in the channel. The bed, moreover, is filled to a considerable depth by "sudd," which has sunk to the bottom and rotted. All this stuff has to be towed out into the stream, and the work is necessarily very slow. In 1900, Lieutenant Drury attempted to force an entrance into his channel. In fourteen days he only cleared 400 metres, which have since closed again (2).

Since 1901, there have been no traces whatever, of the blocks removed by Major Peake. The work was well and thoroughly done and, if continual supervision be given, more especially during the stormy season of the year, there appears to be no reason why the Bahr-el-Gebel should not be kept permanently open.

It is difficult to speak too highly of the work done by him and his staff in 1900. The climate of the region in which this work lay, is extremely unhealthy and the damp heat is very trying. The mosquitoes, at night are almost unendurable. Owing to the exceptionally low river, during the winter and spring months, transport of supplies was rendered extremely difficult and, for several months, the expedition was pratically cut off from all communication with Omdurman. The locality was, moreover, very remote, as Lake No, the point where this work began, is 962 kilometres from Khartoum.

Major Peake, and all who served with him, may well be proud of the results of the season's work. He rendered a great service, both to Egypt and to the Soudan, by opening up this important river.

Since his expedition, steady attempts have been made to complete the clearance of the Bahr-el-Gebel, by removing the block known as No. 15. This, as has been explained, has a length of 36 kilometres and, in reality, consists of many blocks, separated from one another by reaches of open water. Owing to the entire absence of any current in the channel, it is, undoubtedly, the most difficult piece of work in connection with the clearance of the "sudd," in the whole length of the river (3).

(1) See Appendix No. VI.
(2) Idem.
(3) Idem.

In the winter of 1901 and 1902, Major Matthews worked hard to clear this obstruction, and to open up a channel. He succeeded in removing the blocks in rather more than half the length of the closed river, but, owing to the advent of the annual rain, was obliged to stop work before completion. In October 1903, Lieutenant Drury, with a party, started for Lake No, and set to work upon the same tract.

By the end of January 1904, he had succeeded in opening up a passage right through all but the last block, but, even after this was done, no current in the channel resulted. The soundings showed that he was on the true river. Unfortunately, just as success appeared to be assured, Lieutenant Drury was attacked by malarial fever, in its severest form. He became so gravely ill, that is was found necessary to bring him back to Khartoum. As the period of the annual rains was near at hand, it was judged advisable to abandon the work for the present season. Consequently, the Bahr-el-Gebel, in this reach, is still blocked, and steamers, passing north and south, have still to follow the false channel through the shallow lakes. (1)

(1) See Appendix N° VI.

THE BLUE NILE (1)

This river, from Rosaires (where the cataracts commence) to Khartoum, has a length of 426 miles, or 685 kilometres. Between these two places, there is a heavy fall in the bed-levels; the approximate slopes from Rosaires to Senaar being $\frac{1}{5000}$, and between Senaar and Khartoum $\frac{1}{1100}$. The average width of the channel, throughout its course, is 500 metres. Although in the northern reaches, the width increases, it is rarely more than 700 metres at any point. The average height of the banks over summer water-level, is from 9 to 11 metres, for the first 250 kilometres upstream of Khartoum. Further south, they rise, and average over 10 to 12 metres above low water-level. The difference in level between flood and summer is from 8 to 9 metres, and in the first quarter of the year the river is reduced to a succession of deep pools, connected by very shallow reaches. Even native boats can with difficulty navigate the distance between Senaar and Khartoum during this season. The Blue Nile is at its lowest in April, but in the latter half of May, indications of the approaching flood are not wanting. The real rise begins in June, and the maximum height is attained in August. In the latter half of September it begins to fall rapidly.

The velocity of the stream is very great. In winter, the water is very clear and of a beautiful limpid blue colour. In flood, being charged with the scourings of the Abyssinian mountains and forests, it is heavily charged with deposit and is of a deep chocolate colour.

For the first 16 kilometres above Khartoum, the cultivation on both banks is good, although confined to a narrow strip. Sakiehs are numerous. On the west bank, limestone is found, and kilns have been erected for the purpose of obtaining lime for the works at Khartoum.

Soba, on the east bank, at 29 kilometres, was the ancient capital of Alwah, but is now a ruin. Here the cultivation is scattered and patchy, being mostly on the foreshore. From this point, for many miles upstream, the characteristics of the country do not change. The eastern bank is covered with an endless sea, of thick, but low thorn jungle. Here and there, where a village occurs, a few clearances are made, and a little "lubia" is cultivated. The western bank is comparatively open and sandy, but the country is covered with the "halfa" grass. Heavy crops of dhurra, lubia, sesame and vegetables, are grown along the foreshore of the river as the water falls. The area of this cultivation is limited, as the width of the strip is not great. Some of the islands also, are under cultivation, but these are neither numerous, nor of large size. At Maggat (91 kilometres), a largish village on the west bank, the "tukls," or bee-hive-shaped straw houses, take the place of the mud-walled and flat-topped dwellings of the northern districts. The inhabitants at this point seem to be more numerous and the cultivation, especially on the east bank, rather more extensive. From Maggad to Kamlin, the same scenery continues; a strip of low jungle on the east bank and open country on the west bank. Inhabitants and cattle are wanting everywhere. Outside of the thorny belt, the country on either side is treeless and the date palm is conspicuous by its absence. Kamlin (120 kilometres), on the west bank on the river, is a fair-sized village, perched on a high gravelly ridge, overlying a limestone deposit. The inhabitants are chiefly Danagla mixed with a few Jaalin Arabs. This village is the head-quarters of one of the new Mamurias. Behind it, the Ghezireh plain stretches, a flat expanse, without a tree to break its monotony. The soil here, as is the case all over the eastern portion of the Ghezireh (2), is composed of the richest alluvial deposit. In the rains, the entire area is covered with

(1) This note was written in 1899. Since that date, great progress has taken place as regards the extension of the chief towns like Wad Medani, etc. The original text has been, however, left, as I have not visited this river since the year in question. [W.E.G.]

(2) The country lying between the Blue and White Niles used to be called "El Ghezireh es Sennaar." It is now know a "El Ghezireh."

"dhurra." The slope of the country being so high, the inhabitants try to check the rainwater from running off too quickly, by running small banks across, and at right angles to, the general slope. These banks average 0·40 metres in height and, at every 150 metres or so, parallel wings run from them at right angles, thus forming three sides of a maniature basin. This land only requires winter irrigation, to be capable of raising a magnificent wheat crop. The remains of some old indigo vats are still to be seen at Kamlin. These were erected by the Khedive Ismail, at the time that he attempted to introduce the cultivation of this plant into the Soudan. Wild indigo is to be found on the foreshore of the river and there appears to be no reason why, given artificial irrigation, this cultivation should not be a success. From Kamlin to Rufaa, there is no marked change in the features of the country on either side of the river. Cultivation is limited to the flats and the foreshores and the villages are very few and far between.

Rufaa (187 kilometres), on the east bank, is said to be the second largest town on the Blue Nile. It stands some little way back from the river and is a fairly populous place. Its inhabitants are a branch of the Shukriyeh tribe of Arabs and call themselves Rufaa-Shukriyeh. Good crops are raised on the foreshore and islands in the vicinity, and melons are cultivated upon an extensive scale on the flats upstream of the town. The river here is very wide and shallow and navigation in summer is extremely difficult. Still proceeding upstream, the next village of importance met with is Messalamia (241 kilometres from Khartoum), on the western bank. Under the new distribution, a Mamur will be located here. The village must once have been a large one, but is now in ruins, and cultivation is not very extensive. The inhabitants are mostly Halawi Arabs. The river here is narrow, not being more than 400 metres in width. At 216 kilometres from Khartoum, a reef extends along the eastern shore for about 2 kilometres in length; it does not apparently cross the river. At 226 kilometres, the station of Abu Haraz is situated on the eastern bank. From this point, both banks are covered with dense jungle, which might almost be called forest. At Abu Haraz, the trade route to Gedaref starts. All round the camp, the jungle has been cleared, but the place is very malarious. It is difficult to understand why Abu Haraz should be so unhealthy, as it is situated high above the river; the cliffs at the landing place being quite 11 metres over the water. Several "khors," or ravines, run into the river here, which ought effectually to drain the land. The village, which is called Abu Haraz el Bahri, is situated to the north of the camp. The columns and minarets of an old brick mosque, destroyed by the Mahdi, are still standing here. About a kilometre upstream from Abu Haraz, the river Rahad enters the Nile on its eastern bank. This river, which rises in the north-west slopes of the Abyssinian mountains, brings down a large volume of water when in flood. It enters the Nile at an angle of about 70°, and its bed, in February, was one metre higher than the water surface of the Blue Nile at the time. The Rahad, with the exception of a few pools, is dry for many months of the year. Its banks at the junction are steep and high, quite 12 metres over the bed, which has a width of 65 metres. The flood marks show that the rise of the Rahad is from 5 to 6 metres in height. The Blue Nile at this junction forms an "S" curve, taking a sharp bend to the west, and again another to the east. Its width, as measured, is 450 metres. The banks of the Rahad river are covered with thick and dense jungle, as are both banks of the Blue Nile in this reach. Shortly before Wad Medani is reached, the west bank becomes open again, but the forest on the east bank is continuous.

The town of Wad Medani is situated on the west bank of the Blue Nile, at 237 kilometres from Khartoum. It is built on a high ridge, composed of sand and gravel, overlying a limestone formation; it is the largest and most important town upon the Blue Nile, and would almost appear to have taken the place which Senaar once held. The population, which is estimated at from 15000 to 25000, is extremely mixed as to race.

The principal tribes are those of the Medani and Kawaleh Arabs, mingled with a certain number of Jaalin and Shagiyeh. A few Danagla, and even Egyptians, are to be seen, with a sprinkling of Blacks from the Fung and Hamegh country. This town, probably owing to the soil upon which it is built, enjoys the reputation of being the healthiest in the Ghezireh. It is entirely composed of "tukls," built of dhurra straw, and covers a large area. Being the head-quarters of a Mudiria, the new Government buildings are in course of construction. These are built of mud brick, with thatched roofs. The telegraph line passes through Wad Medani. As white ants are very numerous in this locality, it seems probable that iron poles will ere long have to be substituted for the wooden ones now being erected (1).

A large market is held here bi-weekly, on Mondays and on Thursdays. To this, the people flock from long distances, and the scene on market days is a very busy one. Excellent vegetables (tomatoes, onions, brinjals, yams, bahmia) are obtainable in quantities, as are limes and melons. In the market grain of many kinds is exposed for sale, and a small amount of gum, of the red variety. Manchester goods, coloured cottons, coarse sugar, tobacco and cheap Europeon goods such as mirrors, beads, and cutlery, seem to find a ready sale. Soap and sesame oil are manufactured here locally, and the inhabitants are good leather workers, and line skins with ornamental polished leather.

Large flocks of sheep and goats are to be met with, but cattle are rarely seen. The inhabitants explain the absence of these last by the fact, that during the Dervish rule, they used to drive their cattle into the forests to hide them, and this custom has gradually developed into a habit. The Ghezireh land, all round Wad Medani, is of the same description as that described at Kamlin—i.e., a flat plain of alluvial soil. It is covered with "dhurra" in the rainy season. The cultivation along the river is chiefly confined to the foreshore, but is good of its kind. A few sakiehs are at work. Melons are grown upon a large scale. North of the town, the remains of a large brick mosque, built by the founder of the Medani tribe, are to be seen. His tomb is also standing. The mosque was destroyed by the Mahdi. The people here, as elsewhere in the Ghezireh, use the old "Hodgets," or Title deeds for land, granted in the time of the Fung Sultanate, which was destroyed by Mehemet Ali in 1820-1821. Altogether, Wad Medani appears to be the most prosperous town in the whole Sudan, not even excepting Omdurman.

Upstream, from this place, the jungle on the east bank continues, but the west bank is still open and free from bush. The cultivation becomes scantier, and the villages smaller and fewer in number, being mostly hamlets in the jungle. The east bank of the river is generally higher and steeper than the west bank, which is shelving. Throughout its course, the action of the current is more severe on the eastern than on the western bank. Very few palms are to be seen, those which do exist being of the "Deleb" variety (Borassus Ethiopicus). At Gheziret el Fil, a small village on the western bank, there is a grove of these palms. Ascending the river, the trees get larger in size, and the signs of life less and less. At 256 kilometres, the forest covers both banks, and is practically continuous. Except in a few clearances, all cultivation ceases and very few inhabitants are to be seen. At Shilberga (273 kilometres), the cliffs on the east bank are quite 12 metres in height, and very steep. The scenery here is wild and beautiful. The forest trees are covered with dense masses of creepers. Troops of baboons, and small grey monkeys, are to be seen, and bright-plumaged birds abound in the woods. At 200 kilometres from Khartoum, a line of granite reefs, called "Haggar el Guffar," runs right across the river. Further progress in steamers is impossible after the month of January. At 294 kilometres, the village of El Barriab, inhabited by the Kowaleh Arabs, is situated on the west bank, and 5 kilometres

(1) I must repeat that this description was written in 1899, only a few months after the defeat of Khalifa, by Lord Kitchener, at Omdurman. Wad Medani is now a very different place. It is one of the largest and most important trade-centres in the Sudan, and appears to have a great future before it. It is now the head-quarters of the Senaar Mudiria. W.E.G.

further up, the Dinder river enters the Nile from the east. This river is very similar in its characteristics to the Rahad. It is rather larger in section and brings down a greater discharge in flood. It has its source in the same region as the Rahad and runs parallel to it, at a distance of between 100 to 120 kilometres.

The forest on both sides of the Blue Nile is chiefly composed of acacia (Sant), mimosa, tamarisk and " nabbak " (Rhammus Lotus). This last is an evergreen bush, or tree, furnished with numerous and very sharp thorns. It is common all over the African forests, and bears a small fruit like a crab-apple, which the Arabs eat readily. A few tamarind and sycamore trees are also to be seen in these forests. The undergrowth is extremely dense and every variety of thorny bush would seem to flourish here. Except by tracks made by wild animals, or cattle, progress through the bush is almost impossible. The forest belt, on the western bank, is not more than 3 to 5 kilometres in width, and, at Senaar, ceases altogether, only recommencing at Karkauj. On the east bank, it covers a large area; in fact, the whole country, as far as the Gedaref plains, is more or less covered with forest trees and bush. The red gum acacia is met with everywhere here, but the best quality comes from the south of Senaar and round about Karkauj.

PART. II.—DISCHARGES, AND POSSIBLE PROJECTS.

RIVER DISCHARGES.

Since the publication of the last report upon the discharges of the Upper Nile, a considerable amount of additional knowledge has been acquired (1). The information, at that time existing, was limited to the reports of a few travellers, and to a small series of observations, made during a couple of journeys to the frontier of the Egyptian Soudan. These last, however, proved one important point—that the loss of water in the White Nile, during summer, due to the swamps, was enormous. They did little more than this and left unsolved the important question of the relations between the levels of the Equatorial Lakes, and the volume of the Upper Nile. The few records, then existing, of the discharges of the Blue and White Niles at Khartoum, in no way assisted the solution of the complex problems connected with the sources of the river—its annual rise and fall, and its volume at different points of its course.

The study, commenced in the years 1900 and 1901, proved the necessity of obtaining further, and more detailed, information, and it was felt that this could only be satisfactorily obtained, by instituting a systematic series of observations, continued throughout the year, and comprising all the different periods of the fluctuating supply.

In May 1902, a commencement was made, by observing the monthly discharges of both the Blue and the White Niles, at selected sites above Khartoum. These discharges were continued regularly, until the end of the year 1903. The observations were supplemented by flood discharges of the Bahr-el-Gebel (above and below the "sudd") and of the Atbara river—also by sundry discharges of the Sobat, the Bahr-el-Zaraf and the Bahr-el-Ghazal. Further, some useful information was acquired, in the spring of 1903, regarding the volumes issuing from the Equatorial Lakes, in the shape of discharge measurements on the Victoria Nile, at Jinja, and Fajao, and of the Bahr-el-Gebel, at Wadelai. Lastly, early in 1903, the Blue Nile, or Abai, was measured at the point where it leaves Lake Tsana, in Abyssinia.

The foregoing forms a valuable addition to the existing knowledge of the hydrology of the Nile.

It is not pretended that the information, thus collected, is, in any sense of the word, complete, or even that any definite conclusions can be arrived at therefrom. Two years represent an extremely short period of time for observations regarding the regimen of an important river. Nevertheless, it must be admitted that a step in advance has been made, and one in the right direction.

By a fortunate chance, the two years, during which these observations were carried out, were characterized by extreme variations in the volumes of the river when in flood, more particularly so, as regards the White Nile, or, as it is called in its southern reaches, the Bahr-el-Gebel. In 1902, the flood was an exceptionally low one, in both the main branches which unite at Khartoum. In 1903, on the contrary, the flood discharges, in both rivers, were above the average, and in that portion of the White Nile to the south of the "sudd" region the flood was probably a maximum one, or very nearly so. It has thus been possible, even with only two years' observations, to arrive at some idea of the conditions which prevail in seasons of maximum, as well as of minimum supply. The deductions made, formed as they are from two extreme cases, must consequently be based upon a safer foundation than would have been the case had the two years in question been marked by successive floods of similar character.

(1) Foreign Office Blue Book. Egypt No. 2 (1901). "Report as to Irrigation Projects on the Upper Nile, etc."

It must be admitted that the results obtained from the flood of 1903, more particularly as regards the Bahr-el-Gebel, have revolutionized many of the theories previously formed and have necessitated a very considerable change in the general lines of the projects, under study for the improvement of the White Nile. The discharges recorded in this note were all observed by competent observers. The utmost precautions were taken to ensure accuracy. Price's current meters were used, and these instruments were constantly and regularly rated.

The following is a summary of the results of the discharge observations, for each river, separately (1).

The Victoria Nile.

Two discharges of this river have been measured, one, just above the Ripon Falls, where it issues from the Victoria lake, the other, at 19 kilometres downstream of the Murchison Falls, or 24 kilometres above the junction of this river with the Albert Nyanza.

The following are the figures:—

Discharge at the Ripon Falls, on January the 22nd, 1903=548 metres cube per second.
Discharge below the Murchison Falls, on March the 20th, 1903=577 metres cube per second.
Increase= 29 metres cube per second.

Taking into account the velocity of the current and allowing for a reduced velocity through Lake Choga, the water, leaving the Victoria Nyanza when the levels of both lake and river are low, would take some 12 to 13 days to reach Fajao. At this rate of flow, the water which passed the discharge site at the latter place on the 20th of March, must have left Lake Victoria on the 7th or 8th of that month. The Jinja gauge-register shows a rise of 0.19 metres in the lake-level, on the 7th and 8th of March, over that recorded on the 22nd of January; the date on which the first discharge was measured. In other words, the discharge of the Victoria Nile, on the 20th of March, downstream of the Murchison Falls, was due to a lake-level 0.19 metres higher than that of the 22nd of January of the same year, when the discharge of the outlet of the river was measured. According to Mr. Craig's appended discharge-table of the Nile at the Ripon Falls, this rise would be equivalent to a discharge of 567 metres cube a second, at Jinja (2). The increase at Fajao is thus reduced to 10 metres cube per second. As it is practically impossible, even with the most rigid precautions, to obtain exactly similar results from two separate discharges of a river, it may fairly be considered that, in spite of any extra water entering it from the Kafu and other tributaries north of Lake Choga, the volume of the Victoria Nile, downstream of the Murchison Falls, shows no increase, during the dry season, over that passing over the Ripon Falls at Jinja. The regulating effect of the Choga lake is very evident, and it seems even probable that the discharge of the Nile, at the point where it leaves this lake, is less than the amount which enters it, as the Kafu and other streams, all of which join it downstream of Lake Choga, must add, to a certain extent, to its volume.

The discharge of the 20th of March, at Fajao, was probably very nearly a minimum one. The Albert lake, according to the statements of the officials and the natives in the vicinity of Butiabu, was, at that time, at its lowest, for the year in question (3).

According to Mr. Craig's discharge-tables for Fajao, the maximum discharge of the river, at this place, equals 1005 metres cube per second (4). This amount is probably very near the mark, for the reasons given on page 75, where this question is discussed. This

(1) As has been already mentioned, the series of regular monthly discharges was only instituted for the Blue and White Niles, at one single site, in each river, above Khartoum. The want of a special staff for the purpose rendered it impossible to carry out a similar series for the remoter portions of the river. These were measured as often as opportunity presented itself.

(2) See Appendix No. 4.

(3) That is for 1903. The lowest gauge recorded at Wadelai last year, was only 0,07 metres below this. In the year previous, the river at Wadelai, and presumably the Albert lake as well, fell 0.47 metres below the minimum recorded for 1903.

(4) See Appendix No. 4. This is allowing for a maximum rise in flood. of one metre over the level of the 20th of March This rise corresponds to the flood-marks.

discharge is greater, by 355 metres cube per second, than the maximum discharge for the Nile at the Ripon Falls (1). Both these discharge-tables have been calculated from one single discharge at each site. They can consequently only be considered, at best, as approximations.

Nevertheless, there can be little doubt that the volume of water entering Lake Albert, by the Victoria Nile, is, during the flood season, always greater than the amount which leaves Lake Victoria at the Jinja outfall. The distance between the two places is some 408 kilometres, and the catchment basin is of large area. In the rainy season then, the difference must be considerable, as the Kafu, and other rivers, which must add largely to the Nile supply, enter it downstream of its exit from the Choga lake, and are therefore unaffected by this sheet of water.

The Bahr-el-Gebel.

This name comprises the entire length of the river, between the Albert lake, and the junction of the Bahr-el-Ghazal with the White Nile at Lake No; a distance of 1156 kilometres. A reference to the table of discharges, attached to this report, will show that, between the years 1900 and 1903 inclusive, nineteen discharges of the Bahr-el-Gebel have been measured, at different points of its course, and during different seasons of the year (2).

This total includes the discharge at Wadelai, measured on the 20th of March 1903, and this is the sole observation existing, upstream of the Dufilé cataracts. Of the others, six observations were made, south of the 700th kilometre from Lake Albert, i.e., upstream of the point where the stream enters the long expanse of marshes, known by the name of the "sudd." The remaining twelve discharges were measured at different points on the river, in its course through the swamps (3).

The first discharge to be considered, in connection with the Bahr-el-Gebel, is that measured at Wadelai, as mentioned above, this being the nearest discharge site to the outlet from Lake Albert. This observation resulted in a discharge of 646 metres cube per second (4). This figure is greater than the discharge of the Victoria Nile at Fajao, measured two days earlier, by 69 metres cube per second. Apart from the difficulty, already alluded to, of getting two separate discharges to exactly tally, there is a reason for this increase. Between the Albert lake and Wadelai, several streams enter the Nile, such as the Tangi, Achwa and Umi on the east bank, and one or two, of which the names are unknown, upon the west bank. The combined discharges of the Achwa and the Umi, at that period, equalled some 38 metres cube per second. A certain additional volume must be brought in by the Tangi and by the western streams, none of which it was found possible to measure. It is not then unfair to consider that these two discharges correspond satisfactorily, and that the amount of water drawn from the lake, at that period, by the Bahr-el-Gebel, was practically the same as that brought into it by the Victoria Nile. According to the accompanying discharge-table, the minimum and maximum discharges of the Bahr-el-Gebel, at Wadelai, are 538, and 974 metres cube per second, respectively (5).

It will be observed, on comparing the discharge-tables for Fajao and Wadelai, that the maximum, in both cases, corresponds very closely, and that, if the calculations are correct,

(1) See Appendix No. 4. Mr. Craig's discharge-table gives the maximum discharge at Jinja, as equal to 650 metres cube per second.

(2) See Appendix No. 4.

(3) Five other discharges of the Bahr-el-Gebel are given in the appended list, viz, two by Peney, one by de Malzac, one by Poncet, and one by Petherick. All of these refer to the years 1860 and 1861. That of de Malzac appears to be incorrect. The others have not been made use of in the present discussion as they have been superseded by newer, and more precise measurements.

(4) The gauge at Wadelai, on the date of this discharge, i.e., on the 20th March, registered 0.52 metres. In the following month, it fell to 0.45 metres, or 7 centimetres below this level. On the 16th of April 1902, as low a level as 0.05 metres was recorded.

(5) In Appendix No. 4. Mr. Craig has taken as the minimum the lowest level recorded at Wadelai, viz, 0.05 metres, and as the maximum, 2 metres. This last is equivalent to a discharge of 1,000 metres cube per second, but so far as is known, this level has never been yet reached, the highest level registered being 1.93 metres, at the end of November 1903.

the different affluents, entering the Bahr-el-Gebel, add nothing to the volume of this river when in flood. This is impossible to credit. Many of them, particularly the Achwa and the Umi, are fairly important streams, and must, at times, add considerably to the discharge passing Wadelai. Either, then, the discharge-tables are incorrect, or, in flood, the volume leaving the lake is proportionally decreased. The tables are worked out from one single discharge in each case, which is, of course, insufficient to secure exactitude. On the other hand, all accounts go to show that, when the Victoria Nile is in full flood, its waters spread in all directions over the lake surface, and that this reservoir does not necessarily (under such conditions) discharge a volume at the outlet, equivalent to that brought into it by its main tributary ([1]). This is, however, mere speculation. Too little is known, as yet, regarding the rise and fall of either the Albert lake, or of the Victoria Nile, to permit of any safe deductions being made concerning their mutual relations, throughout different seasons of the year. The most that can be said is, that these tables are based upon certain formulae, the reasons for which are described in Mr. Craig's note ([2]).

North of Wadelai, and throughout the cataract region, no observations exist of the volume of the Bahr-el-Gebel, except one, and this contains insufficient detail to permit of its being considered as absolutely reliable ([3]).

The next series of discharges, subsequent to the year 1900, was observed in the vicinity of Lado, 407 kilometres north of the Albert lake. At this point, the cataracts have been passed, and the river flows in a steady stream, rarely, however, in one single channel ([4]). These Lado discharges are most important, as the following pages will show. Their object was to ascertain the volume of water, both when the river was in flood, and at its lowest, and before it entered the "sudd" region. These observations, coupled with a similar series, made downstream of the point where the Nile issues from the "sudd" marshes, prove the enormous loss of water that takes place in this length of river, throughout the year, due to the wastage caused by the evaporation in the swamps upon either side. This loss is increased, by the separation of the stream into many subsidiary channels, in which it loses much of its surface-slope and velocity, and also, by the absorption due to the dense growth of water-weeds, through which its waters have to force their way.

The results obtained from these discharges are surprising, more particularly those arrived at from the measurements made during the high flood of 1903 ([5]).

Four discharges exist for the Nile at Lado. Of these, two were made in the months of March and April, when the river was nearly at its lowest, and two, during the month of September, when the flood was at its highest.

The following are the results:—

(a) *Low season.*

Discharge of the 28th of March 1901—623 metres cube per second.
" " 1st of April 1903—693 " " "

(b) *Flood season.*

Discharge of the 9th of September 1902—1079 metres cube per second.
([6]) " " 9th " 1903—1985 " " "

([1]) Felkin, in 1879, observed a current flowing S.S.-W. up this lake, at the junction of the Victoria Nile, as well as that flowing north into the Bahr-el-Gebel.

([2]) See Appendix IV.

([3]) Peney's discharge at the Makedo Rapids, measured in 1861, is alluded to. He gives the figure as 500 metres cube per second in the dry season of the year.

([4]) Between Lado and Lake No, it is practically impossible to find the Bahr-el-Gebel flowing entirely within one channel. Even here, there are two channels, but this site was selected as being the most likely to give trustworthy results.

([5]) This flood, as far as is known, was, in both the Bahr-el-Gebel and the White Nile, one of exceptional magnitude. It was probably a maximum for these rivers. All observations tend to prove this.

([6]) The accuracy of the discharge of the 9th September 1903, is corroborated by another taken at Mongalla, 37 kilometres downstream of Lado, on the 14th of the same month. This discharge was 2,046 metres cube per second.

No measurements of the Bahr-el-Gebel, at Lado, were made during the spring of 1902, as it was found impossible to despatch a party so far south, in the early portion of that year. The levels of the river, during the months of March and April, were, however, very similar, during the years 1901, 1902 and 1903. The Gondokoro gauge-register bears out this statement (1).

The following were the recorded levels, on the Gondokoro gauge, for the 1st of April for each of these three years :—

1901 = 0.09 metres
1902 = 0.15 „
1903 = 0.49 „

As the discharge of the spring of 1901 was measured on the 28th of March, or only three days earlier than the date in question, it may be considered that the river-levels for the two years, 1901 and 1902, were, on the 1st of April, practically the same (2), and therefore that the discharge for that date, in 1902, was identical with that measured in the year 1901.

The level for April the 1st 1903, is 0.40 metres higher than that for 1901, and 0.34 metres above that for 1902. The discharge of 1903, however, shows an increase over that of the two previous years, equal to 70 metres cube per second (3).

Turning to the flood-levels ; in the month of September, on the Gondokoro gauge, there is a considerable difference in the readings. In this month, the flood attains its maximum.

The following are the readings for the 9th of September for each year :—

1901 = 0.68 metres
1902 = 0.85 „
1903 = 2.39 „

The above shows the extreme difference between the flood of last year, and that of the two years preceding it. The flood of 1901 was an extremely poor one, in fact, it may be doubted if the river levels, during the flood season, ever fell much lower than was the case in September 1901 (4). As the flood of 1903 was an exceptionally high one, the levels of September 9th, in these two years, may be considered as representing those of a minimum, and of a maximum flood (5).

The foregoing levels, for low Nile and for flood, may be conveniently arranged as below:—

Low Nile.			High Nile.	
Year	Date	Gauge Reading metres.	Date	Gauge Reading metres.
1901	—1st April, (28th March)	0·09	9th September	0·68
1902	—1st April	0·15	9th Septemper	0·85
1903	—1st April	0·49	9th September	2·39

Applying to the above, the equivalent discharges, as actually measured, or as calculated from the discharge-table for Gondokoro (6), the following are the results :—

	Gauge Reading metres.		Discharges Metres cubes per second.	How arrived at.
a) *1901.*—1st April, (March 28th)	0·09	=	623	measured
9th September	0·68	=	986	table
b) *1902.*—1st April	0·15	=	667	table
9th September	0·85	=	1079	measured
c) *1903.*—1st April	0·49	=	693	measured
9th September	2·39	=	1985	measured

(1) The present gauge was only erected in the beginning of April 1901. By applying a correction, it is possible to compare it with the levels of the old gauges. A note on the subject, by Captain Lyons, explaining these corrections, is appended to this report.

(2) The difference is only 0.06 metres between them.

(3) The following are the mean levels (as per the Gondokoro gauge) for the first ten days of April, in each of the years in question :—

1901 = 0.11 metres
1902 = 0.12 „
1903 = 0.48 „

(4) The levels of September 1902 were better, but still far below the average.

(5) The following are the mean levels for the first ten days of September, in each year, on the Gondokoro gauge:

1901 = 0.66 metres
1902 = 0.88 „
1903 = 2.24

(6) See Appendix No. IV.

Although the dates of maximum flood at Gondokoro correspond very fairly, occurring in each year during the end of August, or in the month of September, those of the minimum levels of the river differ very considerably for each of the three years.

Thus, in the year 1901, the lowest level recorded was 0·11 metres, on the 27th and 28th of February, while the highest occurs on the 16th of August, when the gauge read 1·25 metres.

In 1902, the lowest level recorded was 0·13 metres on the 23rd of June, and the highest for the year was 1·75 metres, on the 24th of August.

In 1903, the Gondokoro gauge reached its minimum of 0·48 metres, on the 4th of April, and rose to its maximum height of 2·96 metres, on the 23rd of September.

Although this gauge was 0·57 metres higher than that of the 9th September, when the discharge was measured, it is doubtful if the volume of water passing Gondokoro increased in proportion. This rise in the gauge lasted but for a very few days, and much of the discharge must have been wasted in the increased flooding of the marshes.

It may be fairly considered, that the maximum discharge of the river at Lado, is some 2000 metres cube per second, or over, and also, that the average discharge in April is from 625, to 700, metres cube per second. The minimum discharge cannot be very much below this cube, as the lowest gauge-reading recorded at Gondokoro is only 0·22 metres below the level of that of March 28th, 1901. On that date, the discharge was 623 metres cube per second. The minimum volume of the Nile, at Lado, cannot therefore be much below 600 metres cube per second.

The question of the Lado (i.e., Gondokoro) discharges has been treated at some length, as this point on the river is a very important one, being the only place where the volume can be satisfactorily measured, before the stream enters the swamp region, and begins to lose a large portion of its supply (¹).

The series of discharges of the Bahr-el-Gebel, carried out in 1901, although it gave an idea of the loss of water, in summer, due to the marshes, and the "sudd" country, threw no light whatever upon the conditions ruling, at the time when the river was in flood. It was felt that observations of the discharges, during this period, were an imperative necessity, if any real knowledge of the flow of the Upper Nile was to be obtained. It was found impossible, for various reasons, to despatch an expedition so far south in 1901, but in the two following years, Mr. Craig, of the Egyptian Survey Department, visited this region, during two successive floods, and, besides observing the discharges recorded in the preceding pages, made a series of measurements at different points of the Bahr-el-Gebel; as well as in the White Nile and its tributaries, north of Lake No and the "sudd." The results of these observations are of the highest interest. It is now possible to have some idea of what actually takes place in this river during the periods of high, as well as low, water-levels.

Omitting the discharge at Mongalla, measured in 1903, to which allusion has been already made, and which really forms a portion of the Lado series, the next observation of importance is the discharge measured last September at Bor, 570 kilometres from the Albert lake.

(¹) It may be of interest to note here, that the estimate of the flood discharge of the Nile at Lado, made in 1901, was not very far out.

In Foreign Office Blue Book: Egypt Nº 2 (1901) on pages 45 and 46, the following passage occurs :—

" Referring to the cross-section of the river, actually measured at Lado in March last, and applying to it the height marked " " by the previous flood-water, the sectional area arrived at is 1,007 metres square. The flood of 1900, only marked a rise of " " 1·20 metres above low water-level. Chélu states that the Gondokoro gauge, in the high flood of 1878 recorded a rise of " " more than 2 metres above lowest level. This would increase the flood section to 1,191 square metres. The velocity at this " " period can not be much less than 1·5 metres per second and is probably, in a high flood, considerably more. Applying this to " " the area for 1900, the result would be a flood discharge of 1.500 metres cube per second which approaches very nearly to " " Lombardini's figures. It must be recollected, however, that the flood of 1900 was a poor one, and that the total rise was below " " the average. Taking this into consideration, it does not appear to be an over-statement if the *maximum* flood discharge of " " the Upper Nile is estimated at 2,000 metres cube per second. How much of this volume finds its way into the White Nile, and " " how much is lost in the swamps, it is impossible to say. It is difficult, however, to accept Linant Pasha's figure of " " 5,900 metres cube per second, at Khartoum, as being correct."

It has been shown that the discharge at Lado, on the 9th of September 1903, was 1985 metres cube per second, and at Mongalla, on the 14th, was 2046 metres cube. At Bor, on the 15th of the same month, the discharge, as measured, had fallen to 888 cubic metres per second. This does not represent the entire discharge of the river at this point. A certain amount of water passes down a branch from the western, or Eliab, channel which ends in the big lagoon at kilometre 579. This channel is not a very important one, being only 30 metres wide, and shallow. It cannot carry, at most, more than some 100 metres cube per second in flood, and if the Bor discharge be considered to be 1000 metres cube per second, it is probably over, rather than under, the mark (1). Thus, between Mongalla and Bor, in a distance of 133 kilometres only, the river in September 1903 had lost 50 per cent of its volume, and this before entering the "sudd" region at all. There was only one clear day's interval between the two discharges, so there can be no question of an allowance, for a difference of time.

This result is a startling one, and was quite unexpected. Indeed, were it not that the series of discharges, observed further downstream, bear out the steady rate of loss which occurs in the Bahr-el-Gebel, the further north it goes, the correctness of the Bor discharge might well have been questioned. One fact alone does raise a doubt as to whether the observation of the 16th of September really represents the actual loss at Bor, due to the waste on either side of the channel. Previous to his measurements, a gauge was erected by Mr. Craig, at Ghaba Shambé, 205 kilometres north of Bor. This gauge continued to rise slowly for many days after the observation at Bor was made, and the fall in the levels did not commence until the 4th of November (2). It may then have happened that, as the observers made the voyage from Mongalla to Bor in a steamer, they passed ahead of the crest of the flood, and that, when they measured the discharge at the latter place, the river there had not yet felt the full effect of the rise to the south. Against this theory is the fact that the river at Gondokoro, throughout September, had been fairly constant, and the gauge had recorded a level of 2.54 metres on the 4th of that month. It had, further, continued to read over 2 metres, between the 9th and 16th. As the distance between Gondokoro and Bor is only 175 kilometres, and the mean velocity of the stream is 5 kilometres an hour, the rise of the 4th should have reached Bor in less than two days. If, then, the full effect was not felt there in that period of time, it can only have been because the flood-water, instead of flowing forward, was spreading out in all directions over the marshes, and into the lagoons, filling up a huge basin, or reservoir, in the river-valley, as it passed along. That this is what actually happened in 1903, and what actually does happen, in a greater or less degree, in all floods, in this reach of the river, admits of but little doubt. During the month of September of last year, the entire river-valley was flooded, only an occasional narrow ridge being visible above the water anywhere. Even these ridges were frequently interrupted, and the huts erected upon them, during the season of low water, were submerged up to the roofing. The inhabitants had all emigrated to the mainland, and canoes were to be seen, navigating the flooded area in all directions. Trees, also, were immersed to a considerable height. In a flood of such magnitude, it is easy to understand that an enormous quantity

(1) It is a matter of regret to all concerned, that only one discharge exists at Bor, and that for the flood season alone. It would have been of the highest interest to know if the loss of water during summer was at all proportionate to that during the flood. This knowledge would have been invaluable, with regard to further projects for preventing wastage, and making use of the full supply available. That this was not done, was due to misconception of the conditions on the part of those engaged in the study of the river. It was thought, and apparently with good reason, that the real loss of water took place in the marshes to the north of Bor. South of this point, the land on either side is, during the early months of the year, comparatively high and dry, and, although the river is split up into numerous channels, it was imagined that the water, thus temporarily diverted, found its way back into the main stream with comparatively slight loss. It is easy now to see that this supposition was unwarranted, and that the large lagoons, existing on the western bank, must, at all times, absorb a large proportion of the river discharge. This has, unfortunately, been realised too late for the purpose of the present report, and the observations at Bor are incomplete, in as much as they only represent the loss of water between Lado and Bor, when the river is in flood, and show nothing regarding the loss in this reach, during the months of low supply. See Appendix No. VI. Discharges measured in 1904.

(2) The rise at Ghaba Shambé was not great after the 16th of September, being only 0.22 metres. It was, however, both steady and long-continued.

of the water coming from the south, must be lost in filling up the low ground in the valley and that a great portion of the discharge is thus used up, and never finds its way to the north at all. A very simple calculation is sufficient to prove this assertion.

The length of this reservoir may be considered as being that between Gondokoro and the head of the Bahr-el-Zaraf, where the swamp region commences. This distance is 378 kilometres. If the mean width of the flooded area be taken as 5 kilometres, which is under, rather than over, the reality, then the total flooded surface is 1890 square kilometres. Every centimetre of rise over this area would be equivalent to a withdrawal of some 220 cubic metres per second from the volume of the river. A rise of 4.5 centimetres in this great basin would account for a reduction of 1000 metres cube per second in the river discharge.

It may then be asserted, with confidence, that the flood passing Lado fills an immense reservoir and that the effect, as regards withdrawing water from the river, is similar to that produced by the filling of the Upper Egypt basins. Until this reservoir is full, the discharge passing down, is proportionately reduced. This slow filling of the reservoir would satisfactorily account for the steady rise on the Ghaba Shambé gauge (1). It is probable that the higher the flood, the greater is the proportionate loss of water in the river.

This reservoir undoubtedly plays a large part in producing the constancy of supply in the Bahr-el-Gebel. As the river falls, much of the water, thus stored, must slowly drain back into the channel and thus maintain a constant supply. Doubtless a large proportion of it is lost by evaporation, as, the greater the flooded area, the larger the size of the evaporating basin. Still, enough must remain, to largely assist in keeping up the supply during the winter months.

The next point for study is the loss of water in the Bahr-el-Gebel, in its course throughout the great marshes. These commence a little to the north of Ghaba Shambé, at 770 kilometres from the Albert lake, and continue, without a break, for another 390 kilometres until the junction of the Bahr-el-Gebel with the White Nile is reached at Lake No.

A fair number of observations now exist of the volume of the Bahr-el-Gebel, throughout this portion of its length (2).

The following are the discharges observed in the Bahr-el-Gebel, through the "sudd" region :—

No.	Distance of discharge site from Albert lake in kilometres.	Year.	Date.	Discharge in metres cube per second.
1	824	1903	Sept. 18th	532
2	827	1902	„ 4th	398
3	895	1900	April 8th	180
4	941	1903	„ 13th	331 } (3)
5	941	1903	Sept. 1st	375 } (3)
6	941	1903	„ 19th	420 } (3)
7	1027	1902	„ 2nd	314
8	1036	1901	April 1st	262
9	1146	1900	„ 14th	219
10	1146	1903	„ 14th	285
11	1147	1903	Augt. 31st	318
12	1147	1903	Sept. 20th	315

(1) Not far north of Ghaba Shambé, the Bahr-el-Zaraf takes off, and the swamp region commences. It may therefore be considered as the downstream end of the great basin.

(2) An additional discharge, measured in 1904, will be found in Appendix No. VI.

(3) These three discharges were all measured near Hellet en Nuer, a point where the high land on the west, touches the river bank. Here the channel, known as Captain Gage's, takes off.

These may be grouped by years, as follows :—

1900.—Two discharges were measured.

One at kilometre 895, on the 8th of April—180 metres cube per second.
One „ 1146, „ 16th „ —219 „ „

1901.—Only one discharge was measured.

At kilometre 1036, on the 1st April—262 metres cube per second.

1902.—Two discharges were measured.

One at kilometre 827, on the 4th Sept.—398 metres cube per second.
One „ 1027, „ 2nd „ —314 „ „

1903.—Seven discharges were measured.

	One at kilometre	824, on Sept. 18th—532	metres	cube per	second.
(1)	One „	941, on April 13th—331		„	„
(1)	One „	941, on Sept. 1st—375		„	„
(1)	One „	941, on „ 19th—420		„	„
	One „	1146, on April 14th—285		„	„
	One „	1147, on Aug. 31st—318		„	„
	One „	1147, on Sept. 20th—315		„	„

With regard to the discharges for the year 1900, no comparison with the volume in the river, upstream of the "sudd," is possible. In the first place, it was found impossible, in that year, to get through the marsh country to the Upper Nile, and, further, no gauge register for Gondokoro exists. The two discharges for 1900, viz., Nos. 3 and 9, may consequently be omitted from the following discussion. They prove nothing but the fact that the supply in the summer was an extremely scanty one. That the levels both of the Bahr-el-Gebel and of the White Nile, at that time, were abnormally low, admits of no question. The latter river, between Kodok and Khartoum, was so low that through navigation was impossible between the months of January and April. "Portages" were necessitated both at Abu Zeid and Gebelain, as the depth of water in these two reaches was quite insufficient for the steamers (2). The rains failed almost entirely in the north of the Uganda Protectorate, and in the Upper Nile valley, and a famine, more or less severe, visited the entire area.

Turning to the table of discharges on page 154, and omitting Nos. 3 and 9, for the reasons given above, it will be observed that the first points on the Bahr-el-Gebel, at which discharges were measured, were at kilometres 824 and 827. These two sites are so close to one another that they may be considered as one and the same. Both of these observations were made during the month of September, although in different years, i.e., when the flood was at, or near, its maximum. The following is the comparison with the Lado discharge in each of the years in question :—

(3) In 1902, the Lado discharge in September, was	1079	metres cube per second
„ „ the discharge at kilometre 827, in the same month, was	398	„ „ „
and the loss of water was	681	„ „ „
(3) In 1903, the September discharge at Lado, was	1985	„ „ „
„ „ „ „ „ at kilometre 824 was	532	„ „ „
The loss of water was	1453	„ „ „

This means, that, in 1902, a year of low flood, the river, in a distance of 420 kilometres from Lado, had lost 64 per cent of its volume, while in 1903, a year of very high flood, the loss, in the same distance, amounted to 74 per cent of the discharge passing Lado (4).

(1) Measured at Hellet en Nuer.

(2) This was the year in which Egypt experienced a shorter supply of water, during the early summer months, than any of which previous record existed.

(3) In each of these distances, the downstream discharge, i.e., the smaller one, was measured first. The Gondokoro gauge register, however, shows that the readings were steady, throughout this period of time, and for a long time after.

(4) The river Yei, which enters the marshes to the west of the Bahr-el-Gebel, somewhere between this discharge site and Ghaba Shambé, appears to produce no effect whatever upon the volume of the Nile, either in flood or in summer.

The next point on the Bahr-el-Gebel requiring study is Hellet en Nuer, or Eliab Dok, 941 kilometres downstream of the Albert lake. This site is a good one for a discharge, as the high land borders the western bank of the river here.

The results of three observations at this point, are given in the table—all for the year 1903. One of these was in the month of April, when the river, in that year, was at its lowest, and the other two were made in September, when the flood was at its maximum, or nearly so.

The following is the comparison between the discharges at Lado and at Hellet en Nuer, in 1903:—

On the 1st of April, the Lado discharge was... ... ... 693 metres cube per second.
On the 13th of April, the Hellet en Nuer discharge was... 331 " "

The loss of water was ... ... 362 metres cube per second.

Thus, the Bahr-el-Gebel, in April 1903, had, in a distance of 534 kilometres, lost 53 per cent of the volume passing Lado.

In the flood, the loss of water was much more considerable.

Two flood discharges exist for September, at Hellet en Nuer.

The first, on the 1st of that month, was... ... ... 375 metres cube per second
The second on the 19th of that month, was ... ... 420 " "

The latter is the more useful discharge for the purposes of comparison, as it was measured *after* the Lado discharge. In the case of the observations of September the 1st, it is possible that the full effect of the rise in the river had not been felt at Hellet en Nuer.

The comparison then stands thus:—

At Lado, on the 9th of September, the discharge was ... 1985 metres cube per second.
At Hellet en Nuer, on the 19th of September, the discharge was ... ... 420 " "

The loss of water was ... ... 1565 metres cube per second.

In other words, the volume of the river passing Lado, was reduced by 80 per cent, at Hellet en Nuer.

Just above Hellet en Nuer, the channel first described by Captain Gage, of the 7th Dragoon Guards, in the year 1900, takes off the Bahr-el-Gebel on the west. This channel was measured as carrying 22 metres cube per second in summer, and 41 metres cube per second in flood. It is as yet unknown whether this branch returns again to the Gebel, by means of the lagoons and marshes to the north, or whether, as some think, it forms a connection between the Bahr-el-Gebel and the river Rohl, a tributary of the Bahr-el-Ghazal. The discharges are so small, that they have not been taken into account, in the preceding comparisons.

Downstream of Hellet en Nuer, the next sites, at which discharges have been measured in the Bahr-el-Gebel, are at kilometres 1027 and 1036. These two sites are so near to one another that, for the purpose of comparison, they may be assumed to be identical.

One discharge was measured, in the spring of 1901, and the other, during the flood of 1902.

Now, in the end of March 1901, the Lado discharge was... 623 metres cube per second, and, on the 1st of April of the same year, at kilometre 1036 it was. 262 " "

Consequently the loss of water was... ... ... 361 metres cube per second, or, 58 per cent in 629 kilometres.

As regards the flood, the following is the comparison :—

At Lado, the discharge on September the 9th 1902 was. 1079 metres cube per second.
At kilometre 1027, the discharge on Sept. the 2nd 1901 was. 314 „ „

The loss of water was ... ... 765 „ „
or 69 per cent (1).

The last three discharges of this series were measured within 9 or 10 kilometres of the mouth of the river at Lake No, i.e., at kilometres 1146 and 1147 (2).

All three were observed during the year 1903, and therefore afford useful a comparison for that year.

The following are the figures :—

At Lado, on April the 1st 1903, the discharge was... 693 metres cube per second.
At kil. 1147, on April the 14th 1903, the discharge was. 285 „ „

The loss of water was... 408 „ „

or, nearly 59 per cent of the volume, passing Lado, was lost in a distance of 740 kilometres.

The comparison for the flood of 1903 is as follows :—

At Lado, on the 9th of September, the discharge was 1985 metres cubes per second.
At kil. 1147, on the 20th of Sept., „ „ „ 315 „ „ „ (3).
The loss of water was 1670 metres cube per second, or a loss of nearly 85 per cent, in a distance of 740 kilometres.

For the sake of convenience, the above results may be briefly recapitulated.

I.—*Loss in a low flood.*

At 420 kilometres from Lado—64 per cent,
At 629 „ „ „ —69 „ „

II.—*Loss in a high flood.*

At 133 kilometres from Lado—50 per cent,
At 420 „ „ „ —74 „ „
At 534 „ „ „ —80 „ „
At 740 „ „ „ —85 „ „

III.—*Loss in summer.*

At 534 kilometres from Lado—53 per cent,
At 629 „ „ „ —58 „ „
At 740 „ „ „ —59 „ „

From the foregoing, it may be safely asserted, that, in summer, when the river is low, nearly 60 per cent of the volume passing Lado is lost by the time that lake No is reached.

Again, that the loss in a high flood is considerably greater than in a low one, the flood discharges for the years 1902 and 1903 showing a loss of water equal to 69 per cent, and 85 per cent, respectively (4).

Lastly, it may be asserted that the water passing Hellet en Nuer, at all seasons of the year, and under any conditions of the river, is nearly constant, and varies generally between 300 and 450 cubic metres per second, while, at the mouth of the Bahr-el-Gebel, the discharge

(1) This flood-discharge comparison is not absolutely satisfactory, inasmuch as the downstream measurement was made previous to that further up the river. Still, discharges taken lower down the river prove that this heavy loss of water must always exist during the flood. 1902 was a year of low flood.

(2) The Bahr-el Gebel joins Lake No at kilometre 1167, from the Albert lake.

(3) Of the two discharges, of the 1st and 20th September, the latter has been made use of, as being measured subsequent to the Lado discharge. The two correspond so closely, however, only showing a difference of 3 metres cube per second, that it is evident that there was no change in the conditions for a long time previous.

(4) These observations for 1903 are much more complete than for 1902, but even for the latter year, sufficient information exists to prove that the above deduction is a sound one.

is even steadier, the amount entering the White Nile, under any circumstances, only varying between 280 and 320 cubic metres per second.

These observations afford ample proof of the enormous loss of water, caused by the marshes through which the Bahr-el-Gebel passes. The swamps have a powerful regulating influence upon the supply at all seasons, but more particularly so in flood. They retain the water, as in an immense reservoir, returning it gradually back into the river channel, minus the quantity lost by evaporation, and absorbed by the swamp vegetation. This is the real cause of the constancy of the White Nile supply, throughout the winter and summer months ([1]).

Before considering the White Nile discharges, it will be well to examine the information existing, regarding the supply of the two main affluents of this river, viz., the Bahr-el-Ghazal and the Sobat, and also the relations existing between the White Nile, and the secondary branch of the Bahr-el-Gebel, the Bahr-el-Zaraf.

The Bahr-el-Ghazal.

Six discharges have been measured of this river in the present series ([2]).

Of these, three represent the volume during the dry season of the year, and three that of the flood. All of these discharges were measured about the same spot, i.e., upstream of the junction of the Khor Deleb with the Bahr-el-Ghazal, or some 30 kilometres upstream of the point where the Bahr-el-Gebel enters Lake No.

The following are the figures :—

On	March	the	1st, 1900,	the	discharge	was	34	metres	cube	per	second.
„	April	„	3rd, 1901,	„	„	„	27	„	„	„	„
„	April	„	15th, 1902,	„	„	„	23	„	„	„	„
„	Aug.	„	31st, 1902,	„	„	„	15	„	„	„	„
„	Aug.	„	30th, 1903,	„	„	„	12	„	„	„	„
„	Sept.	„	21st, 1903,	„	„	„	20	„	„	„	„

These observations prove clearly that the Bahr-el-Ghazal has no influence, worth mentioning, upon the supply of the White Nile, at any season of the year. Moreover, they show that, when the White Nile is in flood, the volume, passing down the Bahr-el-Ghazal, is even less than is the case when the main stream is at its lowest. This is not difficult to understand. The Bahr-el-Ghazal, for several hundred kilometres, has a very low slope, and a very sluggish stream. Before its waters can reach the Nile, they have to pass through Lake No. This lake is practically a receptacle for the waters of the White Nile, which pass up it, increasing or decreasing its area, according to the level at which they stand. They, consequently, hold back the waters of the feeble stream of the Bahr-el-Ghazal, and, for a long distance upstream, no current at all is apparent in the latter river. In flood, as will be shown later, the waters of the White Nile itself are held back by those of the Sobat, and, at such times, the level of Lake No rises, and the discharge of the Bahr-el-Ghazal is still further reduced. Its volume merely goes to increase the evaporating area of the lake, and its discharge may be neglected altogether, as a factor in that of the White Nile ([3]).

([1]) It is, of course, understood, that a small portion of this loss is compensated by the volume brought in by the Bahr-el-Zaraf into the White Nile. This water is withdrawn from the Bahr-el-Gebel, north of Ghaba Shambé, and a portion of it is restored at the junction north of Lake No.

([2]) Two more discharges are on record, one by de Malzac, measured on the 6th of April 1858 or 1860, equalling 182 metres cube per second. The other, by Petherick, on the 25th of April 1863, gives a volume of 86 metres cube per second. De Malzac's discharge appears to be quite incorrect, and Petherick's was not compiled from direct measurements.

([3]) See Appendix No. VI.

The Bahr-el-Zaraf.

Eight discharges of this branch of the Bahr-el-Gebel have been measured between the years 1900 and 1903; four in the dry season of the year, and four during the flood [1].

The following are the results :—

Dry season.	*Discharges.*
25th of March 1900	= 32 metres cube per second,
3rd of April 1901	= 33 „ „ „ „
16th of April 1903	= 50 „ „ „ „
8th of May 1903	= 61 „ „ „ „

These represent the difference between years of poor, and of good, summer supply. Both 1900 and 1901 were characterized by a very low discharge in the Upper Nile, while 1903 was a year of good average supply.

The same differences are maintained in the flood discharges:—

Flood season.	*Discharges.*
30th of August 1902	= 80 metres cube per second.
4th „ September 1902	= 97 „ „
29th „ August 1903	= 110 „ „
22nd „ September 1903	= 158 „ „

Now 1902 was, again, a year of scanty rainfall and poor flood, while 1903 was marked by a flood of exceptional magnitude in the Upper Nile.

It must not be forgotten, however, in considering the discharge of the Bahr-el-Zaraf, that, previous to the year 1900, the Bahr-el-Gebel was entirely closed by "sudd," almost from the outlet of the Bahr-el-Zaraf, near Ghaba Shambé, to its mouth in Lake No. Observations made on the Bahr-el-Zaraf, in March 1900, proved that in the flood of the previous year, i.e., in 1899, the water in this branch had stood quite one metre above the level of the adjoining country, which must have been flooded to an immense distance upon either side [2]. It is thus fair to conclude that, in that year, a very considerable flood passed down the Bahr-el-Zaraf, and, the deduction is obvious, that this was due to the fact that the Bahr-el-Gebel was closed. It is, then, reasonable to suppose, that, in all years when the Bahr-el-Gebel is blocked, the Bahr-el-Zaraf forms the escape-channel for the waters from the south. When, as at present, the Bahr-el-Gebel is open, the flood discharge of the Zaraf sinks to an insignificant amount [3].

It is not easy to estimate the amount of water which must have passed down the Bahr-el-Zaraf in flood, in a year like 1899. The average sectional area of the channel, if measured to the top of the banks, is, in the lower reaches, from 300 to 350 square metres. The velocity of the stream, in the flood of 1903, was 0.64 metres per second, and, with a large volume passing down as in 1899, it was probably quite 1 metre per second. This would account for a discharge of from 300 to 350 metres cube per second, but, as has been stated, the water stood 1 metre above the banks, so that the volume passing down the river was probably larger than these figures [4].

(1) Three other discharges exist of the Bahr-el-Zaraf. De Malzac, on the 5th of April 1858 or 1860, gives the discharge as 9 metres cube per second.

Petherick, in April 1863, gives the discharge as 47 metres cube per second.

Baker, on the 17th February 1870, gives the discharge as 350 metres cube per second.

The difference is extraordinary, but the explanation probably lies in the fact that, when de Malzac measured the river, the Bahr-el-Gebel was open, and free from "sudd," and when Baker's measurement was made, the reverse was the case.

(2) The marks upon the trees, on the banks, showed this very plainly.

(3) This hypothesis would account for the discharge measured by Baker in 1873, when the Bahr-el-Gebel was closed by "sudd."

(4) See discharge of 1904. Appendix No. VI.

It seems not improbable that, if the Bahr-el-Gebel be permanently kept open, and free from all obstruction, the Bahr-el-Zaraf, not being required, or used as an escape-channel, may eventually disappear, its bed being gradually raised by "sudd," and other marsh grasses.

The Sobat.

A glance at the cross-sections of this river will show how widely it differs in its characteristics from either the Bahr-el-Zaraf or the Bahr-el-Ghazal. It has a well-defined channel, great depth of water and a fair slope. It, moreover, runs between high banks, which, at any rate in the lower portions of its course, are never topped by the water, even in the highest flood. It is essentially a mountain river, and its volume, when in full flood, is considerable, rivalling that of the Victoria Nile, and of the Bahr-el-Gebel, south of Wadelai. It is by far the most important of the White Nile tributary streams, and is, as will be shown, the principal factor in the flood discharge of this river. Indeed, as far as the supply of Egypt is concerned, the Sobat must rank next in importance to the Blue Nile, and the Atbara.

From January to March, its discharge shrinks to very insignificant limits, and the observations show that, even in the latter half of April, the volume added by the Sobat to the Nile is but small. In May, the discharge increases largely, and navigation usually recommences during the month of June. In July and August, it is three-quarters full, and throughout September, October, and very often November, it is in full flood. In the month of December, it begins to fall rapidly.

The recent series of discharges of the Sobat, consists of seven observations (¹).

The following are the details :—

Dry season.

On April	the 16th 1900,	the discharge	was	87	metres	cube	per second
„ „	„ 5th 1901,	„	„	87	„	„	„
„ „	„ 17th 1903,	„	„	45	„	„	„

Flood season.

On Aug.	the 28th 1902,	the discharge	was	572	metres	cube	per second
„ Sept.	„ 15th 1902,	„	„	771	„	„	„
„ Aug.	„ 26th 1903,	„	„	769	„	„	„
„ Sept.	„ 24th 1903,	„	„	895	„	„	„

The discharges taken during the dry season, i.e., in April, are not of much value, as, at this period, the waters of the White Nile hold back those of the Sobat for a long way. For a distance of some 19 to 20 kilometres, no velocity at all is apparent in the latter river, and consequently, the amount of water added to the White Nile is inconsiderable. There is, however, a certain addition caused, even at this period, as the discharges measured in April 1901, and 1903, respectively, show an increased volume in the White Nile, downstream of the Sobat junction, of 87, and 19 metres cube per second, respectively.

In the month of June, the velocity of the Sobat water overcomes the resisting effect of that of the White Nile, and the discharge of the former river increases rapidly, as the observations made at El-Duem bear witness (²).

As regards the flood discharges, that of the 24th of September 1903, cannot be considered to be a maximum, as the river at Nasser continued to rise, until the 7th of November, when a

(¹) Four other discharges of the Sobat are recorded.

One by de Malzac in April 1858 or 1860	equals	80	metres	cubes	per second
One by Petherick „ 1863	„	23	„	„	„
One by „ „ 1862	„	120	„	„	„
One by Pruysenaere on the 15th of June 1862	„	1066	„	„	„

(²) The Duem discharges, in April and May 1903, were 415 and 447 metres cube per second. In June the volume rose to 658 metres cube per second.

slow fall commenced ([1]). The gauge at the American Mission, near the mouth, also records a rise throughout November. Although this gauge, owing to its vicinity to the junction, is not a very reliable one; taken in conjunction with that of Nasser, it proves that the September discharge was not measured when the river had risen to its highest levels. Most probably, a discharge of 1000 metres cube per second was attained, in the latter half of October, and the beginning of November, 1903.

The White Nile.

In considering the conditions of this river, it will be best to divide it into two sections, the one upstream, and the other downstream, of the Sobat junction. In the former, the discharge site was selected at a point below the junction of the Bahr-el-Zaraf. This was necessary in order to ascertain the amount added to the Nile by this branch of the Bahr-el-Gebel.

In order to check the observations, in addition to the measurements of the White Nile, discharges were taken separately of each of the three rivers, whose united waters form the main stream ([2]).

Six discharges, in all, were obtained of the White Nile in its southern section. In the following table, they are given separately and compared with the results obtained from the separate measurements of the Bahr-el-Gebel and el-Zaraf ([3]).

Year.		Month.	Discharge of White Nile.	Discharge of Bahr el-Gebel.	Discharge of Bahr el-Zaraf.	Combined discharge of the two rivers.	Difference.
No. 1.	1901	April	294	262	32	294	Nil.
2.	1902	August	344	314	80	394	+ 50
3.	1902	September	426	398	80	478	+ 52
4.	1903	April	349	285	50	335	— 14
5.	1903	August	417	318	110	428	+ 11
6.	1903	September	483	315	158	473	— 10

As regards Nos. 2 and 3, the discharges of the Bahr-el-Gebel, in 1902, were measured at points rather too far upstream to be satisfactory as a check. That in August was measured at kilometre 824, and that in September at kilometre 1,027. A reference to the percentage of loss of water in this river, given on pages 155 and 157, will show, that, at kilometre 824, some 10 per cent more water passes down the channel than reaches the White Nile at Lake No. At kilometre 1,027, the loss is about 5 per cent less. If then these two discharges be reduced by the above amounts, the totals will more nearly coincide than is shown in the table.

It may then be assumed that the discharges of the White Nile above the Sobat, as given in the table, are fairly correct, and that, while in summer the volume never exceeds 350 metres cube per second, even in a high flood, it does not reach the cube of 500 metres per second ([4]).

Before considering the White Nile discharges in the second section, i.e., downstream of the Sobat, a few words are necessary, as to the effect of this last river upon of the flood of the former, during the period of flood.

([1]) The flood in the Sobat in 1903, was in all probability a good average one, but like that of the Blue Nile, not an exceptional one.

([2]) Although the Bahr-el-Ghazal was measured, its discharges have been neglected, for the reasons already given.

([3]) All the figures, in the different columns of this table, represent metres cube per second.

([4]) As 1903 was an exceptional flood, the discharge of 483 metres cube per second, in September of that year, was most probably a maximum one.

There can be little doubt that the waters of the Sobat, when in flood, hold back those of the White Nile, for a long distance upstream of the junction. This must be so. With an increase in the Sobat discharge, the levels of this river rise rapidly. This rise is communicated to the White Nile, the slope of which, upstream of the junction, is so flat as to be nearly horizontal (1). It seems almost certain that a portion of the Sobat discharge must flow upstream, for a time. At any rate, it causes a rise in the White Nile levels above the junction. The discharge of the White Nile must, of course, continue, but a portion of it is wasted in flooding the marshes and in increasing the area of Lake No. This holding back is entirely due to the increased depth in the White Nile, caused by the flood water of the Sobat. The area of Lake No increases when the Sobat is in flood and its levels rise. That this is not due to an increase in the Bahr-el-Gebel, the discharges of 1903, amply prove (2). It can then only be due to the fact that the water of the White Nile is held back at this period of the year. The Bahr-el-Zaraf may have something to do with this rise, but it enters the Nile some distance downstream of Lake No, and there is no rush of water brought in by this river. It must, however, be admitted that the flood discharges of the White Nile, measured above and below the Sobat junction, do not show that the loss of discharge, in the former river, due to holding back, is a serious one. In August 1903, the White Nile, below the Zaraf junction, but upstream of the Sobat, was discharging 417 metres cube per second. The volume of the Sobat, in that month, was 769 metres cube per second. These two, added together, give a total of 1186 metres cube per second. The White Nile, downstream of the Sobat, and north of Taufikia, was, in August, discharging 1046 metres cube per second, so that the loss, due to the holding back, was only 140 metres cube per second.

In September 1903, this loss was even less.

The discharge of the White Nile, above the Sobat, was	483	metres	cube	per	second.
" " " Sobat, was	895	"	"	"	"
Total...	1378	"	"	"	"

The September discharge of the White Nile, downstream of the Sobat, was 1304 metres cube per second. The loss of water was, therefore, only 74 metres cube. In other words, the White Nile discharges below the junction were reduced in August and September, by 33 and 15 per cent, respectively, from the holding back of its waters by the Sobat.

The next discharge site in the White Nile is at El-Duem, kilometre 1917, from the Albert lake. This point is an important one, as there is a permanent gauge here, which was erected in April 1901, and which has been recorded daily since that date. At this place also, the monthly series of discharges of the White Nile has been observed, commencing from May 1902, and continued to the end of 1903 (3). It is, consequently, possible to arrive at a fairly accurate idea of the conditions existing, with reference to the river levels and supply, at El-Duem, during the different periods of the year. The results obtained from these two years' observations are both curious and interesting.

In order to understand what happens in the White Nile here, it is necessary to study the table of discharges of this river, and, at the same time, those of the Blue Nile, together with the diagrams which have been prepared from the above (4).

(1) The water slope of the White Nile, upstream of the Sobat, worked out from the flood discharges, is only $\frac{1}{17000}$.

(2) The banks of this lake, in April 1903, were some 35 centimetres above the water. The combined discharges of the Bahr-el-Ghazal were at that time 310 metres cube per second. In August and September, the lake-level rose, until the banks were flush with the water, while the discharges of the Gebel and the Ghazal rivers had only increased by 20 metres, i.e., to 330 metres cube per second.

(3) There have been one or two breaks in this series, due to the illness of the observer.

(4) See Appendix V.

The levels given for the White Nile represent those of the El-Duem gauge—those for the Blue are referred to the gauge at Khartoum (1). A reference to these tables shows the following:—

In 1902, the lowest measured discharge of the Blue Nile was 200 metres cube per second, on the 9th of May, the Khartoum gauge reading 0.05. The rise commenced in June, and the maximum measured discharge was taken on the 29th of August, when 7,362 metres cube per second passed down the river. This corresponded to a gauge of 5.32 at Khartoum. The Blue Nile fell slowly through September, but did not drop below 5,000 cubic metres per second, until the beginning of October. It then fell steadily and, on the 28th of December, the recorded discharge was 476 metres cube per second, the Khartoum gauge reading 1.48.

Turning to the White Nile, during this period, the following facts appear:—

On the 13th of May 1902, the Duem gauge read 0.51, with a discharge of 347 metres cube per second. On the 11th of June, this volume had increased to 650 metres cube per second, the gauge standing at 0.95. The increase continued, until, on the 5th of August, 867 metres cube per second were passing El-Duem, with a gauge of 2.20. It must be noted, and this fact is important, that, when the above discharge was measured, the Blue Nile was increasing in volume, from 3500 to 5000 metres cube per second (2).

On the 2nd of September, another discharge of the White Nile was measured. This showed a very heavy drop in the volume at El-Duem, the discharge being reduced to 330 metres cube per second. Meanwhile, the water levels continued to rise and, on this date, the El-Duem gauge read 3·48 (3). At this period, the Blue Nile discharge was somewhere between 6800 and 7300 metres cube per second (4).

On the 1st of October, the White Nile discharge was again measured and showed an increase. The volume was then 870 metres cube per second, or practically the same as that of the 5th of August. The El-Duem gauge remained stationary and, on this date, was 3·50. Referring to the Blue Nile, at the period of this last rise, it will be found that the discharge of this river, at this time, was just 5000 metres cube per second (5). From the 3rd of October, the Blue Nile fell steadily, while the discharge of the White Nile, on the contrary, rose to 930 metres cube per second on the 1st of December, and to 1518 metres cube per second on the 29th of that month. The levels had now steadily fallen. On the 1st of December the gauge read 2·04, and on the 24th of November 2·02. After this last date, the decrease in the discharge of this river commenced, and was continued.

Before considering the reasons for the remarkable drop in the discharge at El-Duem, in the month of September, it will be well to study the discharges for the year 1903. In this year, a complete set of observations, for both Niles, was obtained.

Commencing with the Blue Nile, the table shows that, between the 8th and 23rd of May, there was practically no discharge in the channel at all; nothing but a few pools. The Khartoum gauge read 0·28 centimetres below zero on the 11th of May and, up to the 23rd of that month, the reading was a minus quantity. On the 28th of May, a flush came down and a discharge of 374 metres cube per second is recorded for that date. The Khartoum gauge then read 0·53. This rise was maintained, and the increase in the volume was rapid. On July 31st, with a gauge of 3·45, the discharge was 2800 metres per second and, on the 5th of August, it was 7500 metres cube per second, the gauge at Khartoum reading 4·60(6).

(1) All gauge-readings are in metres, and decimals of metres.

(2) Vide discharges of 1st and 8th of August 1902.

(3) In other words, the discharge of the White Nile in September. was 62 per cent less than it was in August, while the water level rose 1·28 metres.

(4) Vide discharges of 29th of August and 5th of September.

(5) The actual figures were, on the 26th of September, 5040 metres cube per second, and on the 3rd of October, 5060 metres cube per second.

(6) These two discharges are mentioned, because, between these two dates, the river passed the important point, as affecting the White Nile, marked by a discharge of 5000 metres cube per second.

It will be observed that, in 1902, a discharge of 7300 metres cube was equivalent to a water-level of 5·32 on the gauge. In 1903, the Khartoum gauge only registered a level of 4·60, for a discharge of 7500 metres cube. These differences are not easy to understand. They are probably due to some heading up of the water at the junction, which, again, depends upon the relative discharges of the two rivers, prior to the arrival of the Blue Nile flood.

The maximum discharge measured on the Blue Nile in 1903 was 9544 metres cube per second, on the 28th of August, the gauge reading 6·05 (1). After the first few days of September, the fall was a steady one and, on the 4th of December, the discharge was 1102 metres cube per second, with a gauge of 2.35, or some 600 metres cube per second higher than in the same period in 1902.

It now remains to study the figures for the White Nile, and to see what happened in that river during the above period of time.

The discharge of this branch of the Nile, at El-Duem, varied between 400 and 500 metres cube per second between the months of February and May (2). On June the 13th, the rise due to the Sobat was felt, and the discharge, as measured, increased to 658 metres cube per second. The Duem gauge read 1·07. On the 1st of July, the gauge-reading rose to 1·31, and the discharge increased to 884 metres cube per second (3). On the 4th of August, although the Duem gauge had risen to 2.46, the White Nile discharge dropped to 768 metres cube per second and, on the 11th of that month, to 579 metres cube per second. The gauge-reading, notwithstanding, rose to 3·28. On the 18th of August, the discharge was still further reduced, falling to 534 metres cube per second. The gauge rose to 3.70.

Thus, although the water-level in the White Nile in August had risen 2·39 metres above the level in July, the discharge in the latter month had been reduced by some 40 per cent below the volume passing down, on the earlier date (4). Between the 8th of August and the 2nd of September, there were small fluctuations in the discharge, the gauge meanwhile rising steadily. On the 2nd of September, the Blue Nile reached its maximum, and, after this date, began to fall. The White Nile discharge then slowly rose, while the Duem gauge slowly fell. Between the 9th and the 16th of October, the discharge of the Blue Nile fell from 5700 to 3800 metres cube per second, and that of the White Nile rose quickly. On the 24th of September, with a gauge of 4·28 at Duem, the discharge was 763 metres cube and, on the 7th of October, the gauge having fallen to 3.93, the discharge of the White Nile increased to 1588 metres cube per second. This rise continued and, on the 24th of November, with a gauge dropping to 2·44, the discharge passing El-Duem was 1665 metres cube per second (5). Throughout the months of December and January, the discharge was fairly steady—between 1400 and 1500 metres cube per second.

The deductions to be drawn from the foregoing are very evident.

As long as the Blue Nile is low, that is, all through the periods of late autumn, winter and early summer, the White Nile discharge passes Khartoum in an uninterrupted flood, and in fact is, for a great portion of the year, the chief factor in the supply of the river. When, however, the Blue Nile discharge passes a certain point and the water-level exceeds a certain reading on the Khartoum gauge, then its waters hold back those of the White Nile to a very large extent and for a long distance above the junction of the two streams. As the depth increases, the water spreads over the marshes and forms a large reservoir. The raising of the levels decreases the surface slope and reduces the velocity.

(1) The gauge rose to 6·30 on the 2nd of September, 1903.

(2) For actual figures, see the appended table.

(3) At this time, the Blue Nile discharge was only 1200 metres cube per second.

(4) The Blue Nile discharge in the end of July, and beginning of August, i.e., in the period equivalent to the first drop, was somewhere between 2800 and 7100 metres cube per second, with a rapidly rising river. In the latter half of August, it was between 7000 and 9000 metres cube per second.

(5) At this time the Blue Nile discharge had fallen to 1400 metres cube per second. The November discharge at El-Duem was a maximum in 1903.

Under these circumstances, the discharge of the White Nile drops abruptly, but the water-levels continue to rise steadily, as the great pond, upstream of Khartoum and El-Duem, fills up. Until the Blue Nile has fallen again to the point above referred to, the flood of the White Nile is arrested. As soon as this point is passed, its discharge increases very rapidly and the surface-level falls, as the ponded water escapes to the north. The point at which the holding back of the White Nile commences, appears to have occurred, in 1902, when the discharge of the Blue Nile passed 5000 metres cube per second (1). In that year, the discharges and levels prove that, when this volume was surpassed, the discharge of the White Nile was reduced and remained low until the flood had passed, and until the volume of the Blue Nile had again sunk below 5000 metres cube per second. In 1903, the point where the flood of the White Nile was arrested is not quite so clear. As the Blue Nile flood rose, the discharge of that river reached 7000 metres cube per second, before the fall in the White Nile was apparent (2). As the Blue Nile fell, however, the rise in the White Nile commenced, somewhere during the period of time when the Blue Nile discharge was decreasing, from 5700 to 3800 metres cube per second.

Enough has been shown to prove that, when the Blue Nile is in flood and, generally, when its discharge exceeds 5000 metres cube per second, its waters hold back those of the White Nile, and, owing to the increased depth in this river, due to the rise in the water-levels, the volume coming from the south floodst he marshes right and left of the channel and thus reduces the discharge, passing El-Duem, by from 40 to 60 per cent.

Still further evidence was obtained of this holding back of the White Nile water. In 1903, experiments were made with the current meter, above Khartoum, and at El-Duem, with a view to ascertain the velocities of the current at different depths below the surface. These observations were made during the months of August and September, when the holding back was supposed to occur. At El-Duem, from April to July, the mean velocities of the stream varied between 0·30 and 0·40 metres per second. From the 11th of August to the 18th of September, the mean velocity fell to 0·12 and 0·15 metres per second; the average for this period being not more than 0·13 metres per second.

Above Khartoum, the experiment was carried out in still greater detail, as the velocities were measured at every metre of increased depth below the surface, up to a total of eight metres. This was in the months of August and September. It will be seen from the table appended (3), that, although there was a low surface velocity everywhere, this decreased very rapidly and, at the end of August, and again, at the end of September, there was practically no current at all, below the depth of two metres from the surface of the river. It may well be that at one time, during the rise, there may have been a current below the surface, flowing from the junction at Khartoum, upstream, into the White Nile. The current meter would not indicate in which direction the registered velocity was taking place.

One other phenomenon in connection with the Blue Nile flood discharge deserves mention, i.e., that the gauge-readings, both at Wad Medani, and at Khartoum, show a considerable difference between the levels, in a falling, and in a rising flood, for the same discharge in the river. In order to comprehend this, it is advisable to study the diagram of the Khartoum gauge, for the flood of 1902 and 1903 (4).

Taking for example a discharge of 5000 cubic metres per second, in the Blue Nile: in 1902, on the rising river, this volume meant a level of 4.65 metres on the gauge, while in a falling river, the gauge, *for the same discharge*, read 5.15 metres. In 1903, the corres-

(1) A reference to the discharge diagrams will show this very clearly.

(2) It must be remembered that the Blue Nile was then rising very rapidly, and that the discharge increased from 2,870 metres cube. on the 31st of July, to 9340 metres cube. on the 14th of August. The White Nile began to drop on the 4th of August most probably, after the volume of 5000 metres cube had been surpassed.

(3) See Appendix V.

(4) See Appendix V. This phenomenon appears to be common to all torrential rivers.

ponding figures were 4 metres, for the rising flood, and 4.85 metres, for the falling flood. The difference may then be considered to be about 0.90 metres.

It would seem from the above, that there is a ponding up of the water, somewhere after it has passed Khartoum, which prevents the river from falling as quickly as it has risen. In all probability, this holding up takes place at the narrow gorge, or gut, through which the Nile has to pass before it arrives at the Shabluka cataract, 60 kilometres north of Khartoum. This question requires further study, but, until a permanent gauge has been erected, and a permanent discharge site selected at Shabluka, the reason of this stoppage of the flood cannot be definitely determined.

The Blue Nile.

Reference to the discharge of this river will be brief. There is nothing complex about its system of supply, and although but little is as yet known regarding its upper course, and the volume of its main tributaries, there is a considerable amount of information existing, regarding its rise and fall, after it leaves the hills, and of the volume that passes Khartoum throughout the year.

With regard to the discharge of the Abai, as it leaves Lake Tsana, a few facts are available (1).

On the 31st January, 1903, Mr. Dupuis measured this river near the outlet. The discharge at that time was only 42 metres cube per second. The minimum level of Lake Tsana is attained in May, and Mr. Dupuis judged that, between that month and the date when he measured its discharge, a further fall of 15 centimetres was to be expected. This, he estimated, from his measurements of this channel, would reduce the discharge by one half, or to 21 metres cube per second.

As regards the maximum discharge at the lake outfall he makes no estimate, but he calculates the total amount run off by the river, during the 243 days, between the periods of maximum and minimum level (2), to be 1948,000,000 of metres cube. This is equivalent to a daily average discharge of 8 millions of metres cube (3). If these calculations are in any way accurate, and Mr. Dupuis's assumptions are based upon apparently sound arguments, then it is evident that this lake plays a very small part indeed in the flood discharge of the Blue Nile, and that its influence upon the volume of the river is extremely limited. That this is so, appears to be beyond dispute, as the loss of water, due to evaporation over the lake surface, is out of all proportion to the amount discharged at the outlet. The flood supply must be derived from the drainage of the catchment basin, throughout the 700 kilometres traversed by this river, between the lake and the point where it issues from the hills, and also to the supply added to it by its many important affluents, such as the Dudessa, the Dabus, the Dinder and the Rahad. Little is as yet known regarding the course of the Blue Nile, between its exit from Lake Tsana and its last rapid at Rosaires. Its course between these two points has not been yet accurately traced, and the area of its catchment basin, equally with the volume of its tributary rivers, is as yet an unknown quantity. It is, consequently, useless to attempt any estimate of the manner in which its discharge is increased, by the time it arrives at the junction with the White Nile. A considerable amount of information is, however, available as regards its discharge, near, and above Khartoum. A series of observations was commenced in May 1903, and carried on continuously, to the end of December 1903. As a rule, four discharges per month were measured here. A reference to the discharge table will show how complete is the series (4). This table

(1) The Blue Nile is known as the Abai, throughout Abyssinian territory.
(2) That is between October 8th and May 31st.
(3) These calculations will be found in Mr. Dupuis's appended Report.
(4) See Appendix V.

proves that the Blue Nile is at its lowest in the month of May, and attains its maximum during the last days of August, or the first half of September.

Thus, in May 1902, the minimum discharge was 200 metres cube per second.

The maximum of 7362 metres cube per second was reached on the 29th of August (1).

In 1903, the river fell so low, that, from the 8th to the 22nd of May, the discharge, passing Khartoum, was "nil." In the last week of that month, the rise commenced, and, on the 28th of August, the measured discharge was 9544 metres cube per second (2). The flood of 1903 cannot be classed as one of exceptional magnitude—merely as a good average one. In all probability, in years of very high flood, the volume of 12000 metres cube per second, or even more, is attained when the river is at its maximum. It is unfortunately impossible to compare the gauge-readings previous to 1884, at Khartoum, with those subsequent to 1900. All trace of the old gauge is lost. Still, a comparison is possible between the range of the river at this place during different years.

A study of the gauge registers shows that the highest range was 8.06 metres, in 1869, and the lowest was 5.20 metres, in 1877. Also, that, as a rule, although this is not absolute, the range of the Blue Nile in a year of high flood is over 7 metres, and of a low one, below 6 metres. The range for 1903 was only 6.46 metres, while for 1874 and 1878, both years of disastrous flood, the range at Khartoum was, 7.20, and 7.51 metres, respectively.

The discharge of the Nile, north of Khartoum.

A commencement was made in 1902 and 1903 with the discharges of the river between the junction of the two great branches. From November 1902 to July 1903, the discharge site was at Kerreri, but, in August 1903, it was moved to Shabluka, as being a more favourable point for making observations. The flood discharges of the combined rivers do not agree very closely with those of the two Niles, as observed separately. The difference in the totals is most probably due to the filling and emptying of the trough of the river, between the gauge station at Khartoum and the Shabluka pass. Allusion has already been made to the difference in the Khartoum gauge, for a given volume, during a rising and a falling river, and to the ponding up in flood, which most probably takes place, between that place and Shabluka. Until more information is available regarding the rise and fall of the river at this last point, it is of little use to speculate upon the causes of this difference (3). The discharges, however, show that, in 1903, from the 2nd to the 16th of September, a discharge of over 10400 metres cube per second, passed down the river, north of Khartoum.

In order to ascertain the amount of water that reached Egypt, it is necessary to add to the above discharge, the volume added by the Atbara river (4).

The maximum recorded for the Atbara in 1903 was 3088 metres cube per second, on the 30th of August. On the 5th of September, this fell to 2800 metres cube per second. This last date corresponds more nearly than the former with that of the maximum flood passing Shabluka. Adding the two discharges together, it means that a flood of some 13200 metres cube per second passed Berber. Now in Egypt it has, hitherto, been assumed that a flood of 14000 metres cube per second passing Wadi Halfa is an exceptional one (5).

In 1903, a flood of only 800 metres cube per second below this figure, passed Berber, and yet the levels in Egypt were never beyond those of a fair flood, rather inclining to be

(1) The gauge on September the 16th, read 16 centimetres higher than on August the 29th. Probably 8000 metres cube per second represent the maximum for 1902, which was a year of moderate flood.

(2) This discharge is not a maximum, as the gauge on the 2nd of September 1903, stood 0.25 centimetres higher than on August the 28th. The discharge, at this time, must have exceeded 10000 metres cube per second.

(3) The discharges of the Nile at Kerreri, and at Shabluka, are given in a separate table.

(4) The Atbara discharges for 1903, are given in a separate table.

(5) This assumption is not based, apparently, upon any actual discharges, measured during a maximum flood.

a moderate one. The maximum volume, in a flood of exceptional magnitude, must consequently be far greater than had been supposed, and it seems probable that the figure of 16000 metres cubes per second may at times be attained, or perhaps even surpassed.

The Atbara discharges.

Observations were made of the flood discharges of this river, during 1902 and 1903. Although these figures are interesting, as giving a record of the volume during one year of very poor supply, and another of fair average discharge, they do not merit any detailed description.

The discharges, for 1903, show that the Atbara reached its maximum at the end of August, and that the discharge of this river exceeded 1000 metres cubes per second, from the 5th of August to the 25th September [1].

The first waters of the Atbara appear to reach the Nile, with great regularity, during the last week of June and, by the middle of July, the discharge, according to the measurements of the last two years, is from 300 to 400 metres cube a second, increasing to double this amount by the end of the month. The rise in August is very rapid, and the maximum is usually reached between the last week of August, and the first ten days of September. The maximum for 1902 was 2020 metres cube per second, on the 8th of September, and for 1903, 3088 metres cube, on the 30th of August. After this date, the fall was a rapid one and, by the month of November, the flood water had entirely passed away. It seems probable that the Atbara water, when in full flood, holds back that of the Nile to a certain extent, as, during this period, the volume of the former river forces that of the latter across to the western shore. Without permanent gauges, and a series of discharges above and below the junction, it is impossible to verify this supposition.

Concluding remarks upon river discharges.

The foregoing description of the discharges of the Soudan rivers has extended to very considerable length. The importance of the subject must be considered as the excuse.

It may, however, in the interest of those who do not wish to study the question in detail, be useful to give a summary of the information embodied in the foregoing pages, and to recapitulate the more important facts, gathered from the observations of the last two years.

1. *The Victoria Nile.*

The discharge at the Ripon Falls varies between 500 and 650 metres cube per second, with a range of 1.10 metres. Downstream of the Murchison Falls, the range is probably one metre, and the maximum and minimum discharges 1000 and 400 metres cube per second, respectively. The increase in flood is due to the rainfall throughout the catchment area of the river, between these two points, while the decrease, during the low season, is due to the Choga lake, which undoubtedly has a regulating effect upon the supply issuing from Lake Victoria. Lastly, the volume which enters Lake Albert by this river, is generally, in flood, greater than that which leaves it by the Bahr-el-Gebel.

2. *The Bahr-el-Gebel.*

At Wadelai, the first discharge site, the range of the river is about 1.11 metres, while the discharge varies from 550 to 950 metres cube per second. The increase brought in by the streams which feed this river, between Lake Albert and Wadelai, is

(1) The discharges for 1902 are not as reliable as those for 1903, as the site was too near the Nile junction. Last year's discharges were measured 29 kilometres above this point.

compensated by the loss of water, due to a portion of the discharge of the Victoria Nile passing south, up the lake, during the flood season.

At Lado, 381 kilometres, the range is 2·30 metres, and the discharge, in summer, averages from 600 to 700 metres cube per second. The maximum (generally attained in September) varies between 1000 metres cube per second in a low flood, and 2000 metres cube per second in a high one. This increase in the flood supply is due to the rainfall throughout the river valley, and to the volume added by the many important tributaries, such as the Asua, the Kit, etc., which feed the Bahr-el-Gebel between Wadelai and Lado.

At Bor, 559 kilometres, the loss of water in flood is some 50 per cent of the amount passing Lado, and the discharge here can rarely, if ever, exceed 1000 metres cube per second. This loss is due to the filling up of the entire river valley, which thus forms an immense basin, or reservoir, and reduces the discharge passing to the north. This reservoir extends from Lado to the head of the Bahr-el-Zaraf, a distance of some 378 kilometres. As the river falls, the water of this basin, with the exception of the large amount lost by evaporation, slowly filters back through the marshes, into the river, during the winter months, and thus maintains the constancy of supply.

Throughout the "sudd" region, the loss of water in the Bahr-el-Gebel, both in summer and in flood, is very considerable. By the time Lake No (1156 kilometres from Lake Albert, and 749 kilometres from Lado) is reached, 85 per cent of the discharge at Lado has been lost in a high flood, and 70 per cent in a low one. During the summer months the loss at this point varies between 50 and 60 per cent. Lastly, the discharge which enters the White Nile from the Bahr-el-Gebel is nearly constant at all seasons of the year, and never, even in the highest flood, exceeds 300 or 320 metres cube per second (1). The regulating effect of the great marshes is thus very apparent.

3. *The Bahr-el-Ghazal.*

The discharge of this river, as a feeder of the White Nile, may be neglected entirely. Its summer volume, entering Lake No, varies from 20 to 30 metres cube per second, while its flood discharge is even less, equalling from 12 to 20 metres cube per second. None of this water enters the White Nile, merely increasing the flooded area of Lake No. It, however, helps to augment the reservoir area of the main stream.

4. *The Bahr-el-Zaraf.*

This branch of the Bahr-el-Gebel adds to the volume of the White Nile, by an amount varying from 30 to 60 metres cube per second, in summer, and from 80 to 160 metres cube per second, when in flood. If, however, the Bahr-el-Gebel is closed by "sudd," then the discharge of the Bahr-el-Zaraf increases, possibly to from 300 to 400 metres cube per second, during the flood season.

5. *The Sobat.*

This river is the main supply of the White Nile, during the period of flood. The first effects of its waters are felt in May and June, while, as it does not reach its maximum until October and November, the volume of the Blue Nile having then been largely reduced, it maintains the discharge, passing Khartoum, to a very considerable figure. In years of good flood, the discharge of the Sobat varies from 900 to 1000 metres cube per second. In the early months of the year, its discharge shrinks to very low limits, its waters being held back by those of the White Nile. When in flood, the reverse is the case. The volume of the Sobat, being at that time, more than double that of the White Nile, causes a rise in the levels of the latter, upstream of the junction, and holds back its water as far as Lake No.

(1) This is excluding the water brought in by the Bahr-el-Zaraf. Downstream of the junction, the volume of the White Nile, upstream of the Sobat may be considered as varying between 300 and 500 metres cubes per second.

6. *The White Nile.*

The discharge of this river, below the Bahr-el-Zaraf junction, varies from 300 to 500 metres cube per second, according to the season of the year, and the nature of the flood. It is probable that the last figure is a maximum, and is never surpassed (¹). At El-Duem, 637 kilometres below the Sobat junction, the summer supply varies between 350, and 500 metres cube per second. The minimum levels are generally attained in the month of April, and the first half of May. The discharge, owing to the Sobat water, gradually increases until the Blue Nile flood exceeds the volume of 5000 metres cube per second, at Khartoum. As soon as this figure is passed, the discharge of the White Nile is reduced, by an amount varying from 30 to 60 per cent, and this holding back continues until the Blue Nile falls again below the figure above given. This reduction of the White Nile discharge takes place in the months of August and September. As soon as the Blue Nile discharge has fallen below 5000 metres cube per second, that of the White Nile rises very rapidly, attaining its maximum in the months of November and December, when as much as from 1500 to 1700 metres cube per second have been recorded. This increased discharge is, of course, partly due to the Sobat, but also to the draining off of the water which has been ponded up for so long a period. It seems safe to assume that the White Nile discharge at Khartoum, never, under any circumstances, exceeds 1800 cubic metres per second (²).

To sum up:—The White Nile is at its lowest from March to May. It rises in June, is checked again in August and September, and attains its maximum during the months of November and December. Its limits, in a low year, are from 300 to 1,500 metres cube per second, and in one of high flood, from 400, or 500 to 1700 metres cube per second (³).

7. *The Blue Nile.*

The supply of this river is chiefly derived from the drainage of the basin, through which it runs, and from the large tributaries which enter it, downstream of the point where it issues from the Abyssinian hills. The Tsana lake has but a small influence upon its supply, at any period of the year. It is at its lowest in May, when its discharge, at times, shrinks to nothing. It begins to rise in June, and attains its maximum about the end of August. Its discharge, in a year of good flood, is as much as 10000 metres cube per second, and it seems probable that, in a year of exceptional flood, 12000 metres cube may pass Khartoum (⁴). In September, it falls very rapidly, and during the winter months rarely discharges more than from 200 to 400 metres cube per second. The Khartoum gauges prove that a higher reading is recorded, for a given flood discharge, when the river is falling, than is the case when the river is rising. This is probably due to the filling of the valley, between Khartoum and the Shabluka pass.

8.—*The Atbara.*

The first water from this river reaches the Nile in the last week of June, and the maximum is usually reached in the last days of August, or in the first week of September. The Atbara generally attains its maximum, before the full flood from Khartoum has arrived

(¹) The dates of its maximum levels, upstream of the Sobat, coincide with those of the Bahr-el-Gebel.

(²) The flood in the White Nile in 1903 was an exceptionally high one, most probably a maximum, and yet the highest discharge recorded was under 1700 metres cube per second. Linant Pasha de Bellefonds's figure of 5907 metres cube per second, for the end of July, must be utterly wrong. Such a discharge can never have passed down the White Nile, under any circumstances. Chélu Bey's figures in "Le Nil," Paris 1891, for four mouths of 1876, would appear to be very fairly accurate, with one exception, i.e. the cube of 4,351 metres for September. This must be a mistake. Captain Peel's discharge for October 1851, of 1.409 metres cube per second, would also seem to represent the probable volume. but in a year when the Blue Nile had fallen early.

(³) The maximum is never reached until the late autumn, when the Blue Nile flood has passed away.

(⁴) Linant Pasha's discharge of 6104 metres cube per second, must either have been measured in a year of abnormally low flood, or at a date other than that when the river was at its maximum.

at the junction of the two rivers. After the maximum has been reached, the fall of the Atbara is rapid and, by the end of the year the river reverts to its summer state, of a series of pools. The maximum discharge of the Atbara, measured in 1903, was 3088 metres cube per second, but this is probably surpassed in a year of very high flood.

9.—*The Nile, north of Khartoum.*

The discharges of 1903 record a maximum of 10500 metres cube per second in an average year. If to this be added the volume of the Atbara, a total of nearly 14000 cubic metres per second was reached. As, in 1903, the levels, at both Wadi-Halfa and at Cairo, did not pass those of a very ordinary flood supply, it would seem probable that, in very high flood, a volume of quite 16000 metres cube per second must pass Berber.

In conclusion, it may be stated with confidence, that the White Nile contributes practically nothing to the flood which reaches Egypt. This is entirely derived from the Blue Nile, and from the Atbara. On the other hand, the supply passing Aswan during the spring and early summer, is due, almost entirely, to the water of the great lakes, brought down by the White Nile.

The following are the water-slopes of the two rivers, as worked out from the discharges:—

Bahr-el-Gebel.

At Wadelai ... ... $\frac{1}{27000}$ dry season.
At Bor ... ... $\frac{1}{13000}$ flood season.
At 830 kilometres from Lake Albert... $\frac{1}{33000}$ „ „
At Hellet en Nuer ... ... $\frac{1}{40000}$ „ „
At „ „ ... ... $\frac{1}{16000}$ dry season.
At Lake No ... ... $\frac{1}{87000}$ flood season.
At „ ... ... $\frac{1}{54000}$ dry season.

White Nile.

Above Sobat ... ... $\frac{1}{39000}$ dry season.
At Duem ... ... $\frac{1}{100000}$ when Blue Nile has fallen, and the White Nile is at its maximum.
„ ... ... $\frac{1}{80000}$ dry season.

Blue Nile.

At Khartoum ... ... $\frac{1}{11000}$ flood season.

SCHEMES FOR FURTHER UTILIZATION OF THE NILE SUPPLY.

In a previous report, published in 1901, the subject of utilizing the supply of the Upper Nile was treated at some length (1). At the time this report was written, the information existing, with regard to the regimen of the river, did not amount to a very large total, and the remarks which it contained, concerning possible schemes for the control of the Nile head-waters, were made, more with the intention of indicating the general lines upon which future study should be based, than with any idea of presenting definite proposals regarding this very important subject.

The present report is an advance upon its predecessor, in so far as it embodies the results of three years' further observations, and contains a certain amount of data which, in the year 1901, was still wanting. At the same time, the knowledge acquired during these last few years only serves to emphasize the fact, that much information, of the highest importance, is still wanting, and to strengthen the conviction that, before any one of the schemes under consideration can be seriously proposed for execution, a large amount of work is requisite, and much further study of the problems involved must be made.

That such studies should be, as yet, incomplete, is scarcely surprising.

The area traversed by the Nile is an immense one and the difficulties connected with travel in the regions through which it passes, are not inconsiderable.

A period of little more than five years has elapsed since the Dervish power was broken, and the Upper Nile valley was re-opened to travellers. The clearance of the "sudd" in the Bahr-el-Gebel has not yet been entirely completed, and it was not until the end of 1902 that it was found possible to despatch expeditions to the sources of the Blue and the White Niles. Further, previous to 1903, the Egyptian Government had entered upon a great task, namely, the construction of the Nile reservoir at Aswan. Until this work was completed, those controlling the finances of that country did not feel justified in embarking upon other large and far-reaching schemes of irrigation in the Soudan.

Now that the Aswan reservoir is an accomplished fact, it would seem that the time has come when such projects should be seriously examined and an endeavour made to bring some of them to a definite conclusion.

Although the main idea of the present note is to suggest schemes for the improvement of the Nile supply, based upon the experience gained and the observations made, during the past five years, it has another and equally important end in view, namely, to present proposals for the formation of a properly organized irrigation service in the Soudan, whereby the study of the river may be effectively continued and the different projects be presented to the Government of Egypt, in a complete and thoroughly considered form.

The problems to be investigated have two main objects, namely, that of increasing the water supply of Egypt in the summer and that of securing similar advantages to the Soudan during the same period. Both of these ends are of equal importance, although the former is perhaps the more likely to bring in an early return for the expenditure to be incurred.

The best way in which to secure the results aimed at, would appear to be; to reserve the waters of the Blue Nile for the improvement of the countries bordering that river, while Egypt, and the area of the Nile valley lying to the north of Khartoum, shall derive their summer supply from the sister river.

(1) Foreign Office Blue Book, Egypt (No 2) 1901. "Report as to Irrigation Projects on the Upper Nile."

The schemes in connection with the White Nile will be considered first. They are two in number; firstly, the regulation of the great lakes which feed it, and secondly, the prevention of the waste of water, caused by the vast swamps through which it passes in the upper portion of its course.

A reference to those portions of this report, descriptive of the outlets of the Nile from the Victoria and Albert lakes, will show that there should be no exceptional engineering difficulties in connection with the construction of works at either place, for controlling the river water, as it issues from these great reservoirs.

At the Ripon Falls, the construction of a regulator would be a comparatively easy task. The rock, as far as it can be examined on the surface, appears to be sound and good, and the width of the channel would permit of the foundations of the work being completed without any serious trouble.

Sir William Willcocks, in a recent work, has suggested lowering the crest of these falls, and, instead of attempting to raise the lake-surface, drawing upon the immense amount of water annually stored in this lake (¹). This suggestion is a sound one and, should regulation of the Victoria lake outfall ever be undertaken, the necessary works should be carried out upon these lines (²). No object would be attained by raising the water-level of Lake Victoria, even were it possible to do so. This, taking into account the area of the water-surface and the annual loss by evaporation, is extremely doubtful. On the other hand, there is, as an endeavour has been made to prove, an immense volume of water annually available upon which to draw. This volume, even after deducting the loss due to evaporation, is far more than sufficient to meet the wants both of Egypt and the Soudan.

Should, however, such a work ever be undertaken, it would, almost certainly, be necessary to embank the eighty kilometres of its course through Lake Choga. If this were not done, the only result of an increased discharge at the outlet of the river would be an increase of the area of this lake, and a corresponding increase in the loss caused by evaporation.

Beyond the difficulties due to the remoteness of the locality, the scarcity of trained labour, and the cost of transport and supplies, it may be stated with confidence, that there would be no special difficulties involved in the construction of a regulating work at the outlet of the Victoria Nile. Such a work would, in all probability, be far easier to construct than was either the dam at Aswan, or the barrage at Asyut.

Turning to the Albert lake, the best site for a regulator would undoubtedly be at the 15th kilometre downstream of the outlet, at the point where the high land borders the river channel upon either side. Any other point, between Magungo and Dufilé, would necessitate the construction of very heavy embankments, for a considerable length. Here again, no very special difficulties of construction would appear likely to arise. The rock is at some distance below the bed of the river, it is true, and the foundations of the work would have to descend to a considerable depth. Still, there would be nothing to be executed that has not frequently been successfully carried out by hydraulic engineers. The difficulties specified in connection with the work at the Ripon Falls, viz., remoteness of the locality, and the absence of labour and supplies, would be intensified here, as there is no line of railway within any measurable distance. Moreover, all building material would have to be brought from a long way, and the climate of this locality is notorious for its unhealthiness. With these exceptions, there should be no real trouble in executing this work, which is a perfectly feasible one.

It will be seen from the above, that the regulation of both lakes would present no insuperable difficulties, neither would the constructions required be of any colossal size.

(¹) "The Aswan Dam and After" by Sir WILLIAM WILLCOCKS, K.C.M.G. London, 1901.

(²) As the drop below the falls is a very sharp one, there should be comparatively little difficulty in lowering the river bed to the necessary depth by blasting away the rock.

They would merely be regulators of very ordinary dimensions, not larger than many which have been constructed in Egypt within recent years.

The objection to any proposals for augmenting the discharge from the Equatorial lakes, is that, under present conditions, the increased volume would never reach the White Nile, but would be entirely wasted in the marshes through which the Bahr-el-Gebel passes. That this is so will be evident to anyone who may take the trouble to read that portion of this report which more immediately relates to the discharge of that river. It will then be understood that barely 50 per cent of the water which now leaves the Albert lake in summer, ever arrives at the White Nile, while, in the flood, the proportion of loss is very much greater. In other words, the greater the amount of water in the Bahr-el-Gebel, the larger is the proportion of loss; while the discharge entering the White Nile is constant throughout the year. Until, then, some means have been found, whereby the water passing Lado, during the dry season of the year, can be brought down to Khartoum in undiminished volume, it is needless to consider the question of any regulation of the Albert and the Victoria lakes. These projects may therefore be postponed to a possible future, when the existing supply in the Bahr-el-Gebel shall have been made full use of, and when this shall have been found to be insufficient for the requirements of Egypt and the Soudan (1).

The second question to be studied is, how best to improve the channel of the Bahr-el-Gebel, so as to prevent the great wastage of water in the marshes, which, as has been shown, is maintained with but little variation throughout the year.

The solution of this problem is not nearly so easy as, at first sight, it may appear to be.

The discharges of the past few years have proved that, during the summer season, a discharge, varying from 600 to 700 cubic metres a second, passes Lado, while, during the flood, this increases to from 1000 to 2000 cubic metres per second; this last amount, probably, being a maximum. Further, they show, that, at Lake No, where the White Nile commences, i.e., 747 kilometres downstream, the volume discharged by the Bahr-el-Gebel, rarely exceeds 320 metres cube per second, even when the flood in the south is at its maximum. Lastly, they prove that much of this loss, in flood, occurs within a distance of some 163 kilometres from Lado, i.e., between that place and Bor.

Now, although it is of the highest importance so to train and embank the river that the entire summer discharge shall pass on in undiminished volume to the north, it is the reverse of desirable that the same result should be effected in the case of the flood-water. It is true that, in consequence of the holding-back effect of the Blue Nile flood upon that of the White Nile, this extra water could not reach Khartoum, until the Blue Nile had fallen very considerably. Admitting this, the effect of the ponding up of a volume of water, due to a discharge of 2000 metres cube per second, plus the flood discharge of the Sobat, would cause disastrous flooding in the White Nile and Bahr-el-Gebel marshes, and would probably set adrift large areas of the "sudd" grasses, which would float downstream, and possibly block the channel very seriously. It seems, then, most desirable to alter the existing flood-conditions of these rivers as little as is possible and, while securing the full summer discharge, to allow the flood water to waste and evaporate, upstream of Ghaba Shambé, much as it does at present. In other words, the objects of any works undertaken must be to preserve the regulating power of the marshes for the flood water and, at the same time, to find some means of preventing the present wastage in the river during the dry season of the year.

In the report, written in 1901, to which reference has been already made (2), it was suggested that the Bahr-el-Gebel should be embanked between Bor and Lake No, with the object of confining its water, at all seasons of the year, in one single channel. This

(1) If the improvement of the Bahr-el-Gebel, or Bahr-el-Zaraf, as suggested in the latter pages of this report, can be successfully accomplished, then the future alluded to need not necessarily be a very distant one.

(2) Foreign Office Blue Book. Egypt (No. 2) 1901.

suggestion was made with an imperfect knowledge of the conditions of this river during the period of flood. It was, at that time, imagined that the flood discharge found its way into the White Nile, through the marshes, with a scarcely diminished volume. The discharges of the last two years have proved that only from 15 to 25 per cent of this volume ever reaches Lake No. The question consequently has assumed an entirely different aspect. These swamps constitute a natural flood-escape for the waters of the Upper Nile, and it is most desirable that they should continue to do so. It has been shown, in those pages of this report relating to river discharges, that, in the reach, upstream of Ghaba Shambé, the loss of water in summer is chiefly due to the separation of the stream into different channels, many of them leading to large lagoons, and to the numerous spills through the low banks, into the adjoining marshes. Were these spills to be closed, and the subsidiary channels barred across, the summer water would probably arrive at Shambé with a volume but little diminished from that passing Gondokoro and Lado. The question to be considered is, would such measures cause the flood water also to pass on, without reduction in the river discharge? It is most improbable that the closing of the spill channels would have any material effect upon the flood supply, as this, at a very early stage, tops the low banks of the river, spreading over these and flooding the valley. Closing the different branches might, however, produce a marked effect upon the flood discharge. At the same time, unless these branches can be closed during the dry season, the main cause of wastage of water will not have been removed. It seems probable that, if these channels were closed across by low banks, not higher than those of the river itself, the end desired would be secured, i.e., the summer water would be prevented from wasting, and the flood water would rise over them and fill the channels, as at present. A simple method of closure would be to drive two parallel lines of stakes and wattles across the head of each channel, filling the intervening space with earth. Much of this earth would be removed during the flood, but, as the velocity, through these branches, is not great, the staking would probably remain. The banks could be made up again yearly, after the flood had subsided. Another, but much more expensive plan, would be to construct small regulators at the head of each branch channel, closing them during the summer season and opening them during the flood (1).

Sir William Willcocks, in a note written in 1899, proposes closing these channels by planting willows. Now, the willow is not found on the White Nile at all, but there would appear to be a very good substitute for it in the ambatch (2).

Throughout the Upper Nile, this plant grows in great luxuriance and, south of Dufilé, attains to an exceptional height and thickness of stem. The ambatch trees grow in the water, in straight lines bordering the channel, much resembling rows of poplars. North of Bedden, although very numerous, the plant never attains to the same height, or girth—why, it is hard to say, as the climate in both localities appears to be identical. As it thrives in fairly deep water, a line of ambatch, planted across the mouth of a channel, would surely, in time, close the channel altogether. It would very probably be sufficient to take a young tree, give it a sharp point like a stake, and drive it into the bed of the river. It seems almost certain that it would take root and flourish, if planted in this manner. The experiment is well worth a trial. If it succeeded, a very economical and easy method of closing the branch-channels would have been secured. Drifting vegetation and "sudd" would probably be arrested by these lines of trees and, eventually, the channel would be permanently closed. Another plan might be, to plant two rows of ambatch plants, and fill in the space between them with earth, up to the level of the river, during the period of low water.

(1) Such small regulators could probably be effectually constructed in "Béton Armé," which would largely obviate the difficulty of obtaining building materials in this region.

(2) "Herminiera Elaphoxilon."

By some one of these methods, the Nile, south of the Bahr-el-Zaraf outlet, would be confined, in summer, to one single channel. This should not arrest the filling, during flood, of the great reservoir between Lado and Ghaba Shambé, described on page 154 of this report. The water would always rise over the low banks and flood the valley. It could only pass to the north, by means of either the Bahr-el-Gebel, or the Bahr-el-Zaraf. Unless the former were to be widened and deepened its channel could not carry off the extra water, while measures would have to be taken to prevent its escape by means of the latter branch. These measures will be described later.

It would seem then possible, without any very heavy expenditure, to so train the Upper Nile, that, during the dry season, its waters should be delivered at the head of the Bahr-el-Zaraf, without any serious reduction of the volume passing Lado, while during the flood, they would fill the reservoir, upstream of Ghaba Shambé, to the same extent as they do under present conditions.

The next point to be considered is, how best to pass on the summer water, through the great marshes north of Bor, and deliver it into the channel of the White Nile without any serious diminution of the discharge.

The most natural way to effect this, would appear to be, to select one of the two main branches, namely, the Bahr-el-Gebel or the Bahr-el-Zaraf, and to improve its section, so as to render it capable of carrying a discharge of from 600 to 700 metres cube per second. This, as has been said, appears to be the most natural method to adopt, and would most probably be the cheapest. There is, however, another plan which, if it should prove, upon examination, to be feasible, would undoubtedly improve the river to an extent, far beyond any result that could be attained by merely remodelling one or other of the existing channels.

In order to understand this scheme, it will be necessary to refer to the accompanying small-scale map of the river.

It will be seen that a line, drawn through Bor, on the Upper Bahr-el-Gebel, and running due north and south, would cut the White Nile at, or near the point where the Sobat joins this river (¹). The distance between these two points, in a straight line, is approximately 340 kilometres. Were it possible to excavate an entirely new channel for the river, following this line, and to bring down its waters by this means, from the Upper Nile at Bor direct to the White Nile at the Sobat junction, the advantages that would be secured are so great and so obvious, as to outweigh almost every objection that could be made to the proposal; short of the fact that further knowledge might prove that its execution was a sheer impossibility—owing to the levels, or to the conformation of the intervening country.

These advantages may be briefly recounted:—

The entire swamp region would be avoided altogether—the floods in the river might cover these marshes unchecked, as at present, and the channels might be allowed to be blocked by "sudd," without exercising the slightest effect upon the discharge in the new channel—the distance to be travelled by the water would be largely reduced, and navigation would be immensely facilitated by following a direct and straight line—the training works upon the Upper Nile would stop short at Bor, and a distance of some 200 kilometres of such work would be thus economised. As the high land touches the Nile, on the east, at Bor, the new channel would take off in excavation, and much banking would be avoided.

Lastly, the discharge of the new branch would be under complete control, as a regulating head, with a lock, would be built at the point where it left the main river. Another, and larger regulator would be built across the Nile, at Bor, connected with the western high land by an embankment. With these two works, the control of the discharge, at all seasons, would be complete.

(¹) The longitude of this line appears to be, approximately, 31° 40' east of Greenwich.

PLAN II.

MAP

SHEWING PROPOSED NEW CHANNEL

FOR BAHR EL GEBEL.

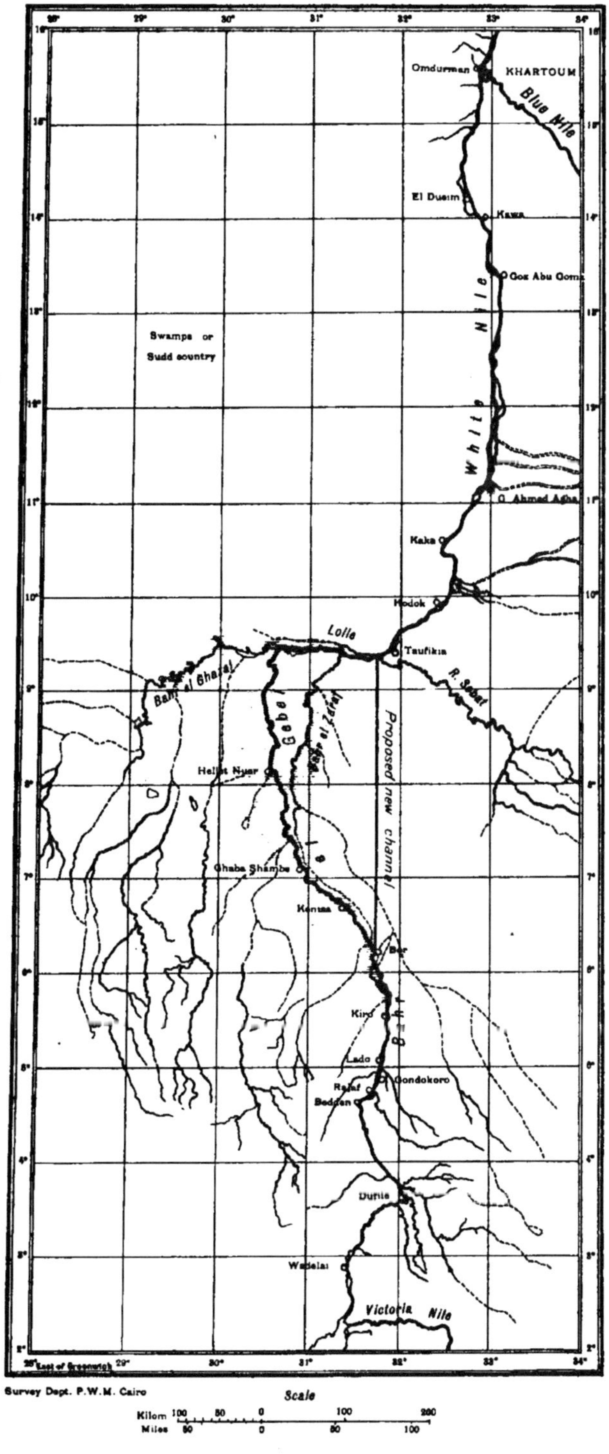

PLAN II.

MAP

SHEWING PROPOSED NEW CHANNEL

FOR BAHR EL GHAZAL

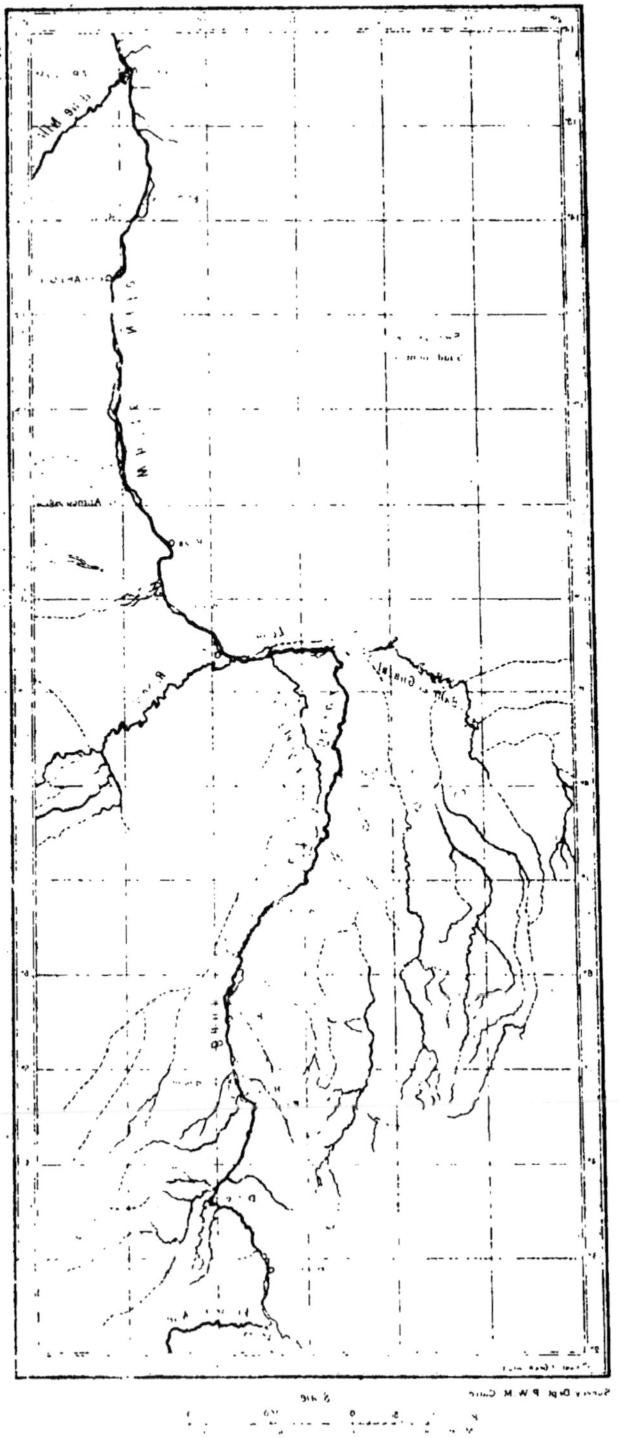

A reference to the chapter upon river discharges will show that, even in an exceptional flood, the discharge passing Bor never, under any circumstances, appears to exceed 1000 metres cube per second. There is no reason why the new channel should not be designed to carry such a volume, in fact, it is very desirable that it should eventually be capable of so doing. With a properly constructed head-regulator, the discharge would be effectively controlled and, during the summer months, it would be an immense advantage could this volume be passed into the White Nile. The only argument against it is that the cost of construction would be largely increased.

Such a discharge is only one-fifth greater than the maximum discharge of the Ibrahimiah Canal at Asyut which, in high floods, carries 800 metres cube per second.

It is true that this amount of water would not pass on to Khartoum, at the time when the Blue Nile discharge exceeded 5000 metres cube per second, but, at such a time, it would not be required, and the supply in the new channel might be reduced, merely keeping a sufficient level to ensure navigation, while the balance in the river might be allowed to escape down the Bahr-el-Gebel, and to flood the marshes. During the summer months, the advantages of having such a supply need no description. The water supply of Egypt would be secured, and the entire needs of the country lying north of Khartoum, as well.

Were a channel to be constructed of this capacity, it would then be most advisable to carry out the proposed schemes for the control of the Equatorial lakes; by constructing regulators at the Ripon Falls, and downstream of the outlet of the Bahr-el-Gebel from the Albert lake. In fact, the one project would be a complement of the other.

This proposal may, perhaps, seem to be so drastic a remedy for the present loss of water as to be inacceptable to some. In reality, it is not so drastic as, at first sight, it may appear to be. The real reason which, given that other conditions are favourable, would render its execution possible, is the power of escape supplied by the Gebel marshes. There is no question of turning the entire Nile flood down an artificial channel. What is proposed amounts to nothing more than the construction of an entirely new channel, not much larger than one of the great canals of Egypt, which would afford a means of delivering the summer water by the shortest and most direct route to the point where it was required and, by avoiding the great swamps, reducing the difficulties of maintenance and the loss of water which is caused by their presence. At the same time, these swamps would act as an effective regulating force to the flood water and would supplement the supply in the winter, in the same proportion as they do at present.

The following is a comparison of the length of the proposed new channel, with those of the Bahr-el-Gebel and El-Zaraf, including the White Nile, upstream of the Sobat junction :—

I.—New channel from Bor to the Sobat, as scaled from the map	340	kilometres.
II.—From Bor to the Sobat junction, via the Bahr-el-Gebel, Lake No, and the White Nile, approximately... ...	710	„
III.—From Bor to the Sobat, via the Bahr-el-Zaraf and the White Nile, approximately...	650	„

The question will naturally arise whether, with such a reduction in the distance traversed by the water, the increase in slope in the new channel would not be so great as to render navigation impossible. This cannot be solved until the difference of level between the two points has been ascertained.

Of course, the proposal is put forward in complete ignorance of this last fact, as well as of the conformation and nature of the country lying between these places. It may be that this difference of level is so great as to render the scheme impossible, except by the construction of a series of locks and regulators which, in such a remote region, could not be recommended. Considering the very flat slopes, both of the Bahr-el-Gebel and the White Nile, this does not seem very probable.

Again, the nature of the intervening country may cause the construction of such a channel to be so difficult, or, at all events, so costly as to render its execution prohibitive. The maps of this region give but little information on this subject except that certain drainage lines cross it, which would have to be provided for. Lastly, the levels may be so high as to enormously increase the cube of excavation, or so low as to necessitate the construction of heavy embankments. All these facts are unknown at present (1).

Such a work as the excavation of this channel, could only, owing to the impossibility of obtaining labour, be executed by machinery. Powerful excavators would be indispensable, and work might be commenced at either end, and be carried on simultaneously. It could probably be completed within a shorter period of time than that requisite for the remodelling of either the Bahr-el-Zaraf, or the Bahr-el-Ghazal (2).

The construction of a regulator in the Nile, below the head of this channel, and of a regulator and lock in the channel itself, would, in a country where neither labour nor building materials exist, be a work of considerable difficulty. Still, it cannot be said that such difficulties render the work impossible. Any estimate of the cost of such a work must be the merest approximation, at present (3).

The first, and the most urgent, necessity is a survey and a line of levels across country, from the Sobat junction to the point where the high bank abuts upon the Nile, at Bor. Until this work has been completed, it is useless to go into any further detail. All that can be said is that, the scheme, upon paper, looks a feasible one, and that, should it prove to be so, the advantages that would result from its execution are so great that it is worth a very considerable sacrifice of money and labour, to secure such a great and lasting benefit to Egypt and to the northern Soudan.

Should the proposals (made later in this report) for a permanent Irrigation Service in the Soudan be accepted by the Egyptian Government, the study of this project should take precedence over all others in that region.

Should the levelled survey prove this scheme to be impossible, then the question of selecting either the Bahr-el-Gebel, or the Bahr-el-Zaraf, for improvement, must be seriously considered, as being the only other possible alternative. At present, the carrying capacity of the Bahr-el-Gebel, is limited to some 400 metres cube per second, while the Bahr-el-Zaraf is, for a long distance downstream of the head, nothing but a line of marshes, and, even in its lower reaches, could not satisfactorily carry this discharge; much less what would be required, were it to be the sole channel for conveying the summer water to the Bahr-el-Abyad. As regards section, slope and general conditions, there is no comparison between the two branches. The Bahr-el-Gebel is undoubtedly the true river, with a depth of from 5 to 6 metres of water, even at its lowest, a strong stream, and an average width of from 70 to 80 metres. The Bahr-el-Zaraf is, in every way, much smaller. Its depth rarely exceeds 2 to 3 metres, its current is feeble, and its average width is between 40 and 50 metres. It more resembles a winding canal, or drainage line, than a great river. Whichever of these channels may eventually be selected, the Bahr-el-Gebel should always be maintained as the line for navigation, and kept open for this purpose. It must always therefore, carry a discharge, varying from 300 to 400 metres cube per second. With properly adapted dredging plant, it would be possible to so enlarge this channel, as to render it capable of carrying the entire summer discharge, of 600 or 700 metres cube per second. Were this to be done, however, it seems almost certain, that a largely increased

(1) The sketch of a portion of this country, made by Bimbashi H.H. Wilson. of the Soudan Service, shows that, for a portion of the distance, at any rate, the country is high, flat and wooded.

Sheet No. 66 N. Middle Sobat, published by the Intelligence Department, War Office, London 1903.

Again, Mr. Grogan in his book "From the Cape to Cairo," describes the country, east of the river, as being an immense plain, but high, and not very swampy.

(2) In all probability, such a work would be best done by giving it to some large contracting firm to execute.

(3) In appendix No. I. an approximate estimate of this work is given. For latest information regarding this project, see Appendix No. VI.

flood discharge would follow and that much of the retention, caused by the marshes, would disappear, while a very probable result would be, the setting adrift of large areas of "sudd" vegetation. It is then advisable to disturb the existing conditions, of this portion of the Bahr-el-Gebel, as little as possible. Some of the worst bends might be cut through and removed, and the connections between the river and the adjacent lagoons, be closed, but this is all that should be done.

In order to provide for the balance of the summer discharge, the Bahr-el-Zaraf should be made use of (1). The knowledge acquired, during the last two years' observation of the flood, has resulted in the conviction, that it is preferable to utilize this branch, in place of embanking, or enlarging, the Bahr-el-Gebel.

The Bahr-el-Zaraf has certain great advantages over the Bahr-el-Gebel, as a channel for the summer supply. In the first place, it is the shorter of the two, by some 60 or 70 kilometres, taking into account the length of the White Nile, between Lake No and the junction of the two rivers. In the second place, throughout the greater portion of its length it is enclosed between dry banks. In the third place, the water, entering the White Nile by the Bahr-el-Zaraf, would do so at a point some 80 kilometres downstream of Lake No. This last is a very strong argument in favour of selecting this line, rather than the Bahr-el-Gebel. It has already been explained that a considerable portion of the water, brought down by this last river, goes to raise the level and increase the limits of Lake No. The area of the evaporating basin is thus augmented. The more water passing down, the greater would be the proportionate loss. By making use of the Bahr-el-Zaraf, such loss would be avoided, as, previous to the arrival of the flood-water in the Sobat, there would be nothing to arrest the flood of the White Nile and, moreover, some 80 kilometres of bad swamp, bordering this river, would be thus avoided. It seems then most advisable to select the Bahr-el-Zaraf for the channel to convey the balance of the summer water from the south, and to so improve its section and capacity, as to render it capable of carrying from 500 to 600 cubic metres per second. The Bahr-el-Gebel would carry the remainder, i.e., its present volume, as its section would be left unchanged. The entire summer supply would be thus provided for, while navigation would follow its present course.

In order to prevent the flood discharge from passing down the Bahr-el-Zaraf, a regulating head would have to be built, at the point where it leaves the Bahr-el-Gebel, upstream of the "sudd." This head would be closed entirely during the flood season, i.e., when the Upper Nile was in flood. The selection of a satisfactory site for this regulator would be, perhaps, one of the most difficult questions in connection with the proposed improvements to the Bahr-el-Zaraf. For some 80 or 90 kilometres from the point where it leaves the Upper Nile, this branch has no defined channel at all, but consists of a long series of lagoons and marshes which are swamps, when the river is in flood, but dry in years of deficient supply.

The high bank approaches the Nile, on the eastern side, at Bor, but this place is 200 kilometres upstream of the point which is generally considered to be the offtake of the Bahr-el-Zaraf and, to make the new head here, would largely add to the length of channel to be improved. On the other hand, Mr. Grogan, in his march from Bor, to the junction of the Zaraf with the White Nile, followed the east bank of a wide branch of the river, which is apparently the boundary of the eastern marshes, and which, according to his sketch-map, joins the Bahr-el-Zaraf lower down (2). This channel he christened the Gertrude Nile. It might then be possible to make use of this, and pass the summer water down it into the Zaraf. If this were possible, then the regulating head could be constructed in the high land, near Bor. This point cannot be decided without further study, and an examination of the channel in question, or without a levelled survey of the proposed

(1) This was suggested as an alternative project, in page 54 of the published Blue Book, Egypt, No , 2, 1901.
(2) "From the Cape to Cairo," by E. S. GROGAN, London, 1900. See Appendix VI, where this channel is described.

alignment (1). If the utilization of the Gertrude Nile be not found feasible, then the only thing to be done will be, to construct a new, embanked channel for the Zaraf, leading from the Nile, through the marshes at the head, and to place the regulator somewhere on this line.

As regards the actual widening of the Bahr-el-Zaraf, this, for the most northerly 200 kilometres of channel, would not be a work of any great difficulty. The banks in this reach are fairly high. The section would require deepening, and the alignment, straightening, rather than any great addition to its width. For the next 70 or 80 kilometres, the banks would require raising, and there would be a considerable amount of straightening to be done, as the course is very twisting. In the last 80 or 90 kilometres, no channel at all exists, and a new one, bounded by good banks, would require to be made throughout.

Provision would have to be made in this channel to carry off the water of the large "khors," which enter the marshes near Bor, from the south-east. The best known of these "khors," are the Khos, the Tu, and the Gianetti. As the Bahr-el-Zaraf would be closed at the head, during flood, and the discharge of these depressions is, at no time, very important, there should be no great difficulty in arranging for this. Inlets might be provided on the east bank, with gates, which could be closed in summer, but opened in flood, to allow of the drainage of these "khors" passing down the Zaraf channel (2).

To estimate the cost of works, such as those outlined for the Bahr-el-Zaraf, with any degree of accuracy, is of course impossible, without cross-sections, or levels. Even the length of the channel is not accurately known, but it cannot be *less* than 360 kilometres, the distance, between Ghaba Shambé and the junction of the Zaraf with the White Nile. With the numerous bends, it is probably more.

In the report already alluded to, published in 1901 (3), an attempt was made, to roughly estimate the cost of remodelling the Bahr-el-Zaraf. This estimate was prepared, on the supposition, that the work would be executed by means of hydraulic dredgers, and completed within a period of five years from the date of its commencement. Owing to the remoteness of the locality, the impossibility of obtaining local labour, and the difficulties, connected with transport and supplies, dredging plant would most undoubtedly have to be made use of for such a work.

The estimate given in 1901, amounted to £E.1,250,000, but, with the information now to hand, it seems probable that this figure would be largely increased (4).

The project for utilizing the Bahr-el-Zaraf has certain disadvantages.

In the first place, this river, at present, acts as a flood-escape for the Bahr-el-Gebel and, in the second place, the length of the new embanked channel to be constructed, would be excessive.

With regard to the first, the closing off of this escape for the flood-water does not constitute a very serious objection to the scheme, provided always that the Bahr-el-Gebel is kept clear of "sudd," and is not permitted to become blocked, as in former times. The flood discharge of the Bahr-el-Zaraf in 1903, namely, in an abnormally high river, only amounted to some 150 metres cube per second. As long as the Bahr-el-Gebel is open, it is most improbable that the volume escaped by the Bahr-el-Zaraf can ever exceed this figure. The retention of this discharge could have but little effect upon the filling up of the great basin, south of Ghaba Shambé, beyond slightly increasing its area. The stoppage of the Zaraf escape would cause no more water to pass down the Gebel, in its course through the

(1) Captain Liddell, of the Egyptian Army, while recently searching for a good route for the telegraph line to Shambé, came across, what was apparently, this channel, to the east of Bor. He describes it as a fine, open piece of water, which the natives informed him, joined the Bahr-el-Zaraf further to the north. It is very possible that this, may eventually prove to be the best line to follow, always supposing that the channel from Bor to the Sobat proves to be impracticable. See Appendix VI.

(2) Although these "khors" are of large section, their slope is feeble. Their discharge can at no time be great. They are large lagoons, rather than streams.

(3) Foreign Office Blue Book—Egypt (N° 2) 1901.

(4) The estimate is given in Appendix No. 1.

swamps, as this channel could not carry the extra discharge, unless increased in section. Consequently, the existing conditions of the river would be practically unchanged.

The second objection to the utilisation of the Bahr-el-Zaraf as a summer discharge channel is more serious, inasmuch as it will involve a heavy expenditure. The task of embanking this branch of the river, throughout its length, is, moreover, one of considerable magnitude, but, by employing dredgers specially adapted to the work, it could undoubtedly be carried to completion.

To the estimate for this work, must be added the cost of training the Upper Nile, i.e., south of Shambé, and the expense entailed by the rectification of the Bahr-el-Gebel through the "sudd" region, by cutting off the worst bends, and by closing off the connections with the lagoons. It is practically impossible to estimate for such a work, without a much more detailed survey of the river than at present exists. Moreover, any such operations must be carried out slowly and tentatively.

As it is proposed, in these projects, to interfere with Nature upon a very considerable scale, such interference can only be attempted safely, if accompanied by great caution. The experience of the engineers upon the Mississippi bears ample testimony to the fact, that, although, in theory, it may be possible to shorten, or straighten a great river—in actual practice, this is impossible over a long distance, beyond a certain point. Any works, having such an end in view, must then be carried out very gradually, and the progressive effect watched with the greatest care.

If either of the schemes suggested can be successfully carried out, the problem of preventing the present wastage of the Upper Nile discharge, in summer, should be satisfactorily solved. The entire volume, of 600 to 700 metres cube per second, which annually passes Lado, during the dry season, should be conveyed to the White Nile with comparatively little loss. In other words, 50 per cent should be added to the discharge of this river at Khartoum (1).

The Sobat would, once its discharge had passed a certain point, hold back this water, as at present, to a certain extent. This would not, however, make any serious difference to Egypt, as such a result could not occur, until the Sobat discharge considerably exceeded that of the White Nile. Consequently, Egypt would obtain the necessary supply, at one time, by means of the White Nile, and at others, by the discharge of the Sobat (2).

It may be useful, at this point of the note, to give a brief "résumé" of the proposals contained in the foregoing pages.

They are as follows:—

(*a*) To prevent waste in summer, by closing of all spills, and barring all branch channels, the latter by earthen dams, or small masonry regulators, between Gondokoro and Ghaba Shambé. Also, to try the experiment of planting ambatch, as a means of closing these channels. The summer water would then be confined to one single stream, while the floods would rise over the valley, and form a great basin, as at present.

(*b*) To study the possibility of excavating a completely new channel, for the summer water of the Upper Nile, on an alignment running nearly due north and south, from Bor, to the Sobat junction with the White Nile. If the levels permit of it, this project should be carried out in preference to any other. The channel should be designed to eventually carry 1000 metres cube per second. A regulator and lock would be built at the head, and another regulator across the Nile, downstream of the new outlet.

(1) The wastage at Lake No would be neither more nor less than at present. 300 metres cube per second pass on north of this lake, and, as the Bahr-el-Gebel would be unaltered, would continue to do so. The extra 300 or 400 metres cube would be brought down by the Bahr-el-Zaraf, and delivered at a point, a long way downstream of Lake No.

(2) These remarks have, of course, reference only to the project for remodelling the Bahr-el-Zaraf. If the channel from Bor to the Sobat were to the constructed, it would be regulated at the head, so as to prevent, as far as possible, its waters from filling up the White Nile channel, upstream of the Sobat junction.

(*c*) If proposal (*b*) should turn out to be impracticable, then, but then only, measures should be taken to improve the Bahr-el-Gebel, through that portion of it which traverses the great marshes, i.e., from Ghaba Shambé to Lake No, by cutting off the worst of the existing bends, and by closing the connections between the river channel and the great lagoons. It is indispensable, under such circumstances, that this river shall be kept free from all blocking by "sudd," not only, because it would have always to remain the navigation channel between the White Nile and Gondokoro, but also, because it would be imperative to prevent any tendency of the flood water to burst out in the direction of the Bahr-el-Zaraf.

The Bahr-el-Gebel would thus, as it does at present, convey about half of the summer discharge at Lado to the White Nile and, even when the river was at its maximum, this discharge would remain constant.

(*d*) Again, if (*b*) is found to be not feasible, then the best project will be to widen, deepen and embank the Bahr-el-Zaraf, throughout its length, by means of powerful dredging plant, thus rendering it capable of carrying the balance of the summer water passing Gondokoro, and discharging it into the White Nile, at the present junction of the two rivers. By this means, the waste which at present occurs at Lake No, would be avoided, and the water would be brought down, from the south to the north, with comparatively little loss. Another great advantage of this scheme would be, that, supposing that the Bahr-el-Gebel did get temporarily blocked by "sudd" during summer, an alternative channel would exist, capable of carrying a considerable, probably the greater, portion of the summer supply. A regulating head would be built for this river, at the point where it leaves the Upper Nile, which, during flood, would be closed entirely. At this period of the year, the Bahr-el-Zaraf would remain dry, except for the drainage water which would enter it, controlled by inlets in the banks, from the right and from the left. If it were found unadvisable, owing to the difficulties caused by the marshes, to construct this head, at the point where Bahr-el-Zaraf takes off from the Upper Nile, it might be possible to utilize the channel, named by Mr. Grogan, the Gertrude Nile, and continue the remodelled Zaraf up to the high land at Bor, where a head could, without difficulty, be constructed.

(*e*) Once the channel for the summer water had been satisfactorily completed, the schemes for regulating on the outlets of the Victoria and Albert lakes, should be put in hand, in order that a constant discharge, of 1000 metres cube per second, should be poured into the White Nile, during the season of lowest supply.

Before leaving the subject of the White Nile, a few words are necessary, as to the method in which the main works should be carried out. These works apply to the proposed new channel from Bor, equally to the work required on the Bahr-el-Zaraf, should the former scheme be rejected. There is no question, that the only practical way would be by the assistance of a fleet of powerful hydraulic dredgers, or excavators, specially designed to meet the various necessities of the case. Several different types would, almost to a certainty, be required, before the work was completed. It would consequently, be advisable to commence with a small number, say with two or three, adding to these, and altering the type, according to the knowledge gained by the experience of the earlier work. To carry out such an undertaking by hand-labour would be practically impossible, and would, almost to a certainty, result in failure (1). The conditions under which the works would have, in this region, to be carried out, constitute the chief difficulty. The local tribes can never be counted upon to provide labour—all supplies would have to be brought from Khartoum, which is more than 950 kilometres from the *nearest* point of the work—fuel for the dredgers and steamers is a difficulty of yearly increasing magnitude—malaria is, at all seasons, prevalent

(1) The advantage of using hydraulic dredgers of high power, for the training and improvement of rivers, has long been recognized in America. On the Mississippi, such dredgers have long been regularly made use of. The Senate Commission's report upon this river, for 1897, states, that such good results have ensued from hydraulic dredging, that ample provision is recommended for continuing the work.

in these marshes—the temperature, even in winter, is high, and the dampness of the atmosphere must be felt to be appreciated. For some months annually, i.e., from June to September, the rainfall is so heavy that continuous work would be well-nigh impossible. Lastly, the mosquitoes of this region are probably more numerous and more ferocious than in any other part of the world. These difficulties constitute a formidable list, and it must be admitted that the task is a heavy one. Still, it is not impossible. It is merely a question of money and time, and possibly of a certain loss of life—the toll levied upon the workers by the climate.

The advantages that would accrue to Egypt, and to the Soudan, north of Khartoum, could an increased discharge of from 600 to 700 metres cube per second be added to the volume of the river, at the period when water is most required, are so great and so obvious, as to warrant an attempt to secure them, even more difficult, and more costly, than that proposed in these pages.

In any such project, the unknown point must, of course, always be, as to how much of this extra water would actually reach Aswan, supposing that the wastage through the "sudd" region could be successfully arrested. The White Nile swamps would doubtless absorb a certain quantity, and evaporation between the Bahr-el-Zaraf and the first cataract, would still further reduce the volume. Allowing that this loss was as much as one-third, which is a high estimate—even so, the balance would form a most important addition to the summer supply of Egypt, and one well worth spending a large sum of money to secure.

It is now necessary to consider the second of the great questions connected with the control of the Nile, viz., the possible utilization of the Blue Nile, as a means of increasing the water supply in summer. The opinion has already been given in these pages that any works undertaken upon this river, should be designed, and carried out, in the interests of the Soudan rather than of Egypt—the latter country deriving its increased discharge from the waters of the White Nile.

There can be no question that by far the best and most certain method of increasing the Blue Nile supply, during the months prior to the annual rise, would be by the construction of regulating works at the outlet of the river from the Tsana lake, using the latter as a storage reservoir, under effective control. No other schemes for this purpose can ever give the same results as this one, and it is more than doubtful whether any one of them will be effectual, except in a very limited degree.

But little is, as yet, known of this river, in the distance between its sources in the Abyssinian plateau and Famaka, where it enters into Soudanese territory. Several attempts have been made, by travellers, to follow this portion of its course, but none of them have been successful. Sites, adapted for the formation of a large reservoir, may exist within this length, although, from the very heavy fall in the bed-levels that must exist throughout, it seems most improbable that such should be the case. Moreover, should suitable sites be found here, they must lie within the Abyssinian boundaries and the objections existing to the construction of works at Tsana, must apply, with equal force, to them.

The waters of the Abai, or Blue Nile, anywhere within the lower portion of its course through the hills, must be so heavily charged with silt, when in flood, that any attempt to store them, at this period, by the construction of a dam across the channel, would inevitably result in such a heavy deposit of the matter in suspension, that the bed would quickly rise and the capacity of the reservoir gradually disappear. The Blue Nile being a torrential river, when the flood subsides, its discharge is largely reduced. At the period then, when its waters are clear and free from deposit, the volume available for storage has been diminished to a very considerable extent. It is just possible that, after the heavily-charged water has passed, the discharge may still be sufficient to permit of a considerable cube of water being stored, given a site possessing the necessary conditions in the valley itself. It is impossible, as yet, to verify this, as, although the average discharge passing Khartoum, throughout the year, is known, it is not known how much of this is due to the Abai, and how much to its different tributaries; notably to its greatest affluent, the Dudessa. Regarding this river, which some travellers have asserted to be even more important, as to volume, than the Abai itself, next to nothing is known—nothing at all events, of which use can be made for studying the relations existing between the two streams and their respective volumes throughout the year.

It seems most unlikely that any site on the Blue Nile, or Dudessa, can be as well situated as is Lake Tsana, for the purpose required and, if a reservoir has to be constructed within foreign territory at all, that spot should certainly be selected for its construction.

Outside of Abyssinian territory, i.e., between Famaka and Rosaires, it may be that a site can be found, whereupon a dam and reservoir might be constructed, but, owing to the heavy slope of this reach of river, the storage capacity of such a reservoir could hardly be great. Such a work might, however, serve a useful purpose, in supplementing the winter supply in the Blue Nile. This point is one requiring early study in connection with projects for this river (1).

Reference has been repeatedly made in these pages to a report upon irrigation projects on the Upper Nile, published in 1901 (2). In that report, the utilization of Lake Tsana as a storage reservoir, was recommended, in preference to any other method of increasing the water-supply of Egypt and of the Soudan. Since it was written, this lake has been visited and studied by an expert, with a view to ascertaining how far it was really suited for this purpose. In December 1902, Mr. Dupuis, of the Egyptian Irrigation Service, visited Lake Tsana, making a complete circuit of its shores. The results of this journey are embodied in a very interesting and able note, which is appended to the present report (3).

Mr. Dupuis's researches do not give quite so favourable a report, as regards the quantity of water that can be stored, as was hoped would be the case. His entire note will well repay perusal, but, for convenience of discussion, the main points contained in it may be briefly mentioned here.

He considers that the following may be assumed, with a fair amount of accuracy:—

The range of the lake varies from 1.25, to 2 metres, according as the year is marked by poor rainfall, or the reverse. In an average year, it may be taken to be 1.5 metres.

The amount of water annually entering the lake, he estimates, at 6500 million of cubic metres, in an unfavourable year, and at considerably more in one of heavy rainfall (4).

The discharge of the Abai, at the outlet, as measured by him, on the 31st of January 1903, was only 42 cubic metres per second. This discharge was observed when the lake level was still 0.50 metres above its minimum level in the month of May. As such a small discharge can in no way account for the fall in the lake-levels, it is evident that the chief factor in lowering the water surface, must be evaporation.

Mr. Dupuis gives the calculations by which he arrives at the average daily account of evaporation throughout the dry season of the year. They appear to be based upon sound reasoning, and it may fairly be assumed that, during the eight dry months, i.e., from October to the end of May, the lake surface is lowered by evaporation alone, at the rate of from 4, to 4.5, millimetres per diem (5). He allows a daily average of 2 millimetres for the four

(1) i.e., as soon as a properly constituted Irrigation Service is organized for the Soudan.

(2) Foreign Office Blue Book — Egypt (N° 2) 1901.

(3) See Part III, of this report.

(4) This is based upon the supposition, that the "run-off," is only 25 per cent of the annual rainfall throughout the catchment basin.

(5) Of course, the value of these calculations depends entirely upon four assumptions; namely, the area of the catchment basin—the amount of the annual rainfall—the mean annual discharge of the Abai, and the range of the lake levels.

The first of these is estimated from the most recent maps—the second, from one year's observation at Gondar—the third from Mr. Dupuis's discharge, and from his measurements of the river channel, while the fourth is calculated from an examination of the flood marks in the vicinity of the lake, and from the statements of the inhabitants. Although then, they cannot be considered as other than approximations, they appear to be justifiable assumptions, based upon a certain amount of fact.

wet months, but this, as he says, is mere assumption. Finally, calculating from an observed fall in the lake, in a given period, and from observed discharges of the in-flowing rivers, as well as of that flowing out, he arrives at a mean daily discharge of the Abai, throughout the year, equal to 8,000,000 metres cube.

The figures thus become :—

	Millions of metres cube.
Total volume received into the lake during the year.	6572
Total volume evaporated during the year...	3648
Total volume discharged by Abai during the year	2924

The annual evaporation then, accepting these figures as fair approximations, amounts to some 55 per cent of the total amount of water entering Lake Tsana in the year; the Abai drawing off the balance, or 45 per cent.

The storage capacity of the lake may therefore be considered to be some 3000,000,000 metres cube ([1]). It is evident that such an amount of water, if it could be stored and discharged, under control, into the Blue Nile during the season of low supply, would render the greatest possible service to the countries which border the river. It would be equivalent to a daily discharge of 30 millions of cubic metres per diem, for 100 days, or of 15 millions of cubic metres, daily, delivered during the months of January to June, inclusive.

As regards the works necessary for the regulation of the lake, Mr. Dupuis does not consider that the construction of a regulator on the Abai would be a work of any supreme difficulty, except for the absence of labour and limestone, and those others connected with transport and supply. He advises that the existing conditions of the lake-levels should be interfered with as little as possible, and that the water surface should not be raised, or the large grazing belts round the lake shores be disturbed. He recommends that the river-bed, for some distance below the outlet, should be lowered, and says that there should be no serious difficulty in the execution of such a work. In this suggestion, Mr. Dupuis is in agreement with the proposals made by Sir William Willcocks, in a recent work ([2]).

There can be no question that these proposals are sound, and that, as in the case of a possible regulator at the Ripon Falls, no attempt at raising the water-levels should be made. The floor of the structure, and the river bed, should be lowered to a depth, sufficient to permit of full use being made of the large supply available, after deducting the amount lost by evaporation.

Finally, Mr. Dupuis estimates that a regulator of 40 openings, of 3 metres each, with the floor sunk to 4 metres below ordinary high-water level in the lake—built in the Abai, at some 10 kilometres below the outlet—would meet the requirements of the case.

There can be no two opinions as to the suitability of Lake Tsana, as a storage reservoir for the Blue Nile. The river, after it leaves the lake, has a heavy fall, and, for a great portion of its course, a rocky bed. The loss of water would be comparatively small and, with a system of weirs constructed in the river bed, between Rosaires and Khartoum, with canals taking off above them, on either side, the summer irrigation, both of the Ghezireh and of the eastern provinces, could be easily and simply effected. Unfortunately, owing to its situation, the political difficulties appear to be so great, that the chance of any such work being carried out must be relegated to a very distant future, if not abandoned altogether. Doubtless, at some period in the world's history, these difficulties will disappear, and advantage will be taken of the obvious suitability of this lake, as a great natural reservoir.

([1]) Mr. Dupuis considers that the above figure represents the capacity for an average year, while, in a low one, it may be reduced to 2,000 millions of metres cube. In his calculations, however, although his range of 1.5 metres is that for a year of mean rainfall, his total of 6,500 millions, entering the lake, is calculated for an *unfavourable* year. As his "run-off," viz 25 per cent of the annual rainfall, appears to be rather low, for a country not very thickly forested, the figure of 3,000 millions may be allowed to stand, as representing the amount that may probably always be counted upon.

([2]) "The Nile Reservoir Dam at Assuan and after" by SIR WILLIAM WILLCOCKS, K.C.M.G., London 1901.

Meanwhile, it is necessary, however reluctantly, to abandon this project and to search for some other means of introducing irrigation into the tracts adjoining the Blue Nile.

Allusion has already been made to the possibility of constructing a dam at the head of the Rosaires rapids, thus forming a reservoir of limited capacity, which would render some assistance to the supply in winter, or in the spring months. Such a scheme, if feasible, would be a useful one, but it will be necessary to go further, and to search in other directions, if any large area of country is to be benefited by an increased water supply. In this connection, the other rivers, which, as well as the Blue Nile, water the eastern Soudan, must be studied, to see if any use can be made of them for this purpose. These rivers are the Dinder, the Rahad and the Atbara, all of which, after issuing from the hills, lie within the frontier of the Soudan. All three are torrential in character—dry during the summer months, with the exception of a few pools, but bringing down large quantities of water, heavily charged with deposit, during the rainy season, when in full flood.

As regards the first two, but little is known of their slope, section or volume. They traverse a tract of country, comprising some of the richest alluvial soil in the Soudan, and could any means be found, by which their flood-waters could be stored and made use of during the months of the spring and early summer, a large area, especially suited for the cultivation of cotton and other valuable crops, could eventually be brought into cultivation. Until, however, these rivers have been studied and facts collected regarding them, no opinion can be formed regarding their suitability for such a purpose, and they must, for the present, be considered merely as possible sources of future supply.

As regards the Atbara, M. Dupuis, in his recent journey, made an inspection of this tributary of the Nile, and his note thereupon is attached to this report (1). His account is not altogether a favourable one.

The Atbara rises in the north-western slopes of the Abyssinian plateau, and leaves the hills, not far from Gallabat. It is formed by the confluence of three large streams, the Goang, the Bubwena and the Gandwaha. On entering the plains, the general course of the Atbara is northerly, until Goz Regeb is reached, when it trends to the north-west, maintaining this general direction until it joins the Nile, south of Berber. It receives the waters of numerous streams from the eastern hills, its principal tributaries being the Salaam and the Settit. This last is probably a more important river than the Atbara.

The tract of country through which the Atbara passes is, at present, unwatered, but the soil is good and, with irrigation, should be capable of producing almost any crop. During the winter and early summer months both the Atbara and the Settit consist of dry stretches of sand, alternating with large, and deep pools (2). They commence to rise in the month of June, and in August and September are in full flood. At this time, their waters contain much deposit—the scourings of the volcanic rocks, and the leaf-mould of the forests. Although clear and limpid when the discharge is low, the water is so heavily laden with silt during the flood, that its colour resembles that of coffee, more than anything else (3). The floods, in both the Atbara and Settit, subside as quickly as they rise, and the question to be studied is, whether there is sufficient water available for storage purposes, after the muddy flood-water has passed away, to make it worth while undertaking the construction of expensive works. Mr. Dupuis is disposed to answer this question in the affirmative, on the grounds that, as the total annual discharge of the Atbara, below the Settit junction, amounts to some 20,000 millions of cubic metres, a comparatively small proportion of this amount would suffice to fill a reservoir of a capacity great enough to irrigate a very large area.

(1) See Part III, of this report.

(2) The Atbara was measured by Mr. Dupuis, in December 1902. The discharge was then only one cubic metre per second. The Settit, in March 1903, was only discharging a quarter of this amount.

(3) The Arabs call the Atbara the "Bahr-el-Aswid" or Black River.

This is true, but, as the flood of the Atbara subsides extremely quickly, it remains to be proved whether, after the muddy water has passed, the discharge available will be sufficient for the required purpose (1). The question can only be tested by observations and discharges, carried out through a series of years.

The discharges of 1902 and 1903 are good, as far as they go, but they do not go far enough. They show the rise, and the maximum flood, for each year, but they do not show how much water is available for storage during the winter months and, of course, give no information as to the time when the water becomes clear and free from deposit.

Mr. Dupuis recommends a dam, of the type of that built at Aswan. This would permit of the passage of the flood water unchecked, and would only be closed when the muddy water had passed away and the stream was clear. He suggests the site of Kashim-el-Girba, as well-suited for the construction of such a dam. This would irrigate the area in the northern reaches of the river, but would leave unwatered the large tract between this place and Gallabat. The only way in which this land could be irrigated would be by a dam much further to the south. According to Mr. Dupuis, such a project would be a very costly one, as the slope of the river, above and below the Settit junction, is very heavy ($\frac{1}{2000}$), while the valley of the river is so deep, that a dam of great height would be necessitated.

There remains one other project for consideration, in connection with Mr. Dupuis's report, which, although not actually connected with the Nile supply, relates to the improvement of a portion of the Soudan and, as such, merits mention in this report. The scheme in question is that of storing and controlling the waters of the river Gash, and thus irrigating the country in the vicinity of Kassala. The study of this project was one of the objects of Mr. Dupuis's late mission (2). The Gash, like the Atbara and Settit, is a torrential stream, having its rise in the northern slopes of the Abyssinian plateau. It flows between well-defined banks, in a north-westerly direction from the hills, until it approaches Kassala. From this point, it begins to spill over the country and eventually loses itself in the sands to the north.

This river is only in flood for some eighty days of the year. It comes down early in July, and dries up towards the end of September. For the rest of the year, it is absolutely dry. While in flood, it runs constantly, rising and falling frequently, though irregularly, but never, or rarely failing altogether. It is occasionally impassable for two or three days at a time (3). Its waters, during the period of flood, are very muddy, and this is one of the chief causes of its disappearance in the sands. The water arrives at the head of the delta, loaded with silt. When the diminishing slope of the country can no longer maintain a velocity in its channel sufficient to keep this material moving, it is thrown down on the bed. The channel is thus blocked, and eventually obliterated, while the clear water spills over the country and sinks into the soil.

Mr. Dupuis proposes to construct a large circular basin, somewhere near the apex of the delta of this river, into which it should be trained by means of banks on either side. The flood water would thus be received into this basin, which it would be allowed to fill up. The clear water, after it had deposited its silt, would be passed through regulators constructed in the basin banks into distributary canals, of which the different regulators would form the heads. In this manner, a complete control would be maintained of the river when in flood. The idea seems to be a good one, but, without more information as to levels, and without some discharges of the Gash during flood, it is impossible to say more

(1) In 1902. the Atbara fell from 2,020 metres cube per second on the 8th of September, to 152 metres cube on the 6th of October. In 1903, the maximum of 3,088 metres cube was measured on the 30th of August. On the 5th of October, i.e., 36 days later, it had fallen to 703 metres cube per second.

(2) See Mr. Dupuis's Report on this river, in Part III.

(3) Mr. Dupuis estimates the ordinary flood discharge of the Gash to be 100 metres cube per second, or 8 millions of cubic metres per diem. It must, however, at times, bring down a larger discharge than this.

about it than that it appears to be a sound, and a feasible, project. As the locality is a very favourable one for irrigation development, and as the difficulties which exist in other portions of the Soudan, as to scarcity of population, are not nearly so great in the country round Kassala, this project should be one of those earliest studied in the future. It has a very great advantage over all others, in the fact, that water thus made use of, would in no way affect the supply of the Nile.

Each of the projects for the eastern Soudan, as described in the foregoing pages, relates to summer, or "Sefi," irrigation alone. Should it be found, upon further and fuller study, that, either on account of expense, or the impossibility of increasing the Blue Nile water-supply, they have to be postponed, or abandoned, there still remains another method of adding to the productive wealth of these areas, to which the objection of an insufficient water-supply does not apply. This method, is the introduction of flood and winter irrigation, for the cultivation of cereals and other winter crops.

Concerning this proposal, the remarks made in a former report, may be quoted here, as the opinions therein expressed, have undergone no material change (1).

On pages 20 and 21 of the report in question, the following passages occur :

" The true agricultural future of the tracts adjoining the Blue Nile, does not, however, lie in the" "direction of summer irrigation, but rather in the development of those crops which can be ripened during" "the winter months. The soil of the Ghezireh, and of a large portion of the lands lying to the east of the" "river, much resembles that of those parts of India which produce the finest wheat. The climate of the" "two countries is very similar, but in the Soudan, one important agent is wanting, viz, a winter rainfall." "Without this, winter crops cannot be raised, except in comparatively small areas adjacent to the river." "Canal, or basin, irrigation must then be supplied as a substitute for the absence of rain in winter." "Were this provided, the Province of Sennar, and the southern portion of the Province of Khartoum," "might become one of the finest wheat-producing areas in the world. Their soil consists, almost every-" "where, of rich alluvial deposit, and the climate, in winter, seems specially suited to the production of" "cereals. Under the hot sun of these latitudes, wheat would ripen early, and be harvested in March." "During the winter months, the supply of water in Egypt, is more than ample for the demands of irriga-" "tion, and the Blue Nile might safely be drawn upon during this period. Were then, irrigation works" "upon this river, to be strictly limited to the development of winter crops, they might, given the necessary" "funds, and a sufficient population, be undertaken at once, as far as Egypt is concerned. The proposed" "railway, connecting Abu Haraz, Gedarif, and Kassala with the Red Sea, would tap these wheat-producing" "districts, and would probably enable them to compete successfully with India in the European markets." "Mecca and the Hedjaz would, almost to a certainty, take large quantities of wheat. It is not possible, in" "a note like the present, to do more than hint at the description of the works necessary for the irrigation" "of these tracts. They would, as has been said, comprise a regulating dam, or set of dams, in the river," "which would raise the water to the level required for the irrigation of the land, on either side. Canals," "of large section, would take off the water from above the dam on either bank, distributing it by means of" "a system of branch canals, or by a combination of canals and basins, according as the slope of the country" "might permit. A combined system of basins and canals would have this advantage over canals alone, in" "that it would permit of the wheat lands being yearly flooded with the rich muddy waters of the Blue" "Nile. The area is so great, comprising many millions of acres, that large tracts might be reserved for the" "cultivation of Dhurra, or Maize, during the rainy season."

At the time that the above was written, the proposed railway, connecting Khartoum with the Red Sea, was merely a possible project for the future, and but little was known regarding the winter discharges of the Blue Nile. At the present moment, work has been commenced on the Suakin-Berber railway and, in a couple of years' time, through communication should be opened between the former port and Khartoum. Once the railway is completed, the situation may be expected to develop rapidly, and facilities for the transport of agricultural produce, from the Blue Nile, to the European and Arabian markets, will have been assured.

(1) Foreign Office Blue Book—Egypt (No. 5) 1899.

As regards the river supply, the discharges of the Blue Nile have been measured regularly since May 1902, and a study of the Khartoum gauges for the last four years shows that the Blue Nile did not fall below a level of 0·50 on the gauge, before the following dates :—

In 1901 on the 25th of February
„ 1902 „ „ 1st „ February
„ 1903 „ „ 9th „ February
„ 1904 it had not reached this level by the 1st of March.

Now, a gauge of 0·50 at Khartoum is equivalent to a discharge of 200 cubic metres per second in the Blue Nile, or to some 17,000,000 cubic metres per diem. Such a discharge would be sufficient for the irrigation of 800,000 acres of winter crops, at the least. All through the month of January, the discharges in the above years were considerably superior to this figure, while, in December, the average volume was above 500 metres cube per second, for each of the years in question. As the winter irrigation would take place principally in the months of December, January, and the first half of February, it appears undeniable that, even in a low year like 1902, there would be a sufficient volume in the river to ensure the watering of a large area of crop (1). The only argument that could be brought against thus making use of the Blue Nile water would be, that the filling of the Aswan reservoir would be spread over a considerably longer period of time than is at present required for this purpose. This is not however a sufficient reason for rejecting the scheme and, should the proposed works on the White Nile prove to be successful in increasing the volume of water brought down to Aswan, this argument would lose its force.

Even should this not be the case, it may be possible, as has already been explained, to form a small reservoir, upstream of Rosaires, which would materially assist in augmenting the winter discharge of the Blue Nile.

For the irrigation of the tracts adjoining this river open weirs, provided with locks, would have to be constructed at suitable sites in the river. In all probability, one such work would be sufficient for the requirements of the country, for a long time to come.

As a commencement, it would seem to be advisable to begin with the irrigation of the northern portion of the Ghezireh, and of those tracts on the eastern bank, lying to the north of Wad Medani. Here, the country is open and comparatively free from bush and forest. Moreover, from its vicinity to Khartoum and the railway, it would appear to be more likely to lend itself to improvement than do the remoter areas to the south. This barrage would most be probably constructed somewhere downstream of the point where the Rahad river joins the Blue Nile, so that the east bank canal could be carried down to the north, without having to cross any stream of importance (2). Should it be found necessary in the future to extend irrigation to the southern tracts, one, or more barrages, further up the river, would have to be constructed, but it does not seem likely that any large development of irrigation, in the country south of Sennar, will be required for many a year to come.

The canal systems would probably entail a considerable expenditure, but these works could be carried out very gradually, and their extension would keep pace with the increase of population, and with irrigation requirements. Should the construction of such a barrage be ever undertaken, it would greatly assist the development of agriculture, were a line of light railway to be constructed on the west bank of the Blue Nile, connecting Khartoum with Wad Medani. Such a line would enable the produce to be brought down to the main line of railway at Halfaya, and thence be conveyed to the port at Suakin (3).

(1) In 1902, by the 15th of February, the level had only fallen 0·17 metres.

(2) As the height to which the water would have to be raised owing to the levels of the country, be considerable, a double weir would most probably be required. It would be a question for study whether it would not be advisable to construct the proposed weir a good deal further up the river. Of course, under such circumstances, the length of the distributary canals would be largely increased.

(3) There appears to be every probability that, if water can be supplied, say, to the middle of February, cotton could be largely grown in these tracts. The experiments made in the Soudan seem to render it a certainty that, cotton planted in the end of June, and watered regularly to the 15th of February, will flourish, and produce a crop.

Before considering the country to the north of Khartoum, it may be as well, as was done for the White Nile, to recapitulate the various projects requiring study on the Blue Nile.

The best and the most complete project in connection with the Blue Nile is, beyond all question, that of constructing a regulator at the outlet of the river, at Lake Tsana, whereby this lake may be converted into a storage reservoir of large size. Were it not for the fact that it lies outside of the Soudan frontier, and that its construction might cause political difficulties, it would be unnecessary to look beyond this scheme, for a means of satisfactorily increasing the volume of the Blue Nile discharge in summer. A reservoir that would store, at a comparatively small cost, 3000 millions of cubic metres of water, would amply suffice for the wants of the Ghezireh and of the eastern Soudan. Unfortunately, the questions involved by its position are so many, and so difficult of adjustment, that the abandonment of this project, to an indefinite future, appears to be a matter of certainty. This being so, it is necessary to search for a project, or projects, involving the construction of works within the territories of the Soudan. The following list gives the different projects requiring study, in this direction, in the order of their importance:—

(1) The selection of a site for an open barrage, in the vicinity of Wad Medani. Such a study would involve that of the projects for the main canals, east and west of the river.

(2) The possibility of making a storage reservoir of limited capacity, within Soudan territory, by means of a dam constructed at or south of the Rosaires rapids. This reservoir would be filled during the months of October and November, and would be made use of for augmenting the river supply, during the months of December, January and February.

(3) The project for improving the irrigation from the river Gash, by means of a basin for controlling the floods, with its subsidiary canals.

(4) The study of the project for constructing a dam and storage reservoir in the Atbara river, near Kashim-el-Girba.

(5) An examination of the rivers Dinder and Rahad, with a view to ascertaining whether the construction of storage reservoirs at any points of their course is practically possible.

(6) An examination of the upper valley of the Atbara, with the same end in view.

As regards the river valley, to the north of Khartoum, and between that place and Berber, the conditions are entirely different from those of the Blue Nile, and more nearly resemble those of Upper Egypt, and of the Dongola Province. The rainfall is irregular, being limited, even south of Shendy, to heavy, but local storms. The strip of good land on either side of the river, bounded by the desert, is not very wide. In this region, the best plan to follow for improving these lands is, undoubtedly, the erection of large pumping stations, capable of irrigating a large area of country. In addition, certain selected tracts might advantageously be turned into basins, but the expenditure would be heavy in proportion to the result to be obtained. The general conditions prevailing in Egypt, between Aswan and Asyut, would thus be reproduced, and the fact that this area, throughout its entire length, is traversed by a line of railway, would greatly facilitate its agricultural development.

Before leaving the question of projects for the development of irrigation, in the countries south of Khartoum, a few words must be said regarding the second object of the present note, to which allusion has been already made, namely, the formation of a properly organized Irrigation Service in the Soudan.

It will be understood from the preceding pages, that the projects to be investigated, are many and varied. Their examination will involve much time and study. The time appears to have now come, when a competent staff should be collected and an annual allotment made in the Budget, sufficient to permit of these schemes being prepared and completed, at as early a date as is consistent with a thorough study of all their details.

Those who have read this report will have observed that, in almost every instance, the proposals made have been subordinate to the results that may be afterwards obtained by actual levelling of the country. This want of levels in the Soudan is a crying one. One of the very first duties of the Irrigation Officers in that country, will be to run lines of levels up either branch of the Nile, with cross-lines across the Ghezireh and to the east of the Blue Nile. Until this has been done, all proposals, regarding works to be carried out, or estimates of their cost, must be mere guess-work, founded upon nothing better than general probabilities. Another necessity is the continuation of the series of river discharges which has been commenced and its extension upon a larger and more complete scale. The erection of good and permanent river-gauges, and their supervision when erected, is also urgently required. Something has been already done in this direction, but much more is required before any real knowledge of the river-levels can be acquired. These three instances have been mentioned among those which must early engage the attention of the staff, but their number could easily be multiplied, as for instance, experiments in river-training, and prevention of wastage of water on the Upper Nile. In this last direction, it will, however, be advisable to attempt nothing upon any large scale, until the level-system has been completed, or, at any rate, very much advanced.

In appendix No. 2 of this report, the details are given, from which the proposals, regarding the necessary staff, and the estimate of cost have been framed. A properly organized Irrigation Service, for the Soudan, would be somewhat as follows:—

An Inspector General of Irrigation should be appointed, having his head-quarters at Khartoum. He would supervise and control the service, as a whole. His chief assistants should consist of two Inspectors, one for the White, and the other for the Blue Nile. It would be advisable to appoint a third, and junior, officer, who would act as a reserve man, and who could be usefully employed upon special works and studies. There should also be appointed a large staff of native engineers and levellers, together with the requisite office establishment. Two steamers would be required for inspection work, one for the White Nile, and another, of very shallow draught, specially designed for work on the Blue Nile.

A considerable expenditure would be entailed, by the purchase of the necessary instruments, and a certain amount of plant, in the shape of tools, tents, etc. Lastly, although it is not proposed that any heavy expenditure should be incurred upon actual works, in the first year, it is imperative that a grant should be provided, sufficient to permit of experiments regarding river-training, etc., being carried out, without any loss of time.

The cost of starting such a service in the Soudan, is estimated at L.E. 24,000, for the first year (¹). This estimate will, most probably require complete re-casting at the end of that period. After twelve months' experience, it will, almost inevitably, show a tendency to increase.

The Egyptian Government must then consider whether it is prepared to incur an annual expenditure, of not less than the above sum, and a possibly heavier charge, for the next few years, without any immediate return in the shape of increased revenue. If its decision is favourable to the proposal, and there can be little doubt that such a decision would be a wise one, then as little time as possible should be lost, and the new Service should be started, by the commencement of the next winter, so as to enable full advantage to be taken of the cool season of the year.

It is not to be expected that projects of any magnitude will be immediately presented for consideration, neither is this to be desired. The fullest study must be given, and the closest observations made of the different schemes, in all their details. This will take time, but it will not be time lost, and it will be far more economical in the end, if a delay, due to

(¹) See Appendix No. 2.

study, occurs *before* a project is presented, than if this occurs *later*, and *after the works have been started.*

Before leaving this subject, a few words must be said upon another point, and one of great importance.

Should it be decided to form an Irrigation Service in the Soudan, it is absolutely necessary that it should be entirely controlled by the Ministry of Public Works in Egypt, and that it should, in fact, form a branch of that Department. This is imperative. The work of such a service will be of a purely technical nature and, moreover, will involve the construction of works which must, more or less, interfere with the supply of the Nile. The control of the flow of this river must remain always, and absolutely, in the hands of one authority. There can be no question of a divided authority in such an important matter, and there can be no two opinions, that such control should be vested in the Egyptian Ministry of Public Works. Doubtless, the Government of the Soudan will be the first to admit this and the last to desire that any other arrangement should be made. It will be, however, in the interests of both Egypt and the Soudan, that this should be clearly laid down, and fully understood.

Consequently, it seems equitable, as its interests are so largely involved in this matter, that Egypt should bear the entire cost of the establishment of such a service, and the Soudan, although it will benefit largely by the measure, should not be called upon to contribute to an expenditure, over which it will have no control.

The officers appointed to the Soudan Irrigation Service, would thus form a portion of the staff of the Egyptian Public Works Department, and be interchangeable with other members of the Service employed in Egypt.

One last word. Although these Officers, as regards all questions relating to the control of the river, or to large and important projects, will be entirely under the orders of the Public Works Minister, it will be a portion of their duties to advise and assist, by all means in their power, the Government of the Soudan. Their services, in this respect, will always be at the disposal of the Governor-General, and his assistants.

There is no reason whatever why such a system should not work well and successfully.

The advantages to the Soudan Government of having a body of technical experts always at hand, to advise on the many questions which must constantly arise in connection with agricultural development, and which are inseparable from irrigation, will, undoubtedly, be very great.

CONCLUDING REMARKS.

In the preceding pages, an attempt has been made, to give some idea of the various questions which must, in the near future, engage the attention of those responsible for the control of the Nile. Before bringing this report to a conclusion, it may be as well to express an opinion regarding the degree of urgency involved in the separate schemes, therein set forth. Moreover, in all projects connected with Nile regulation, the interests of Egypt are so closely linked with those of the Soudan, as to be well-nigh inseparable. Both countries must derive their water supply from the same sources, and the agricultural prosperity of both is mainly dependent upon the one river. It is, therefore, impossible to consider any important irrigation scheme, projected for the one country, without touching upon its possible effects as regards the other.

Again, as the funds required for such measures, would, it is presumed, be found by the Egyptian Treasury, any programme prepared for large irrigation works in the Soudan, should include those proposed, at the same time, for execution in Egypt.

As, however, the discussion of works purely connected with Egypt, will, of necessity, comprise much matter that is foreign to the object of the present report, viz., the improvement of the Upper Nile, this portion of the programme has been separately drawn up, and is attached in the form of an appendix (1).

As regards those projects which more particularly affect the Soudan, although their immediate study is most desirable, it cannot be stated that their execution, upon the scale indicated in the preceding chapter, is a matter of extreme urgency.

In the report upon the Upper Nile, published in 1901, the following remarks were made:—

" The Soudan is scarcely ready yet for the introduction of irrigation works upon a "
" large scale. Were an increased supply of water to be granted at this moment, the country "
" is not in a position to make effective use of the boon. Its chief want, for many years "
" to come, must be population (2)."

These words are almost as applicable to the situation to-day, as they were three years ago. It may well be, that the actual total of the population is considerably larger than was at first supposed, but, even at the most favourable estimate, it must be very small, as compared to the immense areas to be dealt with. It must, moreover, be extremely scattered. Further,—with certain exceptions, the bulk of the population can hardly be classed as an agricultural one (3). It is difficult then to see how, unless labour is imported into the Soudan, full advantage can be taken, in any short period of time, of improved facilities for irrigation, upon an extended scale.

The experiment of imported labour is one that has yet to be tried, and, until such trial has been made, no opinion, regarding probable success or failure, can be worth very much. The natives of India and China, and also the American negro, have all been suggested as possible colonists. Questions such as this are outside of the province of a report like the present, but the fact that population is inseparably connected with agricultural development warrants some allusion to this most important subject, in these pages.

There would seem to be one source, from which immigration to the Soudan, might be usefully encouraged, supposing it were possible to come to an arrangement with the Abyssinian Government. The source alluded to, is the country of the Gallas, in south-western

(1) See appendix No. I.
(2) Foreign Office. Blue Book—Egypt (No. 2) 1901.
(3) These words are meant to apply, chiefly, to the countries lying to the south of Khartoum.

Abyssinia. All travellers, who have visited this region, describe these people as being good agriculturists, and intelligent beyond the average of African races. The climate of their country must be very similar to that of the tracts adjoining the Blue Nile. It would surely be worth while making an attempt to induce the Gallas to settle in the Soudan, before seriously thinking of introducing colonists from another Continent.

Although, in the foregoing remarks, stress has been laid upon the inadequacy of the Soudan population, it must not be imagined that they are intended to advocate a policy of doing nothing towards improving irrigation in that country. The contrary is the case. If nothing is done, no progress is possible, and, until a commencement has been made, no real amelioration in the state of agriculture can be looked for. It is most advisable that all the projects mentioned shall be studied at an early date and that those among them, which may seem to promise even a moderate amount of success, shall be put into execution as soon as funds can be provided.

A reference to the preceding chapter will show that, among the many schemes outlined, there are four, which are recommended as being the most suitable for early examination. Of these, two have reference to the Blue, and two, to the White Nile.

Commencing with the Blue Nile. These projects are: that for controlling the river Gash, and that for a barrage upon the Blue Nile (1). The first of these, as proposed by Mr. Dupuis, does not seem likely to necessitate any very considerable expenditure of money, and there appears to be a population in the locality, sufficient to make good use of the water when supplied.

The other project must necessarily be a costly one, and, for some time at all events, the returns in the shape of revenue are scarcely likely to bear a fair proportion to the capital expended. Nevertheless, if any irrigation scheme is to succeed in the Soudan, this particular one appears to promise the fairest hope of doing so. It has been shown that, even in a year of bad supply, there is sufficient water in the Blue Nile, to permit of the irrigation of a large area of crop during the winter months. If a storage reservoir can be constructed south of Rosaires, the supply will be augmented, but even without the assistance of such a work, the construction of a barrage, to raise the water-level of the river, is well worth a large expenditure. Once this weir was completed, the canal system, upon either side, could be proceeded with slowly and tentatively. The locality, from its vicinity to the two centres of population on the Blue Nile, viz., Khartoum and Wad Medani, is especially well suited for making a commencement with agricultural development, and there would be a good prospect of extending cotton culture upon a large scale. If a line of light railway, connecting the two places, were to be constructed, the prospects of success would be largely enhanced.

Turning to the White Nile, the situation is entirely different. Any schemes connected with the improvement of this river, will, if carried out, be undertaken more in the interests of Egypt, than of the Soudan, although an increased summer supply passing Khartoum would materially assist the irrigation of the Nile valley, north of that place.

A study of the proposals contained in the chapter upon the utilization of the Nile supply will have made it clear that the project recommended for execution, in preference to any other (always supposing that the levelled survey proves it to be a feasible one) is that of the proposed new channel for the Nile, between Bor and the Sobat junction. The arguments in favour of the scheme have been already set forth in full, and there is no occasion to repeat them in detail. The immense advantage to be realised, by leaving the great Swamp Region altogether to one side, and by conveying the water to the north, in a well-constructed, and fully-controlled channel, are so evident, that they can be understood

(1) The scheme for the Gash, is not, properly speaking, a Blue Nile project, but, as it affects the eastern provinces, it has been included as such—merely for the sake of convenience.

by all. The proposal will particularly appeal to those who have ever followed the Bahr-el-Gebel, in its long and winding course through the dreary papyrus marshes. This channel would be by far the best solution of the difficult problem of obviating the present waste of water in the Upper Nile, and the advantages of this scheme are so great, that they are well worth incurring a heavy expenditure to secure.

Should the levels prove the construction of this channel to be impracticable, then the remodelling of the Bahr-el-Zaraf, so as to enable it to carry the required discharge, should be proceeded with. Such a scheme is undoubtedly a possible one, and, if not so effectual a remedy as that first mentioned, in that it would still confine the flow of the river to the marsh country, it is, as far as can be seen, the only alternative possible ([1]).

Once it has been secured, by one or other of these methods, that the summer discharge of the Bahr-el-Gebel shall reach the White Nile in undiminished volume, then the work of regulating the Victoria and Albert lakes, at their outlets, should be proceeded with.

The more important of the projects, demanding immediate attention in the Soudan, have been indicated in the above brief summary. It will be understood that their execution will entail the expenditure of large sums of money. If to this is added the cost of the large irrigation works, required simultaneously in Egypt, this expenditure will reach a very large figure indeed. The appended programme gives an abstract of the approximate cost of such works ([2]).

It is for those who control the finances of Egypt to decide whether such expenditure is desirable, or whether, even with every prospect of a large increase to the annual revenue, as a result of these undertakings, it is not advisable to proceed slowly, and to apply a portion of the surplus available, to the many other necessary reforms alluded to by Lord Cromer, in his yearly Report upon Egyptian Administration. The present high selling and rental value of land in Egypt has engendered a hunger for its acquisition in all classes of the community, and this hunger seems likely to extend to the Soudan. Whether these prices will be maintained, or whether a largely increased production will not, one day, cause a serious fall in the value of all agricultural products, is a question regarding which various opinions are held. Whatever the future may hold, this much is certain, that, at present, land is being urgently sought for everywhere, and that schemes for increasing the cultivated area are being urged upon the Egyptian Government. Fortunately, in the Soudan, equally as in Egypt, there can be no doubt of the eventual return to be obtained from any well-considered, and sound irrigation project. Given a sufficient population, the combination of the sun, the soil and the water renders its success a certainty.

An attempt has been made, in these pages, to explain the utility of the different schemes. Should all, or even a portion of them ever become accomplished facts, it is difficult to estimate the extent of the benefits that will have been secured to a not inconsiderable area of the Continent of Africa. The limits of cultivation in Egypt are far from having been as yet reached. With a Nile under control throughout its entire length, and with the power of adding to its volume, by drawing upon the almost inexhaustible resources of the natural reservoirs which supply it, the agricultural wealth of that country should increase, to an extent beyond the dreams of the most sanguine reformer. The Soudan, it is true, represents an unknown quantity, and its future is one about which it would be, at present, rash to prophesy. That progress, in that country, must be slow is unfortunately certain, but there appears to be no reason why it should not be sure. What has once been, may again be, and there are good grounds for anticipating an eventual return to prosperity— a prosperity, perhaps, even greater than that which excited the astonishment of Nero's envoys, nearly nineteen centuries ago.

([1]) The reasons for rejecting the Bahr-el-Gebel as the main carrying channel, are given in full, in the chapter upon the utilization of the Nile supply.

([2]) See appendix N° I.

Those, to whom the privilege shall be granted of assisting towards this consummation, will have a chance given to them, such as seldom falls to the lot of man. To rescue the Upper Nile from the marshes in which it has lost more than half its volume—to control and regulate the great Equatorial Lakes, making them add to the flow of the river at will—to cause the waters of the Blue Nile to rise, and irrigate the fertile tracts through which they pass—to secure to Egypt a constant and sufficient supply for the entire area between the cataracts and the Mediterranean—to free that country from the ever-present danger of a disastrous flood. These are tasks worthy of comparison with any previously recorded in the world's history, and which, if successfully accomplished, will leave behind them a monument that will probably endure long after all evidence of those erected by an earlier civilization shall have passed away.

W. E. Garstin.

Under Secretary of State for Public Works in Egypt.

Cairo, March the 12th 1904.

Appendix I.

I have been requested to draw up a general programme of the main irrigation projects (in Egypt as well as in the Soudan) which I consider to be advisable for execution within a not very remote future. Before doing so, I have a few words to say. If my observations are to be confined to indicating merely those schemes which, to my mind, merit early study, then there is no great difficulty in the task. If, on the other hand, I am expected to give an idea, however approximate, of the cost of such projects, it is a very different matter. No general estimates, based upon insufficient data, are worth much, and conclusions drawn from such figures are apt to be misleading. Moreover, experience teaches us that estimates thus prepared are, almost invariably, exceeded. I wish it then to be understood, that the figures which I give at the end of this note, are nothing but approximations, based, for the most part, upon rough calculations, and that, consequently, they do not possess much value.

If my general ideas are accepted and certain projects are selected for further and fuller examination, we shall, within a reasonable time, have definite estimates before us, from which accurate ideas of the cost and of the relative value of the different schemes can be obtained.

Before going further, I would also repeat here, what I have so often and at different times stated, that, more especially as regards Egypt, the execution of none of these large works is, with one single exception, a matter of extreme urgency. The exception to which I allude is the provision of escape power for the Nile during an exceptional flood. This question will be discussed later.

As regards the others, although they are doubtless desirable schemes, and although their realisation would largely increase the wealth of Egypt, no one can seriously pretend that the financial stability of that country is dependent upon their immediate execution. Thanks to the work done in the past, Egypt is now practically assured against agricultural disaster, and any future expenditure upon irrigation will be incurred solely with a view of adding still further to the already phenomenal prosperity of the Nile valley. Such an object is of course a highly desirable one and, if the necessary funds are forthcoming, one that an effort should be made to attain. At the same time, I repeat,—such projects are not absolutely vital to the financial security of the country.

The programme, as will be seen, is a very large one and is, as it is meant to be, far-reaching. The Egyptian Government will be free to select from among the different projects those which appear to promise the best returns, and put them into execution as its resources may permit. Meanwhile, I would point out that it is at present spending yearly a sum not far short of L.E.700,000 upon new irrigation works in Egypt. It cannot be asserted then that progress is at a standstill, or that nothing is being done for the development of that country. On the other hand, as I have remarked in my report, the desire to acquire fresh land in Egypt is general, and is becoming keener. An increase to the cultivated area must also increase the revenues. If the Egyptian Government is prepared to face a large expenditure, then I see no reason for delaying the execution of the more important projects, and I have no doubt whatever that the results obtained will fully warrant such a decision, if taken.

As regards the Soudan, matters are rather different. If the annual heavy deficit of that country is ever to be converted into a surplus, it can only be by means of irrigation works and, although I am not sanguine of a speedy return upon the capital expended, I consider that a commencement should be made. Until this is done, there can be no hope of any real improvement.

All that I insist upon is that, under such circumstances, full time shall be given for a thorough study and preparation of each separate project.

I will now outline the different schemes in the programme, discussing each of them briefly.

I will commence with those proposals having reference to Egypt alone.

No examination of the different measures possible for improving the water-supply of Egypt can be complete, without taking into consideration those schemes proposed for this purpose by Sir William Willcocks (¹). These are of such importance that I will give them precedence over all others.

(¹) These proposals have been published in a pamphlet, entitled "The Aswan Reservoir and Lake Mœris" by Sir William Willcocks, K.C.M.G., M.I.C.E., London, 1904.

They are three in number :—

(i) The raising of the Aswan dam, thereby increasing the storage capacity of the Nile reservoir.

(ii) The utilization of the depression known as the Wady Rayan, for a secondary reservoir, to augment the summer supply of northern Egypt.

(iii) The remodelling of the Rosetta branch of the Nile, so as to render it capable of serving as a flood escape for the river.

As regards numbers (i) and (ii), neither of these proposals, as it stands, can be said to be absolutely novel. A dam at Aswan, raised to a height greater than that now suggested, was proposed by Sir W. Willcocks himself, in his original report upon the storage of Nile water (1). Again, the idea of making use of the Wady Rayan as a reservoir is due to Mr. Cope Whitehouse, who, for years, urged this project upon the Government (2). The combination of the two schemes, making the one the complement of the other, as now proposed, is, however, an entirely novel idea.

(i) THE RAISING OF THE ASWAN DAM.

Sir William Willcocks proposes to increase the height of this dam to such a level that the maximum water surface in the reservoir will be raised by six metres, i.e., from R.L. 106, as at present, to R.L. 112, in the future (3). This, he calculates, will double the storage capacity of the reservoir, making it capable of containing 2 milliards of cubic metres of water.

I will commence my remarks by saying that I have, hitherto, opposed the immediate execution of this work. For this attitude on my part I shall afterwards give my reasons. For the present, I will only say that, if this project shall be considered as forming a portion of a definite programme, and *if it be executed in conjunction with others that I shall name*, under such conditions, I withdraw my opposition, and recommend that it be carried out. I will further say that I consider it to be a desirable project, and one that will render undoubted service to Egypt. The scheme has this great advantage over all others, that it is the one from which the earliest returns can be anticipated, and the cost of construction cannot be considered as prohibitive. Use could be made, in Lower Egypt, of the extra water thus stored, in a comparatively short space of time, without waiting until the necessary remodelling of the Upper Egypt basin system had been completed.

I have made it a condition of withdrawing my opposition to this project, that it should be carried out in conjunction with other schemes. These are two in number. The one is the improvement of the Upper Nile, so that an increased summer supply may be brought down, thereby, to Egypt. The other is the provision of sufficient escape power for the river when in flood. Both these schemes are, to my mind, indispensable, and should the Egyptian Government decide to raise the dam, it should, also commit itself to the simultaneous execution of both these works.

My reasons for having opposed the raising of the dam, are as follows :—

In the first place, — there was no special urgency. In the second place, — until the Nile reservoir works were completed, I saw no likelihood of any funds being available for the two projects above mentioned. In the third place, — the filling of a reservoir of largely increased capacity, without any provision for an extra supply of water in the river, would, in years of low discharge, have seriously affected navigation in the Nile, during the winter months. In the fourth place, — there was no existing means for escaping the flood water. The complete suppression of the basins in Upper Egypt would have increased the force of this objection.

In the fifth place, — the raised dam would entail the further submersion of the monuments on the Philæ Island.

As regards my first objection, I have already discussed this point, and I am assuming, in my present remarks, that it is practically decided to undertake certain works in the near future. This assumption applies equally to the second of my objections.

As regards numbers three and four, if the schemes I have proposed are undertaken simultaneously with the raising of the dam, both of these objections vanish.

There then remains only the fifth and last, namely the question of the Philæ monuments. This I will discuss at some length, although I am well aware that in doing so, I am treading upon somewhat delicate ground.

(1) "Perennial Irrigation and Flood Protection of Egypt" Cairo, 1894.
(2) Ibid.
(3) In reality, the gain in height over present conditions, will be only 4·5 metres. We could hold up water to-day, on the dam as it stands, and without any expenditure whatever, to R.L. 107·50, or 1·5 metres above the approved maximum of R.L. 106.

Until actual demonstration had been given, there was no possible means of knowing what would be the effect of the water upon these structures, or to what extent their stability might be endangered by the raising of the water-levels. Now that these temples have been partially submerged throughout one season, it is possible to draw some conclusions regarding these two points. Thanks to the thorough and skilful manner in which their foundations have been consolidated, there have been no signs of subsidence, and there appear to be good grounds for the hope that none will occur in the future. Upon this point, valuable testimony has been given by an authority beyond dispute. This authority is Monsieur Edouard Naville, the eminent Egyptologist. He has lately visited Philæ, and on his return to Europe, expressed his opinion, in very favourable terms, in the columns of a well-known newspaper (1). I will quote a couple of sentences from Monsieur Naville's article. He says :—

"Quel changement d'avec Philé d'autrefois! On ne peut plus guère appeler le temple une ruine;" "il paraît aussi que n'importe quelle construction élevée tout récemment"......

And again :

"On peut même se demander si, à certains égards, le temple de Philé n'est pas aujourd'hui, dans" "des conditions meilleures que la plupart des édifices égyptiens"......

It must be remembered that Monsieur Naville visited the temples after the water had subsided—also, that his opinion is the more important, because, as he says himself, he was one of those who, when the scheme was first proposed, protested most strongly against the submersion of these structures.

We have the further testimony of Monsieur G. Maspero, the Director General of the Antiquities Service in Egypt. He has carefully inspected the ruins, this last winter, and has expressed his opinion regarding their stability in a published pamphlet in favourable, although rather guarded, terms (2). Monsieur Maspero says :—

"Les données en sont consolantes et nous montrent que les travaux entrepris pour permettre" "aux temples d'affronter l'épreuve de l'eau, n'on pas été en vain. La première année s'est bien passée," "et j'espère que la seconde année ne nous apportera pas de mécomptes."

He also says :—

"Le danger d'écroulement par affouillement des eaux, paraît être conjuré, grâce aux travaux" "récents, et le courant est sinon presque nul, du moins si faible, durant la période d'immersion, qu'on" "peut en considérer les effets comme négligeables."

I think then that we may say, with some confidence, that the stability of these temples has, up to the present, not suffered from their submersion.

There is, however, another question to be considered, namely, the effect of the water upon the surface of the stone work. Below the water-level, i.e., in the portion actually submerged, there appears to be no change in the conditions, and all authorities appear to be agreed, that, up to the height reached by the water, everything is as it was. Above the water-line, however, things are different. All along this level, throughout the structures, there is a band of apparently saturated stone, from 0.60 to 0.80 metres in height. The saturation is due to capillary attraction, and, in this band, salts deleterious to the masonry have made their appearance. This is more particularly noticeable round, and on those portions where cement was made use of in repairing the stone-work.

All those who have inspected and reported upon the monuments have drawn attention to this fact, which indeed is evident to anyone visiting the spot.

As regards the remedy for this evil, the general opinion appears to be, that the only one possible is to wash the stone-work thoroughly and carefully, as soon as the water has subsided, thus getting rid of the salts. These are reported as coming away easily. Whether this will effectually preserve the stone from decay, it is impossible to say. Monsieur Maspero considers that it will not be possible to decide this point in a less period of time than from four to five years.

However this may be, the seat of possible damage appears to be limited to this narrow band, situated just above the *maximum level of the reservoir water*. Below water, the salts do not make their appearance. The further raising of the water-surface then, would, apparently, have no other effect than *to transfer* the level of this salted band, to a greater height above the floor of the temples than at present. I do not say that this is not an evil, but I contend that, *as far as damage to the structures is concerned*, the additional height to which the water was raised, would make no practical difference. I hope, moreover, that it will be found that the yearly washing off of the salts will prevent any real injury to the

(1) "Journal de Genève," December the 17th, 1903.
(2) "La protection de Philae, pendant l'hiver de 1902 et l'été de 1903," Cairo, 1904.

stone-work, and that, with the care that will be given to them, these beautiful monuments may be preserved for an indefinite period of time.

From the artistic point of view, I regret that there is nothing to be said in extenuation of the proposed raising of the water-levels. The submersion of the temples, to a further height of six metres, will undoubtedly destroy much of their picturesqueness, and much of the beauty of the present landscape will be spoiled. No one can pretend that this will be otherwise and, unfortunately, this effect will be produced during the time when Philæ is visited by many tourists. That this should be so, must always be a matter for deep regret, but even such a consideration should not be allowed to weigh against the benefits that would result to the Fellahin of Egypt from so large an increase in the storage capacity of the Aswan reservoir.

Reluctant, then, as I am to counsel any measure which may affect the beauty of this unique spot, I am convinced that the raising of the dam is an eventual necessity for Egypt, and one that must, some day, be carried out. Consequently, I think it would be a mistake to postpone the work longer than is absolutely necessary. If then sufficient funds can be obtained, and if the other two schemes, proposed by me, can be taken in hand at the same time, I recommend that the Aswan dam shall be raised, so as to store water in the reservoir to R. L. 112.0.

The cost of this work should not exceed L.E.500,000, a sum which is little enough, in comparison to the value resulting to Egypt from another milliard of cubic metres of water.

I come now to the second of Sir William Willcocks's proposals, i.e., the Wady Rayan.

(ii)—THE WADY RAYAN.

The present project differs very considerably from that submitted by Mr. Cope Whitehouse, in 1894. In that gentleman's scheme, the Aswan reservoir played no part, and the weir at Asyut had no existence. The Rayan depression was to be filled direct from the Nile, when the levels permitted, and the reservoir thus formed was to be used to supplement the river discharge, at the time of lowest volume. This scheme had one great drawback. At the period when the demand for water would have been at its maximum—prior to the arrival of the annual flood, the levels of the great lake would have fallen to such an extent, owing to the withdrawal of a large amount of water to feed the river, that the surface slope of the outlet canal would have been largely diminished and, consequently, the discharge into the Nile by this channel would have been proportionately reduced. Unless, then, the water of the rising flood overtook, and overlapped that issuing from the reservoir at the critical moment, there would, undoubtedly, have been a failure, possibly a disastrous one, of the water supply of Lower Egypt.

Sir William Willcocks's scheme does not contain this defect. His idea is to make use of the Rayan reservoir as a complement to that at Aswan, utilizing the water of the former, during the early portion of the season, and supplementing it from the latter, when, owing to reduced head and slope, the discharge in the outlet canal began to fail.

I cannot do better than quote his own words, which describe his proposal very graphically :—

"When the Assuan dam will have been raised, we shall be standing on the threshold of what it" "will be able to do. The projected Wady Rayan reservoir, or the modern Lake Mœris, will be well" "able to supply the two remaining milliards of cubic metres of water when working in conjunction with" "the Assouan Reservoir. The great weakness of this projected lake has lain in the fact that *by itself* it" "can give a plentiful discharge in April and May, less in June, and very little in July, and it was for" "this reason that in my report of 1894 to the Egyptian Government I had reluctantly to recommend" "that it be not carried out. But when the Assouan Reservoir is capable of supplying two milliards of" "cubic metres of water it will be possible to utilise the Mœris lake to its utmost capacity. The" "Assouan Reservoir, being high above the level of the Nile, can give its supply at the beginning or" "end of the summer; it can give it slowly or with a rush; while the projected Lake Mœris, being" "directly in communication with the Nile, and only slightly above low Nile level, its discharge would" "depend entirely on the difference of level between it and the Nile, and consequently as the summer" "advanced it would gradually fall and would not be able to give at the end of the summer a quarter" "of the discharge it could give at the beginning."

"But let us imagine that the reservoir and the lake are both completed and full of water, and that" "it is the first of April. Lake Mœris will be opened on to the Nile and give all the water needed in" "that month, while the Assouan Reservoir will be maintained at its full level. In May, Lake Mœris" "will give nearly the whole supply and the reservoir will give a little. In June the lake will give" "little and the reservoir much; while in July the lake will give practically nothing and the reservoir" "the whole supply. Working together in this harmonious manner, the reservoir and the lake, which are" "the true complements of each other, will easily provide the whole of the water needed for Egypt (1)."

(1) "The Assuan Reservoir and Lake Mœris," London, 1904, pages 10 and 11.

I have no hesitation in saying that the scheme, as thus presented, is a most attractive one, and one that, if feasible, appears to solve the problem of the best method of increasing the water supply of Egypt.

Further consideration, however, has convinced me that the question is not quite so simple as, at first sight, it may seem to be, and that there are several points connected with it, that will require much consideration, before it can be recommended as the best of all means for attaining the desired end. At the end of this note, I have appended another, written by Mr. Webb, Inspector General of Irrigation in Upper Egypt, and containing a summary criticism of the proposal, together with an approximate estimate of the cost of this work. I may say that I have repeatedly discussed this scheme with him and with Mr. Verschoyle, the Inspector General of Irrigation for Lower Egypt, and that we are agreed upon all points regarding it.

Before going any further, I should draw attention to the fact, that the figures in Mr. Webb's note, showing the amount of water available in the river during winter, differ from those upon which Sir William Willcocks has based his calculations. This difference is due to the amount which I have reserved for irrigation in the eastern Soudan. A reference to the chapter of my report, upon the utilization of the Nile supply, will show that I propose to withdraw 200 metres cubes per second from the river, during the winter months, for the above purpose, and will explain my reasons for so doing. I hold strongly that such a withdrawal should be made, even were no measures for increasing the Nile supply at Khartoum likely to be undertaken. Sir William Willcocks, when he wrote his article, was, of course, unaware of this proposal of mine, and naturally estimated for the entire winter discharge of the Nile reaching Aswan, undiminished, as at present.

It will be seen that this deduction materially affects his project.

Mr. Webb, in his attached note, discusses the two alternative proposals made by Sir William Willcocks, and, making use of Mr. Verschoyle's figures regarding the discharges, he shows that, as regards the smaller project (1), *if the deduction be made for the Soudan*, the Rayan reservoir could not be filled by means of the Bahr Yusuf, during the winter months, in a year of minimum supply. He also shows that even in a mean year this would be very difficult, and would seriously affect navigation in the Nile during the period of filling. Moreover, he points out that in order to supply the Yusufi Canal it would be necessary to put a head of 4·5 metres upon the Asyut Barrage. This would entail the construction of a subsidiary weir, downstream of the work, similar to those recently constructed at the Delta Barrage. It would further necessitate considerable remodelling in both the Bahr Yusuf and the upper reach of the Ibrahimieh canal, in order to permit of the necessary supply being passed down in a bad year. In order then to render the smaller project feasible, it would be necessary either to increase the supply passing Aswan during the winter, or to abandon altogether the idea of benefiting the Blue Nile Provinces.

As regards the second, or larger project (2), Mr. Webb proves that the scheme is a possible one, as the reservoir could be filled, yearly, by the flood water. Even in very low floods like those of 1899 and 1902 this would have been possible, *provided that the inlet canal were made of sufficient large section.*

This last is the important point and, unless the feeder canal be made of sufficient dimensions, it would be impossible to fill the reservoir to the required height in flood, in years of low level. It is here that the main difference of opinions lies between Sir William Willcocks, on the one hand, and Messrs. Webb and Verschoyle, on the other.

The former, in his note, gives the approximate dimensions of his feeder and outlet canals, and bases his estimates thereupon. Mr. Webb and Mr. Verschoyle do not consider these dimensions as, in any way, sufficient, and I agree with them on this point. The consequence is that Mr. Webb's estimate shows a very large increase in the cubes of work that would, in his opinion, be required to be executed (3). He has also increased the rates to be paid for the work, basing his calculations upon his experience in Upper Egypt.

The result is, that his estimate arrives at a total of L.E. 5,700,000, or L.E. 3,100,000 above the figure given by Sir William Willcocks. I confess that I find it difficult to understand how the latter gentleman arrives at such a low estimate of the required expenditure. In the original project, submitted to the Government in 1894, the members of the Technical Commission (4), accepted an estimate of L.E. 3,707,880, as representing the cost of this work (5). This estimate was for one single canal, which was to act both as a feeder

(1) This project is for a reservoir to hold 2 milliards of cubic metres of water. with a single canal for filling and discharging. It is to be supplied during the winter months from the Yusufi Canal. The estimated cost of this project is L. E. 2,000,000.

(2) This is for a reservoir capable of storing 3 milliards of cubic metres of water, with separate inlet and outlet canals, to be filled direct from the Nile. This project is estimated to cost L.E. 2,600,000.

(3) Both estimates are of course approximations, but, as they are both based upon similar data, they can be compared one with another.

(4) Sir Benjamin Baker, K.C.B., Mr. Auguste Boulé and Signor Torricelli.

(5) "Report of the Technical Commission on the Nile Reservoir" Cairo, April 10th, 1894. Chapter I, page 8, article 22.

and an outlet. Sir William Willcocks's project is for two canals, one for feeding the reservoir, and the other discharging from it. These unite at a given point, it is true, but the total length of channel, over that of the original project, is very considerably increased. Taking into account this fact and the increased section of channel required, if the reservoir is to be filled yearly during flood, I consider that Mr. Webb's cubes of excavation very fairly represent the reality.

As regards the rates allowed for work, there is again a difference of opinion. Mr. Webb has based his rates upon the experience of much recent work in Upper Egypt. Even supposing that the earthwork, could be done for 3 P.E., instead of 5 P.E., per cubic metre, it would only mean a reduction of some L.E. 500,000 in the total, which would still show a large excess over that given by Sir William Willcocks's figures.

There is yet another difference between the two estimates, namely, as to the time required to fill the reservoir. Mr. Webb holds by the time calculated in the original estimate, viz, seven years, while Sir William Willcocks considers that this period might be reduced to four years. This point is one of comparatively minor importance, as, if the scheme could be recommended on other grounds, a delay of three years, at the commencement, should not be allowed to affect its execution.

There remains, however, one other point for consideration which is, perhaps, the most important of all; I mean, the uncertainty which must prevail as to whether, when the reservoir is full, the high water-level maintained in the lake will not gradually cause infiltration through the ridge, which separates the Wadi Rayan from the Fayoum, and cause serious damage to the cultivated land of the latter province.

About this there may be many opinions, but there can be no absolute certainty. Reams of paper might be covered with arguments upon one side or the other, but the fact must remain that, until the reservoir has been actually filled and, possibly, until it has been filled for several years in succession, no one can state definitely that infiltration will, or will not result. In order then to arrive at any certainty regarding this question, it will be necessary to complete the work and await the result. As this experiment would cost, at least, L.E.5,000,000, it cannot be classed as other than an expensive one.

That there are differences of opinions I will show. Sir William Willcocks, in his recent article, states definitely that there will be no infiltration. His words are, "unfortunately no water will leak into it," i.e., into the Gharak. He bases his opinion, largely, upon the fact that, when the old Lake Moeris was full of water, there was no question of leakage in the reverse direction, i.e., in the Wadi Rayan from the Fayoum. I must leave it to geologists to state whether this last assertion is capable of definite proof (1).

On the other hand, Sir Benjamin Baker, and his colleagues, on the Technical Commission, expressed a fear that infiltration might result. The following are the words that they used:—

"The Commission is of opinion that the filling of the depression between the levels of—12.00 and" "+27.00, while the Fayoum Province lies between +25.00 and—42.00, might cause the formation of" "springs and marshes in the low lands of the Fayoum. These springs would necessitate the construction" "of special drainage works to minimize the damage to the cultivated lands. The loss from infiltration" "would delay the time of filling the reservoir and also reduce the amount of water available annually" "for irrigation. The Commission cannot calculate with exactitude the extent of these losses. It" "thinks that they will be at first considerable and diminish annually owing to the silting up of the" "smaller springs by the muddy water of the Nile flood, but if there are considerable fissures (as" "appears probable), they will never be diminished" (2).

And in conclusion they say:

"The Commission cannot advise the Government to transform the Wadi Rayan into a reservoir," "as it might be a source of danger for the Fayoum Province, if serious infiltrations and springs were" "to be formed" . . . . (3).

Upon the above, the members of the Commission were unanimous.

These are weighty words, as coming from men of the reputation of the three commissioners, and, in the face of them, any one, I think, would hesitate to recommend this project to the Government, until, at any rate, this matter has been more fully studied (4).

(1) Professor G. Schweinfurth, in a note published in the "Report upon Perennial Irrigation and Flood Protection for Egypt," Appendix XIII, gives his opinion that the Rayan Reservoir will lose a portion of its waters, owing to subterranean clefts or fissures in the bottom of the depression.

(2) "Report of the Technical Commission on the Nile Reservoir," Chapter I, Article 18, page 7, Cairo, 1894.

(3) Ibid. Article 27, page 10.

(4) The general levels of the Fayoum are as follows:—
At Lahun = 24·00.
At Medinet El-Fayoum = 20·00
At Lake Qurun = 44·00.
Lowest point at Fouah = 0·00.
A contour of 17·00 comprises a great portion of the Fayum.
A contour of 10·00 shows the same in the Gharak.
The water in the Rayan basin when just filled, in flood, would stand about 28·50 or perhaps 29·00.

A glance at the map of the locality will show, that, while a ridge of about a kilometre in width separates the Wadi Rayan from the Gharak depression, in the Fayoum, another ridge, some four kilometres in width, separates the Gharak from the rest of the Fayoum.

I find it difficult to believe that, even with the great difference in the levels, the infiltration water could ever pass through the second and wider ridge, even supposing it to be possible that the Gharak might be flooded. Sir William Willcocks says, that if this last were to occur, then the water might be pumped out, and made use of in the Nezleh canal. So perhaps it might, but, in the meantime, the reservoir would be losing water, during the winter months, by the amount of this leakage, together with that lost by evaporation, and it would probably be found necessary to make good this loss by means of the Yusufi canal. This brings us back to the old question, and the objections made to the smaller project.

Taking everything into consideration, all points to the conclusion that a thorough geological examination of the locality, with perhaps a line of shafts sunk through the strata, will be necessary, in addition to a detailed study of the dimensions to be given to the inlet and outlet canals. Until this is done, it is impossible to say more than, that, although the project, as I have said, is, at first sight, a most attractive one, it contains great elements of uncertainty, and that, at best, it will be an experiment—certainly a costly one. It is moreover possible that the doubts as regards future damage to the Fayoum can never be solved until the money has been spent and the project been completed. Until, then, fuller information is available, it is advisable to reserve judgment upon this scheme. Meanwhile I consider that, under any circumstances, the project for improving the Bahr-el-Gebel should be given preference over that of the Wadi Rayan, as I maintain that, if the Aswan dam is to be raised, measures must be taken to increase the water supply passing Aswan. If this is admitted, it will, to my mind, be wiser, and more advantageous in the end, to undertake the work upon a scale sufficiently large to secure, not only for Egypt, but tor the entire Nile valley north of Khartoum, the benefits which such an increased water supply would give.

Even allowing that the cost of the improvement of the Upper Nile will be greater than that of the Rayan scheme, I should still recommend the former, in preference to the latter. Firstly, because it will render service to a much greater area than will the Wadi Rayan. Secondly, because it is necessary, in any case, if the Aswan dam is to be raised, to take measures to increase the river supply to a certain extent. Thirdly and lastly, because there is no risk or uncertainty attendant upon it, when completed.

The Wadi Rayan scheme may then, I think, be given a place secondary to this other. When, at some future time, the question of reclaiming the lakes in the northern Delta, shall, as it surely will, become a pressing one,—then the Rayan project will probably prove to be the best means of securing the increased supply.

Before leaving the question of the Wadi Rayan, I should say a few words regarding its value as a possible flood escape for the Nile. In many respects, this depression would constitute an ideal receptacle for such a purpose, but, as Mr. Webb points out, the section of the inlet canal, to be of any real use in reducing the height of the flood, would require to be even larger than that which would be required merely to fill the reservoir.

The late Colonel J.C. Ross, formerly Inspector General of Irrigation in Egypt, stated as his opinion, that in any calculations for the size of the Nile flood escape channel, the minimum discharge to be allowed for, should be 100,000,000 metres cube per diem.

Such a discharge would necessitate a canal of very large section. Any such work would involve a very heavy expenditure, which would only be warranted, were no other means of providing for the escape of the flood water possible.

Other means do exist, and this brings me to the third and last proposal.

(iii)—THE ROSETTA BRANCH OF THE NILE.

Sir William Willcocks, in his recent paper, urges that both branches ot the river should be put into such order that the danger from a flood passing down would be largely diminished. He further proposes that the section of the Rosetta branch shall be brought to a uniform width, by means of spurs, and the banks thrown back, where necessary, so that this channel shall be able to carry a much larger discharge, without danger to the country, than is at present possible. He would then, in flood, regulate upon the Damietta barrage, treating this branch, as he says, like a large canal, and turning the surplus water down the improved Rosetta branch.

The question of regulating upon the Barrage on the Damietta branch, in a dangerous flood, is one that has long been recognised by us all as a necessity in exceptional cases. All that would however be necessary, with regard to this channel, would be to so regulate it that the discharge passing down did not exceed that of a normal flood. This it could certainly stand, as at present, without any serious risk of danger to the country from a breach in the banks, more especially if a sufficient sum were spent in strengthening them and in improving the training works.

As regards the Rosetta branch, if it is to act as a flood escape, and I agree with Sir William Willcocks in advising that it should be made to do so, then, as he says, it must be put in thorough order, and remodelled throughout its length.

It is needless to enlarge upon the danger to northern Egypt during those times when the flood passing the Delta Barrage assumes exceptional proportions. The question is a most important one. Many years have elapsed since a dangerous flood has occurred, and few of the officers, now in the Irrigation Department, have witnessed one. Another high flood is certain to arrive, and will probably come sooner than later, as all experience shows that the periods of time between dangerous floods do not comprise a large number of years. The damage that a breach in the bank would cause is incalculably greater now than it would have been 20, or even 15 years ago. The improvement in, and the extension of, cultivation, the increase of population, and the rise in the value of the land all make this a certainty. I recommend then that a sum of money be devoted to the improvement of both branches of the river, north of the Barrage, — particularly with the object of so improving the Rosetta branch that it can carry off the surplus water of a dangerous flood without risk to the country.

Sir William Willcocks estimates the cost of these works at L.E.900,000. If an efficient flood escape can be secured for this sum, the result will have been cheaply attained.

It will be seen from the foregoing that I recommend the raising of the Aswan dam and the improvement of the Rosetta branch. I do not recommend the present utilization of the Wadi Rayan as a storage reservoir, for the reasons that I have given in the preceding page.

I further urge, in addition to the two projects mentioned, that the improvement of the Bahr-el-Gebel should be put in hand, and that the water supply of the Nile reaching Egypt in winter and in summer, should be increased by one or other of the methods that I have suggested in my report.

These three works form a portion of the general programme, but not by any means the whole of it. An increased water supply, sufficient for the entire wants of Egypt, will entail the construction of an extensive system of supplementary works, in the shape of canals and drains, in order that the benefits to be derived from the extra water, may be fully secured. Such works will necessitate a very heavy expenditure. This need not be immediate, but may be distributed over a series of years. It must, however, sooner or later be faced, as, until these works are completed, the full results to be anticipated cannot be realised. It is as well therefore that the Egyptian Government should understand that by taking the first step, i.e., by raising the Aswan dam, it is committing itself to a programme which will eventually entail the expenditure of a very considerable capital.

In Upper Egypt, between Asyut and Kena, there are some 750,000 acres of basin land which will be converted to perennial irrigation.

The experience of similar work in Middle Egypt has proved that such conversion cannot be carried out at a less cost than L.E.4 per acre, and, if any great distributary canals have to be constructed or remodelled, this figure will certainly be largely exceeded (¹).

In order to raise the water-level in the river, a barrage, similar in type to that at Asyut, will have to be constructed, between the two places. In order to avoid the necessity of having long, parallel main canals, it will probably be found more economical, and certainly more effectual, to build two of these barrages. Taking into account the conditions of the river, the levels, and the fact that subsidiary weirs will probably be necessitated, such works could hardly be constructed at a much less cost than L.E.1,000,000 each.

The estimate would consequently stand thus :—

Two weirs	L.E.2,000,000
Conversion of 750,000 acres at L.E. 4	„ 3,000,000
Total...	L.E.5,000,000

Again, in order to make full use of the increased supply in Lower Egypt, a considerable amount of canal remodelling and extension, with the construction of new drains, will be necessitated. It is difficult, without fuller detail than I have at present got, to estimate what the total cost of such works would amount to. If I put it at L.E.1,000,000, I shall probably not be giving too high a figure.

Lastly, in order to complete the conversion works in Middle Egypt, connected with the existing reservoir at Aswan, a further expenditure of about L.E.1,000,000 will be required in the course of the next two or three years.

(¹) In Middle Egypt, if the cost of the widening of the Ibrahimieh canal be added to that of the conversion of the basins, the rate of expenditure over the entire area converted, works out to L.E.7 per feddan.

This last sum forms a portion of, what may be called, the existing programme, to which the Government is already, so to speak, committed. I mention it, as it forms a large item in the future expenditure, but, as in my comparison of expenditure with possible returns I do not take into account the revenue to be obtained from the area converted in Middle Egypt, I omit this sum from the comparative table as well.

Turning to the Soudan, the money that may be spent it that region, upon development, is practically unlimited. I have, in my report, attempted to briefly describe the different projects which deserve study. As it would be manifestly impossible and certainly inadvisable, to embark upon them all, or even on the majority of them, in any comparatively short period of time, it only remains for me to select from among them those which I think the most desirable to first carry out. As regards the estimates for these works, I can only repeat what I wrote at the commencement of this note, namely, that the figures given must not be considered as being anything but approximations and, although I have allowed a very large margin for the unforeseen in each case, I can, in no way, guarantee that the actual expenditure will not exceed my present estimate.

The following are those works in the Soudan, which deserve special attention. Of these, the first and last will be undertaken more in the interests of Egypt than of the Soudan, except as regards the Nile valley, north of Khartoum. The others are designed for the benefit of the Soudan alone.

(1) The remodelling of the Bahr-el-Gebel.
(2) The construction of a barrage, in the Blue Nile.
(3) A canal system for the Ghezireh in connection with this barrage.
(4) The regulation of the River Gash.
(5) The construction of a storage reservoir somewhere in Soudan territory, south of Rosaires.
(6) The regulation of the Victoria and Albert Lakes.

I will very briefly discuss the probable cost of each work.

No. 1. There are two alternative proposals for this. The one, is to construct an entirely new channel for the Nile, between Bor and the Sobat; the other, to improve the Bahr-el-Zaraf, rendering it capable of carrying the extra supply.

As regards the first of these, the cost of such a work will undoubtedly be very heavy. I have given my opinion that such a channel, if constructed at all, should eventually be made large enough to carry a discharge of 1000 metres cube per second. For many years to come, however, and, in fact, until the regulation of the lakes is taken in hand, a channel, large enough to carry 700 metres cube per second, will meet all requirements. My present estimate is consequently for a work of such dimensions. It would not be difficult to afterwards enlarge it. As it will, at the same time, be the navigable line, it will be necessary to keep the velocity of the current within manageable limits. I have allowed for a maximum velocity of 2·0 metres per second ([1]). The section necessary to pass this discharge will entail a total cube of earthwork, amounting to some 119,000,000 metres.

This work would all be executed by machinery and, as the cube is enormous, it would probably be possible to find contractors to execute it at a rate not higher than that paid for dredging in Upper Egypt, viz., 3.7 piastres per metre cube.

The total cost of excavation would thus be L.E.4,400,000.

The regulating works would probably cost another L.E.1,000,000, bringing up the total cost to, in round numbers, L.E.5,500,000 ([2]).

The cost of the alternative project, viz., of the Bahr-el-Zaraf, is much less than the above, as the cubes of earthwork are much less. The total for this work, allowing for the same velocity, and for the existing river channel, only amounts to some 85,000,000 of metres cubes.

This at 3.7 piastres the metre cube would be equivalent to an expenditure of	L.E. 3,145,000
Allowing for the head regulator	„ 200,000
Total......	L.E. 3,345,000

or say L.E.3,400,000.

This is considerably less than the cost of the larger project, and yet, the advantages of the latter, if successfully carried out, are so incomparably greater than those to be derived

([1]) Considering how small the amount of navigation is ever likely to be in this reach of the river, (at present there are two steamers a month each way), I do not think it necessary to reduce the velocity below this figure, which is only equivalent to 7 2 kilometres, or 4·5 miles per hour. In flood, the velocity of the Nile is far greater than this.

In the Blue Nile, it is as much as 3 metres per second, and yet navigation suffers no inconvenience.

([2]) It might possibly be found advantageous, on the score of economy, to design the new channel to carry 400 metres cube per second only, allowing the balance, i.e., 300 metres cube per second to pass down the Bahr-el-Gebel as at present. This would reduce the cost of the work to under L.E.3,000,000. This project would not be as perfect a one as the other, inasmuch as a portion of the summer supply would still pass through the swamps. It is, however, worth study.

from the smaller one, that, I should unhesitatingly advise its execution, if the required funds could be provided. The detailed surveys and levels will, however, doubtless largely alter the above figures in both instances.

Project No. 2 is for the construction of a barrage in the Blue Nile, on the type of the Asyut weir. Such a work would almost certainly, taking into account the difficulties of labour and building materials, cost L.E.1,000,000.

For the canal system in project No. 3, I have allowed a figure of L.E.2,000,000. Doubtless a great deal could be done for this expenditure, but how much, without any knowledge of the levels of the country, it is quite impossible to say.

The next proposal on the list is No. 4, the control of the River Gash. Here again, I am met by the same difficulty, viz., absolute ignorance of the levels. I have put down a sum of L.E.500,000 for this work, but this is a mere speculation.

The next project for consideration is No. 5, i.e., a possible storage reservoir at or near Rosaires. It is impossible to give any figures of even moderate accuracy as to the cost of such a work. All that I can say is, that it certainly should not exceed the cost of the Aswan dam, i.e., L.E.2,200,000 and might, I hope, be executed for a very much less figure.

The last project is No. 6, viz., the regulation of the Victoria and Albert lakes. I cannot think that, even allowing for the remoteness of the locality, such works would cost more than L.E.1,000,000 each, or L.E.2,000,000 for the two.

The total expenditure in the Soudan would consequently, using the above figures, amount to one of the following, according to which estimate for the Bahr-el-Gebel were made use of.

	Estimate No. I. L.E.	Estimate No. II. L.E.
Bahr el-Gebel	5,500,000	3,400,000
Reservoir at Rosaires, say	2,000,000	2,000,000
Barrage in Blue Nile	1,000,000	1,000,000
Ghezireh canal system	2,000,000	2,000,000
Gash project	500,000	500,000
Regulation of lakes	2,000,000	2,000,000
Totals	13,000,000	10,900,000

If to the above be added, the expenditure estimated for Egypt, viz :

Raising the Aswan dam...	L.E.	500,000
Remodelling the Rosetta and Damietta Branches	„	900,000
Conversion of Upper Egypt basins	„	5,000,000
Two barrages between Asyut and Kena	„	2,000,000
Total...	L.E.	8,400,000 (¹)

The totals thus become :

	Estimate No. I.	Estimate No. II.
Soudan.	L.E. 13,000,000	L.E. 10,900,000
Egypt	„ 8,400,000	„ 8,400,000
Total... ...	L.E. 21,400,000	L.E. 19,300,000

Both of these are very large figures indeed. There could of course be no question of carrying out such a programme in any very short space of time. In fact, even if the money were available, it is scarcely possible that these works could be executed under a period of 10 to 15 years, under the most favourable circumstances.

The time is not ready for many of them either. If I were asked to point out those which I consider the most urgent and which could probably be carried out in a comparatively short period, I should select the following :

		L.E.
(1)	The raising of the Aswan dam	500,000
(2)	The remodelling of the Rosetta and Damietta branches...	900,000
(3)	„ „ „ Bahr el-Gebel	5,500,000
(4)	A portion of the Lower Egypt canal system	500,000
(5)	„ „ „ Upper „ „ „	2,500,000
(6)	One weir in the Nile between Asyut and Kena	1,000,000
(7)	A weir in the Blue Nile	1,000,000
(8)	A portion of the Ghezireh canal system	500,000
(9)	The Gash project	500,000
	Total	12,900,000

If in No. 3 the smaller project were to be selected, this estimate would be reduced by L.E. 2,100,000, and would amount to L.E. 10,800,000 (²).

(¹) The expenditure of L.E. 1,000,000 for the completion of the conversion of the Middle Egypt basins, is not included in this total, as it belongs to a different programme.

(2) The only really urgent works, to my mind, are Nos. 1, 2 and 3. These involve an expenditure of L.E.6,900,000.

The remaining works, in the list, amounting to a figure of L.E. 8,500,000, could be carried out after the completion of the first portion of the programme.

It now only remains to consider what returns might fairly be expected from the above expenditure. This is not easy to calculate, more especially as far as the Soudan is concerned. It is impossible to say how soon the revenue can be expected to reach its maximum. As, however, in this note, I am dealing with *eventual* expenditure, I can only do the same with *eventual* returns. When they will be realised, no one can tell. In Upper Egypt, the converted basin lands will naturally pay the extra tax, decided upon for land under similar conditions in Middle Egypt, viz., 50 P.E. per acre. South of Kena, where irrigation will be entirely done by pumps, this tax will be reduced to 30 P.E. per acre.

In Lower Egypt, there seems to be no reason why, if good drainage is effected, the reclaimed lands should not *eventually* pay a tax of 100 P.E. per acre, though it is probable that, for many years to come, this tax will not exceed 50 P.E. per acre. The same remark applies to lands in the Soudan, although here the time taken to reach the maximum tax will be very much longer (1).

The approximate annual returns in the shape of revenue from taxation, may thus be set down as follows:

Upper Egypt.

Basin land converted,	— 750,000 acres at 50 P.E.	L.E. 375,000	
Land irrigated by pumps	— 100,000 „ „ 30 „	„ 30.000	

Lower Egypt.

Land brought under cultivation	— 800,000 acres at 100 P.E.... ...	„ 800,000	L.E. 1,205,000

The Soudan.

Ghezireh lands	say 700,000 acres at 50 P.E.	L.E. 350,000	
Lands on the Gash,	„ 100.000 „ „ 50 „	„ 50,000	
Land in the Nile valley, North of Khartoum,	„ 200,000 „ „ 50 „	„ 100,000	
			„ 500,000
	Grand Total		L.E. 1,705,000

Or about 8 per cent upon the capital expenditure, according to the larger estimate.

In this, no account has been taken of the sale of the lands thus brought into cultivation. Both in Lower Egypt and in the Soudan, the area would be considerable. Further, the increase in the Railway and Customs receipts to the Government would naturally be very large.

W. E. Garstin.

March 24th, 1904.

(1) In my estimate I have only taken the smaller figure.

Supplement to Appendix I.

NOTE ON THE PROPOSED WADI RAYAN RESERVOIR

By A. L. Webb, C.M.G.

Inspector General of Irrigation in Upper Egypt.

The completion of the Aswan Dam has revived the very attractive project of utilizing the Wadi Rayan as a storage reservoir for supplementing the summer supply of Lower Egypt, and Sir W. Willcocks has lately brought prominently to the public notice how, by working it in conjunction with a raised Aswan Dam, the wants of the whole of Lower Egypt can be met. The Wadi Rayan Reservoir was amongst the projects submitted to the Technical Commission in 1894: it has been so thoroughly examined and described in the different reports on reservoirs, that it is only necessary to state that it was rejected on account of its excessive cost, and because it could only be of use to Lower Egypt.

Now that the Aswan Reservoir and Asyut Barrage have been completed, conditions have changed, and it is necessary to briefly examine the proposals put forward by Sir W. Willcocks.

There are two projects viz:—

a A reservoir to hold 2 milliards of cubic metres with a single canal for filling and discharging, estimated to cost L.E. 2,000,000.

b A reservoir to hold 3 milliards of cubic metres with separate inlet and outlet canals, estimated to cost L.E. 2,600,000.

Omitting for the present any consideration of the accuracy of the estimated cost, the possibility of the two projects will be briefly examined.

Project A.

Single feeder canal to fill the Reservoir and afterwards to be used as outlet canal: after the Reservoir is full, the Bahr Yusuf is to be utilized for providing the supply of a mean discharge of 230 cubic metres per second from the 15th October to end of February.

Mr. Verschoyle, Inspector General of Irrigation Lower Egypt, has supplied the following statements regarding the supply available for filling the Wadi Rayan by means of the Bahr Yusuf.

MEAN AND MINIMUM RIVER DISCHARGES AT ASWAN

Month	Mean discharge		Minimum discharge	
	Beginning of month	End of month	Beginning of month	End of month
October	7,400	4,650	5,100	3,100
November	4,650	2,700	3,100	1,880
December	2,700	1,880	1,880	1,390
January	1,880	1,390	1,390	930
February	1,390	980	930	610

QUANTITY OF WATER TO BE WITHDRAWN FROM THE RIVER

Locality	October	November	December	January	February
Sudan	200	200	200	200	200
Aswan Reservoir	300	250	200	150	100
Upper Egypt	500	500	416	170	277
Lower Egypt	900	900	750	305	505
Totals	1,900	1,850	1,566	825	1,082

Comparing these two above statements it will be seen that in a mean year no water would be available after 20th February and in a minimum year after the end of January.

It would, therefore, be difficult to obtain sufficient water to fill the Wadi Rayan in ordinary years, and impossible in a minimum year, by means of the Bahr Yusuf.

Again taking the discharge passing Asyut, we have the following, after deducting 230 cubic metres for the Wadi Rayan.

	Mean year.	Minimum year.
At end of December	834 metres cube per second.	344 metres cube per second.
" January	640 " " "	180 " " "
" February	170 " " "	Nil " " "

This shows that in ordinary years navigation would be in difficulties at the end of December, and in low years throughout the winter.

Lastly, in order to supply the Bahr Yusuf it would be necessary to put a head of 4·5 metres on the Asyut Barrage which would mean constructing a subsidiary weir and lock downstream of the barrage at an estimated cost of L.E. 500,000.

The conclusion is that Project *A* would not work.

Project B.

Separate inlet and outlet canals.

Assuming the head of the inlet canal to be near Sharahna, an examination of the flood gauges for the last 5 years shows, according to Mr. Verschoyle's figures that.

(*a*) In very low floods like 1899 and 1902, the reservoir would probably have been filled to R. L. 28·00.

(*b*) In ordinary floods like 1900, 1901 and 1903 the reservoir would probably have been filled to R.L. 29·00.

Now, allowing 1·50 metres in depth for evaporation while the reservoir is full, and assuming no leakage, the reservoir must be filled to R.L. 28·50 in order to draw off two milliards of cubic metres. In low years like 1899 and 1902 the Bahr Yusuf would have to make up the difference of 50 centimetres, which it could easily do between 15th October and end of December.

The conclusion, then, is that Project *B* would work if the inlet canal be made of sufficient dimensions. As designed, the inlet canal has a bed width of 40 metres: it should be, at least, doubled, and instead of 40 and 25 metres respectively in clay and rock, be made 80 and 60 metres. In former reports it has been shown that the outlet canal should have a bed width of 60 instead of 40 metres.

If the Wadi Rayan is to be considered as a flood escape it would be advisable to still further widen the inlet canal, but this consideration may be omitted for the present.

As regards the time required for filling the reservoir there seems no reason to suppose that it will be filled in less time than stated in former reports, viz., 7 years and not 3½ years.

The question of cost may now be considered, assuming the dimensions of the canals as given above: but before doing so it may be as well to state at once that the rates given in the original reports are too low.

The following is an approximate estimate.

Earthwork	25,500.000 metres cube at	0.050	L.E.1,275.000
Marlwork	15,000.000 "	0,080	" 1,200.000
Rock	16,000.000 "	0.120	" 1,920.000
Sand...	1,000.000 "	0.020	" 20.000
Masonry Works	... ...		" 436.000
Diversion of Bahr Yusuf	1,800.000 metres cube at	0.050	" 90.000
Closing depressions...	... ...		" 10.000
Land	4000 acres	L.E.50	" 200.000
	Total		L.E.5,151.000
	Contingencies 10%...		" 515.000
	Grand Total		L.E.5,666,080

The modified project, with inlet and outlet channels of sufficient dimensions to allow of the utilisazion of the Wadi Rayan both as a storage reservoir and a flood escape would cost at least 5½ millions of pounds. It is fascinating and presents no engineering difficulties, but it has its drawbacks. It is costly, it will take 10 years to bring it into working order, and it must not be forgotten that no one can know, nor are there any means of ascertaining, whether it will hold water.

A. L. Webb,
Inspector General of Irrigation Upper Egypt.

Cairo, 21st March, 1904.

Appendix No. II.

ESTIMATE FOR THE FORMATION OF AN IRRIGATION SERVICE IN THE SOUDAN.

General Scheme.

Superior Staff.

One Inspector General of Irrigation with Head Quarters and a central office at Khartoum.

One Senior Director of Works in charge of the White Nile Division; who would also act for the Inspector General during his absence on leave.

One Junior Director of Works in charge of the Blue Nile Division.

One English Assistant Engineer (of the standing of Surveyors of Contracts) to take charge of incidental work and special missions, and as a reserve for vacancies occasioned by leave or sickness; also in training for the occupation of permanent vacancies.

Junior Staff.

Six native Engineers (of the standing of Assistant Engineers on the Egyptian cadres lists) attached to the divisions, or officers, named above. Two to each Division with one to Head Quarters, and one in reserve, for vacancies.

Clerical Staff.

Central Office.

One Accountant at Head Office.
One clerk (speaking English and Arabic) with knowledge of accounts.
One assistant clerk (qualified also as draftsman).

Divisional Offices.

Two correspondence clerks (travelling with the Directors of Works).

Menial Staff.

Orderlies, etc., attached to Engineers and Accountant, and to the different Offices: say 15 in all.

Estimate for Expenses.

(1) Permanent Annual Charges.

Salaries.

		£E.	£E.
Inspector General	1 at 1,500	1,500	
Director of the Works for the White Nile	1 at 800	800	
Director of the Works for the Blue Nile	1 at 600	600	
English Assistant Engineer	1 at 400	400	
Native Engineers	6 at 240	1,440	
Accountant	1 at 240	240	
Clerks	4 at 120	480	
Orderlies	15 at 24	360	
			5,820

Travelling Allowances and Transport.

Estimated, very roughly, at £E.1,000 and £E.1,500 respectively	2,500

Current Expenses.

Office rent	100	
Stationery	100	
Telegrams	100	
Maintenance of instruments, furniture, etc.	100	
Maintenance and working of steamers, with crew	1,000	
Miscellaneous Petty expenses	100	1,500
Contingencies and various items not specially noted ... say		680
Total Permanent Annual Charges		10,500

(2) Special Initial Expenses.

Purchase of two steamers, complete	6,000	
Purchase of instruments	250	
Purchase of office furniture	100	
Purchase of tents and camp furniture for surveying parties	50	
Purchase of tools, etc.	100	
Total		6,500

Working Expenses of Preliminary Survey.

Four levelling parties, of about 6 men each, working continuously, with incidental expenses of messengers, camel hire, etc., etc.	1,000

Purchase of two Barges, or Dahabias.

To serve as depots, and for transport of tools, stores, gangs, etc.	1,000
Total Inital Expenses ... £E.	8,500

(3) Special Grant for preliminary experimental works in river training—construction of shelter houses—wells—piers—erection of gauges—jungle cutting—wood clearance, etc., etc. ... 5,000

Abstract of proposed budget for 1st year.

	£E
(1) Permanent Annual Charges	10,500
(2) Special Initial Expenses	8,500
(3) Special Grant for 1st year's work	5,000
Total	24,000

Cairo, March 24th, 1904.

W. E. Garstin.

Appendix III.

ON THE VARIATIONS OF LEVEL OF LAKE VICTORIA.

The Victoria Nyanza lake occupies the lowest part of a shallow depression situated between the eastern and western rift valleys of East Africa.

It has a water surface of about 68,000 square kilometres and lies at an altitude of 1,129 metres (1) above the sea, and is believed to be of comparatively shallow depth. Situated near the equator, it lies for the greater part of the year in the region of the equatorial rain and cloud belt, and consequently has a considerable rainfall. The surplus water is drained off at the Ripon Falls by the Victoria Nile and the amount so discharged depends on the level of the lake waters. In common with all inland bodies of water this level varies from time to time with more or less regularity and the object of this note is to collect such data as exist, and to endeavour to trace from these data the oscillations of the lake level during the last 20 or 30 years.

The gauge-readings have been considered too contradictory to be of much value (2) but by elimination of certain errors the results are particularly interesting.

Geology.

Of late years a considerable amount of exploration has been undertaken round the lake, and in the German sphere Dantz and others have geologically examined large areas. Generally speaking the west shore of the lake and the country to the west of it consist of crystalline schists, quartzite, etc.; the southernmost parts of the eastern shore are occupied by granite with some crystalline schists, to the north of Speke's Gulf.

Stuhlmann (3) records a well-marked fault line along the western shore of the lake as far as the mouth of the Kagera river, with another parallel to it along the islands. This fault or one of the same series is also said to continue further northwards to meet the north shore of the lake. Recently Dantz (4) has described others as following the openings known as Emin Pasha Gulf, Smith's Sound and Speke Gulf.

Gedge (5) notes the faults on the west side of the lake, in Karagwe, where the shore cliffs descend into deep water close inshore while behind them can be seen a series of parallel faults forming a series of terraces or steps.

Thus it would appear that the Victoria lake is a large, though comparatively shallow, depression of which the larger of the numerous bays and inlets are probably, and in some cases certainly, due to faults.

On the north of the lake no such faults have been described but it does not appear that any very systematic geological examination of Uganda has yet been undertaken.

This part is fundamentally composed of gneissose rocks, frequently covered by laterite, while deposits of sedimentary rocks occur containing iron deposits in places (6). Earthquakes are felt not infrequently and the way that the drainage flows northwards away from the lake suggests probable faulting in the neighbourhood.

In the chart of the northern part of the Victoria lake, published by the Admiralty, from Commander Whitehouse's survey, the grouping of the inlets and islands along certain lines is very marked and though no detailed examination (so far as is known) was then made of the geological structure of this part it is hard to resist the conclusion that the main features have been to a great extent determined by lines of fracture and the accompanying earth movements.

(1) From the Uganda Railway Survey.
(2) RAVENSTEIN; BUCKLEY; Geog. Jour. XXI. 4. p. 359 ; BROWN. Ann. Rep. Pub. Wks. Ministry, Egypt 1902, p. 172.
(3) "Mit Emin Pasha im Herz von Afrika," p. 728, Berlin 1894.
(4) Mittheil. aus den Deutsch. Schutzgebieten XV. 1902, Berlin.
(5) Proc. Roy. Geog. Soc. 1892, p. 322.
(6) SCOTT ELLIOT, "A Naturalist in Mid Africa," London 1896, p. 164.

Climate.

The climate of the Victoria lake basin is typically that which is known as equatorial; two rainy seasons and two dry seasons make up the year, the rains coinciding more or less with the equinoxes and the dry seasons with the solstices, except that the second or minor rains are delayed about 1 to 2 months after the autumn equinox.

It is well shown by tabulating the relative excess of the rainfall according to Angot's method (1).

Entebbe is on the north shore of the lake, Kisumu on the eastern shore, at the head of the Kavirondo Gulf and Mumias is to the north-east of the lake and about 50 kilometres from it. Bukoba is on the western shore, and Tabora is south of the lake, about 280 kilometres distant.

TABLE I.—RELATIVE EXCESS OF RAINFALL.

	JAN.	FEB.	MAR.	APRIL	MAY	JUNE	JULY	AUG.	SEPT.	OCT.	NOV.	DEC.
Mumias.. ..	—37	— 26	— 15	+ **44**	+ 32	+29	+11	— 8	+**23**	— 2	— 2	— 34
Entebbe . ..	—43*	— 3	+ 5	+**115**	+ 20	—22	—51*	—40	—18	—13	+**35**	+ 13
Kisumu.. ..	—12	+ 29	+ 4	+ **55**	+ 15	— 8	—50	—57	—23	— 3	+**31**	+ 22
Bukoba	—40*	+ 3	+ 45	+**184**	+102	—57	—72*	—59	—53	—42	+**15**	— 28
Tabora	+127	+116	+116	+ 83	— 44	—73	—83	—83	—66	—55	+79	+**170**

The amount of rainfall has been recorded at the following places on the lake shores :—

	Shore.	Years of observations.	Mean annual rainfall mm.
Natete..................	N.	7 ½	1200
Entebbe............	N.	7 (2)	1330
Jinja..................	N.	2 (3)	1200 approx.
Kisumu................	N.E.	5	1242
Muanza................	S.	3 (3)	2000 approx.
Bukoba.................	W.	4 (3)	2150

Besides these there are a few other stations in the catchment basin of the lake but their observations only extend over a few years, among these are :—

		Years of observations.	Mean annual rainfall mm
Mumias................	N.E. of lake.	97-03	1832
Tabora................ .	S. » »	5 yrs. (3)	662
Mbarara................	W. » »	2 (3)	800 (5)
Masaka................	W. » »	1 (3)	1000 (4)

The average annual rainfall is difficult to estimate with any accuracy either for the lake area itself or for its catchment basin for, as shown above, it varies greatly in different parts. The records do not extend over many years and are very incomplete so that it is not easy to draw any satisfactory deductions from them. Still from these insufficient data, it may be taken that the average lake rainfall is probably less than 1500 millimetres per annum, since the east shore is said to be comparatively dry. Over the catchment basin any estimate is still more unreliable. The district south and west of the Kagera is said to be one of heavy precipitation but no actual observations exist.

By tabulating for each year the monthly difference from the mean value of the rainfall a better idea of the deficiency or excess in different years is obtained than by dealing with the actual amounts of rain recorded (see Table II). These also show the very local character of the rainfall, as for instance, in April and May 1897. In these months the rainfall at Entebbe was respectively 89 and 127 millimetres above the mean while for the same months at Bukoba there was a deficiency of 180 and 235 millimetres. Thus it does not follow necessarily that exceptional rainfall conditions at any one place are representative of those of the whole lake area.

(1) In this method the rainfall of a month is first expressed in thousandths of the year's total, as if the rain was equally distributed throughout the year. The difference between this and the *actual* rainfall of each month also in thousandths of the total gives the "Relative Excess" of the rainfall of the month. The wet months are + and the dry months —.
The rainfall is heaviest on the west and south of the lake, while on the eastern shore it is comparatively light.
(2) Including 1 year at Navirembo.
(3) These numbers of years are approximate only, as the records are very irregular.
(4) March-December 1903, 949 millimetres.
(5) March-October 1902, 611 millimetres. February and May to December 1903, 915.

TABLE II.

MEAN RAINFALL AND THE DIFFERENCES FROM IT IN MILLIMETRES.

NATETE.

	Jan.	Feb.	Mar.	April	May	June	July	Aug.	Sep.	Oct.	Nov.	Dec.
Mean. 1878-1886.	60	110	114	187	122	72	85	85	98	133	92	42
					Differences from Mean.							
1878	—	—	—	−55	−84	−34	—	—	—	—	−38	+47
1879	+82	−17	+20	−43	+81	−20	−76	−56	+43	−44	−8	−3
1880	−55	+50	+23	—	—	—	—	—	—	—	—	—
1881	+25	+13	+54	+158	−14	−6	−18	+3	−21	−43	+27	+18
1882	−20	+16	−60	+27	−24	−24	−11	−6	+21	+60	−21	−16
1883	+52	−44	−39	−7	−22	+3	+51	+35	−27	−76	+8	−22
1884	−47	−26	−38	−77	−60	+27	+6	−49	+12	+102	+18	−34
1885	−30	+18	+54	−42	+18	+60	+48	+2	−20	+2	+16	+10
1886	−8	−12	−16	+39	+99	−8	—	—	—	—	—	—

ENTEBBE.

	Jan.	Feb.	Mar.	Apr.	May.	June	July	Aug.	Sep.	Oct.	Nov.	Dec.
Mean.	56	98	105	260	140	80	45	60	85	90	155	130
					Differences from Mean.							
1893	—	—	—	− 33	− 40	− 19	−19	−43	+41	+31	− 86	− 76
1896	—	—	—	− 43	− 27	+ 1	−37	+44	−25	+27	+151	− 11
1897	− 12	−34	− 5	+ 89	+127	+ 1	+28	—	—	—	—	—
1900	+ 4	+10	+ 49	+ 85	− 72	+ 68	−34	+14	+ 2	−51	− 3	+188
1901	+ 28	+27	+ 28	− 61	+ 59	—	+57	−55	−68	−41	− 97	− 25
1902	+ 18	+79	− 32	−131	− 35	− 52	+12	+41	+37	+24	+ 42	—
1903	+111	−80	+230	− 39	+ 35	+180	+88	−30	+28	− 7	− 60	+ 9

MUMIAS.

	Jan.	Feb.	Mar.	April	May	June	July	Aug.	Sept.	Oct.	Nov.	Dec.
Mean.	85	104	125	234	211	206	172	138	195	149	150	91
					Differences from Mean.							
1897	+5	+8	+26	−8	−64	+115	−15	+135	+211	+128	+28	−57
1898	−17	−49	−36	+68	−8	+85	+39	−21	−76	−44	+27	−74
1899	—	—	−85	+62	+12	−84	−106	−74	−104	−47	−89	−19
1900	+27	+112	+49	−125	−32	−81	−69	+15	−72	−33	+98	+125
1901	−59	+39	−15	+59	+17	−147	−48	−61	−21	−31	−65	−46
1902	−47	−82	−55	−21	+88	−92	+110	+59	−18	+8	+37	+47
1903	+91	−29	+117	−35	−13	+204	+90	−53	+79	+20	−36	+23

BUKOBA.

	Jan.	Feb.	Mar.	Apr.	May.	June	July	Aug.	Sep.	Oct.	Nov.	Dec.
Mean.	96	172	280	571	403	54	28	56	62	93	209	122
					Differences from Mean.							
1893	—	—	—	—	—	—	—	+1	+ 8	− 7	− 10	+19
1894	−40	—	—	—	− 80	−42	− 1	+4	−57	+17	− 14	−48
1895	− 7	−10	+19	+180	+317	−50	−14	−6	− 6	−19	+121	− 9
1896	+16	—	—	—	—	—	—	—	—	—	—	—
1897	—	—	—	−180	−235	+91	+15	0	+56	+8	− 62	+73
1898	+34	−46	−52	—	—	—	—	—	—	—	—	—
1901	—	—	—	—	—	—	—	—	—	—	− 35	−34
1902	−26	+48	+32	—	—	—	—	—	—	—	—	—
1903	+21	—	—	—	—	—	—	—	—	—	—	—

Winds.

The winds on the lake itself are almost exclusively those due to the presence of the immense water area which gives rise to a lake wind blowing towards the shore from morning to evening, while a reverse wind from the land towards the lake blows from evening until morning (1). This is well shown by the observations taken at Muanza (south shore) and Bukoba (west shore) where these land and lake winds completely mask the effects of the seasonal changes of the trade winds. These latter however blow steadily in places more removed from the lake as at Tabora, (2) to the south where east and south-east winds predominate throughout the year. At this station we are to the south of the true equatorial belt, and there is consequently but one rainy season, December to April, the rest of the year being almost rainless and the humidity is then very low.

In the summer months when the rain-belt lies to the northward the dry south and south-east winds must blow across the lake catchment basin even though the diurnal reversal of winds on the lake itself is not mastered by them, and will greatly increase the evaporation. It will be seen, when the curves of the lake gauge-readings are examined, that this is actually the case and that there is a very marked diminution of the water during the greater dry season, which must be due primarily to greatly increased evaporation from the lake surface.

Variations in level.

The variations in the level of the Victoria lake as of other lakes admit of division into several distinct classes.

Firstly, there is the increase or decrease in size due to climatic or other changes which affect them over long periods ;

Secondly, there are the oscillations due to variations in meteorological conditions having a comparatively short period such as that of about 35 years detected by Brückner (3) and in which a period of high levels is followed by a period of lower levels ;

Thirdly, there are the annual oscillations due, in the case of the Victoria lake, to the April and November rains.

Fourthly, the alteration of lake and land breezes must cause a daily oscillation of the water which will be more noticeable in large landlocked gulfs like Kavirondo (Kisumu) than in more open situations as at Entebbe.

Fifthly, there are minor irregular changes (Seiches) which can only be briefly mentioned, since the evidence available is quite insufficient for any discussion of them.

For the first type, there is much evidence all round the lake that in early times its waters stood at a higher level. Scott Elliot (4) attributes the flat alluvial plains which fill the valleys above the present lake level, to the detritus brought down by the tributary streams and deposited in the still waters of the lake. He puts the upper limit of these alluvial tracts at 30 metres above the present lake level, and notes that the lake apparently remained stationary for a considerable time about 13 metres above its present level.

In any case, seeing at what a small elevation the water-parting on the north shore of the lake is situated, there can have been no very great vertical extension of the lake since the earth movements which turned the drainage of this part towards the Victoria Nile.

Secondly we come to the periodical variation of the lake for which the evidence is furnished by :—

1) observations by travellers and others visiting or residing by the lake ;

2) the series of the lake gauge-readings taken at three points on the northern shore of the lake since 1896.

The French missionaries at Bukumbi on Smith's Sound (south shore) are said to have possessed a record of the level of the lake extending over many years, but it is reported to have been lost with much other scientific material by the sinking of a canoe on the lake.

In discussing the changes in the lake level during a series of years from the observations of travellers there is usually some doubt as to the exact nature of the rise or fall they record. In the case of the Victoria lake, where the average annual range during the years 1896-1903 is $0^{m}\cdot660$ (Table V), it is often uncertain, when a rise of 3 feet is recorded, whether this is a somewhat larger range that usual, or whether a real increase of the mean level of the lake is intended. In the years for which gauge-readings exist the range of the

(1) Maurer, Zur Klimatologie von Deutsch Ostafrika. Archiv. d. Deutsch. Seewarte XXIV. 1901.
(2) Mitt. aus den deutsch. Schutzgebieten, 1903.
(3) Klimaschwankungen. Vienna, 1890.
(4) "A Naturalist in Mid Africa." London, 1896 p. 39.

lake has varied from $0^{m}.46$ to $0^{m}.89$ and variations in range may be indicated to travellers as signs of rising or falling lake level though they may be of a temporary character only; caution therefore is necessary in interpreting isolated observations.

To take the first class of observations:—

In March 1875 Stanley (1) described the island of Ukerewé as separated from the mainland by a narrow channel, at one place only 6 feet wide and 3 feet deep; in June of the same year he punted through it (2).

Wilson (3) notes that in February 1877 there was exceptionally heavy rain to the south of the lake (Uyui), and attributes to this an unusual rise of the lake at this time amounting to 2 feet.

Hutchinson (4) states that Wilson noticed soon after his arrival at Kagehi (south shore), in the middle of February 1877, that the lake was slowly rising. By May, 10 days after the rains had ceased, the level was at its maximum, and then began to recede; the total rise from a point marked on a rock in February was 2 feet. On his arrival again at Kagehi on the 12th January 1878, he found that the water level was within 1 to 1½ inches of the maximum as marked on the rock in the previous May, showing that the November-December rains had been particularly heavy. On revisiting Kagehi on the 15th March 1878, the level was the same as on the 12th January. A few days later at Uganda he obtained evidence of the unusually high level of the lake there also.

Felkin (5) records that the lake rose 3 feet above its normal level in August and September 1878 in consequence of the exceptionally heavy rains. Here it is not clear whether it rose 3 feet above its usual June maximum or above the ordinary January level. In this particular year the January level was about the same as that of the preceding May as already mentioned.

Fischer (6) records a failure of rain to the north-east of the lake near Kisumu in the early part of 1886, and says that two years before the rain had failed, so by this time the fall of the lake seems to have set in.

Stanley, on his second visit to the lake, after the rescue of Emin Pasha, states (7) that by September 1889 the French missionaries at Bukumbi had determined by observation that the lake had fallen 3 feet in the previous 11 years. Here again there is some ambiguity; a fall of the annual mean level should be meant, but perhaps the maxima of different years are referred to. He was also told (7) that Ukerewé was no longer an island.

In April 1891, Dermott (8) noted on the island of Kitaro, south of Ukerewé, that the lake was at a level 5 or 6 feet lower than the high-level marks on the rocks; he also states that the Lugeshi (Rugezi) straits between Ukerewé and the mainland were not passable, there being only a few inches of water.

As in April the lake is usually rising steadily, this observation tends to bear out Stanley's information, and points to the lake having been especially low in 1889-91.

Lugard (9) in June 1892 records an exceptionally heavy rainfall and a marked rise in the lake, "some 6 feet perhaps above its ordinary level." This was due to heavy rainfall between the November and February preceding.

Baumann (10) in 1892 finds Ukerewé an island but the Rugezi strait is fordable, and it is shown as an island in the latest maps: thus there had been a rise of the lake due to the 1891 rains after Dermott's visit.

Baumann (10) collected all information on the subject that he could and was of opinion that the lake level fell from 1880 more than a metre but at the time of his visit, (1892-3) it was rising. This was not the commencement of a period of maxima as seems to be implied, but was due to the heavy rains of November 1891 to February 1892 which caused a higher mean lake level in 1892.

Père Brard (11) states that the lake level on the southern coast rose, in 1895, 1·5 metres in consequence of the heavy rains, and plantations for 200 metres along the southern shores were destroyed. The natives said that no such high level had occurred for 30 years, but that of 1878 was certainly as high or higher.

In this case a high maximum is probably meant as the heavy rains began in March, and were unusually heavy at both Muanza and Bukoba throughout April and May.

(1) "Through the Dark Continent," I p. 160.
(2) Ibid. p. 257.
(3) Proc. Roy. Geog. Soc. 1880, p. 616.
(4) Ibid. 1879, p. 136.
(5) "Uganda and the Sudan," I. p. 396.
(6) Pet. Mitt. 1895, p. 67.
(7) "In Darkest Africa," II, p. 396.
(8) Proc. Roy. Geog. Soc., 1892, p. 120.
(9) Ibid. 1892, p. 827.
(10) Durch "Massai-land Zur Nilquelle," p. 143.
(11) Pet. Mitt. 1897, p. 77.

From the information collected by Sir W. E. Garstin in January 1903 we have :—

a) Père Bresson, of the French Mission at Entebbe, states that there has been a considerable fall in the lake level near Kisibu (between Entebbe and the Murchison Gulf).

b) The natives say that there has been a considerable fall.

c) Mr. Pordage states that the reef in front of Entebbe was covered in 1896, but in February 1903, it was well out of water. The mean level of the lake has fallen about 0·6 metres between these dates according to the gauge readings (see Table IV, p. 29).

d) According to Mr. Wilson since 1894, 3 feet has been the maximum rise of the lake and that was in 1895.

e) Mr. Martin says that since 1889, when he first visited the lake, there has been a distinct fall, and certainly 4 to 5 feet since 1896. At Kisimu there are villages and pasture where in 1889 there was water. He thinks it has fallen 4 to 6 feet.

At the ford above the Ripon Falls the water extended horizontally 30 feet more than at present.

Sessé Islands show shallowing channels and what were formerly separate islands are now connected to the neighbouring land.

Besides these evidences there exists a tradition of a periodical rise and fall of the lake extending over from 25 to 30 years.

Stuhlmann (1) speaks of meeting near Muanza a native some 60 or 70 years old who stated that he was then able to work again the banana plantation which his father had, but which had been abandoned in the speaker's boyhood on account of the rising of the lake level.

Gedge (2) states that according to natives on the north of the lake there is a periodical rise and fall having a period of about 25 years; at the time of writing, apparently, in 1891, the level was between 8 and 9 feet below the highest water mark and they pointed out plantations which were at the time cultivated and which would be again flooded.

Though these various testimonies are not quite concordant, there appears to be, as Stuhlmann also says (3), a general agreement on the part of Europeans and natives that the lake level has sunk recently and particularly from 1878 to 1892, after which, according to Baumann, there was a tendency to rise. This rise, however, appears to have been limited to the years 1892-1895, or perhaps even to 1892 and 1895 only, which were years of heavy rainfall. From this time the fall has been almost continuous up to the end of 1902, as the lake gauges show.

These data may be tabulated as follows :—

1878	Very high in August and September.
1884	Drought N. E. of lake.
1886	Drought N. E. of lake.
1878 / 1890	General fall on southern shore.
1891	Low.
1892	Very high, heavy rainfall, tendency to rise.
1895	Very high.

Comparing these with the fairly complete series of rainfall observations at Natete and Entebbe, 1884 and 1886 were not there very deficient in rainfall; 1884 had a total of 1034 millimetres against a mean for 8 years of 1197, and the early months of 1886 were up to the average. But the eastern shore throughout is much drier, and it is certain that all over the lake basin large variations in rainfall may occur within short distances.

Sieger, (4) after reviewing the evidence for the variations in level of the Central Africa lakes, sums up his results as in the following table :—

Movement.	Period.	Lake.
Minimum	18th Century	Chad and Tanganika
Low	1840-1850	" "
Rapid rise	1853-1855	Chad
Fall	Before 1866	Chad
Rapid rise	1875-76 or 1878	Chad, Nyassa, Tanganika
Fall	1879 to 1886	Nyassa, Tanganika, Kilwa.

Generally speaking 1850 to 1878 was a wet period, and 1879 to 1886 was a dry one for the whole of Central Africa.

Turning now to the recorded readings of the lake level, there are three lake gauges on the Victoria lake, all situated on the northern or north-east shore of the lake; in German

(1) Mitt. d. Deutsch. Schutzgebeit; V. p. 190, 1892.
(2) Proc. Roy. Geog. Soc. 1892 p. 323.
(3) "Mit Emin Pasha ins Herz von Afrika," p 729.
(4) Bericht f. d. XIII Vereins-Jahr (1887) des Verein d. Geographen. a. d. Univ. Wien.

Territory none have yet been established (1). Of these one is at Entebbe on the north shore of the lake, the second at Jinja, just above the Ripon Falls, where the Nile leaves the lake, and the third is at Kisumu, near the railway terminus on the north-east shore of the lake and at the head of the almost land-locked Kavirondo Gulf.

All these gauges have been moved since the daily readings of the lake level were first commenced in 1896 and some considerable gaps occur in the records, still, after eliminating as far as possible these sources of error, there remains a valuable collection of data from which it is possible to obtain a considerable amount of information. The gauges were first fixed at the end of 1895 by Mr. Macalister (2), care being taken to have as firm a foundation as possible to avoid subsidence of the gauge; and observations were commenced 1st January 1896 at Port Alice, which is close to the present site of the Entebbe gauge and at the Luba's gauge which was close to Fort Luba's on the east side of the Napoleon Gulf on the north shore of the lake, not far from the Ripon Falls. The third gauge in 1896 was at Port Victoria at the south-western end of Berkeley Bay, an inlet of moderate size on the north-east shore of the lake.

The changes of the gauge stations since that time must now be mentioned together with the amount of uncertainty which such changes have introduced.

The three gauges at Port Alice, Luba's and Port Victoria were observed regularly until the end of July 1897 when the Sudanese mutiny interrupted the observations. The readings of the Port Alice and Port Victoria gauges were resumed on 1st September 1898 and that at Luba's on 1st May 1898. During this interval there seems to have been no interference with these three gauges but this is now of little importance since on the 1st October 1898, the three gauges were adjusted by Capt. C. N. Fowler (3). On the 30th September 1898 the three gauges stood as follows:—

	ft.	in.
Port Alice	2	4
Luba's	1	7½
Port Victoria	3	3

The lake level had been very steady all September, the range being 2½ inches or less.

It appears that Port Victoria was the gauge to which the others were adjusted, and Capt. C. N. Fowler writes in reply to a query on the subject as follows:—

" In year 1898 I was consulted by Mr. Ernest Berkeley, H.M. Commissioner, as to the fixing of a "Zero" for all stations on the lake; the result of the consultation was as follows:—

" Having fixed a "Zero" at Entebbe (Port Alice) I proceeded in the steam launch *Victoria* at full speed to Luba's station, some 2½ hours' steaming and adjusted the "Zero" at that station to a depth similar to that recorded on Entebbe gauge, no telegraph available. Weather calm during trip. Method primitive, but only one available."

It is seen from the daily observations that on the following day the three gauges were practically in agreement the gauge scales of two having been depressed, so, though Captain Fowler does not definitely say so, Port Victoria was the gauge to which the other two were adjusted.

	Port Alice.	Luba's.	Port Victoria.
30 September 1898...	2 ft. 4 in.	1 ft. 7½ in.	3 ft. 3 in.
Adjustment	+10 „	+1 „ 6 „	0 „ 0 „
1st October 1898 ...	3 ft. 2 „	3 „ 1½ „	3 „ 2½ „ (4)

After this the Port Alice gauge remained until 31st March 1900, when it was removed and set up at Entebbe. These places are close together and this change introduced no appreciable error into the series of observations, for the gauge at Port Alice had been reading 2ft. 8 in. from 19th to the 31st of March; it was erected at Entebbe on the 1st April to read 2ft. 7in. and the same reading was recorded for every day in April so that the lake level was practically stationary during the move of the gauge, as is shown by the following readings of the other gauges:—

	Luba's		Kisumu	
1900.	ft.	in.	ft.	in.
30th March	1	4.0	2	0.0
31st „	1	5.0	2	0.0
1st April	1	4.0	2	2.0
2nd „	1	3.5	2	2.0

Most unfortunately this gauge was knocked down or washed away on the 31st May 1901 and was not replaced until 20th October of the same year so that the fall of the lake at this site from the maximum is not recorded.

(1) One is now being established but the site is not yet known.
(2) Geog. Jour. Oct. 1901 p. 403.
(3) Brit. Assoc. Rep. 1901.
(4) 0.5 inch fall.

After Luba's gauge had been brought into accord with the other two by depressing its zero 1ft. 6 in., on the 1st October 1898, it was regularly observed until 31st July 1901, and on the 1st August 1901, the gauge was transferred to Jinja, close to the head of the Ripon Falls and about 16 kilometres north-west of Luba's. Here again no error has been introduced into the series of observations, for taking the daily readings at the time we have :—

				ft.	in.
Luba's gauge ...	29th	July,	1901	2.	2
	30th	"	"	2.	2
	31st	"	"	2.	1
Jinja gauge ...	1, 2, & 3	August,	"	2.	1

The Kisumu gauge confirms this :

Kisumu				ft.	in.
29th	July	1901	...	2.	6
30th	"	"	...	2.	8
31st	"	"	...	2.	6
1st	Aug.	"	...	2.	8
2nd	"	"	...	2.	8
2nd	"	"	...	2.	6

Thus we have in the Luba's-Jinja series of gauge-readings a practically continuous record from 1st October 1898 to the present time.

The gauge was however altered in December 1901 by having its zero depressed 11 inches. This was done on the advice of Mr. R. B. Buckley, C. S. I., according to information furnished by the Scientific Department of Uganda, who, in reply to a question on this point, telegraphed :—

"Zero of lake level at Jinja was raised (should read "lowered") eleven inches on 21st December 1901 on recommendation Buckley":—

	ft.	in.
On 20th December, 1901 the gauge read	1.	3
On 21st " " " "	2.	1
Difference...	0.	10

This change is shown to be only local by the gauge-readings of the other stations:—

	Entebbe.		Kisumu.	
	ft.	in.	ft.	in.
20th December...	3.	6	1.	3
21st " ...	3.	6	1.	3

The third gauge has had a more chequered career. After readings were resumed in September 1898 at Port Victoria they were continued until the 31st July 1899. This station was then closed and the gauge was transferred to Port Ugowe (Port Florence) on 23rd August 1899. This was a move from a comparatively open situation near the south end of Berkeley Bay to the head of the almost land-locked Kavirondo Gulf. The amount of correction which should be applied to all subsequent readings of the Kisumu gauge in order to bring them into accordance with the Port Victoria readings can be best deduced by a comparison of the readings with those of the Luba's gauge before and after August 1899.

The last readings at Port Victoria were:—

	ft.	in.
29th July, 1899...	2.	5½
30th " " ...	2.	4½
31st " " ...	2.	4

and the first at Port Ugowe were :—

	ft.	in.
23rd August, 1899 ...	2.	6
24th " " ...	2.	6
25th " " ...	2.	5

The lapse of time viz : 23 days, is considerable, and during it we find by reference to the other two gauges that :—

The Luba's gauge showed a fall of 10½ inches and the Port Alice gauge, a fall of 5 inches.

The Port Alice gauge was not at that time furnishing a reliable record of the lake level as will be shown later.

After the gauges had been adjusted on 1st October 1898 the mean readings for that month, in centimetres were (see Table V).

Port Victoria	Luba's	Difference
cm.	cm.	cm.
99	95	+4

In 1899 we have the following comparisons of the monthly means in centimetres :—

	Port Victoria	Luba's	Difference	
April	89	84	+ 5	Mean +3 cm.
January	99	94	+ 5	
June	99	93	+ 6	
July	82	86	— 4	
August 23-31 ...	74[1]	58	+16	+20 cm.
September	69	48	+21	
October	59	38	+21	
November	58	35	+23	

So that a deduction of 17 centimetres should be made from the monthly means of the lake level readings recorded on the Kisumu gauge from 23rd August 1899, to bring them into agreement with those recorded before that date.

At the end of September 1900 the gauge at Port Ugowe (Port Florence) was reading :—

	Ft.	in.
29th September, 1900 ...	1.	11
30th " " ...	1.	11
1st October " ...	1.	8
2nd " " ...	1.	7

but from the 1st October the readings are at Kisumu and have continued to be so down to the present date.

Kisumu is a village on the Kavirondo Gulf but the site of the gauge was not altered when the name of the gauge station was changed. For this third gauge therefore there is fairly continuous series of observations, except the 22 days between the last observation at Port Victoria and the first at Port Ugowe, and as we have seen, a correction of $0^m{\cdot}17$ should be applied to all observations since 23rd August 1899 to bring them into uniformity with the previous observations.

Having shortly detailed the various changes it remains to compare the readings of the three gauges. This is most conveniently done by plotting the monthly mean of the readings of each gauge (See Plan III) and the result may be summarized as follows:—

Throughout 1896 and 1897 the curves of the three gauges, Port Alice, Port Victoria and Luba's keep parallel to each other.

On the 30th September and 1st October 1898 the gauges read :—

	Port Alice	Port Victoria	Luba's
30th September... ...	2 ft. 4 in.	3 ft. 3 in.	1 ft. 7½ in.
1st October	3 " 2 "	3 " 2½ "	3 " 1½ "

being now practically in agreement. In December, however, the mean of the Port Alice gauge was 13 centimetres above that of Luba's and 8 centimetres above that of Port Victoria. The former difference remained fairly constant until August when it rapidly increased to 29 centimetres and by January 1900 it had reached 38 centimetres.

It is unfortunate that the time when this second increase of the difference appears (July-August 1899) is also that when the Port Victoria gauge was moved to Port Ugowe, but as has already been shown above the deduction of 17 centimetres from the Ugowe-Kisumu readings reduces the monthly means to those of the Port Victoria readings with a probable error of 1 or 2 centimetres only. Thus a continuous curve is obtainable with which the fluctuations of Port Alice (Entebbe) gauge can be compared. These corrected values for Kisumu have been plotted in Plan III and will be seen to follow the Jinja curve fairly closely from August 1899 to November 1901.

During this time the Entebbe gauge (up to the time it was destroyed in June 1901) differed considerably from the other two, by about 35 centimetres from September 1899 to October 1900, and afterwards by a less amount up to February 1901.

The most probable explanation of this is that the land at Entebbe was sinking slightly from about October 1898, or indeed earlier, since the difference between mean monthly values of the Port Alice (Entebbe) gauge and Luba's gauge was 23 centimetres in September 1898, although throughout 1896 and 1897 the difference was but 5 to 10 centimetres. In 1899 the

[1] From this date at Port Ugowe (Kisumu).

sinking continued, being marked between August and October, but being on a falling gauge it did not attract attention. At the end of 1900 and the early months of 1901 a slight elevation would seem to have occurred, while in May and probably June a renewed sinking probably took place but the destruction of the gauge renders proof impossible.

So far it appears that there was on the whole a downward movement of the land near Entebbe in 1898 and 1899, which did not affect either Napoleon Gulf or the north-east shore of the lake.

It appears more than probable that there actually was something abnormal at Entebbe in April-May 1901 since a telegram was received at Cairo from Entebbe reporting a rise of 3ft. 3in. in the lake level in six months [1] though the other two gauges showed only about 2 feet rise.

Taking the monthly means from Table V we have in centimetres:—

1901	Entebbe.	Kisumu.	Luba's	Entebbe—Kisumu.	Entebbe—Luba's.
	cm	cm.	cm.	cm.	cm.
January	58	32	35	26	23
February	61	37	36	24	25
March	77	43	48	34	29
April	116	68	66	48	50
May...	153	95	89	58	64

At this point the gauge at Entebbe was destroyed. An additional proof that this rise recorded at Entebbe does not represent the rise of the lake is furnished by Commander B. Whitehouse, R. N., who, in a memorandum on the level of the lake [2], denies that it was unusually high in May 1901 since he points out that in November 1898 it was 16ft. below a bench-mark at Port Florence; in January 1900 the level was low, and 18ft. 1 inch below the same mark; soundings on the entrance line to the harbour showed the same decrease in depth.

By May 1901 the level had risen to 3 ft. 4 in. on the gauge, bringing back the level to what it had been in November 1898. Thus an unusually high level was recorded at Entebbe only. This time the local downward movement of the land occurred during the normal rise of the lake and therefore attracted special attention, but the similar though larger movement in the autumn of 1899 (see p. 27) was on a falling gauge and, as we have seen, was not observed.

These variations of the Entebbe gauge extend over several months so that they cannot be explained by local wind action. The above differences are those between the monthly means of different months and would not be caused by occasional seiches.

Thus of the three gauges, that at Port Alice (Entebbe) records abnormal changes of the lake level which are not borne out by the readings of the other gauges, so that any discussion of the annual oscillation of the lake must be based on one of the others.

The Port Victoria-Kisumu gauge, as has been related above, was the one to which the others were adjusted in October 1898. After August 1899 a correction of about 17 centimetres (see p. 27) has to be made to the readings and they then follow the Jinja readings very closely during 1900 and 1901.

In 1902 and 1903 there are months in which the parallelism between the Kisumu and Jinja gauges is not maintained, e.g. the difference in June 1902 is 30 cm., while in January 1903 it is only 5 cm., but throughout this period the Kisumu curve keeps closely parallel to the Entebbe curve. Thus the Port Victoria-Kisumu series of lake readings furnish the most reliable series of the three gauges and it will be better therefore to study the annual oscillations on this gauge, especially as Whitehouse's observations show that for two and a half years at least the gauge was not interfered with.

These divergences in the curve of the Jinja gauge readings are curious and perhaps if earth-movement is assumed in the case of Entebbe, the same line of argument should be applied to the Jinja gauge from the end of 1901 to 1903. It will be seen that the Jinja curve from November 1901 to February 1902 was on the whole rising while those of Entebbe and Kisumu were falling steadily; again in December 1902 Jinja was steady while Entebbe and Kisumu were rising, and in February 1903 the reverse was the case. Still it is not so marked as in the case of the Entebbe gauge from 1897-1901.

Thus it will be seen that the annual oscillation of the lake level, so far as observations exist, varies between about 1 and 3 feet while absolute range during the last 7 years is 3ft. 9 inches, a considerable difference from the very much larger estimates of travellers and others which have been given on page 23.

(1) Report of Public Works Ministry, Cairo 1901 p. 170.
(2) See p. 35, Appendix III A.

The mean levels of the lake for each year from the Port Victoria-Kisumu gauge (corrected as before) are :—

TABLE III.—ANNUAL MEAN LEVEL OF LAKE.

Years.	Metres.	Feet.	Inches.	Years.	Rate per Annum.	Years.	Total fall of mean level from 1896.
					M.		M.
1896.. ..	0·928	3	0·6	1896–99	—0·065	1896	—
1897.. ..	Incomplete.	..	..	—	—	1897	—
1898.. ..	„	..	..	—	—	1898	—
1899.. ..	0·733	2	4·9	1899–90	—0·342	1899	0·195
1900.. ..	0·391	1	3·4	1900 01	+0·117	1900	0·537
1901.. ..	0·508	1	8·0	1901–02	—0·336	1901	0·420
1902.. ..	0·172	0	6·8	1902–03	+0·559	1902	0·756
1903.. ..	0·731	2	4·8	—	—	1903	0·197

This table gives the mean level of the whole year for each year in which the observations are sufficiently complete. In 1902 the observations for April and May at Kisumu are missing but the Entebbe and Jinja gauges for these months show that the level rose slowly and slightly during these months so that no error is introduced by their omission.

It is evident therefore that there has been steady fall of the average lake level amounting in all to about 76 cm. during the 7 years 1896-1902, followed by a rise of 56 cm. during 1903.

The range for each year and the whole period is as follows :—

TABLE IV.—KISUMU GAUGE.

Year.	Maximum. Reading. Ft.	In.	Maximum. Date	Minimum. Reading. Ft.	In.	Minimum. Date	Range. Ft.	In.	Met.	Remarks
1896	3	8¾	14th Jan.	2	2½	22-29 Oct.	1	6¼	0·46	
1897	3	8	11-14 June	*	*	*	—	—	—	* Observations cease on 31st July.
1898										(No observations before September).
1899	3	7	21st May	0	11¼†	29th Dec.	2	7¼	0·79	† A correction of 6″¾ made to all observations from 23rd Aug. 1899.
1900	2	2¼	10th May	—0	0¾	3-4 Nov.	2	3	0·69	
1901	3	5¼	13th May	0	6¼	5 Feb. & 12 Mar.	2	11	0·89	
1902	—	—	—	—0	0¾	22nd July	—	—	—	Maximum occurred in May, but Kisumu gauge readings for this month were lost, so max. & min. for Jinja are also shown.
„ (Jinja)	1	11¼	23rd May	0	11	24. 27 & 28 Dec.	1	0½	0·32	
1903	3	5¼	17th June 15 & 18 July & 3 Aug.	0	9¼	1-2 Jan.	2	8	0·81	
Absolute 8 year.	3	8¾	14th Jan. 1896.	—0	0¾	3-4 Nov. 1900, and 22 July 1902.	3	9½	1·16	

The conclusions which may be drawn from this study of the lake gauges are the following :—

1. The gauge records are trustworthy when the necessary corrections have been applied as above explained.

2. The Entebbe gauge though of a very great interest in recording a local abnormal movement of the water level, due it is believed, to local intermittent earth movement, is not a true record of the oscillation of the lake level.

3. The Kisumu gauge does truly record the lake oscillation, but about the Jinja gauge there is a slight doubt.

4. The annual oscillation is from 0·30 to 0·90 metres.

5. The period of the secular oscillation cannot be determined from so short a series of observations.

6. Between 1896 and 1902 there has been a fall of 76 centimetres in the average level of the lake, since followed by a rise of 56 cm.

7. 1878 was a high level period.
   1880-90 was a falling level period.
   1892-95 was a temporary high level period.
   1896-1902 was a falling level period.
   1903 was a rise.

TABLE V.—MEAN MONTHLY LEVELS

DATE	STATIONS: Entebbe Maxim.	Entebbe Minim.	Entebbe Mean	Kisumu Maxim.	Kisumu Minim.	Kisumu Mean	Luba's Maxim.	Luba's Minim.	Luba's Mean
1896									
I	**0·64**	0·53	0·58	**1·44**	1·04	1·10	**0·65**	0·58	0·61
II	0·53	0·46	0·51	1·09	0·95	1·03	**0·65**	0·51	0·55
III	0·50	0·41	0·44	1·09	0·91	1·01	0·62	0·47	0·54
IV	0·50	0·44	0·47	1·04	0.95	1·00	0·60	0·46	0·55
V	0·50	0·44	0·47	1·04	0·99	1·01	0·61	0·48	0·56
VI	0·46	0·41	0·43	1·03	0·95	0·99	0.57	0·50	0·53
VII	0·46	0·38	0·42	0·98	0·86	0·92	0·53	0·41	0·47
VIII	0·41	0·36	0·37	0·94	0·86	0 88	0·47	0·39	0·43
IX	0·34	0·23	0 27	0·86	0·74	0 79	0·43	0·27	0·36
X	0·23	**0·13**	0·15	0·76	**0·67**	0·71	0·34	**0·20**	0·26
XI	0·37	0·15	0·26	0·93	0·71	0·83	0·47	**0·20**	0 35
XII	0·39	0·32	0·35	0.91	0·84	0 87	0·44	0·36	0·40
Mean	—	—	0 393	—	—	0·928	—	—	0·468
1897									
I	0·36	0·29	0 33	0·91	0·84	0·86	0·42	0·36	0·40
II	0·36	0·30	0 34	0·93	0·86	0·91	0·48	0·37	0·43
III	0·39	0·34	0·36	0·95	0·91	0·93	0·48	0·36	0·42
IV	0·51	0·38	0·43	1·07	0·94	1 01	0·58	0·43	0·50
V	0·56	0·51	0 53	1·07	0·91	0·99	0·60	0·50	0·57
VI	0·60	0·51	0·56	1·12	1·00	1·07	0·70	0 56	0 61
VII	0·52	0·48	0·50	1·07	1·02	1 04	0·64	0·48	0·56
VIII	—	—	—	—	—	—	—	—	—
IX	—	—	—	—	—	—	—	—	—
X	—	—	—	—	—	—	—	—	—
XI	—	—	—	—	—	—	—	—	—
XII	—	—	—	—	—	—	—	—	—
Mean	—	—	—	—	—	—	—	—	—

DATE	STATIONS: Entebbe Maxim.	Entebbe Minim.	Entebbe Mean	Kisumu Maxim.	Kisumu Minim.	Kisumu Mean	Luba's Maxim.	Luba's Minim.	Luba's Mean
1898									
I	—	—	—	—	—	—	—	—	—
II	—	—	—	—	—	—	—	—	—
III	—	—	—	—	—	—	—	—	—
IV	—	—	—	—	—	—	—	—	—
V	—	—	—	—	—	—	—	—	0·60
VI	—	—	—	—	—	—	—	—	0·51
VII	—	—	—	—	—	—	—	—	0·54
VIII	—	—	—	—	—	—	—	—	0 51
IX	0.76	0·71	0·74	1·03	0·97	0·99	0·54	0·48	0.50
X	1·02	0·97	0 99	1·04	0·95	0·99	0·98	0·91	0·95
XI	1·09	0·96	1·03	1·05	0·95	1·00	0·99	0·91	0 95
XII	1·12	1·04	1·08	1·07	0·94	1·00	0.99	0·88	0·95
Mean	—	—	—	—	—	—	—	—	—
1899									
I	1·03	0·99	1·00	0·99	0·90	0·95	0·95	0·89	0·90
II	**1·09**	0·97	1·01	0·95	0·86	0·91	0·91	0·84	0·87
III	1·03	0·97	0 99	0·95	0·84	0·89	0·89	0·83	0·85
IV	1·07	0·94	0·99	0·97	0·80	0·89	0·94	0·83	0·81
V	**1·09**	1·00	1·04	**1·09**	0·86	0·99	**1·05**	0 85	0·94
VI	1·08	1·02	1·05	1·07	0·91	0·99	1·02	0·86	0·93
VII	1·08	0·98	1·03	0·94	0·71	0·82	0·91	0·79	0·86
VIII	1·00	0·85	0·93	0·62	0·53	0·57	0·85	0·56	0 64
IX	0·85	0·72	0·80	0·68	0·41	0·52	0·56	0·43	0·48
X	0·77	0·72	0 75	0·49	0·34	0·42	0·43	**0·33**	0 38
XI	0·72	**0·67**	0 70	0·49	0·31	0 41	0·36	**0·33**	0·35
XII	0·75	0·69	0 71	0·66	**0·30**	0·44	0·38	**0·53**	0 35
Mean	—	—	0·917	—	—	0·733	—	—	[illegible]

* Minus readings.

)F LAKE VICTORIA *(in Metres).*

DATE	STATIONS											
	ENTEBBE			JINJA			KISUMU			LUBA'S		
	Maxim.	Minim.	Mean	Maxim.	Minim.	Mean	Maxim.	Minim.	Mean	Maxim.	Minim.	Mean
1900												
I	0·77	0·75	0·77	—	—	—	0·57	0·39	0 45	0·44	0·34	0·39
II	0·80	0·77	0·79	—	—	—	0·54	0·34	0·45	0·43	0·33	0·39
III	0·81	0·79	0·80	—	—	—	0·62	0·29	0·43	0·43	0·33	0·38
IV	0·79	0·79	0 79	—	—	—	0·55	0·36	0·48	**0·48**	0·38	0·42
V	0·81	0·79	0·80	—	—	—	**0·67**	0·47	0·56	**0·48**	0·42	0·45
VI	0·85	**0·81**	0 83	—	—	—	0·62	0 44	0·53	0·47	0·41	0 45
VII	**0·88**	0·85	0·86	—	—	—	0·52	0·29	0·48	0·46	0·11	0·15
VIII	0·86	0·81	0·84	—	—	—	0·44	0·29	0·37	0·46	0·43	0·45
IX	0·80	0·64	0·73	—	—	—	0·49	0·29	0·37	0·43	0·30	0 38
X	0·61	0·48	0·53	—	—	—	0·34	0·11	0·19	0·30	0·17	0·24
XI	0·48	**0·43**	0·45	—	—	—	0·24	**0·02***	0·16	0·19	**0·11**	0·16
XII	0·53	**0·43**	0 48	—	—	—	0·45	0 13	0·27	0·38	0·15	0·26
	—	—	0·722	—	—	—	—	—	0·391	—	—	0·368
1901												
I	0·61	0·55	0 58	—	—	—	0·44	0·24	0·32	0·41	0·28	0·35
II	0·65	0·58	0·61	—	—	—	0 49	**0·16**	0·37	0·38	0·30	0·36
III	0·94	0·65	0·77	—	—	—	0·59	**0·16**	0·43	0·58	0·42	0 48
IV	1·33	0·95	1·16	—	—	—	0·97	0·49	0·68	0·89	0·46	0·66
V	1·59	1·42	1·53	—	—	—	**1·05**	0·85	0·95	0·95	0·81	0·89
VI	—	—	—	—	—	—	1·04	0·77	0·88	0·93	0·74	0·83
VII	—	—	—	—	—	—	0·85	0·57	0·65	0·76	0·61	0·68
VIII	—	—	—	0·64	0·46	0·57	0·64	0·44	0·49	—	—	—
IX	—	—	—	0·51	0·27	0·39	0·47	0·34	0·42	—	—	—
X	1·23	1·14	1·18	0·51	0·33	0·45	0·39	0·31	0·35	—	—	—
XI	1·16	1·10	1·13	0.36	0·29	0·33	0·35	0·29	0·32	—	—	—
XII	1·14	1·07	1·10	0·43	0·34	0·40	0·31	0·19	0·24	—	—	—
	—	—	—	—	—	—	—	—	0·508	—	—	—

DATE	STATIONS								
	ENTEBBE			JINJA			KISUMU		
	Maxim.	Minim.	Mean	Maxim.	Minim.	Mean	Maxim.	Minim.	Mean
1902									
I	1·12	1·04	1·07	0·40	0·34	0·38	0·21	0·16	0·18
II	1.07	1·00	1·03	0·43	0·36	0·39	0·17	0·15	0·16
III	1·12	1.03	1·06	0·41	0·34	0·37	0·19	0·15	0·16
IV	1·13	0·99	1 07	0·44	0·39	0·43	—	—	—
V	1·23	1.13	1·20	**0·60**	0·44	0 54	—	—	—
VI	1·22	1.13	1·16	0·55	0·45	0 50	0·30	0·13	0·21
VII	1·14	1·07	1·11	0·46	0·41	0·44	0·30	0·02*	0·17
VIII	1·14	1·04	1·08	0·45	0·38	0·42	0·31	0·02*	0·14
IX	1·13	0·99	1·06	0·41	0·37	0·39	0·21	0·05	0·13
X	1·04	**0·98**	0·99	0·40	0·32	0·35	0·21	0·13	0·14
XI	1·08	0·99	1·03	0·41	0·33	0·37	0·24	0·13	0 16
XII	**1·30**	1·14	1·23	0·43	**0·28**	0·36	0·44	0·16	0·27
	—	—	1·091	—	—	0·412	—	—	0·172
1903									
I	1·37	**1·22**	1·27	0·57	**0·33**	0 42	0·52	**0·24**	0·37
II	1·38	1·29	1·33	0·71	0·62	0·68	0·53	0·26	0·43
III	1·42	1·30	1·36	0·77	0·66	0 71	0·62	0·29	0·44
IV	1·51	1·37	1·42	0·93	0·72	0·78	0·62	0·36	0·52
V	1·75	1·47	1·65	1·10	0·84	1·00	0·85	0·54	0·73
VI	1·88	1·71	1·82	1·22	1·07	1·15	**1·05**	0·80	0·91
VII	1·88	1·80	1·85	**1·37**	1·17	1·24	**1·05**	0·85	0·96
VIII	1·87	1·75	1·81	1·22	1·00	1·14	**1·05**	0·80	0·91
IX	1·83	1·73	1·76	1·03	0·95	0·98	1·02	0·87	0·93
X	1·83	1·75	1·77	1·17	0·99	1·07	0·95	0 34	0·77
XI	**1·90**	1·75	1·81	1·27	1·05	1·16	0·95	0 87	0·90
XII	1·85	1·70	1·80	1·24	1·12	1·16	0·95	0·82	0·90
	—	—	1·638	—	—	0·958	—	—	0·731

The fourth class, daily oscillations, are usually of very small range. All bodies of water are influenced by the attraction of the sun and moon but the tidal effect on inland lakes is usually so slight as to be demonstrated only on the largest lakes and by refined measurements. Lake Michigan which has an area about 25% larger than Lake Victoria has been shown by the U. S. Lake Survey to have a tide with an amplitude of $1^1/_2$ inches for the neap tide, and 3 inches for the spring tide (1). That of Lake Victoria has not yet been investigated with sufficient accuracy to determine its range.

Certainly the effect will be masked by the wind effect caused by the lake breeze by day and the land breeze by night, and this will be much accentuated in a long narrow gulf like the Kavirondo Gulf at Kisumu. Here the gauge shows a daily oscillation which is sometimes very marked.

It comes out also in the monthly means;

KISUMU (2).

	Dec. 1902	Jan.	Feb.	March.	April.	May.	June. 1903
	m.	m.	m.	m.	m.	m.	m.
7 am.... ...	0.44	0.54	0.60	0.61	0.69	0.90	1.08
4 pm.... ...	0.46	0.55	0.67	0.69	0.70	0.89	1.07
Difference...	+02	+01	+07	+08	+01	—01	—01

Further data are not available at the time of writing so the cause of the lower afternoon readings after April cannot be traced.

Pringle (3) says that the maximum rise in a day due to wind and heavy rain was about two feet according to native information.

Gedge (4) notes the occurrence of small temporary rises of the lake at irregular intervals and lasting for an hour or more. Pringle (5) states that he noticed a tidal movement of about 15 centimetres in Kavirondo Gulf, but it is doubtful whether this should not rather be attributed to wind action.

These phenomena are naturally accentuated in gulfs and long inlets, and at Entebbe from June to December 1903 the difference between the 6 a.m. and 6 p.m. observations in the monthly mean varied from $-0^{m}\cdot004$ to $+0^{m}\cdot003$ only.

Similarly Baumann (6) says that at Muanza there was a daily oscillation of 30 centimetres and that in the Rugezi channel the water was $0^{m}50$ lower in the morning than at noon, though no such variation was noticed at Bukoba.

The fifth class of changes of level, viz:—"seiches," certainly occur on the Victoria lake although no precise study of them has yet been made. Lake waters are affected by changes in atmospheric pressure and in some cases variations of level amounting to some feet have occurred in calm weather. Forel (7) has recorded a rise of as much as 1.87 metres on the Lake of Geneva, and on the American lakes even larger ones have been noted (8). Smaller pulsations also occur which are not yet fully understood. It seems probable that the sudden variations shown occasionally by some of the Victoria lake gauges are of the nature of seiches, though the subject cannot be pursued far at present as Entebbe is the only station in Uganda where there is a barometer. All accounts of the lake however mention particularly the violent thunderstorms, the water spouts and cloud bursts which are experienced on the lake, and these all evidence large and rapid variations of atmospheric pressure occurring locally. Thus it is not surprising if the gauges show occasionally irregularities of a somewhat considerable range.

On 1st October 1903 the level recorded by the Kisumu gauge fell suddenly and remained low for 7 days though the other gauges were not affected (9). As only one reading (taken at 7 a.m.) has been received it is not possible to say if the level varied during the day. The monthly mean for October is affected by this week of low levels, as will be seen in Plan III.

(1) Russell. "Lakes of North America." Boston. 1900, p. 33.
(2) The correction $0^{m}\cdot17$ must be subtracted from the 7 a.m. readings in order to make them agree with the values in Table V.
(3) Geog. Jour. Aug. 1893 p. 137.
(4) Proc. Roy. Geog. Soc. 1892, p. 323.
(5) Geog. Jour. Aug. 1893. p. 189. 137.
(6) "Durch Massailand zur Nilquelle," p. 42.
(7) "Handbuch der Seenkunde." Stuttgart 1901 p. 80.
(8) E. A. Perkins. "The Seiche in American Lakes." American Meteor. Jour. Oct 1893.
(9) This has been since (May 1904) explained by there being an error in the reading sent: there was no unusual fall at Kisumu.

	Kisumu		Jinja		Entebbe	
	ft.	in	ft.	in	ft.	in
30th September........	3	8	4	3	5	10
1st October..........	1	8	4	3	5	9 ½
2nd "	1	10	4	2	5	9
3rd "	1	8	4	2	5	9
4th "	1	10	4	2 ½	5	9
5th "	1	10	4	2 ½	5	9
6th "	2	1	4	2 ½	5	11
7th "	2	0	4	2 ½	5	10
8th "	3	0	4	2 ½	5	9

From this short study of the oscillations of the lake some interesting deductions may be drawn.

Though the rise to the May-June maximum is more marked than that due to the November rains nevertheless the effect of the latter is an important one. If the November rains are feeble the lake level continues to fall though slowly, until about April when the heavy rains begin, and cause the lake to rise rapidly. This rise however is followed by a rapid fall since in July, August and September evaporation is at its maximum; the equatorial rain belt lies further to the north and the dry south-east trade winds sweep over the lake catchment basin.

It will be seen that each year in which the November rains were sufficient to cause a rise in the lake as in 1900 and 1902, the mean level of the lake in the following year showed an increase while 1899 and 1901, in which the fall of the lake continued into the following year, were succeeded by lower mean levels. For, of a given amount of water supplied to the lake in November, December and January, a much smaller percentage is lost by evaporation than there is of a similar amount received in the heavy rains of April and May, which are followed by the dry months. This is mentioned specially by Lugard, quoted above, as being the case in the winter of 1891 which was followed by exceptionally high lake levels in 1892.

Seeing that in the latter part of the rainy season this year (1903) the rain has been exceptionally heavy in the Nilotic provinces of Uganda and in the Lake Albert basin, there is every probability that the November rains at the Victoria lake will also be heavy and consequently that the average level of the lake in 1904 will be above that of 1903, unless the April rains should fail entirely.

Taking the average discharge at the Ripon Falls as 575 cubic metres per second, this will give 49·7 million cubic metres per day and 1491 million cubic metres per month, or 17,925 million cubic metres per year. If the area of the lake surface is taken at 65,000 square kilometres the above discharge will represent a fall of the lake surface of about 22·5 millimetres per month. Taking the maximum discharge at the Ripon Falls as 650 metres cube per second, corresponding to the highest level of the lake in 1903 the fall due to the discharge alone would be 25·6 millimetres in a month. If these falls per month are compared with the fall of the curves after the June maximum on Plan III, it will be seen what a powerful factor evaporation is in July, August and September, in that it causes the lake level to fall in some years much faster than the above rate, in spite of all additions to the lake volume by occasional rainfall and what the tributary rivers are bringing in.

If a represents the average rainfall on the lake in a year,
b represents the volume brought in by tributary streams,
c represents the volume lost by evaporation,
and d represents the volume discharged at Ripon Falls, then for 1896-1903 since mean level of the lake has fallen from $0^{m}{\cdot}928$ to $0^{m}{\cdot}731$ or $0^{m}{\cdot}197$ the general condition has been :—$a + b < c + d$

As the average yearly discharge at the Ripon Falls is 17·9 cubic kilometres, and a reduction of the lake level by $0^{m}{\cdot}197$ in 8 years is equivalent to a loss of 12·8 cubic kilometres or a mean yearly diminution 1·6 kilometres; then if the average annual rainfall on the lake is taken at 1,250 mm. for the year,

$$81{\cdot}3 + b = c + 17{\cdot}9 + 1{\cdot}6$$
$$\text{or} \quad c - b = 61{\cdot}8 \text{ cubic kilometres}$$

which is the excess of evaporation over what the tributary streams bring in, showing again how powerful a factor it is. In years of rapid fall this effect is much increased.

H. G. Lyons.

PLAN III.

E VICTORIA N

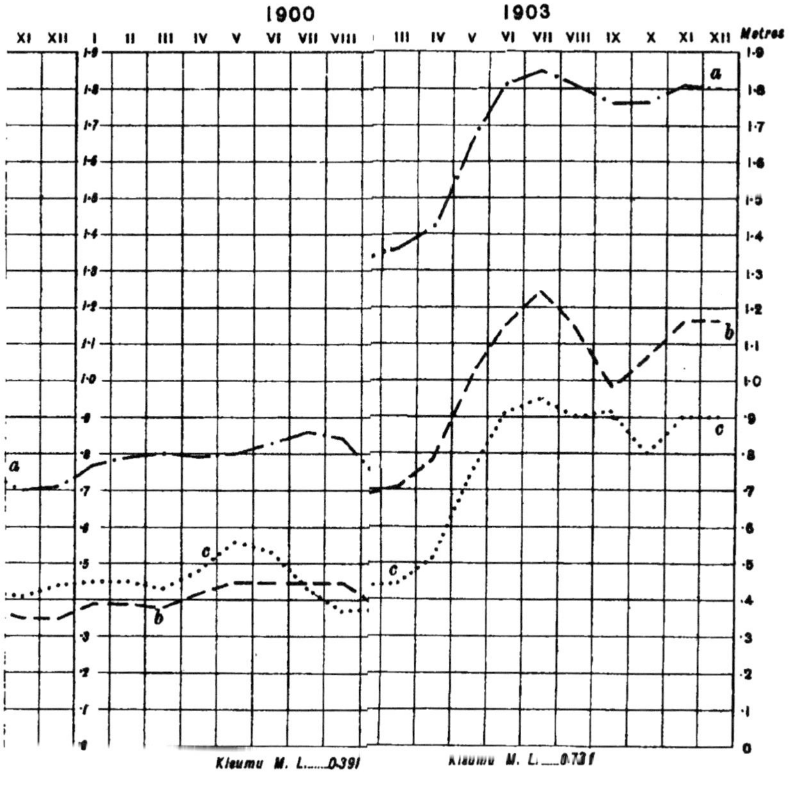

Gauge at Port Alice ... 1 Jan.–31 Mar. } a
" " Entebbe ...... 1 Apr.–31 Dec. }
" " Lubas .... b
" " Kisumu c

Entebbe ...... a
Jinja ...... b
Kisumu c

Appendix III A.

NOTE ON RIPON FALLS.

In accordance with your request of yesterday, I have the honor to forward herewith memo on the level of the Victoria Nyanza together with photographs taken by me in 1900, of the Ripon Falls, Trigonometrical stations, etc.

In Sir William Garstin's Report, as to Irrigation Projects on the Upper Nile, Egypt, N° 2 (1901) page 49, the mean level of the lake (on authority given) is said to average some eight feet lower than it did twenty years previous to June 1897.

In November 1898 the level of the lake was high, and it was then 16 feet below my bench mark at Port Florence.

In January 1900 the level was low and 18 feet 1 inch below the same mark.

There is no doubt that these levels are correct as they were carefully taken over a very short distance only, while the drop is proved by the soundings on the entrance line to the harbour, the level in 1898 giving 11 feet, in 1900 only 9 feet on the same transit line.

During 1901, according to the lowest reading in the Protectorate gauge at Port Florence, a further fall of 1 foot 4 inches took place.

By May 1901 the level had risen 3 feet 4 inches on the same gauge (which it was stated had not been moved in the interval) thus bringing the level back to just what it was in November 1898.

A report was published in the English papers (Weekly Times 31st May) that the lake level was two feet higher than the record in May 1901, but this information must have been given in error, as May level 1901 is shown above to have been only equal to November 1898.

From what I have seen of the lake, it appears to me that the reported fall of 8 feet in the average level since June 1877 is doubtful.

Sir H. M. Stanley's photograph of the Ripon Falls taken in 1875 differed very slightly from mine, my photograph No. 1 (1) taken in June 1900, from the west side of the Nile.

Now in June 1900, the lake level was undoubtedly extremely low, and was so reported by everyone that knew it, both Europeans and natives.

Supposing the fall of 8 feet in 20 years to be correct, which gives about 5 inches fall a year, it would mean that in Sir H. M. Stanley's year the water would have been 8 feet 10 inches higher than when I saw it. In 1898, as I have proved, the level was the same as 1901. There was therefore no permanent fall during that time, but at the time I took my photograph the lake was very low. Two feet can fairly be added to the above 8 ft. 10 in. making a total of 10 feet 10 inches difference between Stanley's time and my own.

The height of the Falls I estimated to be not over 14 feet. Anyone looking at my photographs will see at once that had there been such a drop as that I have calculated, the Falls would have presented an entirely different view to Sir H. M. Stanley's camera and that 10 feet 10 inches more water in the lake would mean that there would be an unbroken fall right across the two right-hand photographs, and the whole character of the view would be changed.

Photograph No. 2 is a view of the Falls taken from the Mission hut on the east side, it can be seen from this view also what a great difference in the appearance of the Falls would be caused by a rise of 10 feet 10 inches in the lake level.

Photographs 3, 4 and 5 shew views of the Falls by which it will be seen that they are of little height, although a great amount of power could be obtained from them. The rapids and cataracts extend for a considerable distance down the river, but I do not know how far, as I have only been about 3 miles below the Falls.

There is a large tree on Buguzi Islet, about 35 miles south of the Ripon Falls (Photograph 6.) The islet is very low, and I estimated the root of the tree to be about 5 feet above the water.

The size of the tree can be estimated from the man standing close to the left of it.

The low height of the island can be seen from the fact of the boat's mast being visible to the right of the tree. The top of the mast would be about 10 feet high, and the boat was lying a short distance off the shore.

(1) These photographs are not reproduced in the report.

As the islet was only 5 feet above the very low level of the lake in 1900, I do not see how such a large tree could have grown on it, had the lake level been steadily falling at the rate of 5 inches a year.

Unless there was a similar rise between 1875 and 1877, which appears unlikely, I fail to see how there could have been such a fall as reported, and if such a fall is going on why should it cease between 1898 and 1901, when levels to bench marks were taken.

B. Whitehouse,
Commander R. N.
Surveyor in Charge, Lake Survey, Uganda Railway.

Nairobi, 31st May 1902.

Appendix IV.

ON THE CALCULATION OF THE DISCHARGE TABLES AND WATER SLOPES.

The following Memorandum deals with the computations involved in drawing up discharge tables for some of the stations on the Bahr-el-Gebel where discharges have been taken, viz:—

(1) Jinja.
(2) The Victoria Nile below the Murchison Falls.
(3) Wadelai.
(4) Gondokoro.

The methods employed for these stations have differed in some respects, but all are based on the application of known hydraulic formulæ to such precise discharge measurements as are available. I propose to offer some remarks on the calculations for each place with a view to estimating the degree of dependence to be placed on the tables.

(1) Jinja.

Here two discharges, one by Mr. C. L. Waring, the second by Sir William Garstin on January 22nd 1903, are available, but I have rejected the former as being based on too few observations of velocity. The second gives as data for further calculations a discharge of 549 metres cube per second with a gauge reading of 0·51 metres (1) at Jinja. Discharges have been first computed to correspond to the highest and lowest readings of the Jinja gauge on two independent assumptions.

Firstly, the problem has been treated as that of a reservoir kept at constant level and discharging over a weir with free fall. The standard formula in this case is $Q = Mb\ H^{3/2}$ where Q is the quantity of water in metres per second flowing over the weir, M is a constant coefficient, b is the effective breadth of the weir. Then b is considered as an unknown quantity to be determined from the given discharge, or better, since the strict theoretical value of M may not apply, Mb is so considered. The depth of water over the sill is assumed to be the same as the mean depth of the nearest of Mr. Waring's sections, taken 60 metres above the Ripon Falls. To this is added the rise from the Falls to Lake Victoria: the sum is then the head of the lake surface above the sill. This will change by the same amount as the Jinja gauge changes from its reading on the date of Mr. Waring's measurement.

The mean depth in question is 7·50 metres.

The rise to the lake surface is 0·17 metres.

Hence on January 12th 1903, when the gauge read 0·41 metres, the head, H, was 7·67 metres. Therefore on January 22nd 1903 when the gauge read 0·51 metres, the head was 7·77 metres and on this date the discharge measured by Sir William Garstin was 549 metres cube per second. Consequently the value of Mb in the above formula is found to be 25·35. With this value, the discharges corresponding to any gauge reading may be found. In particular for the maximum and minimum readings the following values have been found.

With 1·36 metres in July 1903, the discharge was equal to 642 metres cube per second.

And with 0·16 metres in November 1900, the discharge was equal to 512 metres cube per second.

The accuracy of these estimates will depend on the applicability of the formula quoted, a formula deduced from ideal theoretical considerations and applied to an exceedingly complicated practical case. In support of its employment, it may be stated that the formula is known to represent actual discharges in broad deep channels with greater accuracy than can be obtained from its application to narrow shallow weirs where the side and sill frictions have disproportionate effects on the velocities. Further, it does represent the discharge correctly for one value of H and may accordingly be relied upon for values of H not too far distant from the base-value. Also, though Mb is not an absolute constant as assumed above, it varies only very slightly with the head for such a section as is dealt with here. It appears, therefore, that there is considerable justification for applying the formula to the extreme cases of the discharge corresponding to the maximum and minimum readings quoted above. For the former it should be within 10 per cent of the truth while for the latter the agreement should be even closer.

Secondly, the discharge has been computed on the assumption that the mean velocity remains constant and that the sides of the section are vertical. The increase of the

(1) Reduced to the present gauge.

discharge will then be due to the extra layer of water passing when the gauge rises. On January 22nd 1903, the cross section was 2,275 square metres and the breadth 417 metres. A rise of 1 metre above the gauge reading of that date will result in an increment of 417 square metres to the sectional area. Since the mean velocity is 0·24 metres per second, this rise will give an additional discharge of 100 metres cube per second and the increases or decreases in the discharge corresponding to other rises or falls will vary proportionally. For the highest and lowest gauge readings we should accordingly have the following results:

Gauge reading.	Rise above datum(+) Fall below „ (—)	Increment of discharge.	Discharge.
1.36m.	+0.85m.	+85m³ per sec.	634m³ per sec.
0.16m.	—0.35m.	—35m³ „ „	514m³ „ „

These values accord satisfactorily with those calculated on the first assumption, and tend materially to increase the reliability of the figures.

Table I has been drawn up on the basis of these computations.

(2) The Victoria Nile below the Murchison Falls.

In this case the problem is of a totally different nature. It is almost the converse of that at Jinja. For here we have a river discharging over a free fall into a reservoir which is kept practically at constant level. Consequently any change in mean velocity at the discharge site—which was about one third of the distance from the Falls to Lake Albert—must be due to the increase of slope that follows the greater rush of water over the Falls in flood and the consequent heaping up in the narrow channel there. I have decided accordingly to assume that Kutter's well-known formulæ for the mean velocity of a channel are applicable and to apply them to the data provided by Sir William Garstin's discharge to derive a value for the slope at the date when it was measured. The formulæ are:—

$$v = C\sqrt{rs}$$

$$C = \frac{1/n + 23 + 0.00155/s}{1 + n\,(23 + 0.00155/s)\,/\sqrt{r}}$$

where v is the mean velocity in metres per second, s is the slope, r is the hydraulic radius in metres and n is a number dependent on the roughness of the bed.

The measurements made for the discharge give the following data:—

Breadth of the section	309 metres
Sectional area	894 square metres
Wetted perimeter	313 metres
Discharge	576.6 metres cube per second.

Hence $v = 576{\cdot}6/894 = 0.645$ metres cube per second

$r = 894/313 = 2.85$ metres.

On the basis of the discharge at Wadelai I assume n to be 0.025 which is, in point of fact, the value assigned to it by Kutter for "canals and rivers free from stones and weeds," a description that applies aptly enough to the section in question.

Substituting then these values in the formulæ we find:—

$$0.382 = \frac{63 + 0.00155/s}{1 + 0.0148\,(23 + 0.00155/s)}\sqrt{s}$$

By successive approximation a sufficiently exact root of this equation is found to be $s = \frac{1}{18500}$.

Now in flood the river rises here about 1 metre while at the Albert Lake the corresponding rise is 0.84 metre, or an excess of 0.16 metre at the discharge station. The distance to the lake is 22.5 kilometres and the rise from the lake in that distance will be 1.22 metres with a slope of $\frac{1}{18500}$. In flood accordingly, the rise in the same distance will be 1.38 metres which would make the slope then approximately $\frac{1}{16300}$. I have assumed that the slope varies uniformly between these limits as the water rises, and have calculated the various values of the sectional area, wetted perimeter and hydraulic radius corresponding to different heights of the water surface above datum, which has been taken to be the height of the surface at the date of the discharge. With the varying values of the slope it then becomes possible to calculate the different values of the mean velocity, which, multiplied by the sectional area, give the discharge.

Table II gives the result.

(3) Wadelai.

The conditions here are those of a river in regime and little affected by sudden "spates." We may therefore assume that Kutter's formulæ hold in this case also and on that assumption the discharge table has been calculated. Sir William Garstin's discharge, taken on 23rd March 1903, gives the discharge, sectional area and other data relating to the section, while the slope has been deduced from the following considerations. Four very concordant hypsometrical observations were made at different stations between the Albert lake and Nimule and reduced by comparison with the readings of the barometer at Entebbé, kindly supplied by Mr. Mahon, Director of the Botanic Gardens there. As the type and section of the river between the Lake and Nimule vary little, an assumption of uniform slope has been made, the most probable value of which from the observations is $\frac{1}{27000}$.

The data given by the discharge are :—

Discharge	646 metres cube per second
Sectional area	770 square metres
Hydraulic radius	4.80 metres.

Hence the mean velocity is 0.84 metres per second.

Substituting these numbers in the formulæ we obtain :—

$$62.93=\frac{\frac{1}{n}+64.85}{1+29.6n},$$

a quadratic equation for n, the positive root of which gives $n=\frac{1}{42.22}=0.02369$. As remarked above in the discussion of the discharge below the Murchison Falls, this accords with the value of n given by Kutter for such a river channel. With this value a series of values of C in the formulæ may be calculated to correspond with different gauge readings. The slope is considered constant. For this assumption there is warrant in the fact that the range at Lake Albert does not differ much from that at Wadelai. If anything it is less and the average slope of the main stream in flood is less than at low water. It seems probable, however, that the chief effect of the flood on Lake Albert will be to extend its limits towards the north so that the portion which may be looked on as being level will be brought nearer Wadelai and the fall distributed over a shorter length. In the absence of further data it appears most reasonable therefore to consider the slope as being independent of the gauge reading.

As the value of the slope accepted above differs materially from that hitherto regarded as best, the reasons for adopting it may be conveniently indicated here. The hypsometrical observations though few in number derive added weight from the fact that they are the first in this region that have been reduced by comparison with simultaneous barometric readings at a station of known height so near as Entebbé, distant 250 to 400 kilometres. Again the total fall from the Albert Lake at Butiabu to Nimule is 13 metres, which is in better agreement with 6 metres, the value deduced by Zöppritz from Emin Pasha's observations, than with the 33 metres given by Hann. Chavanne (1) rejects Zöppritz's value in favour of that deduced by Hann for reasons which amount to no more than an expression of opinion. Thirdly, the value is confirmed *a posteriori* by the deduced value for Kutter's constant n, which accords well with the standard value given by him for such sections.

The results are given in Table III.

4. Gondokoro.

The data for Gondokoro are the following :—

Dates	28th March 1901.	9th Sept. 1902.	1st April 1903.	8th Sept. 1903.
Gauge readings...	0.08	0.83	0.50	2.33
Discharges... ...	623	1079	693	1985

The computation of a satisfactory table for this station, that would coordinate these data, proved much more difficult than those of the three preceding sections, and this for several reasons. In the first place, there have been four changes of gauge there, and for one period there exists a gap in the readings between the destruction of one gauge and the erection of another (2). It is thus impossible to reduce the earlier readings of one gauge to the present one with any certainty. Secondly, a glance at the appended chart Plan No. IV shows that the river there is subject to great and irregular fluctuations especially about the period of highest flood. Thirdly, the section opposite the gauge is of a complicated nature and different form from that at the sites of the four discharges, which were all within a few hundred metres of each other.

(1) Chavanne "Afrika's Ströme und Flüsse." Vienna, 1883, p. 38.
(2) See below, p. 42.

The observations available show further that the section cannot be considered constant either at the discharge sites or at Gondokoro, but that there must be a continual erosion of the bed with deposit elsewhere. These facts make the application of rational hydraulic formulæ to the discharges a matter of great difficulty. I have tried to coordinate the data on several assumptions, but it is noteworthy that in every case the result gives fair representations of the third and fourth discharges but fails for the first and second except on the assumption of a fall of from 20 to 30 centimetres in the river level between 12th November and 18th November 1902, the dates of the beginning and end of the gap in the readings.

I therefore proceed in the following manner. It is known (¹) that the discharge of a river may be represented approximately by the formula.

$$Q = a\,(x+b)^{3/2}$$

While Q is the discharge, a and b are constants and x is the reading of a vertical gauge. For the reason given above I assume a fall y in the water level between 12th November and 18th November 1902, and accordingly apply y as a correction to the gauge readings prior to the former date. The amended data then become :—

	M.	M.	M.	M.
Readings	0.08+ y	0.83+ y	0.50	2.33
Discharges... ...	623m³ p.s.	1079m³ p.s.	693m³ p.s.	1985m³ p.s.

And with these the constants a, b and y have been computed and their best values found to be 284·8, 1·315 and 0·287 respectively. The fact that the value of y falls between the limits that previous assumptions have indicated gives a presumption that it is about the correct value of the fall in the river surface in the interval alluded to, and that its application as a correction to gauge readings previous to 12th November 1902 is justifiable. The following table shows how close an approximation the formula gives to the observed results.

	M.	M.	M.	M.
Gauge readings... ...	0.367	1.117	0.50	2.33
Observed discharges...	623m³ p.s.	1079m³ p.s.	693m³ p.s.	1985m³ p.s.
Computed discharges..	621 „ „	1080 „ „	696 „ „	1982 „ „

Table IV has accordingly been computed on the basis of the formula

$$Q = 284.8\,(x+1.315)^{3/2}$$

where x is the present gauge reading in metres.

It is well known that the discharge curve for any station on a river is not single-branched but of the nature of a cusped loop, which, if the gauge readings are ordinates, is concave to the axis of abscissae at the cusp. In this case the lower branch would correspond to a rising river. The Gondokoro discharges have all been taken on a falling gauge, and the table probably gives values somewhat too low on the rising gauge. Since, however, there is nothing to indicate the amount of divergence between the branches, no correction has been made to the figures to apply them to the rising stage of the river.

The following table shows the total discharge in millions of metres cube at Jinja, Wadelai and Gondokoro during 1902 and 1903, deduced from the gauge readings and the discharge tables.

	1902	1903
Jinja	17,400	19,200
Wadelai	19,000	24,200
Gondokoro... ...	32,300 (²)	39,200

The catchment basin of the river as discharging at Jinja is approximately 190,000 square kilometres and the annual rainfall about 1·1 m. The discharge at Jinja was therefore 8 per cent of the rainfall in 1902 and 9 per cent in 1903. The catchment basin between Jinja and Wadelai is approximately 132,000 square kilometres and the rainfall about 1·1 m. In 1902 therefore this region contributed only about 1 per cent of the rainfall to the river and in 1908 about 3·5 per cent. The catchment basin of the stretch from Wadelai to Gondokoro is approximately 72,000 square kilometres and the rainfall about 1·1 m. annually. The mean run-off in this region was therefore 17 per cent in 1902 and 19 per cent last year. It is worth mentioning, as confirmatory of some fall in the river at Gondokoro between the dates referred to above, that unless some such

(¹) V. Lombardini, "Essai sur l'Hydrologie du Nil" (Milan 1865) p. 15 etc.

(²) The additional correction +0·287 metres has been applied to the Gondokoro gauge readings before computation of this discharge.

supposition is made the discharges at Wadelai for some rainy months exceed those at Gondokoro, while on the assumption made the former are less, as would naturally be expected.

The diagram of the gauges at Wadelai and Gondokoro for part of 1903 is appended (Plan No IV) as illustrating,

(1) The regulating effect of the lakes at the former station.

(2) The irregularity of the rises and falls at the latter, which shows the local origin of high floods at Gondokoro.

Calculation of Slopes.

In several cases an attempt has been made to calculate the slope of the river at places where discharges have been taken, and in all cases the procedure has been the same. From the data values are calculated for the hydraulic radius and mean velocity. These are substituted in Kutter's formulæ with the value 0·025 for n, and the resulting equation for s, the slope, is solved by successive approximation.

There is one objection to the use of Kutter's formulæ in this way. They are generally recognised as giving too high velocities for small slopes, and inversely with low velocities will give too small values for the slope. Consequently the slopes given by the computations cannot be taken as absolutely correct, but they will certainly give a fair idea of the true gradient, and for comparative purposes may be of considerable value.

In some cases, e.g., the Blue Nile in the low season, the White Nile at Dueim in flood, the White Nile above the Sobat in flood and the Bahr-el-Gebel near Lake No in flood, the values of the slope come out extremely small. I am very strongly of opinion that what is indicated is simply a holding up of the secondary branch by the main branch at the time, and that reverse slopes even may be existent.

As a check on the computation of the slopes the difference of level between Kodok (Fashoda) and Lado has been calculated with the following results :—

Kodok to Lake No	5.5 m.
Lake No to Ghaba Shambe...	18.9 „
Ghaba Shambe to Bor	15.8 „
Bor to Lado	16.0 „

The accepted height of Lado is 465 metres above sea level. If these amounts be taken from this the following table of heights is derived : —

	Heights.	
	Computed.	Accepted (1)
Kodok...	409	404
Lake No	414	—
Ghaba Shambe ...	433	424
Bor	449	441
Lado	465	465

There is thus a satisfactory agreement between the heights deduced from hydraulic considerations and those deduced from barometric observations. This gives a further *à posteriori* verification of the legitimacy of using Kutter's formulæ in this work.

THE NILE GAUGE AT GONDOKORO.

Observations were commenced here on 6th December 1900 after those which had been taken further upstream at Fort Berkeley from 1st September 1899 to 2nd December 1900 were discontinued. The gauge was a light wooden rod graduated in feet and inches. This may be called gauge A. On 27th March 1901 a more substantial gauge of sheet iron screwed to a wooden upright which was strutted from the bank was fixed at the time of Sir W. E. Garstin's visit (2). This may be called B and was divided into metres and centimetres.

(1) Chavanne, op. cit. p. 52.
(2) See Report of the Public Works Ministry, Egypt. 1901, p. 19.

On the 13th November 1902 this was knocked down in the night and lost and another, C, was erected on 18th November 1902 which was graduated in feet and inches.

To avoid the uncertainty caused by such frequent changes of gauge Captain H. G. Lyons on 9th April 1903 fixed a sloping baulk of teak parallel to the slope of the bank and firmly anchored back into it, so as to be out of the way of boats, and hippopotami. This baulk is graduated metrically and has a mark at each 5 centimetres. It is fixed at a slope of 60° so that its readings require to be multiplied by 0.886 to reduce them to vertical metres and by 39.4 × 0.866 or 34.1 to reduce them to vertical inches.

These changes may be tabulated as follows:—

Gauge	In Use.		Reading
	From	To	
A.	6.12.00	27. 3.01	Ft. & in.
B.	28. 3.01	12.11.02	Metric.
C.	18.11.02	8. 4.03	Ft. & in.
D.	8. 4.03	To date.	Metric.

Thus there has been a constant record except from 13-18 November 1902. The connection of these different series of gauge readings with one another is therefore most important.

On the 9th April D gauge was erected and read 0.48 metres or 1 ft. 7 in. while the C gauge which it replaced read 4 in., thus the readings of C gauge require an addition of 0.38 metres to reduce them to those of D gauge.

A difficulty arises now in connecting B gauge with C in consequence of the interval of 5 days between the loss of B gauge and the erection of C gauge.

The recorded readings converted to metres are as follows:—

	M.
10th November 1902... ...	1.37
11th " "	1.42
12th " "	1.50
13th " "	—
14th " "	—
15th " "	—
16th " "	—
17th " "	—
18th " "	0.86
19th " "	0.84
20th " "	0.84

Thus to reduce the B gauge readings to the C gauge the correction will be—0.64 metres *if there was no fall or rise in the river between the 12th and 18th of November.* Mr. Westray who was the observer has stated that he believes the river was stationary between these dates, but no note was made at the time. On the 28th March 1901 B gauge was fixed and read 0.30 when A gauge was reading 1 ft. 6 ½ in. thus the correction to reduce its readings to those of B gauge is —0.16 metre.

These corrections are given in the following table:—

Gauge.	Corrections to Reduce to			
	A.	B.	C.	D.
	M.	M.	M.	M.
A.	0	—0.16	—0.80	—0.42
B.	+0.16	0	—0.64	—0.26
C.	+0.80	+0.64	0	+0.38
D.	+0.42	+0.26	—0.38	0

There is reason to believe, however, as stated above, that the river must have fallen in the interval between gauges B and C. The amount of the fall necessary to render the discharges consistent is 0.287 metre, and the discharge table and total annual discharge at Gondokoro in 1902 are based on the assumption that this quantity is added as an additional correction to the readings of gauges A and B. Since the river is falling in general in November, it is probable that its level was not maintained constant between gauges B and C.

Moreover observations made by the flood discharge party in 1903 at Mongalla, Lado and Gondokoro show that the difference in level between the 1902 and 1903 floods was about 0.90 metre whereas the difference on the gauges is 1.24; thus an additional correction of about 0.30 metre to gauge-readings on B and consequently A is thereby indicated.

J. I. Craig.

TABLE I.

Jinja.

Gauge Reading.	Discharge.	Gauge Reading.	Discharge.
Metres.	Cubic metres per sec.	Metres.	Cubic metres per sec.
0.0	495	0.8	583
0.1	506	0.9	594
0.2	517	1.0	605
0.3	528	1.1	616
0.4	539	1.2	627
0.5	550	1.3	638
0.6	561	1.4	649
0.7	572	1.5	660

TABLE II.

Victoria Nile below Murchison Falls.

Rise Above Datum.	Sectional Area.	Velocity.	Discharge.
Metres.	Square Metres.	Metres per sec.	Cubic metres per sec.
0.0	894	0.645	577
0.1	925	0.664	614
0.2	956	0.683	653
0.3	987	0.702	693
0.4	1018	0.721	734
0.5	1048	0.740	776
0.6	1079	0.759	819
0.7	1110	0.778	864
0.8	1141	0.797	909
0.9	1172	0.816	956
1.0	1203	0.835	1005
1.1	1234	0.854	1054
1.2	1265	0.873	1104

Datum is the height of the water surface at the time of Sir William Garstin's discharge measurement.

TABLE III.

Wadelai.

Gauge	Section	Velocity	Discharge
Metres	Square metres	Metres per sec.	Cubic metres per sec.
0.05*	689.0	0.781	538
0.1	697.1	0.787	549
0.2	713.3	0.799	570
0.3	729.5	0.811	591
0.4	745.7	0.822	613
0.5	761.9	0.833	635
0.6	778.1	0.844	657
0.7	794.3	0.856	680
0.8	810.5	0.867	703
0.9	826.7	0.878	726
1.0	842.9	0.889	749
1.1	859.1	0.900	773
1.2	875.3	0.911	797
1.3	891.5	0.922	822
1.4	907.7	0.933	847
1.5	923.9	0.943	871
1.6	940.1	0.953	896
1.7	956.3	0.964	922
1.8	972.5	0.974	948
1.9	988.7	0.985	974
2.0	1004.9	0.995	1000

* Lowest recorded reading : April 1902.

TABLE IV.

GONDOKORO.

Gauge reading	Discharge	Gauge reading	Discharge
Metres	Cubic metres per sec.	Metres	Cubic metres per sec.
0.0	429	1.4	1274
0.1	479	1.5	1344
0.2	531	1.6	1417
0.3	585	1.7	1491
0.4	640	1.8	1566
0.5	697	1.9	1642
0.6	755	2.0	1718
0.7	815	2.1	1796
0.8	876	2.2	1876
0.9	939	2.3	1957
1.0	1003	2.4	2039
1.1	1069	2.5	2122
1.2	1136	2.6	2205
1.3	1205	2.7	2290

PLAN IV.

BAHR EL GEBEL GUAGES, 1903.

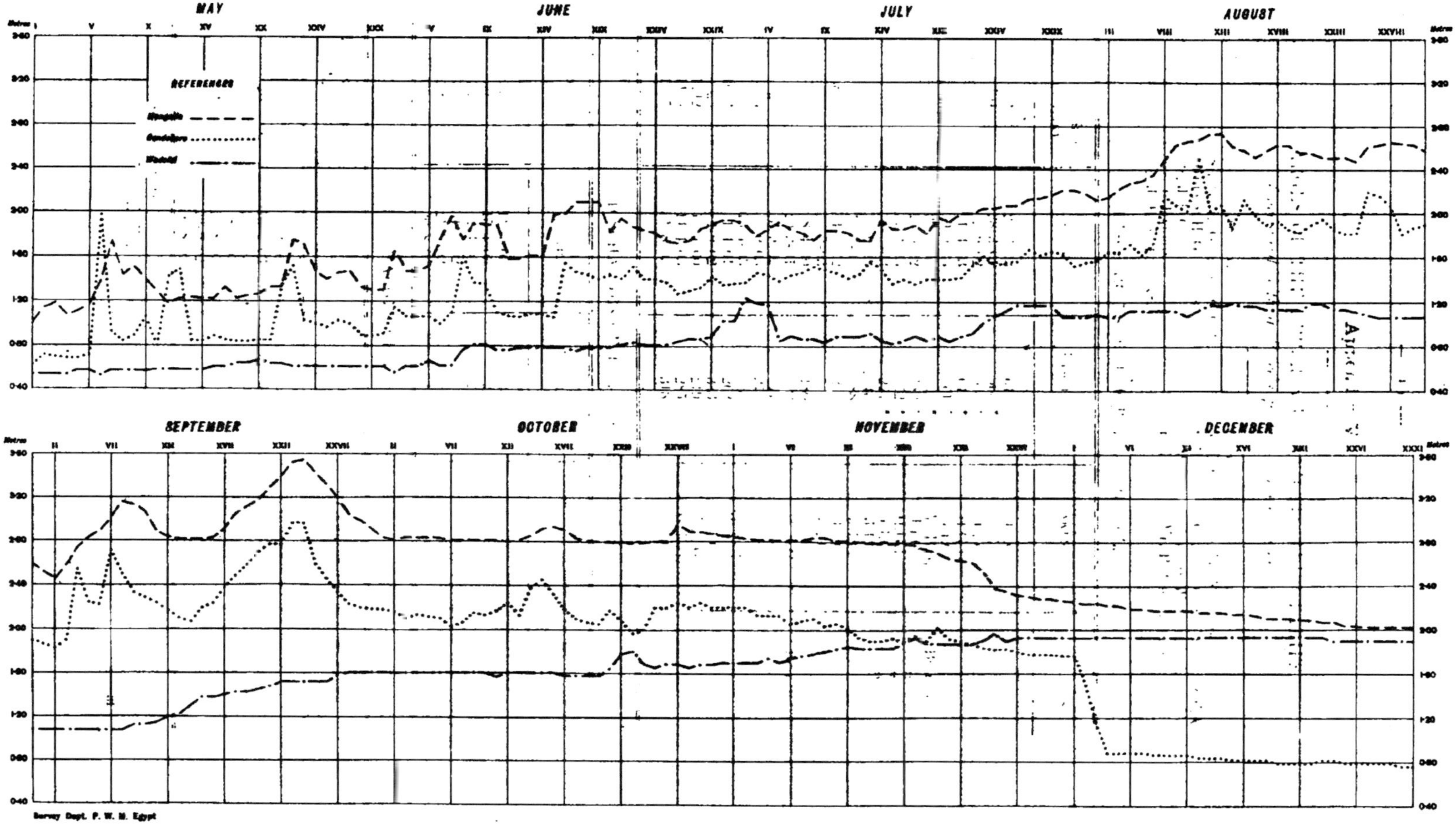

PLAN IV.

BAHR EL GEBEL GUAGES, 1903.

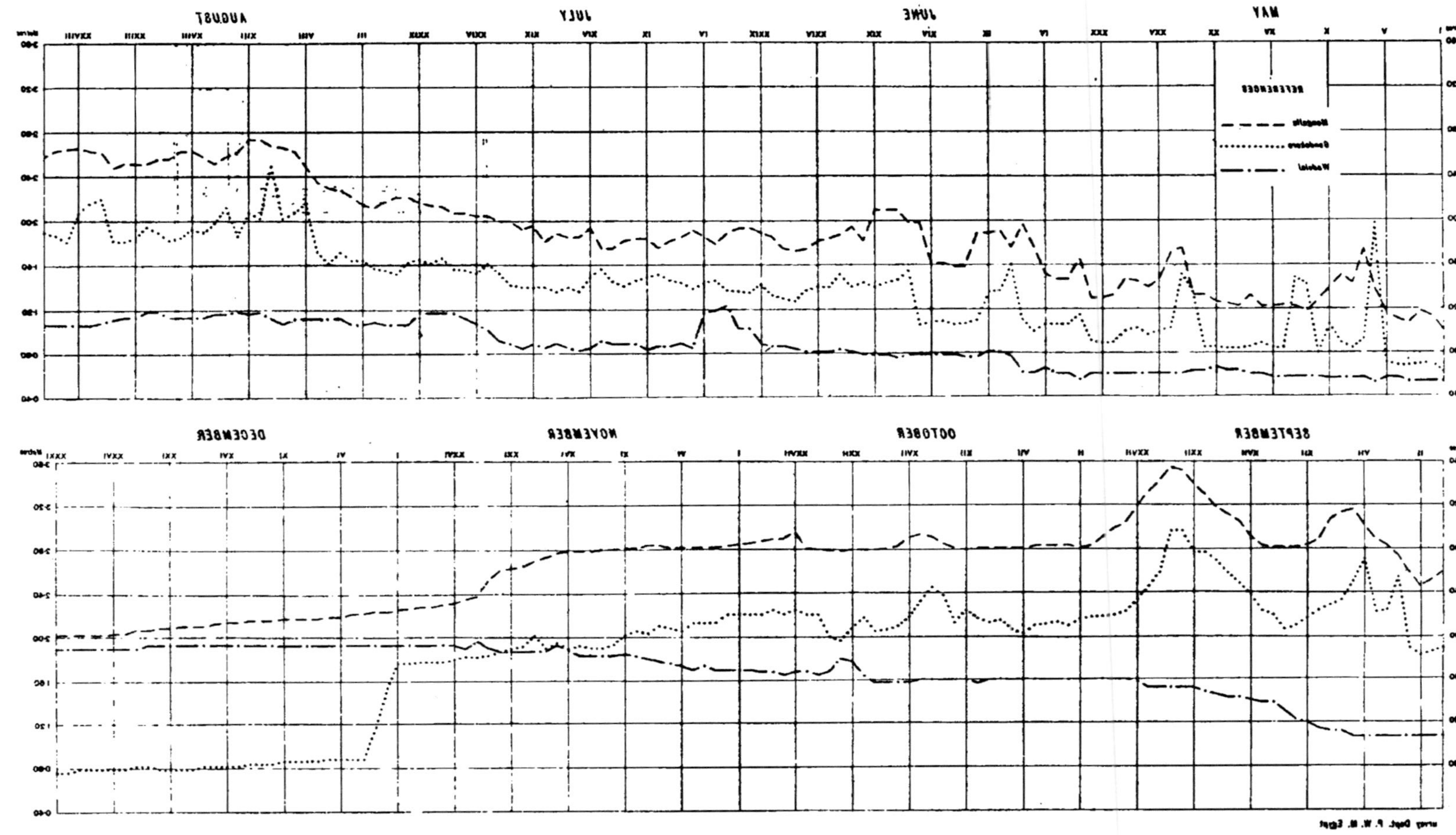

Appendix V.

DISCHARGES OF THE UPPER NILE AND ITS TRIBUTARIES.

(measured with a Price's pattern current meter).

Initials.	Observers.	Initials.	Observers.
W.E.G.	Sir W. E. Garstin, G.C.M.G.	W.F.H.	Dr. W. F. Hume.
H.G.L.	Captain H. G. Lyons.	C.H.W.	Captain C. H. Wood, R.F.A.
J.I.C.	Mr. J. I. Craig.	H.W.	Captain Wilson, R. Lanc. Fus.
T.B.	Mr. T. Barron.	P.E.	Mr. P. Eschelbach.
J.H.L.B.	Mr. J. H. L. Beadnell.		

DISCHARGES OF THE BAHR-EL-GEBEL.

Distance from Albert Lake.	Date.	Discharge.	Taken by.	Remarks.
Kilometres.		Metres cube per sec.		
64	23-3-03	646	J.I.C.	
404	28-3-01	566 *	W.E.G.	
,,	9-9-02	960 *	J.I.C.	
,,	1-4-03	641 *	H.G.L.	
,,	9-9-03	1761 *	J.I.C.	
410	29-3-01	57 *	W.E.G.	Branch.
,,	13-9-02	119 *	J.I.C.	,,
,,	1-4-03	52 *	H.G.L.	,,
,,	8-9-03	224 *	J.I.C.	,,
437	14-9-03	2046	J.I.C.	
561	16-9-03	888	J.I.C.	
820	4-9-02	398	J.I.C.	
,,	18-9-03	532	J.I.C.	
883	8-4-00	180	W.E.G.	
942	20-3-01	22	W.E.G.	Branch.
,,	3-9-02	41	J.I.C.	,,
943	1-9-03	375	J.I.C.	
947	13-4-03	331	W.E.G.	
1003	1-4-01	262	W.E.G.	
,,	2-9-02	333	J.I.C.	
1142	14-4-00	219	W.E.G.	
1146	14-4-03	285	W.E.G.	
1147	31-8-03	318	J.I.C.	

DISCHARGES OF THE BAHR-EL-GHAZAL.

Distance from Lake No.	Date.	Discharge.	Taken by.	Remarks.
Kilometres.		metres cube per sec.		
51	11-4-00	34	W.E.G.	
50	15-4-03	23	W.E.G.	
33	2-4-01	27	W.E.G.	
32	31-8-02	15	J.I.C.	
32	21-9-03	20	J.I.C.	
28	30-8-03	12	J.I.C.	

DISCHARGES OF THE BAHR-EL-ZARAF.

Distance from Mouth.	Date.	Discharge.	Taken by.	Remarks.
Kilometres.		metres cube per sec.		
96	1-3-00	34	W.E.G.	
20	16-4-03	50	W.E.G.	
20	22-9-03	158	J.I.C.	
108	8-5-03	61	H.W.	
14	29-8-03	110	J.I.C.	
8	22-9-02	97	J.I.C.	
20	30-8-02	81	J.I.C.	

* Total discharges at Lado :

28-3-01...........	623	9-9-02...........	1079
1-4-03...........	693	9-9-03...........	1985

DISCHARGES OF THE SOBAT RIVER.

Distance from Mouth.	Date.	Discharge.	Taken by.	Remarks.
Kilometres.		metres cube per sec.		
45	6-4-01	87*	W.E.G.	
40	17-4-03	45	W.E.G.	
25	28-8-02	572	J.I.C.	
25	23-9-02	771	J.I.C.	
25	26-8-03	769	J.I.C.	
25	26-9-03	895	J.I.C.	

(*) By difference between discharges of White Nile above and below the Sobat mouth.

DISCHARGES OF THE WHITE NILE.

Date.	Discharge.	Taken by.	Remarks.
	Above Sobat River.		
30-8-02	336	J.I.C.	7 km. below Zaraf.
22-9-02	419	J.I.C.	6·5 kil. „
22-9-03	450	J.I.C.	21 km. above Lolle.
16-4-03	349	W.E.G.	Just below Lolle.
	Below Sobat River.		
6-4-01	381	W.E.G.	24 km. below Sobat.
17-4-03	368	W.E.G.	14 „ Taufikia.
26-8-03	1046	J.I.C.	14 „ „
25-9-02	1272	J.I.C.	13 „ „
26-9-03	1304	J.I.C.	13 „ „

DISCHARGES OF THE WHITE NILE

TAKEN AT DUEIM 320 KILOMETRES UPSTREAM OF KHARTOUM.

Date.	Discharge.	Taken by.	Date.	Discharge.	Taken by.
	metres cube per sec.			metres cube per sec.	
1902			**1903**		
13 May	347	T.B.	4 Aug.	768	T.B.
11 June	650	T.B.	11 „	579	T.B.
8 July	788	T.B.	18 „	534	T.B.
5 Aug.	867	H.J.L.B.	23 „	654	T.B.
2 Sept.	330	H.J.L.B.	28 „	710	T.B.
1 Oct.	870	W.F.H.	2 Sept.	571	T.B.
28 Oct.	802	W.F.H.	7 „	737	T.B.
1 Dec.	930	W.F.H.	12 „	653	T.B.
29 Dec.	1518	W.F.H.	18 „	840	T.B.
1903			24 „	763	T.B.
			7 Oct.	1588	W.F.H.
27 Jan.	663	T.B.	3 Nov.	1563	H.J.L.B.
24 Feb.	462	T.B.	24 „	1665	H.J.L.B.
24 March	559	T.B.	8 Dec.	1462	P.E.
21 April	415	T.B.	22 „	1403	P.E.
19 May	447	H.J.L.B.			
16 June.	658	H.J.L.B.	**1904**		
1 July.	884	H.J.L.B.	6 Jan.	1508	P.E.
14 July.	835	H.J.L.B.	20 „	1466	P.E.

DISCHARGES OF THE BLUE NILE

TAKEN NEAR KHARTOUM 7 KILOMETRES ABOVE THE JUNCTION WITH THE WHITE NILE.

DATE.	DISCHARGE.	TAKEN BY	DATE.	DISCHARGE.	TAKEN BY
	metres cube per sec.			metres cube per sec.	
1902			**1903**		
9 May	184	T.B.	20 March	201	T.B.
23 "	194	T.B.	3 April	132	T.B.
6 June	604	T.B.	17 "	154	T.B.
20 "	695	T.B.	1 May	121	H.J.L.B.
27 "	837	T.B.	8 "	Nil	H.J.L.B.
4 July	1032	T.B.	15 "	Nil	H.J.L.B.
11 "	1453	T.B.	22 "	Nil	H.J.L.B.
18 "	1612	T.B.	28 " (*)	374	H.J.L.B.
25 "	1885	T.B.	6 June	970	H.J.L.B.
1 Aug.	3420	T.B.	19 "	1500	H.J.L.B.
8 "	4880	H.J.L.B.	26 "	1089	H.J.L.B.
15 "	4720	H.J.L.B.	3 July	1314	H.J.L.B.
22 "	5540	H.J.L.B.	10 "	1952	H.J.L.B.
29 "	7180	H.J.L.B.	17 "	2267	H.J.L.B.
5 Sept.	6580	H.J.L.B.	24 "	3183	H.J.L.B.
12 "	5800	H.J.L.B.	31 "	2870	W.F.H.
19 "	5760	H.J.L.B.	5 Aug.	7584	W.F.H.
26 "	4860	H.J.L.B.	10 "	7100	W.F.H.
3 Oct.	4880	H.J.L.B.	14 "	9340	W.F.H.
10 "	3250	H.J.L.B.	21 "	9519	W.F.H.
17 "	2460	H.J.L.B.	28 "	9544	W.F.H.
24 "	2030	H.J.L.B.	4 Sept.	8474	W.F.H.
31 "	1244	H.J.L.B.	11 "	8385	W.F.H.
7 Nov.	1272	H.J.L.B.	18 "	7070	W.F.H.
14 "	1035	H.J.L.B.	25 "	8965	W.F.H.
21 "	802	H.J.L.B.	2 Oct.	6581	W.F.H.
28 "	787	H.J.L.B.	9 "	5749	W.F.H.
5 Dec.	654	H.J.L.B.	16 "	3812	W.F.H.
12 "	486	W.F.H.	23 "	4198	W.F.H.
23 "	476	W.F.H.	30 "	2893	H.J.L.B.
			6 Nov.	2275	H.J.L.B.
1903			13 "	1790	H.J.L.B.
2 Jan.	348	W.F.H.	20 "	1456	H.J.L.B.
9 "	270	W.F.H.	4 Dec.	1102	H.J.L.B.
16 "	248	W.F.H.	18 "	789	P.E.
23 "	250	T.B.	25 "	722	P.E.
6 Feb.	226	T.B.			
20 "	152	T.B.	**1904**		
6 March	202	T.B.	1 Jan.	604	P.E.
			15 "	488	P.E.

(*) Section henceforth taken 500 metres downstream of former site.
Compare plans Nos. *Va* and *Vb*.

DISCHARGES OF THE ATBARA.

DATE.	DISCHARGE.	TAKEN BY.	DATE.	DISCHARGE.	TAKEN BY.
	metres cube per sec.			metres cube per sec.	
1902			**1903**		
13 July	334	T.B.	5 Aug.	1448	C.H.W.
20 "	600	T.B.	14 "	2318	"
27 "	625	T.B.	15 "	2931	"
10 Aug.	990	H.J.L.B.	27 "	2632	"
24 "	1420	H.J.L.B.	30 "	3088	"
8 Sept.	2020	H.J.L.B.	5 Sept.	2822	"
22 "	690	H.J.L.B.	12 "	2091	"
6 Oct.	152	P.E.	18 "	1672	"
1903			25 "	1267	"
			28 "	902	"
16 July	381	C.H.W.	2 Oct.	925	"
23 "	538	"	4 "	754	"
27 "	780	"	5 "	703	"
2 Aug.	758	"			

The discharges in 1902 were measured near Atbara railway bridge: those in 1903 were measured at Abadar, 29 kilometres up stream from the mouth of the Atbara.

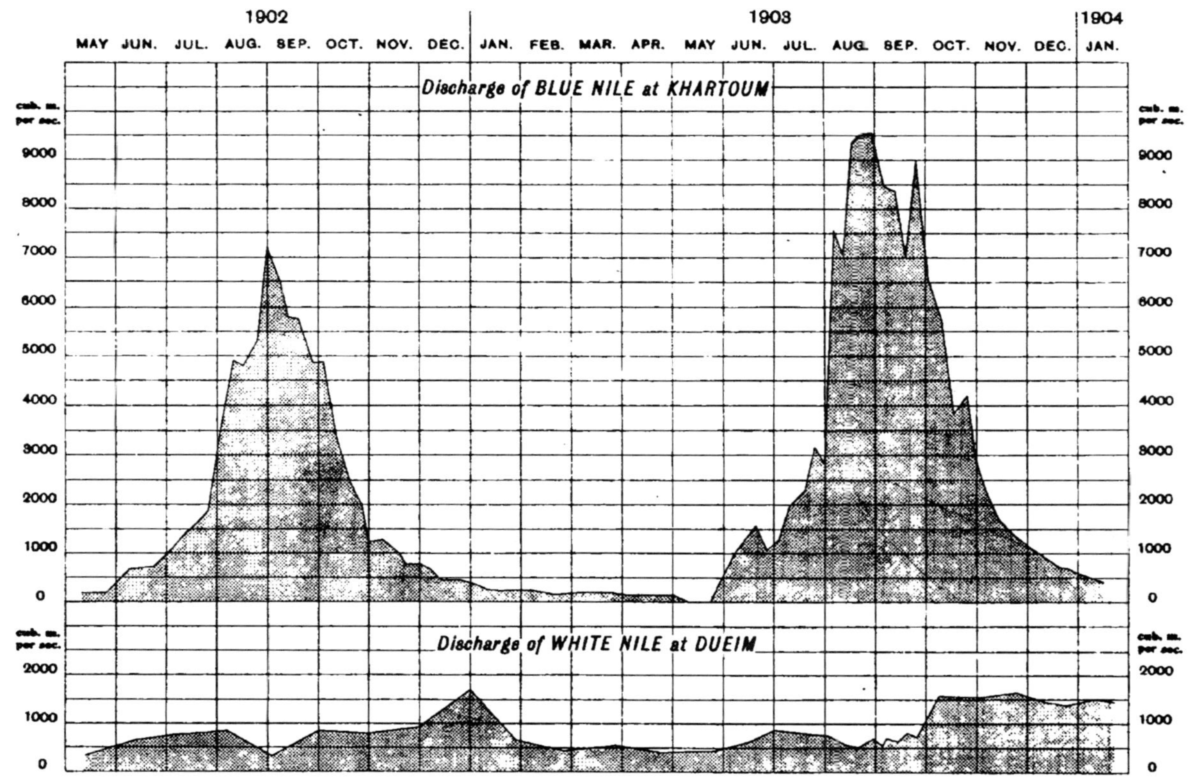

1902
1903
1904
MAY JUN. JUL. AUG. SEP. OCT. NOV. DEC. JAN. FEB. MAR. APR. MAY JUN. JUL. AUG. SEP. OCT. NOV. DEC. JAN.
Discharge of BLUE NILE at KHARTOUM
cub. m. per sec.
9000
8000
7000
6000
5000
4000
3000
2000
1000
0
Discharge of WHITE NILE at DUEIM
cub. m. per sec.
2000
1000
0

Discharge Diagram for the KHARTOUM GAUGE.

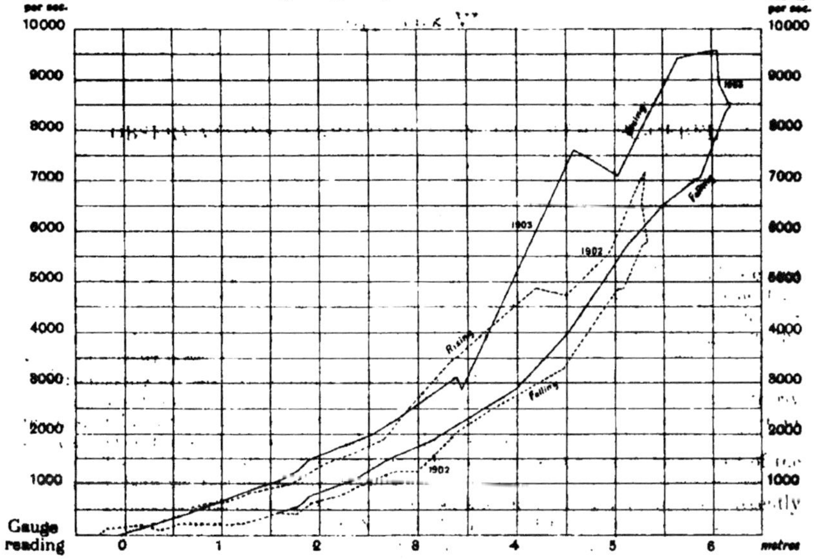

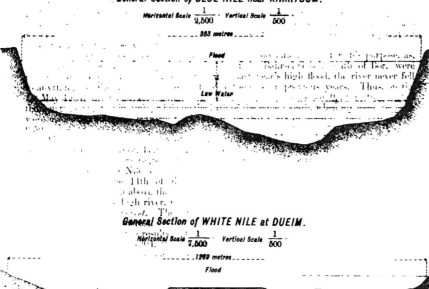

General Section of BLUE NILE near KHARTOUM.

Horizontal Scale $\frac{1}{2,500}$ · Vertical Scale $\frac{1}{500}$

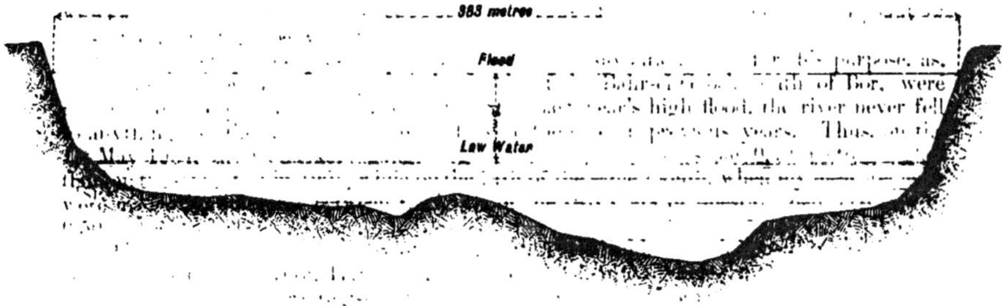

General Section of WHITE NILE at DUEIM.

Horizontal Scale $\frac{1}{7,500}$ Vertical Scale $\frac{1}{500}$

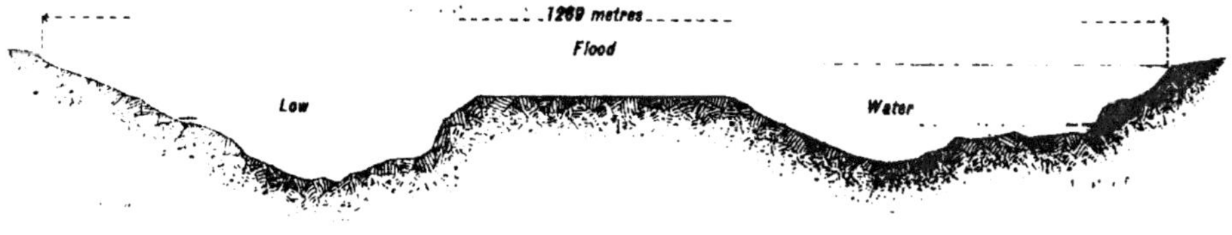

PLAN V.6.

Discharge Diagram for the KHARTOUM GAUGE.

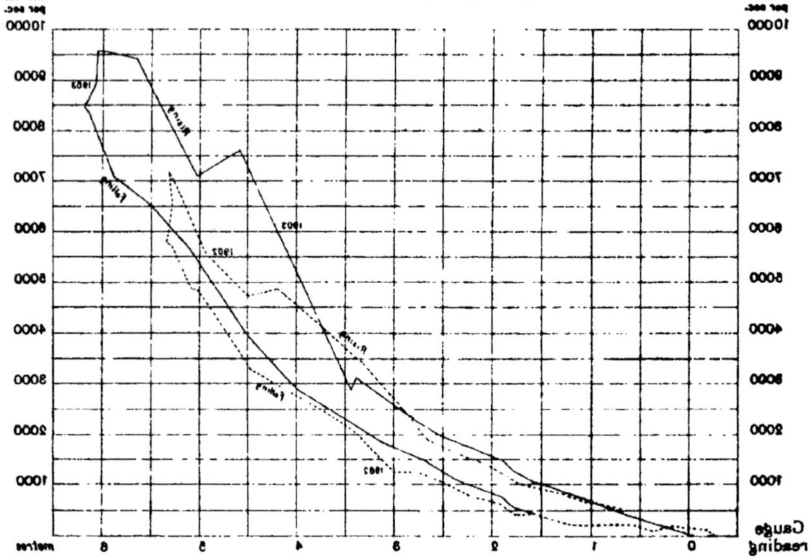

General Section of BLUE NILE near KHARTOUM.

Horizontal Scale $\frac{1}{2,500}$ · Vertical Scale $\frac{1}{500}$ ·

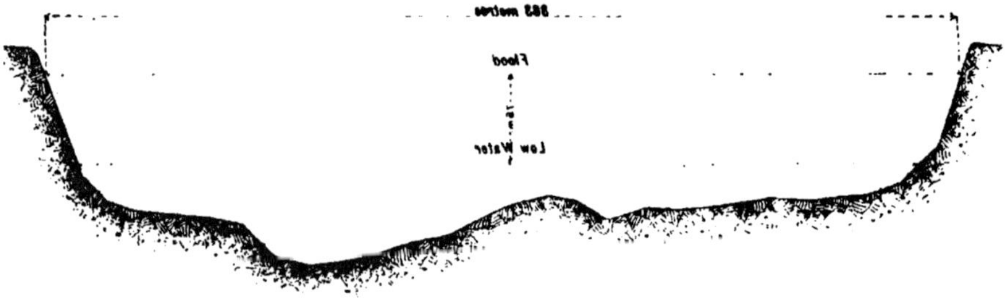

General Section of WHITE NILE at DUEIM.

Horizontal Scale $\frac{1}{7,500}$ · Vertical Scale $\frac{1}{500}$ ·

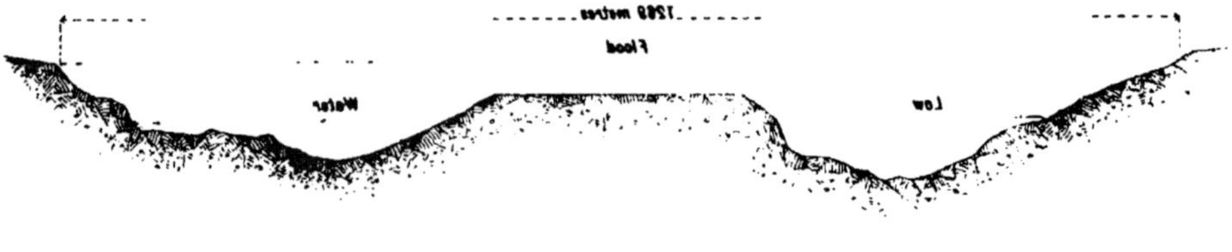

Appendix VI.

OBSERVATIONS CARRIED OUT ON THE BAHR-EL-GEBEL IN MAY 1904.

Since my present report was written, I have again visited the Upper Nile and ascended the river as far south as Gondokoro. During my journey, I collected some supplementary information regarding certain of the points discussed in that report. I have thought this information to be of sufficient value to warrant its introduction into these pages, in the shape of a short note.

In making my late expedition, I had three objects in view, namely:—

(*a*) To obtain further measurements of the volume of the river in its most southerly reaches, and ascertain the loss of water due to the marshes, during the hottest period of the year when the levels were presumably at their lowest.

(*b*) To explore and study the large branch channels said to exist to the east of the main river, between Bor and Ghaba Shambé.

(*c*) To inspect that reach of the Bahr-el-Gebel known as block 15, which was recently cleared of "sudd" by Lieut. Drury, R.N., and Mr. Poole of the Soudan Service.

I will discuss these three questions separately, and as briefly as I can.

(a) *Discharge measurements of the Bahr-el-Gebel and White Nile, in May 1904.*

On page 153 of my report, I explained that the loss of water, occurring between Lado and Bor during the period of lowest Nile, was still unknown; no discharges having been taken at Bor, at that season of the year. One of the main objects of my late journey, was to remedy this omission, and to ascertain, by means of actual discharges, the amount of loss, due to wastage, between these two points.

Unfortunately, the present year was not a very favourable one for this purpose, as, throughout the winter and spring, the levels of the Bahr-el-Gebel, south of Bor, were maintained at a quite exceptional height. Since last year's high flood, the river never fell to anything like the same extent as had been the case in previous years. Thus, on the 1st May 1904, the Gondokoro gauge registered a water level some 0.40 metres higher than on the same date in 1903, while on the 14th of the same month, when my measurements were made, the difference between the levels of the two years in question had increased to 0.50 metres.

Throughout the early months of 1904, high levels had been maintained, the maximum being reached on the 16th, 17th and 18th of April, when the gauges of 0.94, 0.98 and 0.96 metres respectively were registered (1). The rise in April was due to heavy rainfall throughout the Upper Nile valley. Subsequent to these dates, a long break occurred in the rains, and on the 14th of May, the gauge reading was only 0.83 metres. This level is, however, much above the average of previous years for the date in question (2). In consequence of the high river, my most recent discharges do not show the loss of water when the river is at its *lowest*. They do, however, show this loss during a period of *medium* level, and are thus of interest.

The following are the results of the discharges:—

On the 12th of May 1904, the discharge passing down the river at Bor, including the Aliab channel, was *813* cubic metres per second.

On the 14th of the same month, a discharge of *1138* metres cube per second was passing Lado (3).

(1) In April 1903, on the same dates, the gauge readings were 0.56, 0.53 and 0.53 metres.
(2) The Gondokoro gauge register shows that, since the flood of 1903, the levels never fell below 0.62 metres.
(3) It will be observed, by a reference to the chapter on river discharges, that this volume is rather greater than that of he *maximum* flood discharge in September 1902, when 1079 metres cube per second were measured at Lado.

Between the 12th and 14th, the Gondokoro gauge showed a slight rise of 0.16 of a metre. This would slightly reduce the Lado discharge for the date equivalent to the time when the water measured at Bor, had passed the southern discharge site. The difference is so small that I have not taken it into account, but have considered the levels to be steady.

The loss of water between Lado and Bor is, consequently :—

Discharge at Lado	1138	metres cube per second
Discharge at Bor	813	" " " "
Difference	325	metres cube per second

This is equivalent to a loss of some 28 per cent.

It has been shown in my report, that, during the high flood of last year, 50 per cent of the water passing Lado was lost before Bor was reached. It was then explained that this loss was largely due to the flooding of the entire valley and the formation of a large lake, or reservoir. It is not so easy to explain the loss in May last, as the flooded area was comparatively small. A portion of the wastage is no doubt due to evaporation in the broad and shallow channels into which the stream is divided, but, at the time of year in question, the weather was cloudy and the humidity of the atmosphere excessive. In my opinion, much of this loss is caused by the vegetation through which a large portion of the water filters. The dense growth of flooded reeds on both sides of every channel must absorb a very large quantity of water, and I am convinced that to this cause is due the greater portion of the wastage that does occur. In a year of very low supply this loss is undoubtedly less, but, to a certain extent, it must always exist.

The only remedy for this loss will be to select one channel for the stream, and close off all the others by training works, as proposed in my report. Such works south of Bor should not be very difficult to execute, and once this has been done, much of the present waste should be avoided (1).

In order to complete my series of observations for 1904, I measured the amount of water passing down the White Nile, downstream of the junction of the Bahr-el-Zaraf, but upstream of the Sobat junction. Discharges were observed in the Bahr-el-Gebel and in the Bahr-el-Zaraf at the usual sites, a few kilometres upstream of their outlets. The Bahr-el-Ghazal was also visited, with a view to measuring its discharge, but at the ordinary discharge site, upstream of the Khor Deleb, no velocity at all could be observed. The current meter failed to give any indication of a stream, at any depth. This river has therefore been neglected in considering the volume passing down the White Nile, in May 1904.

The following are the figures :—

Discharge of the Bahr-el-Gebel at kilometre 1147, on May the 22nd 1904	=	302	metres cube per second
Discharge of the Bahr-el-Zaraf at 16 kilometres upstream of the junction, on May the 23rd 1904	=	124	" " " "
Therefore the discharge of the White Nile	=	426	metres cube per second

This means that between Lado, and the White Nile, 712 metres cube of water were lost in the marshes, or some 62 per cent of the total volume coming down from the south.

Again, between Bor and the White Nile, the loss was 387 metres cube per second. The loss between these two places was consequently some 47 per cent.

Although these figures only confirm those obtained by previous measurements, they are none the less striking, as showing the appalling waste of water that takes place in this river at all seasons, and that, even a good supply in the Upper Nile, as in the present year, has no effect whatever in increasing the volume passing down the White Nile to the Sobat junction.

To sum up. The results of this year's observations show :—

First. That the Bahr-el-Gebel discharge at Lado, during May 1904, was greater than the *maximum* flood discharge, in September 1902.

Second. That 28 per cent of the water passing Lado was lost by the time Bor was reached, i.e. in a distance of 178 kilometres, while 62 per cent of the volume had disappeared at the junction of the Bahr-el-Zaraf with the White Nile.

Third. That the discharge of the Bahr-el-Zaraf in May 1904, was considerably above the average for that season of the year (2).

Fourth. That, in spite of the high levels of the Bahr-el-Gebel, upstream of the "sudd," the volume passed out into the White Nile below Lake No, was in no way

(1) I refer of course, to the period of low supply. During the flood there will always be a loss, but at that time, it is of no importance.

(2) This increased discharge in the Bahr-el-Zaraf is probably due to the high flood of 1903, which cleared away "sudd" in the supply channels of this branch of the river.

greater than that of preceding years when the southern discharges were much less. This confirms the statement made in my report, namely, that the discharge of the Bahr-el-Gebel, at its outlet, is practically constant between 300 and 500 metres cube per second; never falling below the former, or exceeding the latter figure, no matter what may be the conditions of the river in the vicinity of Gondokoro and Lado.

I will now discuss the second of the objects of my journey :—

(*b*) *The eastern branches of the Bahr-el-Gebel between Bor and Ghaba Shambé.*

Attention was first drawn to the existence of a large channel to the east of the main river, by Mr. E. S. Grogan, in a recent book of travels (1).

In this work he gives a sketch of this channel, which he christens the Gertrude Nile. He followed its right bank for a considerable distance, when marching from Bor to the Bahr-el-Zaraf. Considering the difficulties that he must have experienced in the way of making observations, his sketch of this river is wonderfully accurate, and very fairly represents the general direction and position of the channel. What he could not of course see, were the branch channels to the Nile on its left bank, neither could he follow its course throughout, after it had left the high land and commenced to wander through the marshes.

More recently, Captain Liddell, R.E., the Director of Telegraphs in the Soudan, when endeavouring to find a good line for his wires, crossed a wide stream to the east of Abu Kika. I myself, when making the survey of the Bahr-el-Gebel in 1901, with Captain Lyons, had obtained, from the upper deck of the steamer, occasional glimpses of a wide channel, fringed by tall reeds, running more or less parallel to the east of the main river. As I considered it very desirable that this branch should be investigated, with a view to possible projects for the improvement of the Bahr-el-Zaraf, I decided to visit it in May last. Captain Liddell and I explored it as far as it was possible to do so, and made a compass survey of the different streams visited (2).

The so-called Gertrude Nile is known to the Dinkas as the "Atem," and by this name I shall call it throughout this note. Its head is not traceable at Bor itself, and in this respect Mr. Grogan's sketch plan is incorrect, as the channel only commences at a considerable distance to the north of Bor (3). It is formed by the many spills which leave the Bahr-el-Gebel on its eastern bank, downstream of Bor. These spills are very numerous, but it is impossible to say which of them, if any, is its true head, as no one of them is sufficiently large to justify the assertion that it is the main source of supply (4). In all probability, the Atem river is formed by the combined water of all these spills, which pass through the "sudd" and swamp, and eventually unite into one large channel flowing north, along the line of the high land to the east of the river valley.

Although there is some uncertainty as to where the Atem leaves the Bahr-el-Gebel, there is none whatever, as to the point where its waters rejoin the latter stream. At kilometre 700 of the Bahr-el-Gebel, are two large inlets, some 20 to 25 metres in width, and close together, through which the water coming from the Atem, passes into the Bahr-el-Gebel. At kilometre 755 there is a third (5).

The river Atem, as has been already stated, follows for a great portion of its course, the high land lying to the east of the Nile valley. For some 50 or 60 kilometres below Bor, it is not now navigable, being closed by "sudd" in its upper reaches. North of this point it is open, and is a fine broad stream, averaging from 60 to 80 metres in width. It is occasionally much wider than this, but on the other hand, it, in places, narrows to 20 metres or less. At first sight it appears to be a much more important river than the Bahr-el-Gebel, as it has a strong current, and its general course is straighter than that of the main river. Its depth, however, in the upper portions of its course, is rarely more than 2 to 2.5 metres, and its volume is not considerable (6).

(1) "From the Cape to Cairo," by E. S. Grogan, London, 1900.

(2) The accompanying map, which is a reproduction of that published with my report of 1901, shows the different branches of this channel of the river, as plotted by Captain Liddell from the recent traverse survey.

(3) The impossibility of obtaining fuel for the steamer and the "sudd" blocks at either end, prevented our following this channel throughout its entire length.

(4) We were unable to find any outlet from the Bahr-el-Gebel, large enough to take the steamer through. Between kilometres 590 and 600, there are two spills, which, with a certain amount of clearance, might possibly be made navigable. There must at one time have been an entrance, as the Dinkas are unanimous in asserting that the Dervish Emir, Arabi Dafallah, once entered the Atem in his steamer and passed down it to the north to the point where it separates into two branches. This would be quite impossible now.

(5) In 1901 and 1903, the water was flowing in the reverse direction in these channels, that is, *from* the Bahr-el-Gebel *into* the Atem. Both of these were low years and it seems probable that in such cases, the Atem is lower than the Gebel and the water flows *from* the latter *into* the former, while in a high year like the present, the reverse is the case.

(6) On the 19th of May, I measured the discharge of the Atem above the point where it divides into two branches. Its volume was only 149 cubic metres per second, as against 813 metres per second in the Bahr-el-Gebel at Bor.

The river follows the edge of the forest for about half its course. This forest, although in 1904, it was flooded for a long distance from the river bank, is incomparably the finest that I have yet seen in the Soudan. It is full of large and beautiful trees, many of them being of varieties different to those met with elsewhere. At certain points, the land is high, and above the water level. In such places, Dinka villages are often met with. There must be a large population at no great distance from the river, for, as soon as the people heard of the approach of the steamer, they flocked down in considerable number to the banks. Although very shy and wild a first, they quickly gained confidence, and some of them were induced to come on board the boat. They all recollected the visit of Arabi Dafallah and some of them that of Mr. Grogan. Part of this stream would appear to have never been visited by a white man previous to our arrival. The Dinkas informed us that the flooding in the present year extended for many kilometres back from the river, and that when Mr. Grogan passed along it, the river was exceptionally low and the country dry (1).

Between the Atem and the Bahr-el-Gebel is a sea of swamp, utterly impassable for any thing but an elephant or a hippopotamus. There is little papyrus to be seen, the reeds here being chiefly "Um Soof." Many "mayyehs" wind through these marshes and broad lagoons are now and then to be seen. In this swamp are occasional islands of dry land. The level of these islands is from half a metre to a metre above that of the marshes. Some of them are of considerable extent, and all of them are surrounded by very deep swamp. Their surface is broken by ant-hills and scattered clumps of palms, or of the tree known as "Abu Sidr" (2). The only inhabitants are parties of Dinkas who visit them for the purpose of hunting and fishing. In many places, the Atem widens out into a series of broad and shallow lagoons full of small "sudd" islands. In others, the stream is separated into two or more channels, which, after winding through the grass, unite again and form a single river. The scenery, except where the Atem skirts the forest, is dreary and monotonous to an extreme degree, but is enlivened by an abundant animal life. This river is the haunt of incredible numbers of hippopotami, which swarm in every bay and lagoon, and are bolder and more inclined to dispute the passage of the steamer than in any other part of the Soudan, that I have visited. Elephants are very numerous, and herds are to be seen continually, on both sides of the river, generally feeding in deep swamp. The islands are a favourite retreat of the rare "Cobus Maria" antelope (3).

At some 95 kilometres north of Bor, the Atem river separates into two branches. That to the left, or west, is known as the Awai, while the right-hand bank is called the Myding, or Mydang, by the Dinkas.

I will describe the latter first.

The Myding, where it leaves the Atem, is a fine broad river with a very strong stream. Its general direction is north-easterly, but occasionally it flows due east. Its width, for some distance below the bifurcation, is from 60 to 70 metres and its depth from 2.5 to 3 metres. A few kilometres downstream, however, it decreases rapidly, both in breadth and depth, and at nine kilometres below the junction, it is barely 20 metres wide (4). North of this point, it becomes a very narrow and extremely winding channel through the marshes, and is eventually blocked by "sudd." Its waters must, however, almost certainly, find their way into the Bahr-el-Zaraf, or into the lagoons that go to form the head-waters of that stream. The Dinkas all assert that such is the case. The Myding is characterized by the numerous groups of fine Deleb palms that stand up at intervals out of the surrounding marshes. Except for these palm clumps, the entire area through which this branch passes is a hopeless-looking swamp in every direction. Except at the Meshra of Twi, landing is impossible anywhere, as there are no banks, and even to the east no signs of any continuous high land are visible. When visiting this river, the extent of the Bahr-el-Gebel marshes is realised to the full.

The Awai, or left branch of the Atem, at the head, appears to be much the smaller of the two streams. The channel is narrow and twisting, in places being not more than five metres in width. It was only with difficulty that the steamer was able to force its way through the numerous bends and angles of this branch. Two or three kilometres downstream of the bifurcation, the channel widens out to 20 and 30 metres, with a depth of from 3 to 4 metres, while the stream is very strong. The general direction of the Awai is north-westerly and its course is fairly straight. After the narrow channel below the head has been passed, navigation presents no difficulties, as far as the junction of the Awai with the Bahr-el-Gebel. At the ninth kilometre, the island of Fagak is passed, on the left

(1) This was the case. The Upper Nile in the winter of 1901, was lower than had ever before been known. Otherwise it would have been impossible for any one to have followed the bank of the Atem closely.

(2) The "Abu Sidr" or "Father of Breasts," is common in Uganda, where it is known as the "Rhinoceros tree." The Arabs give it the above name, because the shape of the fruit resembles a woman's breast.

(3) Mrs. Gray's water-buck.

(4) About 2 kilometres below the bifurcation which is marked by a solitary "Abu Sidr" tree, is the "Meshra," or landing place of the district of Twi. Landing is only possible in a dug-out canoe, which has to traverse the swamp for about 1 ½ to 2 kilometres.

hand. This is a low piece of dry land, perhaps 0.40 metres above the general swamp level and covering an area of some 6 or 7 square kilometres. Many ant-hills and a few bushes dot its surface. All round it are limitless marshes (1). At the tenth kilometre, another and larger island, known as Akwoit, is passed on the right-hand side of the river. This island has a length of about 6 kilometres and a breadth of from 3 to 4 kilometres. Beyond it, to the east, the swamp apparently extends into space, but at one point, the dry land of this island touches the bank of the Awai. Akwoit is much frequented by hunting parties of Dinkas, and like Fagak, is covered by ant-hills and clumps of high bush, with occasional Deleb palms. Numerous herds of elephants are to be seen in the vicinity. Downstream of Akwoit, the Awai widens out considerably and becomes an important looking stream, with a width varying from 60 to 100 metres and a depth of from 3 to 4 metres. It passes through broad belts of papyrus, and skirts, or runs through, a series of wide lagoons, all of which are full of "sudd" islands and some of which are several square kilometres in extent, being large enough to merit the name of lakes. From both sides, numerous channels enter it, bringing in water — the drainage of the surrounding swamps. The width of the marshes to the east of the Bahr-el-Gebel (opposite Kanisa and Shambé) must be many kilometres, and it is doubtful whether, at any point in the whole course of this river, they are wider than they are here (2).

At some 36 kilometres downstream of the bifurcation of the Atem, the outlets from the Awai into the Bahr-el-Gebel are arrived at. The two streams, at this point, approach within 200 metres of one another, and the current from the former, into the latter, is extremely strong. Downstream of these outlets the Awai flows on, with a diminished volume, to the north. The width gradually decreases to 30 or 40 metres, and the depth to from 2 to 3 metres. At the 46th kilometre, another channel connects it with the Bahr-el-Gebel and it again loses a portion of its discharge. Some five kilometres below this point, or 51 kilometres from the Atem bifurcation, navigation becomes very difficult, as the river merges into a large "mayyeh," or lagoon, the only outlet from which to the north, is a narrow and shallow channel (3). Beyond this point, we found it practically impossible for the steamer to go. The waters of the Awai, like those of the Myding, eventually find their way into the Bahr-el-Zaraf.

As regards making any practical use of these eastern branches, I do not think that much can be said in favour of such a suggestion. They are undoubtedly fed by the Bahr-el-Gebel spills and while a considerable amount of their water is discharged back into that river, a large amount, at any rate in a year like the present, goes to supply the Bahr-el-Zaraf. In a low year, I feel convinced that the Bahr-el-Gebel feeds the lower reaches of the Awai by the inlets at the 700th kilometre.

Although the Myding and Awai may be considered to be the most southerly sources of the Bahr-el-Zaraf, I should not, from what I have seen of them, recommend their being utilized, should it be eventually decided to remodel that river. The marshes through which they pass are so immense, and so continuous, that the prevention of waste of water would be a work of great difficulty and would entail a large expenditure. I think it would be easier and more economical, under such circumstances, to excavate and embank a new channel for the Zaraf from the Bahr-el-Gebel, following the most direct line, north of Shambé, to the point where its channel runs between dry banks.

It would not be difficult, were it thought desirable, to clear out narrow portions of the Awai and Atem, so as to make a good navigable line between Shambé, to a point not very far to the north of Bor. Such a line would have certain advantages, in-as-much as it would be straighter, and probably shorter, than that at present followed by the steamers. Further, a new and large supply of fuel would be opened up by enabling steamers to reach the eastern forest. On the other hand, it must be recollected that this channel was visited by me, in a year when the river was exceptionally high. To my mind, it is extremely doubtful whether, in summers like those of 1900, 1901, 1902 and 1903, any of these branches would be navigable at all.

Beyond then the opening up of a fresh wood supply, and enabling the district officers to get into touch with the Dinkas of this locality, I can see no advantage to be gained by clearing these rivers. If the Zaraf is to be remodelled, any such scheme should most certainly be prohibited, as it would increase the evaporating area. Under such circumstances

(1) There is said to be a channel, navigable for canoes, from this island to the Bahr-el-Gebel, opposite Abu Kika.

(2) An annoying error has been made by the drawing office, in the map of this portion of the river. This error was unfortunately only discovered, when it was too late to correct it. In sheet No. 11, of the general map of the Bahr-el-Gebel, which accompanies my report, what is apparently a clump of forest, or high land, is shown to the east of the river and at no great distance from it, opposite to the 700th kilometre. This is a mistake made by the draftsman, and no such high land exists. In my map of 1901, this apparent forest was shown as a lagoon, which it is. The swamp to the east is very wide here and no high land is to be found for a great distance from the Gebel. In the map which accompanies this appendix, this error has been adjusted, and the marshes are correctly shown.

(3) This channel must, I think, be the false channel followed in 1901, by Major Peake and Lieut. Drury, when they first forced their way up through the "sudd" into the Upper Nile. It is really one of the many heads of the Bahr-el-Zaraf.

every effort should be made to close the spills on the Bahr-el-Gebel, throughout the entire reach between Bor and Shambé, and confine the whole volume of the river to one single channel.

My late visit to these marshes has confirmed the opinion which I had previously formed, that, if the levels prove the work to be at all feasible, the true solution of the problem of the Upper Nile supply, lies in the construction of the proposed new channel from Bor to the Sobat, leaving the marshes entirely to the west. All the information that I have been able to collect, tends to prove that the country lying between these two places, to the east of the swamps, is a vast, flat plain of grass. It is true that it is flooded during the rainy season for a considerable distance from the marshes, but not to any depth, and by going far enough to the east, this flooding could be avoided.

At the southern end, several large and deep "khors" cross from the east, but none of these "khors" are streams, in the ordinary sense of the word. They are sheets of nearly stagnant water, through which the drainage of the plains filters slowly down to the river. If they were to be closed altogether by the banks of the new channel, I do not think that any serious damage would be caused. In any case, they could be allowed to drain into it by masonry inlets in the banks, and it must not be forgotten that it would be precisely during the rainy season, when the "khors" were full, that the water in the new channel would be regulated at the head, and would be at its lowest.

I inspected the high land at Bor with a view to selecting a site for a possible head of this channel. Almost anywhere between the village and the Dervish Dem, a good site could be found, and the new channel would take off the river in deep excavation which would be a great advantage.

The masonry works in the Nile itself would be difficult of construction, owing to the absence of labour and materials, but would not otherwise constitute an impossible task. The river at Bor has a width of some 146 metres, and a mean depth of 2·50 metres. The regulator would of course have to be designed to stand a considerable head, as, at times, it would be necessary to turn the entire supply down the new channel and practically dry the river itself downstream of the work. A long embankment would also be entailed across the valley with a possible opening and regulator for the Aliab channel, to the west of the main river. These works would probably be carried out by constructing a diversion for the river, and building the regulator in the present channel. I do not pretend that they would be easy of execution, and the unhealthiness of the climate would not tend to make things easier, but I do contend that the advantages to be gained, by the completion of such a project, are so great, that nothing short of actual impossibility, or a prohibitive expenditure, should be allowed to prevent the works from being undertaken(1).

As regards the line of the new channel itself, it would generally run due north from the point selected for the head at Bor. This alignment would avoid the greater part of the flooded area. It may be that, in a portion of its course, it might be found economical to follow the line of the great "khor," which enters the Sobat near the mouth, from the south, and which is known as the "Khor" Filus. Until this channel has been surveyed and the line itself has been levelled, it is useless, however, to speculate upon such a point.

There now only remains to me to give a brief description of my visit to that portion of the Bahr-el-Gebel which, last winter, was cleared of "sudd."

(c) *Block 15 in the Bahr-el-Gebel.*

The channel recently cleared by Messrs. Drury and Poole has again been closed by "sudd" in three places. At the time of my visit, the first two obstructions were small and light, and the steamer had no difficulty in forcing a passage through them. The third, however, was more formidable, and it took us an afternoon, and part of a morning, to cut our way through it. This block was some 150 metres in length and of considerable thickness. It was formed by portions of "sudd" breaking in from a large lagoon on the east bank. I feel certain that the "sudd" blocks which we removed, and which floated downstream, must have closed the river below, probably at the point where a particularly bad and sharp bend exists. In all probability the channel is now blocked at several points. This is not to be wondered at, as the unfortunate illness of Lieut. Drury necessitated the abandonment of the work before completion. Had it not been for this, I feel certain that he would have completed it, and that this portion of the Bahr-el-Gebel would have been now as clear and free from obstruction as any other reach, throughout the course of this river.

(1) During the rainy season, the mosquitoes in the forests immediately south of Bor, are worse than in any other place that I have visited throughout the Upper Nile valley. A small, and peculiarly venomous, variety, is, if possible, more active by day than by night, and, unless there should happen to be a strong wind, makes life in this locality almost intolerable at that time of year.

As regards next season's work, the only thing to be done, in my opinion, will be to commence at the northern end and widen the channel *to its full width throughout*, working steadily upstream.

I should not attempt to go ahead and cut a narrow channel through the blocks. I should work steadily from the downstream end, and, as I say, clear the channel to its full width throughout. If this is done, I think there will be no difficulty in getting the stuff removed to float away without blocking the channel, as there is now a very fair current.

I consider it absolutely necessary to complete the clearance of this channel next winter. The partial removal of the "sudd" has altered the conditions of the shallow lakes at present used for navigation, and signs are not wanting that their levels are slowly falling. It might easily happen that their water surface may fall still more, and in such a case, unless the true river channel is open, communication between Khartoum and the Upper Nile stations might be cut off. If the work of clearance of block 15, be carried out in the way that I suggest, I feel convinced that no serious difficulty will be encountered and that the work can be completed during the winter season.

Before concluding this note, I may observe that the Bahr-el-Gebel, south of Bor, has changed very much since the high flood of last year. New islands have been formed and new channels opened, rendering navigation somewhat bewildering. The great western channel, lying between kilometres 470 and 530, which was formerly the main stream, and which was followed by Baker and by Gordon in their voyages to Gondokoro, has now, after several years of closure, been reopened, and we navigated it without any great difficulty in May last.

In conclusion, I wish to tender my sincere thanks to Sir Reginald Wingate for having kindly placed one of his steamers at my disposal for this journey, and to Captain Liddell and Mr. Crawley for the very great assistance which they rendered me at all times throughout my recent expedition.

W. E. Garstin.

Cairo, June the 10th, 1904.

UGANDA STREAMS

PLAN

No. 1.

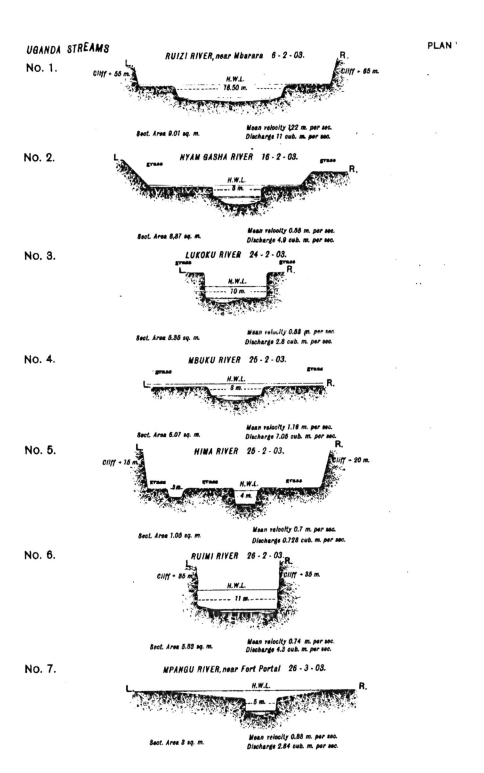

RUIZI RIVER, near Mbarara 6 - 2 - 03.

Sect. Area 9.01 sq. m.

Mean velocity 1.22 m. per sec.
Discharge 11 cub. m. per sec.

No. 2.

NYAM GASHA RIVER 16 - 2 - 03.

Sect. Area 8.87 sq. m.

Mean velocity 0.55 m. per sec.
Discharge 4.9 cub. m. per sec.

No. 3.

LUKOKU RIVER 24 - 2 - 03.

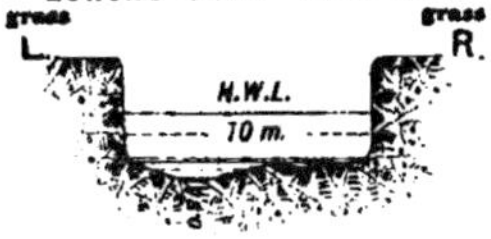

Sect. Area 5.35 sq. m.

Mean velocity 0.53 m. per sec.
Discharge 2.8 cub. m. per sec.

No. 4.

MBUKU RIVER 25 - 2 - 03.

Sect. Area 6.07 sq. m.

Mean velocity 1.16 m. per sec.
Discharge 7.05 cub. m. per sec.

No. 5.

HIMA RIVER 25 - 2 - 03.

Sect. Area 1.05 sq. m.

Mean velocity 0.7 m. per sec.
Discharge 0.728 cub. m. per sec.

No. 6.

RUIMI RIVER 26 - 2 - 03.

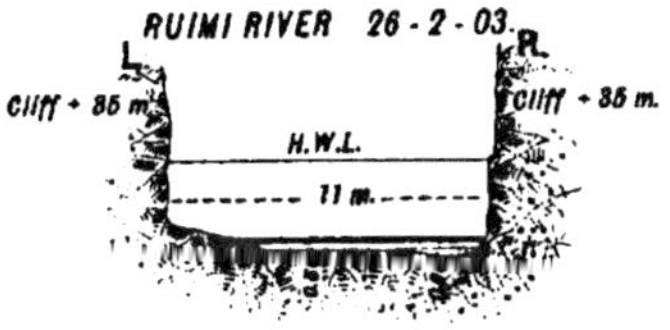

Sect. Area 5.83 sq. m.

Mean velocity 0.74 m. per sec.
Discharge 4.3 cub. m. per sec.

No. 7.

MPANGU RIVER, near Fort Portal 26 - 3 - 03.

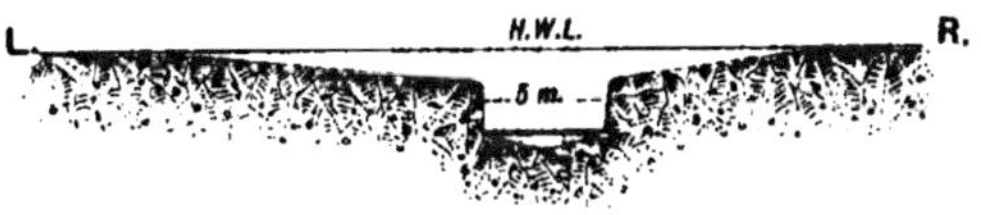

Sect. Area 3 sq. m.

Mean velocity 0.88 m. per sec.
Discharge 2.64 cub. m. per sec.

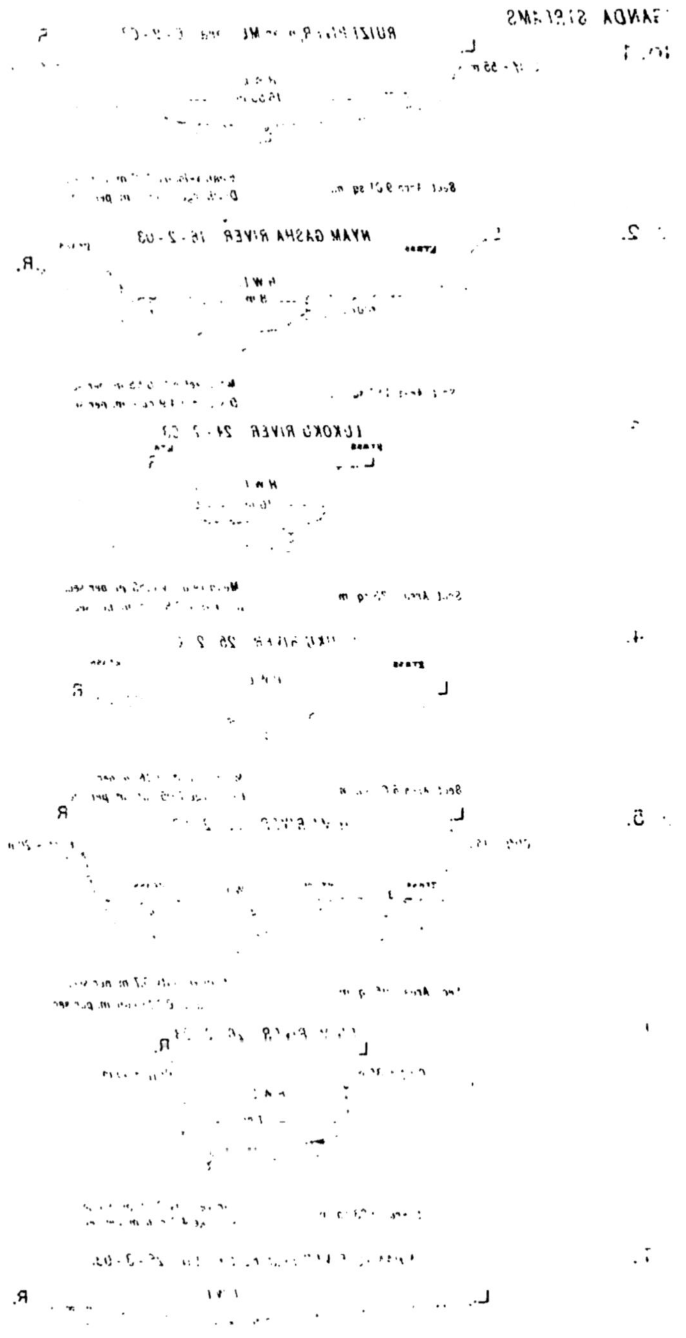
UGANDA STREAMS
No. 1
RUIZI RIVER
L
R
H W L
No. 2
NYAMGASHA RIVER 16-2-63
L
R
H W L
LUKOKO RIVER
H W L
L
R

UGANDA STREAMS

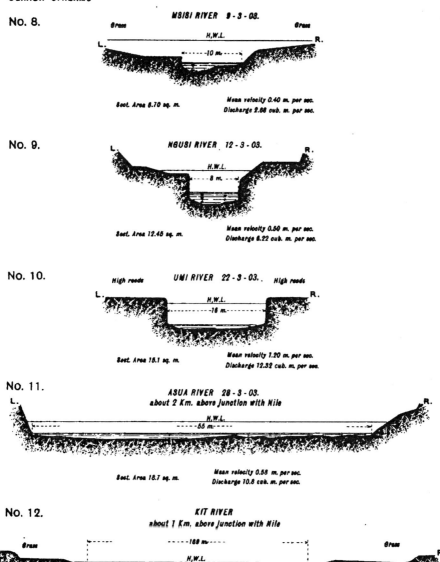

No. 8.

MSISI RIVER 9 - 3 - 03.

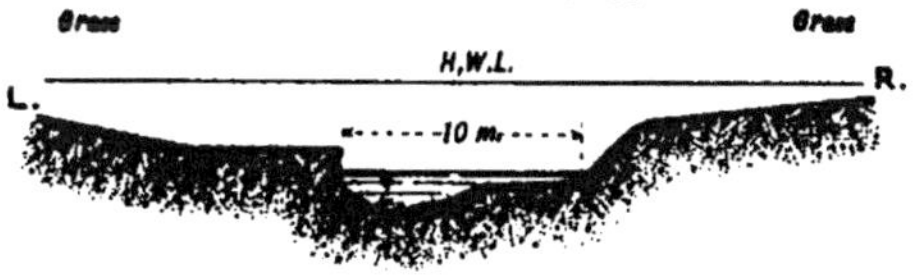

Sect. Area 6.70 sq. m. *Mean velocity 0.40 m. per sec.*
Discharge 2.68 cub. m. per sec.

No. 9.

NGUSI RIVER 12 - 3 - 03.

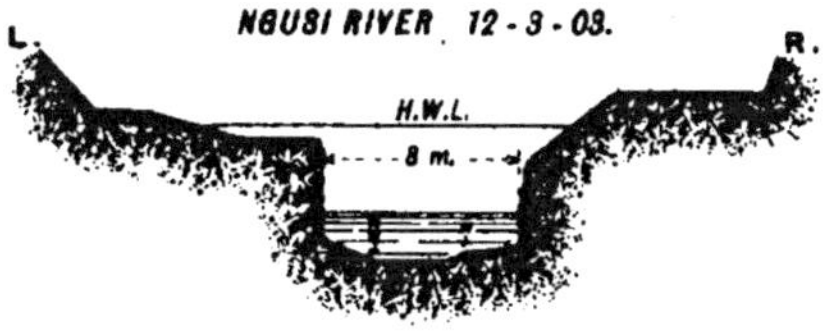

Sect. Area 12.45 sq. m. *Mean velocity 0.50 m. per sec.*
Discharge 6.22 cub. m. per sec.

No. 10.

UMI RIVER 22 - 3 - 03.

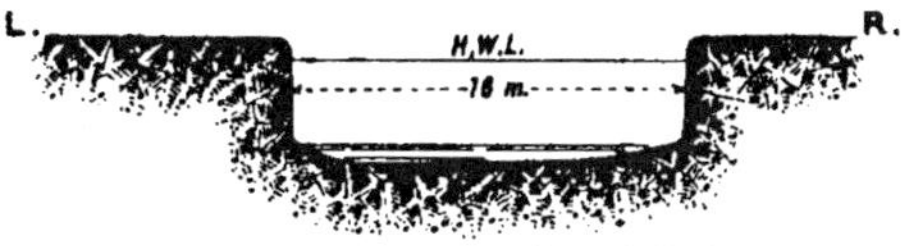

Sect. Area 15.1 sq. m. *Mean velocity 1.20 m. per sec.*
Discharge 12.32 cub. m. per sec.

No. 11.

ASUA RIVER 28 - 3 - 03.
about 2 Km. above junction with Nile

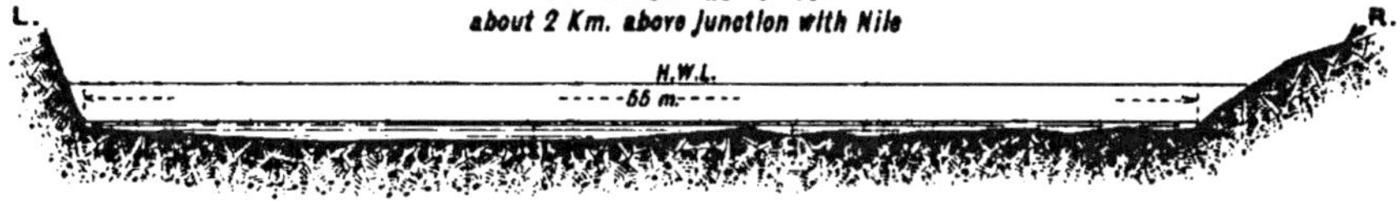

Sect. Area 18.7 sq. m. *Mean velocity 0.58 m. per sec.*
Discharge 10.8 cub. m. per sec.

No. 12.

KIT RIVER
about 1 Km. above junction with Nile

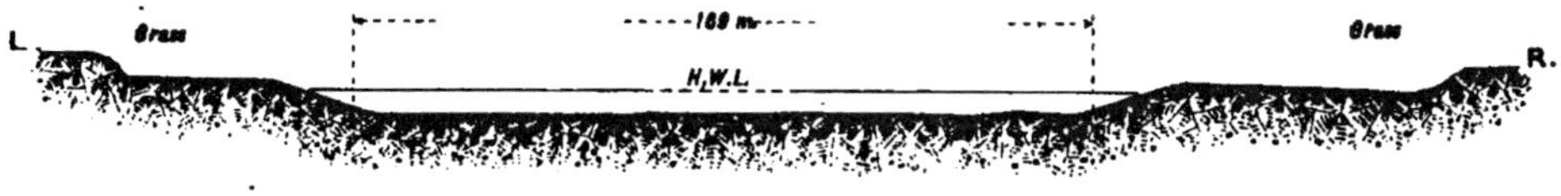

Dry in March 1903. Water 0.03 m. below surface of bed.

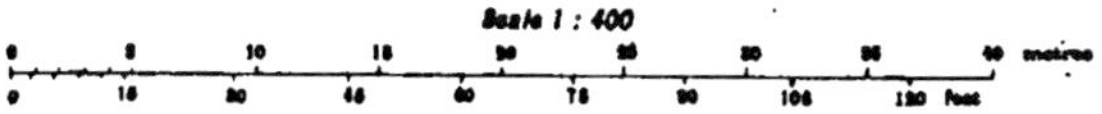

PLAN VIII.b

UGANDA STREAMS

No. 8.

MSISI RIVER 9 - 3 - 03.

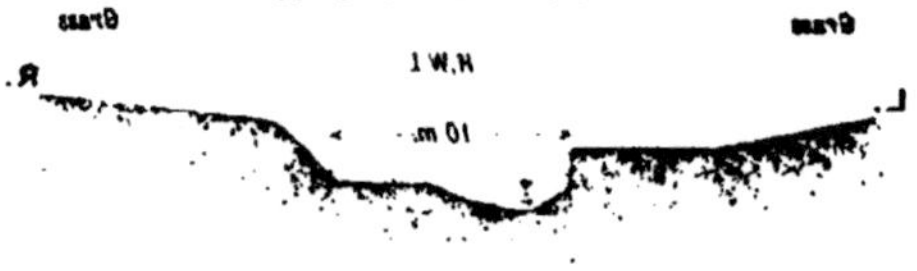

Sect. Area 6.70 sq. m.

Mean velocity 0.40 m. per sec.
Discharge 2.68 cub. m. per sec.

No. 9.

NGUSI RIVER 12 - 3 - 03.

Sect. Area 12.48 sq. m.

Mean velocity 0.50 m. per sec.
Discharge 6.22 cub. m. per sec.

No. 10.

UMI RIVER 22 - 3 - 03.

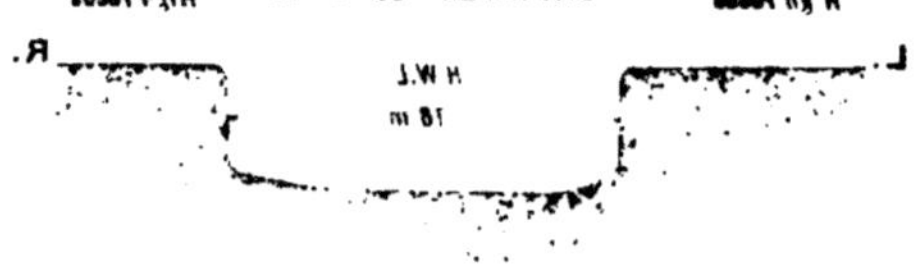

Sect. Area 10.1 sq. m.

Mean velocity 1.20 m. per sec.
Discharge 12.32 cub. m. per sec.

No. 11.

ASUA RIVER 28 - 3 - 03.
about 2 Km. above junction with Nile

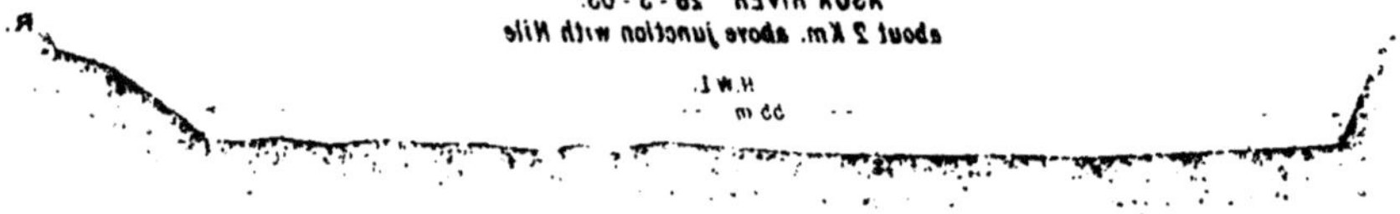

Sect. Area 18.7 sq. m.

Mean velocity 0.58 m. per sec.
Discharge 10.8 cub. m. per sec.

No. 12.

KIT RIVER
about 1 Km. above junction with Nile

Dry in March 1903. Water 0.03 m. below surface of bed

PLAN VIIIa.

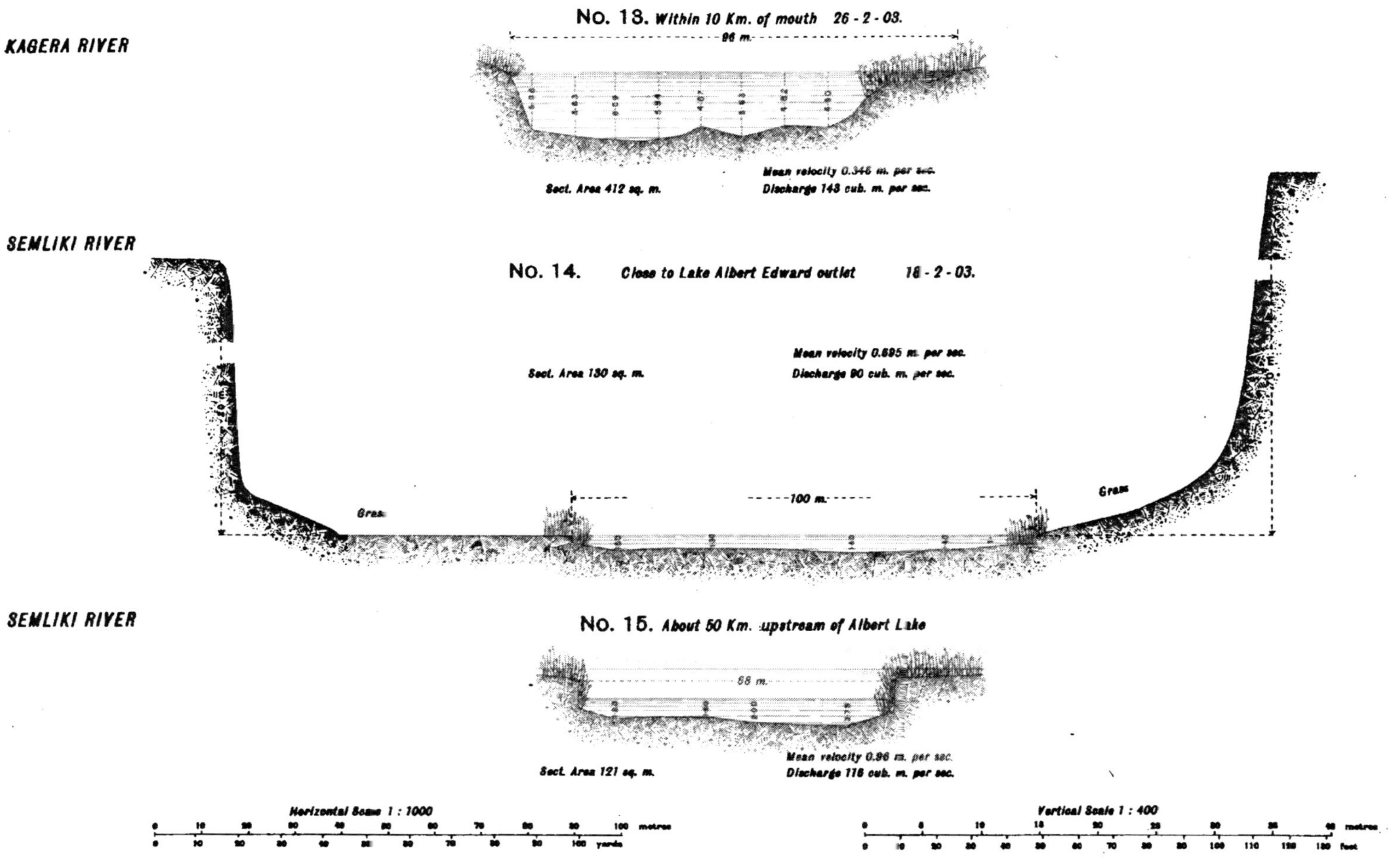
KAGERA RIVER
No. 13. Within 10 Km. of mouth 26 - 2 - 03.
96 m.
Sect. Area 412 sq. m.
Mean velocity 0.346 m. per sec.
Discharge 143 cub. m. per sec.
SEMLIKI RIVER
No. 14. Close to Lake Albert Edward outlet 18 - 2 - 03.
Sect. Area 130 sq. m.
Mean velocity 0.695 m. per sec.
Discharge 90 cub. m. per sec.
100 m.
Grass
Grass
SEMLIKI RIVER
No. 15. About 50 Km. upstream of Albert Lake
68 m.
Sect. Area 121 sq. m.
Mean velocity 0.96 m. per sec.
Discharge 116 cub. m. per sec.
Horizontal Scale 1 : 1000
metres
yards
Vertical Scale 1 : 400
metres
feet

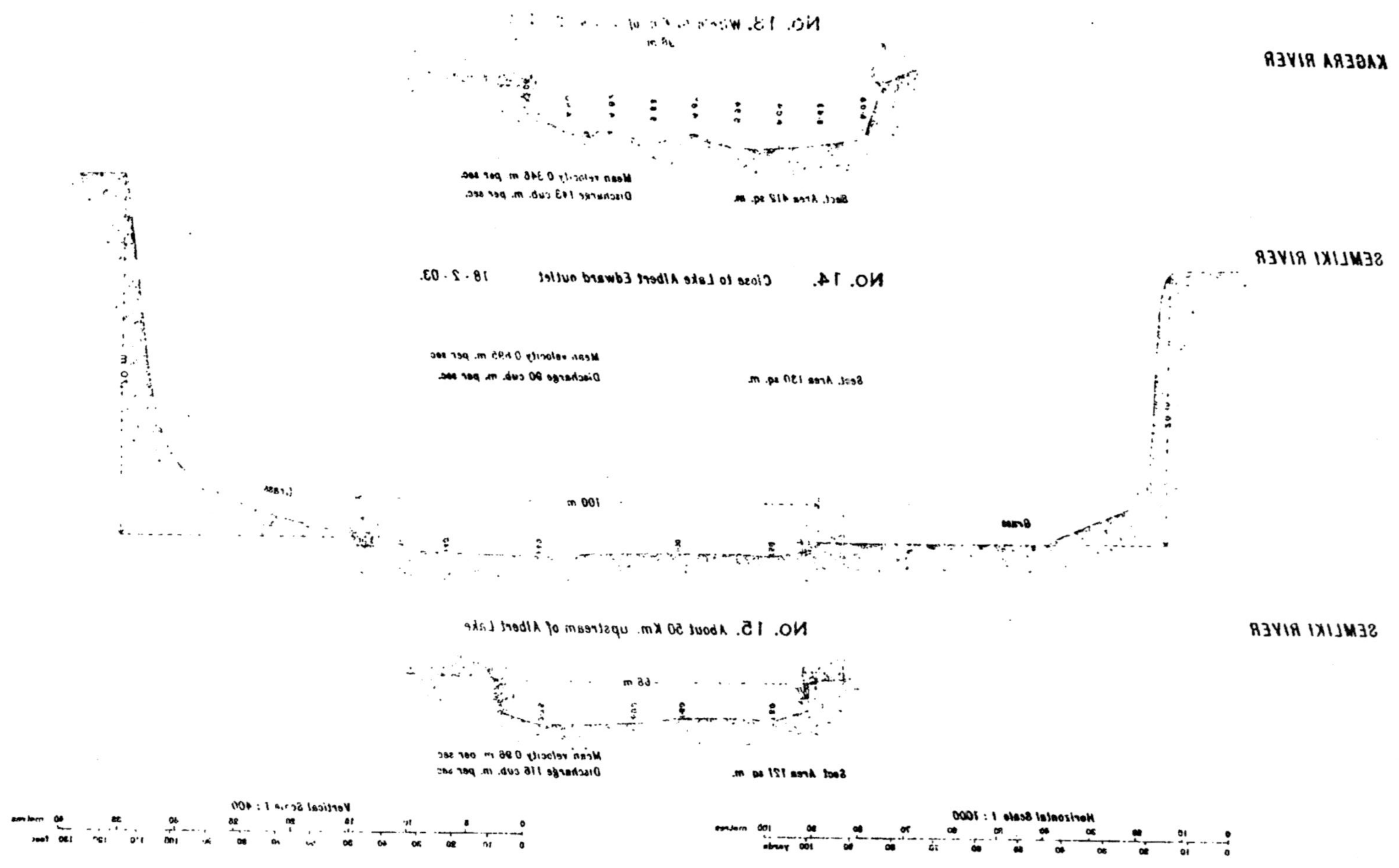
KAGERA RIVER
NO. 13.
Mean velocity 0.346 m. per sec.
Discharge 143 cub. m. per sec.
Sect. Area 412 sq. m.
SEMLIKI RIVER
NO. 14. Close to Lake Albert Edward outlet 18 · 2 · 03.
Mean velocity 0.695 m. per sec
Discharge 90 cub. m. per sec.
Sect. Area 130 sq. m.
100 m
Grass
SEMLIKI RIVER
NO. 15. About 50 Km. upstream of Albert Lake
65 m
Mean velocity 0.96 m. per sec
Discharge 116 cub. m. per sec
Sect. Area 121 sq. m.
Vertical Scale 1 : 400
Horizontal Scale 1 : 1000

PLAN VIIIc.

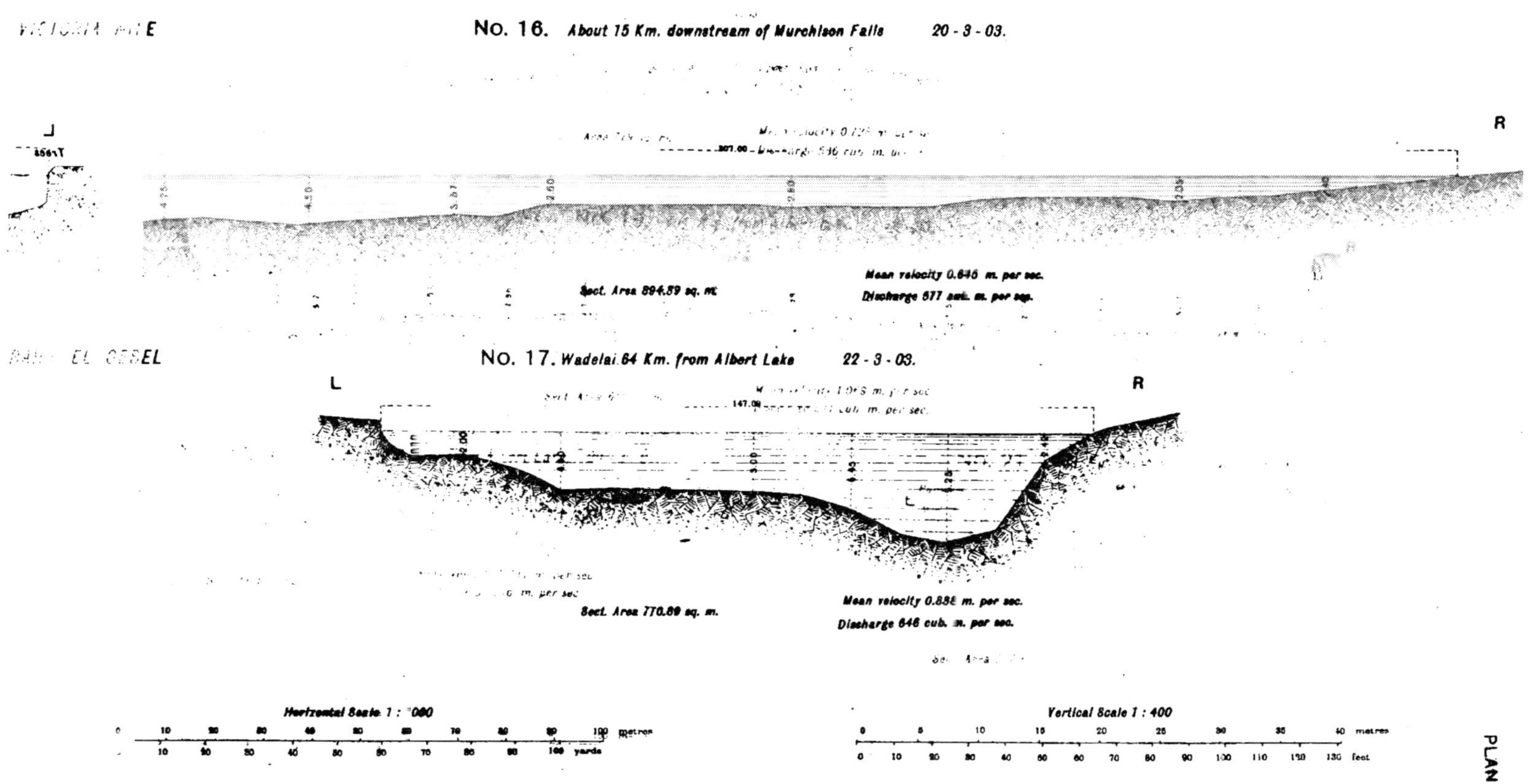
No. 16. About 15 Km. downstream of Murchison Falls 20 - 3 - 03.
L
R
Sect. Area 894.59 sq. m.
Mean velocity 0.645 m. per sec.
Discharge 577 cub. m. per sec.
BAHR EL GEBEL
No. 17. Wadelai 64 Km. from Albert Lake 22 - 3 - 03.
L
R
147.09
Sect. Area 770.69 sq. m.
Mean velocity 0.838 m. per sec.
Discharge 646 cub. m. per sec.
Horizontal Scale 1 : 1000
0 10 20 30 40 50 60 70 80 90 100 metres
10 20 30 40 50 60 70 80 90 100 yards
Vertical Scale 1 : 400
0 5 10 15 20 25 30 35 40 metres
0 10 20 30 40 50 60 70 80 90 100 110 120 130 feet

PLAN VIII. d.

PLAN VIII.

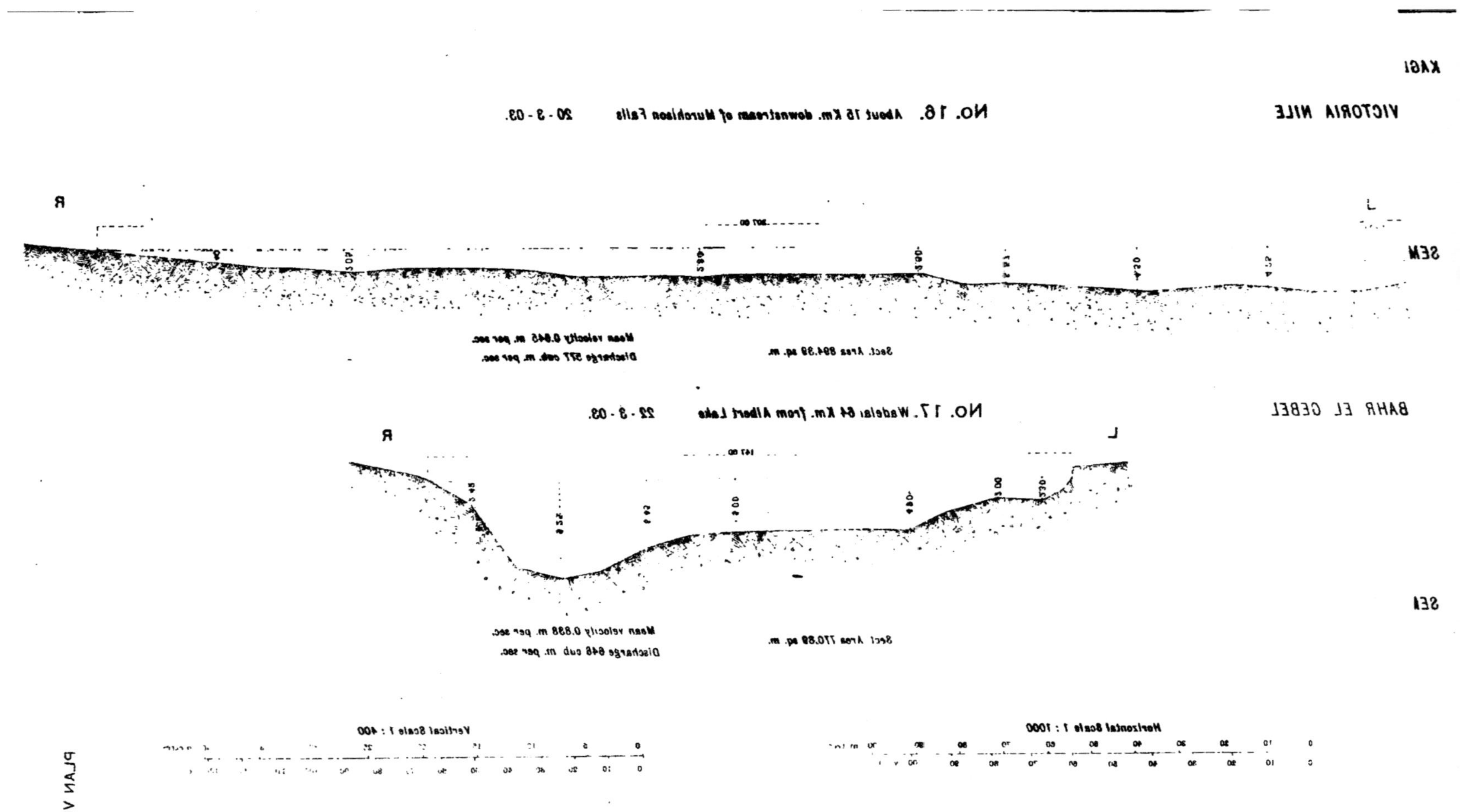
KAGI
VICTORIA NILE
NO. 16. About 15 Km. downstream of Murchison Falls 20 - 3 - 03.
SEM
R
L
Mean velocity 0.645 m. per sec.
Discharge 577 cub. m. per sec.
Sect. Area 894.38 sq. m.
BAHR EL GEBEL
NO. 17. Wadelai 64 Km. from Albert Lake 22 - 3 - 03.
SEA
R
L
Mean velocity 0.838 m. per sec.
Discharge 646 cub. m. per sec.
Sect. Area 770.89 sq. m.
Vertical Scale 1 : 400
Horizontal Scale 1 : 1000

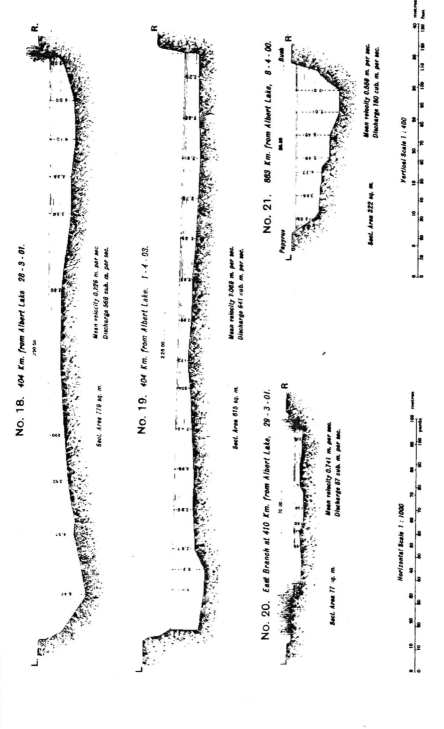

No. 18. *404 Km. from Albert Lake 28 - 3 - 01.*

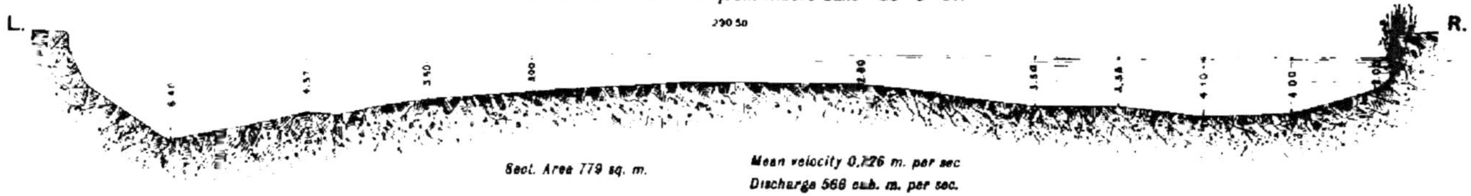

Sect. Area 779 sq. m.

Mean velocity 0.726 m. per sec
Discharge 566 cub. m. per sec.

No. 19. *404 Km. from Albert Lake. 1 - 4 - 03.*

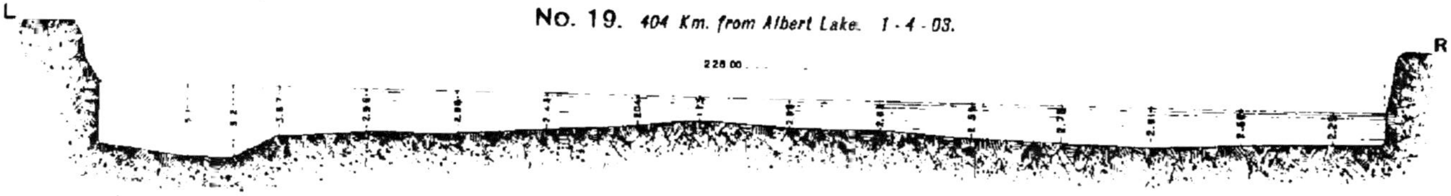

Sect. Area 615 sq. m.

Mean velocity 1.069 m. per sec.
Discharge 641 cub. m. per sec.

No. 20. *East Branch at 410 Km. from Albert Lake, 29 - 3 - 01.*

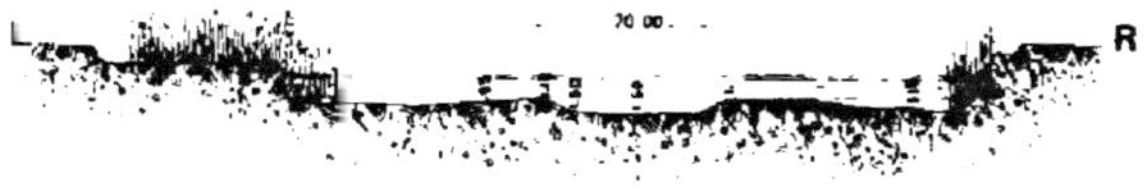

Sect. Area 77 sq. m.

Mean velocity 0.741 m. per sec.
Discharge 57 cub. m. per sec.

No. 21. *883 Km. from Albert Lake, 8 - 4 - 00.*

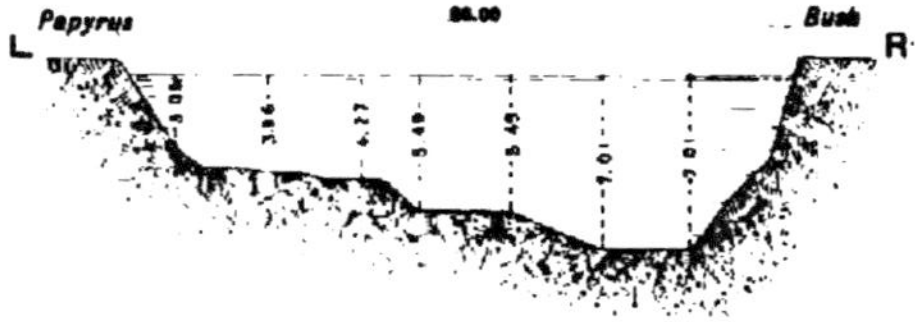

Sect. Area 322 sq. m.

Mean velocity 0.559 m. per sec.
Discharge 180 cub. m. per sec.

Horizontal Scale 1 : 1000

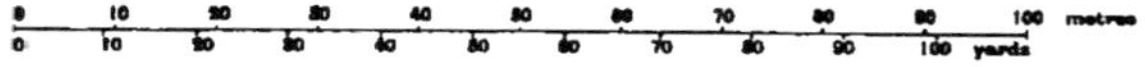

Vertical Scale 1 : 400

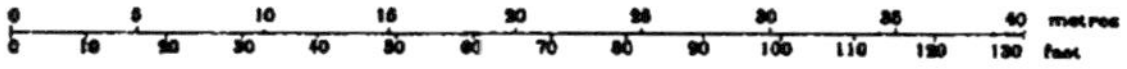

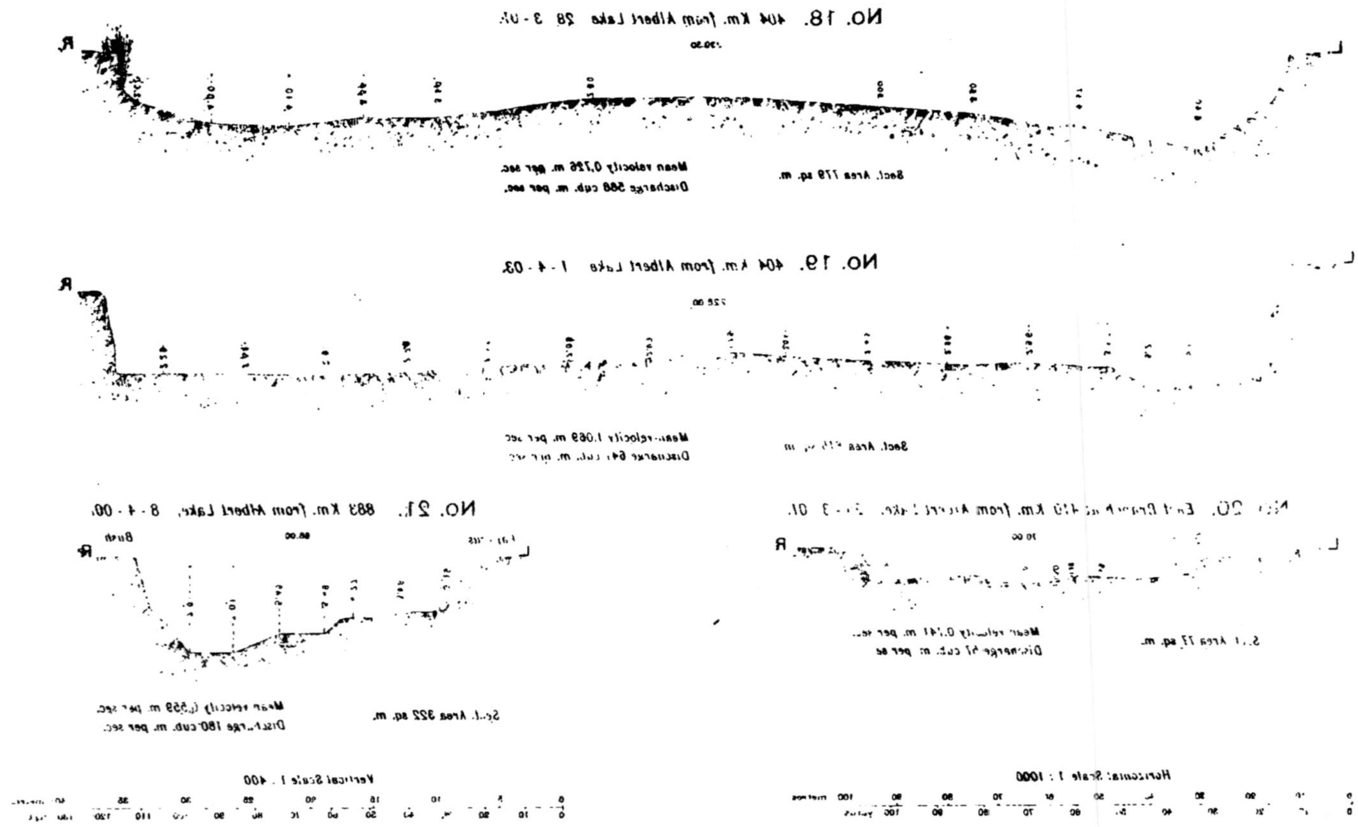
NO. 18. 404 Km. from Albert Lake 28 - 3 - 03.
Mean velocity 0,726 m. per sec.
Discharge 568 cub. m. per sec.
Sect. Area 779 sq. m.
NO. 19. 404 Km. from Albert Lake 1 - 4 - 03.
Mean velocity 1.069 m. per sec.
Sect. Area
NO. 21. 883 Km. from Albert Lake. 8 - 4 - 00.
Bush
Mean velocity 0,559 m. per sec.
Discharge 180 cub. m. per sec.
Sect. Area 322 sq. m.
NO. 20.
Mean velocity 0,741 m. per sec.
Sect. Area 72 sq. m.
Vertical Scale 1 : 400
Horizontal Scale 1 : 1000

BAHR EL GEBEL

. 22. *West Branch 942 Km. from Albert Lake. 20 - 3 - 01.*

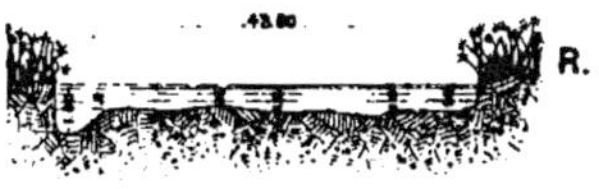

Sect. Area 43,5 sq. m. *Mean velocity 0,505 m. per sec.* *Discharge 22 cub. m. per sec.*

NO. 22. *947 Km. from Albert Lake, 13 - 4 - 03.*

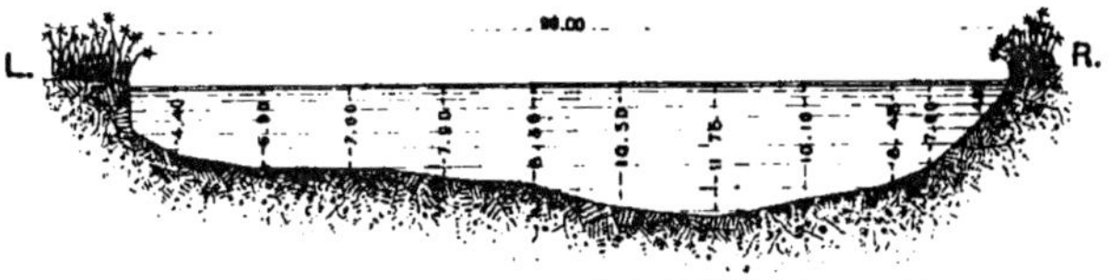

Sect. Area 392 sq. m. *Mean velocity 0.888 m. per sec.* *Discharge 881 cub. m. per sec.*

NO. 23. *1003 Km. from Albert Lake, 1 - 4 - 01.*

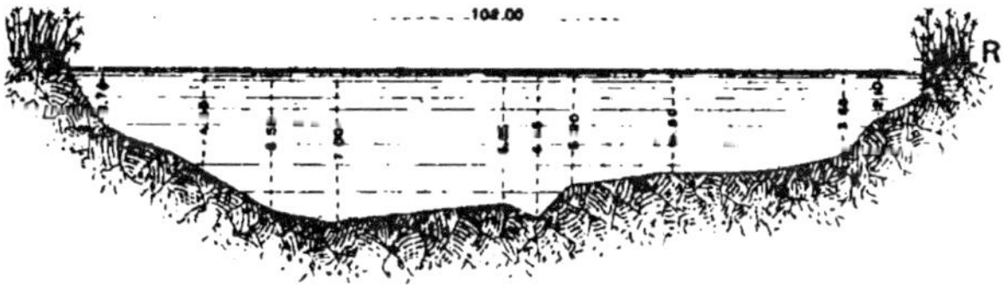

Sect. Area 485 sq. m. *Mean velocity 0.540 m. per sec.* *Discharge 282 cub. m. per sec.*

NO. 24. *1142 Km. from Albert Lake, 14 - 4 - 00.*

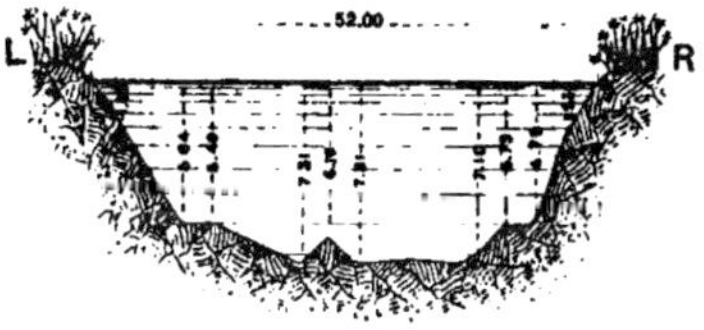

Sect. Area 262 sq. m. *Mean velocity 0.836 m. per sec.* *Discharge 219 cub. m. per sec.*

NO. 25. *1146 Km. from Albert Lake 14 - 4 - 03.*

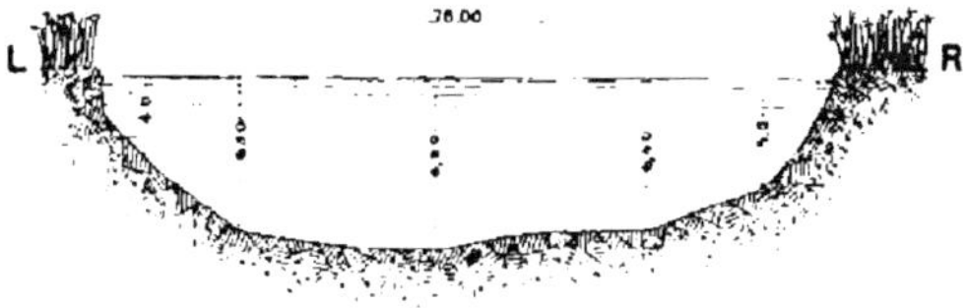

Sect. Area 474 sq. m. *Mean velocity 0.706 m. per sec.* *Discharge [illegible] cub. m. per sec.*

Horizontal Scale 1 : 1000

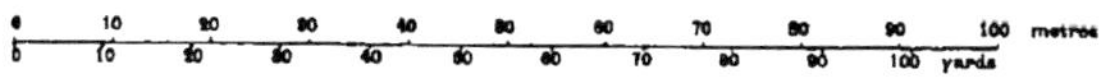

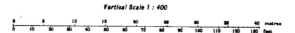

Vertical Scale 1 : 400

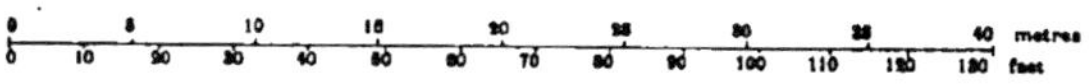

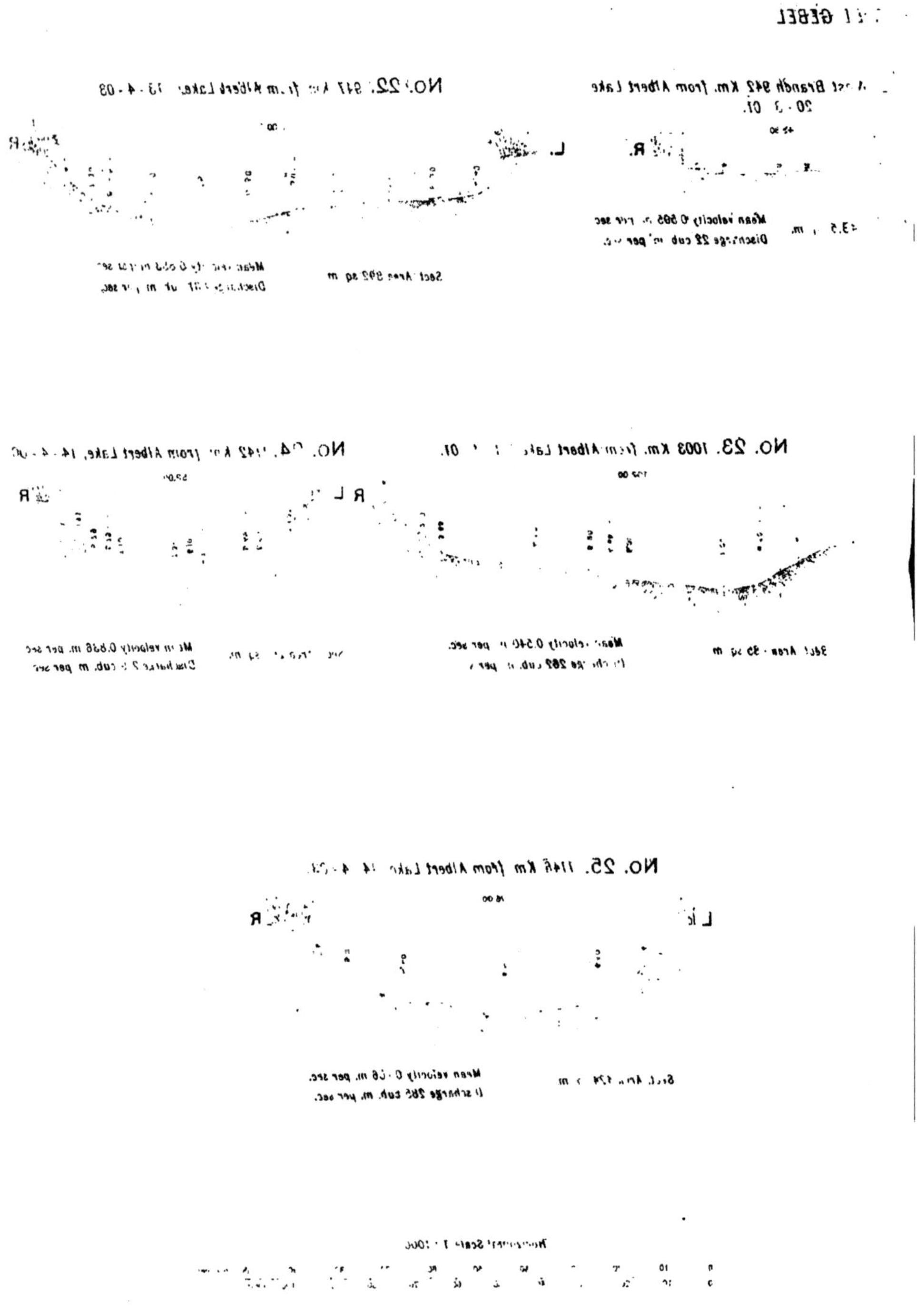

EL GEBEL
NO. 22. 947 Km. from Albert Lake
Sect. Area 992 sq. m.
West Branch 942 Km. from Albert Lake
20 - 3 - 07.
Mean velocity 0.595 m. per sec.
Discharge 22 cub. m. per sec.
NO. 23. 1003 Km. from Albert Lake
Sect. Area 95 sq. m.
Mean velocity 0.540 m. per sec.
NO. 24. 1142 Km. from Albert Lake, 14 - 4 - 06
NO. 25. 1146 Km. from Albert Lake
Sect. Area 524 sq. m.
Mean velocity 0.56 m. per sec.
Discharge 285 cub. m. per sec.
Horizontal Scale 1 : 1000

BAHR EL GEBEL

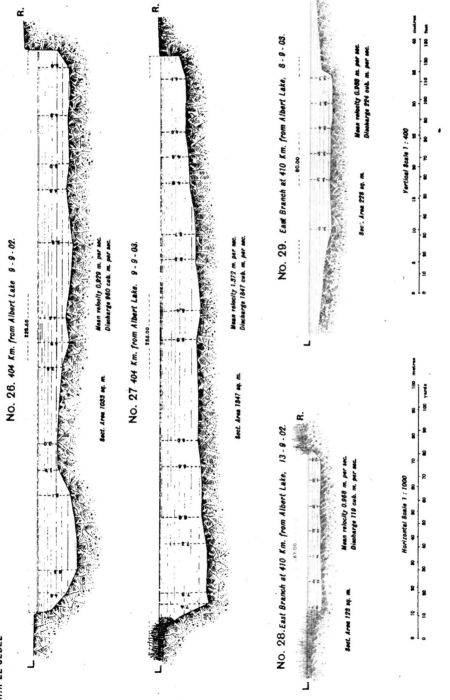

No. 26. *404 Km. from Albert Lake 9 - 9 - 02.*

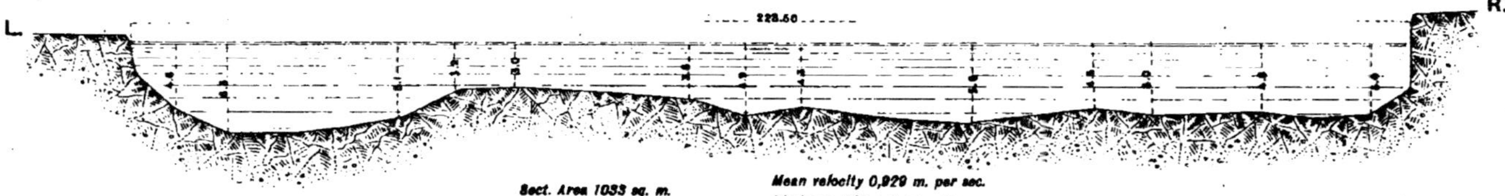

Sect. Area 1033 sq. m.

Mean velocity 0,929 m. per sec.
Discharge 960 cub. m. per sec.

No. 27 *404 Km. from Albert Lake. 9 - 9 - 03.*

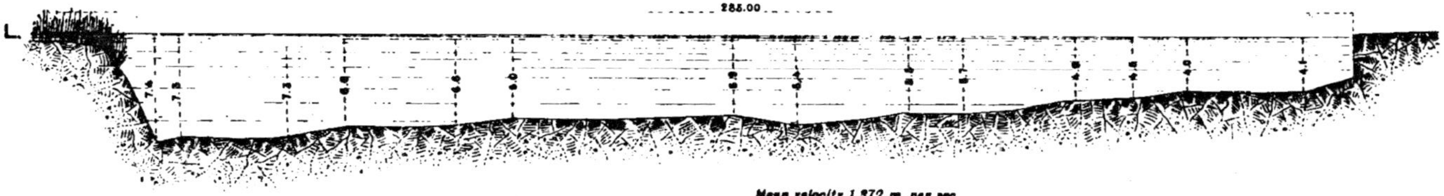

Sect. Area 1847 sq. m.

Mean velocity 1.372 m. per sec.
Discharge 1847 cub. m. per sec.

No. 28. *East Branch at 410 Km. from Albert Lake, 13 - 9 - 02.*

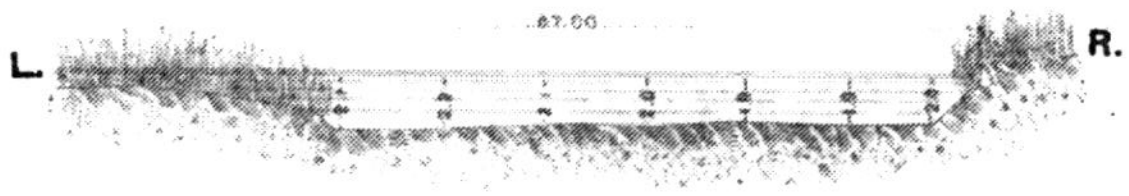

Sect. Area 123 sq. m.

Mean velocity 0.968 m. per sec.
Discharge 119 cub. m. per sec.

No. 29. *East Branch at 410 Km. from Albert Lake, 8 - 9 - 03.*

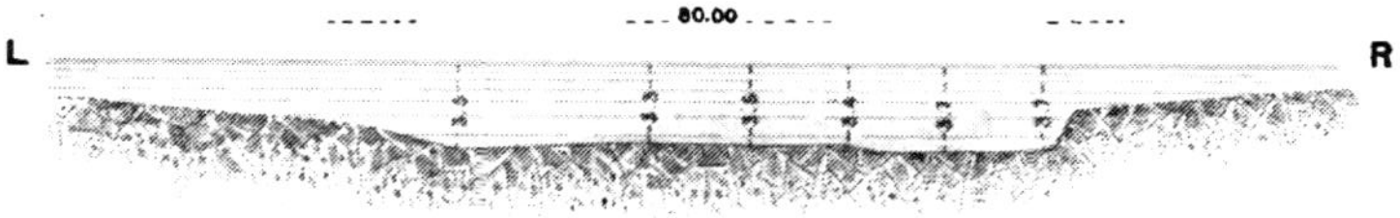

Sect. Area 228 sq. m.

Mean velocity 0.988 m. per sec.
Discharge 224 cub. m. per sec.

Horizontal Scale 1 : 1000

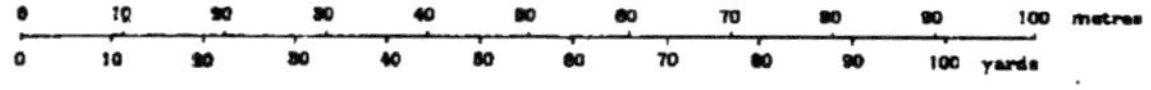

Vertical Scale 1 : 400

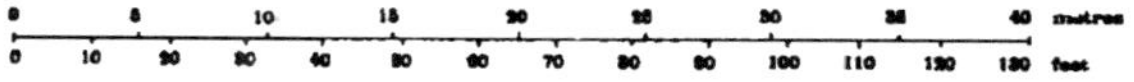

PLAN VIII. g.

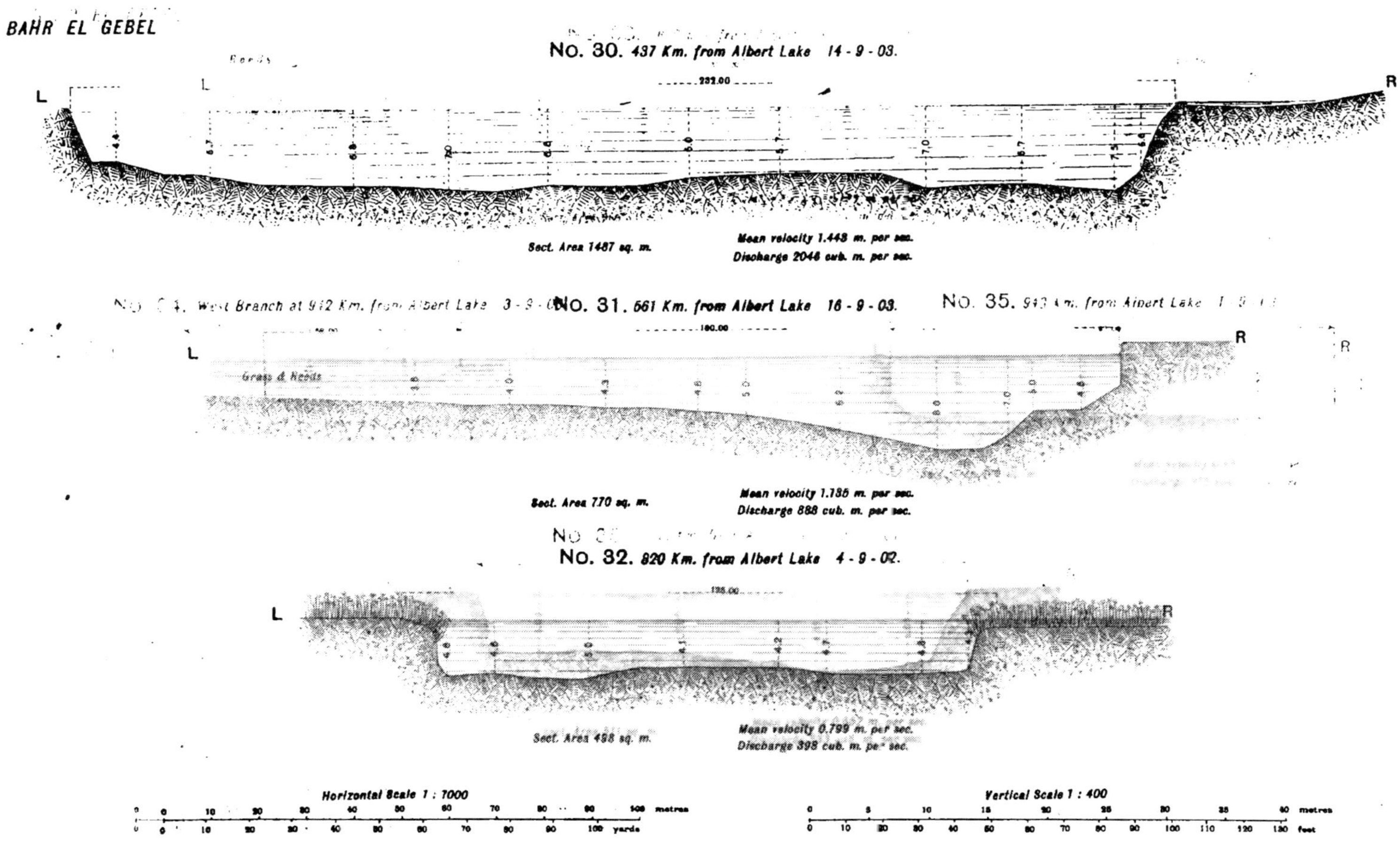
BAHR EL GEBEL
NO. 30. 437 Km. from Albert Lake 14 - 9 - 03.
232.00
Sect. Area 1487 sq. m.
Mean velocity 1.443 m. per sec.
Discharge 2046 cub. m. per sec.
NO. 31. 561 Km. from Albert Lake 16 - 9 - 03.
160.00
Grass & Reeds
Sect. Area 770 sq. m.
Mean velocity 1.135 m. per sec.
Discharge 888 cub. m. per sec.
NO. 32. 820 Km. from Albert Lake 4 - 9 - 02.
Sect. Area 498 sq. m.
Mean velocity 0.799 m. per sec.
Discharge 398 cub. m. per sec.
Horizontal Scale 1 : 7000
metres
yards
Vertical Scale 1 : 400
metres
feet

PLAN VIII. h.

BAHR EL GEBEL

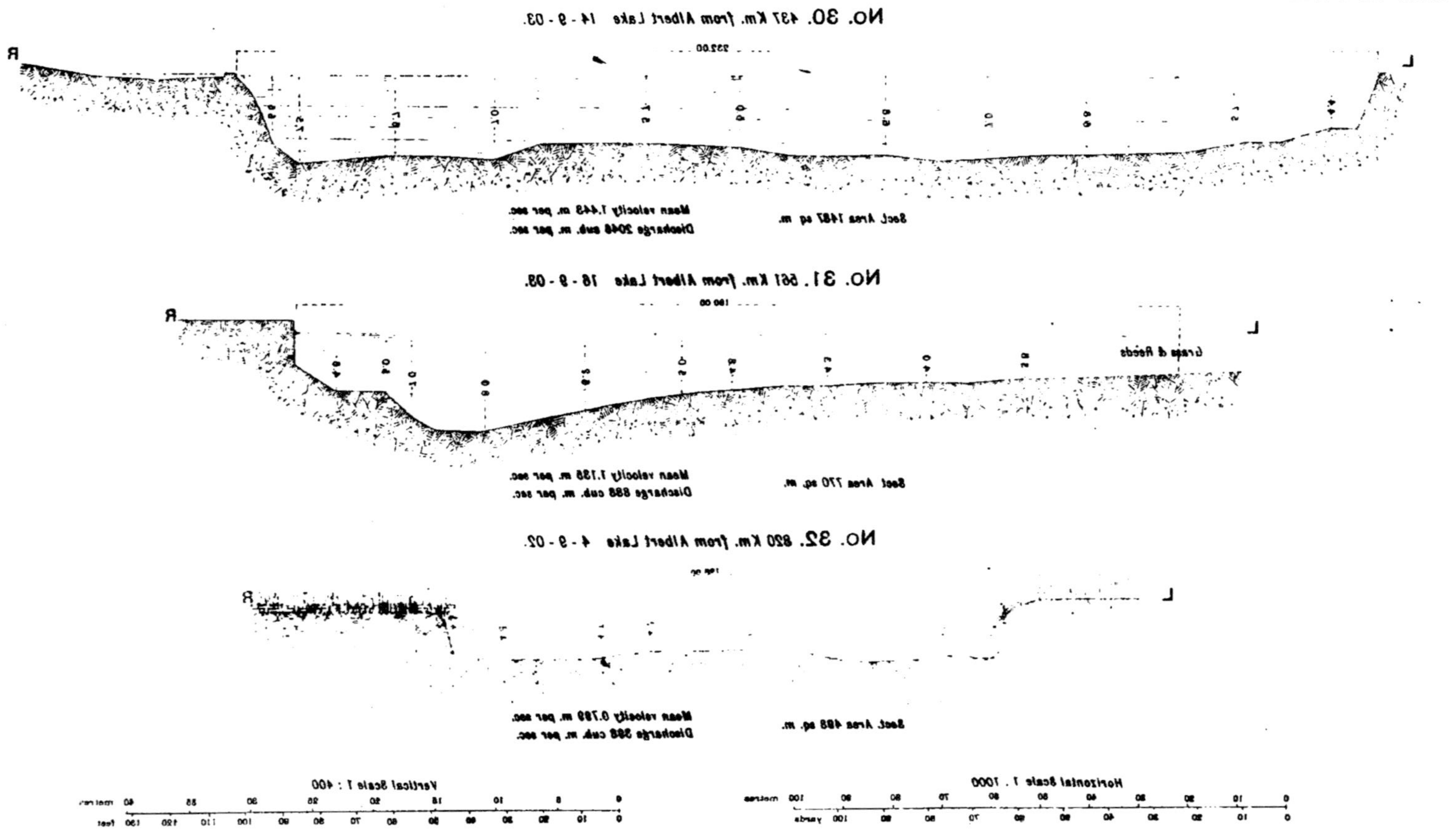

BAHR EL GEBEL

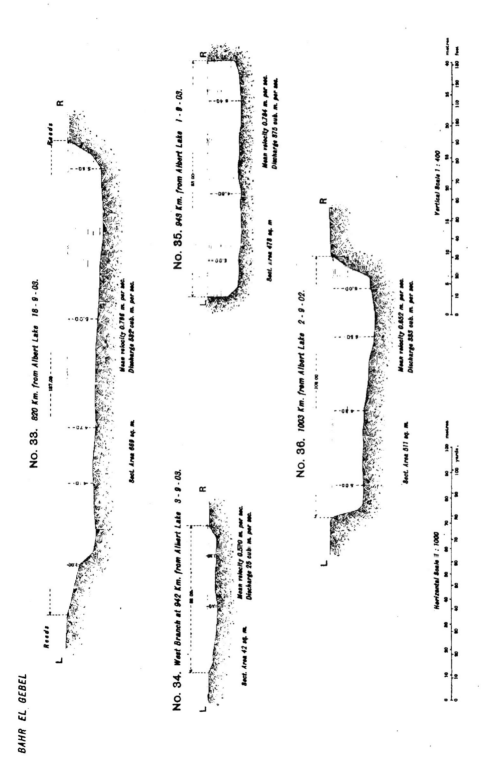

NO. 33. *820 Km. from Albert Lake 18 - 9 - 03.*

Sect. Area 669 sq. m.

Mean velocity 0.796 m. per sec.
Discharge 532 cub. m. per sec.

NO. 34. *West Branch at 942 Km. from Albert Lake 3 - 9 - 03.*

Sect. Area 42 sq. m.

Mean velocity 0.520 m. per sec.
Discharge 25 cub. m. per sec.

NO. 35. *943 Km. from Albert Lake 1 - 9 - 03.*

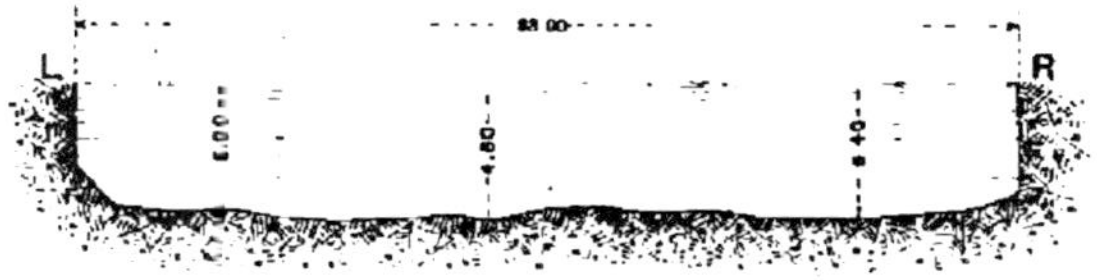

Sect. Area 478 sq. m

Mean velocity 0.784 m. per sec.
Discharge 375 cub. m. per sec.

NO. 36. *1003 Km. from Albert Lake 2 - 9 - 02.*

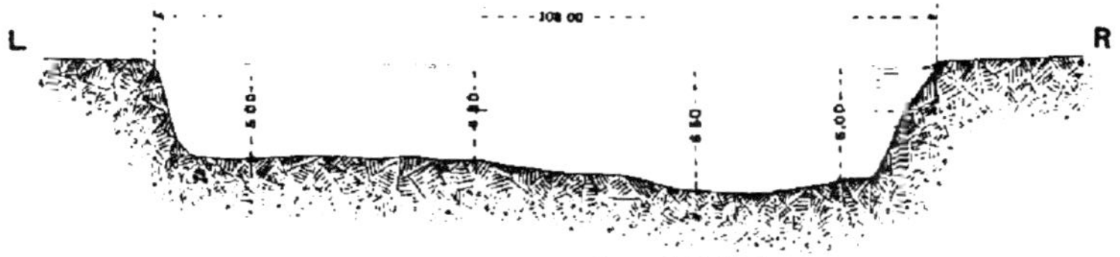

Sect. Area 511 sq. m.

Mean velocity 0.652 m. per sec.
Discharge 333 cub. m. per sec.

Horizontal Scale 1 : 1000

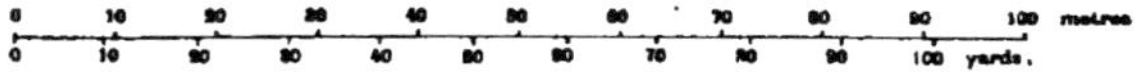

Vertical Scale 1 : 400

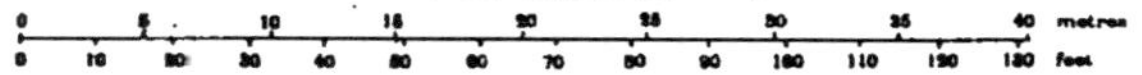

PLAN VIII. i.

BAHR EL GEBEL

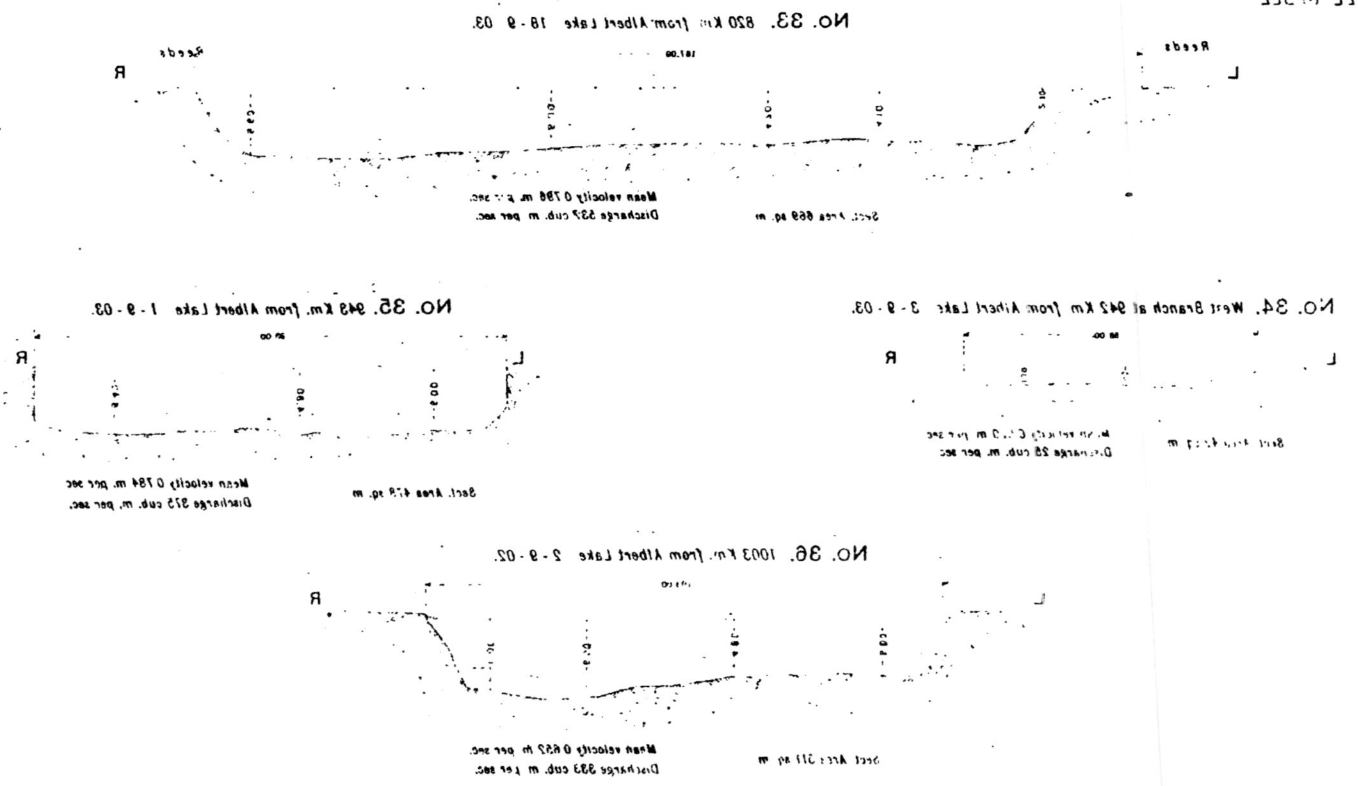

BAHR EL GEBEL

No. 37. *1147 Km. from Albert Lake. 31-8-03.*

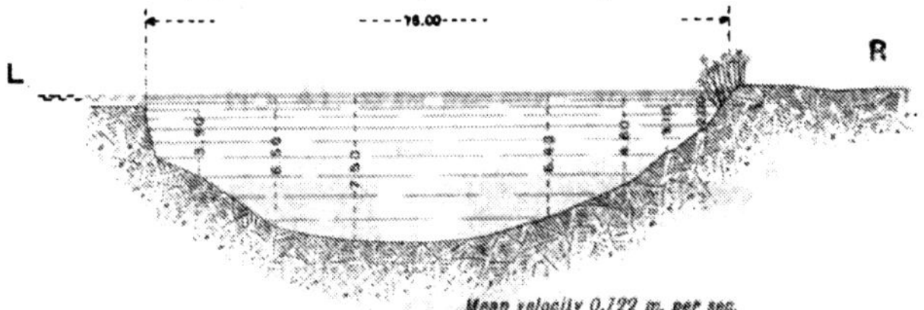

Sect. Area 441 sq. m.

Mean velocity 0.722 m. per sec.
Discharge 318 cub. m. per sec.

BAHR EL GHAZAL

No. 38. *51 Km. from mouth 1-4-00.*

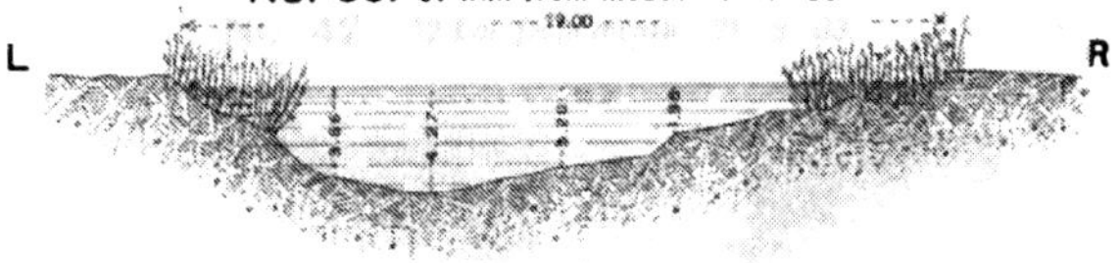

Sect. Area 161 sq. m.

Mean velocity 0.211 m. per sec.
Discharge 34 cub. m. per sec.

No. 39. *50 Km. from mouth 15-4-03.*

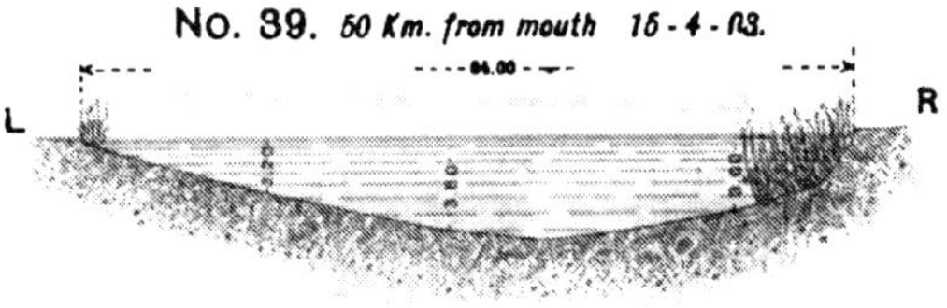

Sect. Area 200 sq. m.

Mean velocity 0.195 m. per sec.
Discharge 23 cub. m. per sec.

No. 40. *33 Km. from mouth 2-4-01.*

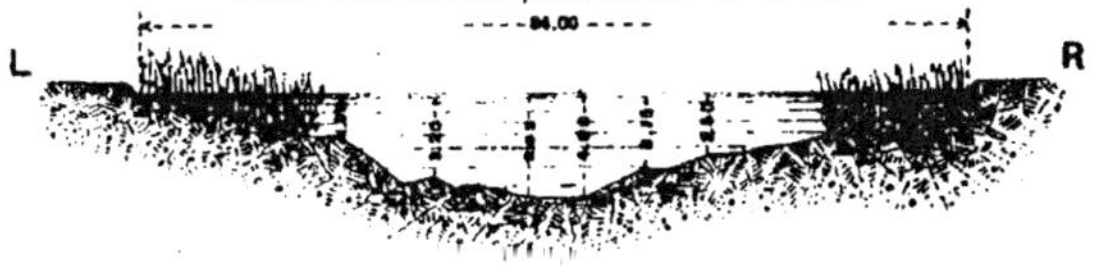

Sect. Area 149 sq. m

Mean velocity 0.181 m. per sec.
Discharge 27 cub. m. per sec.

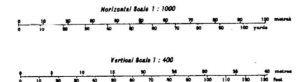

Horizontal Scale 1 : 1000

Vertical Scale 1 : 400

No. 37. 1147 Km. from Albert Lake 31-8-03.

Mean velocity 0.722 m. per sec.
Discharge 318 cub. m. per sec.

Sect. Area 441 sq. m.

BAHR EL GHAZAL

No. 38. 51 Km. from mouth 1-4-00

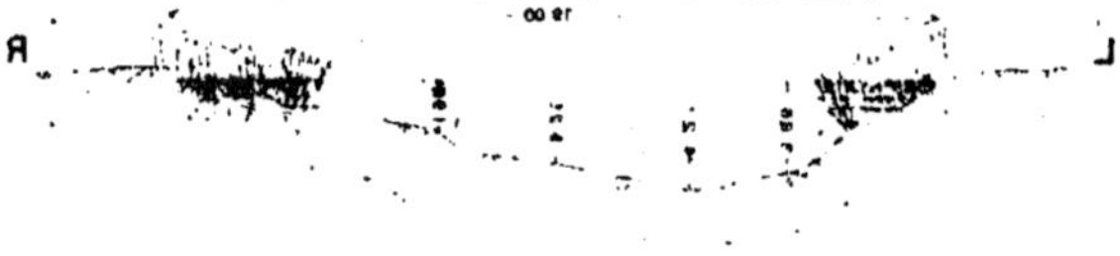

Mean velocity 0.211 m. per sec.
Discharge 34 cub. m. per sec.

Sect. Area 161 sq. m.

No. 39. 50 Km. from mouth 15-4-03.

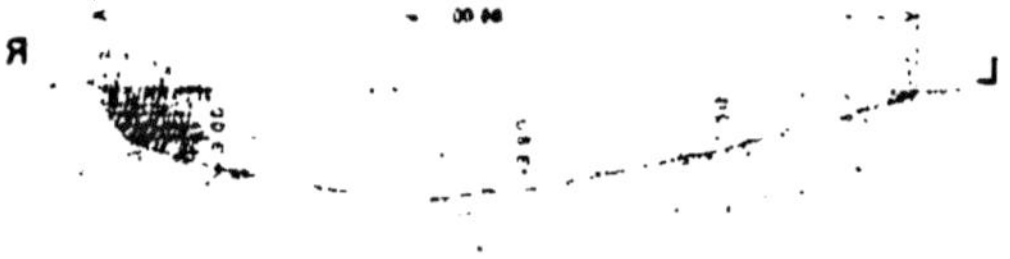

Mean velocity 0.195 m. per sec.
Discharge 23 cub. m. per sec.

Sect. Area 200 sq. m.

No. 40. 33 Km. from mouth 2-4-01.

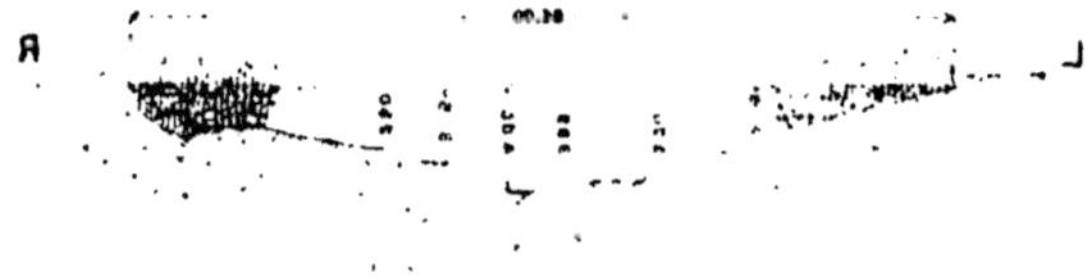

Mean velocity 0.181 m. per sec.
Discharge 27 cub. m. per sec.

Sect. Area 149 sq. m.

Horizontal Scale 1 : 1000

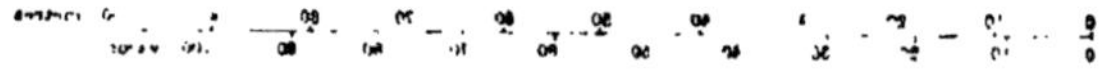

Vertical Scale 1 : 400

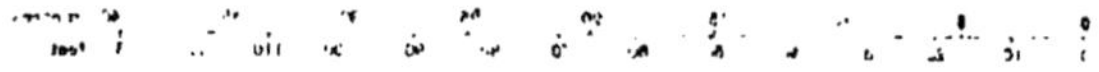

BAHR EL GHAZAL

No. 41. *33 Km. from mouth 31 - 8 - 02.*

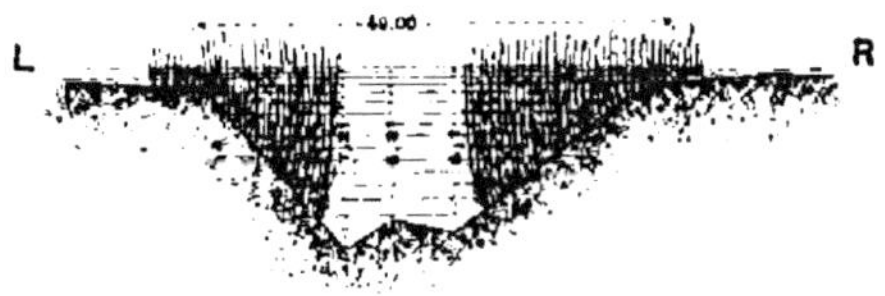

Sect. Area 88 sq. m.

Mean velocity 0.172 m. per sec.
Discharge 15 cub. m. per sec.

No. 42. *32 Km. from mouth 21 - 9 - 03.*

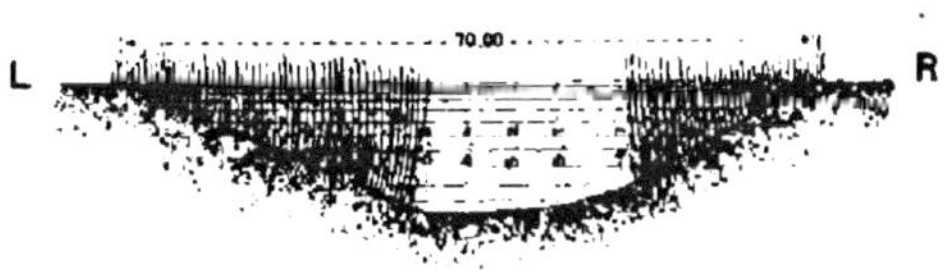

Sect. Area 104 sq. m.

Mean velocity 0.192 m. per sec.
Discharge 20 cub. m. per sec.

No. 43. *28 Km. from mouth 30 - 8 - 03.*

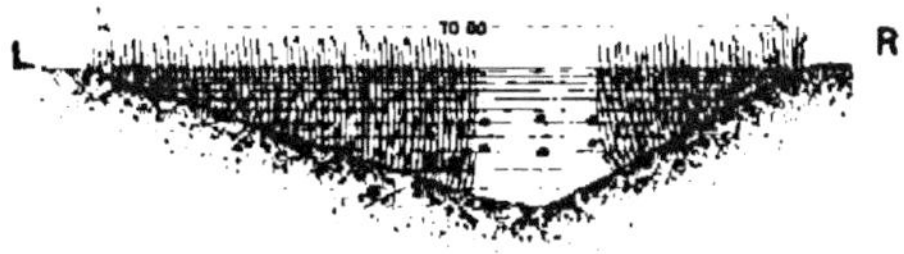

Sect. Area 52 sq. m.

Mean velocity 0.231 m. per sec.
Discharge 12 cub. m. per sec.

Horizontal Scale 1 : 1000

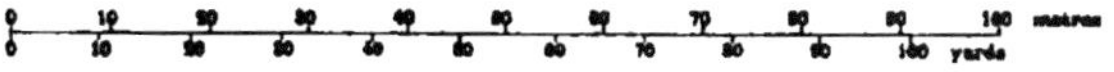

Vertical Scale 1 : 400

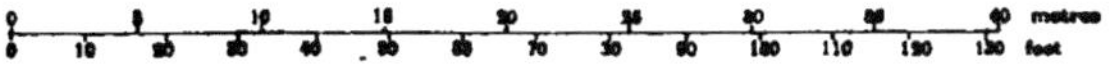

BAHR EL ZARAF

NO. 44 *96 Km. from mouth 25 - 3 - 00.*

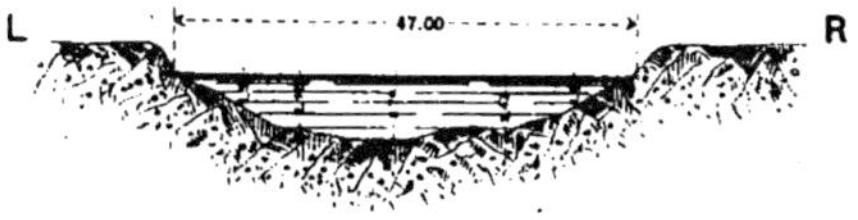

Sect. Area 91 sq. m.

Mean velocity 0.353 m. per sec.
Discharge 32 cub. m. per sec.

NO. 45. *About 20 Km. from mouth 16 - 4 - 03.*

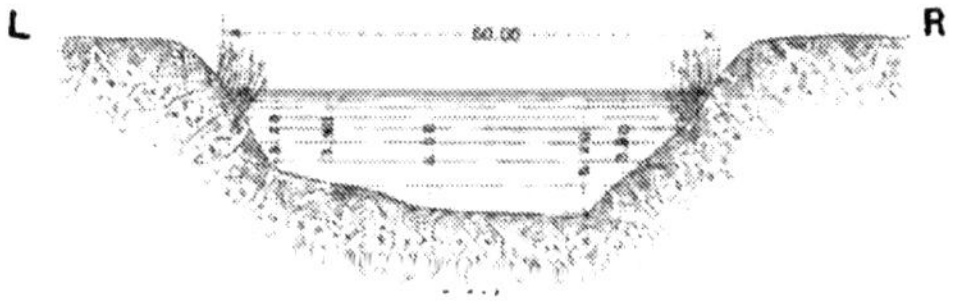

Sect. Area 179 sq. m.

Mean velocity 0.304 m. per sec.
Discharge 50 cub. m. per sec.

NO. 46. *19 Km. from mouth 3 - 4 - 01.*

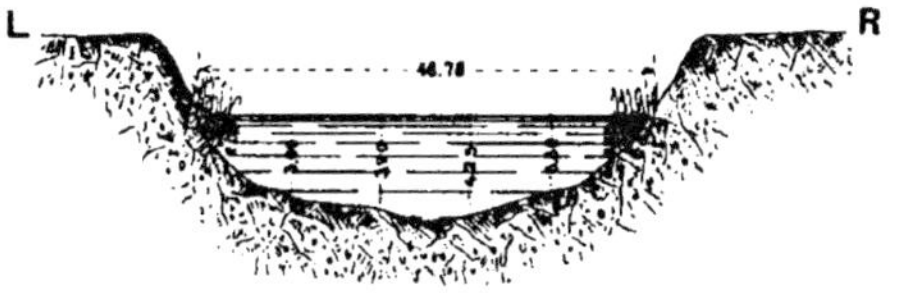

Sect. Area 138 sq. m.

Mean velocity 0.239 m. per sec.
Discharge 33 cub. m. per sec.

NO. 47. *20 Km. from mouth 22 - 9 - 03.*

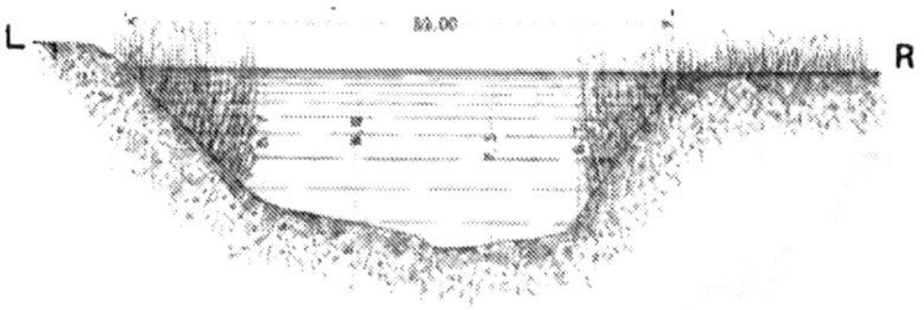

Sect. Area 232 sq. m.

Mean velocity 0.658 m. per sec.
Discharge 158 cub. m. per sec.

Horizontal Scale 1 : 1000

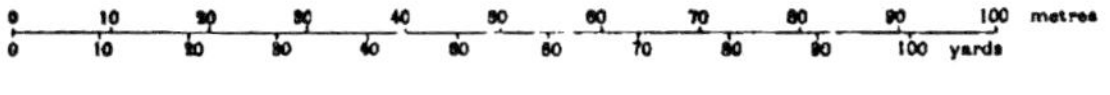

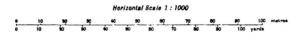

Vertical Scale 1 : 400

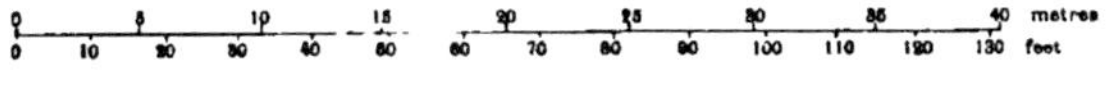

PLAN VIII. m.

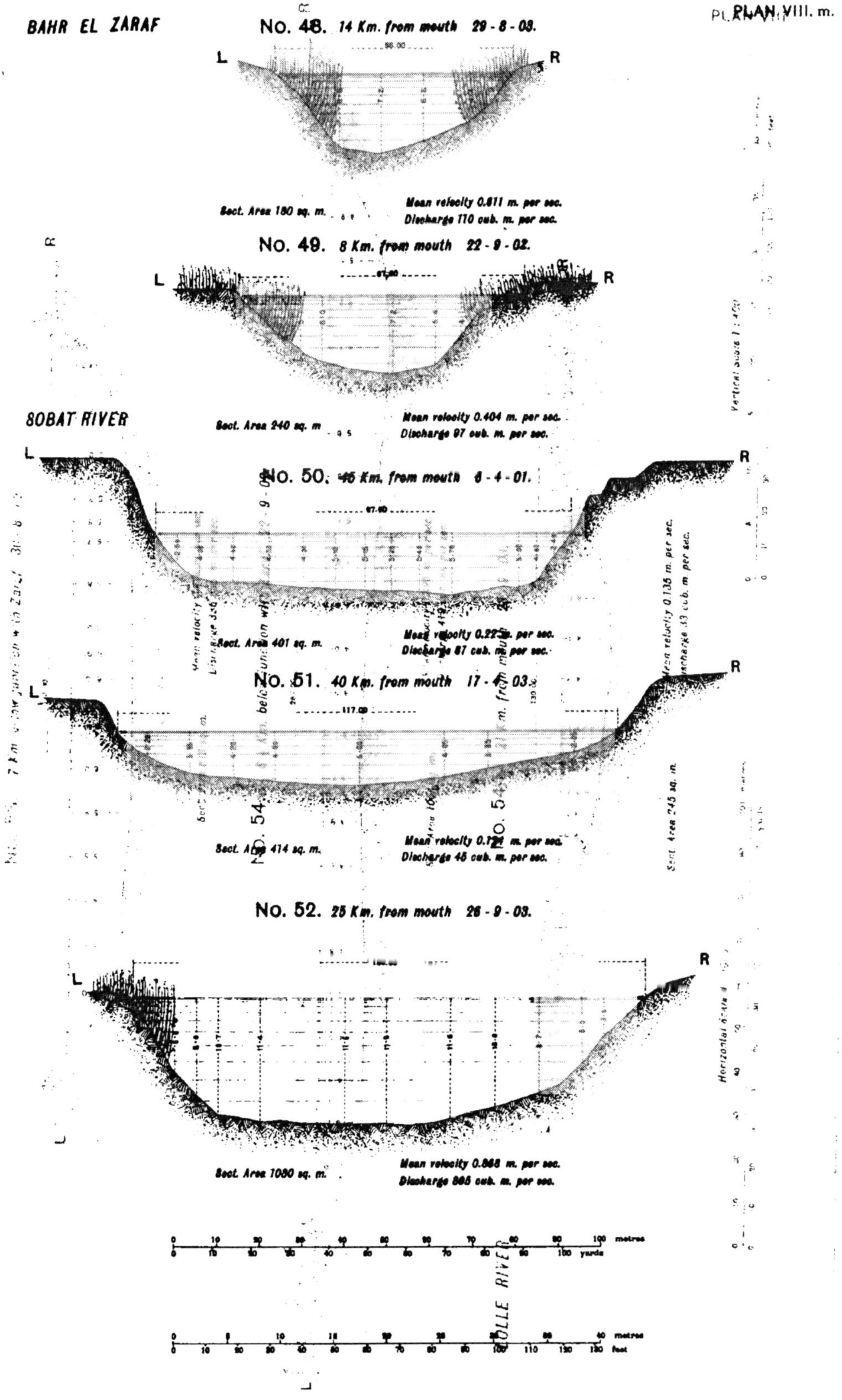
BAHR EL ZARAF
No. 48. 14 Km. from mouth 29 - 8 - 03.
L
R
Sect. Area 180 sq. m.
Mean velocity 0.611 m. per sec.
Discharge 110 cub. m. per sec.
No. 49. 8 Km. from mouth 22 - 9 - 02.
L
R
Sect. Area 240 sq. m
Mean velocity 0.404 m. per sec.
Discharge 97 cub. m. per sec.
SOBAT RIVER
No. 50. 45 Km. from mouth 6 - 4 - 01.
L
R
Sect. Area 401 sq. m.
Mean velocity 0.22 m. per sec.
Discharge 87 cub. m. per sec.
No. 51. 40 Km. from mouth 17 - 4 - 03.
L
R
117.00
Sect. Area 414 sq. m.
Mean velocity 0.1 m. per sec.
Discharge 45 cub. m. per sec.
No. 52. 25 Km. from mouth 26 - 9 - 03.
L
R
Sect. Area 1050 sq. m.
Mean velocity 0.868 m. per sec.
Discharge 885 cub. m. per sec.
0 10 20 30 40 50 60 70 80 90 100 metres
0 10 20 30 40 50 60 70 80 90 100 yards
0 5 10 15 20 25 30 35 40 metres
0 10 20 30 40 50 60 70 80 90 100 110 120 130 feet
Vertical Scale 1 : 400
Horizontal Scale

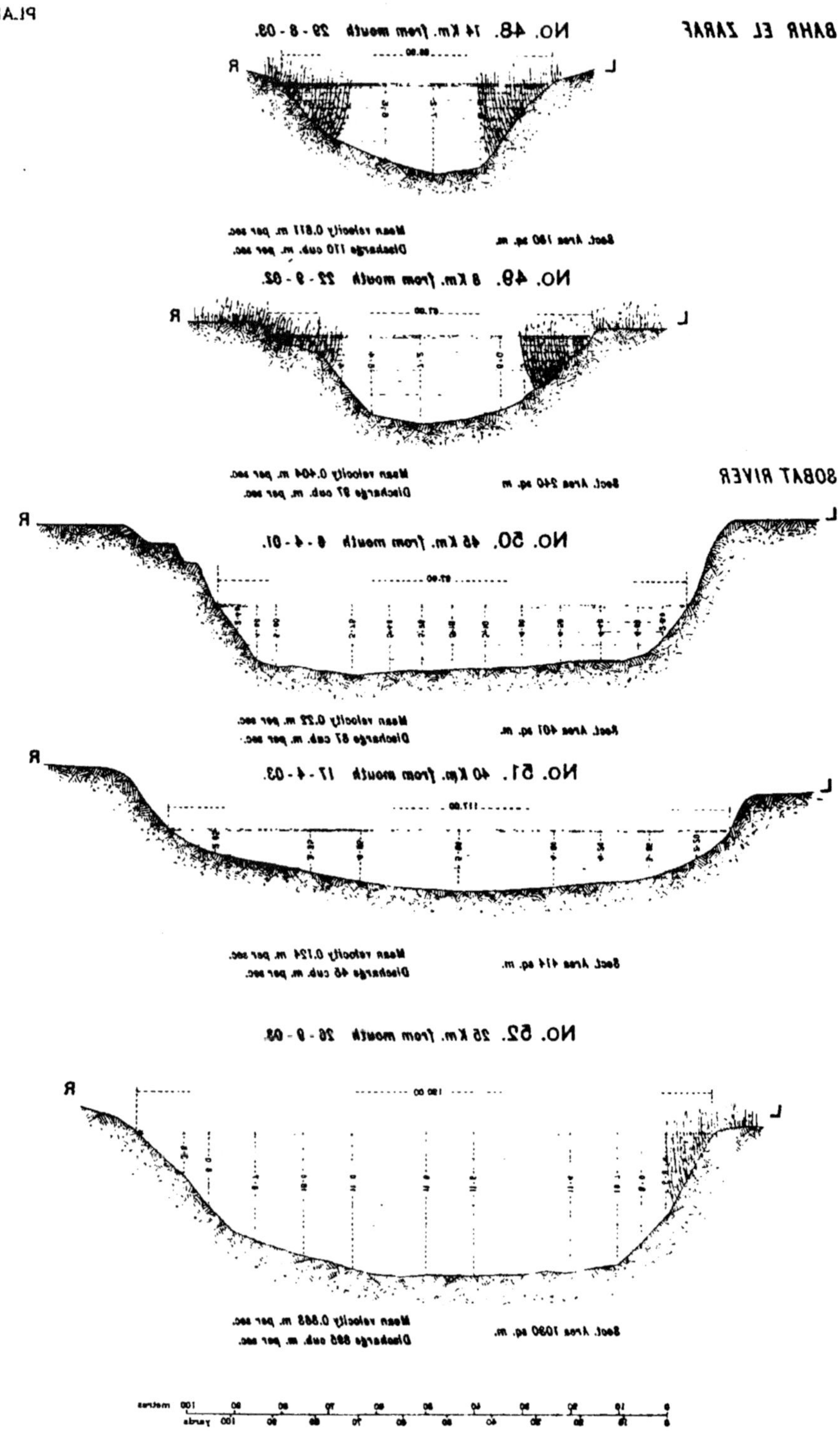

PLAN
BAHR EL ZARAF
NO. 48. 14 Km. from mouth 29-8-03.
R
L
Mean velocity 0.611 m. per sec.
Discharge 110 cub. m. per sec.
Sect. Area 180 sq. m.
NO. 49. 8 Km. from mouth 22-9-02.
R
L
Mean velocity 0.404 m. per sec.
Discharge 97 cub. m. per sec.
Sect. Area 240 sq. m
SOBAT RIVER
NO. 50. 45 Km. from mouth 6-4-01.
R
L
Mean velocity 0.22 m. per sec.
Discharge 87 cub. m. per sec.
Sect. Area 401 sq. m.
NO. 51. 40 Km. from mouth 17-4-03.
R
L
Mean velocity 0.124 m. per sec.
Discharge 45 cub. m. per sec.
Sect. Area 414 sq. m.
NO. 52. 25 Km. from mouth 26-9-03.
R
L
Mean velocity 0.858 m. per sec.
Discharge 885 cub. m. per sec.
Sect. Area 1030 sq. m.
metres
yards

WHITE NILE

No. 53. *7 Km. below junction with Zaraf 30 - 8 - 02.*

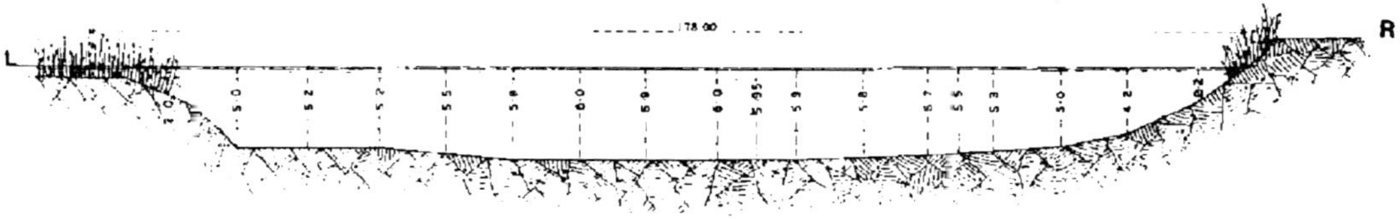

Sect. Area 813 sq. m.

Mean velocity 0.414 m. per sec.
Discharge 336 cub. m. per sec.

No. 54.a. *6 ½ Km. below junction with Zaraf 22 - 9 - 02.*

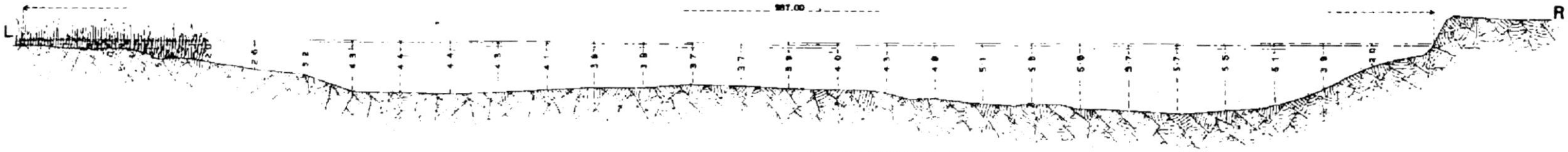

Sect. Area 1054 sq m.

Mean velocity 0.398 m. per sec.
Discharge 419 cub. m. per sec.

LOLLE RIVER

No. 54.b. *21 Km. from mouth 23 - 9 - 03.*

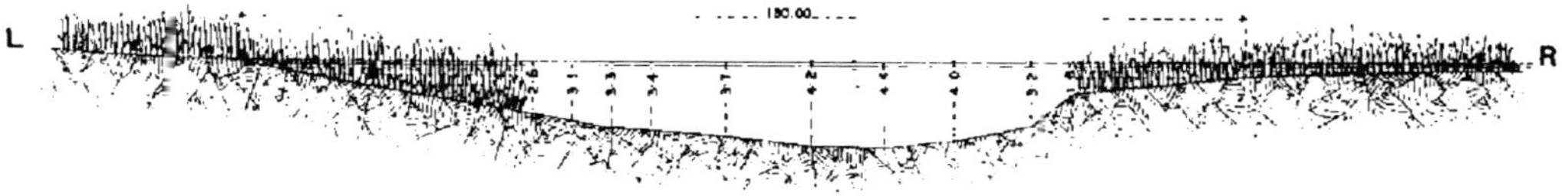

Sect. Area 245 sq. m.

Mean velocity 0.135 m. per sec.
Discharge 33 cub. m. per sec.

Horizontal Scale 1 : 1000

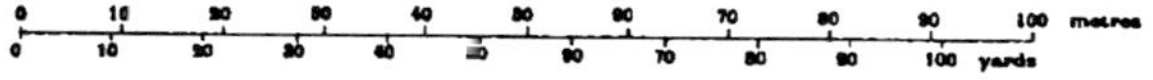

Vertical Scale 1 : 400

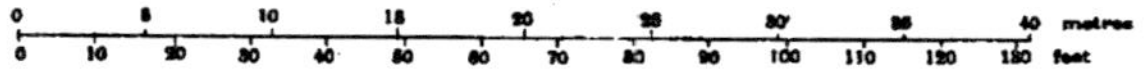

PLAN VIII. n.

WHITE NILE

PLAN VIII.o.

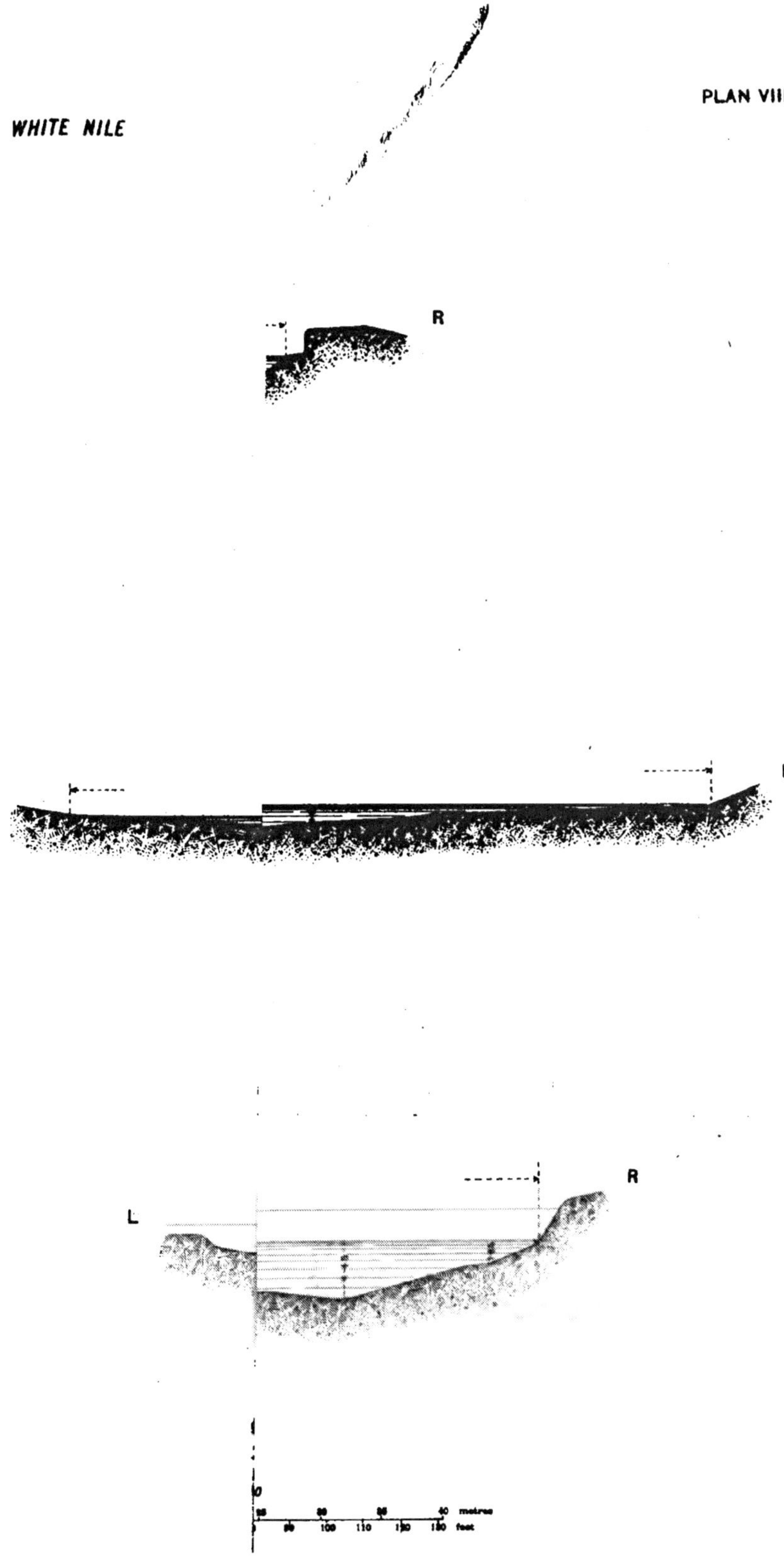

WHITE NILE

No. 55.

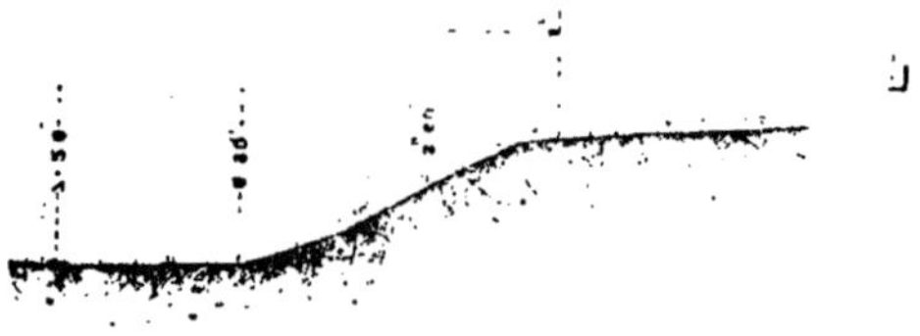

Sect. Area

No. 56.

Sect. Area

No. 57.

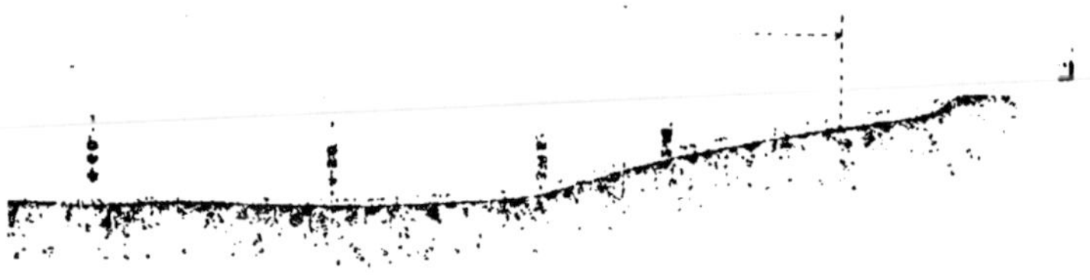

Sect. Area

Horizontal Scale 1 : 1000

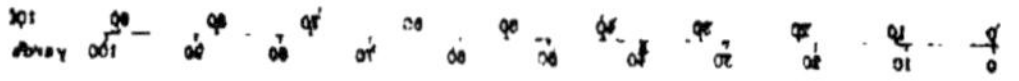

PLAN VIII. p.

WHITE NILE

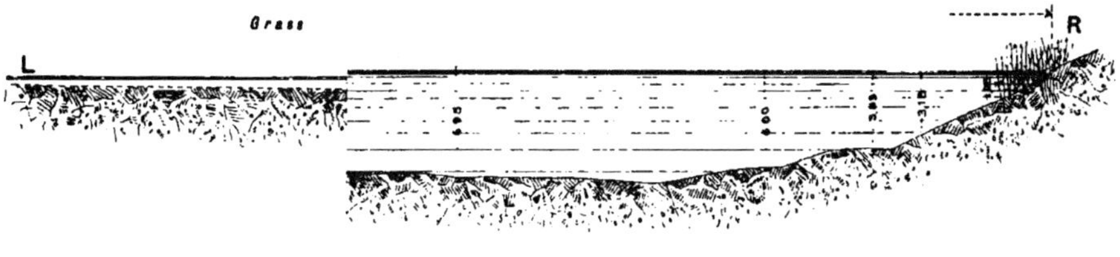

Vertical Scale 1 : 400

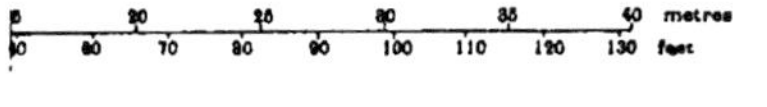

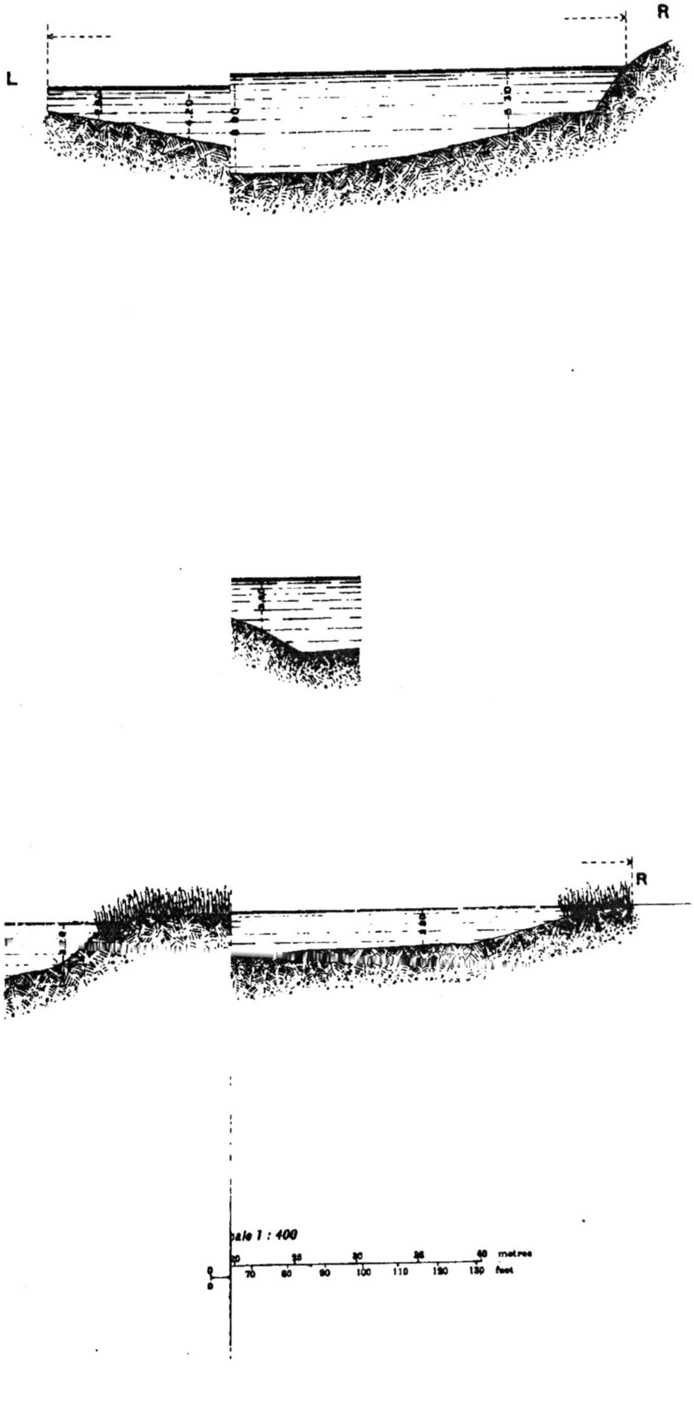

PLAN VIII. q.

No. 6C

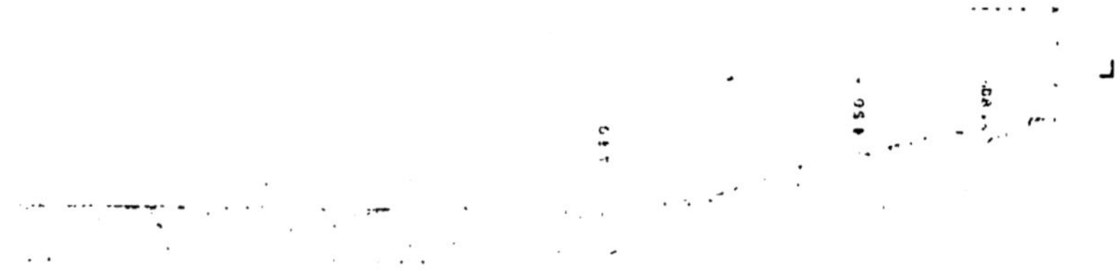

No. 6

R

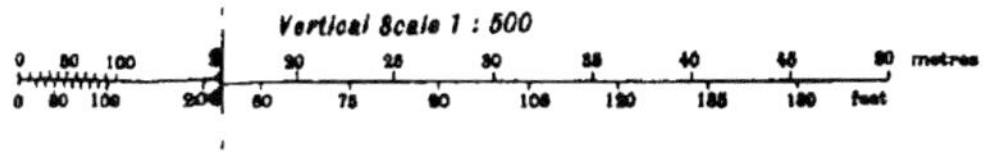

REPORT UPON LAKE TSANA

AND

THE RIVERS OF THE EASTERN SOUDAN

BY

Mr. C. DUPUIS
Egyptian Irrigation Service.

REPORT BY MR. C. E. DUPUIS.

GENERAL REPORT ON THE JOURNEY.

I received orders to prepare for the expedition in October 1902, the date by which the expedition should reach the Abyssinian border being given as December 15th.

The objects of the expedition as explained to me by Sir William Garstin were:

(1) To visit and collect all possible information concerning Lake Tsana in Abyssinia with a view to deciding whether it could be effectively utilized as a reservoir for the Nile, should such a proposal ever come within the range of practical politics.

(2) To examine the rivers Atbara, Settit and Salaam as far as possible in the time available, taking discharge observations and cross sections whenever the opportunity offered, with a view to determining the actual existing conditions of those rivers, and the possibility of utilizing their waters.

(3) To examine the conditions and irrigation possibilities of the River Gash at Kassala.

(4) To look at the waste culturable lands near the Nile and Athara in the neighbourhood or Berber, and report on existing conditions and the possibility of constructing irrigation works.

(5) To arrange if possible to erect a gauge and reporting station on the River Atbara where the Gedaref-Kassala telegraph line crosses it near Fasher.

The European party composing the expedition consisted of myself in charge, assisted by Mr. C. G. Crawley, with Dr. A. J. Hayes as Medical Officer.

Owing to some delay in the correspondence with Colonel Harrington concerning the Emperor Menelik's permission, the expedition did not leave Cairo till the 26th of November and reached Khartum on December 3rd.

After two or three days spent in completing arrangements we left Khartum on December 6th, and marched up the right bank of the Blue Nile to Abu Haraz, a distance of one hundred and twenty miles, in six days.

This portion of the journey might have been done by steamer, but, as there was some uncertainty in Cairo about the condition of the river, camels had been arranged for, and the arrangement was adhered to.

By marching in this way a better idea of the country was obtained than would have been possible from the steamer, but observations were necessarily limited to a narrow strip along one side of the river, and I was only able to obtain hearsay information concerning the very interesting Gezireh tract, which every one seems to be agreed is the most prosperous and promising area in this part of the Soudan, and offers the most likely field for remunerative irrigation works on a large scale.

But I may say that everything I heard about the Gezireh makes it seem probable that a large canal system could be introduced there without much difficulty, and that the whole area is, comparatively speaking, so well populated, and contains so many considerable villages with wells and large areas of cultivation, that there is every reason to hope that the introduction of a dependable canal system to assist, if not to replace, the light and precarious rainfall, would be followed by rapid and striking developments.

It it impossible to estimate the difficulties or cost of any such scheme without an elaborate survey involving a great deal of levelling work, but it seems probable that a large canal could be constructed at reasonable cost, taking off the Blue Nile somewhere near Sennaar and running down through the heart of the Gezireh to Khartum; such a canal could be used for six months in the year, from say July 1st to the end of December, without affecting the Nile supply to an extent that would be injurious to Egypt, to the immense benefit of the area served; under present conditions a perennial supply is out of the question, but that is a further development that would involve larger and more expensive works, and can well afford to wait.

The country adjacent to the Blue Nile along its right bank, through which our route lay, forms part of the Gezireh Mudirieh for administrative purposes, and though generally regarded as of small value or account compared to the richer tract of the Gezireh proper, nevertheless struck me as fairly well peopled and prosperous, and as containing vast possibilities of development.

In the immediate neighbourhood of Halfaya the country is practically desert, but the soil does not seem to be by any means hopelessly sterile, and, marching southwards, it improves rapidly.

Generally speaking the Blue Nile has no wide level berm lands at about flood level, such as are found in other places along the Nile, and lend themselves so well to the formation of basins : the river runs in an eroding section with a fringe of broken raviney ground, lightly covered with bush and scrub, and about a mile wide on either side; the ravines are shallow and ill-defined, and lead up on to an immense level plain extending as far as can be seen; this plain is generally about fifteen metres feet above flood level, and very large tracts of it are cultivated with "rain-crops" of durra (sorghum), the success of which depends absolutely on the very uncertain rainfall; this year these crops seem to have done well in this Mudirieh.

The great level plain above the ravines is generally nearly bare, but is lightly covered with grass and scrub in places, the amount of vegetation increasing as you proceed southwards. The soil is almost entirely cracked black cotton soil and looks, and apparently is, extremely fertile.

Excepting the purely local ravines there are no defined tributary streams falling into the Blue Nile between Halfaya and the mouth of the Rahad at Abu Haraz, but one or two well-defined depressions do apparently run a long distance back into the upper plain lands, and these probably carry a considerable flow of water at times of unusually heavy rainfall.

Villages are numerous and are generally situated at the top of the ravines, on the edge of the plain, about a mile from the river; Rufaa is the most considerable, and is at present the Mudirieh town of the Gezireh province; the area cultivated in rain crops about Rufaa is very large.

From Rufaa on to Abu Haraz the country is similar, but there are fewer villages, more bush, and less cultivation.

At Abu Haraz we halted one day, and then started on December 13th for Gedaref, which we reached on December 19th, the estimated distance from Abu Haraz being 150 miles. For the first forty miles the route lay along the river Rahad through a continuation of very similar country, but there are only two or three villages with small areas of cultivation. The Rahad, which was quite dry except for isolated pools in its bed, is a purely torrential river, with a bed width of about thirty metres, surface width of fifty metres, and flood depth of five metres; it only flows for three or four months, coming down in July and drying up in November.

The river is very tortuous, but has a clean cut, well defined and uniform section, the channel being bounded on either side by a fringe of shallow ill defined ravines more or less overgrown with bush and grass, and rising gradually to the usual plain, fifteen metres or more above flood level.

These ravines are full of small kunkar and in places gravelly, but generally the soil is a good loamy clay merging into cracked cotton soil on the upper plain; except at one place

BLUE NILE, AT SUBA, 20 KILOMETRES ABOVE KHARTOUM

RIVER RAHAD AT SHERIF YAKUB

KHOR ARUB, NEAR GALLABAT

in the Rahad, close to its junction with the Blue Nile, no rock outcrops or stone formations of any kind were seen in this reach.

At forty miles from Abu Haraz, at Ain el Lueiga, the road leaves the Rahad, and makes for the north-eastern end of the long low range of hills known as Jebel Arang.

In about a mile it is clear of the ravines, and then lies across an absolutely level open plain covered with tall dry grass and dotted with thorn bushes: this plain is entirely uncultivated and uninhabited.

From this point to within a mile or two of Gedaref, a distance of over one hundred miles, the country is exactly similar, and consists of an immense plain of black cotton soil of the greatest fertility, dotted with small isolated granitic hills at long intervals, and covered with grass and scrub; in the neighbourhood of the hills there is generally a good deal of extremely thorny bush, which is often practically impenetrable off the track, but by far the greater portion of the plain is open grass prairie with scattered bushes. Except for petty scour lines in the immediate neighbourhood of the hills, not a single defined drainage channel is seen until the Khor Faraka is reached a few miles out of Gedaref. In the whole of this length there is only one dependable well, at El Fau, where the road passes through a low gap in the Gebel Arang range near its north-eastern end: there is no doubt that other wells used to exist, as there were formerly several small villages with fair tracts of cultivation; these villages were situated as a rule at the foot of one or other of the small hill masses, and the old wells could no doubt be reopened, and new ones dug in many places, were it considered worth while to do so.

From El Fau to Gedaref, seventy miles, there is no water at all, the road running through the same endless plain of rich soil with a few small hills in sight in various directions. Were the population available it seems highly probable that wells could be sunk in many places in this area, and villages established for the cultivation of rain crops: the rainfall is said to be dependable but the absence of water makes the country uninhabitable for at least six months in the year.

The level of the plain as determined from aneroid readings shows a gradual rise towards Gedaref, which is about 600 feet higher than Khartum.

Could canal irrigation be introduced into this tract its possibilities would seem to be almost unlimited; as usual a great deal of levelling work is required before any definite proposals on such a large object could be put forward for consideration: but it looks as if the level of the country would preclude the construction of a canal from the Blue Nile at Abu Haraz, such as has been suggested from a study of the map alone.

A canal taking off from the Rahad about fifty miles above its junction with the Blue Nile near the western end of Jebel Arang is probably quite feasible; this canal might run roughly parallel to the Nile at some distance from it, and would protect and develope the strip of country so enclosed.

The existing villages and areas of cultivation along the Nile bank would form nuclei from which rapid development and extension might be confidently anticipated.

The Rahad would of course only afford a supply for three months in the year, but even that would secure an immense area of rain crops, and the extra moisture in the soil should render the well supply much more abundant and dependable, and possibly available for winter and summer cultivation.

The Rahad supply might eventually be supplemented by storage reservoirs higher up its course, or perhaps by a cut from the Dinder, or even from the Blue Nile itself further up: but in this as in other cases in the Soudan, the consideration of a perennial supply to any canals that it may be found possible to construct is premature for the present. Flood canals that would secure the rain crops, and soak the soil, improving the well supply, and perhaps rendering winter and summer cultivation possible, would be a large enough advance on the present hap-hazard system to satisfy the requirements of the people for some time.

The upper part of the Gedaref plain is probably quite out of the reach of any possible canal from the Rahad side, and if anything ever can be done for it, it must be from the Atbara. This is considered later in a special note on the Atbara, but the case is not a promising one.

The great plain comes to an end within a few miles of Gedaref, the ground becomes uneven and rocky, and Gedaref itself is situated in an open valley surrounded by bare hills of basaltic rock.

We arrived at Gedaref on the afternoon of the 19th of December, and remained there two days to rest our camels, during which time we saw as much as we could of the neighbourhood.

Gedaref consists of a collection of small villages or hamlets in a large irregular open valley; the soil is fertile and almost everything planted seems to grow well: the water-supply is generally represented as abundant, but that is not the impression that I received; there seem to be a limited number of wells yielding a scanty supply which suffices, with economy, for the needs of the population.

Gedaref has obtained, what seems to me a rather exaggerated reputation as the "granary of the Soudan." There is no doubt that the country is highly fertile, but so is practically the whole of the eastern Soudan, and Gedaref's pre-eminence would seem to be due chiefly to the fact that owing to the existence of a few dependable wells, it is habitable, while other places are not.

Canal irrigation, even were a supply of water available, is out of the question in the immediate vicinity of the town, owing to the rocky uneven surface of the land, but I should say that more and better wells are here as everywhere urgently needed, and that the construction of tanks by damming the valleys of some of the large khors would be of great benefit to the neighbourhood, both in affording facilities for cattle-watering, and many other purposes for which a plentiful supply of water is essential, and in relieving the drain upon the wells that tends to exhaust them early in the season.

In fact I am strongly of opinion that for the Gedaref neighbourhood the construction of small reservoirs by damming the natural khor lines, and the digging of wells, are the best forms that work for improving agricultural conditions could take. The nature of the country would make the construction of such reservoirs fairly easy, and unless the amount of rain falling has been greatly exaggerated there should be no doubt about their filling up during the rains, if constructed in well selected places; it is of course essential that any such tanks should be constructed under proper professional supervision, or there will inevitably be failures and accidents, and it is probably the difficulty of constructing such works in the absence of proper supervision that accounts for their non-existence in a country where they would seem to be singularly desirable; the nature of the soil and other conditions are generally remarkably similar to those of Bundelkund and other portions of the great central plain of India, where such tanks are one of the most conspicuous and important features of the country.

The expedition left Gedaref on the 22nd of December and reached Gallabat on the 26th, the estimated distance being ninety-four miles, making the total distance from Khartum 364 miles.

The character of the country in this length is considerably different, the road follows roughly the watershed line dividing the catchment areas of the rivers Atbara and Rahad, the country is broken and rocky in places, especially about Doka, and on approaching Gallabat, but the highest hills are only a few hundred feet above the level of the surrounding plains. Where the road leaves the watershed decidedly, the country levels out into a great plain of black cotton soil with well-defined khors at intervals of two or three miles apart.

For some fifteen miles after leaving Gedaref the country is undulating and bare, with rocky ridges, and valleys consisting of large irregular tracts of rich soil, in many of which are small villages with wells and considerable areas of cultivation.

The forest country then begins, and this continues almost unbroken over the whole area drained by the upper waters of the Rahad and Atbara, and may indeed be said to extend up to and all round Lake Tsana also, though naturally its character varies a good deal from place to place.

Generally speaking this forest is composed of very poor trees, and is more of the character of bush; in the Soudan plains the trees consist almost wholly of different kinds of mimosa and acacia, the kittar thorn and the white and red-barked acacias being the most common, these latter average about twenty feet high with stems six inches to a foot in diameter, and though excellent fuel, are quite useless as timber. A good deal of gum is collected and exported from the forests between Gedaref and Gallabat.

In addition to the trees there is generally an overpowering growth of coarse jungle grasses, which are annually burnt over the greater part of the country during the winter months.

Where the grass has not been burnt, the tract is much shut in by vegetation and the view extremely restricted, so that the character of the country can be judged only by what is seen along the road itself; and even where it has been burnt, the view is lost in the surrounding bush in all directions at a very moderate distance. This limited power of observation is a very noticeable and inconvenient feature of travelling through this country.

A striking feature of this waterless forest is the extraordinary abundance of bees, which are a great nuisance when halting during the day-time, as in their mad search for moisture they settle in clouds on every damp surface, including the face and hands of travellers, until every water vessel becomes a hive, and rest is impossible. One cannot avoid being stung frequently, but fortunately the sting is not very severe.

Only two or three small villages and patches of cultivation are passed in the forest between Gedaref and Gallabat, but many traces of the comparative prosperity of former times are seen in ruined village sites and old wells, now mere names.

There are obvious signs of an increased rainfall as one proceeds south, but wells are few and far between, and the water supply is still precarious and scanty.

At Khor Otrub, about five miles out from Gallabat, there is a little water and a trickling flow in the bed of the channel, and from here onwards water is as often as not to be found in the beds of the larger streams, but generally only in pools or very small springs.

As regards the possibilities of agricultural development in this tract, they are undoubtedly very great indeed, but there is no opening for large irrigation works; much might be done by digging more and better wells, and all about this part I think that the construction of reservoir tanks by damming the natural drainage lines would be likely to prove indirectly a most remunerative form of public investment.

Considerable herds of cattle and flocks of sheep and goats exist, but they are absolutely nothing to what the forest could support were not the greater part of the area practically useless owing to the want of water.

Even where wells exist they are generally very small and shallow and quickly exhausted, and the labour of watering any considerable number of cattle from them is very great indeed, and takes much time, so that the number of cattle that one of these small wells can support is strictly limited.

The advantage of large open tanks where any number of cattle could water in a few minutes at their own time are too obvious to need discussion. Such tanks even if they did not hold water throughout the year, would almost certainly ensure a dependable supply to wells in their neighbourhood; and would form local centres of population, at first perhaps principally pastoral, and largely migratory, but which would probably soon develope into permanent villages with extending areas of cultivation.

I saw several fields of cotton in the neiggbourhood of Gallabat, grown of course without artificial irrigation, and it is well-known that formerly a great deal was grown about here and exported to Abyssinia.

What I saw was rather small and stunted but apparently healthy, and the quality of the cotton was said to be very fair; some samples of different varieties of cotton grown experimentally in the Kassala Mudirieh were given us by Colonel Henry, Mudir of Kassala, and brought down to Cairo.

Of course here, as everywhere, the want of population is the dominant feature of the economy of the country, but that is a matter which will almost certainly right itself gradually, and is indeed apparently doing so in excess of anticipations.

Gallabat is a pleasantly situated place on hilly ground, where the Soudan plains finally merge into the Abyssinian mountains. Up to within a few miles of Gallabat though there is a good deal of rocky broken ground the country is still essentially a plain country, the area of level or gently undulating ground greatly exceeding the hilly areas; after Gallabat it is essentially a hill country, though for some distance large tracts of comparatively level culturable land are found, gradually becoming more and more broken and stoney.

The old fort of Gallabat which is being adopted as the site of the official headquarters of the place, stands on a hill about one hundred and fifty feet above the village, a pleasant, open healthy looking site commanding extensive views over a great tract of hilly forest. The town is situated well to the east of the Atbara-Rahad watershed line and the Atbara lies about five miles to the north-east at some three hundred feet lower level, its general course is uncertainly traceable from the fort as a wide shallow depression of irregular ground buried in the usual dense forest growth.

We visited the river one day and found it to be a fine torrential stream a little over a hundred metres wide, running about five metres depth of water in flood, with a bed consisting of a succession of large deep pools, rocky ridges, and boulder-strewn shallows. The jungle growth along the river was extremely dense, and forcing a way through it down to the water was most laborious and exhausting in the great heat.

At the end of December the flow of the river amounted only to one cubic metre per second and was diminishing rapidly; by the end of February this flow had ceased entirely.

At Gallabat we were met by Mr. Johannis, the interpreter sent by Colonel Harrington from Addis Abeba with the King's letter permitting the party to visit Abyssinia. Mr. Johannis also brought some mules and a few Abyssinian followers.

Here also we found the seventy donkeys purchased on our account at Gedaref, and the escort of eleven men of the Arab Battalion who were to accompany us. We had also engaged seventeen men in Gedaref to act as donkey drivers and brought them up with us, making in all a party of about forty-five persons.

After three days spent chiefly in arranging our kit to suit the donkey transport, and collecting sundry items of supplies that had been overlooked, we left Gallabat on December 30th and entered Abyssinia.

In nine days' easy marching we reached Lake Tsana, at Delgi, at its extreme north-western corner, the estimated distance from Gallabat being 92 miles.

Our route which bore almost due south-east, followed up the course of the Gandwaha river, one of the chief tributaries, if not the main head channel, of the Atbara itself, for about two-thirds of the distance.

It then turned slightly to the south, and crossing the Atbara-Rahad watershed ridge, descended into the valley of the Gira, which is apparently the head of the river Scimfa.

This was rather surprising and unexcepted, as it had seemed from the maps more probable that we should cross the head-waters of the Upper Goang flowing northwards and westwards to the Atbara.

The Gira is a typical mountain river in a country consisting almost wholly of impervious basaltic and granitic rocks; it is evidently a furious torrent after rain, but dry except for the merest trickle at other times; it runs in a deep narrow valley, shut in, hot, and airless, and probably very unhealthy.

It has a very variable section averaging about fifteen metres bed-width with three metres depth of water in flood, and a tremendous slope; in full flood its discharge must be very large, and all about here the evidences of violent tropical rains are exceedingly marked.

It will be noted from the longitudinal section of this portion of the route that the Gira river lies relatively at a lower level than the Gandwaha, that is the upper waters of the Rahad have a steeper slope, and more rapid drainage than those of the Atbara.

Near to the point at which we struck the Gira are some hot springs in the river bank, which have a reputation for healing properties, and are somewhat resorted to by the scanty population of this part of Abyssinia. The water has no appreciable taste or smell but is beautifully clear and soft, and issues freely so hot that the hand cannot be kept in it.

Following up the Gira valley, the road ascends rapidly and the hills close in upon the river and become more and more lofty, at last the track leaves the valley and climbs up a projecting shoulder between profound ravines; these rapidly rise up and die out as the track emerges on an open grassy upland showing a considerable change of character and climate. Up to this point the general characteristics of the country continue the same as at Gallabat, an unbroken forest of dense grass and inferior trees covering an extremely rugged broken land surface.

Very soon after emerging on the plateau the slope of the ground changes; it descends towards the east somewhat rapidly, and Lake Tsana is seen at a distance of a few miles, some five or six hundred feet below.

The road winds down, steeply a first, then gently, over undulating plains covered with high grass and cultivated in patches, to the edge of the lake.

From Gallabat to the edge of the plateau, within seven miles of the lake, the country appears to be utterly uninhabited; and except for a very occasional party of traders met on the road, generally carrying down coffee, not a single human being is to be seen; but the whole tract has a most unenviable reputation as a happy hunting ground for brigands and robbers, which so far as I could ascertain is well-deserved.

Hidden away in the forest amidst the tangle of hills and valleys are a few petty villages, which are nothing but nests of robbers, who live by levying blackmail from the passing caravans.

The road is undoubtedly most unsafe and insecure except for large well-armed parties, and its insecurity must militate seriously against the development of trade between Abyssinia and the Soudan. The road itself is a tolerable fair-weather foot-path: it is very bad and rough in places, and donkeys and mules give much trouble by catching up their loads in trying to pass between trees and rocks too close together, or by jambing in narrow places where the track has scoured down into a deep V-shaped channel in clayey soil: inclined surfaces of hard slippery rock also caused us one or two accidents, but no serious loss.

The road could be vastly improved at very moderate cost by simply cutting down obstructing trees and bushes, and rolling stones out of the way; it would take a good deal of money to do anything with the really bad bits; but these only amount altogether to a very few miles out of the total of nearly one hundred: the rivers, being dry, give no trouble except during the rainy seasons, but the ascents from and descents to the numerous ravines are often very bad going.

Until we reached the edge of the plateau no Abyssinians met us or questioned our right to proceed; on arriving there we were somewhat roughly directed to halt until orders could be received concerning us from Ras Guksa. In the absence of the local chief we had some little trouble in overruling the objections of his locum tenens in spite of our showing the King's letter, but eventually got our way as regards proceeding to the edge of the lake, where we had always intended to stop for a day or two.

The demeanour of the people was suspicious and unfriendly until a man arrived next day who had been specially deputed by Ras Guksa to meet and accompany us, but who had been waiting at another place, and so missed us for the moment: after his arrival everything was easy, and we did exactly as we liked.

Delgi is the natural point of arrival and departure between Lake Tsana and Gallabat; the village is situated on a low projecting rocky promontory, and is a small port without a harbour, to which the coffee grown on the south-eastern shores of the lake and destined for export to the Soudan is brought, in frail-looking papyrus boats.

The promontory commands a beautiful and characteristic view of the lake, with the mountains of the Gorgora peninsular and its islands in front, and the lake extending to a water horizon from east round to south.

Distant mountains are visible to the north and north-east, and also to the south and west, but to the south-east only the faint outline of the conical hill on Dega Island can be seen on a clear day.

The general impression obtained is that the lake is larger and its surroundings less mountainous than would be imagined from a study of the map.

The depression occupied by the lake is, generally speaking, saucer-shaped, the land rising from the edge of the water in gentle undulating plains getting steeper and steeper and terminating in considerable hills or mountains of some importance. In several places as at Gorgora on the north, Mitraha and Korata on the east, Zegi on the south, and Dengelber on the west, the hills come right down to the lake and descend more or less abruptly into the water, but more often they stand back at some distance from it.

The geological formation is almost everywhere of the same primitive character that seems to be universal in the eastern Soudan, granite, gneiss, and quartz, varied only by tracts of lava, basalt, and eruptive rocks. Sandstone is reported by some travellers, and lime-stone is said to be found near Gondar, but I saw neither myself.

The large tracts of comparatively level land, consist almost entirely of the cracked black cotton soil usually found associated with igneous rocks.

At the mouths of all the larger rivers flowing into the lake are extensive alluvial plains generally composed wholly of this same cotton soil, and of the greatest fertility, though nine-tenths of their area now grows nothing more valuable than coarse grass.

Perhaps the most characteristic feature of this portion of Abyssinia is the universal luxuriant grass growth; not the extremely coarse reedy flags of the hotter Soudan, but a close uniform growth of tall straight grass generally six to eight feet high, but often more, especially in low ground.

This grass though fairly dry is not of the tinder-like consistency of that found on the lower plains, and is consequently to a large extent unburnt, and constitutes a very formidable obstacle to getting about. The more level portions of the country are generally open, but there are a good many trees, many of them fair-sized flat-topped acacias with a cedar-like habit of growth, giving a pleasant park-like appearance at a distance, though the illusion is somewhat dispelled at close quarters by the difficulty of forcing a way through the matted grass. The rougher ground is generally more or less bushy, and the hills are covered with scrub forest.

Wherever observed the lake was found to be shallow for a considerable distance out from the shore, the bed shelving gradually with a slope of about one in a hundred, and a firm sandy bottom.

The border of the lake consists almost everywhere of a reedy fringe standing in the water, with a strip of short, damp, succulent grass behind it, rising on a gentle incline to a small bank that forms the edge of the lake at high water; above this bank begin the usual level or undulating grass-grown plains.

These features of the lake are considered in more detail in the special note on the subject, but for general descriptive purposes it may be added that except for limited areas of papyrus swamp on the southern borders, the lake edge is generally sharply defined, and

LAKE TSANA, ROCKY ISLANDS AT OUTLET

KORATSA VILLAGE

SIEDEVER, RUINED CHURCH

the land along its borders comes down cracked, dry, and grass-grown to within a hundred metres or so of the water's edge.

The mouths of the streams flowing into the lake are marked by muddy, reedy swamps, often difficult to cross, but except in the stream lines, the valley plains along the rivers consist of firm hard and dry soil, in the winter months, right down to the edge of the lake.

It is possible, and indeed probable, that the conditions are considerably different in the rainy season, when the heavy rainfall, the overflowing of the streams and rivers, and the drainage off the higher ground behind, must convert much of the flat low-lying land near the lake border into something very like swamp, but the area actually flooded by the rise of the lake must be relatively inconsiderable.

We decided to march round the lake by the north and east as this gave us a clear route through Ras Guksa's territory right up to the lake outlet, and with his representative accompanying us we had no fear of detention or of an unfriendly reception.

We left Delgi on January 10th. We wished to keep along the lake's edge as much as possible, but the irregular coast line and the necessity of avoiding the swampy river mouths, compels the path to keep away from it in many places. The track is almost everywhere a narrow and obscure footpath in dense grass, constantly bifurcating and changing direction, and impossible to follow without a guide.

The most serious obstacles were muddy streams in which the loaded donkeys floundered, and occasionally got badly bogged, but the streams were quite narrow and easily bridged by a rough causeway of branches and grass.

We halted a day to rest and collect supplies at Mitraha on the east shore, a beautiful spot, where we visited the island and ruined church that mark the limit of the Dervish invasion of Abyssinia on this side.

We had a good deal of trouble crossing the river Reb, which, though carrying no appreciable discharge, had a width of over fifty metres and a depth of a metre and a half, at the so-called ford: but we got across without loss with the aid of our Berthon boat, in which we ferried all our luggage, while the donkeys were driven or rather dragged over.

It may be noticed here that the most serious inconvenience of this crossing was the fact that it took place in the afternoon, followed by the usual penetrating night cold, coupled with the fact that there was no firewood available, the whole country being open grass land.

In the neighbourhood of the lake the temperature used to fall regularly every night to about the freezing point, the lowest observed being 29° F. (the thermometer being exposed on a camp-stool outside my tent,) and to rise to about 80° in the shade in the afternoon, giving a very excessive and trying range for our lightly clothed followers. This extreme range of temperature was even more marked in the Soudan plains, 45° and 104° having been observed on the same day, and is apparently characteristic of the whole of this part of the world in the dry winter months.

The Gumara river which is of about equal size and importance to the Reb, was crossed without difficulty at an easy ford formed by a bar of coarse kunkar. The discharge of the Gumara river was estimated at two cubic metres per second; that of the Reb could not even be estimated as the current was imperceptible in the large section, but the two rivers are so similar in character and area drained that it is probable that it was of about the same amount.

From here we decided to pay a flying visit to Debra Tabor to thank Ras Guksa for the facilities he had afforded us in our travels. Leaving Dr. Hayes in charge of the camp, Mr. Crawley and I proceeded with a minimum of following and equipment to Debra Tabor, which we reached in two days.

This trip took us up to a considerable height above sea level, the estimated level of Debra Tabor being 8,829 feet, but the needle of my aneroid having run beyond the end of the scale I could not determine it exactly.

The formation of the country consisted throughout of granitic and other forms of crystalline rocks, with yellowish clays near the hills, and cotton soil in the more open plains.

On this trip we unfortunately lost one of our escort, who fell ill and died within thirty-six hours, of acute dysentery : when we found it impossible to get him into Debra Tabor, we left him at a roadside cottage where he was kindly tended by two Abyssinian women till he died the next day.

We were well received by Ras Guksa who had had a letter concerning our visit from King Menelik, and showed considerable interest in its object.

We stayed only one day at Debra Tabor, and then returned in two more to the main body of the expedition.

At Korata we first saw the coffee plantations for which the south-eastern shores of the lake are noted; here also was the first papyrus, which is very plentiful to the south but is not found on the north side of the lake.

We had considerable difficulty owing to the conflicting and unreliable information in deciding where to strike the Abai river, and how to attempt its passage.

Eventually we camped at a place called Woreb, two or three miles from the river, and made daily excursions for the purpose of exploration and survey.

The rough broken country made the collection of information by the only reliable method, namely personal observation, slow work ; but a good deal was done, and a fair idea obtained of the leading features of the locality.

We crossed the river successfully on the 30th of January, and camped again on the lake's edge at Bahrdar Georgis.

Observations made on the discharge of the lake outlet on January 31st, determined it as 42 m^3. per second, or about three and a half millions of cubic metres per day. This is perhaps the most important definite result of the expedition, and I am quite satisfied as to the substantial correctness and reliability of the observation : it confirms the suspicion already entertained that the discharge would prove to be considerably less than had been estimated from the reports of previous travellers.

It must however be remembered that 1902 was a year of very light rainfall, and this discharge is probably considerably below the average; but as is explained at greater length in the special note on this object, there is no doubt but that owing to the large extent of the lake's surface compared to the area that it drains, evaporation is a more important factor in maintaining the equilibrium of its level than the discharge of the outlet.

The value of the lake as a possible reservoir depends solely on the total amount of water discharged by the outflowing river during the year, and this unfortunately depends chiefly on the discharge in the comparatively short time during which the water is at a high level, which can only be guessed at, and to a comparatively small extent on that during the remainder of the year.

The discharge on the 31st of January must almost certainly be considerably less than the mean daily discharge of the year, which can therefore hardly be less than five million cubic metres, and remembering that 1902 was a dry year, the total annual discharge of the outflowing river can hardly average less than two thousand million cubic metres ; it is probably more, and I estimate it at about three thousand millions, which is therefore the limiting effective capacity of any reservoir that could be constructed.

The river Abai leaves the lake by an extremely irregular arrangement of channels and light rapids over rocky barriers, uniting into a fine broad stream about two hundred metres wide with a moderate but ill-distributed slope for some kilometres; it then becomes narrower and more rapid.

From Bahrdar Georgis Mr. Crawley and I made another flying excursion to the old Portugese bridge over the Abai (Blue Nile) at Agam Deldi, and the falls of Tis Esat.

RIVER ABAI, AND S.E. CORNER OF LAKE TSANA

RIVER REB

RIVER ABAI, 7 KILOMETRES FROM LAKE

RIVER ABAI, RAPIDS NEAR THE FORD

RIVER ABAI, FORD, 10 KILOMETRES FROM LAKE

RIVER ABAI, BRIDGE AGAM DELDI, 30 KILOMETRES FROM LAKE

RIVER ABAI, LOOKING UPSTREAM
FROM BRIDGE

RIVER ABAI, LOOKING DOWNSTREAM
FROM BRIDGE

RIVER ABAI, FIRST RAPID, WHERE IT LEAVES LAKE

This excursion was a long day's march out, and the same back, the estimated distance being twenty-one miles.

The bridge and the falls, and the general idea obtained of the upper valley of the Blue Nile were all very interesting. The bridge is a quaint, half ruinous old structure, very remarkable as being still the only one spanning the Blue Nile in its whole length.

The gorge crossed by the bridge is pershaps more striking than the bridge itself, the whole river being confined in a channel which it would be quite possible for an active man to jump across in places; down this the water foams and roars in a furious torrent.

The falls are really exceedingly fine, they are situated at the head of the gorge crossed by the bridge, and the river descends fully 150 feet in a single leap into a profound abyss; they are difficult to find and approach, and we nearly missed seeing them.

The gorge below the falls has been alluded to as a possible site for a reservoir dam affecting Lake Tsana; this is quite out of the question, as the crest of the falls is some hundreds of feet below the level of the lake, and lies in a wide open valley.

As regards the valley of the Blue Nile and the possibility of obstructing or diverting the river, I can only say that from the furthest point reached, near the bridge, the valley further on was an immense cleft, hemmed in on either side by mountains of great height, into the heart of which it appeared to be descending deeper and deeper; the level of the river must be some three thousand feet below that of the mountains on either side of it, and the idea of diverting such a stream bodily out of its natural valley is simply absurd.

As we wished to complete the circuit of the lake, and this involved passing through the territory of Ras Mangasha, to whom no letter had been sent by the King concerning the expedition, I despatched messengers to him at his capital at Buré, some sixty miles to the south-west, with the King's letter of introduction; and received in return friendly messages, and letters of introduction from the Ras to the local chiefs, with a man to escort and assist us.

This we immediately found to be necessary, as pending the return of the messengers, the local chief at Zegi was not at all inclined to be friendly.

We left Bahrdar Georgis on the 4th of February, and halted two days at Zegi awaiting our messengers.

Zegi is the centre of the coffee-growing district, and the most flourishing and populous locality on the borders of the lake, though even here by far the larger proportion of the surrounding country is covered with grass and forest.

The whole of the hilly peninsular is practically one large coffee estate, the coffee bushes growing under the shade of finer trees than are generally seen hereabouts.

Numerous narrow shady paths wind about the hills from village to village, and the condition of the whole place is in pleasant contrast to the extreme wildness and abandonment of most of the country round Lake Tsana.

Leaving Zegi on February 7th we completed the return journey to Delgi in four days: the chief object of interest in this portion of the journey was the Abai river. This we found to be, as expected, considerably the largest and most important feeder of the lake. It is a fine-looking stream with a clean well-defined section of about eighty metres width, and not less than four metres average depth. It runs in a flat-bottomed valley nearly a mile wide, which is said to be generally flooded for three months in the rainy season, and reaches the lake through a large area of marsh and papyrus swamp. We crossed it at a very good ford some miles above its mouth, where the river runs swiftly in a well-distributed stream over some rocky shallows, with an estimated discharge of nearly one million cubic metres per day.

None of the streams falling into the lake on its western side carry any appreciable perennial discharge, and almost all are absolutely dry during the greater part of the year:

it seems probable that the catchment area of the lake in this direction has been over-estimated, and that the watershed is even closer to the lake than in generally shown in the maps.

The ground descends more steeply to the lake hereabouts than in most places, and the irregular hills, bays, and islands about Dengelber are very picturesque. Dengelber was the limit of the Dervish raids on the west side of the lake.

After two days' halt at Delgi we returned by exactly the same route that we had followed in coming up, to Gallabat, which we reached on February 20th.

Throughout our march round the lake we were able to buy sheep, cattle and grain in most places at very reasonable prices. Flour was always rather more difficult, and generally involved a halt of a day and special arrangements for grinding by the women in several houses; this could only be arranged for in the larger villages.

Vegetables were difficult to obtain, and practically only potatoes and onions were obtainable, and these only at Zegi.

The crops chiefly grown round the lake are durra, teff, gram, and barley; a little cotton was seen in one or two places but seemed stunted and poor. Teff flour is the standard food of the people, made up into large flat soft cakes of about the appearence and consistency of the English "crumpet." Presents of these cakes, milk, eggs, fowls, and tej, or honey wine, were generally brought to us by the headman of the nearest village on our arrival at any camp, but by no means always.

There was some difficulty about paying for these things, and in knowing who to pay, the headman always insisting that they were presents from his master Ras Guksa, whilst in reality they were collected, presumably under pressure, from the villagers.

Except under the influence of the Ras's representative, I do not think that much would have been forthcoming, nor would it have been possible to buy necessary supplies easily.

Large herds of cattle are pastured round the lake border, and cattle-breeding should be capable of development into a large and profitable industry, and trade with the Soudan, when communications are improved.

Donkeys and mules are plentiful, cheap, and good in Abyssinia, though very small; in these also there might be a considerable export trade.

There was no incident of interest on the return journey to Gallabat, but in this portion of the march we lost the only three donkeys that we did not bring back with us to Gallabat.

At Gallabat we parted with the interpreter and other Abyssinians, left out escort, and dismissed our donkey drivers; and sent back the donkeys, donkey-saddles, and some of the mules to Gedaref, to be disposed of in the most convenient way.

On February 23rd we started again with camel transport, and marched down the Atbara along the new road.

For about forty miles the road runs nearly due north parallel to and at a distance of a mile or two from the Atbara. The country is rough and uneven, densely covered with grass and scrub forest, and abounding with game.

The Atbara is one hundred to one hundred and twenty metres wide with a bed of coarse shingle and occasional bars and outcrops of granitic rock. There was no flow of water in the river bed, but large pools are always to be found at short intervals, and the flood marks of last year's rainy season showed a fairly uniform depth of about four metres above low-water level. In years of heavy rainfall, the river must rise fully two metres higher.

At Sharafa the river turns to the east to round a hilly ridge running eastwards from the rough ground about Doka, and the road leaves it, continuing in a generally northerly direction to Tabrakhalla, marked by a small conical hill, and a gap in the range.

Here there is a small well with a precarious supply, and a break in the road, but we found our way, with the aid of a guide, by a circuitous route, to Goresha, a large and comparatively flourishing village, with a good well, in open, undulating ground.

LAKE TSANA. S.E. BAY FROM ZEGI

LAKE TSANA. THE WESTERN SHORE FROM SIEDEVER

LAKE TSANA. THE WESTERN SHORE FROM SIEDEVER

RIVER GANDAWAHA, 80 KILOMETRES FROM SOURCE

RIVER ATBARA, NEAR GALABAT

RIVER ATBARA AT WAD ABU SIMAN

From Goresha Mr. Crawley and I started on March 1st on a flying expedition to try and find the junction of the Salaam river with the Atbara, but after a very long and tiring march through trackless bush over badly-cracked ground, we came down upon the Atbara, (presumably above the junction), in a very wild place, and found our guides completly at fault.

This place was a remarkable gorge in coarse sandstone rock, where the river forces its way through a narrow cleft about twenty metres wide, between cliffs rising vertically from a profoundly deep pool.

We camped for the night on the edge of the river, and on the following morning made an excursion in search of the junction on foot, but failed to locate it. In our absence one of the camels was killed by a lion quite close to the camp.

We then returned to Goresha, and continued our march through Aradib and Sofi to the Atbara-Settit junction.

Throughout this section of our route there were occasional villages, with considerable areas of crops, and obvious traces of much more extensive cultivation in former times.

The greater part of the Kassala Mudirieh, and the Gedaref-Gallabat tract more particularly, has suffered this year from a most disastrous blight of the durra crop, known as "asal" or "honey," from the sticky deposit formed all over the plant and leaves.

About Goresha, Aradib and Sofi the main crop appears to have failed totally, to the great distress of the population.

South of Tabrakhalla the Atbara runs in a rough raviney valley about one hundred feet below the general plain level, but the plain itself is broken and undulating.

North of Tabrakhalla this plain becomes more uniformly level, and the river runs in a deep trench about one hundred and fifty feet below it, with a well-defined fringe of ravines a mile or more wide on either side.

At the Settit junction and for a considerable distance northwards the valley must be nearly two hundred feet deep, and the ravine fringe nearly two miles wide on either side; above the ravines is a perfectly level bush-covered plain of rich cotton soil.

Near Goresha the forest thins out and its place is taken by extensive open grassy plains, which were probably once largely cultivated, but are now for the most part waterless, and entirely uninhabited.

Two or three large well defined khors are passed hereabouts flowing down to the Atbara from the hilly ground to the west, on which favourable sites could no doubt be found for the construction of reservoir tanks of the kind advocated for this neighbourhood.

At Aradib and Sofi the Atbara is about 150 metres wide on the average, and ran about six metres of water in the 1902 flood; there was still a trickle from pool to pool at the beginning of March 1903.

The river runs with a shingly bed through a rather curious formation of coarse gritty sandstone, which forms fine cliffs and numerous rocky bars and barriers, but it is poor stuff, and would offer but a bad foundation for works of any size. The sandstone stratum extends up through about two-thirds of the height of the ravines, the upper third consisting of the usual black cotton soil.

At the junction with the Settit, the Atbara is the wider stream, but it is comparatively shallow. Opinions vary as to which is the more important river, but I think it probable that the Settit is the larger and steadier stream, though the Atbara may have fiercer floods.

The Settit was carrying a trifling flow of water on March 8th, the Atbara a mere trickle, the combined discharge amounting to only one quarter of a cubic metre per second.

The sandstone formation ceases above this point, and the occasional rocks in the river bed near the junction are of a granitic character.

From this point the road, though it follows the river, does so at a distance of a couple of miles or so to the west, generally along the edge of the upper plain, to avoid the rough ground of the ravines; and the river is not seen again until Khashim el Girba is reached.

This is a very remarkable spot, and the probable site of large canal works in the future, if such are ever undertaken on the Atbara.

Just above the "meshra," or watering-place, the Atbara flows in a narrow deep trench, perfectly straight for a couple of miles or so, with a width of little over 100 metres, and a depth of about 10 metres all across the pool when at summer level.

The sides of this trench are nearly vertical cliffs of extremely hard granitic rock rising twenty metres or more from the water.

At the meshra this trench suddenly fans out into a wide shallow channel, the pool ceases, and the river breaks up into three or four separate branches, amidst a confusion of rocky islands, and is not fully re-united into a single stream for several miles.

The rocky substratum through which the river has cut its way here, gives little or no indication of its presence in the level uplands, which continue as before to form an unbroken bush-covered plain of black soil up to within a couple of miles or so of the river, where it suddenly breaks into ravines.

The telegraph line from Kassala to Gedaref crosses the river where it runs in this narrow trench, and it is here that arrangements were made for erecting a river gauge and reporting station.

The road to Kassala crosses the river a few miles further on at Fasher, where it has a wide shallow and uniform section with a pebbly bed.

There was still a small discharge, estimated at a tenth of a metre per second, rippling over the stones in the centre of the channel as this point, but where the river was next seen, at Goz Regeb some eighty miles further north, all flow had ceased.

From Fasher to Kassala is a waterless march of forty miles over a perfectly level bush-covered plain of rich soil. With the exception of some temporary Arab huts near Fasher, and the police-post at Mogatta, no habitation was seen from the Settit junction to Kassala; the whole of this magnificent stretch of rich country is utterly desolate and uninhabited. Game is fairly abundant, and lions are numerous along the river.

At Kassala there are any number of wells, depending ultimately on the river Gash, which runs close to the town in a shallow sandy channel on the level of the plain; but the river is absolutely dry for nine months of the year.

We reached Kassala on the evening of March 15th and stayed there four days.

Colonel Henry, Mudir of Kassala, and Major Dwyer were very kind in supplying information concerning the river Gash, and in showing us the various points of interest, and the works in hand.

Leaving Kassala on March 20th we marched by a route somewhat to the north of the direct route to Goz Regeb, following the most westerly branch of the Gash river to within about 30 miles of that place; Colonel Henry and Major Dwyer accompanied us to this point.

The direct route is a waterless march of 70 miles; we found wells at about 25 miles and 50 miles from Kassala and others could no doubt be sunk at intermediate places.

The irrigation possibilities of the Gash are treated in a separate note; they are undoubtedly very great.

From Goz Regeb to within a few miles of Berber the road follows the Atbara, but as usual little is seen of the river itself except at the halting places, and not always then.

The river has a clean well defined and uniform section three hundred and fifty to four hundred metres wide, with a flat sandy bed and steep clay banks rising six to eight metres above low-water level. The flood of 1902 only rose about five metres.

Large pools occupy a considerable portion of the river bed in many places, some of these are of great extent and depth; the usual length being about a kilometre with a width of one hundred metres or so; they contain many large fish and crocodiles, but hippopotami which were formerly numerous are now nearly if not quite extinct.

RIVER ATBARA. SANDSTONE GORGE NEAR SALAAM JUNCTION

JUNCTION OF ATBARA WITH SETTIT

JUNCTION OF ATBARA WITH NILE

ATBARA. ROCKY GORGE NEAR SALAAM JUNCTION

ATBARA AT FASHER, LOOKING DOWNSTREAM

ROCK ON GEBEL ERIMBAT, GOZ REGEB

JEBEL KASSALA FROM THE MUDIRIA

RIVER GASH AT THE BERBER ROAD-CROSSING

The river is bounded on either side by the usual fringe of ravines but the rise to the level uplands is less than it is further south, and probably does not exceed one hundred feet above flood level anywhere.

The country becomes rapidly drier as one advances northwards, and sandhills begin to be a feature of the plain, but it is still lightly scrub-covered, and only a very mild kind of desert, until within fifty miles of Berber, where the real shingly barren lands begin.

The river has a narrow fringe of rich berm lands in the last hundred miles of its course, its immediate edge being occupied by an extremely dense and practically impenetrable belt of dom palms. In places these berms widen out into considerable stretches, and a system of basin cultivation might be possible, but without a tolerably correct plan, and some levels, it is not easy to speak definitely.

The possibilities of the Atbara as a whole are treated separately, but generally speaking the case is not very promising; the river is too torrential in character, and the way in which it persistently flows in a trench of great depth, would make any works for its utilisation extremely expensive.

On the other hand I do not believe that the silt carried by the river would be such a serious obstacle to the construction of reservoirs in its channel as has been thought; the river is undoubtedly a very dirty one in flood, but it would seem to be fairly free from the heavier forms of deposit, such as drifting shale, shingle, and coarse sand, owing to the stable geological formation through which it runs.

The immense plains of the Kassala Mudirieh consist almost uniformly of the richest cotton soil, it is not till north of Goz Regeb in the Berber Mudirieh that the quality of the land begins to fall off, and even here I understand that very extensive isolated areas of rich soil are found amongst the barren sand and shingle, especially in the tongue of land between the Atbara and the Nile, which would be comparatively easily reached by a canal.

We reached Berber on April 2nd and left on the 4th, arriving at Cairo on the morning of April 9th.

The health of the expedition was excellent throughout, and we enjoyed a singular immunity from accidents, complications, or disagreable incidents of any kind, and can, I think, congratulate ourselves on a very decidedly successful trip.

The five matters to which my attention was specially directed were all given careful consideration, and are separately dealt with in the accompanying notes.

My thanks are due to Mr. Crawley for his assistance, and to Dr. Hayes, whose abilities I am glad to say were really never seriously tested on behalf of the expedition, but whose readiness to place them at the disposal of the numerous casual applicants was undoubtedly of much assistance in securing the expedition a friendly reception in Abyssinia.

We are all also much indebted to the many Soudan officials with whom we came in contact, and who were without exception most helpful, and ready to take any amount of trouble on our behalf.

SPECIAL NOTE ON LAKE TSANA
AND THE POSSIBILITY OF ITS UTILIZATION AS A RESERVOIR.

The existing accepted maps of Lake Tsana appear to be correct in all their main features.

That prepared from the observations made by Dr. Anton Stecker during his travels in 1881 in particular, is a remarkably good representation of the lake, and was most useful to the expedition throughout, and though no doubt capable of correction in detail, especially as regards its southern and south-eastern portions, may, for all practical purposes concerning the storage of water, be accepted as correct.

As regards the country surrounding the lake also, all observations made only went to confirm the substantial correctness of the features shown on the best available maps of the locality, though possibly the extent of the catchment area on the west and south-west sides of the lake has been slightly over-estimated.

Those maps make the area of the lake surface approximately 3,000 square kilometres, and of the catchment area 14,000 square kilometres, exclusive of the lake area.

The only available records (Bruce 1770 and 1771 and d'Abbadie 1838) make the rainfall of Gondar between 0·90 and 1·00 metre.

From the nature of the country, and the appearance of the drainage lines, as well as from local report, it would seem that the rainfall of the south and east of the lake is considerably heavier than that of the north and west, and it is at least highly probable that the average rainfall of the whole lake basin is somewhat greater than that of Gondar.

The mean rainfall of the catchment area can therefore be safely assumed at one metre per annum, falling almost wholly in the four months June, July, August and September.

The greater part of the drainage area feeding the lake consists of cracked black cotton soil in undulating plains, but there are also large tracts of clayey soil, and in the more hilly portions extensive outcrops of rock and stone.

The rock formation apparently consists almost wholly of lava, basalt, and primitive crystalline rocks.

This arrangement is highly unfavourable to the formation of springs, and tends to exaggerate the character of the season in its effect upon the flow of the rivers, which are almost purely torrential.

In a year of light and well distributed rain the moisture is largely absorbed by the soil and re-evaporated between the showers; and in a year of persistent heavy rainfall the comparatively thin layer of spongy soil on an impervious bed, becomes wholly saturated, and a very high proportion of the fall is run off.

The general impression is that, on the whole, the basin of Lake Tsana is not a good gathering ground for a reservoir, and that the run-off must be very variable in amount, and cannot safely be estimated at over twenty-five per cent of the average rainfall in unfavourable years.

Adopting this figure and an average rainfall of one metre the following calculation gives a first rough estimate of the total volume of water reaching the lake.

Owing to the large proportion borne by the area of the lake to the total catchment area, it is necessary to consider the land and water areas separately, and we have:—

1 metre depth over the lake area of 3,000 square kilometres = 3,000 million m^3 + 25 per cent of 1 metre depth over the land area of 14,000 square kilometres = 3,500 million m^3.

Total 6,500 million cubic metres in an unfavourable year, and considerably more in favourable years.

Considering the matter in another way, with the aid of observations made on the lake itself.

Numerous observations and enquiries all round its borders enable it to be asserted with some confidence that the highest level of the lake in the autumn of 1902 was just about seventy-five centimetres above its level at the end of January 1903, and that its lowest level in May 1903 will be very approximately fifty centimetres lower, showing a total range of one and a quarter metres this season.

All accounts agree in representing 1902 as a year of very light rainfall and the 1902 flood marks were obviously below the average flood level.

It is rather difficult to say exactly what that level is, but it would seem to be about twenty-five centimetres above the 1902 level, giving a mean annual range of one and a half metres, as the low summer level in all seasons must be very nearly the same.

In years of very heavy rainfall the level of the lake is reported to rise considerably higher, by an amount that may be roughly estimated at fifty centimetres.

We can thus I think assume with fair accuracy that the normal annual range of the lake's level is about one and a half metres, with an exceptional minimum of one and a quarter metres, and an exceptional maximum of two metres.

Observations on the discharge of the river Abai, or Blue Nile, where it leaves the lake, made it 42 cubic metres per second on the 31st January 1903; with a further fall of fifty centimetres in the level of the lake, this discharge would almost certainly be reduced by more than a half; and the total outflow between that date and the middle of May, when the lake ceases to fall, would not suffice to lower the level of the lake by more than ten centimetres, even were there no inflow into the lake; it is clear therefore that the principal factor in reducing the level of the lake must be evaporation.

This is only what might be expected, the air being very dry, with light northerly and westerly winds and uniformly fine bright weather.

The dryness of the air is shown by the great range of temperature, which in winter rises daily from near the freezing point at sunrise to nearly eighty degrees Farenheit in the shade in the early afternoon: there is however generally a fairly heavy dew on the lake border, which shows that the dryness is not absolute.

Under the circumstances a daily evaporation of about half a centimetre might be expected, which would mean a loss of fifteen millions of cubic metres of water to the lake daily, or more than four times the observed discharge of the outflowing river.

A further interesting check on the above rough estimates is afforded by the following observations.

It was noticed that the level of the lake at Delgi fell approximately fifteen centimetres in the interval of 33 days between the two visits paid to that place.

The observation made on the discharge of the Abai river, at about the middle of the period, must give very approximately the mean discharge of the outflowing river during that time, which may therefore be taken as three and a half millions of metres cube per day

The sum of the discharges of the inflowing rivers is estimated from rough observations as follows:—

River Abai 9.0 m^3 per second, Reb 2.0 m^3, Gumara 2.0 m^3, Magetch 0.3 m^3. Arno Garno 0.3 m^3, Gelda 0.5 m^3, Unfraz 1.2 m^3, and many petty streams say 1.7 m^3, total 17 m^3 per second, or one and a half millions a day.

The excess of the discharge of the outflowing over that of the inflowing rivers can therefore only account for a loss of two million cubic metres of water per day, or sixty six millions in the thirty-three days.

But the observed fall of level of fifteen centimetres represents a loss of 450 millions.

Evaporation and absorption (which is probably inconsiderable) must therefore account for a loss of 450 − 66 = 384 millions of cubic metres of water, equivalent to a depth of 128 millimetres over the whole lake area in 33 days, or say 4 millimetres per day.

Again considering the anticipated fall of fifty centimetres in the lake level between the end of January and the middle of May, i.e., in a period of just about 100 days; as noted above, the discharge of the outflowing river, even if the inflow be neglected, could not account for as much as 10 centimetres of this, and considering the inflow, it can hardly account for more than 5 centimetres; therefore evaporation must account for a fall of 45 centimetres in 100 days, or 4.5 millimetres per day.

We shall therefore probably not be far wrong in assuming evaporation to average 4 millimetres a day for the eight dry months of the year (October 1st to May 31st).

To complete the calculation we may assume it to average 2 millimetres a day in the four wet months (June 1st to September 30th,) though this is a mere guess.

We can then estimate the conditions of the rise and fall of the lake, and the discharge of its outlet as follows:—

From October 1st when the lake is assumed full, to May 31st when it is assumed dead low, i.e. in 243 days, its level falls on the average 1.500 metres, of which 0.972 metres is due directly to evaporation; the remaining 0.528 metres, equivalent to a volume of 1,584 millions of cubic metres, plus the discharge of the inflowing rivers, estimated to amount to 364 millions (at one and a half millions a day,) or a total amount of 1,948 millions, must be run off by the river in the 243 days.

This gives a mean daily discharge of eight millions a day.

From June 1st to September 30th, i.e. in 122 days, the lake rises 1.500 metres, that is, it increases in volume by 4,500 million cubic metres, in spite of the evaporation of 2 millimetres depth, equal to six million cubic metres, per day, and the discharge of the river, which may be assumed to average much the same during the four months during which it is rising, at it does during the eight months in which it is falling.

We have then the following figures:

Total volume of water received into the lake during the year ...	6,572	millions of cubic metres.
Total volume evaporated during the year...	3,648	„
Total volume discharged by the river during the year	2,924	„

It is interesting to note how closely these figures agree with those obtained by simple assumptions regarding rainfall, run-off and evaporation, made on general grounds.

It is also worth while pointing out that a discharge of three and a half millions in the outflowing river on January 31st, after a season of very poor rainfall, with the lake at only fifty centimetres above its low summer level, is hardly compatible with a mean daily discharge of much less than eight millions in normal years.

On the other hand an average of eight millions involves the acceptance of a rather larger discharge in the river during the comparatively short time for which the lake is at a high level, than I should have been inclined to estimate from the appearance of the channel, but such an estimate is necessarily little more than a guess.

I think therefore that the effective reservoir capacity of the lake may be assumed to amount to about three thousand million cubic metres in an average year, though in years of very light rainfall it might be found impossible to store much more than two thousand, and in years of heavy rainfall perhaps as much as five thousand would be available, if the means of storing it existed.

The most that any system of regulation could attempt to do would be to concentrate this total available volume into a comparatively short period of flow, the outlet of the lake being kept entirely closed during the remainder of the year.

Assuming the reservoir designed for a capacity of three thousand million cubic metres, with its full supply level at present normal high water level, and assuming that the whole supply was required to be drawn off in the hundred days immediately preceding June 1st, when the normal rise of the lake commences, the effect of such regulation would be that, starting with the reservoir full as at present on October 1st, its level would fall under the influence of evaporation alone, more slowly than at present, until the draw off commenced in the latter part of February, when it would become more rapid, and at the end of May when the sluices were closed the lake would be some thirty-two centimetres lower than at present ; then with the outlet closed the lake would rise during the rainy season, more rapidly than at present, regaining its full supply level on September 30th.

The whole effect of such regulation would thus only be to increase the range of levels in the lake by thirty-two centimetres, giving a slightly higher level from October to March, and slightly lower level from April to September.

Such an arrangement would hardly constitute an appreciable modification of existing conditions, and would be more than compensated for by the facilities that the necessary works would afford for keeping down the level of the lake in exceptional floods.

A work of the kind required to control the waters of the lake to this extent would be a simple matter from an engineering point of view, the range of levels (under two metres) is small, and the discharge dealt with though large (thirty million cubic metres a day) is not excessive, and there is no doubt but that such a work could be constructed.

As regards the site for its construction, the modified range of levels in the lake would require that the water should fall to thirty-two centimetres below its present ordinary annual minimum, and with the lake at that level the regulator should be capable of passing its full normal discharge of thirty million cubic metres a day.

This would necessarily involve the cutting down and lowering of the bed of the channel by which the water now naturally leaves the lake.

The actual features of the outlet site become thus of particular interest.

The river Abai may be considered to leave Lake Tsana at the first place where the outlet channel becomes sufficiently contracted or obstructed to cause an obvious velocity of flow.

This point is very definitely fixed by a heavy rapid over a bar of volcanic rock, with an estimated drop of one and a half metres, within a couple of kilometres of the open lake.

The place was only found with some difficulty, and is not easy of access, owing to the numerous side channels and patches of boggy ground, and the overpowering growth of grass, reeds, and trees.

It is difficult to get a clear view of the individual rapids and channels from any point, and quite impossible to get anything like a general view of the arrangement.

But broadly speaking, it may be said that the surplus waters of the lake pass in the first instance through one or two fairly large channels in a narrow rocky bar into a lagoon of considerable extent and depth which is nearly separated from the lake by the bar in question, and pass out from this lagoon into the commencement of the river proper by two or three heavy and distinct rapids, with a drop of about one and a half metres when the lake is low.

The water flowing from these rapids is collected by a complicated network of channels and pools enclosing islands, into one distinct and well-defined river in the course of a kilometre or two, which then flows forward with an average width of about two hundred metres, and a very varying and irregular section, forming a succession of light rapids and papyrus-fringed pools; the drop at each rapid is small, varying up to fifty centimetres, and the rapids occur at irregular intervals from a few hundred metres up to two or three kilometres apart; in the wide and deep sections of the river the current is quite imperceptible.

After the first eight or ten kilometres, the rapids become more numerous and important, and the large pools cease, and the river runs for some twenty-five kilometres in a narrow section, as a rapid stream hugging the foot of the hills bounding a wide open valley on its northern side.

The valley then narrows in, and the river plunges over the falls of Tis East into a profound gorge in which it passes under the old bridge at Agam Deldi, and flows away to the south-east in a deep cleft in a mountainous country.

For the question under consideration it is only the first few metres of fall from the lake which are of any interest.

The existence of a considerable rapid at the lake exit and its occurrence over a kind of bar with deep water above and below it, is a very important feature, and there is no doubt but that by cutting or blasting this bar away the water of the lake could be run off to at least fifty centimetres below its present normal low water level.

But to make the river carry off a discharge of anything like thirty millions with the water at that level, would mean a good deal of work in clearing the channel below that rapid, and possibly above it also, the amount of which cannot be estimated with any approach to accuracy without a careful detailed survey.

But it is probable that a moderate amount of work in blasting away the bars forming rapids and in removing small islands, rocks and boulders in the shallows would make a great difference to the discharging capacity of the river at reasonable expense.

The bar forming the first rapid consists of shattered volcanic rock in loose angular fragments, and resembles a rubble breakwater, the water passing freely through as well as over it.

From its nature it would be comparatively easy to remove but it would not offer a convenient or safe foundation for a work of any size.

Assuming that it was decided to construct some kind of work for controlling the outflow from the lake, it would almost certainly be desirable to go some little way down the river, and construct the regulator on one of the bars forming rapids in the stream, as such a work could be constructed almost in the dry, and the necessary clearance of the channel would not be materially affected by its position.

It is probable that a good site could be found in the neighbourhood of the ford, about ten kilometres from the lake.

A regulator of forty openings of three metres each, with its floor at four metres below ordinary high water level in the lake would seem suitable.

Such a work might be constructed of stone found in the immediate vicinity, and bricks burned on the spot.

Lime would be rather a difficulty. I only saw three or four buildings constructed with lime mortar in Abyssinia, concerning which I was informed, that the lime used in constructing the church at Mitraha, on the east side of the lake, came from the neighbourhood of Gondar; and that that used in constructing the church at Bahrdar Georgis, near the lake outlet, came from a considerable distance amongst the mountains to the south, where lime is said to be abundant.

The lime used in the construction of the old Portugese bridges over the Abai no doubt came from the same neighbourhood.

I saw no limestone or signs of limestone formation anywhere round the lake, but it almost certainly exists to the south, and probably also near Gondar.

Kunkar is plentiful in the ravines of the Atbara and Gira rivers up to within thirty or forty kilometres of the lake, but I saw little or none round about the lake itself, except one bar of coarse inferior stuff at the ford on the Gumara river, it is however not improbable that kunkar would be found on careful search.

It would be very desirable to design the regulator so as to reduce the materials that it would be necessary to import to a minimum, and it is for this reason that a regulator with comparatively small openings; which could be worked by hand by means of simple horizontal planks, is suggested.

The grooves could be cut in hard stone, and even wood for the planks might possibly be obtained locally, but this is doubtful.

Throughout the above it has been assumed that the present average high water level of the lake must be accepted as the future high water level of the reservoir.

From the engineering point of view it would no doubt be simpler to accept the outlet channel as it is, and obtain the required discharging capacity by raising the level of the lake, but it then becomes necessary to consider the character of the lake shore, and how a raising of the level of the water would affect the adjacent lands.

The borders of the lake consist generally of a fringe of reeds from twenty to fifty metres in width standing on the edge of the water, behind which is a belt of about the same width of gently-inclined ground covered with thick, short, marshy grasses and weeds and affording excellent grazing.

This open belt forms a sort of grassy beach to the lake, protected from wave-wash by the tall reeds in front, and rises gently to the foot of a steep little bank about one metre in height, the toe of which is at normal high water level.

This bank is the true edge of the lake, and from it the damp grasses and reeds at once give place to the tall dry grass and scrub characteristic of the country.

The above description is typical and of very general application, but the width of the reed and grazing belts vary greatly from place to place, disappearing entirely where the hills come down to the water, and spreading out into wide strips of swampy ground near the mouths of some of the rivers, and more especially the Abai.

That is, generally speaking, the lake border is sharply defined, but there is a belt of gently-inclined ground of moderate width, consisting almost entirely of good grazing ground, that is covered and uncovered annually by the rise and fall of the lake.

From the bank forming the true lake edge the rise of the land away from the lake is exceedingly variable; except in the deltaic plains of the larger rivers it is so rapid that the area that would be flooded by any probable increase of the lake's level would be inconsiderable, and consisting, as it almost always does, of uncultivated scrub jungle, would be unimportant.

In the deltaic plains however it would seem that the land slope cannot be more than about 1 in 5,000 for some miles back from the lake edge, and there are numerous patches of cultivation and small villages, which would feel the effect of a very moderate raising of the water; and the disturbance of existing conditions would occasion many minor inconveniences to the inhabitants of the shore, and would almost certainly be bitterly resented.

It would obviously be undesirable to complicate a sufficiently difficult position by incurring the hostility of the local population, and I am strongly of opinion that if anything is done, the existing regime of the lake should be disturbed as little as possible; and, as already pointed out, the lake could be fully utilized as a reservoir with an almost inappreciable amount of disturbance, by a suitable treatment of the outlet channel.

Three thousand million cubic metres of water is a very large volume, but it is doubtful if a reservoir of that capacity would be of sufficient value, having regard to the inconvenience of the immense distance, and the probable loss of water by evaporation on the way down, to justify its construction being undertaken in the interests of Egypt alone, in the face of the serious difficulties and political complications involved.

As a reservoir for the Blue Nile feeding canals irrigating the Gezira, and the rich lands to the east of that river in the Soudan, the suitability of Lake Tsana is so great and obvious that it seems almost inevitable that sooner or later in the world's history some solution of the political difficulties must be found, and advantage taken of it.

The Soudan is certainly not yet in a sufficiently advanced state to profit by the construction of such a work, but it would be a great pity if Egypt were to appropriate and utilize inefficiently natural facilities apparently destined to play an important part in regenerating the Soudan, in which Egypt is so greatly interested.

A large canal irrigating the Gezira seems an almost obvious and inevitable work of the near future.

The average discharge of the outlet of Lake Tsana under present conditions can hardly be as much as five million cubic metres a day between January 1st and June 30th; it was actually three and a half millions on January 31st this year, and it was estimated that it would probably fall to under two millions in May.

Assuming the political difficulties solved, and Lake Tsana converted into a reservoir, it could be relied on to provide a discharge of fifteen million cubic metres a day for the six months January to June inclusive, equivalent to a total capacity of 2,715 millions, of which five millions would be more than equal to the present natural discharge to which Egypt and the lower Nile may be considered to have a claim, and the remaining ten millions would be available for the spring and early summer discharge of the Gezira and other Soudan canals.

During the remainder of the year those canals could draw upon the natural supply of the river without appreciably affecting other interests.

The utilization of Lake Tsana as a reservoir to discharge fifteen million cubic metres a day for 181 days, instead of thirty millions a day for 100 days as originally considered, would simplify the works required.

The increase in the range of the lake levels would be reduced from 32 to 26 centimetres, a smaller regulator would suffice, and much less work would be necessary in the outlet channel.

It would seem therefore that though Lake Tsana is suitable for conversion from a natural into an artificial reservoir, the advantages offered are hardly sufficient to justify the work being undertaken in the interests of Egypt alone, and that to do so would be to deprive the Soudan of one of its main hopes for future development.

The Soudan is not however yet ready to utilize the water that would be afforded by such a work, but when it is, a comparatively simple work could be constructed that would be of great value to that country and would also be of some slight benefit to Egypt.

Further that, if ever and whenever such a work is undertaken, it should be designed so as to disturb existing conditions as little as possible, and the details of the work should be as simple as possible, avoiding all heavy important material to the utmost.

In conclusion it may be pointed out that Lake Tsana is too large in proportion to its catchment area to make a really satisfactory reservoir.

Evaporation from the lake's surface accounts for more than half the total volume of water received into it in an ordinary year; were the area of the lake to be doubled there would probably be no outflow from it at all; could it be halved its storage capacity would be increased by fifty per cent.

From its peculiar position it happens that the waters of the lake could be drawn off, and its area reduced to any desired extent, by boring a tunnel under the western watershed.

Such a tunnel would be at least seven or eight miles long, and would be enormously expensive; it would convey the waters of the lake into the ravines of the Gira river, a tributary of the Rahad.

The drainage of the lake and the diversion of its waters is probably quite out of the range of practical politics, and it is not certain that there would be any great gain from effecting it, but it is worth noting that it is perfectly feasible, and presents certain advantages from the purely technical point of view.

The political difficulties in the way of constructing and maintaining any work of control for utilizing the water of Lake Tsana have only been referred to in a general way throughout this note; but they would undoubtedly require very serious attention in detail, in organizing and executing any such works, above and beyond the broader issues that would be arranged diplomatically. I do not think that it would do to count much on the good-will of the local inhabitants, and certainly not upon their assistance.

The country is poor and sparsely inhabited, and the people are independent and indifferent to strangers, whom they look upon with considerable suspicion.

Supplies in small quantities are cheap if the people choose to bring them, but labour would probably be unobtainable.

Without the cordial support of the King and local Rases, emphasized by some show of force, I have no doubt but that work would be quite impossible, and it would certainly be unwise to attempt it except on a most complete understanding on all points.

SPECIAL NOTE ON THE RIVER ATBARA.

The route followed by the expedition in going to and returning from Abyssinia was such as to give a very good general idea of the leading physical features and character of the eastern Soudan.

The whole country from the Gash to the Rahad, and probably on to the Dinder and Nile also, consists of a vast plain of rich black soil sloping gently north-westwards from the foot of the Abyssinian hills on the south-east, which corresponds approximately with the Abyssinian frontier.

The plain is broken at irregular intervals by little hill groups, formed by outcrops of the underlying stratum of granitic rock, but these are for the most part small and isolated, and have not much effect on its general level and character.

The rainfall which determines the character of the vegetation and the appearance of the country, is heavy in the south-east, where the country is clothed in unbroken forest; light over the central portion, which consists chiefly of grassy plains varied by tracts of small thorney bush; and almost entirely absent along the Nile to the north-west, where the occasional showers are insufficient to maintain any vegetation worth the name, and except for the strips of cultivated land along the Nile itself, the country is practically desert.

The whole of this vast area is, with the exception of an insignificant fraction round about the few small villages, utterly uncultivated and uninhabited, and suffers almost everywhere from want of water in an acute form.

The enormous area of these plains, their uniform level, and their extreme fertility, at once suggest the introduction of canals and irrigation, as a remedy for their waterless and waste condition.

The slope of the country being generally towards the Nile, it is clear that, excepting perhaps a strip along their western edge, these plains cannot look for help to that river.

There remain then the Gash, Rahad, and Atbara: the two former are small torrential rivers, of which the Gash already does, and the Rahad can very likely be made to do much useful work, but their whole available volume would not suffice to irrigate more than a fraction of the area under consideration, and from their position the possibility of their utilization is limited to small areas on the fringe of the main tract.

The Atbara on the other hand is a much larger river, its course lies conveniently adjacent to the largest section of the great plain on its higher edge, and it would seem at first sight to promise well.

We will proceed then to consider in detail the observed features of that river, and how far it does or does not offer facilities for utilization.

According to the best available maps the river Atbara is formed by the confluence of three large streams, the Goang, Bulwena and Gandwaha, a little above Gallabat, near the border of Abyssinia.

Of these rivers only the Gandwaha was seen by the expedition, but that river was followed up to within fifty miles of its source, and the general features of the country about its extreme head were distantly viewed from various points: it is probably the main channel, to which the Goang and Bulwena are tributary branches.

Opposite Gallabat the Atbara has a section one hundred and twenty metres wide, and runs about five metres depth of water in flood.

The bed of this channel consists of boulders and coarse shingle varied by rocky outcrops, and the banks are of firm loamy soil; all the rock hereabouts is of the usual crystalline character, granite, gneiss, basalt and allied forms.

At this point there was a flow of water estimated to amount to one cubic metre per second at the end of December 1902; two months later there was no flow at all.

A considerable proportion of the bed of the river is occupied by a succession of large deep pools fringed with grass, and bushes of a kind of willow, which must be entirely submerged in flood.

From near Gallabat the river runs about one hundred miles northwards without much change of character or section to near the junction of the River Salaam.

Here the occurrence of some strata of coarse gritty sandstone in the valley have compelled the river to cut its way through as best it could in a series of narrow deep gorges, giving it a very varying and peculiar section.

The Salaam, which unfortunately we could not manage to see, is from all accounts of about equal size and importance to the Atbara itself, and carries a small perennial flow, amounting however this year to no more than a mere trickle of water.

From the Salaam to the Settit junction the Atbara has a width of from one hundred and fifty to two hundred metres with a normal flood depth of about six metres, the section varying greatly from place to place, the bed, where exposed, is uniformly composed of small boulders and coarse shingle with occasional bars and ridges of rock.

Throughout this length the river channel lies in the sandstone substratum.

The Settit at the junction again appears to be of about equal size and importance to the Atbara, but is probably the larger and steadier stream; it carries an appreciable but very small perennial discharge, amounting on March 8th to one quarter of a cubic metre per second.

Below the Settit junction the river lies in a deep valley with a wide fringe of very rough raviney ground and is not easy of access; but where next seen at Khashim el-Girba the channel was a deep narrow trench through a substratum of granitic rock forming a long and profoundly deep pool with a width of about 125 metres and a flood depth of about 15 metres all across the section.

At Khashim el-Girba the river breaks up into several channels amidst a group of rocky islands, forming a heavy rapid in flood, and a few miles lower down, a little below the point at which the channels reunite into a single stream, is the important Fasher ford, where the Gedaref-Kassala road crosses the river.

The channel here is some four hundred metres wide with a shallow section barely six metres deep in the centre in ordinary floods.

The river bed is still composed of shingle and small boulders at this point, and carried a trivial discharge of about one-tenth of a cubic metre per second on March 14th.

Where next seen at Goz Regeb, some eighty miles further down, the character of the river had considerably changed and it had become more a river of the plains with a flat sandy bed some three hundred and fifty metres wide, steep clayey banks, and a flood depth of about seven metres.

With the exception of some bars and outcrops of coarse kunkar no rock was seen from Goz Regeb onwards, and all perennial flow had ceased.

The section does not vary materially from Goz Regeb down to the Nile, and is comparable to that of the Damietta branch of the Nile in Egypt, though perhaps not quite so deep, but even here the current in flood is always described as very strong.

A sheet of cross sections of the river in different parts of its course is appended to this report and illustrates the above description.

A rough longitudinal section of the river has also been prepared from numerous observations with a small aneroid, and though such a section cannot pretend to accuracy, the observations are sufficiently consistent to give grounds for supposing that the levels deduced are relatively fairly accurate, and give very approximately the true absolute altitudes of the different places.

The levels of a few places on the plain at some distance from the river are plotted on the section, and give at a glance some idea of what is and what is not possible in the way of irrigation so far as levels are concerned.

It is well known that the character of the Atbara is markedly torrential.

As noted in the above description the river has, for all practical purposes, no discharge at all for several months in the year in any part of its course.

The rains begin in the upper part of its basin in the latter part of May, and early in June the river about Sofi and Tomat (near the Settit junction) begins to show signs of being affected.

This first effect is rather curiously described by the local inhabitants as the "swelling of the springs"; what it is is no doubt the pushing forward of the clear water filling the numerous large pools along its course by the first flow of flood water down the river from the hilly country near its source.

This increase of the clear water discharge is followed in a few days by the arrival of the dirty red water and a more marked and rapid rise.

The Settit is said to come down before the Atbara, but only by a few days.

The increasing violence of the rains, spreading northwards over a rapidly extending area of the river basin, causes the first feeble flows of water, creeping slowly down its bed from pool to pool, to be successively overtaken by stronger and stronger flushes, till in the lower reaches of the river the flood in some years becomes piled up into a regular wave of considerable height, and advances down the dry channel like a bore.

The first waters of the Atbara flood appear to reach the Nile in the last week of June with great regularity.

The flood once established the Atbara runs at a high level very steadily, it is at its highest in August at which time the normal discharge in the lower reaches is estimated at at least 2,500 metres cube per second.

During September it falls rapidly, by the end of October it becomes fordable in many places, and by the end of November it is practically dry.

It is clear from the above that the Atbara is not a river that lends itself readily to utilization for irrigation purposes, except possibly in the form of flood canals or some development of the basin system.

A supply could only be obtained for a perennial canal system by the construction of storage reservoirs on a large scale.

Next to its torrential character perhaps the most marked characteristic of the Atbara is the way in which it persistently flows in a narrow valley or trench of great depth, which it has cut in the plain through which its course lies.

This plain was no doubt originally formed by the river itself from the wash-down of the Abyssinian mountains, but owing to some change of conditions, possibly the gradual wearing down of the rocky barriers forming the cataracts of the Nile, the bed of the Atbara has for a long time past been gradually lowering itself into a channel of its own making, through the old alluvium, and in places into the rock below, and it now lies almost throughout its course in a narrow deep valley with an eroding section, fringed by a belt of extremely rough raviney ground, rising gradually to the plain level on either side.

The slopes of the river bed and of the upland plain are roughly parallel, and the difference of level between them is about two hundred feet near Gedaref, and diminishes gradually northwards; the width of the ravine belt is rather variable, but generally from a mile and a half to two miles on either side of the river channel.

As can be seen from the longitudinal section of the river the estimated slope of its bed is about $\frac{1}{2000}$ for a long distance above and below the Settit junction, that is, a canal with a longitudinal slope of say $\frac{1}{10000}$, taking off the river at its natural level would have a course of nearly one hundred miles on sidelong ground in the ravines before it could gain the two hundred feet necessary to enable it to emerge upon the plain.

Close to the Abyssinian border the slope of the river is steeper, but the country there is very rough, and the river is a small one.

Gedaref is about one hundred miles from the Abyssinian border, it also marks the limit of the forest, and rather broken ground, and the commencement of the great grassy plains.

Above Gedaref the rainfall is fairly heavy, and irrigation works on a large scale are hardly necessary, even were they possible.

An ideal canal from the Atbara would issue on to the great plains in the neighbourhood of Gedaref; but the alignment that would have to be followed by any canal leading off the river in the usual way would be prohibitively difficult and expensive.

The only chance of producing a really satisfactory work would appear to consist in the construction of a masonry dam of very large proportions, the greater portion of the height of which would consist merely of a solid obstruction raising the water of the river much above its present level, and so enabling a canal to take off at a height that would greatly reduce the length of the expensive and difficult supply channel; combined with a reservoir superstructure to store water for the supply of the canal during the summer months.

The expense of constructing such a work would be very great, but the section of the river valley would provide an efficient and suitable reservoir with large capacity.

It would probably not be much use attempting to construct such a work above the Salaam junction, as the country is so rough that the canal would still be very difficult to construct, the capacity of any possible reservoir would be but small, and the sufficiency of the supply afforded by the river doubtful.

Were a suitable site available, the best possible place for a dam of the kind indicated would be just below the Salaam junction, but the only rock seen in that portion of the river's course was a gritty sandstone of inferior quality; the alignment of the canal also would be difficult.

Below the Settit junction the supply would be ample, and a good site is known to exist at Khashim el-Girba, but this is very far down.

A canal system starting from any convenient point below the Settit junction could, however, still be made to command an enormous area of land, and the country about the lower part of the river has some advantages over the upper country in its more open character and the absence of the seroot fly.

As regards the possibility of constructing large reservoirs on the Atbara, in view of the enormous quantity of silt that it is said to carry. There is no doubt but that all accounts agree in representing the Atbara as an exceptionally dirty river in flood.

The Settit is said to be more particularly responsible for this, but the fact hardly requires any explanation; the universal prevalence of friable easily eroded black soil, and the great number of scouring ravines draining directly to the river, are quite sufficient to account for it; and there is evidently also an immense quantity of vegetable trash carried by the water, as again was only to be expected seeing that almost the whole area drained is clothed in unbroken forest.

The material held in suspension must however be almost entirely silt of a very light kind, as the existence of old established belts of grass and bush, growing along the edges of the pools in the river bed, in positions where they must be exposed to the full violence of the flood, and wholly submerged for days if not weeks at a time, as well as the obvious permanence of the pools themselves, show clearly that there can be but little movement of the heavy shingle forming the river bed, or drift of the coarser kinds of sand and other deposit along it.

For this reason I am of the opinion that the silt difficulty is not by any means prohibitive, especially if reservoirs of the Assouan type were designed allowing the free passage of the earlier and dirtier portion of the flood water, and storing only the later and clearer portion.

The total annual discharge of the river may be roughly estimated as at least twenty thousand million cubic metres, and a very small proportion of this, obtained entirely from the comparatively clear water of the latter portion of the flood would suffice to fill any reservoirs that it is likely to be found practically possible to construct.

In the last hundred miles of its course the Atbara begins to develope a fringe of berm lands on either bank at about ordinary high flood level.

These lands undoubtedly consist of very rich soil, and are favourably situated for cultivation, but they are densely overgrown in many places with scrub jungle and dom palms, and would want a goot deal of clearance before they could be fully cultivated.

The width of the berms varies greatly and is difficult to estimate owing to the amount of vegetation, but they seem to be continuous, and up to a kilometre or more in width in places, though generally less, and sometimes quite narrow.

Beyond the fringe of rich berm lands rises the broken raviney ground which everywhere bounds the course of the Atbara, but here the ravines are shallow and ill-defined and the upper lands are practically desert.

Here as elsewhere, nothing but a systematic survey and a lot of levelling work can determine the possibilities of the case, but the conditions so far as it was possible to observe them, seemed not unfavourable to the development of a small basin system, which, on the right bank, might be continued down the Nile after the Atbara junction to past Berber where there is a lot of good land on a rather high level including the Hassa lands specially referred to in another note.

The value of such lands flooded by exceptional rainfall or by unusually high flood, is fully recognized by the people about Berber, who would not be long in taking advantage of rich basin lands annually and dependably irrigated.

This development of a small tract of basin irrigation is practically the only project for the utilisation of the waters of the Atbara that I am able to suggest as worthy of serious consideration under present conditions, and even that should not be undertaken without a much more careful study of the locality than I was able to make.

It will be seen from the above description that the Atbara is a very unsatisfactory river from the irrigation point of view, for, in addition to the extremely torrential character of its supply, it has a further great additional disability in the way in which it persistently flows in a narrow deep valley far below the level of the surrounding country, and in the fact that at no part of its course do the natural features appear to afford the slightest facility for leading canals off it.

The slope of the river bed is too slight to give a ready command of the country to a canal taking off it some way up, and too great to afford facilities for reservoir construction except by means of works on a very large scale.

At the same time it flows through the heart of a country covered with soil of the richest and most fertile description, but which is almost uninhabitable owing to the deplorable deficiency of water everywhere.

It is possible that a more accurate and detailed survey of the ground may show the conditions to be rather more favourable than they appeared to me, and the river valley and channel are well worth careful study, for the need of water is so urgent that very large expenditure will almost certainly be incurred some day to obtain it; but as the result of a personal reconnaissance it would seem that the only way in which it would be possible to make use of the waters of the Atbara for irrigation on any scale would be by the construction of enormous dams which would convert considerable reaches of the river valley above them into lakes of which only a comparatively small depth would be available for utilisation for irrigation purposes, the canals supplied taking off at a high level.

Such dams would have to pass the floods of the Atbara with a heavy fall, and would require to be very bold and special works of their kind; the Periyar Dam in Madras may be instanced as typical of the kind of work suggested.

Could a suitable site be discovered, the best position for such a work would be a little below the Atbara Salaam junction; with a secondary dam and system of canals below the Settit junction, but in the present state of the Soudan it is useless to discuss such ambitious schemes further.

As regards the possibility of constructing reservoirs in the Atbara valley for the benefit of Egypt; such works are probably quite practicable, but the Atbara valley would not appear to offer any special advantages over the broader valley of the Nile, and has the disadvantage of being further off.

Admitting the practical impossibility of doing anything for the greater part of these plains of the eastern Soudan by means of canals, at any rate for the present, it would seem that the only thing to do is to improve the well supply, and construct local storage tanks wherever possible.

With permanent villages established on good permanent wells, a good deal of rain cultivation could be effected, and the cattle-breeding industry, already fairly large and important, could be enormously developed.

A small grant for well-sinking and the experimental construction of a few tanks would probably be money well spent; the people seem to be singularly inexpert in well construction, considering the overwelming importance of the subject to them, and it might be worth while to import a few professional Indian well-sinkers. Personally I cannot but think that water would be much more generally found than seems to be believed, and the want of it would certainly be much less acutely felt if the wells were habitually made larger and deeper.

NOTE ON THE RIVER GASH.

The River Gash or Mareb issues from the Abyssinian hills on to the Soudan plains in the form of a wide shallow sandy torrent on much the same level as the plains themselves.

At the point where it rounds the southern end of Jebel Kassala, some five miles to the south of Kassala town, it has a channel averaging about one hundred and fifty metres wide with a depth of not more than one metre, between the low banks that ordinarily bound the stream.

In a very high flood the river flows to some extent over the adjacent berms, for one hundred metres or more on either side of the true channel, amongst the grass and scrub; these berms are scored and furrowed by spill channels, returning at intervals to the main stream.

Beyond the berms the river is confined on the right by the rocky spurs of Jebel Kassala itself, and on the left by a rise of the ground which is however very slight, probably not more than two or three metres at most, and is apparently soon followed by a gentle slope towards the west and north-west, i.e., away from the river, merging into the almost dead-level plain that extends right away to the Atbara, some forty miles off.

The section of the river is in fact deltaic.

The whole country about here is entirely uncultivated, and is densely overgrown with trees and bush.

These general characteristics are maintained down to Kassala, which is situated on low ground on the east bank, very little above the river level, opposite a gap in the hills (here some two or three miles off) between Jebel Kassala and Jebel Mokran.

Below Kassala the section of the river becomes more and more distinctly deltaic, and it begins to spill over its banks on either side.

At the same time the channel proper becomes somewhat narrower and deeper, and is lined along the ridge of both banks by a continuous belt of fair sized tamarisk trees, with patches of cultivation amongst and behind them.

The spills become more numerous and continuous, with several fairly large and defined channels amongst them; the river section rapidly dwindles, and at six or seven miles from Kassala disappears entirely.

All this overspill area is thickly coated with the mud deposit of last year's flood, and large areas of durra cultivation exist upon it; where not cultivated it is generally more or less thickly overgrown with tamarisk, and various kinds of acacia, as well as many smaller shrubs.

The cultivation and denser jungle is succeeded by an irregular belt of tussocky grass with fewer trees and bushes furrowed by many more or less ill-defined scour channels, which have a tendency to unite and grow deeper again, and eventually collect into two or three considerable and distinct drainage lines leading in a northerly or north-westerly direction; these are the lines of flow ordinarily marked on the maps as the branches into which the river Gash divides.

They flow for from fifty to one hundred miles, irrigating large areas of grazing ground and supporting a succession of small semi-permanent villages with patches of cultivation.

The most important of these branches appears to flow almost due north past the comparatively important village of Fillik, and to eventually lose itself in a sandy desert tract to the north of that place, but this I did not see.

Water can be obtained almost anywhere within the area affected by the Gash flood by sinking wells; those that I measured had a depth of between six and seven metres to the water surface, and a diameter of about one metre; they are mostly temporary affairs sunk in the bed of the river, or of one of the spill channels, and re-dug annually. They are carried but very little below spring level, and the supply of the outlying wells is liable to fail in the summer.

The Gash only flows for about eighty days in the year, coming down early in July and drying up in the latter part of September; throughout the remainder of the year the river bed is absolutely dry.

Whilst in flood the river runs constantly, rising and falling frequently and irregularly but rarely or never falling entirely, and generally running with such strength as to form a tolerably formidable and troublesome ford opposite Kassala town, which is occasionally impassable for two or three days at a time.

The channel is some two hundred and fifty yards wide at the ford, and its mean flood depth is probably about fifty centimetres, and the current is described as very rapid.

The ordinary flood discharge might be estimated from the above at about one hundred cubic metres per second or say eight million cubic metres per day, but I think it more probable that it is less, and that it does not often exceed five million cubic metres per day; as I doubt the possibility of fording a larger stream of the character described, in the way that I understand that it is habitually crossed during the flood season.

Exceptional floods, or periods of continued high water, must no doubt represent very much larger discharges, and it is probably on these that the success of the Gash flood as a whole is chiefly dependent.

In any case I think that it is evident that the river is a comparatively small one, and incapable under any circumstances of irrigating satisfactorily the whole of the immense area that it commands; it is therefore very desirable that the available supply of water should be economized to the utmost.

It must however be remembered that there is a fair amount of rain at Kassala during the period of the Gash flood, this amounted to 7·8 inches in 1902, an exceptionally dry year, and has averaged between nine and ten inches for the last three years.

Almost all the maps represent the Gash as a tributary of the Atbara; replies to many enquiries on this point make it tolerably certain that if any of the Gash water ever reaches the Atbara, it is only in extremely wet years, and as a very unusual and exceptional occurrence; and with even an elementary system of control and regulation, no such waste of invaluable water would ever be allowed to occur.

The point at which the Gash is supposed to fall into the Atbara is just north of the village of Adarama; about halfway between Goz Regeb and Berber; there is a depression, with a flat bottom nearly a mile wide of excellent soil, densely covered with bush, running down to the Atbara at that point, but its connection with the Gash is at least doubtful, and it shows no sign of a strong flow of water in any part of its width.

The system of cultivation in the neighbourhood of Kassala embraces three principal classes of crop.

(1) *The rain crop*, of early white durra, sown on the higher ground and depending for its success on the character of the weather during the rainy season; this crop is usually sown in July and reaped in October, but in 1902 it failed completely.

(2) *The Gash flood crop*, of late white durra, sown in the autumn on areas that have been thoroughly saturated by the Gash flood, and usually reaped in March; in 1902-3 this crop promised well, but was very seriously damaged by the "asal" blight.

(3) *The garden crop*, comprising any crop grown with the aid of perennial irrigation from wells, at present practically confined to vegetable gardens in Kassala itself, but formerly widely extended and including a considerable area of cotton and other high class crops.

With the exception of the rain crop, which is precarious at best and comparatively unimportant, the whole agricultural prosperity of the fertile tract round Kassala depends absolutely on the river Gash, which feeds the springs that supply the wells, floods and refreshes a large portion of the most valuable grazing grounds, and irrigates directly on a system corresponding approximately to an uncontrolled basin system a considerable area (capable of very large extension), upon which are grown most valuable and productive crops of durra.

It is essential that in any scheme of treating the river, no one of these main functions that its waters perform should be lost sight of, or unduly sacrificed to the others.

There is no doubt but that in its present uncontrolled state the Gash does not do its work at all efficiently, and it should not be difficult to devise some scheme by which the cultivated area could be largely developed without either injuring the grazing or the all-important well supply.

Under present conditions the Gash, like any other uncontrolled deltaic river, is given to troublesome vagaries.

The cultivated areas and best grazing grounds shift about with the changing directions of flow of the flood waters, while the wells are liable to be affected by the same cause, involving a constant migration of the population, and a feeling of insecurity that militates against any expenditure on improvements; not to mention the trouble and complications involved in the administration of the country under such conditions.

Moreover, the waters of the Gash, spreading in a thin sheet over very extensive areas of nearly level ground, offer the largest possible surface for evaporation, whilst often flooding considerable areas of hard unproductive soils, which neither absorb water readily for the benefit of the springs, nor grow good grazing grasses; and in other cases it is only by keeping large areas continuously flooded, which have been thoroughly irrigated already, and suffering a continuous heavy loss from evaporation, that water can be passed forward to more distant places.

Undoubtedly what would seem to be required is some system of canalization and basin construction by means of which certain defined and selected areas could be given water in the manner, to the amounts, and at the times desired, so far as the supply of water available in the river might permit, whether for the purpose of growing durra, irrigating grazing grounds, or replenishing the springs.

The way in which the Gash obliterates itself in its own silt a few miles north of Kassala is very curious, and shows the necessity for great caution in any attempt to canalize the river.

It is highly probable that its muddy waters would treat an artificially constructed canal with as little ceremony as they do their own large and well-defined natural channel, if turned directly into it.

But we can, I think, take a hint from the behaviour of the river in its natural state.

The waters arrive at what may be called the head of the delta loaded with sand and silt, and when the diminishing slope of the country can no longer maintain the velocity necessary to keep this material moving, it is thrown down as a deposit which entirely blocks and obliterates the channel in a short distance; and the river breaks up and overflows in all directions.

Once freed from the heavier portions of the suspended water, the comparatively clear water flows forward with a tendency to scour rather than to silt and to amalgamate rather than to disperse, if one may judge from general descriptions and a hurried view of a small part of the tract affected.

The area situated about the head of the delta is thus one of intense and concentrated deposit, and the soil is, as might be expected, extremely rich. It is here that best durra lands are situated. These lands cannot however be sown until the Gash flood is over, owing to their liability to inundation, and the crops grown on them are therefore late in ripening; a fact which has this year involved them in the disastrous "asal" blight, which earlier sown crops escaped almost entirely.

Some system of control of the river would appear to be necessary under which the waters would continue to deposit their heavy silt over a limited area near the head of the delta, and to pass forward in a comparatively clear condition along a series of defined lines in various directions.

This would seem to point strongly to something in the nature of a basin or system of basins about the apex of the delta feeding canals leading in various directions through regulators in the retaining banks.

Under present conditions a good deal of work is done under Government control every year in making and maintaining sadds across the heads of some of the larger spill channels near the delta head; as these channels have a tendency to open out and develope into important branches, carrying an undue proportion of water in new directions to the detriment of the established cultivation and interests on the older lines of flow, while at the same time they lower the level of the water in the river itself, so that the valuable areas of cultivated land situated about the delta head are incompletely or insufficiently flooded.

A sort of fight is in fact maintained to preserve the existing conditions, against the natural tendency of a markedly deltaic river to keep continually opening out new lines of flow, and silting up and abandoning old ones.

In the absence of any very definite plan of campaign, and with the rather meagre resources available, this fight is almost necessarily a losing game, and in any particular instance the river is pretty sure to get the best of it sooner or later; causing considerable temporary loss and inconvenience, gradually passing off as the new channel in its turn chokes and destroys itself.

If works can be constructed on any scale it would seem that what is required is a large circular basin enclosing the tract about the delta head, into which the river would be guided by small retaining banks running some little distance up the main river on either side.

The river would be received into this basin and allowed to overflow and spread about in the area enclosed, throwing down the greater portion of its heavy silt just as it does at present, and passing off through several regulators in the surrounding bank.

Until the end of the flood the regulators in this bank would not be used to a greater extent than was necessary to secure the partition of the water in the way desired, so that existing conditions would be but very slightly disturbed; at the end of the flood, when the river began to fall, the regulators would be closed, and the whole basin given a last thorough soaking, and the stored water could then be run off and utilized lower down.

The various regulators would form the heads of different canals, or might feed a second system of basins forming a more or less concentric ring round the first circular basin, or one or more of them might be used merely as escapes to pass any excess of water forward down the existing lines of flow: at first the last named would probably be the most important function performed by them, but it is clear that the single ring bank would at once give absolute control of the river with a minimum of disturbance of existing conditions; and canals of exact section and carefully considered alignment could be developed from it; or some of the old lines of flow could be improved into canals, though it would probably be necessary to maintain the largest of them as escapes, at any rate for some time.

Without plans or levels it is impossible to say what the size of the first basin should be, or what depth of water the bank should be designed to hold up, or to give any idea of the number, size or position of the regulators required, but it would probably be found better to provide a large number of comparatively small regulators than a few large ones, and as the estimated discharge of the river is of moderate amount, these works would not be individually very expensive or difficult to construct, and they might be built gradually, if funds were not available for all at once.

But before any definite scheme could be prepared more information is absolutely essential; it is impossible to form an even moderately correct conception of such a peculiar river and arrangement of channels from one or two rides over a small portion of the area affected, along tortuous paths, through thick bush and high crops.

It is worth noting that the proposed basin bank would provide a means of crossing the Gash in flood not far off the line of the Kassala-Berber road, a great advantage, as the difficulty and danger of fording the river is often a serious inconvenience, especially to postal arrangements.

The canals distributing the waters of the river would take the place of the present ill-defined depressions and khor lines; and the available supply would be concentrated upon selected areas, by which means much waste and loss by evaporation would be avoided.

The grazing grounds could be systematically irrigated by occasional floodings, instead of being as at present the accidental result of large areas of marshy overflow.

Distant villages could get their irrigation in regular rotation, instead of depending as now upon the ability of occasional flushes in the river to overpower the losses from absorption and evaporation through a long series of swamps and areas of shallow flood, and reach them irregularly in uncertain amount.

Areas around important well groups would be given a thorough and prolonged soaking with a good depth of water, and the wells themselves enlarged, deepened and improved.

Proceeding in this way it is hardly possible to doubt but that a very great and fairly rapid development of the country could be effected, and the works are of a kind that could be constructed gradually, as the increase of population and the cultivated area justified their being undertaken.

In addition to the main deltaic system, there was once a canal taking off the Gash at the southern foot of Jebel Kassala, and irrigating a considerable tract of the great plain to the west of the river opposite Kassala town, where much cotton was grown, and several well-sakias existed, with garden cultivation; the whole tract is now entirely uncultivated, overgrown with bush, and destitute of human habitations.

I visited the site of the head of the old canal, and saw the remains of the old channels and banks, still fairly intact, and also obtained a good deal of information concerning it from an old Government clerk resident in Kassala.

It appears that the canal was first made about sixty years ago, and was last used about thirty years ago.

The Gash was completely dammed across, just below the off-take, before the arrival of the flood, and the whole supply of the river diverted into the canal for thirty days.

The dam was then formally and ceremoniously cut, and the waters of the river allowed to flow forward along their natural channel for the rest of the flood.

The old canal and the ends of the old bank could easily be repaired and utilized, and this would be one way of helping to restore the ancient prosperity of the district, though I rather doubt the wisdom of the old method of working.

It is not clear why the canal was abandoned and it may have been due to difficulties with silt, though more probably it was because it was found to be injurious to other and larger interests further down the river.

The agricultural possibilities of the Gash area in Kassala Mudirieh cannot fail to strike any visitor interested in such matters, the fertility of the soil is unquestionable, and there is no doubt as to the former prosperity of the country.

Present conditions are in sad and striking contrast, but there have been considerable developments in the last two or three years, and the want of population is not such an acute difficulty in the neighbourhood of Kassala as elsewhere in the mudirieh.

The cultivated area has extended and is extending rapidly, and very large herds of cattle and flocks of sheep and goats exist all over the Gash area.

More and better wells are everywhere urgently needed, and the extension of garden cultivation deserves every encouragement that can be given to it.

Nothing would give a greater impetus to the restoration of the district than works for the control of the Gash flood, by means of which definite conditions could be guaranteed to definite tracts of country; and under such circumstances I have little doubt but that the necessary cultivators would soon be forthcoming.

Here, as elsewhere in the Soudan, startling developments must not be looked for, but the conditions do appear more favourable than in most places for doing a great deal of good by means of very moderate expenditure on irrigation works.

Before anything can be done a rough plan and chart of levels must be prepared for the tract specially under consideration, and it is urgently desirable that a competent engineer or surveyor should be deputed to collect the information required, and submit it for definite and detailed proposals to some irrigation expert.

That information would be sufficiently well given, and quickly obtained by running a a single straight line of levels due north from Kassala for say twenty kilometres and taking long cross-section lines at right angles to this line at every kilometre.

It is probable that a very useful beginning in the construction of works of control could be made by building three or four kilometres of bank of light section, and two or three small regulators, which could probably be done for a few thousand pounds, but it is impossible to speak with any certainty until the survey has been made.

Even if there is no immediate prospect of funds being forthcoming, it would seem highly desirable to obtain accurate information, from a study of which the general lines to be followed in dealing with the Gash could be laid down.

The cost of the survey would probably be indirectly recovered many times over in the first year, and much improvement work of a permanent nature, such as bank construction, could be gradually accomplished in the same way, and by the same agency as that by which the present purely temporary works of control are executed.

NOTE ON THE HASSA LANDS NEAR BERBER.

The section of the Nile valley and the general physical conditions of the country about Berber are very similar to those of the narrower parts of Upper Egypt.

There are, however, minor points of difference, notably in the facts that in the Soudan the culturable areas are more irregular and uneven both in surface and quality, and in that they are situated in a region liable to be visited occasionally by heavy storms of rain, throwing large quantities of water down the khors and depressions draining the adjacent desert, both of which facts would have to be considered in any scheme of irrigation, and would probably increase the difficulty and expense of constructing the necessary works as compared with Egypt.

In most places there is a well-defined alluvial berm to the river, of recent formation and very varying width, up to perhaps a couple of kilometres, the general level of which is at or about high flood level.

Much of this berm is already highly cultivated with crops of durra, wheat, barley, lubia etc., the necessary irrigation being effected by means of sakias and shadoufs along the river's edge.

The uncultivated parts are generally more or less covered with tufts of coarse grass and small scrubby bushes, and their surface is often much cut up and rendered uneven by sand-drift.

Behind this berm, on a higher level by two or three metres, and forming a secondary terrace also of very varying width, is found in many places another similar berm of much older formation, now well above the reach of the highest floods.

This upper terrace has in places become more or less covered with stones, and in others has had its surface so much cut up and covered by sand-drift that it is not always easily distinguishable from the true desert into which it merges.

It is as a rule dotted with scrub and wholly uncultivated, but considerable stretches are planted with durra in years of favourable rainfall and yield good crops.

In places the areas available for cultivation are very extensive and consist apparently of excellent soil; of this the Hassa lands of some six thousand feddans, situated about 10 kilometres north of Berber, are an excellent example.

The true desert consists generally of pure barren shingle, rising with a gentle inclination for a long distance, and is of no agricultural value whatever.

The railway runs approximately along the toe of the desert slope on the dividing line between the culturable and unculturable lands, some little way from the river.

Berber is situated forty kilometres north of the mouth of the Atbara.

The Nile in this length has a rather heavy slope owing to the existence of several rocks in the channel, and a succession of light rapids for some distance below the Atbara junction.

Some levels taken in connection with the original proposal for the reclamation of the Hassa lands are said to have shown a fall of between nine and ten metres in the river level from the Atbara mouth to Berber; and some levels that I saw in connection with a project for the construction of a small system of basins on the west bank of the river in this reach supported this estimate.

I think that any scheme involving pumping for perennial irrigation on a large scale for this tract may be dismissed at once as out of the question, both on account of its cost, and the doubt as to whether the country is ready for it, not to mention the question arising from Egypt's interest in the matter.

It would in my opinion almost certainly be wiser, in this as in all similar instances, to follow the lines of development followed by Egypt itself, and commence with the comparatively cheap and simple basin system, for which water would always be available in abundance, without raising the thorny question of summer supply; and when a certain degree of prosperity has been established it will be time enough, should the water difficulty have been solved, to proceed to a conversion to the perennial system.

The people of Berber and the neighbourhood are thoroughly awake to the value of such lands as these when flooded, as they occasionally are, by unusually heavy rainfall or an exceptionally high Nile, and under such circumstances large areas of crop are sown and big returns realized, off lands that in most years are barely distinguishable from the surrounding deserts.

They would almost certainly be ready to at once take advantage of lands regularly and dependably flooded by artificial means under the basin system.

I understand that the proposal originally entertained concerning the Hassa lands contemplated a canal taking off the Nile at the Atbara junction, and running down alongside the river in the usual way with a less slope than the river itself till it commanded the lands to be irrigated, also the erection of large pumps to feed the canal when the river was not high enough to do so direct.

As regards the canal this is probably quite practicable, the distance is about fifty kilometres, and the fall in the river about ten metres — five metres would be ample for the fall in the canal, which could therefore command and irrigate lands up to five metres above river level in the neighbourhood of Hassa village, and a good deal of land at lower levels further up.

The difficulties of construction would not be serious except for the existence of a series of villages, including the town of Berber itself, along the edge of the upper terrace, which any such canal must almost necessarily follow.

These are unquestionably serious obstacles, especially the town of Berber, the principal buildings in which are along the edge of a steep bank of considerable height which descends abruptly into a branch channel of the river.

In the absence of detail levels it is difficult to discuss a point which is solely a question of levels, but I think the difficulty is a serious one, and could only be overcome by heavy expenditure.

Through the town of Berber also runs a large and formidable desert khor, now provided for on the railway by a girder bridge of several metres' span, at the site of a bad "washout" some two or three years ago.

This channel would undoubtedly give serious trouble to the canal at intervals, unless provided for by an expensive syphon or super-passage.

The length of the canal is considerable and the amount of earthwork would be large; a good many bridges would also be required owing to the number of villages adjacent to its line.

I was only able to make a very hasty visit to Hassa, and was certainly given to understand that much of the land is of very superior quality, but what I was able to see of it did not impress me very favourably.

The possibility of dealing with this tract in a way likely to prove financially remunerative in a reasonably short time, would, I think, depend largely on the area that could be brought within the scope of one canal system, and the extent to which the canal could be made to consist of a series of shallow basins involving only light earthwork in the form of a retaining bank along the river's edge.

This would probably be best effected by means of a canal or basin system starting some little way up the Atbara on its right bank, and continued past the junction of the Atbara with the Nile down the right bank of the latter river.

In this way the feeding canal could be brought in at a comparatively high level, and following as nearly as might be the line of the railway, it could pass behind Berber and the other villages that form the most serious obstacle to the constructton of a canal on the lines originally contemplated.

If fuller information and a detailed survey showed it to be possible and worth while, the proposals here outlined might be elaborated into an extensive canal system or chain of basins extending all down the lower Atbara and for a considerable distance down the Nile past Berber.

Without such a survey it is quite impossible to say what area of land might be brought within the scope of such a scheme, or how much money it would be worth while to spend upon it.

There is no doubt that the strip of culturable land is on the average but a narrow one, and there would be one or two short lengths of high rough ground to cut through, where projecting spurs of the desert run right down to the river, but otherwise the difficulties of construction should not be serious.

In any case the first thing required is a reasonably correct plan and a few lines of levels, and if any money is forthcoming for work of the kind under discussion, it could not be better spent in the first instance than in preparing rough survey and level charts of any tracts which casual observation or local report suggest as likely to offer suitable fields for irrigation works of a simple and inexpensive kind.

Without some central office in the Soudan for the control and direction of such surveys and the collection of the necessary information, I do not see how anything can be done, except in the way of small local works of a tentative and experimental kind the results of which are not likely to be very satisfactory, and may be very misleading.

But speaking very broadly it seems probable that the Hassa lands, and all other similar tracts in the Berber Mudiria would be best dealt with under present conditions by the introduction of a basin system modelled very much on the lines of the systems in the southern parts of Upper Egypt, and that there would not seem to be any great difficulty in introducing such a system so far as can be judged from a casual visit.

But much more exact and detailed information is required before any comprehensive scheme could be even entertained, and such information could only be collected by parties of surveyors working for a considerable time under the direction of some competent central authority specially charged with the investigation.

ATBARA GAUGE

In accordance with instructions I made certain arrangements concerning the erection of a gauge on the Atbara near Fasher.

I ascertained before arriving there that the telegraph line from Kassala to Gedaref crosses the Atbara at Khasim el-Girba, about seven miles above Fasher, where the river runs through a rocky gorge.

Colonel Henry, Mudir of Kassala, kindly arranged to send out a mason from Kassala to meet me there with tools for cutting a gauge in the rock.

We arrived there a day earlier than had been expected, and Mr. Crawley and I took advantage of the opportunity to mark out the gauge in red pencil and scratches, on a nearly vertical rock face.

On the arrival of the mason we found that his tools were quite unequal to the task of cutting the exceedingly hard water-worn rock face, and that no better tools were available in Kassala.

We therefore elaborated our marks a little, and then continued our march to Kassala, from where I telegraphed to Cairo for better tools.

The rock on which we marked the gauge rises out of a deep pool about a quarter of a mile above the usual halting place at Khashim el-Girba, where the Kassala-Gedaref road touches the river—an excellent site.

The gauge is designed so that a reading of ten metres is the normal low water level of the river, corresponding to a trickling discharge out of the pool in which it stands, (which was the condition of things at the time of our visit), and the marks were carried up to a reading of twenty metres, though ordinary floods do not apparently rise more than six or seven metres, and the flood marks of 1901 showed a rise of little over five.

The telegraph line crosses the river about a mile above the gauge site.

With Colonel Henry's assistance I arranged in telegraphic correspondence with Captain Liddell, Director General of the Soudan Telegraphs, to erect a tap wire from the main line to a hut to be erected on the roadside within two or three hundred metres of the gauge.

Colonel Henry also promised to arrange for the erection of the necessary hut at a cost not exceeding ten pounds.

At the same time I arranged provisionally for the erection of rain-gauges at Gallabat, Gedaref and Khasim el-Girba, which arrangement was subsequently confirmed by Mr. Webb, as Acting Under-Secretary.

On my arrival in Cairo I discussed the matter with Mr. Webb, and the tools and rain-gauges not having yet been sent off, it was decided to send up a mason from Assouan with them.

I wrote various letters accordingly to the different people concerned, and the file of correspondence on the subject is submitted with this report for record and reference.

The present state of the matter is therefore as follows:—

A gauge was marked out in a temporary manner in a good site on the Atbara at Khashim el-Girba.

An experienced mason was sent up to Kassala with suitable tools to cut the gauge in the rock in a permanent manner, which was apparently completed about the end of May.

A hut has been constructed on the Kassala-Gedaref road near the gauge and a tap wire laid to it from the existing telegraph line.

Captain Liddell was asked to complete the fitting of the hut as a reporting telegraph station, and if possible to find a man to take up his station there from June 1st, and to let us know on what terms he would consent to do so.

Captain Liddell agreed to do all that he was been asked to do in this matter, and estimated the monthly expense at about £10, in addition to the cost of the first installation, which will be quite small.

The arrangements have since been completed, and the gauge is now being reported daily but details are not yet fully known.

Three rain-gauges have also been sent up, to be erected at Gallabat, Gedaref and Khashim el-Girba.

The rain-gauge at Khashim el-Girba will be read daily by the signaller stationed there, as well as the river gauge, as part of his regular duties.

Captain Liddell has agreed to allow the telegraph signaller at Gallabat to look after the rain-gauge there, he receiving in consideration an honorarium of £1 a month.

Colonel Henry and Dr. Ensor, P.M.O. of Kassala Mudirieh, were asked if they had any objection to the local medical officer at Gedaref observing and reporting the rainfall there on the same terms, and said they had none.

Dr. Ensor has kindly promised to exercise a friendly supervision over these gauges in the course of his tours, and to see that they are suitably placed, and that the men understand how to use them.

The arrival of the rain-gauges has not yet been reported and I fear that the arrangements can hardly have been in full working order for the begining of this rainy season, but a good definite start has been made, and the information when obtainable should be of the greatest value and interest.

C. Dupuis.

15 June 1903.

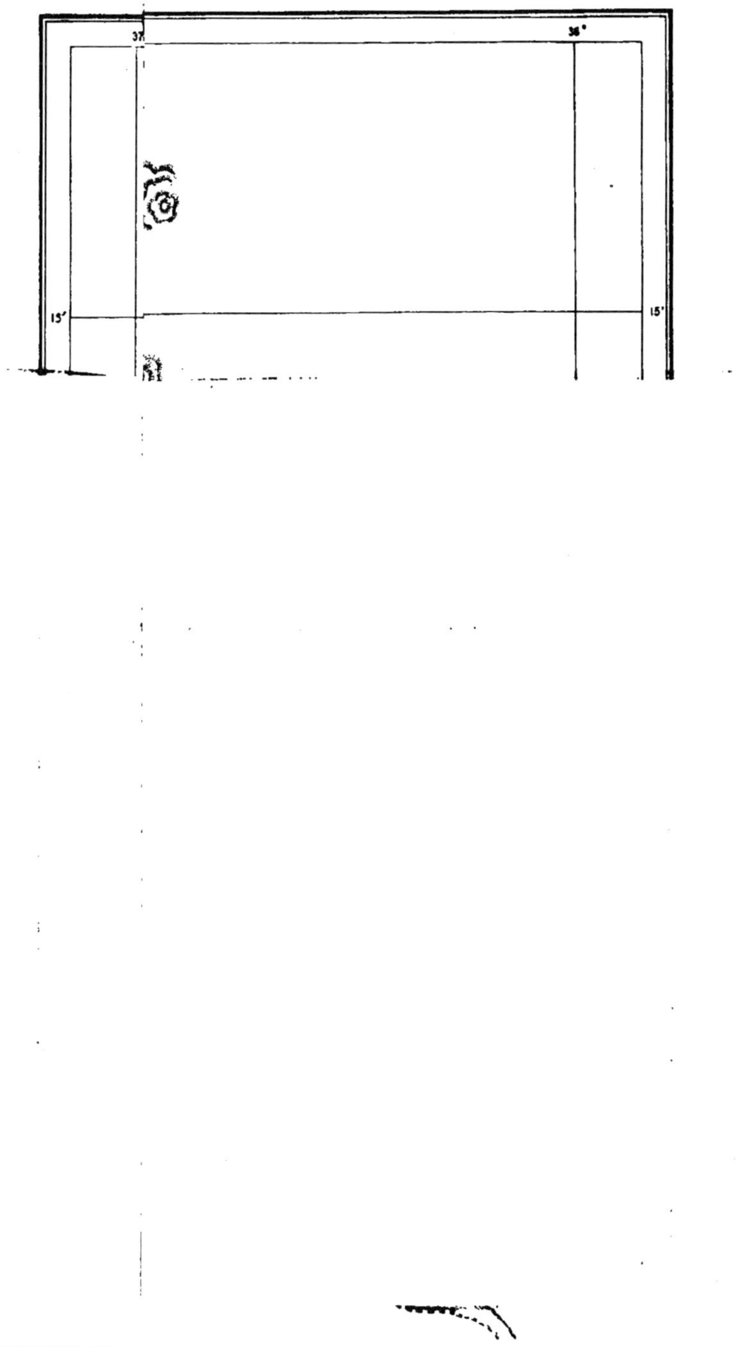

Survey Dep. P.W.M. Cairo.

PLAN XI.

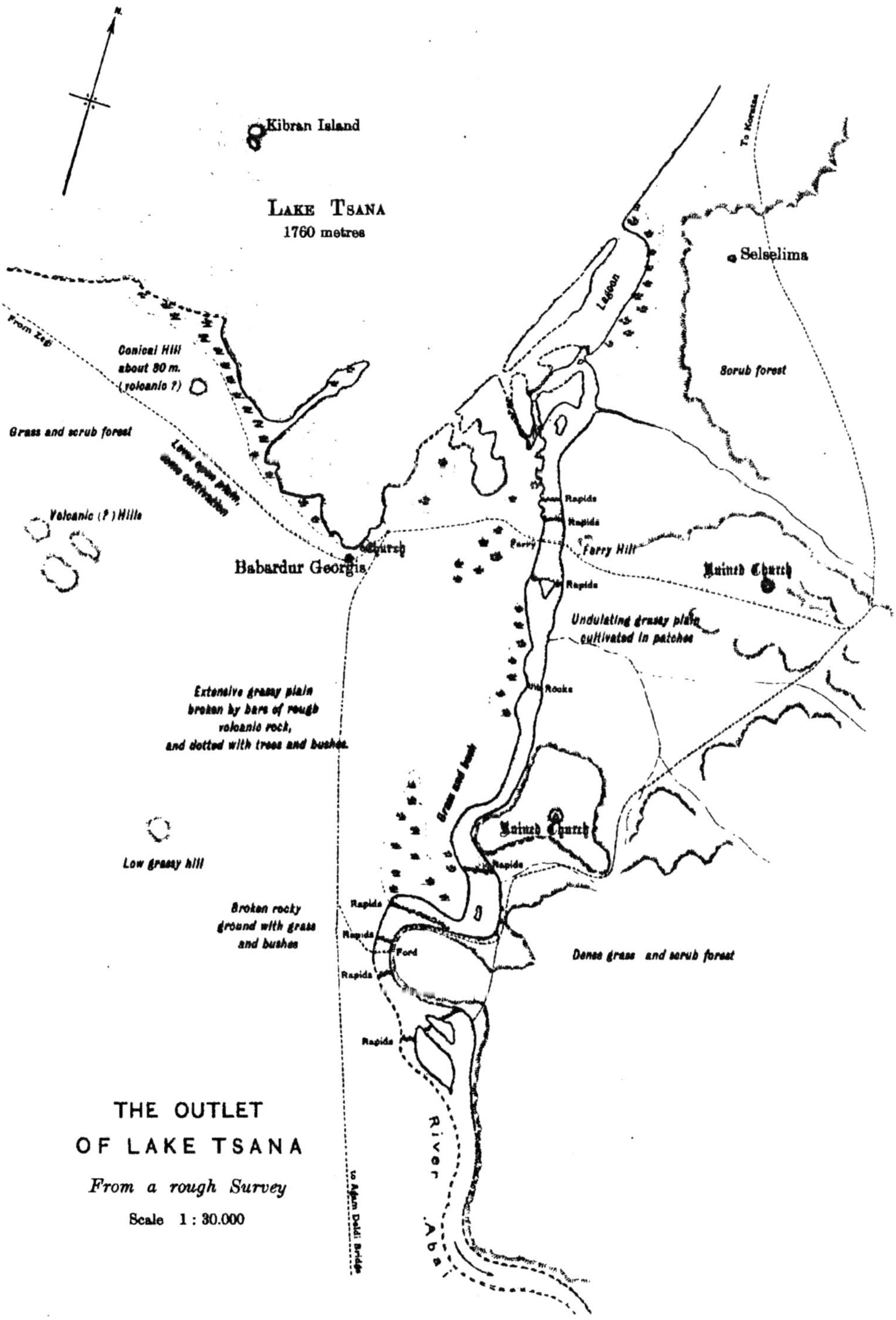

THE OUTLET
OF LAKE TSANA
From a rough Survey
Scale 1 : 30.000

Survey Dep. P. W. M. Cairo.

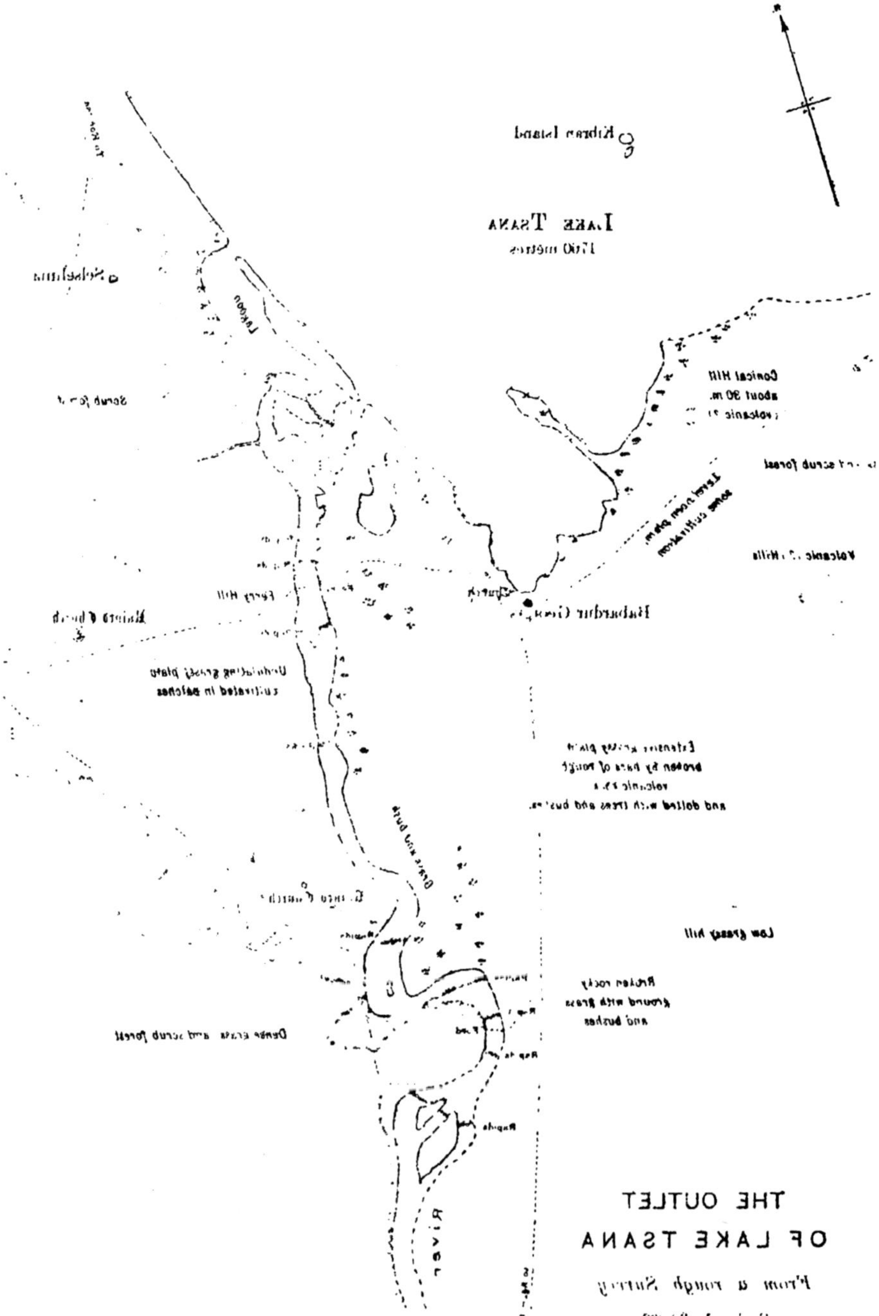
THE OUTLET
OF LAKE TSANA
From a rough Survey
Scale 1 : 30,000
Lake Tsana
1760 metres
Kibran Island
Lagoon
Scrub forest
Conical Hill
about 30 m.
volcanic
Level open plain
some cultivation
Volcanic Hills
Church
Ferry Hill
Undulating grassy plain
cultivated in patches
Extensive grassy plain
broken by bars of rough
and dotted with trees and bushes
Grass and bush
Low grassy hill
Broken rocky
ground with grass
and bushes
Dense grass and scrub forest
Rapids
River
Survey Dep. P.W.M. Cairo

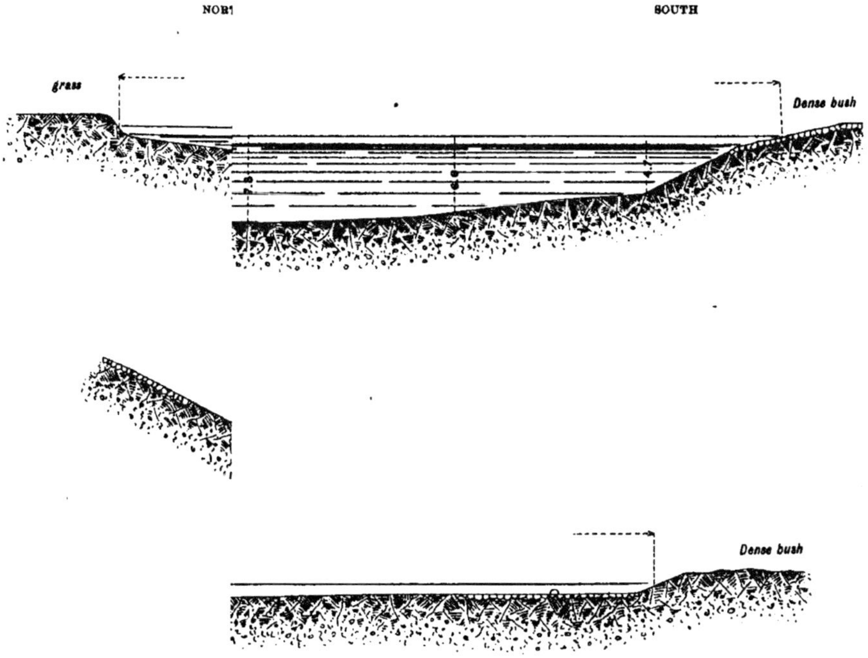
NOR
SOUTH
grass
Dense bush
Dense bush

LAKE TSANA
TRIBUTARIES

NO. 4. *RIVER MAGETSCH 12 - 1 - 03.*

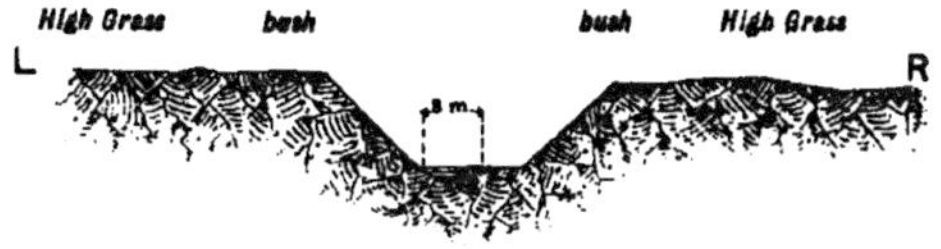

NO. 5. *RIVER ARNO GARNO 15 - 1 - 03.*

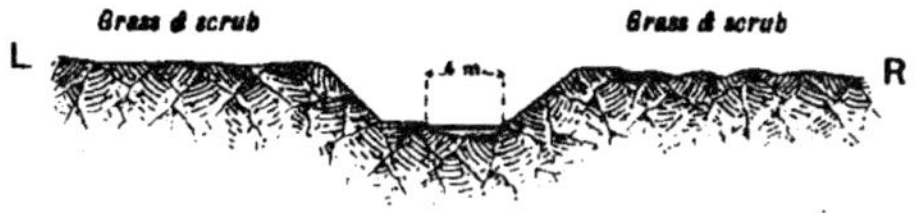

NO. 6. *RIVER REB 16 - 1 - 03.*

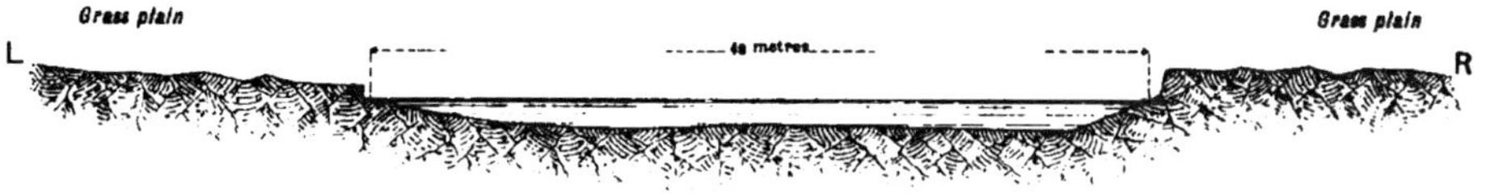

NO. 7. *RIVER GUMARA 17 - 1 - 03.*

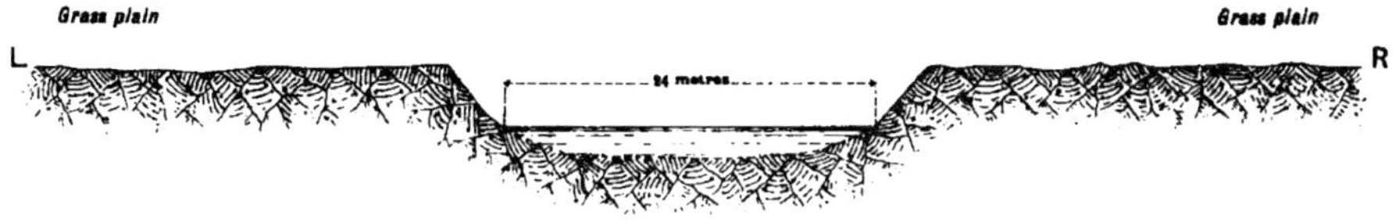

NO. 8. *RIVER GELDA 24 - 1 - 03.*

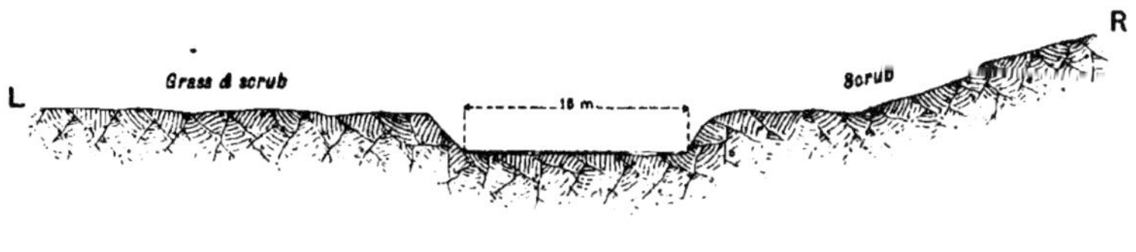

NO. 9. *RIVER ABAI 7 - 2 - 03.*

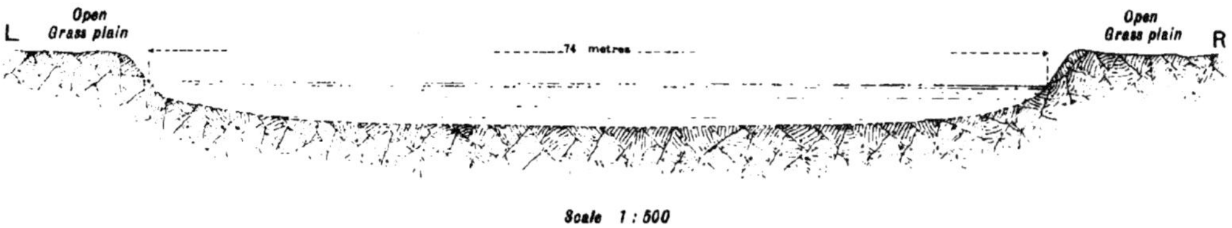

Scale 1 : 500

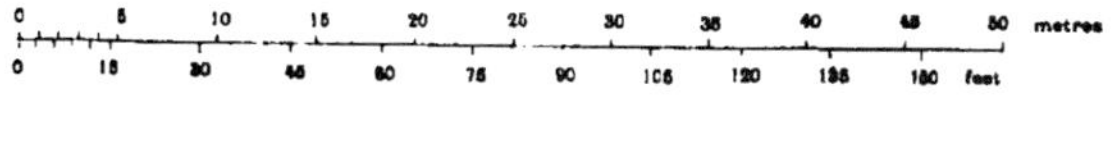

PLAN XII.1

LAKE TSANA
TRIBUTARIES

NO. 4. RIVER MAGETSCH 12-1-03.

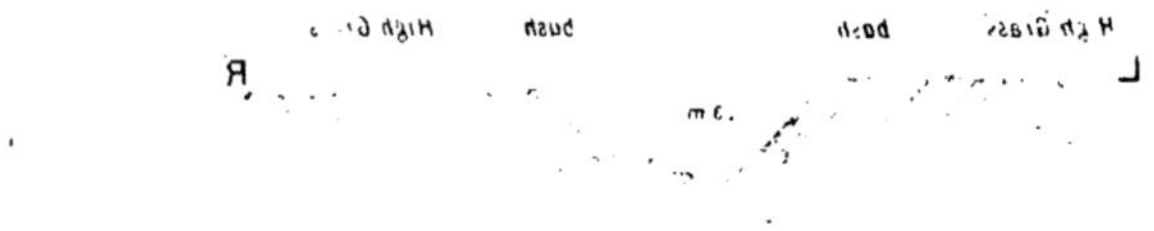

NO. 5. RIVER ARNO GARNO 15-1-03

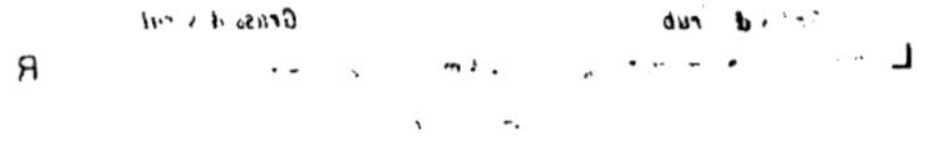

NO. 6. RIVER REB 16-1-03

NO. 7. RIVER GUMARA 17-1-03

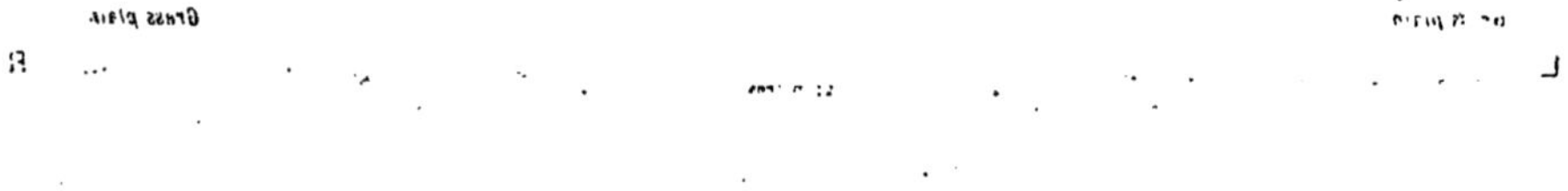

NO. 8. RIVER GELDA 24-1-03

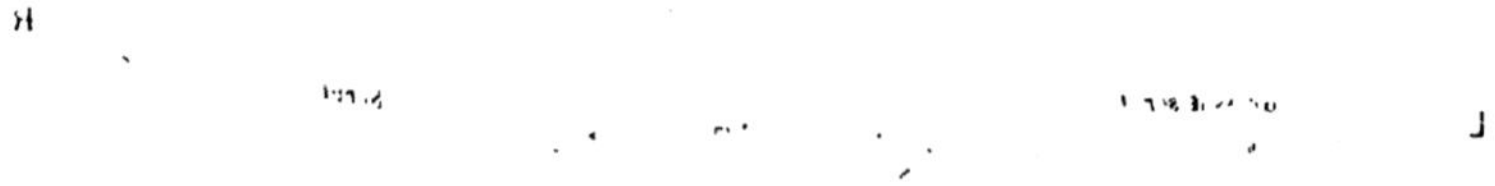

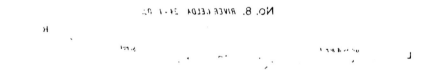

ATBARA RIVER

NO. 10. *At River Gandwaha, 850 Km. from Nile junction 3 - 1 - 03.*

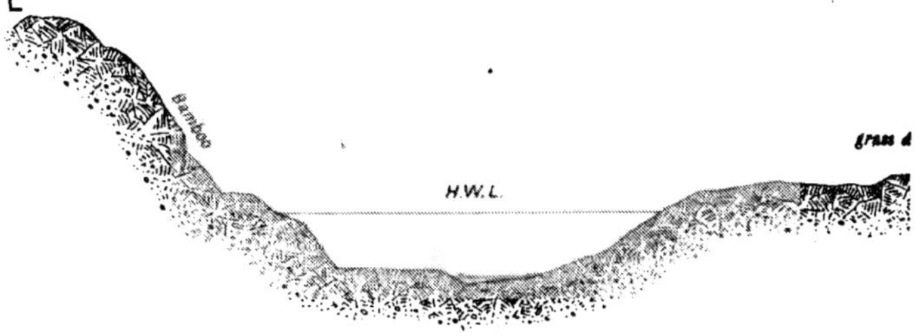

NO. 11. *At Gallabat, 850 Km. from Nile junction 28 - 12 - 02.*

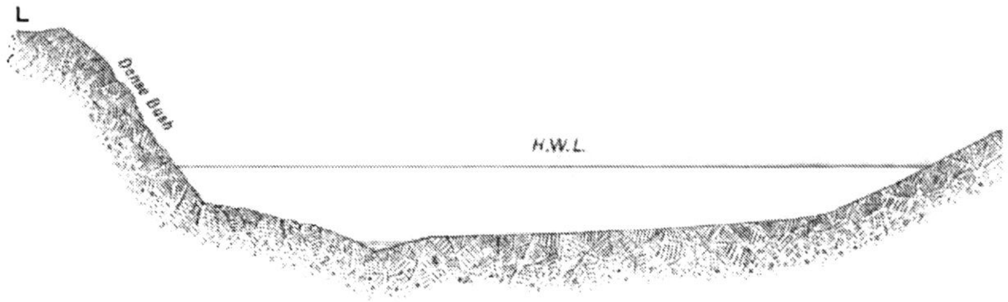

NO. 12. *At Mohammed Osman 750 Km. from Nile 24 - 2 - 03.*

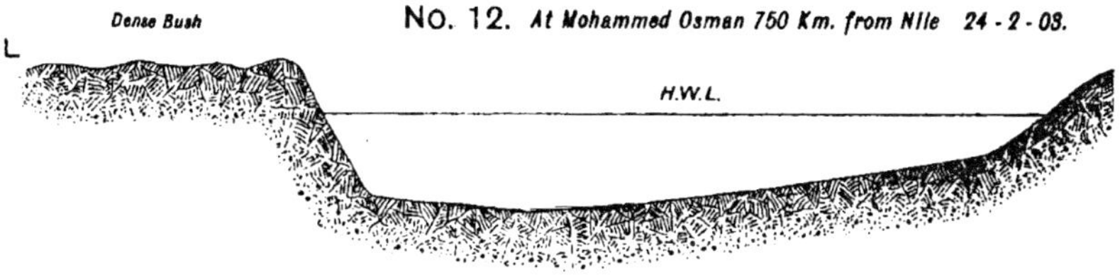

Horizontal Scale 1 : 1000

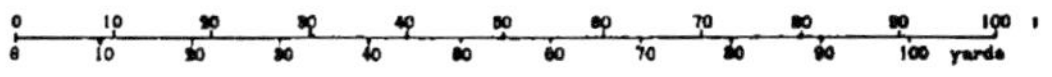

Vertical Scale 1 : 400

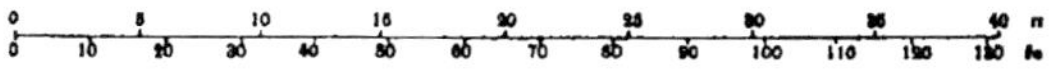

ATBARA RIVER

No. 13. *Near Salaam Junction 650 Km. from Nile 2 - 3 - 03.*

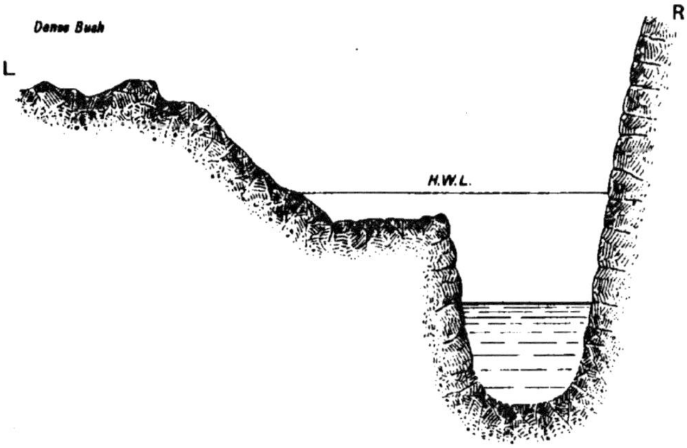

No. 14. *At Aratib. 600 Km. from Nile 5 - 3 - 03.*

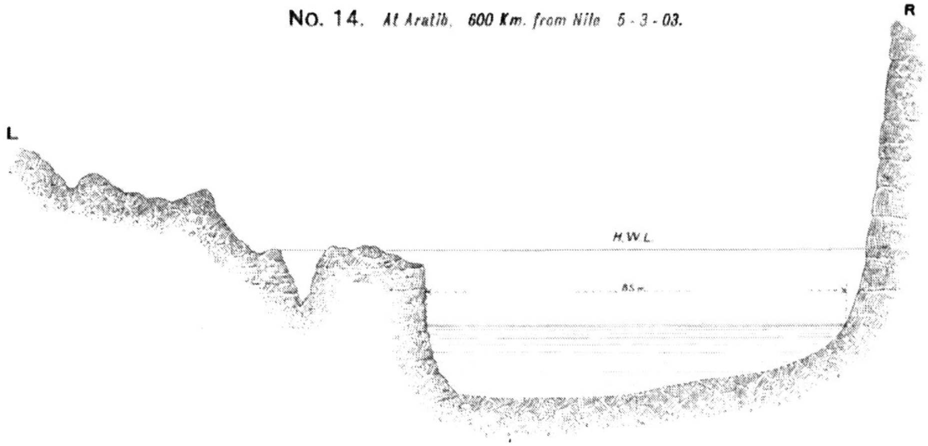

Horizontal Scale 1 : 1000

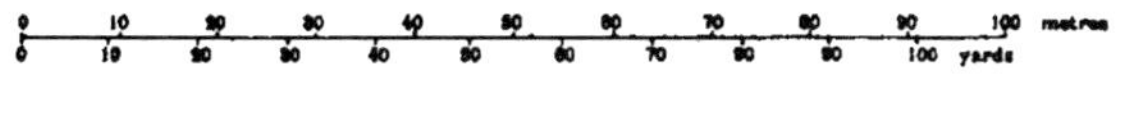

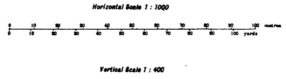

Vertical Scale 1 : 400

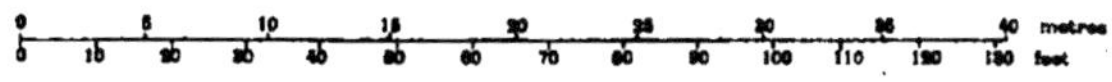

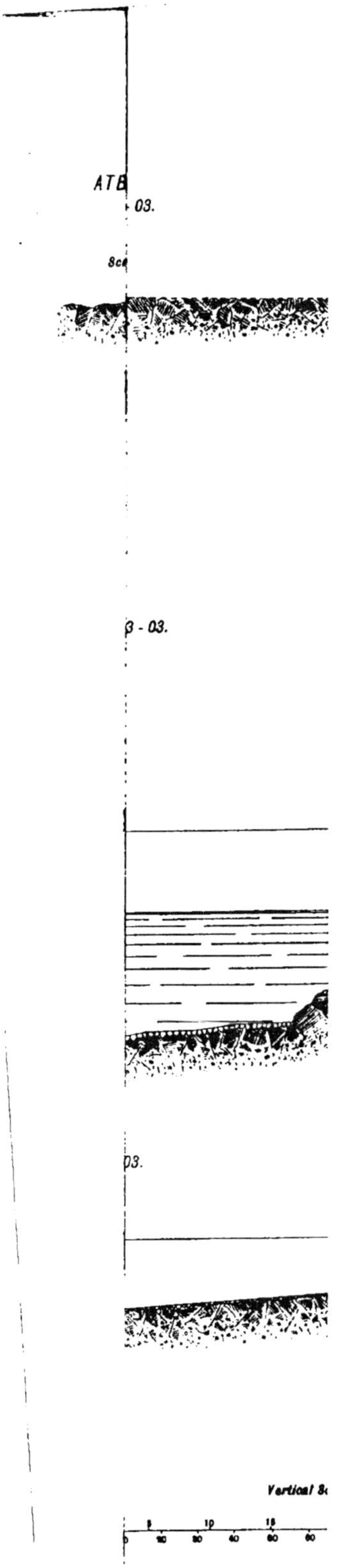
ATB
03.
Sc
β - 03.
03.
Vertical S
5
10
15
10
20
40
60
80

ATBAR

PLAN XII.F.

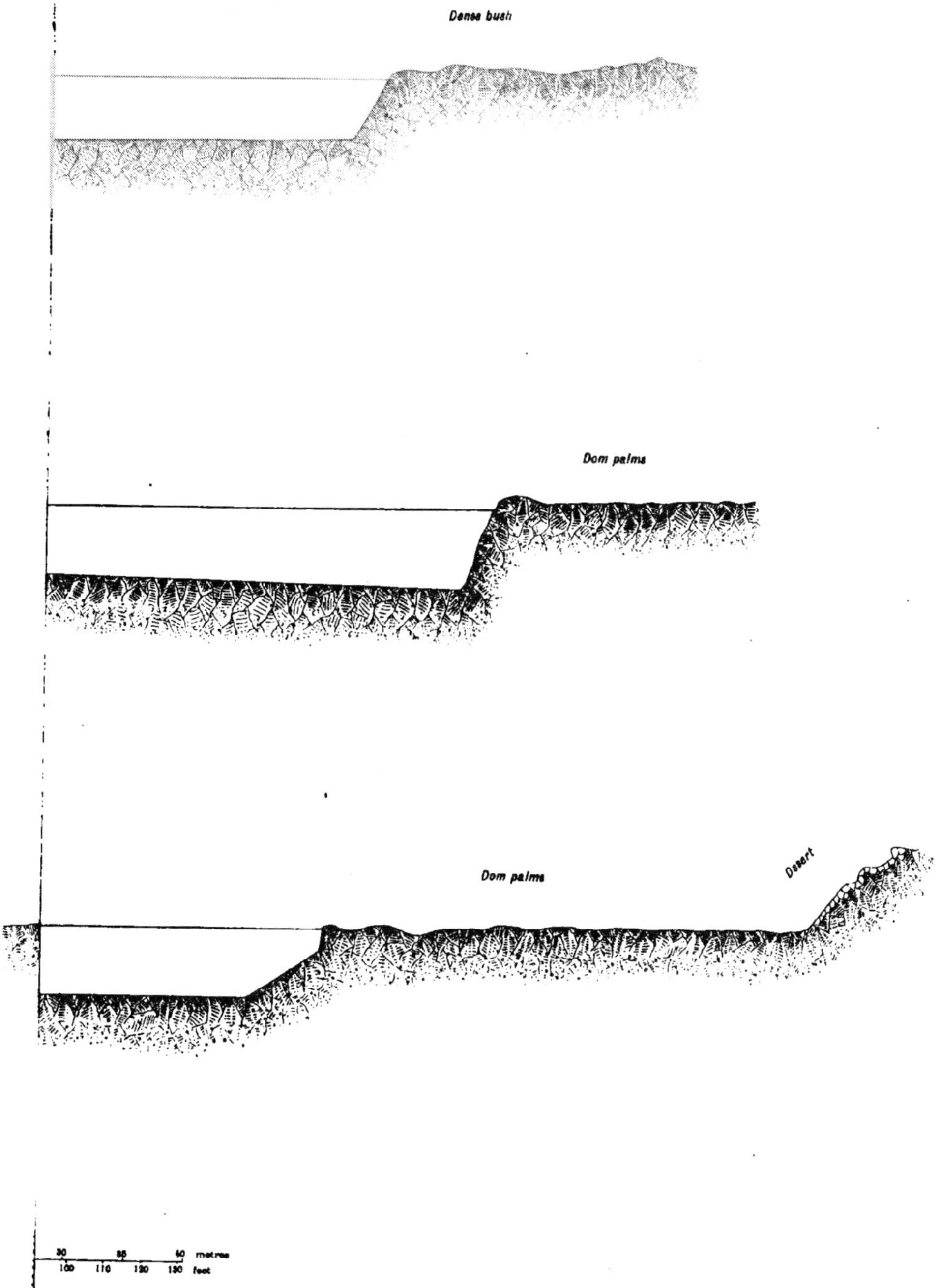

PLAN XII.

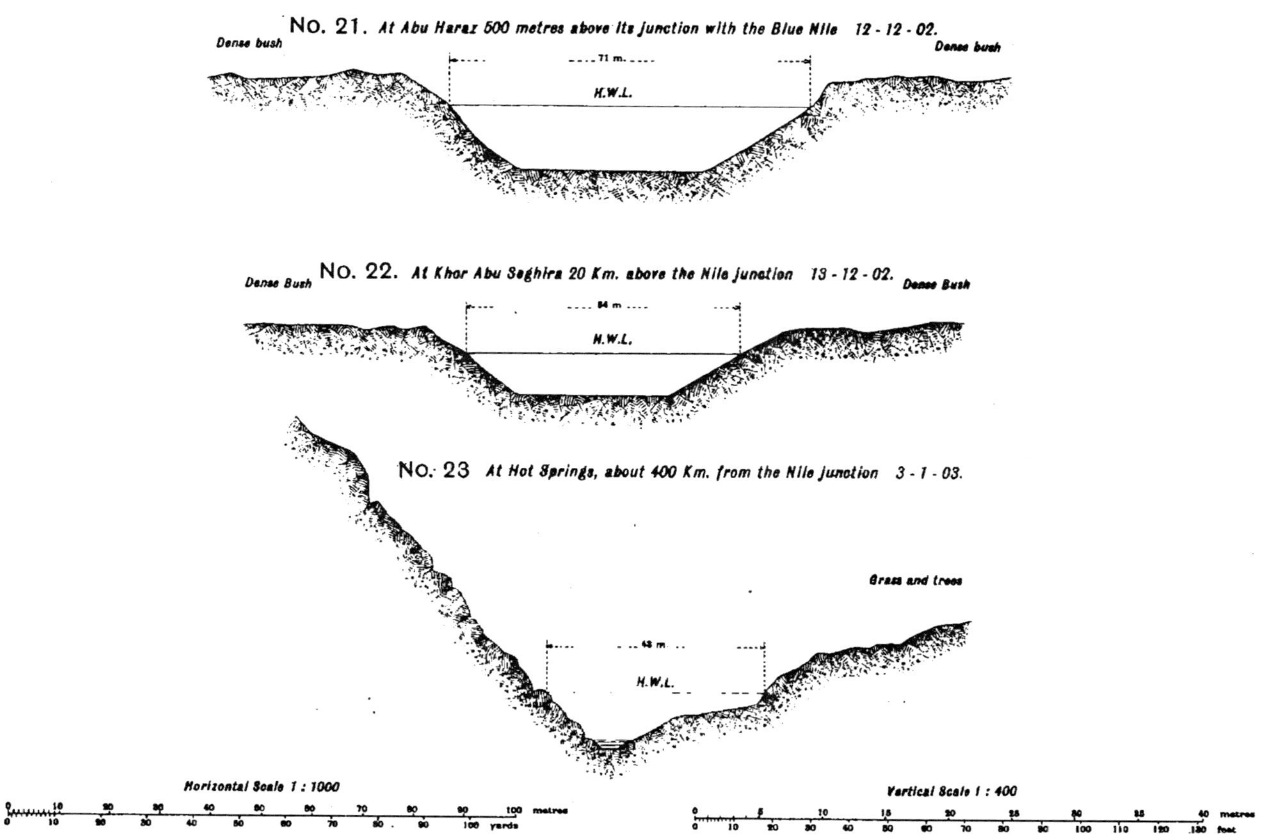
No. 21. At Abu Haraz 500 metres above its junction with the Blue Nile 12 - 12 - 02.
Dense bush
Dense bush
71 m.
H.W.L.
No. 22. At Khor Abu Seghira 20 Km. above the Nile junction 13 - 12 - 02.
Dense Bush
Dense Bush
84 m
H.W.L.
No. 23 At Hot Springs, about 400 Km. from the Nile junction 3 - 1 - 03.
Grass and trees
43 m
H.W.L.
Horizontal Scale 1 : 1000
metres
yards
Vertical Scale 1 : 400
metres
feet

RIVER RAHAD

NO. 21. At Abu Haraz 500 metres above its junction with the Blue Nile 12-12-02.

NO. 22. At Khor Abu Saghira 20 Km. above the Nile junction 13-12-02.

NO. 23. At Hot Springs, about 400 Km. from the Nile junction 3-1-03.

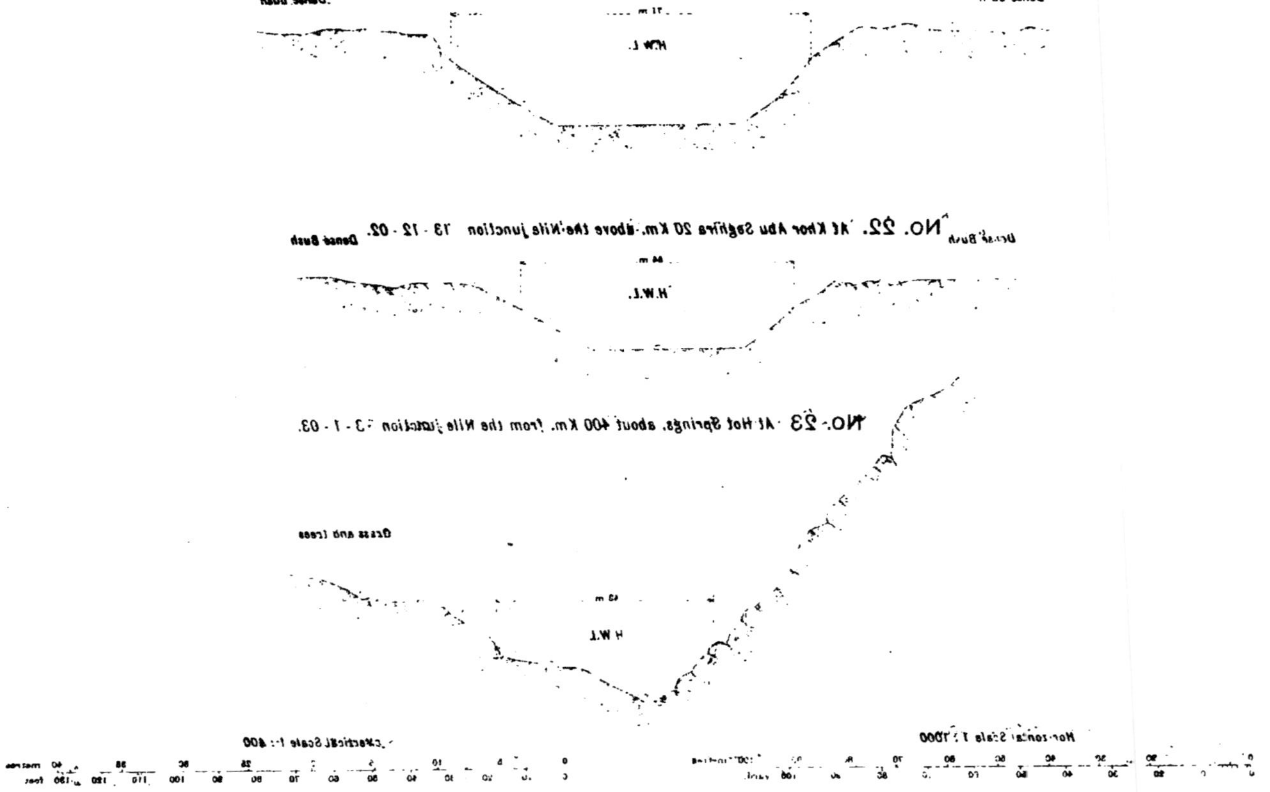

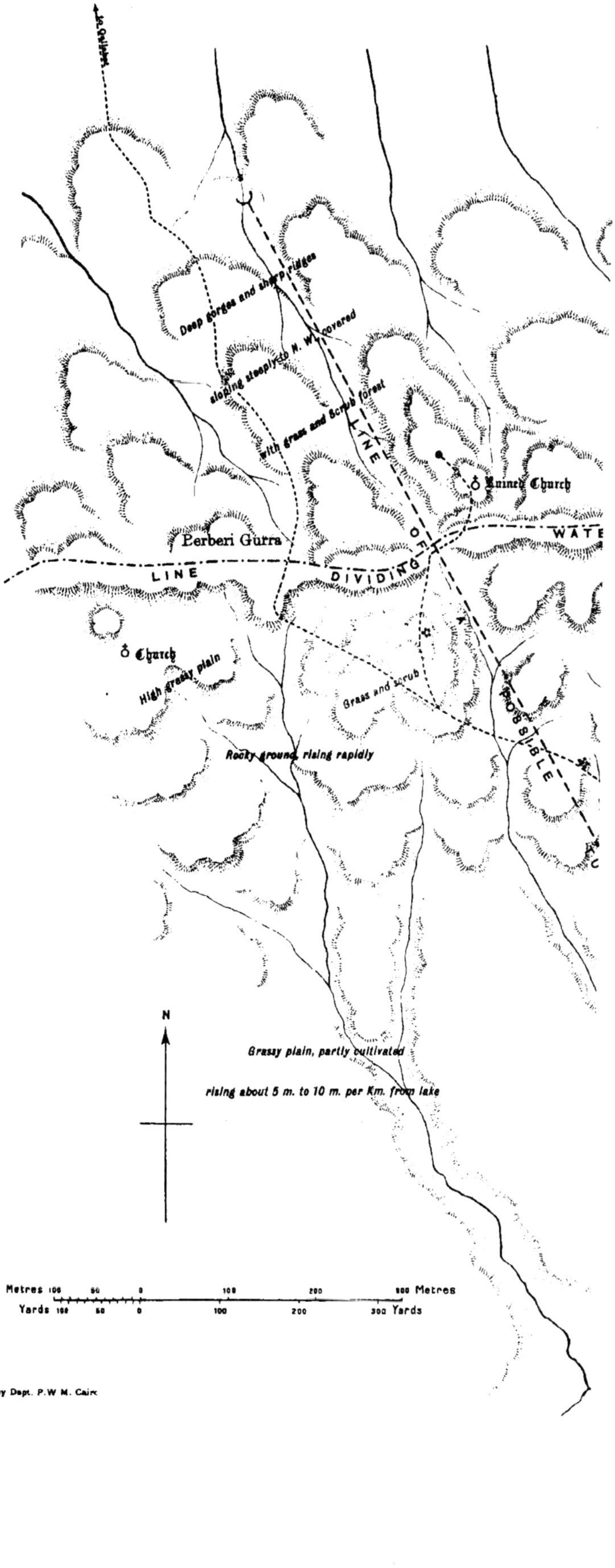

rvey Dept. P.W M. Cairc

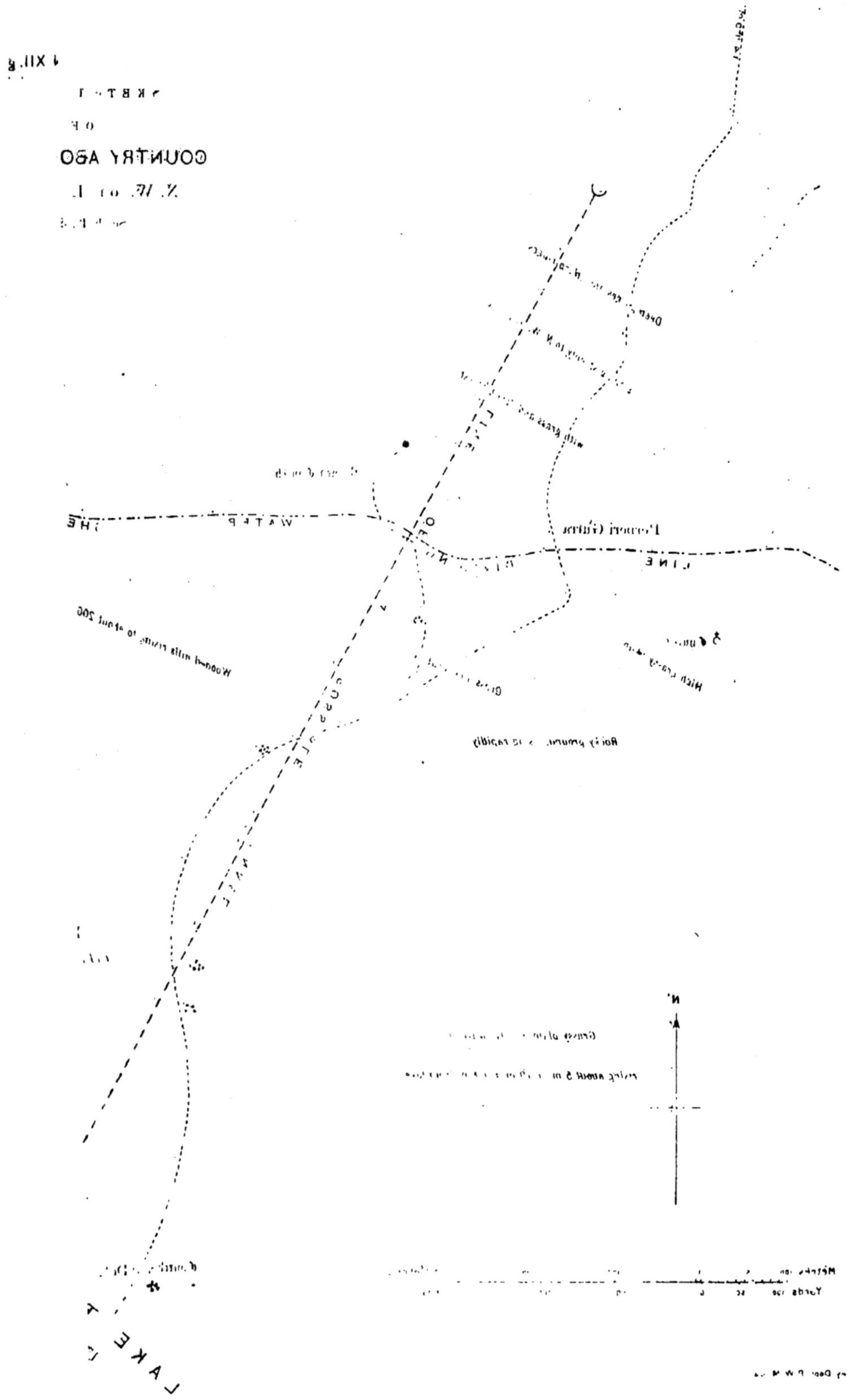

PLAN XIV.

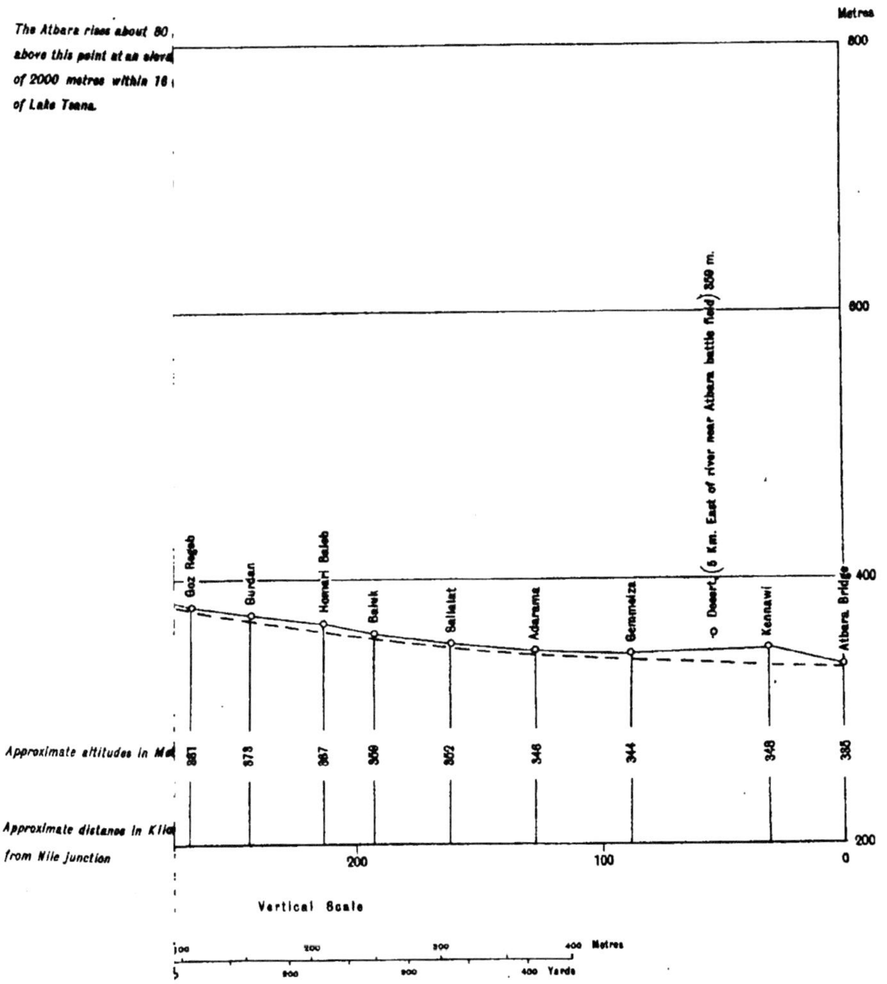
The Atbara rises about 80
above this point at an eleva
of 2000 metres within 16
of Lake Tsana.
Metres
800
600
400
200
Goz Regeb
Burdan
Hawari Baleb
Balek
Sallalat
Adarama
Geramelza
Desert (5 Km. East of river near Atbara battle field) 359 m.
Kennawi
Atbara Bridge
Approximate altitudes in Me
381
373
367
359
352
346
344
348
335
Approximate distance in Kil
from Nile junction
200
100
0
Vertical Scale
100 200 300 400 Metres
200 300 400 Yards

LaVergne, TN USA
22 October 2010
201992LV00003B/41/P

9 781143 101960